DI112865

Narratives of Exploration and Adventure

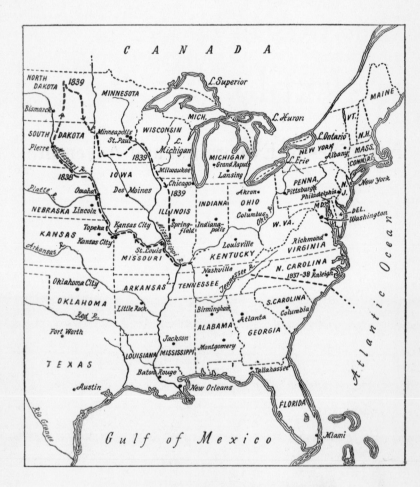

Frémont's Earliest Explorations, 1837–1839

NARRATIVES OF
Exploration
and Adventure

BY
JOHN CHARLES FRÉMONT

Edited by ALLAN NEVINS
DeWitt Clinton Professor, Columbia University

Maps by James MacDonald

LONGMANS, GREEN & CO.
NEW YORK · LONDON · TORONTO
1956

LONGMANS, GREEN AND CO., INC.
55 FIFTH AVENUE, NEW YORK 3

LONGMANS, GREEN AND CO. LTD.
6 & 7 CLIFFORD STREET, LONDON W 1

LONGMANS, GREEN AND CO.
20 CRANFIELD ROAD, TORONTO 16

77237

NARRATIVES OF EXPLORATION AND ADVENTURE

PUBLISHED SIMULTANEOUSLY IN THE DOMINION OF CANADA BY
LONGMANS, GREEN AND CO., TORONTO

FIRST EDITION

LIBRARY OF CONGRESS CATALOG CARD NUMBER 56-7867

Printed in the United States of America

Preface

"It appears to be no more than a just tribute to your exertions," wrote J. J. Abert, head of the Topographical Bureau, to Frémont on April 26, 1843, "that I should express my great personal pleasure as well as official satisfaction with your report which has now been printed, reflecting credit . . . upon your good taste as well as intelligence. It is by efforts like these that officers elevate their own character while they also render eminent public service; and while they also contribute to the standing and usefulness of their particular branch of service. Perseverance in the course you have commenced cannot fail to lead to distinction. . . ." This commendation of young Frémont's report on his first trans-Missouri expedition, that through South Pass to the Wind River chain of the Rockies, is part of the extensive correspondence between Frémont and Abert in the National Archives. On one side the letters show Frémont making careful estimates of costs for his work (low estimates, too; that for the second expedition, 1842–43, was only $10,500); buying materials—chronometers, sextants, barometers, drawing instruments; recruiting his parties; and worrying about his map work. He was obviously a strange combination of impulsive enterprise and businesslike caution, the enterprise predominating. On the other side the letters show the Bureau giving him singularly vague directions, exhibiting a certain nervousness about his headstrong traits, and taking marked pride in his achievements.

Much was expected of Frémont; he always accomplished more than was anticipated. It is illuminating to compare the Topographical Bureau's "Sketch of Duties" for his second trans-Missouri expedition with the actual result. Abert's instructions (March 10, 1843) ran:

To proceed to the main forks of the Kansas river, determine their position, and thence survey the main stream to its head. From the head of the

v

Kansas to fall directly on to the Arkansas and survey it to its head, crossing the mountains by that prong which forms the *boundary between the
United States and Mexico.* Continuing along the western base of the
mountains and crossing the heads of all the streams which take their rise
in that portion of the mountains, join on to your positions of 1842 on the
Colorado of the Gulf of Mexico. Thence continuing northwestwardly
across the waters of the Columbia, turn westwardly into the Flat-Head
country, and join on to Lieut. Wilkes's Survey. From that point to return
by the *Oregon road,* and on again reaching the mountains, diverge a little
and make a circuit of the Wind River chain, which is about eighty miles
long. This circuit would embrace within its limits the heads of the
Colorado, the Columbia, some of the heads of the Missouri proper, the
Yellowstone and the Platte.

But Frémont, responsive to the wishes of an expansionist group of
Western senators, did not tamely return from the Columbia River
by the Oregon Trail. Instead, with both political and geographical
motives, he boldly proceeded southward, mapped an unknown ter-
rain, and by a reckless winter passage of the Sierras entered Alta
California, ultimately coming back by a route of his own. His report
on this second journey created a sensation, and was circulated in
uncounted thousands of copies both as a Congressional document
and as a book issued by various publishers.

Doubtless it is because of the wide currency of Frémont's *Report
of the Exploring Expedition to the Rocky Mountains in the Year
1842, and to Oregon and North California in 1843–44,* as the book
combining his accounts of his first two Far Western tours was called,
that his graphic record of his journeys has found no modern re-
publication. He made five trans-Missouri expeditions in all. Of the
first two he wrote official reports; the third he described in full
in his *Memoirs of My Life* (1886); the fourth and fifth he left without record, though S. N. Carvalho has given us a graphic narrative
of the last. All editions of the reports have become somewhat difficult to obtain, and the *Memoirs* are rarely found. The time seemed
ripe for a volume which would combine the reports, the relevant
material in the *Memoirs,* and the important description of the Great
Basin in Frémont's *Geographical Memoir* accompanying the Frémont-Preuss map of that region, in one consecutive record of his
explorations. This record will, it is hoped, be as interesting to the
general reader as it is valuable to the student.

I have attempted to present an accurate text, with footnotes which will elucidate certain of its more difficult features. Frémont's own treatment of capitalization and italics, and even at times his spelling of proper names, is far from uniform; I have therefore felt justified in reducing them to a general modern form. I have searched the National Archives and other repositories in vain for the sketchbooks mentioned on page 75. For a fuller commentary on the explorations than it has been possible to furnish in the introduction and the notes, the reader is referred to my book, *Frémont: Pathmarker of the West.*

ALLAN NEVINS

Contents

Frémont as an Explorer

by Allan Nevins

ROLLING plains covered with dry bunch grass stretch for miles on every side. Far on the northern horizon lifts an enormous square-topped butte, giving individuality to that quarter of the landscape. Westward, faint in the distance but brought into hard relief as the sun sets, are penciled the snowy peaks of an isolated mountain chain; and close inspection shows that near their base the country dips into a narrow valley, with cottonwoods indicating a stream whose waters are fed by these distant summits. Nowhere is any sign of life or motion visible except that on the south, far along the rolling swells, certain black specks slowly change their position, sometimes coagulating into a mass, sometimes scattering widely; they are buffalo. It is an uninhabited, untraversed country, bare of track or meaning—a page on which the first hieroglyphs of history are still to be inscribed.

In this solitude suddenly appears a party of thirty men, moving slowly on foot, and leading a larger number of animals; some horses with saddlebags, more of them pack mules and pack ponies laden with all kinds of gear from tents to frying pans. At a distance the group, tattered, dusty, burned black by the sun, wild-looking, might be taken for dismounted Tatars or Beduins. They are long-haired, gaunt, and hawk-eyed. But their arms are short carbines, with heavy knives and revolvers at their belts; and close at hand, it is plain that apart from a few Indians assisting as guides, they are Americans. Most of them speak English, some a French patois. They are all young; all steel-muscled and determined-looking; all alert and disciplined—no straggling is permitted. At their head walks a lithe, well-proportioned man, clad in deerskin shirt, blue army trousers, and thick-soled moccasins, with a cotton handkerchief bound around his head. His remarkable feature is not his curling

1

black beard, aquiline nose, or high forehead, and not even his piercing eyes, but his air of intense energy.

What was the true character, and what the precise training, of John Charles Frémont as he thus appeared on the Western stage? He described himself as an officer of topographical engineers. What was the history of this special corps, and what were its functions? He obviously had various duties in relation to such a landscape as we have described. Was he simply to wander through it, take some random notes on hills and watercourses, jot down the state of the weather, and camp and cook buffalo meat whenever he felt tired? If that were so, we might wonder at the fact that his name has been given to so long and varied a list of places—rivers, peaks, counties, towns, streets—in the United States. What relation did he bear to exploring expeditions before him and after him?

I

The character of John Charles Frémont has been much misapprehended. He has usually been described as of a romantic temperament. But although the romance of his career, with its unending adventure and wild vicissitudes of golden and leaden fortune, can hardly be exaggerated, and although the quality of common-sense tough-minded judgment sometimes deserted him, he was essentially steady, patient, and industrious. Particularly as an explorer he was painstaking and persistent. Few men were better inured to drudgery and hardship. He had dash and brilliance, to be sure, but he made his way upward in his profession primarily by close application and sheer toil. Another common misapprehension paints him as flamboyant, fond of the dramatic, and eager for publicity. Nothing could be further from the fact. He was, in reality, a man of quiet, retiring temper; using few words, and specially averse to talking of himself; anxious to play his part, but inclined to underrate his accomplishments.

Even that unsympathetic observer Josiah Royce found reserve a principal characteristic, and speaks of his "gracious and self-possessed bearing." S. N. Carvalho, the gifted painter, daguerreotypist, and writer who accompanied him on his fifth expedition, emphasizes the same trait. "I found him reserved, almost to taciturnity," he writes, adding later:

It is worthy of remark that in all the varied scenes of vicissitude, of suffering and excitement, from various causes, during a voyage when the natural character of a man is sure to be developed, Col. Frémont never forgot he was a gentleman; not an oath, no boisterous ebullitions of temper, when, heaven knows, he had enough to excite it, from the continued blunders of the men. Calmly and collectedly, he gave his orders, and they were invariably fulfilled to the utmost of the men's abilities. . . .

Although on the mountains and away from civilization, Col. Frémont's lodge was sacred from all and everything that was immodest, light or trivial; each and all of us entertained the highest regard for him. The greatest etiquette and deference were always paid to him, although he never ostensibly required it. Yet his reserved and unexceptionable deportment demanded from us the same respect with which we were always treated, and which we ever took pleasure in reciprocating.

Professional assiduity, readiness to endure any amount of monotonous hard work, deprivation, and exhaustion, unusual self-control—these were traits of Frémont that we should not allow his many adventures, and the picturesqueness of the scenes in which he moved, to obscure. Other qualities, however, some of them virtues and some grave faults, come nearer the core of his personality.

He was a lover of action, a man of intensely kinetic temperament, craving outdoor pursuits as much as did William Clark or Kit Carson; as restless, in fact, as any frontiersman. In boyhood he had snatched pleasure from risks in the waters around Charleston from which most lads would have recoiled. He had ardently turned from professional opportunities—the pulpit, the bar—to the joys of surveying in the forested valleys and mountains of the southern Appalachians. He loved to sail, to ride, to climb, to swim, to skate, to spend his time with dogs and horses. He was a marksman of such unerring eye that he could kill a weasel at twenty paces with a sightless pistol. His hearing was so acute that when, in Indian country, a man in his camp snapped a cap of his gun, "the quick ear of Col. Frémont" caught it at a distance, and he came up instantly with a merited rebuke. It is significant that Carson, like that other expert frontiersman Alexis Godey, regarded him with deferential respect. To both he was as efficient a man of action as they could desire—and in addition a scientist. Godey speaks of "his daring energy, his indomitable perseverance, and his goodness of heart." Carson writes that he shared indescribable hardships with Frémont

from 1842 to 1847, "and the credit which he deserves I am incapable
to do him justice in writing."

This passion for activity in the open gave him a single-minded
devotion to the work of exploration. As he put it in his *Memoirs,*
his life was of his own choosing, "occupied in one kind of work, and
had one chief aim." It was "full of purpose." It completely failed to
train him for the stern tasks of civilized communities; for politics,
war, and business, which he later confronted, and in which he
lamentably failed. He admits that he was unequipped to deal with
"the poisoned atmosphere and jarring circumstances of conflict
among men, made subtle and malignant by clashing interests." But
because his Western labors had a congenial simplicity he could
throw into them his whole heart. His love of action found just the
theater he wanted:

. . . .The obstacles which I had to encounter were natural ones, and
I could calculate unerringly upon the amount of resistance and injury I
should have to meet in surmounting them. Their very opposition roused
strength to overcome them. The grand mountains stood out fairly in
their armor of ice and snow; the sterile face of the desert warned the
traveler off; and if he ventured there it was with full knowledge of his
danger. No treachery lurked behind the majesty of the mountain or lay
hidden in the hot glare of the inhospitable plain. And though sometimes
the struggle was hard, it was an honest one and simple; and I had my
own free will how to combat it. There was always the excitement which
is never without pleasure, and it left no griefs behind.

His years of exploration, 1838–54, from the time he was twenty-
five until he was forty-one, did not cultivate in him the qualities of
a thinker or even those of a careful planner. They did not give him
breadth or insight in dealing with complex human situations. Nor
did they greatly curb the impetuosity that was one of his marked
defects—which as a young man led him to risk and almost lose the
records of his first independent expedition (1842) by trying to
descend the rapids of the flooded Platte in a rubber boat, and which
as a much older man caused him to issue one of the most injudicious
proclamations of the Civil War. He had inherited from one or both
of his parents—the erratic, artistic French émigré who was his
father, the unhappy Virginia girl who was his mother—a certain
opportunism which, as in so many greater men, flawed his general

integrity. But these years of exploration did most happily use his abounding energy, his quick mind, his scientific aptitudes, and his tremendous enthusiasm for nature.

Of all our American explorers, no other had anything like his zest for the work he was doing: a zest compounded of delight in wild scenes, excited hope of new discoveries, and the thrill of peril. He makes us share his pride in his instruments; a specially fine thermometer, for example, raises bright anticipations of experiments in determining altitudes. He first sees the northern Rockies with a throb of elation: "I looked forward to an exploration of their snowy recesses with great pleasure." He lies long awake in his camp on the shores of Great Salt Lake enjoying "the strangeness of our situation, and the excitement we felt in the associated interest of the place." When he descended into California after his midwinter passage of the Sierras, he writes that the evergreen trees, the singing birds, and the sweet summer wind "nearly intoxicated us with delight."

Scene after scene he draws with captivating gusto; for example, a landscape in southern Oregon which still bears the names he gave it. The party had traveled through a gloomy pine forest clogged with three feet of crusted snow, the air dark with another heavy, gusty snowfall. Suddenly they came to the verge of a vertical precipice of rock:

At our feet—more than a thousand feet below—we looked into a green prairie country, in which a beautiful lake, some twenty miles in length, was spread along the foot of the mountains, its shores bordered with green grass. Just then the sun broke out among the clouds, and illuminated the country below, while around us the storm raged fiercely. Not a particle of ice was to be seen on the lake, nor snow on its borders, and all was like summer or spring. The glow of the sun in the valley below brightened up our hearts with sudden pleasure; and we made the woods ring with joyful shouts to those behind; and gradually, as each came up, he stopped to enjoy the unexpected scene. Shivering on snow three feet deep, and stiffening in a cold north wind, we exclaimed at once that the names of Summer Lake and Winter Ridge should be applied to these two proximate places of such sudden and violent contrast.

His feeling for landscape, for trees and flowers, and for wild life sometimes blended in one rapturous whole. Thus he describes one unexplored glade in the Rockies with a rich undergrowth of plants, and numerous flowers in brilliant bloom—"a place to delight the heart of a botanist"; beavers and mallard ducks in the stream; small brown squirrels leaping about in the branches; and air fragrant with pine. "I realized this delightful morning the pleasure of breathing that mountain air which makes a constant theme of the hunter's praise, and which now made us feel as if we had been drinking some exhilarating gas." His record is filled with sunlight. The toil, the discomfort, the danger, never dull his quick, sentient pleasure in the wild, the new, and the beautiful.

Gifted as Frémont was with this dynamic, exuberant temper, it was the more creditable to him that in fields of knowledge connected with his calling he was a model of application. He felt from childhood, as he writes, a love of mathematics. He was a close student of botany, who long after his exploring days were over delighted to go on botanical excursions in the Hudson Valley. He made himself a good geologist, collecting specimens with discrimination, and taking special pride in some types, such as rocks showing fossil infusoria. Of his mastery of the difficult art of topographical surveying, and his partial mastery of cartography, more will be said later. He did enough general reading and enough work in Greek and Latin to form a sound literary style—in later years he even wrote verse. Only a well-read man, on reaching San Francisco Bay, would have given the "Golden Gate" its name, with the Greek equivalent; would have spoken of a narrow Rocky Mountain pass with hot springs as "this Thermopylae of the West"; or would have written of an old woman of the Snake tribe as "desirous, like Naomi of old, to return to her people." When he saw wide scattered columns of smoke sent up in the Nevada desert by alarmed Indians, he knew something of which most early explorers were ignorant: "It is a signal of ancient and very universal application among barbarians."

It was also creditable to Frémont that with his zest in exploration he united the qualities of a sound disciplinarian. While this fact must be read between the lines of his narrative, it is perfectly plain. His expeditions moved by fixed hours and rules. To be up at daybreak, the animals grazing (if possible) while the men snatched a quick breakfast; to march all day; to camp an hour before sunset, giving the animals that much more time to pasture; to put the packs under rubber cloths or other shelter; to stack the rifles, muzzles tied together, a knife laid on the rope to cut it if an alarm occurred; to place a three-man guard, relieved every two hours—these were the primary regulations. Frémont trained the men in firing at marks; he assigned the tasks—this man to cook, that to hunt, another to gather fuel. Carvalho, Godey, and others testify that he was singularly successful in preventing quarrels and maintaining a healthy morale, and that he took care to share all specially dirty or risky tasks.

Meticulous carefulness and industry were part of his discipline, for he himself bore the heaviest responsibilities. As chief scientific observer he was often awake at midnight making astronomical calculations, his feet freezing in slush and snow, his face cut by a parching wind, and awake again while the morning stars still shone brilliantly. He had to write the journal, no matter how cold, tired, or hungry he might be. He was the chief medical officer. He was responsible for every piece of government equipment, every animal, every human life. One evidence of his carefulness is that he took a small cart for carrying instruments from the Missouri to the very foot of Mount Hood. "In all our long traveling," he writes, "it had never been overturned or injured by any accident of the road." When any emergency occurred, from a flight of the camp animals to an impromptu negotiation with the Indians, he had to meet it.

Carvalho makes much of his humanity; "the finer feelings of his heart seemed to govern all his actions, as well towards man as beast." One of his rules was never to shoot an animal except for food or scientific examination. His attitude toward Indians was exceptionally considerate. In the Oregon-California expedition of 1843–44 he reached a Shoshone camp and, needing food, sent several men to trade tobacco, cloth, knives, and other articles for it. But the tribe had no game and few roots. "Several of the Indians drew aside their blankets, showing me their lean and bony figures; and I would not any longer tempt them with a display of our merchandise to part with their wretched subsistence."

He showed always a peaceable mien, and on one occasion forbade any reprisal even upon irresponsible young braves who had talked of killing white emigrants. Kit Carson was always quick enough to kill, and we repeatedly read of white trappers who slew Indians as a form of sport. Frémont, however, was struck with pity by the wretched lot of some tribes. Describing the miserable Indians near Fort Boise, who lived on salmon in summer but often died of outright starvation in winter, he adds: "Many little accounts and scattered histories, together with an acquaintance which I gradually acquired with their mode of life, had left the aboriginal inhabitants of this vast region pictured in my mind as a race of people whose great and constant occupation was the means of procuring a subsistence." At the Falls of the Oregon he made an old man a generous present of tobacco, "and was struck with the impression which my unpropitiated notice made on the Indians"; they hastened to assure him he need no longer guard his animals. His sketch of the Klamath Indians strikes a note of compassion, and still more does that of the Diggers in the Nevada sagebrush wastes:

From all that I saw and heard, I should say that humanity here appeared in its lowest form, and in its most elementary state. Dispersed in single families; without firearms; eating seeds and insects; digging roots (and hence their name)—such is the condition of the greater part. Others are a degree higher, and live in communities upon some lake or river that supplies fish, and from which they repulse the miserable Digger. The rabbit is the largest animal known in this desert; its flesh affords a little meat; and their baglike covering is made of its skins. The wild sage is their only wood. . . . It serves for fuel, for building material, for shelter to the family, and for some sort of covering for the feet and legs in cold weather.

Another trait of character, which partly accounts for the gusto he brought to exploration, was intellectual curiosity. His wide range of interests gives his reports no small part of their value, and inspires a wish that he had indulged still more frequently in divagatory comment.

Sometimes he deals with amusing trivia, like the shades of meaning attached to the words "butte," "knob," and "cerro." Sometimes he turns to economic geography, as in the entry for August 30, 1843, discussing the wide range of the buffalo in the 1820s, their subsequent diminution and almost complete disappearance from the Pacific slopes, and the numbers annually slain in recent times. Sometimes his disquisitions have a political interest, as in the paragraph for May 23, 1844, on the importance of keeping the Columbia River under the American flag. Having little power of abstract thought, Frémont seldom indulges in theories or generalizations. Now and then, nevertheless, an incisive sentence goes straight to its mark, as in his statement on the character of the more treacherous Indians: "Like tigers, their first spring is the dangerous one."

Finally, and in some ways most importantly, Frémont developed an imaginative largeness of outlook which lifted him quite above the level of a plodding though efficient army officer like Zebulon M. Pike. Possessing an eye for grand geographical features, he never let the trees obscure the forest. Without this trait, he would not have been the first to name and describe the Great Basin. It was developed rather than bred in him, however, and to understand it we must turn to a fuller view of his training.

II

From Charleston College, which he left in 1831 without quite completing his work, but where he was well grounded in mathematics and the classics, he went on a naval cruise to South America, teaching midshipmen; then he helped survey a railway route in the Carolina and Tennessee mountains; immediately thereafter he accompanied his superior in the United States Topographical Corps (to which the influential Joel R. Poinsett got him appointed) in a military reconnaissance of the Cherokee country in Georgia. This was all good practice. He learned much of surveying, mapping, and woodcraft. But his tuition really began when in 1838 he was made assistant to a distinguished scientist, J. N. Nicollet, who had been chosen by the War Department to execute a scientific examination of the wide plateau between the Upper Mississippi and the Upper Missouri.

This brought Frémont under the influence of the vital French tradition in topographical studies. In Great Britain and France alike military and civil engineering had developed side by side, fostered by the government for defensive purposes. Henry VIII had employed numerous engineers, some of eminence; Charles II had increased the English engineering force, and had made the chief engineer Surveyor-General of the King's Works; in the eighteenth

century British military engineering had become very important
both in the motherland and North America. The Indian engineers
(under first the East India Company, later the Crown) were to
write a lustrous page in exploration, surveying, mapping, and civil
works. Meanwhile, in France Vauban in 1690 had founded the Corps
de Génie, which became the best body of military engineers anywhere. The principal French school of civil engineering, the Ecole
des Ponts et Chaussées, had been established in Paris in 1747, and
placed twenty-one years later in the quarters (Hôtel de Fleury)
where it still flourishes.

Nicollet, the brilliant Savoyard whose mathematical talents lifted
him from poverty (he was a herdsmen's son) to modest fame in the
France of Napoleon while he was still only in his twenties, was not
a product of the great Ecole; he had been lucky to get a scholarship
in a provincial college at Cluses. But when he went to Paris, becoming secretary and librarian of the Observatory in 1817, he knew
many of its staff and graduates. A little later, made an astronomical
assistant in the Bureau of Longitude, he was temporarily immersed
in the French government service, and in touch with all its scientific activities. Europe had no scientist who knew more about means
of making mathematics, astronomy, and meteorology useful to
mariner, explorer, and civil engineer. When he suddenly determined
to emigrate to the United States in 1832, he was received by scientific circles as well as French families as a man of high distinction.
In 1836 the officers at Fort Snelling were delighted to assist him in
traveling to the Upper Mississippi and in studying the Chippewa;
and the next year Poinsett, now Secretary of War, invited him to
Washington.

The methods he used in his government survey of the Minnesota
and Dakota country in 1838–39 are interestingly set forth in his
*Report Intended to Illustrate a Map of the Hydrographical Basin
of the Upper Mississippi River* (1843). As they were in advance of
the methods used by previous government and private expeditions
in America, Frémont was fortunate to be the chief assistant of so
skilled a teacher.

Nicollet was the first explorer to make careful use of the barometer in calculating interior altitudes in America. Fortin's barometer,
improving upon the instrument long before invented by Torricelli,

had not come into use until early in the nineteenth century—the earliest barometer easily portable. The still better Kew barometer was yet to come. "Now that science has placed within the reach of everybody the admirable instrument known as the barometer," writes Nicollet in his report, "has rendered it so applicable to the measurement of heights, and has so perfected it as to be capable of results whose precision can be all that is desired, observations by it are being multiplied everywhere." But he hastened to add that its use was far from easy:

There is, in fact, a crowd of considerations to be reflected upon, of attentions and care to be given, arising from and dependent upon the construction of the instruments employed, and on the circumstances in which the observer finds himself placed—particularly which cannot be foreseen, much less prescribed in advance—that he only can estimate, and without the due estimation of which, observations apparently well made are in reality good for nothing.

A user of the barometer, he continued, must know every part of the instrument, and be ready to repair it, however inadequate his facilities, if necessary. (Frémont's ingenious repair of a broken barometer by scraping thin a buffalo horn and bending it in tubular form to replace the glass exemplifies Nicollet's point.) He must, Nicollet says, be familiar with all the meteorological laws relating to these instruments, so that when variations occur, he will know which are periodic, which accidental. He must be able to apply corrections as between syphon and cistern barometers. He must exercise sleepless care of his treasures. "Indeed, chronometers and barometers are inexhaustible sources of anxiety for the traveling geographer. I do not know moments of greater annoyance then those when one finds a chronometer stopped, or a barometer broken, just when he is about confidently to use them." How many notes of worry over his instruments Frémont interjects into his narratives!

And when the time comes for final calculations, Nicollet writes, tedious analysis is required. "In this the correspondence and simultaneity of readings have to be settled; care must be taken to compare with one another only those observations made under conditions of the atmosphere as nearly as may be similar."

But compared with some other tasks, barometrical observations were easy. The scientific explorer had constantly to ascertain the azimuth (point or quarter of the horizon), the time, the latitude, and the longitude. He had to make exact observations on geology, botany, ornithology, and zoology. He had to note the weather, with precise temperatures. He had to collect specimens—the right specimens. He had to make contributions to ethnology by notes on Indian life. If he were worth his literary salt (and few were), he had to record scenes and incidents that would commend his narrative to the general reader. In short, he had to be alert to everything all the time.

On all this Nicollet, supplementing others, gave quickly absorbed lessons to the ardent young Frémont. Never did scientist have a more eager learner. The best mode of ascertaining the true time, Nicollet writes, "is to measure the absolute altitudes of the sun, or of some principal stars, taken both east and west of the meridian of the spot where the observation is made." Two or three series of observations are requisite, the stars being selected "to fulfill the theoretical conditions required for good hour-angles." Of course for two or three series, the sentries must awaken the tired observer; and precise detailed calculations must follow. But to determine time in this way, the azimuth must be known. And so must the latitude, for without it the hour-angle of the spherical triangle could not be ascertained.

To find the latitude, Nicollet informs us, two good series of observations should be taken in the course of the night, "one to the north, the other to the south of the zenith, and each of from ten to fifteen readings." But it was important to observe the stars in pairs of nearly equal distance, north and south, for this eliminated constant instrumental errors. Then, using the tables in the *Ephemerides of the Heavens*, and applying due corrections for refraction, the result would be trustworthy. Most difficult of all was the determination of longitude. Some methods required a theodolite, impossible to use on long expeditions. Nicollet preferred telescopic observations of occultations (roughly, eclipses) of the planets and the fixed stars by the moon, or observations of the eclipses of the satellites of Jupiter, which is blessed with eleven moons. Once more the *Ephemerides* was used. The astronomical telescope had to be very good; the observations had to be extremely precise; the time had to be exact, for any error was translated into longitudinal error. All long exploring expeditions, including Frémont's, ran into trouble with longitude, chiefly because the chronometers became inexact.

It will be seen that measurements of time, place, distance, and direction, the basic elements of exploration, were exceedingly difficult. But not only was exploration largely worthless without them; life itself might depend on their accurate determination. On his fifth expedition Frémont, deep in January snows east of the Wasatch Range, sent an experienced Delaware to reconnoiter possible paths ahead. He returned in gloom, saying that all were impossible. "We *must* cross," quietly replied Frémont. "The question is how." Writes Carvalho:

After the council, Col. Frémont told me there would be an occultation that night, and he wanted me to assist in making observations. I selected a level spot on the snow and prepared the artificial horizon. The thermometer indicated a very great degree of cold; and standing almost up to our middle in snow, Col. Frémont remained for hours making observations, first with one star, then with another, until the occultation took place. Our lantern was illuminated with a piece of sperm candle. . . .

The next morning, Col. Frémont told me that Parowan, a small settlement of Mormons, forty rods square, in the Little Salt Lake Valley, was distant so many miles in a certain direction, immediately over this great mountain of snow; that in three days he hoped to be in the settlement, and that he intended to go over the mountain, at all hazards.

With terrible toil, they beat out a path over and through the Wasatch Mountains, Frémont leading. And, writes Carvalho:

On the very day and hour previously indicated by Col. Frémont, he conducted us to the small settlement of Parowan, in Little Salt Lake Valley, which could not be distinguished two miles off, thus proving himself a most correct astronomer and geometrician. Here was no chance work—no guessing—for a deviation of one mile, either way, from the true course would have plunged the whole party into certain destruction. An island at sea may be seen for forty miles. . . . Not so with a winter travel over trackless mountains of eternal snow, across a continent of such immense limits, suffering the privations of cold and hunger, and enervated by disease. It seems as if Col. Frémont had been endowed with supernatural powers of vision, and that he had penetrated with his keen and powerful eye through the limits of space, and saw the goal to which all his powers had been concentrated to reach.

But we return to Nicollet and his tuition. His report shows that he made careful observations, Frémont assisting, of physical geography—Frémont drew many sketches for him; that he took fairly expert notes on geology; and that he recorded as much as possible of Indian life and Indian place names. He knew little about botany, but Charles Geyer went with Nicollet's party to fill that gap, bringing back collections which Dr. John Torrey, long an eminent figure at Princeton and in the College of Physicians and Surgeons in New York, catalogued. From Geyer, too, whom the generous Nicollet employed at his own expense, Frémont learned a great deal.

When the Nicollet expedition ended, young Frémont became a working member of a small scientific group in Washington which taught him more than he could have gained from the laboratories and seminars of a great modern university. It is clear that the lonely bachelor Nicollet looked on Frémont almost as a son. He took the young man on a vacation to Baltimore. Then the two became housemates of the Swiss-born scientist Ferdinand Rudolph Hassler, trained at the University of Berne, an old-time friend of Jefferson, and the virtual founder of the Coast Survey. Frémont listened to the endless discussions between Nicollet and Hassler on mathematics, astronomy, topography, and other subjects; Hassler abrupt and dogmatic, Nicollet polite and flexible—"the one flint and the other steel, fire flashing out in every argument." In the observatory atop Hassler's house the three—often joined by J. J. Abert, head of the Topographical Corps—spent endless hours in observations and calculations. "Frémont and I have had eleven good series of astronomical observations this week," Nicollet once wrote.

Out of the partnership of Nicollet and Frémont grew the map that the former bound with his *Report*; "one of the greatest contributions ever made to American geography," writes Lieutenant G. K. Warren in his history of Western explorations before 1855.

III

It was a marvelous training for a scientific explorer, at once precise and broad; far better than that which West Point at this time gave young officers of the Topographical Corps. Granting that great explorers are born, not made—David Livingstone had but a medical education—we must nevertheless regard training as important. Frémont was as well equipped as any predecessor and better than most, and should in some respects have improved upon their work. What comparisons can we draw between his achievements and those of others?

Lewis and Clark are in a sense *hors concours,* defying rivalry. They had the advantage of being the first comers in most of the great area they traversed. They were men not merely of exceptional gifts, but of complementary talents—Clark the administrator, engineer, and practiced woodsman, Lewis the scientist, artist, and writer. Each, nevertheless, was versatile and adaptable. Though Clark was the more experienced frontiersman, Jefferson correctly says in his memoir of Lewis that the latter was "intimate with the Indian character, customs, and principles; habituated to the hunting life; guarded by exact observation of the vegetables and animals of his own country against losing time in the description of objects already possessed; honest, disinterested, liberal, of sound understanding, and a fidelity to truth so scrupulous that whatever he should report would be as certain as if seen by ourselves." Jefferson adds that "he possesses a great mass of accurate observation on all the subjects of observation which present themselves." Both had served in the army, fighting the Indians under Anthony Wayne.

As scientific explorers they set a mark which Frémont—who undoubtedly read with admiring care both Patrick Gass's *Journal* of the expedition (1807 and later editions) and Nicholas Biddle's *History* of it (1814 and later)—might well envy. They made careful observations of temperature and weather; records of the miles traveled; and notes on flora and fauna. Lewis in particular wrote descriptions of the natural scenery—for example, the Great Falls of the Missouri—possessing vividness and charm. They drew outline maps, plans, and miscellaneous sketches of high value. They were keenly observant of Indian customs, dress, and economy; Lewis's description of how an Indian teepee was made, erected, and used is almost a model piece of exposition. They took skins of some animals not before known—a badger, for example—and described others so closely that identification became easy. They collected botanical and geological specimens.

Lewis and Clark stand at the head of our explorers; but (and it is no derogation of their merits to say this—they suffered from some unescapable limitations. Their scientific instruments—only a sextant, a chronometer, and a spirit-level—and their mathematical and astronomical knowledge were alike inadequate for the accurate fixing of positions. Of necessity their measurements of distance were rough. A comparison of their record for one stretch of 210 miles—from Whitebear Island in the Missouri to the junction of the Madison and Jefferson rivers—with the measurements made by the Missouri River Commission, shows that they exaggerated the distance by twenty per cent. Their smattering of geology being slight, their interest in it was restricted. They passed over areas rich in gold and silver, the region of the Montana gold rush, without noting the gold flecks in the sands and the nuggets on the bars. They had no such knowledge of botany as Geyer taught Frémont. After all, they were pathbreakers; specialized work had to come later.

Zebulon M. Pike, too, was a pathbreaker, one whose much greater deficiencies were partly beyond his control. His bold Southwestern expedition of 1805–07 had in view an apparent object, the reconnoitering of Spanish borderlands for the benefit of a possible future American expeditionary force, which was not scientific, and which he could not avow in the book he later published. Probably he was not displeased when the Spanish authorities seized him and sent him from the Rio Grande down to Chihuahua. But Pike's narrative (1810), compared with Frémont's, is scientifically thin and literarily dull. He had no instruments to reckon latitude or longitude; no talent for map making; no real interest in wild life—little beyond a narrow military outlook. His descriptions of natural scenes are flatter than the Llanos Estacados of the Texas Panhandle. Compare Frémont's stirring account of the Royal Gorge of the Arkansas with the single sentence which Pike gives that magnificent gateway: "I marched for about five miles on the river, which was one continued fall through a narrow channel and immense cliffs on both sides."

This ill-educated army officer had his qualities; an extraordinary man, he was bravery itself, as he showed by dying later on the field of battle. But though he blazed one of the trails that multitudes of emigrants were to follow, he was no important explorer. He even lost his way with facility. The Spanish officer who first intercepted him offered guides to the Red River. "What," exclaimed Pike in consternation, "is not *this* the Red River?" "No, sir," rejoined the officer. "It is the Rio Grande del Norte!"

More could be said for the expedition of Lewis Cass (then territorial governor of Michigan) in 1820 along the shores of Lake Superior and to the headwaters of the Mississippi, for objects partly political (he wished to treat with Indian tribes) and partly geographical. He suggested to the War Department that it give him an officer of engineers to make a correct chart, and "some person acquainted with zoology, botany, and mineralogy," the result being that Henry R. Schoolcraft and David B. Douglass accompanied him to care for these interests. Douglass made a handsome collection of plants for Dr. John Torrey to classify and describe; Schoolcraft penned an enthusiastic report on the resources of the country, calling special attention to the evidences of large iron and copper deposits. Though limited in extent, this was a highly successful piece of exploration—which failed, however, to discover the true source of the Mississippi.

Meanwhile, the Corps of Topographical Engineers (of which, curiously, no history has ever been written) had come into existence. Its origin dates from 1813, when topographical officers were first authorized by law, to be attached to the general staff of the Army. Ten officers were at once appointed. They worked at first in conjunction with the older Corps of Engineers (established 1802) in special charge of the fortifications of the country. Gradually, however, it became evident that two distinct engineering groups were needed, one for defense, and one for civil tasks—river and harbor work, roadmaking, and exploration. In 1831, therefore, the Topographical Bureau was made a distinct unit, to report directly to the Secretary of War and receive orders from him. Complaint soon arose that its functions and authority were vague. A new law of 1838 therefore gave the Topographical Corps clearer rank and form, and the War Department at once issued explicit regulations dividing civil engineering from military engineering. By 1843 the Corps of Engineers boasted of one colonel, one lieutenant colonel, four majors, and thirty-two lesser officers.

One Dartmouth-educated officer of this corps, Stephen H. Long, seemed for a time about to establish a reputation like that later made by Frémont. He had helped chart some Upper Mississippi Valley waters. Then, in 1819, the War Department assigned him to lead an expedition to the Rockies. He ascended the Platte and the South Platte the next year, discovered the peak that bears his name, and did valuable work in the upper valley of the Arkansas River. With him, as botanist, geologist, and surgeon, went Edwin James, a graduate of Middlebury College and a former student of John Torrey's. It was James who, with two companions, was the first white man to ascend Pikes Peak; and using notes furnished by Long, who made no report, James furnished a vigorous two-volume *Account* of the journey with an atlas. Though this contained some useful data on fauna and Indians, it failed to hit the mark at which it was aimed.

It did so for a reason which was probably not lost on Frémont, who undoubtedly read the volumes with care. Long and James gave an unfavorable description of the trans-Mississippi country, which chilled readers and furnished ammunition to Daniel Webster and other foes of rapid Western growth. The expansive American people demanded optimism, not pessimism. Long turned to railroad construction, which he made his real career. When Frémont first joined Nicollet in 1838, Long was chief engineer of the Atlantic & Great Western.

These were the principal scientific explorations of the West under government auspices—Lewis and Clark's, Pike's, Lewis Cass's, Long's, Nicollet's—thrown upon the record when Frémont, like a trained and eager athlete, strode forward to begin his independent work. Eager to surpass them all, he had some reason to believe he could do it. He was but twenty-eight in the year of his trial flight, the Des Moines survey, and but twenty-nine in that of his first expedition, 1842. He was brilliant of mind, ardent of heart, fearless of temper. He had made the most of half a dozen years of active training, and four years of superb tuition under Nicollet, Geyer, and Hassler. With the westward migration mounting like a torrent, and national expansion into California and Oregon a general hope, he could be sure of keen public interest in whatever he accomplished. His father-in-law Thomas Hart Benton and other men of power were ready to support him.

Other government explorers were still to come forward:—W. H.

Emory with his military reconnaissance of 1846–47; Howard Stansbury with his exploration of the Great Salt Lake region in 1849–50; R. B. Marcy with his work on the Red River in 1852; the men, including J. W. Gunnison and John Pope, who conducted the Pacific Railroad surveys of 1853–55. They were not destined to equal their predecessors. Of all those who came after Lewis and Clark, Frémont made much the greatest mark. How and why is it the greatest?

IV

Taking account merely of his first three expeditions, he covered much more ground than any other man. Without carrying along any special technical assistants except Charles Preuss on the second expedition as map maker, and E. M. Kern on the third or Oregon-California expedition as map maker and sketcher, he dealt with a wider range of scientific subjects, and treated them, in general, more expertly. He united practical with scientific objects, striving to give useful information to emigrants, traders, and travelers. He imparted to his reports a higher literary quality (to which his wife Jessie contributed) than any other man we have mentioned; Meriwether Lewis wrote vividly, and Howard Stansbury penned a colorful narrative which has been unjustly neglected, but they did not reach Frémont's consistent level. No other explorer after Lewis and Clark was half, nay, one-tenth as widely read or eagerly quoted; none exerted half as much influence on the westward exodus. In short, Frémont's exploratory work combined numerous types of excellence.

Any comparison of his reports with others brings his comprehensive scientific findings into clear distinction. Take his observations for four days, September 12, 13, 14, 17, 1843, just after leaving Great Salt Lake. He gives two calculations of longitude and latitude, with a record of the means used in making them. He furnishes the altitude of a peak, the altitude of the pass above Bear River, and Snake River, and the width and altitude of the Bannock River Valley. He identifies, with both English and Latin names, six varieties of trees found along Clear Creek, and one in the pass. He describes also a number of plants—"purple fields of *Eupatorium purpureum*, with helianthi, a handsome solidago (*Solidago canadensis*)," a thistle (*Circium Virginianum*) whose carrot-like roots the Indians were using for food, and the kooya plant, which he identifies as *Valeriana edulis.* He gives the temperature of some hot springs. He records thermometer readings at various hours, chiefly sunrise and sunset, but once at midnight. He notes significant bits of geology, as of the hot springs—"gushing out together, beneath a conglomerate, consisting principally of fragments of a grayish-blue limestone, efflorescing a salt." At eight points he inserts comments on the quality of the soil. Indeed, these four days include an emphatic statement on the fertility of the river-and-creek system in the Great Salt Lake area that powerfully swayed Brigham Young and the Mormons in their migration of 1846–47:

> The bottoms . . . form a natural resting and recruiting station for travelers, now, and in all time to come. The bottoms are extensive; water excellent; timber sufficient; the soil good, and well adapted to grains and grasses suited to such an elevated region. A military post, and a civilized settlement, would be of great value here, grass and salt so much abound. The lake will furnish exhaustless supplies of salt. All the mountains here are covered with a valuable nutritious grass, called bunch grass from the form in which it grows, which has a second growth in the fall. The beasts of the Indians were fat upon it; our own found it a good subsistence; and its quantity will sustain any amount of cattle, and make this truly a bucolic region.

These notes are typical of his reports as a whole. Can we wonder that such a work as Joseph E. Ware's *The Emigrants' Guide to California* (1849), much used in gold-rush days, was largely founded on Frémont's narratives, reproducing whole sentences verbatim? While Frémont's reports gave scientists a wealth of new information, they served also—circulated in tens of thousands of copies—as the readiest popular source of information on the trans-Missouri West.

Frémont submitted his botanical collections for his first and second expeditions, like Nicollet before him, to Dr. John Torrey, who in his descriptive catalogue (published by the Smithsonian) pays warm tribute to their value. He named a new genus of *Chenopodiaceae* for Frémont "as a well-merited compliment for the services he has rendered North American botany." [1] Torrey speaks of the "many

[1] It was Frémont who gave us our first description of two important western trees which bear his name, the Fremont cottonwood, which he calls the sweet cottonwood, because his animals could browse on its sweet inner bark, and the Frémont nut pine, often called the one-leaved nut pine. He was also the first writer in English to describe the Joshua tree.

interesting plants" he gathered. The geological specimens gathered in Oregon and California Frémont sent to James Hall, New York State Paleontologist, perhaps the greatest living master of stratigraphic geology. Hall's report commends Frémont not only for the care he took to collect suites of rocks of significant mineral and fossil content—"no survey of any unknown region should be made without at the same time preserving collections of the prevailing rocks, minerals, and fossils"—but for the precise geological information included in the Oregon-California report. "The attention given to this subject in the foregoing report renders the information of the highest value, and perfectly reliable in reference to opinions or calculations regarding the resources of the country." Hall was always chary of praise; but he named a new species of fossil fern for Frémont, "as a testimony of the benefits that science has derived from his valuable explorations on the west of the Rocky Mountains."

It should be added that Lieutenant G. K. Warren in his monograph on Western exploration terms the Frémont-Preuss map of the Oregon-California expedition one which "in most respects may serve as a model." This dry, exact government document for once grows warm in praising Frémont's general correctness in astronomical observations, and Preuss's skill in sketching topography in the field and representing it on the map. For a striking description of the methods used in cartographical work, the reader need only turn to page 75 of the present book.

It was Frémont who did most to dispel the impression, created by Long and others, that the trans-Missouri plains were barren. He writes repeatedly that the land is generally excellent, that water alone is needed, and that adequate moisture is often available. "The soil of all this country," he writes July 11, 1843—meaning the wide region between the Mississippi and the Rockies—"is excellent, admirably adapted to agricultural purposes, and would support a large agricultural and pastoral population." The first scientifically trained man to reach the shores of the Great Salt Lake, he supplied the earliest adequate account of it. He was first to reach Pilot Peak on a short cut across the Nevada desert upon the general line later defined as the Hastings Cutoff. He did some very real pathfinding in southern Oregon, northern California, and the Sierras. He was the first man, as Humboldt noted, to describe the volcanic character of certain Rocky Mountain areas, and to dilate on the vulcanicity of the Cascades.

His greatest geographical contribution, however, lay in his identification and description of the Great Basin, the huge region whose special peculiarity had escaped B. L. E. Bonneville and others. Frémont invented the term still used for the basin, or collection of small basins, between the Wasatch Range on the east and the Sierra on the west—a mountain-rimmed region with no outlet for its streams. Even yet, a better description of its major characteristics than that given by Frémont's reports (see especially October, 1843, and the *Geographical Memoir*) would be difficult to find. The image of the Great Basin haunted Frémont from the moment he first seized and broadly sketched it. He had explored much of its high periphery on the Utah, the northern, and the California sides. "It cannot be less than 400 or 500 miles each way," he writes, "and must lie principally in the Alta California [then including Nevada-Utah]. . . . Of its interior but little is known. It is called a desert, and from what I have seen of it, sterility may be its principal character; but where there is so much water, there must be some oasis."

Frémont's estimate of distances was fairly correct. The Sierras and the Wasatch, their steep faces fronting each other, lie 400 to 500 miles apart. The mountain and plateau country between is much eroded, but since the streams cannot run to the sea, the eroded materials fill the space between the barren peaks to a great depth. An artesian-well driller near Huxley, Nevada, has brought up well-preserved redwood from a depth of 1900 feet. During the glacial period, when rains were heavy, two great bodies of water filled the basin; one, covering much of present-day Nevada, now termed by geologists Lahontan Lake, the other in Utah (with Great Salt Lake its vestige) called Lake Bonneville. Frémont's reference to an oasis is echoed by modern writers who have called the settled fertile parts of Utah "an oasis at the foot of the Wasatch." When Humboldt in his final volume adopted the explorer's term, he remarked: "Our knowledge of this configuration is one of the chief points of Frémont's great hypsometrical investigations in 1843–44."

He fulfilled his youthful dream of assisting in "the opening up of unknown lands, the making unknown countries known." And his record of this fulfillment derives its appealing zest and vividness from the fact that, as he writes, "the learning at first hand from Nature herself, the drinking first at her unknown springs, became a source of never-ending delight to me."

V

While we cannot call Frémont a great man, we can maintain that as an explorer—the first distinctively scientific explorer produced by the United States—he had qualities of greatness. As the English student E. W. Gilbert says in *The Exploration of Western America 1800–1850*, his work can be ranked with that of Livingstone, Burton, and Sven Hedin. Alas that his career was warped into inferior channels, while he was yet in his early prime, by the Mexican War! The sun that rose so auspiciously on the well-equipped young man marching purposefully and joyously into the West of 1838 sank into the dust and commotion of California in 1846. The smoke of battle hid complications and frustrations that Frémont, turning back from Oregon on what he deemed an imperative summons, could never have guessed; and before it cleared away the quarrel with General S. W. Kearny had forced him from the Army and deprived him of government support in further exploration. His scientific labors were virtually ended, for the two privately equipped expeditions which he later led failed of significant results.

A new America emerged from the Mexican War, enlarged by one-third in extent, and faced by an exigent problem in tying East and Far West together by road, telegraph, and railway. It needed scientific explorers and map makers; it needed just such dedicated skill and rich experience as Frémont could have supplied. Had fate been kinder, he might have done much to examine the new resources, assist emigrants, and find the best paths of transcontinental commerce. All the glitter and adventure of his later career—the California Senatorship, the Mariposa fortune, the Republican Presidential nomination in 1856, the major-generalship in the Civil War, the railroad presidency—were a poor compensation for what he and the country lost. But the high achievement of the eight years, in which he not only kept the field of Western investigation but led it, remains a permanent possession; and his record of those years may be counted one of our proud American stories.

CHAPTER 1

Youth: A Railroad Survey:
The Cherokees *

Looking back over the years of the life which I am about to transfer to the blank pages before me, I see in its earlier part but few things worthy of note. The lights and shadows of schoolboy life are like April weather. There is much sunshine and the clouds pass quickly. Farther along the shadows darken and lengthen. But the current events which belong to early life make slight impressions and have no consequences. They do not extend their influence into

* The material of this chapter is from *Memoirs of My Life*, by John Charles Frémont, Belford, Clarke & Company, Chicago & New York, Vol. I (no other published), 1887, pp. 18–26. Frémont had reasons for passing rapidly over his earliest years and saying nothing of his parentage, for he was of illegitimate birth. His mother, Anne Beverley Whiting, had married a citizen of Richmond, Virginia, Major John Pryor, who was old enough to be her father; childless and unhappy, she eloped in July, 1811, with a Frenchman named Charles Frémon, who had painted frescoes and taught first in William and Mary College and then in a Richmond academy. This union with Frémon was permanent. John Charles, the first of their three children, was born in Savannah January 21, 1813. The family went to Nashville for a time, and then to Norfolk. In or about 1818, Frémon died; and John Charles's mother, in straitened circumstances, soon removed to Charleston, S. C., where the boy grew up.

Young Frémont (for a *t* had been added to the name) soon attracted attention by the brilliance of his mind, his physical quickness and vigor, and his charm of personality. As his story indicates, he was as impulsive as he was courageous, as rash as he was generous. At sixteen he was confirmed in St. Philip's Church, and his mother for a time hoped he would become an Episcopalian clergyman. A Charleston attorney, John W. Mitchell, met the cost of sending him to a preparatory school kept by Dr. Charles Robertson, the "Scotch gentleman" here mentioned. This was in 1827, and so rapid was the lad's progress in Latin, Greek, and mathematics that in 1829 he was admitted, as he says, to the junior class of Charleston College. Robertson years later described the youthful Frémont in enthusiastic terms. He was of "middle size, graceful in manners, rather slender, but well formed, and upon the whole what I should call handsome; of a keen piercing eye and a noble forehead, seemingly the very seat of genius." And Robertson added: "Whatsoever he read, he retained."

the time when life begins in earnest. Looking back over the misty road I dwell with mixed feelings upon the pictures that rise up in my memory. Not upon all with pleasure.

Yet they are part of myself and represent pleasant scenes and faces that were dear, now dim in the obscurity of years. But on these pages I recur only to those passages in my early life which had some connection with its after part and were a governing influence in it. Throughout, at different periods it has been my good fortune to be in familiar relations with men who were eminent, each in his own line, all of whom were individualized by character and some distinguished by achievement. Even if insensibly, such associations influence the course of life and give its coloring to it. The early part of mine was desultory. "The path that men are destined to walk" had not been marked out for me. Later events determined this, and meantime I had freedom of choice in preparatory studies.

At sixteen I was a good scholar. My teacher, who became my friend as well, was a Scotch gentleman who had been educated at Edinburgh; he was thoroughly imbued with classic learning, and lived an inner life among the Greeks and Latins. Under his enthusiastic instruction I became fond as himself of the dead languages, and to me also they became replete with living images. I entered upon the study of Greek with genuine pleasure and excitement. It had a mysterious charm for me as if behind the strange characters belonging to an ancient world I was to find things of wonderful interest. I loved to pore over the volumes of old Greek plays in their beautiful Edinburgh print that were among my teacher's cherished books, and the fresh ones that occasionally came to him from Scotland. Filled with the figures of that ancient world into which I had entered, they remain stamped as pleasing bits into the recollections of that time, and show how completely my mind was possessed by my work. The years spent in this way gave me habits of study and laid the foundation for a knowledge of modern languages which long afterward became valuable in important events.

Upon the strength of these studies I now entered at once into the junior class at the Charleston college, though far behind it in other branches and especially in mathematics. But this new field interrupted the close relations with my friend and teacher Dr. John

Robertson. Many years afterward, in reading the introduction to his translation of Xenophon's *Anabasis,* I had the pleasure to find him speaking of me as "his once beloved and favorite pupil—his prodigious memory and enthusiastic application."

I was fond of study, and in what I had been deficient easily caught up with the class. In the new studies I did not forget the old, but at times I neglected both. While present at class I worked hard, but frequently absented myself for days together. This infraction of college discipline brought me frequent reprimands. During a long time the faculty forbore with me because I was always well prepared at recitation, but at length, after a formal warning neglected, their patience gave way and I was expelled from college for continued disregard of discipline. I was then in the senior class. In this act there was no ill-feeling on either side. My fault was such a neglect of the ordinary college usages and rules as the faculty could not overlook and I knew that I was a transgressor.[1]

A few years afterward the faculty voluntarily revised their decision and conferred on me the degree of Bachelor and Master of Arts, so taking me back into the fold. Meantime I had my compensation. The college authorities had wrapped themselves in their dignity and reluctantly but sternly inflicted on me condign punishment. To me this came like summer wind, that breathed over something sweeter than the "bank whereon the wild thyme blows." I smiled to myself while I listened to words about the disappointment of friends—and the broken career. I was living in a charmed atmosphere and their edict only gave me complete freedom. What the poets dwell on as "the rarest flower of life" had bloomed in my path—only seventeen, I was passionately in love. This was what had made me regardless of discipline and careless of consequences. This was the true rebel that carried me off to pleasant days and returned me buoyant at night to hard work in order to catch up with my class next morning. With my memory full of those days, as the recollection rises to the surface I put it down here. This is an autobiography and it would not be true to itself if I left out the bit of sunshine that made the glory of my youth—what Schiller calls "his glorious youth." It is only a few lines, a tribute which as they reappear around me I give to the pleasant companions who made

[1] Numbered notes will be found at the end of the section.

life gay at that time. There will be enough hereafter of grave and hard, conflict and dissension, violence and injury and fraud; but none of these things were known to us, that little circle of sworn friends, who were gathering our spring flowers. We took no thought for the harvest but gathered our cornflowers from the upspringing grain.

I remember, once along the banks of the Des Moines, a botanist with me stooped down and grasped the clustered head of a low flowering plant. Under the broad leaves lay coiled a rattlesnake, close to his hand. Geyer escaped, but it gave him a spasm that made him dig his heels into the ground and jerk his arms nervously about as he threw off the shock.

Always afterward he looked for snakes among his flowers. With ours there were never any. Some thorns perhaps, as I had just found, but these go with the sweetest flowers.

Since I was fourteen years old I had been intimate with a Creole family who had escaped from the San Domingo massacre.[2] With the mother and grandmother, there were two boys and three girls. The elder of the boys was older than I, the girls all younger. The eldest of the three girls was Cecilia. They were all unusually handsome; clear brunette complexions, large dark eyes, and abundant blue-black hair.

The grandmother was the head of the family and its autocratrice. She was a tall, stern old woman, with iron-gray hair, over seventy years of age, and held absolute rule over us all, from the mother down. Often when the riot was at the highest or we had kept it up late, her sudden appearance would disperse us like a flock of quail. The house children would scamper off to bed and the visitors make a prompt escape. The house stood on a corner and there was a room at the rear which is daguerreotyped on my memory. This room opened directly on the street and belonged to us by squatters' right. It was by this door that we were accustomed to make a sudden exit when the grandmother made one too many for us.

But her ill humor of the moment never lasted until the next time came for us to meet. The severe lines imprinted on her face by trials, after repose had not smoothed away. But often when we were in full flight before her I have seen the lurking smiles break into a pleased laugh that cleared away the sternness. In a manner

I grew up with the children. Before and after I left college they, but especially one, were the companions with whom I was always happy to spend what time I could seize upon. The boys and I made a restless trio.

The days went by on wings. In the summer we ranged about in the woods, or on the now historic islands, gunning or picnicking, the girls sometimes with us; sometimes in a sailboat on the bay, oftener going over the bar to seaward and not infrequently when the breeze failed us getting dangerously near the breakers on the bar. I remember as in a picture, seeing the beads of perspiration on the forehead of my friend Henry as he tugged frantically at his oar when we had found ourselves one day in the suck of Drunken Dick, a huge breaker that to our eyes appeared monstrous as he threw his spray close to the boat. For us it really was pull Dick pull Devil.

Those were the splendid outside days; days of unreflecting life when I lived in the glow of a passion that now I know extended its refining influence over my whole life. The recollection of those days has never faded. I am glad that it was not required of me to come back as an enemy among those scenes.

This holiday time could not last, but it was beautiful, although I was conscious that I could not afford it. I had not entirely neglected my studies. Sometimes, seized with a temporary remorse for time lost I gathered up my books and overworked myself for awhile, only to relapse with keener zest into the more natural life.

The accidents that lead to events are often hardly noticeable. A single book sometimes enters fruitfully into character or pursuit. I had two such.[3] One was a chronicle of men who had made themselves famous by brave and noble deeds, or infamous by cruel and base acts. With a schoolboy's enthusiasm I read these stories over and over again, with alternate pleasure or indignation. I please myself in thinking they have sometimes exercised a restraining or inspiring influence. Dwelling in the memory they were like the ring of Amasis.

The other was a work on practical astronomy, published in the Dutch. The language made it a closed book but for the beautifully clear maps of the stars and many examples of astronomical calculations. By its aid I became well acquainted with the night skies and familiarized myself with the ordinary observations necessary to determine latitude and longitude. This was the beginning of the astronomical knowledge afterwards so essential to me.

Soon now the day for care and work came. We were only two, my mother and I. We had lost my sister. My brother was away, making his own career, and I had to concern myself for mine. I was unwilling to leave my mother. Circumstances had more than usually endeared us to each other and I knew that her life would be solitary without me. I was accustomed to be much at home and our separations had been slight. But now it was likely to be for long and the hard part would be for the one left alone. For me it was very different. Going out into the excitement of strange scenes and occurrences I would be forced out of myself and for long intervals could forget what I left behind. For her in the sameness of daily life there would be a blank not easily filled. But my mother had an experience of sacrifice which with her true womanly nature it had been hard to learn. Realizing that now the time had come for another, she, but not cheerfully, sent me forward on my way.

The necessity for exertion was making itself felt and the outlook for my future was vague. But among the few men whom I had come to know as friends there was one whose kindly aid and counsel was often valuable to me, then and afterward.

Mr. Poinsett was one of the distinguished men of the day, of broad and liberal mind, refined by study and much travel. While Minister to Mexico his cultivated taste led him to interest himself in the luxuriant flora of that country. Known in a graver way through his public works and service, it has chanced that his name has been kept familiarly present and most popularly known by the scarlet Poinsettia which he contributed to botany.

I knew him after he returned from Mexico, and before and during the time when he was Secretary of War. By his aid, but not with his approval, I went to the South American coast as teacher on board the U. S. sloop of war *Natchez*, Captain Zantzinger.[4] Admiral Farragut was one of the lieutenants. The voyage had its advantages. I saw more of the principal cities and people than a traveler usually does on passing through a country, though nothing of the interior. But the time spent was long and had no future bearing. Among the few events that occurred to break the routine of ship life there was one in which I was concerned that I remember with satisfaction.

While lying at Rio de Janeiro a duel had taken place between two
of the midshipmen in which one lost his life. Both were men of high
character and had been friends. The fatal termination of the meeting was deeply regretted, and by no one more than the survivor.
A trivial misunderstanding shortly after resulted in another. The
principals on this occasion were Mr. Lovell, of South Carolina, and
Mr. Parrott, of Massachusetts. Decatur Hurst was Lovell's second,
and I Parrott's. Lovell was a nephew of Mr. Poinsett and Hurst a
nephew of Commodore Decatur. Hurst and I were friends. He
proposed to put only powder in the pistols for the first fire. If then
another should be insisted on we would give them lead. In this we
incurred some personal risk, but were quite willing to take it for
the sake of the persons principally interested in the result.

This being agreed upon, we succeeded in leaving the ship without having attracted any attention to our movements, and crossing
the bay quietly, landed on the north shore. Leaving the boat, we
found a narrow strip of sandy beach about forty yards long between
the water and the mountain. In such a place men could hardly miss
each other. The few preparations made, we placed our men twelve
paces apart and gave the word. Both looked sincerely surprised
that they remained standing upright as before. Going up each to
his man, we declared the affair over; the cause of quarrel in our
opinion not justifying a second shot. There was some demur, but
we insisting carried our men triumphantly back to the ship, nobody
hurt and nobody wiser. Hurst and I greatly enjoyed our little *ruse
de guerre*.

Of the four men three are dead. Just when Lovell died I do not
know. Admiral Parrott died in New York about seven years
ago. Hurst too is dead. While on the African coast he was badly
wounded in a duel, which ultimately caused his death not long
afterward.

When the cruise was over I returned to Charleston. In the meantime Congress had created the post of Professor of Mathematics in
the Navy.[5] I applied for a commission and was ordered before an
examining board, to be convened shortly at Norfolk. Then came for
me another pleasant month, for I was back among my old friends,
and the strong motive I had now added to the pleasure I always
found in study. All day long I was at my books, and the earliest

dawn found me at an upper window against which stood a tall poplar, where the rustling of the glossy leaves made a soothing accompaniment. The surroundings go for a great deal in intellectual work.

My examination was successfully over and I had received, and declined, my appointment.

Just then an opportunity was offered me to go under Captain W. S. Williams, of the U. S. Topographical Corps, as one of the assistant engineers on surveys to be made for a projected railway from Charleston to Cincinnati.[6] I gladly accepted the chance that fell to me, and spent a summer in congenial work among the mountains of South Carolina and Tennessee. There were several parties, each under an able engineer. That to which I belonged was under the direction of Lieutenant [Richard M.] White, a graduate of West Point, who knew well how to make our work agreeable. We were engaged in running experimental lines, and the plotting of the field notes sometimes kept us up until midnight. Our quarters were sometimes at a village inn and more frequently at some farmer's house, where milk and honey and many good things were welcome to an appetite sharpened by all-day labor on foot and a tramp of several miles backward and forward, morning and evening. It was cheery, wholesome work. The summer weather in the mountains was fine, the cool water abundant, and the streams lined with azaleas. As often is with flowers of that color, the white azaleas were fragrant. The survey was a kind of picnic with work enough to give it zest, and we were all sorry when it was over.

The surveys being suspended, I returned home and only casually if ever met again the men with whom I had been associated. General Morrell, with whom many years afterward I lived as neighbor on the Hudson, was the only one I remember to have met.

It had been the policy of President Jefferson, suggested by his acquisition of the Louisiana territory, to remove all the Indian tribes from the Eastern States to the west of the Mississippi. This policy was adopted and carried forward by Mr. Monroe, and completed under President Jackson.

The last to be removed were the Cherokees who inhabited a district where the States of North Carolina, Tennessee, and Georgia cornered together. This territory was principally in Georgia, and

consisted in greater part of a body of land ceded to the Cherokees
by Georgia in 1783.

For the good of the bordering States, and for the welfare of the
Indians as well, this was a wise and humane measure. But the
Cherokees were averse to the change. They were unwilling to leave
the homes where they had been domiciled for half a century.

The country was mountainous and the face of it not accurately
known. Looking to the contingency of hostilities already threatening with the Indians, Captain Williams was ordered to make a
military reconnaissance of the territory they occupied. I went with
him again as one of his assistants.[7]

The accident of this employment curiously began a period of
years of like work for me among similar scenes. Here I found the
path which I was "destined to walk." Through many of the years
to come the occupation of my prime of life was to be among Indians
and in waste places. Other events which intervened were incidents
in this and grew out of it. There were to be no more years wasted
in tentative efforts to find a way for myself. The work was laid out,
and it began here with a remarkable continuity of purpose.

This was a winter survey made hurriedly. When we entered the
Indian territory we were three together, Archie Campbell, Hull
Adams and I. About dark we reached the Nantahéylè River,[8] at an
Indian village. The Indians were having a feast and a carouse and
were all drunk. The squaws hid us in a log out-cabin, half filled with
shucked corn. We did not pass a comfortable night. The shouts of
the drunken Indians and rats running over us kept us awake; and
we were glad when morning came. The night had been cold and
our bathtub was the Nantahéylè River. There was ice along the
banks and the water in my hair froze into fretful quills.

With the beginning of the reconnaissance our little party was
scattered, each to separate work. The Indians, after their usual way
of living, occupied the country sparsely. In parts, this was beautifully fertile; broad level valleys, with fine streams and forest land. I
had a guide named Laudermilk, a very intelligent, good-tempered
man, intimately acquainted with the territory to be surveyed. In
true pioneer spirit he had built his cabin at a spot in the woods as
much out of the way and isolated as he could well find. He was
about thirty years old and his wife twenty. It was comfortable

quarters. Occasionally we would spend a night there, making a hard ride through snow to reach it. Sometimes we were alone, making a sketch of some stream, and stopping at night at an Indian cabin. At other times, when the work was in a more uninhabited part of the territory, we had a small party of men, with pack saddles to carry our tents and provisions.

It was a forest country thinly occupied by Indian farms. At night we slept in half-faced tents, with great fires of hickory logs at our feet. Pigs which ranged during the fall and fattened on chestnuts made our *pièce de résistance* on these occasions.

As it sometimes chanced, I was present at Indian feasts, where all would get wild with excitement and some furious with drink. Bloody frays were a certain accompaniment, slashing with knives, hands badly cut from clutching the blades, and ugly body wounds. Their exhibition of brute courage and indifference to pain compelled admiration, with regret for the good material wasted. But these were the exceptional occasions. In their villages and in their ordinary farming life they lived peaceably and comfortably. Many of their farms were much the same as those that are to be met with everywhere on our remote frontier. The depreciating and hurtful influence was the proximity of the whites. One of the pieces of work assigned to me was a reconnaissance of the Hiwassee River.[9] It was over very rough and tangled ground. The first day's work of twenty miles on foot made me so stiff next morning that I moved like a foundered horse, and I suppose I was foundered for the time. In getting over the trunks of fallen trees I had to sit down upon them and lift over first one leg and then the other. But this was only for the first day. That night we had stopped at the log house of an Indian. It was a handsome specimen of forest architecture; a square-built house standing on a steep bank of the Hiwassee, with glass-paned windows. But the striking feature in such surroundings was that all the logs were evenly hewed so that they laid solidly together and presented a smoothly even surface. Its finish, in its own way, made quite an agreeable impression from its unexpectedness in such a place. Below, the riverbanks fell away, leaving a little valley, in which he had made his cornfield.

In much travel among Indians I have had a fair opportunity to become acquainted with different tribes and learned to appreciate and comprehend the results of the differing influences brought to bear upon them. Here in the Cherokee country, as in different regions afterward, I saw how their differing conditions depended upon their surroundings. In the Great Basin I saw them in the lowest stage of human existence where it was in its simplest elements, differing from that of wild animals only in the greater intelligence of the Indians. Sage bush sheltered them; seeds, bush squirrels and hares, grasshoppers, worms, anything that had life made their food.

Going upward, I saw them on the great prairie plains in the higher stages to which the surrounding facilities for a more comfortable and easier life had raised them. Nomadic, following the game and the seasons but living in villages, buffalo and large game gave them good food and clothing, and made for them dry warm lodges. And afterward in the nearer approach to the civilized life to which the intermittent efforts of the Government at agencies and reservations, and the labor of the Protestant and Catholic churches, had brought them.

FOOTNOTES

1. The date of Frémont's expulsion was February 5, 1831, when he was within three months of graduation. The faculty journal gives the grounds as "habitual irregularity and incorrigible negligence." Charleston College had strict rules, which required students to be on the premises seven hours daily. Its new president, Dr. Jasper Adams, had declared he would make the place "a fountain of intelligence and virtue."

2. Frémont's father had been a refugee from the Santo Domingo uprising.

3. For a time Frémont taught in John A. Wooten's private school in Charleston; for a time also he worked in the Apprentices' Library, which combined classes with a collection of books. While teaching, he read widely.

4. Joel R. Poinsett returned to Charleston from his ministerial service in Mexico in the summer of 1830. He liked to help young men of promise, and as a member of St. Philip's Church and a friend of Charleston College, he naturally took an interest in Frémont. Poinsett's strong attachment to the Union —he supported Jackson in the Nullification controversy—probably had its effect on Frémont's views. The sloop *Natchez* sailed on its South American voyage in May, 1833. Frémont was employed as teacher of mathematics; as yet no naval academy existed, and the midshipmen who were assigned to cruising ships required such instructors.

5. By the Act of March 3, 1835, Congress authorized several such professorships. It is evident that Frémont was proficient in mathematics.

6. Once more Poinsett befriended Frémont; he was leader of a committee to promote the projected Louisville, Cincinnati & Charleston Railroad.

7. This expulsion of the Cherokees at the instance of Southwestern interests

greedy for their lands was one of the cruellest acts in the history of the Federal Government. The survey in which Frémont participated occupied the winter of 1836–37. He would naturally, at the time, share the views of Southern white folk on the desirability of transferring the Indians west of the Mississippi.

8. The Nantahala River flows out of the Nantahala Mountains in western North Carolina into the Little Tennessee River.

9. The Hiwassee River in southeastern Tennessee, near the Georgia and North Carolina boundaries, flows northwest into the Tennessee River.

CHAPTER 2

Nicollet:
*Surveying the Minnesota-Dakota Country

THE Cherokee survey was over. I remained at home only just long enough to enjoy the pleasure of the return to it, and to rehabituate myself to old scenes. While I was trying to devise and settle upon some plan for the future, my unforgetful friend, Mr. Poinsett, had also been thinking for me. He was now Secretary of War, and, at his request, I was appointed by President Van Buren a second lieutenant in the United States Topographical Corps, and ordered to Washington. Washington was greatly different then from the beautiful capital of today. Instead of many broad, well-paved, and leafy avenues, Pennsylvania Avenue about represented the town. There were not the usual resources of public amusement. It was a lonesome place for a young man knowing but one person in the city, and there was no such attractive spot as the Battery by the sea at

* This chapter is taken from Frémont's *Memoirs*, pp. 31–54. It might well be called the Nicollet chapter of Frémont's life. Joseph Nicolas Nicollet, often mistakenly called Jean, was fifty-two when he made the survey of the upper Missouri country on which Frémont accompanied him (1838). A musician, an accomplished mathematician—he had been professor of mathematics at the Collège Louis-le-Grand in Paris—a man well read in all the sciences, he was just the mentor Frémont needed. He had been born in Savoy, had attracted attention by the brilliance of his mind, and had rapidly advanced to the position of secretary and librarian of the Observatory, where he worked with Laplace. At the time of the Revolution of 1830 he emigrated to New Orleans. The Chouteau family in St. Louis helped him in his plans for exploring the upper Mississippi and its headwaters, and in 1836–37 he spent the winter at Fort Snelling. Secretary Poinsett then asked him to come to Washington. Frémont's enthusiastic account of his personality is the fullest we possess. A man of slight physique, ill adapted to hardship, his years of exploration were destined to be few. For his part, he became warmly attached to Frémont. When the young man left him for a special survey, he wrote of the pain the separation had given him, and added: "I shall await you with open arms to embrace you, and congratulate you."

Charleston, where a stranger could go and feel the freedom of both eye and thought.

Shut in to narrow limits, the mind is driven in upon itself and loses its elasticity; but the breast expands when, upon some hilltop, the eye ranges over a broad expanse of country, or in face of the ocean. We do not value enough the effect of space for the eye; it reacts on the mind, which unconsciously expands to larger limits and freer range of thought. So I was low in my mind and lonesome until I learned, with great relief, that I was to go upon a distant survey into the West. But that first impression of flattened lonesomeness which Washington had given me has remained with me to this day.

About this time, a distinguished French savant had returned from a geographical exploration of the country about the sources of the Mississippi, the position of which he first established. That region and its capabilities were then but little known, and the results of his journey were of so interesting a nature that they had attracted public notice and comment. Through Mr. Poinsett, Mr. Nicollet was invited to come to Washington, with the object of engaging him to make a complete examination of the great prairie region between the Mississippi and Missouri rivers, as far north as the British line, and to embody the whole of his labors in a map and general report for public use.

Mr. Nicollet had left France, intending to spend five years in geographical researches in this country. His mind had been drawn to the early discoveries of his countrymen, some of which were being obliterated and others obscured in the lapse of time. He anticipated great pleasure in renewing the memory of these journeys, and in rescuing them all from the obscurity into which they had fallen. A member of the French Academy of Sciences, he was a distinguished man in the circles to which Arago and other savants of equal rank belonged. Not only had he been trained in science, but he was habitually schooled to the social observances which make daily intercourse attractive, and become invaluable where hardships are to be mutually borne and difficulties overcome and hazards met. His mind was of the higher order. A musician as well as a mathematician, it was harmonious and complete.

The Government now arranged with him to extend his surveys

south and west of the country which he had already explored. Upon this survey I was ordered to accompany him as his assistant.[1]

It was a great pleasure to me to be assigned to this duty. By this time I had gone through some world-schooling and was able to take a sober view of the realities of life. I had learned to appreciate fully the rare value of the friendly aid which had opened up for me such congenial employment, and I resolved that, if it were in me to do so, I would prove myself worthy of it. The years of healthy exercise which I had spent in open air had hardened my body, and the work I had been engaged in was kindred to that which I was now to have. Field work in a strange region, in association with a man so distinguished, was truly an unexpected good fortune, and I went off from Washington full of agreeable anticipation.

At St. Louis I joined Mr. Nicollet. This was the last large city on the western border, and the fitting-out place for expeditions over the uninhabited country. The small towns along the western bank of the Missouri made for two or three hundred miles a sort of fringe to the prairies. At St. Louis I met for the first time General Robert E. Lee, then a captain in the United States Engineer Corps, charged with improvements of the Mississippi River. He was already an interesting man. His agreeable, friendly manner to me as a younger officer, when I was introduced to him, left a more enduring impression than usually goes with casual introductions.

In St. Louis Mr. Nicollet had a pleasant circle of friends among the old French residents. They were proud of him as a distinguished countryman, and were gratified with his employment by the American Government, which in this way recognized his distinction and capacity. His intention, in the prosecution of his larger work to revive the credit due to early French discoverers, was pleasing to their national pride.

His acquaintances he made mine, and I had the pleasure and advantage to share in the amiable intercourse and profuse hospitality which in those days characterized the society of the place. He was a Catholic, and his distinction, together with his refined character, made him always a welcome guest with his clergy. And I may say in the full sense of the word, that I "assisted" often at the agreeable suppers in the refectory. The pleasure of these grew in remembrance afterward, when hard and scanty fare and sometimes starvation and consequent bodily weakness made visions in the mind, and hunger made memory dwell upon them by day and dream of them by night.

Such social evenings followed almost invariably the end of the day's preparations. These were soon now brought to a close with the kindly and efficient aid of the Fur Company's officers.[2] Their personal experience made them know exactly what was needed on the proposed voyage, and both stores and men were selected by them; the men out of those in their own employ. These were principally practiced voyageurs, accustomed to the experiences and incidental privations of travel in the Indian country.

The aid given by the house of Chouteau was, to this and succeeding expeditions, an advantage which followed them throughout their course to their various posts among the Indian tribes.

Our destination now was a trading post on the west bank of the Mississippi, at the mouth of the St. Peter's, now better known as the Minnesota River. This was the residence of Mr. Henry Sibley,[3] who was in charge of the Fur Company's interests in the Mississippi Valley. He gave us a frontier welcome and heartily made his house our headquarters. This was the point of departure at which the expedition began its work. It was on the border line of civilization. On the left or eastern bank of the river were villages and settlements of the whites, and the right was the Indian country which we were about to visit. Fort Snelling was on the high bluff point opposite between the Minnesota and the Mississippi. Near by was a Sioux Indian village, and usually its Indians were about the house grounds. Among these I saw the most beautiful Indian girl I have ever met, and it is a tribute to her singular beauty that after so many years I remember still the name of "Ampetu-washtoy"—"the Beautiful Day."

The house had much the character of a hunting lodge. There were many dogs around about, and two large wolfhounds, Lion and Tiger, had the run of the house and their quarters in it. Mr. Sibley was living alone, and these fine dogs made him friendly companions, as he belonged to the men who love dogs and horses. For his other dogs he had built within the enclosure a lookout about fifteen feet high. Around its platform the railing was usually bordered with the heads of dogs resting on their paws and looking wistfully out over the prairie, probably reconnoitering for wolves. Of the two hounds Tiger had betrayed a temper of such ferocity, even against his master, as eventually cost him his life. Lion, though a brother, had, on the contrary, a companionable and affectionate disposition and almost human intelligence, which in his case brought about a separation from his old home.

On the marriage of Mr. Sibley, Lion so far resented the loss of his first place that he left the house, swam across the Mississippi, and went to the fort, where he ended his days. Always he was glad to meet his master when he came over, keeping close by him and following him to the shore, though all persuasion failed to make him ever recross the river to the home where he had been supplanted; but his life-size portrait still hangs over the fireplace of Mr. Sibley's library. These dogs were of the rare breed of the Irish wolfhound, and their story came up as an incident in a correspondence, stretching from Scotland to Minnesota, on the question as to whether it had not become extinct, growing out of my happening to own a dog inheriting much of that strain.

Cut off from the usual resources, Mr. Sibley had naturally to find his in the surroundings. The prominent feature of Indian life entered into his, and hunting became rather an occupation than an amusement. But his hunting was not the tramp of a day to some neighboring lake for wild fowl, or a ride on the prairie to get a stray shot at a wolf. These hunting expeditions involved days' journeys to unfrequented ranges where large game was abundant, or in winter to the neighborhood of one of his trading posts, where in event of rough weather the stormy days could be passed in shelter. He was fully six feet in height, well and strongly built, and this, together with his skill as hunter, gave him a hold on the admiration and respect of the Indians.

In all this stir of frontier life Mr. Nicollet felt no interest and took no share; horse and dog were nothing to him. His manner of life had never brought him into their companionship, and the congenial work he now had in charge engrossed his attention and excited his imagination. His mind dwelt continually upon the geography of the country, the Indian names of lakes and rivers and their signification, and upon whatever tradition might retain of former travels by early French explorers.

Some weeks had now been spent in completing that part of the outfit which had been referred to this place. The intervening time had been used to rate the chronometers and make necessary observations of the latitude and longitude of our starting-point.

At length we set out. As our journey was to be over level and unbroken country, the camp material was carried in one-horse carts, driven by Canadian voyageurs, the men usually employed by the Fur Company in their business through this region. M. de Montmort, a French gentleman attached to the legation at Washington, and Mr. Eugene Flandin, a young gentleman belonging to a French family of New York, accompanied the party as friends of Mr. Nicollet. These were pleasant traveling companions, and both looked up to Mr. Nicollet with affectionate deference and admiration. No botanist had been allowed to Mr. Nicollet by the Government, but he had for himself employed Mr. Charles Geyer, a botanist recently from Germany, of unusual practical knowledge in his profession and of companionable disposition.

The proposed surveys of this northwestern region naturally divided themselves into two: the present one, at this point connecting with Mr. Nicollet's surveys of the upper Mississippi, was to extend westward to the waters of the Missouri Valley; the other, intended for the operations of the succeeding year, was to include the valley of the Missouri River, and the northwestern prairies as far as to the British line.

Our route lay up the Minnesota for about a hundred and fifteen miles, to a trading post at the lower end of the Traverse des Sioux; the prairie and river valley being all beautiful and fertile country. We traveled along the southern side of the river, passing on the way several Indian camps, and establishing at night the course of the river by astronomical observations. The Traverse des Sioux is a crossing place about thirty miles long, where the river makes a large rectangular bend, coming down from the northwest and turning abruptly to the northeast; the streams from the southeast, the south, and southwest flowing into a low line of depression to where they gather into a knot at the head of this bend, and into its lowest part as into a bowl. In this great elbow of the river is the Marahtanka or Big Swan Lake, the summer resort of the Sissiton Sioux.[4] Our way over the crossing lay between the lake and the river. At the end of the Traverse we returned to the right shore at the mouth of the Waraju or Cottonwood River, and encamped near the principal village of the Sissitons. Their lodges were pitched in a beautiful situation, under large trees. It needs only the slightest incident to throw an Indian village into a sudden excitement which is startling to a stranger. We were occupied quietly among the Indians, Mr. Nicollet, as usual, surrounded by them, with the aid of the interpreter getting them to lay out the form of the lake and the course of the streams entering the river near by, and, after repeated pronunciations, entering their names in his notebook; Geyer, followed by some Indians, curiously watching him while digging up plants; and I, more numerously attended, pouring out the quicksilver for the artificial horizon, each in his way busy at work; when suddenly everything started into motion, the Indians running tumultuously to a little rise which commanded a view of the prairie, all clamor and excitement. The commotion was caused by the appearance of two or three elk on the prairie horizon. Those of us who were strangers, and ignorant of their usages, fancied there must be at least a war party in sight.

From this point we traveled up the Waraju River and passed a few days in mapping the country around the Pelican Lakes, and among the lower spurs of the Coteau des Prairies, a plateau which separates the waters of the Mississippi and Missouri rivers. This is the single elevation separating the prairies of the two rivers. Approaching it, the blue line which it presents, marked by wooded ravines in contrast with the green prairie which sweeps to its feet, suggested to the voyageurs the name they gave it, of the Prairie Coast. At this elevation, about fifteen hundred feet above the sea, the prairie air was invigorating, the country studded with frequent lakes was beautiful, and the repose of a few days was refreshing to men and animals after the warmer and moister air of the lower valley. Throughout this region, the rivers and lakes, and other noticeable features of the country, bear French and Indian names, Sioux or Chippewa, and sometimes Shayan (Cheyenne). Sometimes they perpetuate the memory of an early French discoverer, or rest upon some distinguishing local character of stream or lake; and sometimes they record a simple incident of chase or war which in their limited history were events.

We now headed for our main object in this direction, the Red Pipe Stone Quarry,[5] which was to be the limit of our western travel; from there we were to turn directly north. All this country had been a battleground between the Sioux and Sacs and Foxes. Crossing the high plains over which our journey now lay, we became aware that we were followed by a party of Indians. Guard at night was necessary. But it was no light thing, after a day's work of sketching the country, to stand guard the night through, as it now fell to me among others to do. When we would make the noon halt I promptly took my share of it under the shade of a cart in deep sleep, which the fragrant breeze of the prairie made delightful.

Our exaggerated precautions proved useless, as the suspected hostile party were only friendly Sioux who, knowing nothing about us, were on their side cautiously watching us.

The Indians have a belief that the Spirit of the Red Pipe Stone speaks in thunder and lightning whenever a visit is made to the Quarry. With a singular coincidence, such a storm broke upon us as we reached it, and the confirmation of the legend was pleasing to young Renville and the Sioux who had accompanied us.

As we came into the valley the storm broke away in a glow of sunshine on the line of red bluff which extended for about three miles. The day after our arrival the party of Indians we had been watching came in. We spent three friendly days together; they were after the red pipestone, and we helped them, by using gunpowder, to uncover the rock.

It was in itself a lovely place, made interesting by the mysterious character given to it by Indian tradition, and because of the fact that the existence of such a rock is not known anywhere else. It is on the land of the Sissiton Sioux, but the other Indians make to it annual pilgrimages, as it is from this they make their images and pipes. This famous stone, where we saw it, was in a layer about a foot and a half thick, overlaid by some twenty-six feet of red-colored indurated sandrock, the color diminishing in intensity from the base to the summit. The water in the little valley had led the buffalo through it in their yearly migration from north to south, and the tradition is that their trail wore away the surface and uncovered the stone.

There was a detached pedestal standing out a few feet away

from the bluff, and about twenty-five feet high. It was quite a feat to spring to this from the bluff, as the top was barely a foot square and uneven, and it required a sure foot not to go further. This was a famous place of the country, and nearly all of us, as is the custom in famous places the world over, carved our names in the stone. It speaks for the enduring quality of this rock that the names remain distinct to this day.

When the position had been established and other objects of the visit accomplished, we took up the northern line of march for the Lac Qui Parle, the trading post and residence of the Renville family.[6]

On our way we passed through and mapped the charming lake country of the Coteau des Prairies.

The head of the Renville family, a French Canadian, was a border chief. Between him and the British line was an unoccupied region of some seven hundred miles. Over all the Indian tribes which ranged these plains he had a controlling influence; they obeyed himself and his son, who was a firm-looking man of decided character. Their good will was a passport over this country.

The hospitable reception which is the rule of the country met us here. I take pleasure in emphasizing and dwelling on this, because it is apart from the hospitality of civilized life. There is lively satisfaction on both sides. The advent of strangers in an isolated place brings novelty and excitement, and to the stranger arriving, there is great enjoyment in the change from privations and watchful unrest to the quiet safety and profusion of plenty in such a frontier home. Our stay here was made very agreeable. We had abundance of milk and fresh meat and vegetables, all seasoned with a traveler's appetite and a hearty welcome.

To gratify us a game of Lacrosse was played with spirit and skill by the Indians.[7] Among the players was a young half-breed of unusual height, who was incomparably the swiftest runner among them. He was a relation of the Renvilles and seemed to have some recognized family authority, for during the play he would seize an Indian by his long hair and hurl him backward to the ground to make room for himself, the other taking it as matter of course.

Some time was spent here in visiting the various lakes near by, fixing their position and gathering information concerning the character of the country and its Indians. This over, and the limit of the present journey attained, we turned our faces eastward and started back to the mouth of the St. Peter's.

While Mr. Nicollet was occupied in making a survey of the Lesueur River, and identifying localities and verifying accounts of preceding travelers, I was sent to make an examination of the Mankato or Blue Earth River, which bore upon the subjects he had in view. The eastern division of the expedition now closed with our return to Mr. Sibley's.

Among the episodes which gave a livelier coloring to the instructive part of this campaign was a hunting expedition on which I went with Mr. Sibley. With him also went M. Faribault,[8] a favorite companion of his on such occasions. It was a royal hunt. He took with him the whole of Red Dog's village—men, women, and children. The hunting ground was a number of days' journey to the south, in Iowa, where game was abundant; many deer and some elk. It was in November, when the does are in their best condition. The country was well timbered and watered, stretches of prairie interspersed with clumps and lines of woods.

Early in the morning the chief would indicate the camping ground for the night, and the men sally out for the hunt. The women, with the camp equipage, would then make direct for the spot pointed out, ordinarily some grove about nine miles distant. Toward nightfall the hunters came in with their game.

The day's tramp gave a lively interest to the principal feature which the camp presented; along the woods bright fires, where fat venison was roasting on sticks before them, or stewing with corn or wild rice in pots hanging from tripods; squaws busy over the cooking and children rolling about over the ground. No sleep is better or more restoring than follows such a dinner, earned by such a day.

On the march one day, a squaw dropped behind, but came into camp a little later than the others, bringing a child a few hours old. By circumstance of birth he should have become a mighty hunter, but long before he reached man's age he had lost birthright, he and his tribe, and I doubt if he got even the mess of pottage for which Esau bartered his. During the hunt we had the experience of a prairie fire. We were on a detached excursion, Sibley, Faribault, and I. After midnight we were aroused from a sound sleep by the crackling noise, and springing to our feet, found ourselves surrounded, without a minute to lose. Gathering in our animals, we set fire to the grass near our tent, transferring quickly animals and baggage to the cleared ground. The fire swept past, and in a few seconds struck a grove of aspens near by and leaped up the trees, making a wall of flame that sent a red glow into the sky brighter even than the waves of fire that rolled over the prairie. We lost nothing, only tent and belongings a little blackened with the smoldering grass; but the harm was to the woods and the game.

The work of the year and in this quarter was now finished, and we returned to St. Louis, to prepare for the survey of the more western division in the succeeding year.

A partial equipment for the expedition to the northwest prairies was obtained in St. Louis. Arrangements had previously been made at Lac Qui Parle, during the preceding journey for a reinforcement of men to meet the party at an appointed time on Rivière à Jacques, a tributary to the Missouri River. At St. Louis five men were engaged, four of them experienced in prairie and mountain travel; one of them Etienne Provost, known as *l'homme des montagnes*.[9] The other man was Louis Zindel, who had seen service as a noncommissioned officer of Prussian artillery, and was skilled in making rockets and fireworks. We left St. Louis early in April, 1839, on board the *Antelope*, one of the American Fur Company's steamboats which, taking its customary advantage of the annual rise in the Missouri from the snows of the Rocky Mountains, was about starting on its regular voyage to the trading posts on the upper waters of the river.

For nearly two months and a half we were struggling against the current of the turbid river, which in that season of high waters was so swift and strong that sometimes the boat would for moments stand quite still, seeming to pause to gather strength, until the power of steam asserted itself and she would fight her way into a smooth reach. In places the river was so embarrassed with snags that it was difficult to thread a way among them in face of the swift current and treacherous channel, constantly changing. Under these obstacles we usually laid up at night, making fast to the shore at some convenient place, where the crew could cut a supply of wood for the next day. It was a pleasant journey, as little disturbed as on the ocean. Once above the settlements of the lower Missouri, there were no sounds to disturb the stillness but the echoes of the high-pressure steam pipe, which traveled far along and around the shores, and the incessant crumbling away of the banks and bars, which the river was steadily undermining and destroying at one place to build up at another. The stillness was an impressive feature, and the constant change in the character of the river shores offered always new interest as we steamed along. At times we traveled by high perpendicular escarpments of light-colored rock, a gray and yellow marl, made picturesque by shrubbery or trees; at others the river opened out into a broad deltalike expanse, as if it were approaching the sea. At length, on the seventieth day we reached Fort Pierre,[10] the chief post of the American Fur Company. This is on the right or western bank of the river, about one thousand and three hundred miles from St. Louis. On the prairie, a few miles away, was a large village of Yankton Sioux. Here we were in the heart of the Indian country and near the great buffalo ranges. Here the Indians were sovereign.

This was to be our starting-point for an expedition northward over the great prairies, to the British line. Some weeks were spent in making the remaining preparations, in establishing the position and writing up journals, and in negotiations with the Indians. After the usual courtesies had been exchanged, our first visit to their village was arranged. On our way we were met by thirty of the principal chiefs, mounted and advancing in line. A noble-looking set of men showing to the best advantage, their fine shoulders and breasts being partly uncovered. We were conducted by them to the village, where we were received with great ceremony by other chiefs, and all their people gathered to meet us. We were taken into a large and handsome lodge and given something to eat, an observance without which no Indian welcome is complete. The village covered some acres of ground, and the lodges were pitched in regular lines. These were large, of about twenty skins or more. The girls were noticeably well clothed, wearing finely dressed skins nearly white, much embroidered with beads and porcupine quills dyed many colors; and stuffs from the trading post completed their dress. These were the best-formed and best-looking Indians of the plains, having the free bearing belonging with their unrestrained life in sunshine and open air. Their mode of life had given them the uniform and smooth development of breast and limb which indicates power, without knots of exaggerated muscle, and the copper-bronze of their skins, burnt in by many suns, increased the statuelike effect. The buffalo and other game, being near, gave them abundant food and means to obtain from the trading posts what to them were luxuries.

Having made the customary and expected presents which ratified the covenants of good will and free passage over their country, we left the village, escorted halfway by the chiefs.

A few days after our visit to the village, one of the chiefs came to the fort, bringing with him a pretty girl of about eighteen, handsomely dressed after the manner I have described. Accompanied by her and the interpreter, he came to the room opening on the court where we were employed over our sketchbooks and maps, and formally offered her to Mr. Nicollet as a wife for him. This placed our chief for a moment in an embarrassing position. But, with ready and crafty tact, he explained to the chief that he already had one, and that the Great Father would not permit him to have two. At the same time suggesting that the younger chief, designating me, had none. This put me in a worse situation. But being at bay, I promptly replied that I was going far away and not coming back, and did not like to take the girl away from her people; that it might bring bad luck; but that I was greatly pleased with the offer, and to show that I was so, would give the girl a suitable present. Accordingly, an attractive package of scarlet and blue cloths, beads, a mirror, and other trifles was made up, and they left us; the girl quite satisfied with her trousseau, and he with other suitable presents made him. Meantime we had been interested by the composure of the girl's manner, who during the proceedings had been quietly leaning against the doorpost, apparently not ill-pleased with the matrimonial conference.

All was now ready. The rating of the chronometers had been verified. Our observations had placed Fort Pierre in latitude 44°23′28″, longitude, 100°12′30″, and elevation above the sea 1,456 feet. Horses, carts, and provisions had been obtained at the fort and six men added to the party; Mr. May, of Kentucky, and a young man from Pembinah had joined us. They were on their way to the British colony of the Red River of the North. William Dixon and Louison Frenière had been engaged as interpreters and guides.[11] Both of these were half-breeds, well known as fine horsemen and famous hunters, as well as most experienced guides. The party now consisted of nineteen persons, thirty-three horses, and ten carts. With Mr. Nicollet, Mr. Geyer, who was again our botanist, and myself, was an officer of the French army, Captain Belligny, who wished to use so good an occasion to see the Indian country. We reached the eastern shore with all our equipage in good order, and made camp for the night at the foot of the river hills opposite the fort. The hills leading to the prairie plateau, about five hundred feet above the river, were rough and broken into ravines. We had barely reached the upland when the hunters came galloping in, and the shout of *"la vache! la vache!"* rang through the camp, everyone repeating it, and everyone excited.

A herd of buffalo had been discovered, coming down to water. In a few moments the buffalo horses were saddled and the hunters mounted, each with a smooth-bore, single or double-barrelled gun, a handkerchief bound filletlike around the head, and all in the scantiest clothing. Conspicuous among them were Dixon and Louison. To this latter I then, and thereafter, attached myself.

My horse was a good one, an American, but grass-fed and prairie-bred. Whether he had gained his experience among the whites or Indians I do not know, but he was a good hunter and knew about buffalo, and badger holes as well, and when he did get his foot into one it was not his fault.

Now I was to see the buffalo. This was an event on which my imagination had been dwelling. I was about to realize the tales the mere telling of which was enough to warm the taciturn Renville into enthusiastic expression, and to rouse all the hunter in the excitable Frenière.

The prairie over which we rode was rolling, and we were able to keep well to leeward and out of sight of the herd. Riding silently up a short slope, we came directly upon them. Not a hundred yards below us was the great, compact mass of animals, moving slowly along, feeding as they went, and making the loud incessant grunting noise peculiar to them. There they were.

The moment's pause that we made on the summit of the slope was enough to put the herd in motion. Instantly as we rose the hill, they saw us. There was a sudden halt, a confused wavering movement, and then a headlong rout, the hunters in their midst. How I got down that short hillside I never knew. From the moment I saw the herd I never saw the ground again until all was over. I remember, as the charge was made, seeing the bulls in the rear turn, then take a few bounds forward, and then, turning for a last look, join the headlong flight.

As they broke into the herd the hunters separated. For some instants I saw them as they showed through the clouds of dust, but I scarcely noticed them. I was finding out what it was to be a prairie hunter. We were only some few miles from the river, hardly clear of the breaks of the hills, and in places the ground still rough. But the only things visible to me in our flying course were the buffalo and the dust, and there was tumult in my breast as well as around me. I made repeated ineffectual attempts to steady myself for a shot at a cow after a hard struggle to get up with her, and each time barely escaped a fall. In such work a man must be able to forget his horse, but my horsemanship was not yet equal to such a proof. At the outset, when the hunters had searched over the herd and singled out each his fattest cow, and made his dash upon her, the herd broke into bands which spread over the plain. I clung to that where I found myself, unwilling to give up, until I found that neither horse nor man could bear the strain longer. Our furious speed had carried us far out over the prairies. Only some straggling groups were in sight, loping slowly off, seemingly conscious that the chase was over. I dismounted and reloaded, and sat down on the grass for a while to give us both rest. I could nowhere see any of my companions, and, except that it lay somewhere to the south of where I was, I had no idea where to look for the camp. The sun was getting low, and I decided to ride directly west, thinking that I might reach the river hills above the fort while there was light enough for me to find our trail of the morning. In this way I could not miss the camp, but for the time being I was lost.

My horse was tired and I rode slowly. He was to be my companion and reliance in a long journey, and I would not press him. The sun went down, and there was no sign that the river was near.

While it was still light an antelope came circling round me, but I would not fire at him. His appearance and strange conduct seemed uncanny but companionable, and the echo to my gun might not be a pleasant one. Long after dark I struck upon a great number of paths, deeply worn, and running along together in a broad roadway. They were leading directly toward the river, and I supposed, to the fort. With my anxieties all relieved I was walking contentedly along, when I suddenly recognized that these were buffalo trails leading to some accustomed great watering place. The discovery was something of a shock, but I gathered myself together and walked on. I had been for some time leading my horse. Toward midnight I reached the breaks of the river hills at a wooded ravine, and just then I saw a rocket shoot up into the sky, far away to the south. That was camp, but apparently some fifteen miles distant, impossible for me to reach by the rough way in the night around the ravines. So I led my horse to the brink of the ravine, and going down I found water, which, *à plusieurs reprises*, I brought up to him, using my straw hat for a bucket. Taking off his saddle and bridle, and fastening him by his long lariat to one of the stirrups, I made a pillow of the saddle and slept soundly until morning. He did not disturb me much, giving an occasional jerk to my pillow, just enough to let me see that all was right.

At the first streak of dawn I saddled up. I had laid my gun by my side in the direction where I had seen the rocket, and riding along that way, the morning was not far advanced when I saw three men riding toward me at speed. They did not slacken their pace until they came directly up against me, when the foremost touched me. It was Louison Frenière. A reward had been promised by Mr. Nicollet to the first who should touch me, and Louison won it. And this was the end of my first buffalo hunt.

The camp gathered around, all glad to see me. To be lost on the prairie in an Indian country is a serious accident, involving many chances, and no one was disposed to treat it lightly. Our party was made up of men experienced in prairie and in mountain travel, exposed always to unforeseen incidents.

When Frenière left the camp in search of me he had no hesitation about where to look. In the rolling country over which the hunt lay it would have been merely an accident to find either camp or water. He knew I would not venture the chance, but would strike directly for the river; and so in leaving camp he kept the open ground along the heads of the ravines, confident that he would either find me or my trail. He was sure I would remain on the open ground at the first water I found. He knew, too, as I did not, that from the fort the valley of the river trended to the northwest, by this increasing the distance I had to travel; still farther increased by a large bend in which the river sweeps off to the westward. On the maps in common use it was nearly north and south, and had it really been so in fact I should have reached the breaks while it was still light enough for me to see the fort or recognize our crossing place, and perhaps to find my way to the camp. All the same I had made an experience and it had ended well.

The camp equipage being carried in carts, and not packed upon mules, the gearing up was quickly done; but meanwhile I had time for a fine piece of fat buffalo meat standing already roasted on a stick before the fire, and a tin cup of good coffee. My horse and I did a fair share of walking on this day's march, and at every unusually good spot of grass I took the bit from his mouth and let him have the chance to recruit from the night before.

We were now on the upland of the Coteau du Missouri, here 1,960 feet above the sea. Traveling to the northeastward, our camp for the night was made by a fork of the Medicine Bow River, the last running water our line would cross until we should reach the waters of the Rivière à Jacques [12] on the eastern slopes of the plateau. On the open plains water is found only in ponds, not always permanent, and not frequent.

From the top of the hill which gives its name to the stream where we had encamped the view was over great stretches of level prairie, fading into the distant horizon, and unbroken except by the many herds of buffalo which made on it dark spots that looked like groves of timber, here and there puffs of dust rising from where the bulls were rolling or fighting. On these high plains the buffalo feed contentedly, and good buffalo grass usually marks the range where they are found. The occasional ponds give them water, and, for them, the rivers are never far away.

This was the Fourth of July. I doubt if any boy in the country found more joy in his fireworks than I did in my midnight rocket with its silent message. Water and wood tonight were abundant, and with plenty in camp and buffalo all around we celebrated our independence of the outside world.

Some days were now occupied in making the crossing of the plateau, our line being fixed by astronomical positions, and the level prairie required no sketching. I spent these days with Frenière among the buffalo. Sometimes when we had gotten too far ahead of our caravan it was an enjoyment to lie in careless ease on the grass by a pond and be refreshed by the breeze which carried with it the fragrance of the prairie. Edged with grasses growing into the clear water, and making a fresh border around them, these resting spots are rather lakelets than ponds.

The grand simplicity of the prairie is its peculiar beauty, and its occurring events are peculiar and of their own kind. The uniformity is never sameness, and in his exhilaration the voyager feels even the occasional field of red grass waving in the breeze pleasant to his eye. And whatever the object may be—whether horseman, or antelope, or buffalo—that breaks the distant outline of the prairie, the surrounding circumstances are of necessity always such as to give it a special interest. The horseman may prove to be enemy or friend, but the always existing uncertainty has its charm of excitement in the one case, and the joy of the chase in the other. There is always the suspense of the interval needed to verify the strange object; and, long before the common man decides anything, the practiced eye has reached certainty. This was the kind of lore in which Frenière was skilled, and with him my prairie education was continued under a master. He was a reckless rider. Never troubling himself about impediments, if the shortest way after his buffalo led through a pond, through it he plunged. Going after a band on one of these days, we came upon a long stretch of shallow pond that we had not seen, and which was thickly sown with boulders half hidden in tall grass and water. As I started to go around he shouted, "In there—in! *Tout droit! faut pas craindre le cheval.*" And in we went, floundering through, happily without breaking bones of ourselves or our horses. It was not the horse that I was afraid of; I did not like that bed of rocks and water.

Crossing the summit level of the plateau we came in sight of the beautiful valley, here about seventy miles broad, of the Rivière à Jacques, its scattered wooded line stretching as far as the eye could reach. Descending the slope, we saw in the distance ahead moving objects, soon recognized as horsemen, and before these could reach us a clump of lodges came into view. They proved to be the encampment of about a hundred Indians, to whom Dixon and Frenière were known as traders of the Fur Company. After an exchange of friendly greetings our camp was pitched near by. Such a rare meeting is an exciting break in the uneventful Indian life; and the making of presents gave a lively expression to the good feeling with which they received us, and was followed by the usual Indian rejoicing. After a conference in which our line of travel was indicated, the chief offered Mr. Nicollet an escort, the country being uncertain, but the offer was declined. The rendezvous for our expected reinforcement was not far away, and Indians with us might only prove the occasion for an attack in the event of meeting an unfriendly band. They had plenty of good buffalo meat, and the squaws had gathered in a quantity of the *pommes des prairies,* or prairie turnips (*Psoralia esculenta*), which is their chief vegetable food, and abundant on the prairie. They slice and dry this for ordinary and winter use.

Traveling down the slope of the coteau, in a descent of 750 feet we reached the "Lake of the Scattered Small Wood," a handsome but deceptive bit of water, agreeable to the eye, but with an unpleasant brackish taste.

About two years ago I received a letter, making of me some inquiries concerning this beautiful lake country of the Northwest. In writing now of the region over which I had traveled, I propose to speak of it as I had seen it, preserving as far as possible its local coloring of the time, shutting out what I may have seen or learned of the changes years have wrought. But since the time of which I am writing, I have not seen this country. Looking over it, in the solitude where I left it, its broad valleys and great plains untenanted as I saw and describe them, I think that the curiosity and interest with which I read this letter, will also be felt by any who accompany me along these pages. Under this impression, and because the writer of the letter had followed our trail to this point—the "Lake of the Scattered Small Wood"—I give it here:

Iowa City, Ia., February 13, 1884

. . . This I write feeling that as you have devoted your life to engineering and scientific pursuits, it will be at least a gratification to receive a letter upon such subjects as are connected with what you have done. It has been my fortune to locate and construct railway lines for the Chicago & Northwestern Railway in Minnesota and Dakota, in doing which I have surveyed not less than three thousand miles of line, and in so doing have passed over a very large extent of the surface of that region. While doing this work I have been led to inquire into the climate of that remarkable region. I visited many places which you in 1838 discovered and named. Among these are Lakes Benton and Hendricks, the first about twenty miles north of the famous 'Red Pipe Stone Quarry,' a very fine sheet of water, along the south shore of which I located the railroad, and there has sprung up a fine town called Lake Benton. West of this, in Dakota, and on the west side of the Big Sioux River, is a lake region, to many of the lakes in which you gave names, and it is to this locality that I wish to particularly call your attention. These lakes bear the names of Thompson, Whitewood, Preston, Te-tonka-ha, Abert (now changed to Albert), Poinsett, and Kampeska. The last-named is at the head of the Big Sioux, and Poinsett a few miles to the southward.

When I constructed the Dakota Central Railway in 1879–80, all these lakes excepting Thompson, Poinsett, and Kampeska, were dry; and it took me a long time and no small research to ascertain when they last held water. They had been known to be dry for the twenty-five years preceding 1879, or at least persons who had lived there or in the vicinity for twenty-five years said that the lakes were dry when they came into the locality, and had, with numerous smaller ones, been dry ever since; and all who knew about them had a theory that they had dried up long since, and that they never would fill again; but I found old Frenchmen who had seen these lakes full of water in 1843–46, and I, in studying over the matter, found that you had seen and named them in 1836–38, and I would thank you very much if you will take the time and trouble to describe them to me as you saw them then.

I came very near locating the railroad line through Lake Preston, for the head men of the railroad company believed that it had dried up for all time; but on my presenting the testimony of certain reliable voyageurs, they allowed me to go around it. It was well that they did, for the winter of 1880–81 gave a snowfall such as had not been seen since the years 1843–44, and in the spring of 1881 all these lakes filled up, bank full, and have continued so ever since. I had the pleasure of comparing my engineer's levels for elevation above the sea with your barometer determination at Fort Pierre on the Missouri River. Your altitude was 1,450 feet, mine was 1,437, the difference 13 feet. My determination is within the limits of ± 6 feet. The distance over which my levels were taken was 680 miles, and were well checked. I also followed up your trail as you marched from Fort Pierre northeasterly to the 'Scattered Small Wood Lake.' I was so successful as to verify your barometer readings in several instances by checking with mine, and in no case found over 15 feet difference between us, and that always in the same relation as at Fort Pierre. Hoping that you will excuse this long letter, and that you may be able to tell me if those lakes were dry when you saw them, or otherwise, and add any other information you see fit.

I am, truly yours,

C. W. IRISH, C. E.

The next day we reached the Rivière à Jacques, at the Talle de Chênes, a clump of oaks which was the rendezvous where our expected reinforcement was to meet us. The river valley here is about seventy miles wide. Observations made during the four days that we remained at the Talle de Chênes place it in latitude 45° 16′ 34″, longitude 98° 7″ 45, and the elevation above the sea 1,341 feet. At the end of this time, no one appearing, the party again took up the line of march, and, following the right bank, on the evening of the 14th encamped near the mouth of Elm River. This river and its forks are well timbered, and for the reason that they furnish fire-wood and shelter, Indian hunting parties make it their winter crossing place on the way westward after buffalo on the Missouri plateau.

On the high plains the winter storms are dangerous. Many tales are told of hunters caught out in a *poudrerie* with no timber near, when it is impossible to see one's way, and every landmark is obliterated or hidden by the driving snow. At such times the hunter has no other resource than to dig for himself a hole in the snow, leaving only a breathing-place above his head, and to remain in it wrapped in his blankets until the storm passes over, when, putting on the dry socks and moccasins which he always carries, he makes for the nearest wood.

The buffalo herds, when caught in such storms and no timber in sight, huddle together in compact masses, all on the outside crowding and fighting to get to the inside; and so, kept warm by the struggling, incessant motion, the snow meanwhile being stamped away under their feet, protect themselves from the fiercest storms.

For several days we traveled up the valley of the Jacques, making astronomical stations, and collecting material for Mr. Nicollet's map. Occasionally, to the same end, I was detached, with Dixon or Frenière, on topographical excursions, which gave me a good general knowledge of the country along the route. At the Butte aux Os (Bone Hill), in latitude 46° 27′ 37″, longitude 98° 8′, elevation above the sea 1,400 feet, we left the Rivière à Jacques, or Chansansan, its valley extending apparently far in a course to west of north, and in a few miles we reached the height of land which separates it from the Shayen River.[13] This is a tributary to the Red River of the North, and was formerly the home of the Shayens, today written Cheyennes. In the incessant wars between the various tribes of this region the Shayens were driven from their country over the Missouri River south to where they now are.

The summit of the plateau was only 1,460 feet above the sea. Here we regained the great prairie plains, and here we saw in their magnificent multitudes the grand buffalo herds on their chief range. They were moving southwestwardly, apparently toward the plains of the upper Missouri. For three days we were in their midst, traveling through them by day and surrounded by them at night. We could not avoid them. Evidently some disturbing cause had set them in motion from the north. It was necessary to hobble some of our animals and picket them all, and keep them close in to prevent any of them from making off with the buffalo, when they would have been irretrievably lost. Working through the herds, it was decided, in order to get more out of their way, to make a temporary halt for a day or two on the Tampa, a small stream flowing into the Shayen. On the second day after, Dixon and Frenière came in with three Indians from a party which had been reconnoitering our camp. They belonged to a hunting village of some three hundred lodges, who were out making buffalo meat and were just about arranging for a grand "*surround.*" It would have been dangerous to risk breaking in upon this, as might easily happen in our ignorance of the locality and their plans. To avert mischief Frenière, on the third day, rode over to the village with a message requesting their chiefs to indicate the time and route for our march. In consequence we were invited to come on to their encampment. Pushing our way through the crowds of buffalo, we were met in the afternoon by two of the chiefs, who escorted us to the village and pointed out the place for our camp. We found the encampment made up of about three hundred lodges of various tribes—Yanktons, Yanktonons, and Sissitons— making about two thousand Indians.

The representations of our guides had insured us a most friendly reception. We were invited to eat in the lodges of different chiefs, the choicest, fattest pieces of buffalo provided for us, and in return they were invited to eat at our camp. The chiefs sat around in a large circle on buffalo robes or blankets, each provided with a deep soup plate and spoon of tin. The first dish was a generous pot-au-feu, principally of fat buffalo meat and rice. No one would begin until all the plates were filled. When all was ready the feast began. With the first mouthful each Indian silently laid down his spoon, and each looked at the other. After a pause of bewilderment the interpreter succeeded in having the situation understood. Mr. Nicollet had put among our provisions some Swiss cheese, and to give flavor to the soup a liberal portion of this had been put into the kettles. Until this strange flavor was accounted for the Indians thought they were being poisoned; but, the cheese being shown to them, and explanation made, confidence was restored; and by the aid of several kettles of water well sweetened with molasses, and such other tempting delicatessen as could be produced from our stores, the dinner party went on and terminated in great good humor and general satisfaction.

The next day they made their surround. This was their great summer hunt when a provision of meat was made for the year, the winter hunting being in smaller parties. The meat of many fat cows was brought in, and the low scaffolds on which it was laid to be sun-dried were scattered over all the encampment. No such occasion as this was to be found for the use of presents, and the liberal gifts distributed through the village heightened their enjoyment of the feasting and dancing, which was prolonged through the night. Friendly relations established, we continued our journey.

Having laid down the course of the river by astronomical stations during three days' travel, we crossed to the left bank and directed our road toward the Devil's Lake, which was the ultimate object of the expedition. The Indian name of the lake is Mini-wakan, the Enchanted Water; converted by the whites into Devil's Lake.

Our observations placed the river where we left it in latitude 47° 46′ 29″, longitude 98° 13′ 30″, and elevation above the sea 1,328 feet, the level of the bordering plateaus being about one hundred and sixty feet above the river.

In our journey along this river, mosquitoes had infested the camp in such swarms and such pertinacity that the animals would quit feeding and come up to the fires to shelter themselves in the smoke. So virulent were they that to eat in any quiet was impossible, and we found it necessary to use the long green veils, which to this end had been recommended to us by the fur traders. Tied around our straw hats, the brims kept the veils from our faces, making a space within which the plates could be held; and behind these screens we contrived to eat without having the food uncomfortably flavored by mosquito sauce piquante.

After a short day's march of fourteen miles we made our first camp on this famous war and hunting ground, four miles from the Mini-wakan. Early in the day's march we had caught sight of the woods and hills bordering the lake, among them being conspicuous a heart-shaped hill near the southern shore. The next day after an hour's march we pitched our camp at the head of a deep bay not far from this hill. To this the Indians have given the name of The Heart of the Enchanted Water, by the whites translated Heart of the Devil's Lake.

At a wooded lake of fresh water near last night's camp on the plateau we had found traces of a large encampment which had been recently abandoned. The much-trodden ground and trails all round showed that a large party had been here for several weeks. From many cart-wheel tracks and other signs our guides recognized it as a hunting camp of the Métis, or Boisbrûlés,[14] of the Red River of the North; and the deep ruts cut by the wheels showed that the carts had received their full load, and that the great hunt of the year was over. It was this continuous and widespread hunt that had put in motion the great herds through which we had passed.

Among other interesting features of the northwest we had heard much from our guides about these people and their buffalo hunts, and to have just missed them by a few days only was quite a disappointment.

The home of the Half-breeds is at Pembina in British North America. They are called indifferently Métis or Half-breeds, Boisbrûlés, and Gens libres or Free People of the North. The Half-breeds themselves are in greater part the descendants of French Canadian traders and others who, in the service of the Fur Company, and principally of the Northwest Company of Montreal, had been stationed at their remote forts, or scattered over the northwest Indian country in gathering furs. These usually took local wives from among the Indian women of the different tribes, and their half-Indian children grew up to a natural life of hunting and kindred pursuits, in which their instincts gave them unusual skill.

The Canadian *engagés* of the company who had remained in the country after their term of service had expired were called Free Canadians; and, from their association with the Half-breeds came also the name of Gens libres. They were prominently concerned in a singular event which occurred in British America about a quarter of a century before the time of which I am writing. In the rivalry between the Hudson's Bay Company and the Northwest Fur and Trading Company of Montreal, the Half-breeds were used by the Northwest Company in their successful attempts to destroy a Scotch colony which had been planted by the Earl of Selkirk on the Red River of the North at its confluence with the Assiniboine, about forty miles above Lake Winnipeg. The colony was founded upon a grant of land made to the Earl by the Hudson's Bay Company in 1811, and about a hundred immigrants were settled at the Forks in 1812, reaching to some two hundred in 1814. This was called the Kildonan settlement, from a parish in the County of Sutherland which had been the home of the immigrants. In August of 1815 it was entirely broken up by the Northwest Company, and the settlers driven away and dispersed. During the following winter and spring the colony was re-established, and in prosperous condition when it was attacked by a force of Half-breeds, under officers of the Northwest Company, and some twenty unresisting persons killed; including Mr. Semple, the Governor of the Hudson's Bay Company and five of his officers. In the course of this contest there were acts of a savage brutality not repugnant, perhaps, to the usages of the Indian country where they were perpetrated, but unknown among civilized men. The opposition made to the colony by the Northwest Company was for the declared reason that "colonization was unfavorable to the fur trade;" their policy was to hold the great part of a continent as a game preserve for the benefit solely of their trade.

The colony was revived when the Northwest was merged in the Hudson's Bay Company, and reoccupied its old site at the Forks of Red River, the settlements extending gradually southward along the banks of the river. The grants of land which had been made to the colonists by the Earl of Selkirk held good under the general grant made to him by the Hudson's Bay Company in 1811, and have been so maintained.[15]

Meantime the Half-breeds had been increasing in number; and, as the buffalo have receded before the settlements in British America, they make their hunting expeditions to the plains around the Devil's Lake. With them, the two important events of the year are the buffalo hunts which they come to these plains to make. They bring with them carts built to carry each the meat of ten buffalo, which they make into pemmican. This consists of the meat dried by fire or sun, coarsely pounded and mixed with melted fat, and packed into skin sacks. It is of two qualities: the ordinary pemmican of commerce, being the meat without selection, and the finer, in small sacks, consisting of the choicest parts kneaded up with the marrow. Buffalo tongues, pemmican, and robes constitute chiefly their trade and support.

When making their hunts the party is usually divided, one-half to hunt, the other to guard the camp. Years ago they were much harassed by the Indians of the various tribes who frequented these buffalo grounds as much to fight as to hunt. But as a result of these conflicts with the Half-breeds the Indians were always obliged to go into mourning, and gradually they had learned to fight shy of these people and of late years had ceased to molest them. They are good shots and good riders, and have a prairie-wide reputation for skill in hunting and bravery in fighting.

We remained on the Devil's Lake over a week, during which three stations were made along the southern shore, giving for the most northern latitude 47° 59′ 29″, and for longitude 98° 28′. Our barometer gave for the top of the "Enchanted Hill" 1,766 feet above the sea, for the plateau 1,486 feet, and for the lake 1,476 feet. It is a beautiful sheet of water, the shores being broken into pleasing irregularity by promontories and many islands. As in some other lakes on the plateau, the water is brackish, but there are fish in it; and it is doubtless much freshened by the rains and melting snows of the spring. No outlet was found, but at the southern end there are low grounds by which at the season of high waters the lake may discharge into the Shayen River. This would put it among the sources of the Red River. The most extended view of its waters obtainable from any of the surrounding hills seemed to reach about forty miles in a northwesterly direction. Accompanied by Dixon or Frenière, I was sent off on several detached excursions to make out what I could of the shape and size of the lake. On one of these I went for a day's journey along the western shore, but was unable in the limited time to carry my work to the northern end. Toward nightfall we found near the shore good water and made there our camp in open ground. Nothing disturbed our rest for several hours, when we were roused by a confused heavy trampling and the usual grunting sounds which announced buffalo. We had barely time to get our animals close in, and to throw on dry wood and stir up the fire, before the herd was upon us. They were coming to the lake for water, and the near ones being crowded forward by those in the rear and disregarding us, they were nigh going directly over us. By shouting and firing our pieces, we succeeded in getting them to make a little space, in which they kept us as they crowded down into the lake. The brackish, salty water is what these animals like, and to turn the course of such a herd from water at night would be impossible.

Unwieldy as he looks, the buffalo bull moves with a suddenness and alertness that make him at close quarters a dangerous antagonist. Frenière and I being together one day, we discovered a bull standing in the water of a little lake near the shore, and we rode up to see what he was doing there alone. "He may be sick," said Frenière. As we approached we noticed that he was watching us inquiringly, his head high up, with intention, as a bull in an arena. As we got abreast of him within a few yards, he made two or three quick steps toward us and paused. *"Oho! bonjour camarade,"* Frenière called out, and moved his horse a little away. My attention for an instant was diverted to my riata, which was trailing, when the bull made a dash at us. I made an effort to get out of his range, but my horse appeared to think that it was in the order of proceeding for me first to fire. A rough graze to his hind quarters which staggered him made him see that the bull had decided to take this particular affair into his own hands, or horns, and under the forcible impression he covered a rod or two of ground with surprising celerity, the bull meanwhile continuing his course across the prairie without even turning his head to look at us. Concluding that it was not desirable to follow up our brief acquaintance, we too continued our way. A good hunter does not kill merely for the sake of killing.

The outward line of the expedition being closed, our route was now turned eastward across the plateau toward the valley of the Red River of the North. The first night was passed at a small freshwater lake near the Lake of the Serpents, which is salt; and on August 7th we encamped again on the Shayen-oju. Continuing east, we crossed next day the height of land at an elevation of 1,500 feet above sea level, and a few miles farther came in view of the widespread valley of the Red River, its green wooded line extending far away to the north on its way to British America. From this point, traveling southerly, a week was spent in sketching and determining positions among the headwaters of its tributaries; and on August 14th we descended again to the valley of the Shayen and recrossed that river at an elevation of 1,228 feet above the sea, its course not many miles below curving northeast to the Red River. Two days later we reached the Lake of the Four Hills, about a hundred feet above the river. This lake is near the foot of the ascent to the Réipahan, or Head of the Coteau des Prairies. We ascended the slope to the highest point at the head of the Coteau, where the elevation was 2,000 feet above the sea and the width of the Coteau about twenty miles. In its extension to the south it reaches, in about a hundred and fifty miles, a breadth of forty miles; sloping abruptly on the west to the great plains of the Rivière à Jacques, and on the east to the prairies of the Minnesota River. Here we spent several days in the basin of the beautiful lakes which make the headwaters of the Minnesota, of the Mississippi River, and the Tchankasndata or Sioux River of the Missouri. The two groups of lakes are near together, occupying apparently the same basin, with a slight rise between; the Minnesota group being the northern. They lie in a depression or basin, from 150 to 300 feet below the rim of the Coteau, full of clear living water, often partially wooded; and, having sometimes a sandy beach or shore strewed with boulders, they are singularly charming natural features. These were pleasant camping grounds—wood was abundant, the water was good, and there were fish in the lakes.

From the lake region we descended 800 or 900 feet to the lower prairies, and took up our march for the residence of our friends the Renvilles.

Some well-employed time was devoted here to make examinations of the Big Stone and other lakes, and to making observations and collecting materials to render Mr. Nicollet's projected map of this region as nearly complete as practicable. In all these excursions we had the effective aid of the Renvilles, whose familiar knowledge of the country enabled us to economize both labor and time.

The autumn was far advanced when we took our leave of this post. That year the prairie flowers had been exceptional in luxuriance and beauty. The rich lowlands near the house were radiant with asters and goldenrod, and memory chanced to associate these flowers, as the last thing seen, with the place. Since then I have not been in that country or seen the Renvilles; but still I never see the goldenrod and purple asters in handsome bloom without thinking of that hospitable refuge on the far northern prairies.

Some additional examinations on the watershed of the Minnesota and along the Mississippi closed the labors of these expeditions; and at nightfall early in November I landed at Prairie du Chien in a bark canoe, with a detachment of our party. A steamboat at the landing was firing up and just about starting for St. Louis, but we thought it would be pleasant to rest a day or two and enjoy comfortable quarters while waiting for the next boat. But the next boat was in the spring, for next morning it was snowing hard, and the river was frozen from bank to bank. I had time enough while there to learn two things: one, how to skate; the other, the value of a day.

After some weeks of wagon journey through Illinois, in a severe winter, we reached St. Louis; when, after the party had been cared for, I went on to Washington to assist Mr. Nicollet in working up the material collected in the expeditions.

FOOTNOTES

1. Careful map making in America is as old as the seventeenth-century explorers, Champlain and Lescarbot having been responsible for important maps of the ground they covered. The Jesuit and Recollect missionaries, introducing

compass and astrolabe, did excellent cartographical work. Really scientific and detailed topographical activity on a large scale, however, began with the engineers and officers of the British Army in America. After the Seven Years' War and the conquest of Canada, well-trained men attached to British posts conscientiously surveyed much of the newly gained interior territory. Jefferson's purchase of Louisiana inaugurated governmental exploration and mapping of the regions west of the Mississippi. The Lewis and Clark Expedition (Clark being a specially good cartographer) resulted in excellent maps; so did the expedition of Zebulon Pike into New Spain. When Nicollet undertook the survey of the upper Missouri in 1838, the Santa Fe Trail had recently been surveyed and mapped (1825–27) by a government expedition under Joseph C. Brown, while Captain B. L. E. Bonneville, supported by men interested in the fur trade, had explored a considerable part of the Rocky Mountain region (1832–35), and, though his exploits have been much exaggerated, published two useful maps. Nicollet's private explorations among the headwaters of the Mississippi made him the proper person to survey and map the upper Missouri and the region northwest of the Mississippi.

2. Frémont refers to the American Fur Company. In 1822 this company, founded by John Jacob Astor, had established a branch in St. Louis which became known as its Western Department. Another and earlier branch, called the Northern Department, had been established at Mackinac. In 1827 the Columbia Fur Company joined the larger organization, and was termed the Upper Missouri Outfit of the American Fur Company. Astor, growing old, sold out his interests in 1834. The Western Department went to Pratte, Chouteau & Co.; the Northern Department, which inherited the name of American Fur Company, to a group headed by Ramsay Crooks. It was this last-named company which controlled the fur trade of the whole area between Detroit and the Red River of the North, the region Nicollet and Frémont were now to explore. It also handled marketing operations for Pratte, Chouteau & Co., which this year (1838) became Pierre Chouteau, Jr., & Co.

3. Henry Hastings Sibley (1811–1891), born in Detroit, had joined the American Fur Company at Mackinac in 1828, and six years later had reached Fort Snelling to take charge of the extensive fur trade with the Sioux in the area running north to the Canadian boundary and west to the crest of the Rockies. The roomy stone house which Frémont describes became a recognized haven for explorers, army officers, missionaries, and traders. Indian chiefs were hospitably entertained there. Sibley, a man of commanding physique and vigorous personality, was elected the first delegate in Congress when Minnesota became a Territory (1849) and the first governor when it became a State (1858). No white man knew the Sioux better, and none had a wider influence among them.

4. The city of Mankato now lies at the point of this elbow; and within the bend lies the town of Nicollet, in the county of Nicollet.

5. In present-day Pipestone County, Minnesota, which lies on the South Dakota boundary, in the valley of the Big Sioux River.

6. Lac Qui Parle is a broad enlargement of the Minnesota River near the South Dakota boundary, bounded on the west by Lac Qui Parle County, Minnesota.

7. Lacrosse was originally an Indian game, played widely by North American tribes, and given its name by the French from the crooked stick (fitted with a net) used in playing it. Natural goals—rocks or trees—were often used,

but in the more formal matches a pole or poles were erected. As the goals were from a quarter-mile to half a mile or more apart, scores or hundreds could play; Catlin saw from 600 to 1000 Indians engaged. The game often lasted for hours.

8. It is not clear whether this was Jean Baptiste Faribault (1775–1860) or his son Alexander, born 1806. The elder Faribault, a French Canadian, had been apprenticed in 1796 to the North West Fur Company, and sent to the posts of this British establishment in Illinois. Later, living at Prairie du Chien, he took the side of the British in the War of 1812. American army officers induced him to remove to the neighborhood of Fort Snelling in 1819, where at first he farmed, but later entered the employ of the Columbia Fur Company. Trading with the Sioux, he gained great influence among them. Minnesota has named a county for him, and the city of Faribault for his son Alexander. Sibley wrote a life of the father.

9. The preferred spelling is Provôt. One of the ablest "mountain men," a match almost for Kit Carson or Jim Bridger, Provôt was able to teach young Frémont a great deal about the West, and unquestionably did so. Some students of Western history assert that Provôt reached Great Salt Lake in 1820, four years before Jim Bridger is said to have discovered it. According to Hiram Chittenden, he was the discoverer of South Pass.

10. The first settlement at Fort Pierre, South Dakota, was a little trading post opened by Joseph LaFramboise in 1817. Presently the Columbia Fur Company occupied it and renamed it Fort Tecumseh. Then in 1828 the Astor interests took possession, and four years later named it Fort Pierre Chouteau. For a long period it was the only civilized spot in what is now South Dakota.

11. Frenière, an experienced "mountain man" and plainsman, also taught Frémont much. He was noted for his vision, and at far distances could determine whether a faint moving dot was buffalo, Indian, or antelope. William Dixon was an expert guide. Nicollet in his report of this expedition relates how, traversing the Coteau de Missouri, he brought them out at just the spot desired, a headland commanding a magnificent view of the James River. "You wanted geography," he told the explorers, who gazed in admiration; "look—there's geography for you!"

12. That is, the James River. The expedition was heading toward Devil's Lake, in what is now northeastern North Dakota.

13. The Sheyenne River, which runs from the Devil's Lake district south and east to empty into the Red River near Fargo, all in North Dakota, is of course not to be confused with the Cheyenne River, which runs through western South Dakota to empty into the Missouri not far above Fort Pierre.

14. These Half-breeds of the Red River Valley were hunting in the Dakota country because buffalo were growing scarce in Canada. They were descendants of French and British fur traders and adventurers who had intermarried with Sioux, Chippewa, and other tribes. Their huge carts, drawn by oxen, would hold the meat of ten or twelve buffalo apiece.

15. The Highland and other settlers under Selkirk's protection established themselves securely at Fort Garry in what is now Manitoba. Here, at the confluence of the Red and the Assiniboine rivers, grew up the city of Winnipeg.

CHAPTER 3

Hassler:
Courtship of Jessie Benton: Oregon *

THE official report of our return to Washington was duly made.
I accompanied Mr. Nicollet in his visit to the President and Mr.
Poinsett, by whom he was received with marked cordiality and
assured of their great satisfaction in the success of the expedition.
It had brought back valuable knowledge concerning a region of
great agricultural capacities, little known to the people at large, and
which opened to them a new field to occupy. Mr. Poinsett told me of
his gratification with the good report which Mr. Nicollet gave him
concerning myself; and his kind reception and approval were to me
the culminating pleasure of a campaign which had been full of
novel interest.

Some pleasant days were spent in welcomes to Mr. Nicollet by
his friends in Baltimore, in which I was usually included. Among
the agreeable acquaintances made at this time the most interesting
to me was Bishop Chanche, of St. Mary's College. Here, as in St.
Louis, Mr. Nicollet's relations with the upper clergy were intimate
and friendly; and with him I had in this way the advantage of
seeing in intimacy men of secluded and dignified lives and large
impersonal aims. They received him as the abbots of old welcomed
a congenial traveler into their calm retreats when monasteries were
seats of learning. The security and peace and orderly comfort made
for them a grateful refreshment and relief.

At the college, Mr. Nicollet had his quarters, which were always
kept ready for him. He used to take pleasure in showing me in his
wardrobes the wealth of linen and other luxuries of his former
civilized life; which were all in amusing contrast with that which
we had lately been leading, where the chief luxury we could com-

* From Frémont's *Memoirs*, pp. 55-72.

mand was a clean skin. It is an uncommon pleasure in a man's life to have such an interior welcome and so real a home in many places as Mr. Nicollet had. The sight of these things usually recalled to him other scenes and events, and led him in confidential intercourse to tell them over to me as they came up in his mind, and so carried my knowledge of him back into his former life.

The loss of friends marks our path through life with crosses which tell us of griefs, as in unfrequented countries a wayside cross or heap of stones marks the spot where some traveler had suddenly come face to face with death on his road. Involuntarily one looks around as if the hidden danger still lurked there. The cross gives a warning impress, and imagination lends its aid to recall the tragedy which had left its shadow on the ground. I had returned to Washington in a condition of happy thoughtlessness, relieved from work, and my mind not burdened with a care. The campaign was over and its objects accomplished. What now remained to be done was merely the giving a definite shape to its results, so interesting that it could not be called labor, but pleasure only. And so I was already enjoying the fruitful repose, in expectation.

But now there came to me the news that our little circle had been broken by the loss of my only brother, who had returned to die at home. So soon as the requirement of immediate duty permitted I obtained leave. The short time which had been given me I spent with my mother. The years had been made lonely by the absence of both, and now still more by the loss of one of us, and I was happy for her sake in the unusual brightness my presence brought with it; and for a while it was almost the old time again.

But the brief leave was soon over, and I returned to Washington. Among Mr. Nicollet's scientific affiliations, one of the most intimate and the most interesting, because of the opposite characters of the two men, was that with Mr. Hassler, the chief of the United States Coast Survey.[1] Both were indurated in science, and so far congenial, but both entirely opposite in complexion of mind and in manner; the one flint, and the other steel, fire flashing out in every argument. Mr. Nicollet was urbane, forbearing, rounding off obstructions in intercourse; polished and persuasive, and careful of the feelings of others. Mr. Hassler was abrupt, full of sharp edges and intolerant of pretentious mediocrity. Going directly to the heart of his subject and in language the most direct, he was almost a distinct species, where the exterior photographed the inner man. What he did, or the manner in which he did it, was absolutely without reference to outside opinion or outside effect. What he intended to do he did in what seemed to him the best way, and that was all. His life had been the pursuit of science, and his occupation now was its application; and for this he was exceptionally qualified, and any interference with his work he resented with indignant promptitude.

To a member of a committee who complained to him of a delay in his report to Congress, with the remark that when he had a report to write he did it in a day, Mr. Hassler replied: "That is time enough for such reports, but before you could write one of mine, your days would be numbered." He would not allow the prefix of "Honorable," merely because of usage. A Cabinet officer who had offended him he addressed: "Mr. ——, the Honorable Secretary, etc." The place was honorable, he conceded—not the man.

All Washington of that date remembers the figure dressed in white flannel, which habitually was driven through the streets in a large foreign-built carriage, commonly called "the ark." In this he was used to go to the field of his operations along the coast, where his surveying parties were occupied. The ark was so arranged that in it on these occasions were always packed some of the essentials for clean and comfortable sleeping and toilet needs; together with red and white German wines, and some such provision as was good for the health of a man who knew that good food was essential to good brainwork. He was both abstemious and fastidious. When he accepted an invitation to dinner, which was seldom, his habit was to carry with him some bottles of these German wines, as he would drink of no other kind, and only of his own. But his abruptness never degenerated into common rudeness. The thin, intellectual face and tall, slight figure contradicted any idea of that kind. It was always intellect speaking, not passion; and withal there was a kindly disposition.

Mr. Nicollet's work was to be done in Washington, which was also Mr. Hassler's headquarters. These two men were naturally happy of the occasion that enabled them to come together, and it was decided that we three should make our bachelor quarters at Mr. Hassler's own house on Capitol Hill. In this arrangement there was some disparity of purse as well as of age. It was interesting to see the manner in which these two proceeded to organize the establishment. Of one thing they were aware, as many otherwise good housekeepers in our country are not, that the essential element in a household for economy and health is the cook. In this, accident favored us. A chef recently arrived from France had just been rejected by President Van Buren, on account of the high salary which he considered proportioned to his skill. Somehow he found his way to us. An examination, noncompetitive, resulted in showing him regularly trained to his occupation. He was a man of middle age, of imposing presence, and opened the interview by the production of a long sheet of paper with this heading: *"Pour un cuisinier Français il faut une batterie de cuisine,"* and, following this, an enumeration incomprehensible even to Mr. Nicollet. This was the beginning and end of his examination, and made him master of the situation. A man who knew so much about his tools was likely to know how to use them, and he did. For Mr. Nicollet delicate food had become a necessity. His health had been impaired by the discomforts and exposures in his expeditions, seriously so in that to the sources of the Mississippi. During this he had been long and dangerously ill when off alone with only his guide, and now it pleased him to have this opportunity to nurse his injured health. The first dinner was a fete to me, to whom for two years the *batterie de cuisine* had been a *chaudière,* the camp kettle of the Canadian voyageur.

It was a summer evening, and, going to the front of the house, we found our new chef, in white cap and apron, quietly installed on the porch enjoying the evening air. Mr. Nicollet was taken aback by the unexpected vision, and in his quiet way suggested to him, *"Mon garçon, c'est pas comme il faut, ceçi."* The man on his part was equally surprised, for he said that he had understood that in this country all were on terms of equality. But he was sensible, and took it, as it was meant, in good part, and our ménage worked on smoothly, to Mr. Nicollet's great benefit.

Our work was to be done in the Coast Survey building on the hill. Here Mr. Hassler had appropriated to us several rooms, some of which were for the work, and others for our more private use. I had here with me a congenial companion of my own age, and of the same corps, Lieutenant Scammon, who had been assigned to duty with Mr. Nicollet in working up astronomical observations and the construction of the map. Both of us had unusual facility in figures. Like myself, he was a lover of chess, and this engrossed much of our leisure time. In fact, the time was divided between work and chess. He was also a man of varied and large reading for one so young, and had the gift of a pleasant and companionable temper; this rounded the circle of my daily associates.

The house on the hill overlooked the Potomac, and the breeze from the valley swept away the summer heat. Mr. Nicollet profited by the situation and the command of fine instruments to put up an observatory here, where he and I spent many interesting nights in observations. The night watches were sometimes long, after the day spent among figures which required care, but there is something in the tranquil movements of the great bodies, endless through space, which impresses patience on those watching. Mr. Nicollet's mind was fruitful of interesting things, so that the hours never dulled into sleep. I remember, one night, lying by my lantern when we were engaged in some outside work, a beetle lit on the open book in which I was recording observations made by him from time to time. I was glad to have something to do, and before the insect flew off I made a sketch of him which happened to be lifelike. Coming to the lantern to read off his instrument, Mr. Nicollet struck at the drawing to brush away the beetle. He was vexed by the hearty laugh which expressed my pleasure at his testimony to the accuracy of my drawing, and reproached me for the frivolity, which was really lightheartedness that goes soon enough.

To him an astronomical observation was a solemnity, and required such decorous preparation as an Indian makes when he goes where he thinks there are supernatural beings. "*C'est toujours comme ça chez vous,*" he said. "Instead of occupying your mind with these grand objects, you give your attention to insect things." "But," I reply, "that is because my mind is not large enough to get those enormous bodies into it. I try, but I get lost in the size of them; my mind has not yet got to comprehend them. I can reach a certain distance or a certain size, and then my mind stops and falls back upon itself. I get baffled in the mental effort to imagine a hugeness which the sight is always contradicting. With you it is very different. You have been studying these things so long and so deeply that your mind has become broadened and takes them in comfortably. You have gotten to comprehend this infinity—I not yet. Perhaps if I remain long enough with you I shall." And with the implied compliment his irritation was soothed, and our talk turned into strange and kindred, and always interesting, speculations on discoveries yet to come.

And in this way, or something like it, our nights were often passed.

Mr. Benton was a disciple of Jefferson. He was familiar with all that had been said and done by him concerning the region on the North Pacific, and the subject had been dwelt upon, made personal to him by the explorer, General Clarke. With a mind full of the subject, he wished to confer with Mr. Jefferson, and made a visit to him at his home in the winter of 1825. The ideas in reference to overland communication which had grown up in the mind of Mr. Jefferson were based upon the acquisition of the Louisiana territory. He talked these over with Mr. Benton, and they became his in the way that he assimilated information which he recognized to be good. To such a mind, of which the chief bias was to utilize material, this vast unused region had already presented itself as an object of immediate and accumulating interest. In area it was an empire; shut off from the new, it opened to the ancient East by one great harbor, at which all the avenues to interior communication concentrated. And this empire, ours of right, was in the hands of an old enemy whose firm grasp was unrelenting.

From the moment he realized the situation, he had resolved to wrest back this region and hold it where it belonged, in the American empire.

In his position of Senator he had now a standpoint from which to work, and thenceforward he devoted his energies to carrying through the plans which these two statesmen had the forecast to initiate. Taking part as he did in all the great questions that came before Congress, the rigorous maintenance of our title to the Columbia was with him continuously the greater question, because the interests of his State demanded it; in this as in all the important passages of his life he certainly earned recognition as exceptionally the man "tenacious of purpose."

The occupation of the Lower Columbia by an American emigration, and the enforcing of our title to its whole valley and the Pacific coast north to the 49th parallel, had already become the aim of his persistent effort before he entered political life.

In 1820, the first proposition made in Congress for the occupation of the Columbia was introduced through Mr. Floyd, who was a member of the House from Virginia. Mr. Floyd was a near relation of Mrs. Benton. The old "Indian Queen," on what was called by way of distinction "the Avenue," was a headquarters for Western and Southwestern men. Mr. Floyd and Mr. Benton were staying there; and with them were Mr. Ramsay Crooks and Mr. Russell Farnham, both concerned in the American Fur Company, and at that time representing its interests at Washington.

Mr. Farnham had recently returned from a visit to the Lower Columbia. Mr. Benton the year before had written and published, in St. Louis, a series of essays in relation to the treaty of 1818, directed to show that the joint occupation must result in possession by England if our own occupation of the river valley were longer delayed. These essays had been read by Mr. Floyd, and were fully agreed in by him. Mr. Benton had not yet been admitted to his seat in the Senate because of the long debate on the Missouri Compromise, which virtually settled the question of slavery extension.

After reviewing and consulting together over the Oregon situation, Mr. Floyd took up the subject and moved for a committee to consider and report upon it. A select committee of three was granted by the House, which within six days reported a bill "to authorize the occupation of the Columbia River, and to regulate trade and intercourse with the Indian tribes thereon.". . .*

I was with Mr. Nicollet in his official visit of duty to the Missouri Senators, Mr. Benton and Mr. Linn.[2] He knew of the comprehending interest which both, especially Mr. Benton, had in the results of the expedition as being directly in the line of Western progress. Through the Chouteaus and other leading men in St. Louis, with whom he was on intimate terms, Mr. Nicollet knew of Mr. Benton's unwearied

---

* A small amount of political detail is here omitted. Frémont notes that Benton continued to labor fruitlessly (so far as this period went) for the termination of the joint Anglo-American occupation of Oregon. But he did not join the chauvinists who presently set up a clamor with "Fifty-four Forty or Fight"; on the contrary, he always insisted that the 49th parallel was the true boundary.

74 NARRATIVES OF EXPLORATION AND ADVENTURE

interest in furthering knowledge of our Western possessions and bringing them into occupation.

The essential importance to the country of the great band of unoccupied territory which lay between the Mississippi and the Pacific coast had been one of the chief subjects which Western members were endeavoring to force upon the early action of Congress. The farming value of the country over which the surveys of Mr. Nicollet extended impressed them still more strongly with the importance of the trans-Missouri region, and gave fresh impulse to their efforts. Oregon was now coming to the forefront among political questions which were tending to embitter party politics. But the presidential elections were absorbing attention, and for a period suspended effort on other questions.

The Democratic party, which had been so strong and masterful under Jackson, was nearing the end of its powerful reign. As foreigners and men of science, Mr. Hassler and Mr. Nicollet had but little interest in passing political affairs. To them the recurring party struggles were in the established order of things. They looked upon their own work as belonging with the material development of the country, disconnected from the political changes which to them meant only a change in the personnel of the Government. National questions which affected the whole country they looked at in their large aspect, and followed with the close attention of thinking and farsighted men. As for myself, neither then nor afterward had I any interest in merely party contests, but naturally I was deeply interested in their frequent discussion of questions which grew out of the progress of the country. These gave shape and solidity to my own crude ideas. The one question to which I had given any serious thought was outside of politics and above party.

Mr. Poinsett had lived much abroad. His education had been finished in England, and he had traveled in Asia as well as in Europe. He had been our Minister to revolutionary Mexico, and to the new South American republics.

In the midst of these surroundings he was able to compare their political elements with the new growth of government which promised a grand future to his own country; but, looking at it from a distance so great that only the salient points were visible, he saw the dark spot on the sun which was ominous of evil, and under the impressions then made he formed the opinions which determined and guided his political course.

I was one of his devoted adherents. My education and condition of life had left me disinterested and unprejudiced as to the question which was the root of discord, and I had never given thought to its material side. My opinions on this subject grew out of my education, which had inculcated intolerance of oppression in every form and that love of the common country which in America was part of a boy's growth. In this condition of mind when General Jackson's course drew the line in South Carolina, I had joined the party of Mr. Poinsett and gave unwavering allegiance to the Union.

I was now settled down to regular work. There was always in this the interest of a problem to be worked out. There is pleasure in labor which is sure of a result, and this was as sure as the stars which had their part in it.

I have said that our settlement was near the Capitol, and some of the leading subjects of discussion there had special interest for us as being kindred to our own occupation and looking to its continuation.

Members of both houses occasionally came to see the progress of Mr. Hassler's coast surveys, and usually extended their visit to our rooms. We were not yet at work on the map. There was a mass of astronomical and other observations to be calculated and discussed before a beginning on this could be made. Indeed, the making of such a map is an interesting process. It must be exact. First, the foundations must be laid in observations made in the field; then the reduction of these observations to latitude and longitude; afterward the projection of the map, and the laying down upon it of positions fixed by the observations; then the tracing from the sketchbooks of the lines of the rivers, the forms of the lakes, the contours of the hills. Specially is it interesting to those who have laid in the field these various foundations to see them all brought into final shape—fixing on a small sheet the results of laborious travel over waste regions, and giving to them an enduring place on the world's surface.

Mr. Benton had expected to find the map in progress, and was disappointed to see only the blank projection. But his disappointment gave way to interest of another kind when he saw spread out on the tables the evidences of the material first to be digested. His visit was not simply one of intelligent curiosity, but there was purpose in it, as indeed, I found when afterward I came to know him, there was in all that he did. The character of his mind was to utilize, and what he could not assimilate he did not touch. He knew well to use information and give it point. The results of our journeys between the two great rivers had suggested to him the same work for the broader field beyond the Missouri. His inquiries on this occasion were all of distinct pertinency. They were directed to know about our means and manner of traveling, the nature of the work required to be done, and the instruments employed. In the course of his inquiries he dwelt on the unoccupied country beyond the Missouri and the existing uncertain and incomplete knowledge concerning it. The interview left on me a profound impression and raised excited interest. The ideas suggested remained fixtures in my mind. The thought of penetrating into the recesses of that wilderness region filled me with enthusiasm—I saw visions. Formerly I had been entirely devoted to my intended profession of engineering. The lives of great engineers had been my treasured exemplars. But strict engineering had lost its inspiration in the charm of the new field into which I had entered during the last few years.

In this interview with Mr. Benton my mind had been quick to see a larger field and differing and greater results. It would be travel over a part of the world which still remained the New—the opening up of unknown lands; the making unknown countries known; and the study without books—the learning at first hand from Nature herself; the drinking first at her unknown springs—became a source of never-ending delight to me. I felt that it was an unreasonable pleasure to expect that it might happen to me to be among the very few to whom the chance had fallen to work with Nature where in all her features there was still aboriginal freshness.

This interview with Mr. Benton was pregnant of results and decisive of my life. In what way it brought these results about, and how important they were, will be seen as we go on.

His visit, returned by Mr. Nicollet and myself, led into others and grew into intimacy. Congress was in session, and at his house I often met Western members, all, at that time, being "West" which lay beyond Pennsylvania. Often, on such evenings, we being present, the conversation turned upon our surveys, and naturally led to the subjects which so much interested Mr. Benton and his Western colleagues. Among those who were more especially his personal and political friends were his fellow Senator from Missouri, Lewis F. Linn, and Senator Dodge,[4] the elder half-brother of Mr. Linn—a man with such composure of natural dignity, in aspect and manner, that he was known among his friends as "the Sachem." There was great love and unity between the brothers, who were in appearance very different: Senator Dodge, of powerful build and unusual height, his quiet strength of manner indicating the thoughtful, commanding habit of his mind; Senator Linn, of moderate size, but with a beauty as complete as it was remarkable—a head and features resembling the young head of Byron, but made winning by the expression of kind feelings and the play of a quick mind.

In these unpremeditated talks, where unstudied expression gave the color of every man's mind and bits of information found receptive place, plans were of easy digestion. And in this way measures were conceived and perfected which, by the strength behind them, carried their own fulfillment. And gradually, as being kindred with our thoughts and present occupations, they engrossed our minds and settled into practical shape.

The months passed, and carried with them labor done. Our preliminary work had been in greater part completed, and we had begun on the map, Mr. Scammon and I. Meantime, Mr. Nicollet's health was being steadily undermined. He had grown restless, and made frequent visits away from Washington—I think usually to some quiet retreat among his friends in Baltimore, where, too, was a physician who had his confidence. He was not in condition to reduce into shape the materials for his report, which were varied and interesting and embraced the labor of years of thought and study following upon most interesting travel. And, waiting for the return of nerve and strength which were slow in coming, his writing was delayed. No second hand can do this like the first. The impressions made by the visible objects, the pleasure of the first experience and the anticipations of roused curiosity, the sense of danger threatened and met, the relief from obstacles overcome, cannot be transfused into a mind that is cold and unexcited. The lights and shadows are all lost on the level plane; and to such physical description, the eye that has not seen cannot bring a mind to feel and comprehend. And so Mr. Nicollet waited, hoping for the health that did not return.

In the family of Mr. Benton were four sisters and but one son, Randolph, then twelve years old. It fell to each of the sisters to have a marked life; and, as they grew into womanhood, they were separated far apart, as often happens in this large country of ours. All of them had strong, high character, and capacities carefully cultivated; and among them rare musical talent. Randolph died when just entering into what promised to be a distinguished life.

Jessie was the second daughter. I went with the eldest of the sisters to a school concert in Georgetown, where I saw her. She was then just in the bloom of her girlish beauty and perfect health effervesced in bright talk which the pleasure of seeing her sister drew out.

Naturally, I was attracted. She made the effect that a rose of rare color or beautiful picture would have done. Months passed before, in the vacation time, I saw her again, at her father's house, which already I had come to frequent. She was happy in the return to her home, and my first impressions of her were made in the unreserve of family life, where the real nature most readily expresses itself. Her beauty had come far enough down from English ancestry to be now in her that American kind which is made up largely of mind expressed in the face; but it still showed its Saxon descent. At that time of awakening mind the qualities that made hers could only be seen in flitting shadows across the face, or in the expressions of incipient thought and unused and untried feeling. So in writing here I give what afterknowledge made known to me. Nor would it be possible to disentangle the interwoven threads of memory and confine impressions to the time when they were made. There are features which convey to us a soul so white that they impress with instant pleasure, and of this kind were hers. As, too, in the daily contact there are others from which to receive pleasant words or kindly acts gives the sort of agreeable surprise we feel when suddenly we come upon patches of bright, particolored phlox growing on naked rocks. The phlox loves the naked sand or rock, but the difference is in the warmth it finds there. In the human rock there is no heart to replace the sun.

Her qualities were all womanly, and education had curiously preserved the down of a modesty which was innate. There had been no experience of life to brush away the bloom. She had inherited from her father his grasp of mind, comprehending with a tenacious memory; but with it a quickness of perception and instant realization of subjects and scenes in their completed extent which did not belong to his; and with these, warm sympathies—a generous pity for human suffering, and a tenderness and sensibility that made feeling take the place of mind; so compelled was every impulse to pass through these before it could reach the surface to find expression. There was a rare union of intelligence to feel the injury of events, and submission to them with silence and discretion; and withal a sweet, and happy, and forbearing temper which has remained proof against the wearing of time.

Insensibly and imperceptibly, in these frequent meetings, there came a glow into my heart which changed the current and color of daily life and gave beauty to common things. And so it came that there was no room for reason, which found a cold and dull ear that heard, but did not listen. . . .*

The winter work of making up charts required the rooms we had been using at the Coast Survey building. This, with the frequent and prolonged absences of Mr. Nicollet, brought about a change in our establishment to smaller but comfortable quarters at the foot of the Capitol. And so there the work was continued through the winter, without event, until the death of President Harrison. For the day of the funeral ceremonies, I cleared our workroom and made it gay with plants and flowers; for from its windows the family of Mr. Benton had consented to view the procession. The death of a President so suddenly following his accession to power was a shock to the community. As yet no President had died in office, and there was sincere personal feeling for General Harrison, who was a brave and amiable man. The funeral pageant was something to see and remember, as an event of the time. I was to take part with my corps in the ceremonies, but I procured leave and went back to be with my friends, for to me the funeral occasion proved, as I had hoped, to be my red-letter day.

* A paragraph about the difficulty of writing on "The intimate relationships of life" is omitted.

All this time Mr. Nicollet's health was not mending. The writing of his report was still delayed.

In the surveys that had been made during his last expedition, the upper part only of some of the larger rivers had been embraced. The Des Moines was one of these; and at his request I was sent, in July, to make such a reconnaissance of its lower course as would nearly complete it. Whether or not this detachment of myself from Washington originated with Mr. Nicollet I do not know, but I was loath to go.

I had again with me on this survey one of my companions of the former expedition in Mr. Charles Geyer, who accompanied me as botanist. I established the course of the river upward from its mouth about two hundred miles, which brought the survey to the Raccoon Forks; and Mr. Geyer did all that the season and time allowed for botany. It was here that Geyer found the snake under his flowers. There were many snakes along the river, and botany became a hazardous pursuit. As had been proposed, our examination was confined to the immediate valley of the river, but we frequently ranged into the woods, where deer and wild turkey were abundant; and the survey was a health-giving excursion, but it did not cure the special complaint for which I had been sent there.

The influence of women is a force sometimes dangerous. Mrs. Benton was not friendly to my suit, though to me she always was. She thought her daughter much too young—she was but sixteen—and, beyond this, that the unsettled life of an army officer was unfavorable to making such a home as she wished for her. She had herself, for seven years, delayed to marry Colonel Benton until he resigned from the army.

Mrs. Poinsett and Mrs. Benton were on friendly terms, and Mr. Poinsett was Secretary of War and my friend. The charge of this reconnaissance, in connection with Mr. Nicollet's important work, was an advance for me, and accordingly I was sent. But it did not take long to get through with it. I returned to Washington and set about reducing to shape the new material just collected, in order to add the results to Mr. Nicollet's map.

I was leading a busy, working life; what was immediately at hand and what projected should have been enough to occupy my thoughts and time. A probation of a year had been agreed upon, but, as sometimes happens, the most important events of our individual life come upon us suddenly and unpremeditatedly; and so it was with our marriage, which was on October 19, 1841.

Mr. Nicollet was ill in Baltimore, and we went there to see him at the house of his friend Professor Ducatel. Our visit pleased and roused him. The nervous exhaustion which was a feature of his illness made everything seem a task. He had come to remain late in bed, sometimes doing his writing there and not rising at all during the day. He had formed an ideal to himself for his work, which he was never satisfied to have reached when he got his thoughts on paper.

In reality, the material which his science had enabled him to gather was so interesting that to barely set down the facts in the light of his own knowledge would have made a great work.

In intervals of revived health he came to Washington, coming always to us—to him we were "*mes enfants*." But he was fixedly morbid about the impediments and discouragements which he fancied in the way of getting out his work.

I was now busily occupied in office-work every day while the light lasted, hurrying to put in good order what remained for me to do in connection with Mr. Nicollet's surveys. As I have said, the discussions among the Western members had taken shape; they were agreed that the time had come to put into action their views concerning Oregon.

I knew that Mr. Benton was decided that an expedition ought to be sent to open the way for the emigration through the mountains; and I knew, also, he intended Mr. Nicollet should be at his head, and that I should be his assistant.

This expedition was intended to be "auxiliary and in aid to the emigration to the Lower Columbia"; it was to indicate and describe the line of travel, and the best positions for military posts; and to describe, and fix in position, the South Pass in the Rocky Mountains, at which this initial expedition was to terminate. At this time the South Pass, at the head of the Platte River, was the one most available for our emigration, and already used.

With this knowledge, and the hope of having part in such an expedition, I worked unremittingly to have the way cleared of previous work; leaving only the brief evening hours for the new home just begun for me.

I felt I was being drawn into the current of important political events: the object of this expedition was not merely a survey; beyond that was its bearing on the holding of our territory on the Pacific; and the contingencies it involved were large.

One stormy evening near Christmas, when we were quietly enjoying the warm glow of firelight, a note was brought in to me from Mr. Hassler. The bearer was a strange figure—a shock of light curly hair standing up thick about his head, and a face so red that we attributed it to a wrong cause instead of to the cold and the nervousness and anxiety which turned his speech into stammering. Under the first impression I went outside with him. I found that he was a German, a skilled topographer, who came to me with this letter from Mr. Hassler requesting employment for him if we had any to give. I brought him in again, and sat him down by the fire while I thought over what might be done to have the pleasure of meeting Mr. Hassler's wish. I found that he was actually without means of support. The failure of an appropriation had thrown him out of his regular work, and the needs of his little family were immediate. He was divided between their want and his own natural pride, and asked of me to go with him to verify their condition, which I did; and their Christmas was made comfortable.

There were astronomical observations remaining unreduced. That work, I told him, I could get for him. This he said he was not able to do. His profession was topography—in this he excelled, but that was all. The only thing I could devise was to get for him this astronomical work and do it myself, which I could by working in the evenings. It troubled him greatly that I should have to do this for him, but it was the only way I could come in aid; and so it was done. This was Preuss;[4] and this was the beginning of our long friendly comradeship. The little service which I was able to render him he amply repaid by years of faithful and valuable service as topographer on my journeys, during which his even temper and patient endurance of hardship earned my warm regard. Preuss had the endurance in working with an aim that so characterizes his nation, and with it a cheerful philosophy of his own which often brightened dark situations. He was of those who were comrades, and part with me, in the life of which I am writing.

Therefore I give them their place, not content to leave them on the page merely as a bodiless name which awakens no interest. I wish to give enough of their personality to individualize them, and make them known as I came to know them, so that hereafter when from time to time they reappear in the narrative, it will be as familiar figures in whom something of the interest of old acquaintance may be felt.

The year which had been so eventful to me was drawing to its close, and the Christmas time which smooths its end was at hand. Mr. Hassler offered us his carriage to make the New Year's visit of ceremony to the President, and to please him we accepted it. But it took some nerve to drive up in the ark among the holiday crowd, who were familiar enough with its Noah, but looked and smiled on the young lady in full dress and officer in uniform. Mrs. Frémont disembarked at her father's to assist in the reception there, and that evening in the intimacy of after-dinner talk there came to me the probability of my being the head of the proposed expedition.

Mr. Nicollet's health did not improve; but was steadily failing. My mind was unwilling to see this. But the larger experience of Mr. Benton made him sure Mr. Nicollet could not again take charge of an expedition.

The evening was passed in considering this contingency, and with the New Year began my joint work with Mr. Benton in behalf of our Western territories.

The months immediately following were occupied in preparation. The object of the expedition, as "ordered by the Topographical Bureau with the sanction of the Secretary of War," was simply to explore the country between the Missouri River and the Rocky Mountains; but its real purpose, the objects which were had in view in designing it, were known only to the circle of its friends. It was not until long after that it was avowed to be "in aid of and auxiliary to the Oregon emigration."

General Harrison, as a Western and military man, would most probably have entered heartily into the ultimate motive of the expedition. With him Mr. Benton was on friendly terms. President Harrison's Secretary of War, John Bell of Tennessee, was also a Western man. But the death of the President made different conditions. Mr. Tyler threw the weight of his administration against any measure to encourage and aid the emigration to Oregon. His Secretary of War [Mr. John Canfield Spencer] was from the East, and a lawyer. These were the altered circumstances which required prudence and reserve in avoiding any check to the projected movement to settle the Oregon question by emigration. The amount appropriated was small. In obtaining this it was necessary to use caution, in order to avoid the opposition which for various reasons might be expected. This Mr. Benton's parliamentary experience enabled him to do successfully. But the limited means exacted a close economy in the outfit. With the plan fully settled I went in March to New York to obtain necessary instruments and other essentials. Among these I had made an indiarubber boat, with airtight compartments, to be used in crossing or examining watercourses. So far as I know, this was the first boat of the kind made or used in such work. When finished it was brought to Washington by Mr. Horace Day, who took much pride in it.[5] It was the early day of indiarubber, when its preparations were not "odorless." Mr. Day himself unpacked it at the house, on a broad gallery opening from the dining room, saying that there "might be some odor from the chemicals." There was; to such a degree that it was promptly transferred to the stable, but not in time to avoid a long-contested battle between his "chemicals" and the obligatory disinfectants. Notwithstanding, it proved of valuable service, until finally it came to a violent end in the line of its duty.

The unreserve of daily intercourse under his own roof had given me a familiar knowledge of Mr. Benton's plans. Recognizing fully his forceful energy, and the certainty of success this carried with it, I gave henceforward to him and the work confided to me unstinted devotion.

FOOTNOTES

1. Ferdinand Rudolph Hassler (1770–1843), a Swiss by birth, educated at the University of Bern, had come to the United States in 1805. His devotion to scientific pursuits recommended him to members of the American Philosophical Society. When that body urged Jefferson to survey the coasts of the United States, Hassler became interested. He drafted a plan, and, Congress having authorized the survey, was named to undertake the work. Delays occurred, however, and it was not until 1816 that he was appointed the first superintendent of the Coast Survey, and not until 1832 that he was able to place the enterprise on the high plane that he desired. A truly eminent scientist, satisfied with nothing but the best standards of geodetic surveying, he was deficient —as Frémont notes—in tact, and impatient of the interference of auditing officers and politicians. His path was naturally full of thorns. It is significant

that his wife, after bearing him nine children, left him. But in the eleven years preceding his death he placed the Coast Survey on the sound basis which it has always since maintained.

2. Lewis Fields Linn (1795–1843), a Kentuckian by birth, was Senator from Missouri from 1843 until his death. He was a Jacksonian Democrat, a close friend of Benton, and a strong believer in expansion to the Pacific. Despite his intense belief in Manifest Destiny, he was moderate in speech and action.

3. Senator Linn's father had married the widowed mother of Henry Dodge (1782–1867), who in 1836 was appointed the first governor of the Territory of Wisconsin, and who in 1841 was elected delegate to Congress. Later, when Wisconsin became a State, he was one of its first Senators.

4. Charles Preuss, a German of fine personal qualities, was to prove invaluable to Frémont on the second and fourth expeditions; and though he did not go on the eventful third expedition, he drew from Frémont's data the map of the Oregon country and the area west of the Colorado River, which in its day was the best map of this great region.

5. Horace H. Day (1813–1878) became noted as a manufacturer of rubber articles, a rival of Charles Goodyear, and an experimenter in the use of compressed air. He had opened a factory at New Brunswick, New Jersey, in 1839, for making rubber goods.

CHAPTER 4

First Expedition:
From Missouri to Fort Laramie *

ALL was now ready. I left Washington for the West on May 2d, 1842, Mrs. Frémont remaining at home with her family during my absence.

Arriving at St. Louis, I was received at her home with cordial hospitality by Mrs. Sarah Benton Brant, the favorite niece of Mr. Benton and wife of an old friend and army officer. In all my journeys from St. Louis, and in my visits to it in later years, I have been always welcomed by her with an affectionate regard which I have reciprocated and cherished to the present hour as among the most satisfactory of my recollections.

This expedition, directed as it was toward the opening of the Western territory, was pleasing to the people of St. Louis, who furthered my preparations with prompt and willing aid.

For this journey, which would be exposed to serious contingencies, good men and fitting animals were a first necessity. The getting these together—the necessary equipment which it needs experienced foresight to provide—required time; but at the end of several weeks this had been done, and a party of valuable and experienced men selected. Among these I had engaged as hunter Lucien Maxwell,[1] a son-in-law of one of the principal merchants in New Mexico, Mr. Beaubien, and brother-in-law of Christopher Carson, better known as "Kit Carson,"[2] who also had his home in Taos. Maxwell was about twenty-eight years of age, about five feet ten inches in

---

* The first three pages are from Frémont's *Memoirs*, pp. 73–75, which give his fullest account of preparations for the first expedition. The remainder of the chapter is from his *Report on an Exploration of the Country Lying between the Missouri River and the Rocky Mountains, on the Line of the Kansas and Great Platte Rivers* (1843).

height, and strongly built. He was personally known, by trading among them, to the tribes who ranged the country toward New Mexico, accustomed to the life of the prairies, and a resolute man and good hunter. Carson and he were close friends.

My journey from St. Louis was by steamboat up the Missouri to a point near the mouth of the Kansas River, where a few houses were the nucleus of a future town, but then called Chouteau's or Kansas Landing.

On the boat I met Kit Carson. He was returning from putting his little daughter in a convent school at St. Louis. I was pleased with him and his manner of address at this first meeting. He was a man of medium height, broad-shouldered and deep-chested, with a clear steady blue eye and frank speech and address; quiet and unassuming.

It will be anticipating to speak here of Carson in connection with after events, but I give one incident to illustrate the simple honesty of his character.

He had gone to Washington with despatches from me in 1847, and was staying at the house of Senator Benton, welcomed there as my friend. Mr. Benton was in the West, but Carson's modesty and gentleness quickly made him a place in the regard of the family, to whom he gave back a lasting attachment. At one time during his stay he was seen to be troubled in mind, and our young friend, Midshipman Beale, being asked to find what had quenched Carson's good spirits, ascertained that he felt it was wrong to be among such ladies when they might not like to associate with him if they knew he had had an Indian wife. "She was a good wife to me. I never came in from hunting that she did not have the warm water ready for my feet." She had died long since, and he was now married to a daughter of Beaubien. But his straightforward nature would not let him rest while there was anything concealed which he thought ought to be known to the family who were receiving him as a friend. It was the child of his Indian wife that he had just placed in the shelter of the St. Louis convent school when we first met.

I had expected to engage as guide an old mountaineer, Captain Drips, but I was so much pleased with Carson that when he asked to go with me I was glad to take him. Now, he has become so familiarly known that I will let the narrative tell of the life we had together, out of which grew our enduring friendship.

From the Landing I went ten miles up the Kansas River to the trading post of Mr. Cyprian Chouteau, where we were already on Indian ground. This was one of the friendly contributions by the St. Louis Chouteaus,[3] which were to come in aid on this and future journeys. We were delayed here some twenty days in fitting men and animals, arms and equipment, into place and good order; but the time used in this was regained in the strength of the animals, as the spring grass was improving with every day.

This was now to be their only food, and in a measure regulated the travel, which depended on their condition.

At length we set out. It was like a ship leaving the shore for a long voyage, and carrying with her provision against all needs in her isolation on the ocean.

Bad weather, which interfered with astronomical observations, delayed us several days in the early part of June at this post, which is on the right bank of the Kansas River, about ten miles above the mouth and six beyond the western boundary of Missouri. The sky cleared off at length, and we were enabled to determine our position—in longitude 94° 25′ 46″, and latitude 39° 5′ 57″. The elevation above the sea is about seven hundred feet. Our camp, in the meantime, presented an animated and bustling scene. All were busily occupied in completing the necessary arrangements for our campaign in the wilderness, and profiting by this short delay on the verge of civilization to provide ourselves with all the little essentials to comfort in the nomadic life we were to lead for the ensuing summer months. Gradually, however, everything—the matériel of the camp, men, horses, and even mules—settled into its place, and by the 10th we were ready to depart; but before we mount our horses, I will give a short description of the party with which I performed this service.

I had collected in the neighborhood of St. Louis twenty-one men, principally Creole and Canadian voyageurs, who had become familiar with prairie life in the service of the fur companies in the Indian country. Mr. Charles Preuss, a native of Germany, was my assistant in the topographical part of the survey. Maxwell, as has already been said, had been engaged as hunter; Carson was our guide. The persons engaged in St. Louis were:

Clément Lambert, J. B. L'Esperance, J. B. Lefêvre, Benjamin Potra, Louis Gouin, J. B. Dumés, Basil Lajeunesse, François Tessier, Benjamin Cadotte, Joseph Clément, Daniel Simonds, Leonard Benoit, Michel Morly, Baptiste Bernier, Honoré Ayot, François Latulippe, François Badeau, Louis Ménard, Joseph Ruelle, Moïse Chardonnais, Auguste Janisse, Raphael Proue.

In addition to these, Henry Brant, son of Colonel J. B. Brant, of St. Louis, a young man nineteen years of age, and Randolph, a lively boy of twelve, son of Mr. Benton, accompanied me, for the development of mind and body which such an expedition would give. We were all well armed, and mounted, with the exception of eight men, who conducted as many carts, in which were packed our stores, with the baggage and instruments, and which were each drawn by two mules. A few loose horses, and four oxen which had been added to our stock of provisions, completed the train. We set out on the morning of the 10th, which happened to be Friday—a circumstance which our men did not fail to remember and recall during the hardships and vexations of the ensuing journey. Mr. Cyprian Chouteau, to whose kindness during our stay at his house we were much indebted, accompanied us several miles on our way, until we met an Indian whom he had engaged to conduct us on the first thirty or forty miles, where he was to consign us to the ocean of prairie, which, we were told, stretched without interruption almost to the base of the Rocky Mountains.

From the belt of wood which borders the Kansas, in which we had passed several good-looking Indian farms, we suddenly emerged on the prairies, which received us at the outset with some of their striking characteristics; for here and there rode an Indian, and but a few miles distant heavy clouds of smoke were rolling before the fire. In about ten miles we reached the Santa Fe road, along which we continued for a short time and encamped early on a small stream, having traveled about eleven miles.

During our journey, it was the customary practice to encamp an hour or two before sunset, when the carts were disposed so as to form a sort of barricade around a circle some eighty yards in diameter. The tents were pitched, and the horses hobbled and turned loose to graze; and but a few minutes elapsed before the cooks of the messes, of which there were four, were busily engaged in preparing the evening meal. At nightfall the horses, mules, and oxen were driven in, and picketed—that is, secured by a halter, of which one end was tied to a small steel-shod picket, and driven into the ground, the halter being twenty or thirty feet long, which enabled them to obtain a little food during the night. When we had reached a part of the country where such a precaution became necessary, the carts being regularly arranged for defending the camp, guard was mounted at eight o'clock, consisting of three men, who were relieved every two hours; the morning watch being horse guard for the day. At daybreak the camp was roused, the animals turned loose to graze, and breakfast generally over between six and seven o'clock, when we resumed our march, making regularly a halt at noon for one or two hours. Such was usually the order of the day, except when accident of country forced a variation; which, however, happened but rarely.

We traveled the next day along the Santa Fe road, which we left in the afternoon, and encamped late in the evening on a small creek, called by the Indians Mishmagwi. Just as we arrived at camp, one of the horses set off at full speed on his return, and was followed by others. Several men were sent in pursuit, and returned with the fugitives about midnight, with the exception of one man, who did not make his appearance until morning. He had lost his way in the darkness of the night, and slept on the prairie. Shortly after midnight it began to rain heavily, and as our tents were of light and thin cloth, they offered but little obstruction to rain; we were all well soaked and glad when morning came. We had a rainy march on the 12th, but the weather grew fine as the day advanced. We encamped in a remarkably beautiful situation on the Kansas bluffs, which commanded a fine view of the river valley, here from three to four miles wide. The central portion was occupied by a broad belt of heavy timber, and nearer the hills the prairies were of the richest verdure. One of the oxen was killed here for food.

We reached the ford of the Kansas late in the afternoon of the 14th, where the river was two hundred and thirty yards wide, and commenced immediately preparations for crossing. I had expected to find the river fordable; but it had been swollen by the late rains, and was sweeping by with an angry current, yellow and turbid as the Missouri. Up to this point, the road we had traveled was a remarkably fine one, well beaten, and level—the usual road of a prairie country. By our route, the ford was one hundred miles from the mouth of the Kansas River. Several mounted men led the way into the stream, to swim across. The animals were driven in after them, and in a few minutes all had reached the opposite bank in safety, with the exception of the oxen, which swam some distance down the river, and returning to the right bank, were not got over until the next morning. In the meantime, the carts had been unloaded and dismantled, and an indiarubber boat, which I had brought with me for the survey of the Platte River, placed in the water. The boat was twenty feet long and five broad, and on it were placed the body and wheels of a cart, with the load belonging to it, and three men with paddles.

The velocity of the current, and the inconvenient freight, rendering it difficult to be managed, Basil Lajeunesse, one of our best swimmers, took in his teeth a line attached to the boat, and swam ahead in order to reach a footing as soon as possible, and assist in drawing her over. In this manner, six passages had been successfully made, and as many carts with their contents, and a greater portion of the party, deposited on the left bank; but night was drawing near, and, in our anxiety to have all over before the darkness closed in, I put upon the boat the remaining two carts, with their accompanying loads. The man at the helm was timid on water, and, in his alarm, capsized the boat. Carts, barrels, boxes, and bales were in a moment floating down the current; but all the men who were on the shore jumped into the water, without stopping to think if they could swim, and almost everything—even heavy articles, such as guns and lead—was recovered.

Two of the men, who could not swim, came nigh being drowned, and all the sugar belonging to one of the messes wasted its sweets on the muddy waters; but our heaviest loss was a bag of coffee, which contained nearly all our provision. It was a loss which none but a traveler in a strange and inhospitable country can appreciate; and often afterward, when excessive toil and long marching had overcome us with fatigue and weariness, we remembered and mourned over our loss in the Kansas. Carson and Maxwell had been much in the water yesterday, and both, in consequence, were taken ill. The former continuing so, I remained in camp. A number of Kansas Indians visited us today. Going up to one of the groups

who were scattered among the trees, I found one sitting on the
ground, among some of the men, gravely and fluently speaking
French with as much facility and as little embarrassment as any of
my own party, who were nearly all of French origin.

On all sides was heard the strange language of his own people,
wild, and harmonizing well with their appearance. I listened to him
for some time with feelings of strange curiosity and interest. He
was now apparently thirty-five years of age; and, on inquiry, I
learned that he had been at St. Louis when a boy, and there had
learned the French language. From one of the Indian women I
obtained a fine cow and calf in exchange for a yoke of oxen. Several
of them brought us vegetables—pumpkins, onions, beans, and let-
tuce. One of them brought butter, and from a Half-breed near the
river I had the good fortune to obtain some twenty or thirty pounds
of coffee. The dense timber in which we had encamped interfered
with astronomical observations, and our wet and damaged stores
required exposure to the sun. Accordingly the tents were struck
early the next morning, and, leaving camp at six o'clock, we moved
about seven miles up the river, to a handsome, open prairie, some
twenty feet above the water, where the fine grass afforded a luxurious repast to our horses.

During the day we occupied ourselves in making astronomical
observations, in order to lay down the country to this place, it being
our custom to keep up our map regularly in the field, which we
found attended with many advantages. The men were kept busy
in drying the provisions, painting the cart covers, and otherwise
completing our equipage, until the afternoon, when powder was
distributed to them, and they spent some hours in firing at a mark.
We were now fairly in the Indian country, and it began to be
time to prepare for the chances of the wilderness.

Friday, June 17th. The weather yesterday had not permitted us
to make the observations I was desirous to obtain here, and I therefore did not move today. The people continue their target firing.
In the steep bank of the river here were nests of innumerable swallows, into one of which a large prairie snake had got about half
his body, and was occupied in eating the young birds. The old ones
were flying about in great distress, darting at him, and vainly endeavoring to drive him off. A shot wounded him, and, being killed,
he was cut open, and eighteen young swallows were found in his

body. A sudden storm that burst upon us in the afternoon, cleared away in a brilliant sunset, followed by a clear night, which enabled us to determine our position, in longitude 95° 38′ 05″, and in latitude 39° 06′ 40″.

A party of emigrants to the Columbia River, under the charge of Dr. White, an agent of the Government in Oregon territory, were about three weeks in advance of us.[4] They consisted of men, women, and children. There were sixty-four men, and sixteen or seventeen families. They had a considerable number of cattle, and were transporting their household furniture in large heavy wagons. I understood that there had been much sickness among them, and that they had lost several children. One of the party, who had lost his child, and whose wife was very ill, had left them about one hundred miles hence on the prairies; and as a hunter, who had accompanied them, visited our camp this evening, we availed ourselves of his return to the States to write to our friends.

The morning of the 18th was very unpleasant. A fine rain was falling, with cold wind from the north, and mists made the river hills look dark and gloomy. We left our camp at seven, journeying along the foot of the hills which border the Kansas Valley, generally about three miles wide, and extremely rich. We halted for dinner, after a march of about thirteen miles, on the banks of one of the many little tributaries to the Kansas, which look like trenches in the prairie, and are usually well timbered. After crossing this stream, I rode off some miles to the left, attracted by the appearance of a cluster of huts near the mouth of the Vermilion. It was a large but deserted Kansas village, scattered in an open wood, along the margin of the stream, on a spot chosen with the customary Indian fondness for beauty of scenery. The Pawnees had attacked it in the early spring. Some of the houses were burnt, and others blackened with smoke, and weeds were already getting possession of the cleared places. Riding up the Vermilion River, I reached the ford in time to meet the carts, and, crossing, encamped on its western side. The weather continued cool, the thermometer being this evening as low as 49°; but the night was sufficiently clear for astronomical observations, which placed us in longitude 96° 04′ 07″, and latitude 39° 15′ 19″. At sunset the barometer was at 28.845, thermometer 64°.

We breakfasted the next morning at half-past five, and left our

encampment early. The morning was cool, the thermometer being
at 45°. Quitting the river bottom, the road ran along the uplands,
over a rolling country, generally in view of the Kansas, from eight
to twelve miles distant. Many large boulders, of a very compact
sandstone, of various shades of red, some of them four or five tons
in weight, were scattered along the hills; and many beautiful plants
in flower, among which the *Amorpha canescens* was a characteristic,
enlivened the green of the prairie. At the heads of the ravines I
remarked, occasionally, thickets of *Salix longifolia,* the most common willow of the country. We traveled nineteen miles, and pitched
our tents at evening on the headwaters of a small creek, now nearly
dry, but having in its bed several fine springs. The barometer indicated a considerable rise in the country—here about fourteen
hundred feet above the sea—and the increased elevation appeared
already to have some slight influence upon the vegetation. The
night was cold, with a heavy dew; the thermometer at 10 P.M. standing at 46°, barometer 28.483. Our position was in longitude 96° 14'
49", latitude 39° 30' 40".

The morning of the twentieth was fine, with a southerly breeze,
and a bright sky; and at seven o'clock we were on the march. The
country today was rather more broken, rising still, and covered
everywhere with fragments of siliceous limestone, particularly on
the summits, where they were small, and thickly strewed as pebbles
on the shore of the sea. In these exposed situations grew but few
plants; though whenever the soil was good and protected from the
winds, in the creek bottoms and ravines and on the slopes, they
flourished abundantly; among them the amorpha still retaining its
characteristic place. We crossed, at 10 A.M., the Big Vermilion,
which has a rich bottom of about one mile in breadth, one-third of
which is occupied by timber. Making our usual halt at noon, after a
day's march of twenty-four miles, we reached the Big Blue, and
encamped on the uplands of the western side, near a small creek,
where was a fine large spring of very cold water. This is a clear and
handsome stream, about one hundred and twenty feet wide, running, with a rapid current, through a well-timbered valley. Today
antelope were seen running over the hills, and at evening Carson
brought us a fine deer. Longitude of the camp 96° 32' 35", latitude
39° 45' 08". Thermometer at sunset 75°.

A pleasant southerly breeze and fine morning had given place to a gale, with indications of bad weather when, after a march of ten miles, we halted to noon on a small creek, where the water stood in deep pools. In the bank of the creek limestone made its appearance in a stratum about one foot thick. In the afternoon, the people seemed to suffer for want of water. The road led along a high dry ridge; dark lines of timber indicated the heads of streams in the plains below; but there was no water near, and the day was very oppressive, with a hot wind, and the thermometer at 90°. Along our route the amorpha has been in very abundant but variable bloom—in some places, bending beneath the weight of purple clusters; in others, without a flower. It seems to love best the sunny slopes, with a dark soil and southern exposure. Everywhere the rose is met with, and reminds us of cultivated gardens and civilization. It is scattered over the prairies in small boskets, and when glittering in the dews and waving in the pleasant breeze of the early morning, is the most beautiful of the prairie flowers. The artemisia, absinthe, or prairie sage, as it is variously called, is increasing in size, and glitters like silver, as the southern breeze turns up its leaves to the sun. All these plants have their insect habitants, variously colored, taking generally the hue of the flower on which they live. The artemisia has its small fly accompanying it through every change of elevation and latitude; and wherever I have seen the *Asclepias tuberosa,* I have always remarked, too, on the flower a large butterfly, so nearly resembling it in color as to be distinguishable at a little distance only by the motion of its wings. Traveling on the fresh traces of the Oregon emigrants relieves a little the loneliness of the road; and tonight, after a march of twenty-two miles, we halted on a small creek which had been one of their encampments. As we advance westward, the soil appears to be getting more sandy, and the surface rock, an erratic deposit of sand and gravel, rests here on a bed of coarse yellow and gray and very friable sandstone. Evening closed over with rain and its usual attendant, hordes of mosquitoes, with which we were annoyed for the first time.

June 22d. We enjoyed at breakfast this morning a luxury, very unusual in this country, in a cup of excellent coffee, with cream from our cow. Being milked at night, cream was thus had in the morning. Our midday halt was at Wyeth's Creek, in the bed of which were numerous boulders of dark ferruginous sandstone, mingled with others of the red sandstone already mentioned. Here a pack of cards, lying loose on the grass, marked an encampment of our Oregon emigrants; and it was at the close of the day when we made our bivouac in the midst of some well-timbered ravines near the Little Blue, twenty-four miles from our camp of the preceding night. Crossing the next morning a number of handsome creeks, with clear water and sandy beds, we reached at 10 A.M. a very beautiful wooded stream, about thirty-five feet wide, called Sandy Creek, and sometimes, as the Otos frequently winter there, the Oto Fork. The country has become very sandy, and the plants less varied and abundant, with the exception of the amorpha, which rivals the grass in quantity, though not so forward as it has been found to the eastward.

At the Big Trees, where we had intended to noon, no water was to be found. The bed of the little creek was perfectly dry, and on the adjacent sandy bottom cacti, for the first time, made their appearance. We made here a short delay in search of water; and, after a hard day's march of twenty-eight miles, encamped at five o'clock on the Little Blue, where our arrival made a scene of the Arabian desert. As fast as they arrived, men and horses rushed into the stream, where they bathed and drank together in common enjoyment. We were now in the range of the Pawnees,[5] who were accustomed to infest this part of the country, stealing horses from companies on their way to the mountains, and, when in sufficient force, openly attacking and plundering them, and subjecting them to various kinds of insult. For the first time, therefore, guard was mounted tonight. Our route the next morning lay up the valley, which, bordered by hills with graceful slopes, looked uncommonly green and beautiful. The stream was about fifty feet wide, and three or four deep, fringed by cottonwood and willow, with frequent groves of oak tenanted by flocks of turkeys. Game here, too, made its appearance in greater plenty. Elk were frequently seen on the hills, and now and then an antelope bounded across our path, or a deer broke from the groves. The road in the afternoon was over the upper prairies, several miles from the river, and we encamped at sunset on one of its small tributaries, where an abundance of prêle (equisetum) afforded fine forage to our tired animals.

We had traveled thirty-one miles. A heavy bank of black clouds in the west came on us in a storm between nine and ten, preceded by a violent wind. The rain fell in such torrents that it was difficult to breathe facing the wind; the thunder rolled incessantly, and the whole sky was tremulous with lightning, now and then illuminated by a blinding flash, succeeded by pitchy darkness. Carson had the watch from ten to midnight, and to him had been assigned our young *compagnons de voyage* Messrs. Brant and R. Benton. This was their first night on guard, and such an introduction did not augur very auspiciously of the pleasures of the expedition. Many things conspired to render their situation uncomfortable; stories of desperate and bloody Indian fights were rife in the camp; our position was badly chosen, surrounded on all sides by timbered hollows, and occupying an area of several hundred feet, so that necessarily the guards were far apart; and now and then I could hear Randolph, as if relieved by the sound of a voice in the darkness, calling out to the sergeant of the guard to direct his attention to some imaginary alarm; but they stood it out, and took their turn regularly afterward.

The next morning we had a specimen of the false alarms to which all parties in these wild regions are subject. Proceeding up the valley, objects were seen on the opposite hills, which disappeared before a glass could be brought to bear upon them. A man who was a short distance in the rear came spurring up in great haste, shouting, "Indians! Indians!" He had been near enough to see and count them, according to his report, and had made out twenty-seven. I immediately halted, arms were examined and put in order, the usual preparations made; and Kit Carson, springing upon one of the hunting horses, crossed the river, and galloped off into the opposite prairies, to obtain some certain intelligence of their movements.

Mounted on a fine horse, without a saddle, and scouring bareheaded over the prairies, Kit was one of the finest pictures of a horseman I have ever seen. A short time enabled him to discover that the Indian war-party of twenty-seven consisted of six elk,[6] which had been gazing curiously at our caravan as it passed by, and were now scampering off at full speed. This was our first alarm, and its excitement broke agreeably on the monotony of the day. At our noon halt, the men were exercised at a target; and in the evening we pitched our tents at a Pawnee encampment of last July.

They had apparently killed buffalo here, as many bones were lying about, and the frames where the hides had been stretched were yet standing. The road of the day had kept the valley, which is sometimes rich and well timbered, though the country is generally sandy. Mingled with the usual plants, a thistle (*Carduus leucógraphus*) had for the last day or two made its appearance; and along the river bottom, *Tradescantia virginica* and milk plant (*Asclepias syriaca* *), in considerable quantities.

Our march today had been twenty-one miles, and the astronomical observations gave us a chronometric longitude of 98° 22′ 12″, and latitude 40° 26′ 50″. We were moving forward at seven in the morning, and in about five miles reached a fork of the Blue,[7] where the road leaves that river, and crosses over to the Platte. No water was to be found on the dividing ridge, and the casks were filled, and the animals here allowed a short repose. The road led across a high and level prairie ridge, where were but few plants, and those principally thistle (*Carduus leucógraphus*), and a kind of dwarf artemisia. Antelope were seen frequently during the morning, which was very stormy. Squalls of rain, with thunder and lightning, were around us in every direction; and while we were enveloped in one of them, a flash, which seemed to scorch our eyes as it passed, struck in the prairie within a few hundred feet, sending up a column of dust.

Crossing on the way several Pawnee roads to the Arkansas, we reached, in about twenty-one miles from our halt on the Blue,[8] what is called the coast of the Nebraska, or Platte, River. This had seemed in the distance a range of high and broken hills; but on a nearer approach were found to be elevations of forty to sixty feet, into which the wind had worked the sand. They were covered with the usual fine grasses of the country, and bordered the eastern side of the ridge on a breadth of about two miles. Change of soil and coun-

---

* "This plant is very odoriferous, and in Canada charms the traveller, especially when passing through woods in the evening. The French there eat the tender shoots in the spring, as we do asparagus. The natives make a sugar of the flowers, gathering them in the morning when they are covered with dew, and collect the cotton from the pods to fill their beds. On account of the silkiness of this cotton, Parkinson calls the plant Virginian silk."—*Loudon's Encyclopedia of Plants*.

The Sioux Indians of the Upper Platte eat the young pods of this plant, boiling them with the meat of the buffalo. [Frémont's note]

try appeared here to have produced some change in the vegetation. Cacti were numerous, and all the plants of the region appeared to flourish among the warm hills. Among them the amorpha, in full bloom, was remarkable for its large and luxuriant purple clusters. From the foot of the coast, a distance of two miles across the level bottom brought us to our encampment on the shore of the river, about twenty miles below the head of Grand Island, which lay extended before us, covered with dense and heavy woods. From the mouth of the Kansas, according to our reckoning, we had traveled three hundred and twenty-eight miles; and the geological formation of the country we had passed over consisted of lime and sandstone, covered by the same erratic deposit of sand and gravel which forms the surface rock of the prairies between the Missouri and Mississippi rivers. Except in some occasional limestone boulders, I had met with no fossils. The elevation of the Platte Valley above the sea is here about two thousand feet. The astronomical observations of the night placed us in longitude 98° 45' 49", latitude 40° 41' 06".

June 27th. The animals were somewhat fatigued by their march of yesterday, and, after a short journey of eighteen miles along the river bottom, I encamped near the head of Grand Island,[9] in longitude, by observation, 99° 05' 24", latitude 40° 39' 32". The soil here was light but rich, though in some places rather sandy; and, with the exception of a scattered fringe along the bank, the timber, consisting principally of poplar (*Populus monilifera*), elm, and hackberry (*Celtis crassifolia*), is confined almost entirely to the islands.

June 28th. We halted to noon at an open reach of the river, which occupies rather more than a fourth of the valley, here only about four miles broad. The camp had been disposed with the usual precaution, the horses grazing at a little distance attended by the guard, and we were all sitting quietly at our dinner on the grass, when suddenly we heard the startling cry, "*Du monde!*" In an instant every man's weapon was in his hand, the horses were driven in, hobbled, and picketed, and horsemen were galloping at full speed in the direction of the newcomers, screaming and yelling with the wildest excitement. "Get ready, my lads!" said the leader of the approaching party to his men, when our wild-looking horsemen were discovered bearing down upon them; "*Nous allons attraper des coups de baguette.*" They proved to be a small party of fourteen, under the charge of a man named John Lee, and, with their baggage and provisions strapped to their backs, were making their way on foot to the frontier. A brief account of their fortunes will give some idea of navigation in the Nebraska. Sixty days since, they had left the mouth of Laramie's Fork, some three hundred miles above, in barges laden with the furs of the American Fur Company. They started with the annual flood, and, drawing but nine inches water, hoped to make a speedy and prosperous voyage to St. Louis, but, after a lapse of forty days, found themselves only one hundred and thirty miles from their point of departure. They came down rapidly as far as Scott's Bluffs, where their difficulties began. Sometimes they came upon places where the water was spread over a great extent, and here they toiled from morning until night, endeavoring to drag their boat through the sands, making only two or three miles in as many days. Sometimes they would enter an arm of the river, where there appeared a fine channel, and, after descending prosperously for eight or ten miles, would come suddenly upon dry sands, and be compelled to return, dragging their boat for days against the rapid current; and at others they came upon places where the water lay in holes, and, getting out to float off their boat, would fall into water up to their necks, and the next moment tumble over against a sand bar. Discouraged at length, and finding the Platte growing every day more shallow, they discharged the principal part of their cargoes one hundred and thirty miles below Fort Laramie, which they secured as well as possible, and, leaving a few men to guard them, attempted to continue their voyage, laden with some light furs and their personal baggage. After fifteen or twenty days more struggling in the sands, during which they made but one hundred and forty miles, they sunk their barges, made a cache of their remaining furs and property in trees on the bank, and, packing on his back what each man could carry, had commenced, the day before we encountered them, their journey on foot to St. Louis.

We laughed then at their forlorn and vagabond appearance, and in our turn, a month or two afterward, furnished the same occasion for merriment to others. Even their stock of tobacco, that sine qua non of a voyageur, without which the night fire is gloomy, was entirely exhausted. However, we shortened their homeward journey by a small supply from our own provision. They gave us the welcome intelligence that the buffalo were abundant some two days' march in advance, and made us a present of some choice pieces, which were a very acceptable change from our salt pork. In the interchange of news and the renewal of old acquaintanceships we found wherewithal to fill a busy hour; then we mounted our horses, and they shouldered their packs, and we shook hands and parted. Among them I had found an old companion on the northern prairie, a hardened and hardly served veteran of the mountains, who had been as much hacked and scarred as an old "Moustache" of Napoleon's "Old Guard." He flourished in the soubriquet of La Tulipe, and his real name I never knew. Finding that he was going to the States only because his company was bound in that direction, and that he was rather more willing to return with me, I took him again into my service. We traveled this day but seventeen miles.

At our evening camp, about sunset, three figures were discovered approaching, which our glasses made out to be Indians. They proved to be Cheyennes—two men and a boy of thirteen. About a month since, they had left their people on the south fork of the river, some three hundred miles to the westward, and, a party of only four in number, had been to the Pawnee villages on a horse-stealing excursion, from which they were returning unsuccessful. They were miserably mounted on wild horses from the Arkansas plains, and had no other weapons than bows and long spears, and had they been discovered by the Pawnees, could not, by any possibility, have escaped. They were mortified by their ill success, and said the Pawnees were cowards who shut up their horses in their lodges at night. I invited them to supper with me, and Randolph and the young Cheyenne, who had been eying each other suspiciously and curiously, soon became intimate friends. After supper we sat down on the grass, and I placed a sheet of paper between us, on which they traced rudely, but with a certain degree of relative truth, the watercourses of the country which lay between us and their villages, and of which I desired to have some information. Their companions, they told us, had taken a nearer route over the hills; but they had mounted one of the summits to spy out the country, whence they had caught a glimpse of our party, and, confident of good treatment at the hands of the whites, hastened to join company. Latitude of the camp, 40° 39' 51".

We made the next morning sixteen miles. I remarked that the ground was covered in many places with an efflorescence of salt, and the plants were not numerous. In the bottoms was frequently seen tradescantia, and on the dry benches were carduus, cactus, and amorpha. A high wind during the morning had increased to a violent gale from the northwest, which made our afternoon ride cold and unpleasant. We had the welcome sight of two buffaloes on one of the large islands, and encamped at a clump of timber about seven miles from our noon halt, after a day's march of twenty-two miles.

The air was keen the next morning at sunrise, the thermometer standing at 44°, and it was sufficiently cold to make overcoats very comfortable. A few miles brought us into the midst of the buffalo, swarming in immense numbers over the plains, where they had left scarcely a blade of grass standing. Mr. Preuss, who was sketching at a little distance in the rear, had at first noted them as large groves of timber. In the sight of such a mass of life, the traveler feels a strange emotion of grandeur. We had heard from a distance a dull and confused murmuring, and when we came in view of their dark masses there was not one among us who did not feel his heart beat quicker. It was the early part of the day, when the herds are feeding, and everywhere they were in motion. Here and there a huge old bull was rolling in the grass, and clouds of dust rose in the air from various parts of the bands, each the scene of some obstinate fight. Indians and buffalo make the poetry and life of the prairie, and our camp was full of their exhilaration. In place of the quiet monotony of the march, relieved only by the cracking of the whip, and an "*Avance donc! enfant de garce!*" shouts and songs resounded from every part of the line, and our evening camp was always the commencement of a feast which terminated only with our departure on the following morning. At any time of the night might be seen pieces of the most delicate and choicest meat, roasting *en appolas*, on sticks around the fire, and the guard were never without company. With pleasant weather and no enemy to fear, an abundance of the most excellent meat, and no scarcity of bread or tobacco, they were enjoying the oasis of a voyageur's life. Three cows were killed today. Kit Carson had shot one, and was continuing the chase in the midst of another herd, when his horse fell headlong, but sprang up and joined the flying band. Though considerably hurt, he had the good fortune to break no bones; and Maxwell, who was mounted on a fleet hunter, captured the runaway after a hard chase. He was on the point of shooting him, to avoid the loss of his bridle (a handsomely mounted Spanish one), when he found that his horse was able to come up with him. Animals are frequently lost in this way, and it is necessary to keep close watch over them in the vicinity of the buffalo, in the midst of which they scour off to the plains and are rarely retaken. One of our mules took a sudden freak into his head, and joined a neighboring band today. As we were not in a condition to lose horses, I sent several men in pursuit, and remained in camp, in the hope of recovering him, but lost the afternoon to no purpose, as we did not see him again. Astronomical observations placed us in longitude 100° 05′ 47″, latitude 40° 49′ 55″.

July 1st. Along our road today the prairie bottom was more elevated and dry, and the hills which border the right side of the river higher and more broken and picturesque in the outline. The country, too, was better timbered. As we were riding quietly along the bank a grand herd of buffalo, some seven or eight hundred in number, came crowding up from the river, where they had been to drink, and commenced crossing the plain slowly, eating as they went. The wind was favorable; the coolness of the morning invited to exercise; the ground was apparently good, and the distance across the prairie (two or three miles) gave us a fine opportunity to charge them before they could get among the river hills. It was too fine a prospect for a chase to be lost; and, halting for a few moments, the hunters were brought up and saddled, and Kit Carson, Maxwell, and I started together. They were now somewhat less than half a mile distant, and we rode easily along until within about three hundred yards, when a sudden agitation, a wavering in the band, and a galloping to and fro of some which were scattered along the skirts, gave us the intimation that we were discovered. We started together at a hand gallop, riding steadily abreast of each other, and here the interest of the chase became so engrossingly intense that we were sensible to nothing else. We were now closing upon them rapidly, and the front of the mass was already in rapid motion for the hills, and in a few seconds the movement had communicated itself to the whole herd.

A crowd of bulls, as usual, brought up the rear, and every now and then some of them faced about, and then dashed on after the band a short distance, and turned and looked again, as if more than half inclined to stand and fight. In a few moments, however, during which we had been quickening our pace, the rout was universal, and we were going over the ground like a hurricane. When at about thirty yards, we gave the usual shout (the hunter's *pas de charge*) and broke into the herd. We entered on the side, the mass giving way in every direction in their heedless course. Many of the bulls, less active and less fleet than the cows, paying no attention to the ground, and occupied solely with the hunter, were precipitated to the earth with great force, rolling over and over with the violence of the shock, and hardly distinguishable in the dust. We separated on entering, each singling out his game.

My horse was a trained hunter, famous in the West under the name of Proveau, and, with his eyes flashing and the foam flying from his mouth, sprang on after the cow like a tiger. In a few moments he brought me alongside of her, and, rising in the stirrups, I fired at the distance of a yard, the ball entering at the termination of the long hair, and passing near the heart. She fell headlong at the report of the gun, and checking my horse, I looked around for my companions. At a little distance Kit was on the ground, engaged in tying his horse to the horns of a cow which he was preparing to cut up. Among the scattered bands, at some distance below, I caught a glimpse of Maxwell; and while I was looking a light wreath of white smoke curled away from his gun, from which I was too far to hear the report. Nearer, and between me and the hills toward which they were directing their course, was the body of the herd, and giving my horse the rein we dashed after them. A thick cloud of dust hung upon their rear, which filled my mouth and eyes and nearly smothered me. In the midst of this I could see nothing, and the buffalo were not distinguishable until within thirty feet. They crowded together more densely still as I came upon them, and rushed along in such a compact body that I could not obtain an entrance—the horse almost leaping upon them. In a few moments the mass divided to the right and left, the horns clattering with a noise heard above everything else, and my horse darted into the opening. Five or six bulls charged on us as we dashed along the line, but were left far behind; and, singling out a cow, I gave her my fire, but struck too high. She gave a tremendous leap, and scoured on swifter than before. I reined up my horse, and the band swept on like a torrent, leaving the place quiet and clear. Our chase had led us into dangerous ground. A prairie-dog village, so thickly settled that there were three or four holes in every twenty yards square, occupied the whole bottom for nearly two miles in length. Looking around, I saw only one of the hunters, nearly out of sight, and the long dark line of our caravan crawling along, three or four miles distant. After a march of twenty-four miles, we encamped at nightfall one mile and a half above the lower end of Brady's Island. The breadth of this arm of the river was eight hundred and eighty yards, and the water nowhere two feet in depth. The island bears the name of a man killed on this spot some years ago. His party had encamped here, three in company, and one of the number went off to hunt, leaving Brady and his companion together. These two had frequently quarreled, and on the hunter's return he found Brady dead, and was told that he had shot himself accidentally. He was buried here on the bank; but, as usual, the wolves had torn him out, and some human bones that were lying on the ground we supposed were his. Troops of wolves that were hanging on the skirts of the buffalo kept up an uninterrupted howling during the night, venturing almost into camp. In the morning they were sitting at a short distance, barking, and impatiently waiting our departure to fall upon the bones.

July 2d. The morning was cool and smoky. Our road led closer to the hills, which here increased in elevation, presenting an outline of conical peaks three hundred to five hundred feet high. Some timber, apparently pine, grow in the ravines, and streaks of clay or sand whiten their slopes. We crossed during the morning a number of hollows, timbered principally with box elder (*Acer negundo*), poplar, and elm. Brady's Island is well wooded, and all the river along which our road led today may, in general, be called tolerably well timbered. We passed near an encampment of the Oregon emigrants, where they appear to have reposed several days. A variety of household articles were scattered about, and they had probably disburdened themselves here of many things not absolutely necessary. I had left the usual road before the midday halt, and in the afternoon, having sent several men in advance to reconnoiter, marched directly for the mouth of the South Fork.[9] On our arrival, the horsemen were sent in and scattered about the river to search the best fording places, and the carts followed immediately. The stream is here divided by an island into two channels. The southern is four hundred and fifty feet wide, having eighteen or twenty inches water in the deepest places. With the exception of a few dry bars, the bed of the river is generally quicksands, in which the carts began to sink rapidly so soon as the mules halted, so that it was necessary to keep them constantly in motion.

The northern channel, two thousand two hundred and fifty feet wide, was somewhat deeper, having frequently three feet of water in the numerous small channels, with a bed of coarse gravel. The whole breadth of the Nebraska, immediately below the junction, is five thousand three hundred and fifty feet. All our equipage had reached the left bank safely at six o'clock, having today made twenty miles. We encamped at the point of land immediately at the junction of the North and South forks. Between the streams is a low rich prairie, extending from their confluence eighteen miles westwardly to the bordering hills, where it is five and a half miles wide. It is covered with a luxuriant growth of grass, and along the banks is a slight and scattered fringe of cottonwood and willow. In the buffalo trails and wallows I remarked saline efflorescences, to which a rapid evaporation in the great heat of the sun probably contributes, as the soil is entirely unprotected by timber. In the vicinity of these places there was a bluish grass, which the cattle refuse to eat, called by the voyageurs "*herbe salée*" (salt grass). The latitude of the junction is 40° 04′ 47″, and longitude, by chronometer and lunar distances, 100° 49′ 43″. The elevation above the sea is about two thousand seven hundred feet. The hunters came in with a fat cow; and, as we had labored hard, we enjoyed well a supper of roasted ribs and boudins, the chef d'œuvre of a prairie cook. Mosquitoes thronged about us this evening; but, by ten o'clock, when the thermometer had fallen to 47°, they had all disappeared.

July 3d. As this was to be a point in our homeward journey, I made a cache (a term used in all this country for what is hidden in the ground) of a barrel of pork. It was impossible to conceal such a proceeding from the sharp eyes of our Cheyenne companions, and I therefore told them to go and see what it was they were burying. They would otherwise have not failed to return and destroy our cache, in expectation of some rich booty; but pork they dislike, and never eat. We left our camp at nine, continuing up the South Fork,[10] the prairie bottom affording us a fair road; but in the long grass we roused myriads of mosquitoes and flies, from which our horses suffered severely. The day was smoky, with a pleasant breeze from the south, and the plains on the opposite side were covered with buffalo. Having traveled twenty-five miles, we encamped at six in the evening, and the men were sent across the river for wood, as there is none here on the left bank. Our fires were partially made of the bois de vache, the dry excrement of the buffalo, which, like that of the camel in the Arabian deserts, furnishes to the traveler a very good substitute for wood, burning like turf. Wolves in great numbers surrounded us during the night, crossing and recrossing from the opposite herds to our camp, and howling and trotting about in the river until morning.

July 4th. The morning was very smoky, the sun shining dimly and red, as in a thick fog. The camp was roused with a salute at daybreak, and from our scanty store a portion of what our Indian friends called the "red firewater" served out to the men. While we were at breakfast a buffalo calf broke through the camp, followed by a couple of wolves. In its fright it had probably mistaken us for a band of buffalo. The wolves were obliged to make a circuit around the camp, so that the calf got a little the start, and strained every nerve to reach a large herd at the foot of the hills, about two miles distant; but first one, and then another and another wolf joined in the chase, until its pursuers amounted to twenty or thirty, and they ran him down before he could reach his friends. There were a few bulls near the place, and one of them attacked the wolves and tried to rescue him, but was driven off immediately, and the little animal fell an easy prey, half devoured before he was dead. We watched the chase with the interest always felt for the weak; and had there been a saddled horse at hand, he would have fared better.

Leaving camp, our road soon approached the hills, in which strata of a marl like that of the Chimney Rock, hereafter described, make their appearance. It is probably of this rock that the hills on the right bank of the Platte, a little below the junction, are composed, and which are worked by the winds and rains into sharp peaks and cones, giving them, in contrast to the surrounding level region, something of a picturesque appearance. We crossed this morning numerous beds of the small creeks which, in the time of rains and melting snow, pour down from the ridge, bringing down with them always great quantities of sand and gravel, which have gradually raised their beds four to ten feet above the level of the prairie which they cross, making each one of them a miniature Po. Raised in this way above the surrounding prairie, without any bank, the long yellow and winding line of their beds resembles a causeway from the hills to the river. Many spots on the prairie are yellow with sunflower (helianthus).

As we were riding slowly along this afternoon, clouds of dust in the ravines, among the hills to the right, suddenly attracted our attention, and in a few minutes column after column of buffalo came galloping down, making directly to the river. By the time the leading herds had reached the water the prairie was darkened with the dense masses. Immediately before us, when the bands first came down into the valley, stretched an unbroken line, the head of which was lost among the river hills on the opposite side; and still they poured down from the ridge on our right. From hill to hill, the prairie bottom was certainly not less than two miles wide; and, allowing the animals to be ten feet apart, and only ten in a line, there were already eleven thousand in view. Some idea may thus be formed of their number when they had occupied the whole plain. In a short time they surrounded us on every side, extending for several miles in the rear, and forward as far as the eye could reach, leaving around us, as we advanced, an open space of only two or three hundred yards. This movement of the buffalo indicated to us the presence of Indians on the North Fork.

I halted earlier than usual, about forty miles from the junction, and all hands were soon busily engaged in preparing a feast to celebrate the day. The kindness of our friends at St. Louis had provided us with a large supply of excellent preserves and rich fruit cake; and when these were added to a macaroni soup and variously prepared dishes of the choicest buffalo meat, crowned with a cup of coffee, and enjoyed with prairie appetite, we felt, as we sat in barbaric luxury around our smoking supper on the grass, a greater sensation of enjoyment than the Roman epicure at his perfumed feast. But most of all it seemed to please our Indian friends, who, in the unrestrained enjoyment of the moment, demanded to know if our "medicine days came often." No restraint was exercised at the hospitable board, and, to the great delight of his elders, our young Indian lad made himself extremely drunk.

Our encampment was within a few miles of the place where the road crosses to the North Fork, and various reasons led me to divide my party at this point. The North Fork was the principal object of my survey; but I was desirous to ascend the South Branch, with a view of obtaining some astronomical positions, and determining the mouths of its tributaries as far as St. Vrain's Fort,[11] estimated to be some two hundred miles farther up the river and near to Long's Peak. There I hoped to obtain some mules, which I found would be necessary to relieve my horses.

In a military point of view, I was desirous to form some opinion of the country relative to the establishment of posts on the line connecting the settlements with the South Pass of the Rocky Mountains, by way of the Arkansas and the South and Laramie forks of the Platte. Crossing the country northwestwardly, from St. Vrain's Fort to the American Company's Fort at the mouth of Laramie, would give me some acquaintance with the affluents which head in the mountains between the two; I therefore determined to set out the next morning, accompanied by Mr. Preuss and four men— Maxwell, Bernier, Ayot, and Basil Lajeunesse. Our Cheyennes, whose village lay up this river, also decided to accompany us. The party I left in charge of Clément Lambert, with orders to cross to the North Fork; and at some convenient place, near to the Coulée des Frênes, make a cache of everything not absolutely necessary to the further progress of our expedition. From this point, using the most guarded precaution in his march through the country, he was to proceed to the American Company's Fort at the mouth of Laramie's Fork, and await my arrival, which would be prior to the 16th, as on that and the following night would occur some occultations which I was desirous to obtain at that place.

July 5th. Before breakfast all was ready. We had one led horse in addition to those we rode and a pack mule, destined to carry our instruments, provisions, and baggage, the last two articles not being of very great weight. The instruments consisted of a sextant, artificial horizon, etc., a barometer, spyglass, and compass. The chronometer I of course kept on my person. I had ordered the cook to put up for us some flour, coffee, and sugar, and our rifles were to furnish the rest. One blanket, in addition to his saddle and saddle blanket, furnished the materials for each man's bed, and everyone was provided with a change of linen. All were armed with rifles or double-barreled guns; and, in addition to these, Maxwell and myself were furnished with excellent pistols. Thus accoutered, we took a parting breakfast with our friends, and set forth.

Our journey the first day afforded nothing of any interest. We shot a buffalo toward sunset, and, having obtained some meat for our evening meal, encamped where a little timber afforded us the means of making a fire. Having disposed our meat on roasting sticks, we proceeded to unpack our bales in search of coffee and sugar and flour for bread. With the exception of a little parched coffee, unground, we found nothing. Our cook had neglected to put it up, or it had been somehow forgotten. Tired and hungry, with tough bull meat without salt (for we had not been able to kill a cow) and a little bitter coffee, we sat down in silence to our miserable fare, a very disconsolate party; for yesterday's feast was yet fresh in our memories, and this was our first brush with misfortune. Each man took his blanket, and laid himself down silently; for the worst part of these mishaps is that they make people ill-humored. Today we had traveled about thirty-six miles.

July 6th. Finding that our present excursion would be attended with considerable hardship, and unwilling to expose more persons than necessary, I determined to send Mr. Preuss back to the party. His horse, too, appeared in no condition to support the journey; and accordingly, after breakfast, he took the road across the hills, attended by one of my most trusty men, Bernier. The ridge between the rivers is here about fifteen miles broad, and I expected he would probably strike the fork near their evening camp. At all events, he would not fail to find their trail, and rejoin them the next day.

We continued our journey, seven in number, including the three

Cheyennes. Our general course was southwest, up the valley of the river, which was sandy, bordered on the northern side of the valley by a low ridge; and on the south, after seven or eight miles, the river hills became higher. Six miles from our resting place we crossed the bed of a considerable stream, now entirely dry—a bed of sand. In a grove of willows near the mouth, were the remains of a considerable fort, constructed of trunks of large trees. It was apparently very old, and had probably been the scene of some hostile encounter among the roving tribes. Its solitude formed an impressive contrast to the picture which our imaginations involuntarily drew of the busy scene which had been enacted here. The timber appeared to have been much more extensive formerly than now. There were but few trees—a kind of long-leaved willow—standing; and numerous trunks of large trees were scattered about on the ground. In many similar places I had occasion to remark an apparent progressive decay in the timber. Ten miles farther we reached the mouth of Lodge Pole Creek, a clear and handsome stream, running through a broad valley. In its course through the bottom it has a uniform breadth of twenty-two feet, and six inches in depth. A few willows on the banks strike pleasantly on the eye, by their greenness, in the midst of the hot and barren sands.

The amorpha was frequent among the ravines, but the sunflower (helianthus) was the characteristic; and flowers of deep warm colors seem most to love the sandy soil. The impression of the country traveled over today was one of dry and barren sands. We turned in toward the river at noon, and gave our horses two hours for food and rest. I had no other thermometer than the one attached to the barometer, which stood at 89°, the height of the column in the barometer being 26.235 at meridian. The sky was clear, with a high wind from the south. At two, we continued our journey; the wind had moderated, and it became almost unendurably hot, and our animals suffered severely. In the course of the afternoon, the wind rose suddenly, and blew hard from the southwest, with thunder and lightning, and squalls of rain; these were blown against us with violence by the wind; and, halting, we turned our backs to the storm until it blew over. Antelope were tolerably frequent, with a large gray hare; but the former were shy, and the latter hardly worth the delay of stopping to shoot them; so, as evening drew near, we again had recourse to an old bull, and encamped at sunset on an island of the Platte.

We ate our meat with a good relish this evening, for we were all in fine health, and had ridden nearly all of a long summer's day, with a burning sun reflected from the sands. My companions slept rolled up in their blankets, and the Indians lay in the grass near the fire; but my sleeping place generally had an air of more pretension. Our rifles were tied together near the muzzle, the butts resting on the ground, and a knife laid on the rope, to cut away in case of an alarm. Over this, which made a kind of frame, was thrown a large indiarubber cloth, which we used to cover our packs. This made a tent sufficiently large to receive about half of my bed, and was a place of shelter for my instruments; and as I was careful always to put this part against the wind, I could lie here with a sensation of satisfied enjoyment, and hear the wind blow, and the rain patter close to my head, and know that I should be at least half dry. Certainly, I never slept more soundly. The barometer at sunset was 26.010, thermometer 81°, and cloudy; but a gale from the west sprang up with the setting sun, and in a few minutes swept away every cloud from the sky. The evening was very fine, and I remained up to take some astronomical observations, which made our position in latitude 40° 51′ 17″, and longitude 103° 07′ 00″.

July 7th. At our camp this morning, at six o'clock, the barometer was at 26.183, thermometer 69°, and clear, with a light wind from the southwest. The past night had been squally, with high winds, and occasionally a few drops of rain. Our cooking did not occupy much time, and we left camp early. Nothing of interest occurred during the morning; the same dreary barrenness, except that a hard marly clay had replaced the sandy soil. Buffalo absolutely covered the plain on both sides the river, and whenever we ascended the hills, scattered herds gave life to the view in every direction. A small drove of wild horses made their appearance on the low river bottoms, a mile or two to the left, and I sent off one of the Indians (who seemed very eager to catch one) on my led horse, a spirited and fleet animal. The savage maneuvered a little to get the wind of the horses, in which he succeeded—approaching within a hundred yards without being discovered. The chase for a few minutes was animated and interesting. My hunter easily overtook and passed the hindmost of the wild drove, which the Indian did not attempt to lasso, all his efforts being directed to the capture of the leader. But the strength of the horse, weakened by the insufficient nourishment of grass, failed in a race, and all the drove escaped. We halted at noon on the bank of the river, the barometer at the time being 26.192, and the thermometer 103°, with a light air from the south, and clear weather.

In the course of the afternoon, dust rising among the hills at a particular place attracted our attention; and, riding up, we found a band of eighteen or twenty buffalo bulls engaged in a desperate fight. Though butting and goring were bestowed liberally and without distinction, yet their efforts were evidently directed against one —a huge gaunt old bull, very lean, while his adversaries were all fat and in good order. He appeared very weak, and had already received some wounds, and while we were looking on, was several times knocked down and badly hurt, and a very few moments would have put an end to him. Of course we took the side of the weaker party, and attacked the herd; but they were so blind with rage that they fought on, utterly regardless of our presence, although on foot and on horseback we were firing in open view within twenty yards of them. But this did not last long. In a very few seconds we created a commotion among them. One or two which were knocked over by the balls jumped up and ran off into the hills; and they began to retreat slowly along a broad ravine to the river, fighting furiously as they went. By the time they had reached the bottom, we had pretty well dispersed them, and the old bull hobbled off to lie down somewhere. One of his enemies remained on the ground where we had first fired upon them, and we stopped there for a short time to cut from him some meat for our supper. We had neglected to secure our horses, thinking it an unnecessary precaution in their fatigued condition; but our mule took it into his head to start, and away he went, followed at full speed by the pack horse, with all the baggage and instruments on his back. They were recovered and brought back, after a chase of a mile. Fortunately everything was well secured, so that nothing, not even the barometer, was in the least injured.

The sun was getting low, and some narrow lines of timber four or five miles distant promised us a pleasant camp, where, with plenty of wood for fire, and comfortable shelter, and rich grass for our animals, we should find clear cool springs, instead of the warm water of the Platte. On our arrival, we found the bed of a stream fifty to one hundred feet wide, sunk some thirty feet below the level of the prairie, with perpendicular banks, bordered by a fringe of green cottonwood, but not a drop of water. There were several small forks to the stream, all in the same condition. With the exception of the Platte bottom, the country seemed to be of a clay formation, dry, and perfectly devoid of any moisture, and baked hard by the sun. Turning off toward the river, we reached the bank in about a mile, and were delighted to find an old tree, with thick foliage and spreading branches, where we encamped. At sunset the barometer was at 25.950, thermometer 81°, with a strong wind from S. 20° E., and the sky partially covered with heavy masses of cloud, which settled a little toward the horizon by ten o'clock, leaving it sufficiently clear for astronomical observations, which placed us in latitude 40° 33′ 26″, and longitude 103° 30′ 37″.

July 8th. The morning was very pleasant. The breeze was fresh from S. 50° E. with few clouds, the barometer at six o'clock standing at 25.970, and the thermometer at 70°. Since leaving the forks, our route had passed over a country alternately clay and sand, each presenting the same naked waste. On leaving camp this morning, we struck again a sandy region, in which the vegetation appeared somewhat more vigorous than that which we had observed for the last few days; and on the opposite side of the river were some tolerably large groves of timber.

Journeying along, we came suddenly upon a place where the ground was covered with horses' tracks, which had been made since the rain, and indicated the immediate presence of Indians in our neighborhood. The buffalo, too, which the day before had been so numerous, were nowhere in sight—another sure indication that there were people near. Riding on, we discovered the carcass of a buffalo recently killed—perhaps the day before. We scanned the horizon carefully with the glass, but no living object was to be seen. For the next mile or two, the ground was dotted with buffalo carcasses, which showed that the Indians had made a surround here, and were in considerable force. We went on quickly and cautiously, keeping the river bottom, and carefully avoiding the hills; but we met with no interruption and began to grow careless again. We had already lost one of our horses, and here Basil's mule showed symptoms of giving out, and finally refused to advance, being what the Canadians call *resté*. He therefore dismounted, and drove her along before him; but this was a very slow way of traveling. We had inadvertently got about half a mile in advance, but our Cheyennes, who were generally a mile or two in the rear, remained with him. There were some dark-looking objects among the hills about two miles to the left, here low and undulating, which we had seen for a little time, and supposed to be buffalo coming in to water; but, happening to look behind, Maxwell saw the Cheyennes whipping up furiously, and another glance at the dark objects showed them at once to be Indians coming up at speed.

Had we been well mounted, and disencumbered of instruments, we might have set them at defiance; but as it was, we were fairly caught. It was too late to rejoin our friends, and we endeavored to gain a clump of timber about half a mile ahead; but the instruments and the tired state of our horses did not allow us to go faster than a steady canter, and they were gaining on us fast. At first they did not appear to be more than fifteen or twenty in number, but group after group darted into view at the top of the hills, until all the little eminences seemed in motion, and, in a few minutes from the time they were first discovered, two or three hundred, naked to the breechcloth, were sweeping across the prairie. In a few hundred yards we discovered that the timber we were endeavoring to make was on the opposite side of the river; and before we could reach the bank, down came the Indians upon us.

I am inclined to think that in a few seconds more the leading man, and perhaps some of his companions, would have rolled in the dust; for we had jerked the covers from our guns, and our fingers were on the triggers; men in such cases generally act from instinct, and a charge from three hundred naked savages is a circumstance not well calculated to promote a cool exercise of judgment. Just as he was about to fire, Maxwell recognized the leading Indian, and shouted to him in the Indian language, "You're a fool, God damn you, don't you know me?" The sound of his own language seemed to shock the savage, and, swerving his horse a little, he passed us like an arrow. He wheeled as I rode out toward him, and gave me his hand, striking his breast and exclaiming "Arapaho!" They proved to be a village of that nation among whom Maxwell had resided as a trader a year or two previously, and recognized him accordingly. We were soon in the midst of the band, answering as well as we could a multitude of questions; of which the very first was, of what tribe were our Indian companions who were coming in the rear? They seemed disappointed to know that they were Cheyennes, for they had fully anticipated a grand dance around a Pawnee scalp that night.

The chief showed us his village at a grove on the river six miles ahead, and pointed out a band of buffalo, on the other side of the Platte immediately opposite us, which he said they were going to surround. They had seen the band early in the morning from their village, and had been making a large circuit, to avoid giving them the wind, when they discovered us. In a few minutes the women came galloping up, astride on their horses, and naked from the knees down and the hips up. They followed the men, to assist in cutting up and carrying off the meat.

The wind was blowing directly across the river, and the chief requested us to halt where we were for a while, in order to avoid raising the herd. We therefore unsaddled our horses, and sat down on the bank to view the scene; and our new acquaintances rode a few hundred yards lower down, and began crossing the river. Scores of wild-looking dogs followed, looking like troops of wolves, and having, in fact, but very little of the dog in their composition. Some of them remained with us, and I checked one of the men, whom I found aiming at one, which he was about to kill for a wolf. The day had become very hot. The air was clear, with a very slight breeze; and now, at twelve o'clock, while the barometer stood at 25.920, the attached thermometer was at 108°.

Our Cheyennes had learned that with the Arapaho village were about twenty lodges of their own, including their own families; they therefore immediately commenced making their toilet. After bathing in the river, they invested themselves in some handsome calico shirts, which I afterward learned they had stolen from my own men, and spent some time in arranging their hair and painting themselves with some vermilion I had given them. While they were engaged in this satisfactory manner, one of their half-wild horses, to which the crowd of prancing animals which had just passed had recalled the freedom of her existence among the wild droves on the prairie, suddenly dashed into the hills at the top of her speed. She was their pack horse, and had on her back all the worldly wealth of our poor Cheyennes, all their accouterments, and all the little articles which they had picked up among us, with some few presents I had given them. The loss which they seemed to regret most were their spears and shields, and some tobacco which they had received from me. However, they bore it all with the philosophy of an Indian, and laughingly continued their toilet. They appeared, however, a little mortified at the thought of returning to the village in such a sorry plight.

"Our people will laugh at us," said one of them, "returning to the village on foot, instead of driving back a drove of Pawnee horses."

He demanded to know if I loved my sorrel hunter very much; to which I replied he was the object of my most intense affection. Far from being able to give, I was myself in want of horses; and any suggestion of parting with the few I had valuable was met with a peremptory refusal.

In the meantime the slaughter was about to commence on the other side. So soon as they reached it, the Indians separated into two bodies. One party proceeded directly across the prairie toward the hills in an extended line, while the other went up the river; and instantly, as they had given the wind to the herd, the chase commenced. The buffalo started for the hills, but were intercepted and driven back toward the river, broken and running in every direction. The clouds of dust soon covered the whole scene, preventing us from having any but an occasional view. It had a very singular appearance to us at a distance, especially when looking with the glass. We were too far to hear the report of the guns, or any sound; and at every instant through the clouds of dust which the sun made luminous, we could see for a moment two or three buffalo dashing along, and close behind them an Indian with his long spear, or other weapon, and instantly again they disappeared. The apparent silence, and the dimly seen figures flitting by with such rapidity, gave it a kind of dreamy effect, and seemed more like a picture than a scene of real life. It had been a large herd when the *cerne* commenced, probably three or four hundred in number; but, though I watched them closely, I did not see one emerge from the fatal cloud where the work of destruction was going on. After remaining here about an hour, we resumed our journey in the direction of the village.

Gradually, as we rode on, Indian after Indian came dropping along, laden with meat; and by the time we had neared the lodges, the backward road was covered with the returning horsemen. It was a pleasant contrast with the desert road we had been traveling. Several had joined company with us, and one of the chiefs invited us to his lodge. The village consisted of about one hundred and twenty-five lodges, of which twenty were Cheyennes, the latter pitched a little apart from the Arapahoes. They were disposed in a scattering manner on both sides of a broad irregular street, about one hundred and fifty feet wide, and running along the river.

As we rode along, I remarked near some of the lodges a kind of tripod frame, formed of three slender poles of birch, scraped very clean, to which were affixed the shield and spear, with some other weapons of a chief. All were scrupulously clean, the spearhead was burnished bright, and the shield white and stainless. It reminded me of the days of feudal chivalry; and when, as I rode by, I yielded to the passing impulse, and touched one of the spotless shields with the muzzle of my gun, I almost expected a grim warrior to start from the lodge and resent my challenge. The master of the lodge spread out a robe for me to sit upon, and the squaws set before us a large wooden dish of buffalo meat. He had lit his pipe in the meanwhile, and when it had been passed around, we commenced our dinner while he continued to smoke. Gradually five or six other chiefs came in, and took their seats in silence. When we had finished, our host asked a number of questions relative to the object of our journey, of which I made no concealment; telling him simply that I had made a visit to see the country, preparatory to the establishment of military posts on the way to the mountains. Although this was information of the highest interest to them, and by no means calculated to please them, it excited no expression of surprise, and in no way altered the grave courtesy of their demeanor. The others listened and smoked. I remarked that in taking the pipe for the first time, each had turned the stem upward, with a rapid glance, as in offering to the Great Spirit, before he put it in his mouth.

A storm had been gathering for the past hour, and some pattering drops on the lodge warned us that we had some miles to go to our camp. Some Indian had given Maxwell a bundle of dried meat, which was very acceptable, as we had nothing; and springing upon our horses, we rode off at dusk in the face of a cold shower and driving wind. We found our companions under some densely foliaged old trees, about three miles up the river. Under one of them lay the trunk of a large cottonwood, to leeward of which the men had kindled a fire, and we sat here and roasted our meat in tolerable shelter. Nearly opposite was the mouth of one of the most considerable affluents of the South Fork, La Fourche aux Castors (Beaver Fork), heading off in the ridge to the southeast.

July 9th. This morning we caught the first faint glimpse of the Rocky Mountains, about sixty miles distant. Though a tolerably bright day, there was a slight mist, and we were just able to discern the snowy summit of "Long's Peak" ("Les Deux Oreilles" of the Canadians), showing like a small cloud near the horizon. I found it easily distinguishable, there being a perceptible difference in its appearance from the white clouds that were floating about the sky. I was pleased to find that among the traders and voyageurs the name of "Long's Peak" had been adopted and become familiar in the country. In the ravines near this place, a light brown sandstone made its first appearance. About eight, we discerned several persons on horseback a mile or two ahead, on the opposite side of the river. They turned in toward the river, and we rode down to meet them. We found them to be two white men, and a mulatto, named Jim Beckwith,[12] who had left St. Louis when a boy, and gone to live with the Crow Indians. He had distinguished himself among them by some acts of daring bravery, and had risen to the rank of a chief but had now, for some years, left them. They were in search of a band of horses that had gone off from a camp some miles above, in charge of Mr. Chabonard. Two of them continued down the river, in search of the horses, and the American turned back with us and we rode on toward the camp. About eight miles from our sleeping place we reached Bijou's Fork, an affluent of the right bank. Where we crossed it, a short distance from the Platte, it has a sandy bed about four hundred yards broad, the water in various small streams, a few inches deep.

Seven miles farther brought us to a camp of some four or five whites (New Englanders, I believe), who had accompanied Captain Wyeth [13] to the Columbia River, and were independent trappers. All had their squaws with them, and I was really surprised at the number of little fat buffalo-fed boys that were tumbling about the camp, all apparently of the same age, about three or four years old. They were encamped on a rich bottom, covered with a profusion of fine grass, and had a large number of fine-looking horses and mules. We rested with them a few minutes, and in about two miles arrived at Chabonard's camp, on an island in the Platte. On the heights above, we met the first Spaniard I had seen in the country. Mr. Chabonard was in the service of Bent and St. Vrain's company, and had left their fort some forty or fifty miles above, in the spring, with boats laden with the furs of the last year's trade. He had met the same fortune as the voyageurs on the North Fork, and, finding it impossible to proceed, had taken up his summer's residence on this island, which he had named St. Helena. The river hills appeared to be composed entirely of sand, and the Platte had lost the muddy character of its waters, and here was tolerably clear. From the mouth of the South Fork, I had found it occasionally broken up by small islands; and at the time of our journey, which was at a season of the year when the waters were at a favorable stage, it was not navigable for anything drawing six inches water. The current was very swift—the bed of the stream a coarse gravel.

From the place at which we had encountered the Arapahoes, the Platte had been tolerably well fringed with timber, and the island here had a fine grove of very large cottonwoods, under whose broad shade the tents were pitched. There was a large drove of horses in the opposite prairie bottom; smoke was rising from the scattered fires, and the encampment had quite a patriarchal air. Mr. Chabonard received us hospitably. One of the people was sent to gather mint, with the aid of which he con-

cocted very good julep; and some boiled buffalo tongue, and
coffee with the luxury of sugar, were soon set before us. The
people in his employ were generally Spaniards, and among them
I saw a young Spanish woman from Taos, whom I found to be
Beckwith's wife.

July 10th. We parted with our hospitable host after breakfast
the next morning, and reached St. Vrain's Fort, about forty-five
miles from St. Helena, late in the evening.[14] This post is situated
on the South Fork of the Platte, immediately under the mountains, about seventeen miles east of Long's Peak. It is on the
right bank, on the verge of the upland prairie, about forty feet
above the river, of which the immediate valley is about six hundred yards wide. The stream is divided into various branches by
small islands, among which it runs with a swift current. The bed
of the river is sand and gravel, the water very clear, and here
may be called a mountain stream. This region appears to be
entirely free from the limestones and marls which give to the
Lower Platte its yellow and dirty color. The Black Hills lie between the stream and the mountains, whose snowy peaks glitter
a few miles beyond. At the fort we found Mr. St. Vrain, who
received us with much kindness and hospitality. Maxwell had
spent the last two or three years between this post and the village
of Taos; and here he was at home, and among his friends. Spaniards frequently come over in search of employment, and several
came in shortly after our arrival. They usually obtain about six
dollars a month, generally paid to them in goods. They are very
useful in a camp, in taking care of horses and mules; and I engaged one, who proved to be an active, laborious man, and was
of very considerable service to me. The elevation of the Platte
here is five thousand four hundred feet above the sea. The neighboring mountains did not appear to enter far the region of perpetual snow, which was generally confined to the northern side
of the peaks. On the southern, I remarked very little. Here it
appeared, so far as I could judge in the distance, to descend but
a few hundred feet below the summits.

I regretted that time did not permit me to visit them; but the
proper object of my survey lay among the mountains farther
north, and I looked forward to an exploration of their snowy

recesses with great pleasure. The piny region of the mountains to the south was enveloped in smoke, and I was informed had been on fire several months. Pike's Peak is said to be visible from this place, about one hundred miles to the southward, but the smoky state of the atmosphere prevented my seeing it. The weather continued overcast during my stay here, so that I failed in determining the latitude, but obtained good observations for time on the mornings of the 11th and 12th. An assumed latitude of 40° 22′ 30″ from the evening position of the 12th enabled me to obtain, for a tolerably correct longitude, 105° 12′ 12″.

July 12. The kindness of Mr. St. Vrain had enabled me to obtain a couple of horses and three good mules; and with a further addition to our party of the Spaniard whom I had hired, and two others, who were going to obtain service at Laramie's Fork, we resumed our journey at ten, on the morning of the 12th. We had been able to procure nothing at the post in the way of provision. An expected supply from Taos had not yet arrived, and a few pounds of coffee was all that could be spared to us. In addition to this, we had dried meat enough for the first day; on the next, we expected to find buffalo. From this post, according to the estimate of the country, the fort at the mouth of Laramie's Fork, which was our next point of destination, was nearly due north, distant about one hundred and twenty-five miles.

For a short distance, our road lay down the valley of the Platte, which resembled a garden in the splendor of fields of varied flowers which filled the air with fragrance. The only timber I noticed consisted of poplar, birch, cottonwood, and willow. In something less than three miles, we crossed Thompson's Creek, one of the affluents to the left bank of the South Fork—a fine stream, about sixty-five feet wide, and three feet deep. Journeying on, the low dark line of the Black Hills [15] lying between us and the mountains to the left, in about ten miles from the fort we reached Cache à la Poudre, where we halted to noon. This is a very beautiful mountain stream, about one hundred feet wide, flowing with a full swift current over a rocky bed. We halted under the shade of some cottonwoods, with which the stream is wooded scatteringly. In the upper part of its course, it runs amid the wildest mountain scenery, and, breaking through the Black Hills, falls into the Platte, about ten miles below this place. In the course of our late journey, I had managed to become the possessor of a very untractable mule—a perfect vixen—and her I had turned over to my Spaniard. It occupied us about half an hour today to get the saddle upon her; but, once on her back, José could not be dismounted, realizing the accounts given of Mexican horses and horsemanship; and we continued our route in the afternoon.

At evening we encamped on Crow (?) Creek, having traveled about twenty-eight miles. None of the party were well acquainted with the country, and I had great difficulty in ascertaining what were the names of the streams we crossed between the North and South forks of the Platte. This I supposed to be Crow Creek. It is what is called a salt stream, and the water stands in pools having no continuous course. A fine-grained sandstone made its appearance in the banks. The observations of the night placed us in latitude 40° 42′, longitude 104° 57′ 49″. The barometer at sunset was 25.231; attached thermometer at 66°. Sky clear, except in the east, with a light wind from the north.

July 13th. There being no wood here, we used last night the bois de vache, which is very plentiful. At our camp this morning the barometer was at 25.235; the attched thermometer 60°. A few clouds were moving through a deep-blue sky, with a light wind from the west. After a ride of twelve miles, in a northerly direction, over a plain covered with innumerable quantities of cacti, we reached a small creek in which there was water, and where several herds of buffalo were scattered about among the ravines, which always afford good pasturage. We seem now to be passing along the base of a plateau of the Black Hills, in which the formation consists of marls, some of them white and laminated; the country to the left rising suddenly, and falling off gradually and uniformly to the right. In five or six miles of a northeasterly course, we struck a high ridge, broken into conical peaks, on whose summits large boulders were gathered in heaps. The magnetic direction of the ridge is northwest and southeast, the glittering white of its precipitous sides making it visible for many miles to the south. It is composed of a soft earthy limestone and marls, resembling that hereafter described in the neighborhood of the

Chimney Rock, on the North Fork of the Platte, easily worked by the winds and rains, and sometimes molded into very fantastic shapes.

At the foot of the northern slope was the bed of a creek, some forty feet wide, coming, by frequent falls, from the bench above. It was shut in by high perpendicular banks, in which were strata of white laminated marl. Its bed was perfectly dry, and the leading feature of the whole region is one of remarkable aridity, and perfect freedom from moisture. In about six miles we crossed the bed of another dry creek; and, continuing our ride over a high level prairie, a little before sundown we came suddenly upon a beautiful creek, which revived us with a feeling of delighted surprise by the pleasant contrast of the deep verdure of its banks with the parched desert we had passed. We had suffered much today, both men and horses, for want of water, having met with it but once in our uninterrupted march of forty miles, and an exclusive meat diet creates much thirst.

"*Las bestias tienen mucha hambre,*" said the young Spaniard, inquiringly. "*Y la gente tambien,*" said I: "*amigo,* we'll camp here." A stream of good and clear water ran winding about through the little valley, and a herd of buffalo were quietly feeding a little distance below. It was quite a hunter's paradise, and while some ran down toward the band to kill one for supper, others collected bois de vache for a fire, there being no wood; and I amused myself with hunting for plants among the grass.

It will be seen, by occasional remarks on the geological formation, that the constituents of the soil in these regions are good, and every day served to strengthen the impression in my mind, confirmed by subsequent observation, that the barren appearance of the country is due almost entirely to the extreme dryness of the climate. Along our route the country had seemed to increase constantly in elevation. According to the indication of the barometer, we were at our encampment five thousand four hundred and forty feet above the sea.

The evening was very clear, with a fresh breeze from the south, 50° east. The barometer at sunset was 24.862, the thermometer attached showing 68°. I supposed this to be a fork of Lodge Pole Creek, so far as I could determine from our uncertain means of information. Astronomical observations gave for the camp a longitude of 104° 39′ 37″, and latitude 41° 08′ 31″.

July 14th. The wind continued fresh from the same quarter in the morning; the day being clear, with the exception of a few clouds in the horizon. At our camp at six o'clock the height of the barometer was 24.830, the attached thermometer 61°. Our course this morning was directly north by compass, the variation being 15° or 16° easterly. A ride of four miles brought us to Lodge Pole Creek, which we had seen at its mouth on the South Fork; crossing on the way two dry streams, in eighteen miles from our encampment of the past night, we reached a high bleak ridge, composed entirely of the same earthy limestone and marl previously described. I had never seen anything which impressed so strongly on my mind a feeling of desolation. The valley, through which ran the waters of Horse Creek, lay in view to the north, but too far to have any influence on the immediate view. On the peak of the ridge where I was standing, some six or seven hundred feet above the river, the wind was high and bleak; the barren and arid country seemed as if it had been swept by fires, and in every direction the same dull ash-colored hue, derived from the formation, met the eye. On the summits were some stunted pines, many of them dead, all wearing the same ashen hue of desolation. We left the place with pleasure, and after we had descended several hundred feet, halted in one of the ravines, which, at the distance of every mile or two, cut the flanks of the ridge with little rushing streams, wearing something of a mountain character. We had already begun to exchange the comparatively barren lands for those of a more fertile character. Though the sandstone formed the broken banks of the creek, yet they were covered with a thin grass; and the fifty or sixty feet which formed the bottom land of the little stream were clothed with very luxuriant grass, among which I remarked willow and cherry (*Cerasus virginiana*); and a quantity of gooseberry and currant bushes occupied the greater part.

The creek was three or four feet broad, and about six inches deep, with a swift current of clear water, and tolerably cool. We had struck it too low down to find the cold water which we should have enjoyed nearer to its sources. At two P.M. the barometer was at

25.050, the attached thermometer 104°. A day of hot sunshine, with clouds, and a moderate breeze from the south. Continuing down the stream, in about four miles we reached its mouth, at one of the main branches of Horse Creek. Looking back upon the ridge, whose direction appeared to be a little to the north of east, we saw it seemed at frequent intervals with the dark lines of wooded streams, affluents of the river that flowed so far as we could see along its base. We crossed, in the space of twelve miles from our noon halt, three or four forks of Horse Creek, and encamped at sunset on the most easterly.

The fork on which we encamped appeared to have followed an easterly direction up to this place; but here it makes a very sudden bend to the north, passing between two ranges of precipitous hills, called, as I was informed, Goshen's Hole. There is somewhere in or near this locality a place so called, but I am not certain that it was the place of our encampment. Looking back upon the spot, at the distance of a few miles to the northward, the hills appear to shut in the prairie, through which runs the creek, with a semicircular sweep, which might very naturally be called a hole in the hills. The geological composition of the ridge is the same which constitutes the rock of the Courthouse and Chimney, on the North Fork, which appeared to me a continuation of this ridge. The winds and rains work this formation into a variety of singular forms. The pass into Goshen's Hole is about two miles wide, and the hill on the western side imitates, in an extraordinary manner, a massive fortified place, with a remarkable fullness of detail. The rock is marl and earthy limestone, white, without the least appearance of vegetation, and much resembles masonry at a little distance; and here it sweeps around a level area two or three hundred yards in diameter, and in the form of a half-moon, terminating on either extremity in enormous bastions. Along the whole line of the parapets appear domes and slender minarets, forty or fifty feet high, giving it every appearance of an old fortified town.

On the waters of White River, where this formation exists in great extent, it presents appearances which excite the admiration of the solitary voyageur, and form a frequent theme of their conversation when speaking of the wonders of the country. Sometimes it offers the perfectly illusive appearance of a large city, with numerous streets and magnificent buildings, among which the Canadians never fail to see their cabaret; and sometimes it takes the form of a solitary house, with many large chambers, into which they drive their horses at night, and sleep in these natural defenses perfectly secure from any attack of prowling savages. Before reaching our camp at Goshen's Hole, in crossing the immense detritus at the foot of the Castle Rock, we were involved amid winding passages cut by the waters of the hill; and where, with a breadth scarcely large enough for the passage of a horse, the walls rise thirty and forty feet perpendicularly. This formation supplies the discoloration of the Platte. At sunset, the height of the mercurial column was 25.500, the attached thermometer 80°, and wind moderate from S. 38° E. Clouds covered the sky with the rise of the moon, but I succeeded in obtaining the usual astronomical observations, which placed us in latitude 41° 40′ 13″, and longitude 104° 24′ 36″.

July 15th. At six this morning the barometer was at 25.515, the thermometer 72°; the day was fine, with some clouds looking dark on the south, with a fresh breeze from the same quarter. We found that in our journey across the country we had kept too much to the eastward. This morning, accordingly, we traveled by compass some 15° or 20° to the west of north, and struck the Platte some thirteen miles below Fort Laramie. The day was extremely hot, and among the hills the wind seemed to have just issued from an oven. Our horses were much distressed, as we had traveled hard, and it was with some difficulty that they were all brought to the Platte; which we reached at one o'clock. In riding in toward the river, we found the trail of our carts, which appeared to have passed a day or two since.

After having allowed our animals two hours for food and repose, we resumed our journey, and toward the close of the day came in sight of Laramie's Fork. Issuing from the river hills, we came first in view of Fort Platte, a post belonging to Messrs. Sybille, Adams & Co., situated immediately in the point of land at the junction of Laramie with the Platte. Like the post we had visited on the South Fork, it was built of earth, and still unfinished, being enclosed with walls (or rather houses) on three of the sides, and open on the fourth to the river. A few hundred yards brought us in view of the post of the American Fur Company, called Fort John, or Laramie.[16]

This was a large post, having more the air of military construction than the fort at the mouth of the river. It is on the left bank, on a rising ground some twenty-five feet above the water; and its lofty walls, whitewashed and picketed, with the large bastions at the angles, gave it quite an imposing appearance in the uncertain light of evening. A cluster of lodges, which the language told us belonged to Sioux Indians, was pitched under the walls, and, with the fine background of the Black Hills and the prominent peak of Laramie Mountain, strongly drawn in the clear light of the western sky where the sun had already set, the whole formed at the moment a strikingly beautiful picture. From the company at St. Louis I had letters for Mr. Boudeau, the gentleman in charge of the post, by whom I was received with great hospitality and an efficient kindness which was invaluable to me during my stay in the country. I found our people encamped on the bank, a short distance above the fort. . . . *

FOOTNOTES

1. Lucien Bonaparte Maxwell (1818–1875) combined the blood of a Scottish American father and a Franco-American mother. He got some schooling at Kaskaskia, Illinois, where he was born. But he was off at an early age to Taos, where he met Kit Carson. Sometime around 1840 he worked at Fort St. Vrain on the South Platte. He was destined to do Frémont good service, especially in the stirring events of the conquest of California. He was also destined to figure in some of the most spectacular land litigation of the century, that revolving around the huge Maxwell Grant in New Mexico, a tremendous tract which he obtained partly by inheritance and partly by purchase.

2. Kit Carson attained such fame that it is difficult to remember that at this time he was practically unknown, and that indeed Frémont's writings were first to bring him to wide public notice. Born in Kentucky in 1809, he died in 1868. He had received no schooling when, after being apprenticed to a saddler, he ran away from his Missouri home in 1826 and joined an expedition to Santa Fe. Years of fighting Indians and trapping beavers in the Far West followed. He hunted buffalo, too, to supply meat for Bent's Fort. He had thus become thoroughly familiar with a great part of the Rocky Mountains and the Southwestern plains when, after a trip to Missouri to put his five-year-old half-breed daughter in school, he met Frémont. The two immediately became fast friends. On the first three expeditions Frémont found Carson almost indispensable. Kit

* Frémont's *Report* at this point includes nearly five pages from the journal kept by Charles Preuss on the journey of his separate party. Their trip up the North Platte to Fort Laramie had been uneventful except for a meeting with a large party of traders and trappers led by Jim Bridger, who warned them of hostile bands of Sioux, Cheyenne, and Gros Ventre. These pages are omitted.

never wavered in his devotion to Frémont, while the latter paid his guide the highest possible tribute in saying: "With me Carson and truth are one." His integrity and modesty matched his expert knowledge of the West.

3. The two leading members of the Chouteau family at this time were Jean Pierre Chouteau (1758–1849), who had retired to an estate on the outskirts of St. Louis, and Pierre Chouteau, his son (1789–1865), head of a firm which, as has been noted, had taken over the Western Department of Astor's American Fur Company.

4. This party of perhaps 120 emigrants, headed by Dr. Elijah White, successfully made the long journey from Missouri to Oregon.

5. The Pawnee Indians inhabited the valley of the Platte, easiest of the hunting grounds of the Cheyenne and Arapahoe. The Otos, mentioned above, occupied lands south of the Pawnee. No other tribe suffered so much from the migration to Oregon as the Pawnee, who quickly wasted away under disease and dissipation.

6. The elk or wapiti, once common over the whole country, was now being driven off to the Rocky Mountain region.

7. The Big Blue River flows down from southeastern Nebraska through northeastern Kansas to empty into the Kansas River at the present city of Manhattan.

8. Not far from the present city of Grand Island in eastern Nebraska.

9. The two forks of the Platte join in Lincoln County, Nebraska, near the present-day city of North Platte, and about seventy miles from the Colorado boundary at its nearest point.

10. Frémont's party was now moving south by west up the South Platte, toward what is now the Colorado boundary at Julesburg.

11. St. Vrain's Fort was on the headwaters of the South Platte, north of Denver, and not very far from what is now Greeley, Colorado. Fort Laramie was well to the northwest, across mountainous country in what is now Wyoming; a post flanked on the east by the Laramie Range. Frémont was giving his picked party an arduous route to blaze.

12. Properly Jim Beckwourth, a noted scout and trapper, whose narrative of his life and adventures, written from his own dictation, is a minor Western classic. Born 1798, he had joined William H. Ashley's company of fur traders. Then he abandoned life among the whites to live with the Indians, spending half a dozen years with the Crows, and contracting unions with various Indian women. By this time he was once more with the whites. He died in or about 1867.

13. Nathaniel J. Wyeth (1802–1856), a Massachusetts man much excited about Oregon, had tried to establish on the Columbia River a colony which was to catch and ship salmon, trade for furs, and grow farm produce. He built a fort where the Willamette empties into the Columbia, and a much more important post, Fort Hall, on the line of the Oregon and California Trail. All this was fairly ancient history now; for Wyeth's second and last party had reached Oregon in 1834. Some of the Yankees he had taken out had gone native.

14. St. Vrain's Fort or trading post was a small adobe structure near what is now Evans, Colorado, on the south bank of the South Platte. Ceran St. Vrain (1802–1870) had sprung from the French in Missouri, and had lost no time in getting into the fur trade. He maintained direct relations with the Mexican Southwest, carrying on commercial affairs with Taos, Santa Fe, and Sonora; and he became a Mexican citizen. While he held this status he received from

the Mexican Government a land grant of four million acres. His hospitality to such visitors as Frémont became famous. A large man of fine appearance, great courage, and amiable deportment, he became much beloved in wide Western circles.

15. These were the Laramie Mountains, and are not to be confused with the Black Hills of Dakota. Frémont was in southeastern Wyoming.

16. Fort Platte, here mentioned, was a rough unfinished adobe post belonging to a fur-trading company. Fort Laramie, near at hand, belonged to the American Fur Trading Company. First built in 1834 as Fort William, by William Sublette and Robert Campbell, it had been taken over by the powerful corporation in 1836. Its log stockade had been replaced by adobe walls. The fort was a trading center for a wide mountain area, and was famous among both Indians and whites.

CHAPTER 5

From Fort Laramie
to the Wind River Range *

I WALKED up to visit our friends at the fort, which is a quadrangular structure, built of clay, after the fashion of the Mexicans, who are generally employed in building them. The walls are about fifteen feet high, surmounted with a wooden palisade, and form a portion of ranges of houses which entirely surround a yard of about one hundred and thirty feet square. Every apartment has its door and window—all, of course, opening on the inside. There are two entrances, opposite each other and midway the wall, one of which is a large and public entrance, the other smaller and more private—a sort of postern gate. Over the great entrance is a square tower with loopholes, and, like the rest of the work, built of earth. At two of the angles, and diagonally opposite each other, are large square bastions, so arranged as to sweep the four faces of the walls.

This post belongs to the American Fur Company, and, at the time of our visit, was in charge of Mr. Boudeau. Two of the company's clerks, Messrs. Galpin and Kellogg, were with him, and he had in the fort about sixteen men. As usual, these had found wives among the Indian squaws; and, with the usual accompaniment of children, the place had quite a populous appearance. It is hardly necessary to say that the object of the establishment is trade with the neighboring tribes, who, in the course of the year, generally make two or three visits to the fort. In addition to this, traders, with a small outfit, are constantly kept among them. The articles of trade

* From Frémont's *Report on an Exploration of the Country Lying between the Missouri River and the Rocky Mountains,* continued. His course now lay from Fort Laramie, in what today is southeastern Wyoming, northwestward to the west-central part of the present-day State. Following the North Platte to its junction with the Sweetwater, he took a somewhat circuitous route. On the way he inspected Independence Rock, a great landmark on the Oregon Trail, and went through South Pass, one of the main objectives of his journey.

consist, on the one side, almost entirely of buffalo robes; and, on the other, of blankets, calicoes, guns, powder, and lead, with such cheap ornaments as glass beads, looking glasses, rings, vermilion for painting, tobacco, and principally, and in spite of the prohibition, of spirits, brought into the country in the form of alcohol and diluted with water before sold.

While mentioning this fact, it is but justice to the American Fur Company to state that, throughout the country, I have always found them strenuously opposed to the introduction of spirituous liquors. But, in the present state of things, when the country is supplied with alcohol, when a keg of it will purchase from an Indian everything he possesses—his furs, his lodge, his horses, and even his wife and children—and when any vagabond who has money enough to purchase a mule can go into a village and trade against them successfully, without withdrawing entirely from the trade it is impossible for them to discontinue its use. In their opposition to this practice the company is sustained, not only by their obligation to the laws of the country and the welfare of the Indians, but clearly, also, on grounds of policy; for, with heavy and expensive outfits, they contend at manifestly great disadvantage against the numerous independent and unlicensed traders who enter the country from various avenues, from the United States and from Mexico, having no other stock in trade than some kegs of liquor, which they sell at the modest price of thirty-six dollars the gallon. The difference between the regular trader and the coureur des bois (as the French call the itinerant or peddling traders), with respect to the sale of spirits, is here, as it always has been, fixed and permanent, and growing out of the nature of their trade. The regular trader looks ahead, and has an interest in the preservation of the Indians and in the regular pursuit of their business, and the preservation of their arms, horses, and everything necessary to their future and permanent success in hunting; the coureur des bois has no permanent interest, and gets what he can and for what he can, from every Indian he meets even at the risk of disabling him from doing anything more at hunting.

The fort had a very cool and clean appearance. The great entrance in which I found the gentlemen assembled, and which was floored, and about fifteen feet long, made a pleasant, shaded seat, through which the breeze swept constantly; for this country is famous for high winds. In the course of conversation I learned the following particulars, which will explain the condition of the country.

For several years the Cheyennes and Sioux had gradually become more and more hostile to the whites, and in the latter part of August, 1841, had had a rather severe engagement with a party of sixty men under the command of Mr. Frapp, of St. Louis. The Indians lost eight or ten warriors, and the whites had their leader and four men killed. This fight took place on the waters of Snake River; and it was this party, on their return under Mr. Bridger,[1] which had spread so much alarm among my people. In the course of the spring, two other small parties had been cut off by the Sioux—one on their return from the Crow nation, and the other among the Black Hills. The emigrants to Oregon and Mr. Bridger's party met here, a few days before our arrival. Division and misunderstandings had grown up among the emigrants; they were already somewhat disheartened by the fatigue of their long and wearisome journey, and the feet of their cattle had become so much worn as to be scarcely able to travel. In this situation they were not likely to find encouragement in the hostile attitude of the Indians, and the new and unexpected difficulties which sprang up before them. They were told that the country was entirely swept of grass, and that few or no buffalo were to be found on their line of route; and, with their weakened animals, it would be impossible for them to transport their heavy wagons over the mountain.

Under these circumstances, they disposed of their wagons and cattle at the forts; selling them at the prices they had paid in the States, and taking in exchange coffee and sugar at one dollar a pound and miserable worn-out horses which died before they reached the mountains. Mr. Boudeau informed me that he had purchased thirty, and the lower fort eighty, head of fine cattle, some of them of the Durham breed.

Mr. Fitzpatrick,[2] whose name and high reputation are familiar to all who interest themselves in the history of this country, had reached Laramie in company with Mr. Bridger; and the emigrants were fortunate enough to obtain his services to guide them as far as the British post of Fort Hall,[3] about two hundred and fifty miles beyond the South Pass of the mountains. They had started for this post on July 4th and, immediately after their departure, a war party of three hundred and fifty braves set out upon their trail. As their principal chief or partisan had lost some relations in the recent fight, and had sworn to kill the first whites on his path, it was supposed that their intention was to attack the party should a favorable opportunity offer; or, if they were foiled in their principal object by the vigilance of Mr. Fitzpatrick, content themselves with stealing horses and cutting off stragglers.

These had been gone but a few days previous to our arrival.

The effect of the engagement with Mr. Frapp had been greatly to irritate the hostile spirit of the savages; and immediately subsequent to that event the Gros Ventre Indians had united with the Oglalas and Cheyennes, and taken the field in great force—so far as I could ascertain, to the amount of eight hundred lodges. Their object was to make an attack on a camp of Snake and Crow Indians and a body of about one hundred whites, who had made a rendezvous somewhere in the Green River Valley or on the Sweet Water. After spending some time in buffalo-hunting in the neighborhood of the Medicine Bow Mountain, they were to cross over to the Green River waters, and return to Laramie by way of the South Pass and the Sweet Water Valley. According to the calculation of the Indians, Mr. Boudeau informed me they were somewhere near the head of the Sweet Water.

I subsequently learned that the party led by Mr. Fitzpatrick were overtaken by their pursuers near Rock Independence, in the valley of the Sweet Water; but his skill and resolution saved them from surprise, and, small as his force was, they did not venture to attack him openly. Here they lost one of their party by an accident, and, continuing up the valley, they came suddenly upon the large village. From these they met with a doubtful reception. Long residence and familiar acquaintance had given to Mr. Fitzpatrick great personal influence among them, and a portion of them were disposed to let him pass quietly; but by far the greater number were inclined to hostile measures, and the chiefs spent the whole of one night, during which they kept the little party in the midst of them, in council, debating the question of attacking them the next day; but the influence of "The Broken Hand," as they called Mr. Fitzpatrick (one of his hands having been shattered by the bursting of a gun), at length prevailed, and obtained for them an unmolested passage; but they sternly assured him that this path was no longer open, and that any party of whites which should hereafter be found upon it would meet with certain destruction. From all that I have been able to learn, I have no doubt that the emigrants owe their lives to Mr. Fitzpatrick.

Thus it would appear that the country was swarming with scattered war parties; and when I heard, during the day, the various contradictory and exaggerated rumors which were incessantly repeated to them, I was not surprised that so much alarm prevailed among my men. Carson, one of the best and most experienced mountaineers, fully supported the opinion given by Bridger of the dangerous state of the country, and openly expressed his conviction that we could not escape without some sharp encounters with the Indians. In addition to this, he made his will; and among the circumstances which were constantly occurring to increase their alarm, this was the most unfortunate; and I found that a number of my party had become so much intimidated that they had requested to be discharged at this place. I dined today at Fort Platte, which has been mentioned as situated at the junction of Laramie River with the Nebraska. Here I heard a confirmation of the statements given above. The party of warriors which had started a few days since on the trail of the emigrants was expected back in fourteen days, to join the village with which their families and the old men had remained. The arrival of the latter was hourly expected; and some Indians have just come in who had left them on the Laramie Fork, about twenty miles above. Mr. [Joseph] Bissonette, one of the traders belonging to Fort Platte, urged the propriety of taking with me an interpreter and two or three old men of the village, in which case he thought there would be little or no hazard in encountering any of the war parties. The principal danger was in being attacked before they should know who we were.

These Indians had a confused idea of the numbers and power of our people, and dreaded to bring upon themselves the military force of the United States. Mr. Bissonette, who spoke the language fluently, offered his services to accompany me so far as the Red Buttes. He was desirous to join the large party on its return, for purposes of trade, and it would suit his views, as well as my own, to go with us to the Buttes; beyond which point it would be impossible to prevail on a Sioux to venture, on account of their fear of the Crows. From Fort Laramie to the Red Buttes, by the ordinary road, is one hundred and thirty-five miles; and, though only on the threshold of danger, it seemed better to secure the services of an interpreter for the partial distance than to have none at all.

So far as frequent interruption from the Indians would allow, we occupied ourselves in making some astronomical calculations and bringing up the general map to this stage of our journey; but the tent was generally occupied by a succession of our ceremonious visitors. Some came for presents, and others for information of our object in coming to the country; now and then one would dart up to the tent on horseback, jerk the trappings from his horse, and stand silently at the door, holding him by the halter, signifying his desire to trade him. Occasionally a savage would stalk in with an invitation to a feast of honor—a dog feast—and deliberately sit down and wait quietly until I was ready to accompany him. I went to one; the women and children were sitting outside the lodge, and we took our seats on buffalo robes spread around. The dog was in a large pot over the fire, in the middle of the lodge, and immediately on our arrival was dished up in large wooden bowls, one of which was handed to each. The flesh appeared very glutinous, with something of the flavor and appearance of mutton. Feeling something move behind me, I looked round and found that I had taken my seat among a litter of fat young puppies. Had I been nice in such matters, the prejudices of civilization might have interfered with my tranquillity; but, fortunately, I am not of delicate nerves, and continued quietly to empty my platter.

The weather was cloudy at evening, with a moderate south wind, and the thermometer, at six o'clock, 85°. I was disappointed in my hope of obtaining an observation of an occultation which took place about midnight. The moon brought with her heavy banks of clouds, through which she scarcely made her appearance during the night.

The morning of the 18th was cloudy and calm, the thermometer at six o'clock at 64°. About nine, with a moderate wind from the west, a storm of rain came on, accompanied by sharp thunder and lightning, which lasted about an hour. During the day the expected village arrived, consisting principally of old men, women, and children. They had a considerable number of horses, and large troops of dogs. Their lodges were pitched near the fort, and our camp was constantly crowded with Indians, of all sizes, from morning until night, at which time some of the soldiers generally came to drive them all off to the village. My tent was the only place which they respected. Here only came the chiefs and men of distinction, and generally one of them remained to drive away the women and children. The numerous strange instruments, applied to still stranger uses, excited awe and admiration among them, and those which I used in talking with the sun and stars they looked upon with especial reverence as mysterious things of "great medicine."

Of the three barometers which I had brought with me thus far successfully, I found that two were out of order, and spent the greater part of the 19th in repairing them—an operation of no small difficulty in the midst of the incessant interruptions to which I was subjected.[4] We had the misfortune to break here a large thermometer, graduated to show fifths of a degree, which I used to ascertain the temperature of boiling water, and with which I had promised myself some interesting experiments in the mountains. We had but one remaining on which the graduation extended sufficiently high; and this was too small for exact observations. During our stay here the men had been engaged in making numerous repairs, arranging pack saddles, and otherwise preparing for the chances of a rough road and mountain travel. All things of this nature being ready, I gathered them around me in the evening, and told them that "I had determined to proceed the next day. They were all well armed. I had engaged the services of Mr. Bissonette as interpreter, and had taken, in the circumstances, every possible means to insure our safety.

"In the rumors we had heard I believed there was much exaggeration, and then they were men accustomed to this kind of life and to the country; and that these were the dangers of everyday occurrence, and to be expected in the ordinary course of their service. They had heard of the unsettled condition of the country before leaving St. Louis, and therefore could not make it a reason for breaking their engagements. Still, I was unwilling to take with me, on a service of some certain danger, men on whom I could not rely; and as I had understood that there were among them some who were disposed to cowardice, and anxious to return, they had but to come forward at once, and state their desire, and they would be discharged with the amount due to them for the time they had served." To their honor be it said, there was but one among them who had the face to come forward and avail himself of the permission. I asked him some few questions, in order to expose him to the ridicule of the men, and let him go. The day after our departure he engaged himself to one of the forts, and set off with a party for the Upper Missouri. I did not think that the situation of the country justified me in taking our young companions, Messrs. Brant and Benton, along with us. In case of misfortune it would have been thought, at the least, an act of great imprudence, and therefore, though reluctantly, I determined to leave them. Randolph had been the life of the camp, and the *petit garçon* was much regretted by the men, to whom his buoyant spirits had afforded great amusement. They all, however, agreed in the propriety of leaving him at the fort, because, as they said, he might cost the lives of some of the men in a fight with the Indians.

July 21st, 1842. A portion of our baggage, with our field notes and observations, and several instruments, were left at the fort. One of the gentlemen, Mr. Galpin, took charge of a barometer, which he engaged to observe during my absence; and I entrusted to Randolph, by way of occupation, the regular winding up of two of my chronometers, which were among the instruments left. Our observations showed that the chronometer which I retained for the continuation of our voyage had preserved its rate in a most satisfactory manner. As deduced from it, the longitude of Fort Laramie is 7h. 01' 21", and from lunar distance 7h. 01' 29"; giving for the adopted longitude 104° 47' 43". Comparing the barometrical observations made during our stay here with those of Dr. G. Engelmann at St. Louis, we find for the elevation of the fort above the Gulf of Mexico four thousand four hundred and seventy feet. The winter climate here is remarkably mild for the latitude; but rainy weather is frequent, and the place is celebrated for winds, of which the prevailing one is west. An east wind in summer, and a south wind in winter, are said to be always accompanied with rain.

We were ready to depart; the tents were struck, the mules geared up, and our horses saddled, and we walked up to the fort to take the stirrup cup with our friends in an excellent home-brewed preparation. While thus pleasantly engaged, seated in one of the little cool chambers, at the door of which a man had been stationed to prevent all intrusion from the Indians, a number of chiefs, several of them powerful, fine-looking men, forced their way into the room in spite of all opposition. Handing me the following letter, they took their seats in silence. . . .*

Fort Platte, July 1, 1842

Mr. Frémont: The chiefs having assembled in council, have just told me to warn you not to set out before the party of young men which is now out shall have returned. Furthermore, they tell me that they are very sure they will fire upon you as soon as they meet you. They are expected back in seven or eight days. Excuse me for making these observations, but it seems my duty to warn you of danger. Moreover, the chiefs who prohibit your setting out before the return of the warriors are the bearers of this note.

I am, your obedient servant,
JOSEPH BISSONETTE,
BY L. B. CHARTRAIN

Names of some of the chiefs—The Otter Hat, the Breaker of Arrows, the Black Night, the Bull's Tail.

After reading this, I mentioned its purport to my companions, and, seeing that all were fully possessed of its contents, one of the Indians rose up, and, having first shaken hands with me, spoke as follows:

"You have come among us at a bad time. Some of our people have been killed, and our young men, who are gone to the mountains, are eager to avenge the blood of their relations, which has been shed by the whites. Our young men are bad, and if they meet you they will believe that you are carrying goods and ammunition to their enemies, and will fire upon you. You have told us that this will make war. We know that our Great Father has many soldiers and big guns, and we are anxious to save our lives. We love the whites, and are desirous of peace. Thinking of all these things, we have determined to keep you here until our warriors return. We are glad to see you among us. Our father is rich, and we expected that you would have brought presents to us—horses and guns and blankets.

* The French translation omitted.

But we are glad to see you. We look upon your coming as the light which goes before the sun; for you will tell our Great Father that you have seen us, and that we are naked and poor, and have nothing to eat; and he will send us all these things." He was followed by the others to the same effect.

The observations of the savage appeared reasonable; but I was aware that they had in view only the present object of detaining me, and were unwilling I should go farther into the country. In reply, I asked them, through the interpretation of Mr. Boudeau, to select two or three of their number to accompany us until we should meet their people—they should spread their robes in my tent and eat at my table, and on our return I would give them presents in reward of their services. They declined, saying that there were no young men left in the village, and that they were too old to travel so many days on horseback, and preferred now to smoke their pipes in the lodge, and let the warriors go on the warpath. Besides, they had no power over the young men, and were afraid to interfere with them. In my turn I addressed them:

"You say that you love the whites; why have you killed so many already this spring? You say that you love the whites, and are full of many expressions of friendship to us; but you are not willing to undergo the fatigue of a few days' ride to save our lives. We do not believe what you have said, and will not listen to you. Whatever a chief among us tells his soldiers to do, is done. We are the soldiers of the great chief, your father. He has told us to come here and see this country, and all the Indians, his children. Why should we not go? Before we came, we heard that you had killed his people, and ceased to be his children; but we came among you peaceably, holding out our hands. Now we find that the stories we heard are not lies, and that you are no longer his friends and children. We have thrown away our bodies, and will not turn back. When you told us that your young men would kill us, you did not know that our hearts were strong, and you did not see the rifles which my young men carry in their hands. We are few, and you are many, and may kill us all; but there will be much crying in your villages, for many of your young men will stay behind, and forget to return with your warriors from the mountains. Do you think that our great chief will let his soldiers die and forget to cover their

graves? Before the snows melt again, his warriors will sweep away
your villages as the fire does the prairie in the autumn. See! I have
pulled down my white houses, and my people are ready; when the
sun is ten paces higher we shall be on the march. If you have anything to tell us, you will say it soon."

I broke up the conference, as I could do nothing with these people; and, being resolved to proceed, nothing was to be gained by
delay. Accompanied by our hospitable friends, we returned to the
camp. We had mounted our horses, and our parting salutations had
been exchanged, when one of the chiefs (the Bull's Tail) arrived to
tell me that they had determined to send a young man with us; and
if I would point out the place of our evening camp, he should join
us there. "The young man is poor," said he; "he has no horse, and
expects you to give him one." I described to him the place where
I intended to encamp, and, shaking hands, in a few minutes we
were among the hills, and this last habitation of whites shut out
from our view.

The road led over an interesting plateau between the North Fork
of the Platte on the right, and Laramie River on the left. At the
distance of ten miles from the fort we entered the sandy bed of a
creek, a kind of defile, shaded by precipitous rocks, down which we
wound our way for several hundred yards to a place where, on the
left bank, a very large spring gushes with considerable noise and
force out of the limestone rock. It is called the Warm Spring, and
furnishes to the hitherto dry bed of the creek a considerable rivulet.
On the opposite side, a little below the spring, is a lofty limestone
escarpment, partially shaded by a grove of large trees, whose green
foliage, in contrast with the whiteness of the rock, renders this a
picturesque locality. The rock is fossiliferous, and, so far as I was
able to determine the character of the fossils, belongs to the carbo-
niferous limestone of the Missouri River, and is probably the western limit of that formation. Beyond this point I met with no fossils
of any description.

I was desirous to visit the Platte near the point where it leaves
the Black Hills, and therefore followed this stream, for two or three
miles, to the mouth; where I encamped on a spot which afforded
good grass and *prêle* (equisetum) for our animals. Our tents having
been found too thin to protect ourselves and the instruments from

the rains, which in this elevated country are attended with cold and unpleasant weather, I had procured from the Indians at Laramie a tolerably large lodge, about eighteen feet in diameter, and twenty feet in height. Such a lodge, when properly pitched, is, from its conical form, almost perfectly secure against the violent winds which are frequent in this region, and, with a fire in the center, is a dry and warm shelter in bad weather. By raising the lower part so as to permit the breeze to pass freely, it is converted into a pleasant summer residence, with the extraordinary advantage of being entirely free from mosquitoes, one of which I have never seen in an Indian lodge. While we were engaged very unskillfully in erecting this, the interpreter, Mr. Bissonette, arrived, accompanied by the Indian and his wife. She laughed at our awkwardness, and offered her assistance, of which we were frequently afterward obliged to avail ourselves, before the men acquired sufficient expertness to pitch it without difficulty. From this place we had a fine view of the gorge where the Platte issues from the Black Hills, changing its character abruptly from a mountain stream into a river of the plains. Immediately around us the valley of the stream was tolerably open; and at the distance of a few miles, where the river had cut its way through the hills, was the narrow cleft, on one side of which a lofty precipice of bright red rock rose vertically above the low hills which lay between us.

July 22d. In the morning, while breakfast was being prepared, I visited this place with my favorite man, Basil Lajeunesse. Entering so far as there was footing for the mules, we dismounted, and, tying our animals, continued our way on foot. Like the whole country, the scenery of the river had undergone an entire change, and was in this place the most beautiful I had ever seen. The breadth of the stream, generally near that of its valley, was from two to three hundred feet, with a swift current, occasionally broken by rapids, and the water perfectly clear. On either side rose the red precipices, vertical, and sometimes overhanging, two and four hundred feet in height, crowned with green summits, on which were scattered a few pines. At the foot of the rocks was the usual detritus, formed of masses fallen from above. Among the pines that grew here, and on the occasional banks, were the cherry (*Cerasus virginiana*), currants, and *grains de bœuf* (*Shepherdia argentea*).

Viewed in the sunshine of a pleasant morning, the scenery was of a most striking and romantic beauty, which arose from the picturesque disposition of the objects, and the vivid contrast of colors. I thought with much pleasure of our approaching descent in the canoe through such interesting places; and, in the expectation of being able at that time to give to them a full examination, did not now dwell so much as might have been desirable upon the geological formations along the line of the river, where they are developed with great clearness. The upper portion of the red strata consists of very compact clay, in which are occasionally seen embedded large pebbles. Below was a stratum of compact red sandstone, changing a little above the river into a very hard silicious limestone. There is a small but handsome open prairie immediately below this place, on the left bank of the river, which would be a good locality for a military post. There are some open groves of cottonwood on the Platte. The small stream which comes in at this place is well timbered with pine, and good building rock is abundant.

If it is in contemplation to keep open the communications with Oregon territory, a show of military force in this country is absolutely necessary; and a combination of advantages renders the neighborhood of Fort Laramie the most suitable place, on the line of the Platte, for the establishment of a military post. It is connected with the mouth of the Platte and the Upper Missouri by excellent roads, which are in frequent use, and would not in any way interfere with the range of the buffalo, on which the neighboring Indians mainly depend for support. It would render any posts on the Lower Platte unnecessary; the ordinary communication between it and the Missouri being sufficient to control the intermediate Indians. It would operate effectually to prevent any such coalitions as are now formed among the Gros Ventre, Sioux, Cheyenne, and other Indians, and would keep the Oregon road through the valley of the Sweet Water and the South Pass of the mountains constantly open. . . . It lies at the foot of a broken and mountainous region, along which, by the establishment of small posts in the neighborhood of St. Vrain's Fort, on the South Fork of the Platte, and Bent's Fort, on the Arkansas, a line of communication would be formed, by good wagon roads, with our southern military posts, which would entirely command the mountain passes, hold some of the most troublesome tribes in check, and protect and facilitate our intercourse with the neighboring Spanish settlements. The valleys of the rivers on which they would be situated are fertile; the country, which supports immense herds of buffalo, is admirably adapted to grazing; and herds of cattle might be maintained by the posts, or obtained from the Spanish country, which already supplies a portion of their provisions to the trading posts mentioned above.

Just as we were leaving the camp this morning, our Indian came up and stated his intention of not proceeding any farther until he had seen the horse which I intended to give him. I felt strongly tempted to drive him out of the camp; but his presence appeared to give confidence to my men, and the interpreter thought it absolutely necessary. I was, therefore, obliged to do what he requested, and pointed out the animal, with which he seemed satisfied, and we continued our journey. I had imagined that Mr. Bissonette's long residence had made him acquainted with the country, and, according to his advice, proceeded directly forward, without attempting to regain the usual road. He afterward informed me that he had rarely ever lost sight of the fort; but the effect of the mistake was to involve us for a day or two among the hills, where, although we lost no time, we encountered an exceedingly rough road.

To the south, along our line of march today, the main chain of the Black or Laramie Hills rises precipitously. Time did not permit me to visit them; but, from comparative information, the ridge is composed of the coarse sandstone or conglomerate hereafter described. It appears to enter the region of clouds, which are arrested in their course, and lie in masses along the summits. An inverted cone of black cloud (cumulus) rested during all the forenoon on the lofty peak of Laramie Mountain, which I estimated to be about two thousand feet above the fort, or six thousand five hundred above the sea.[5] We halted to noon on the Fourche Amère, so called from being timbered principally with the *liard amère* (a species of poplar), with which the valley of the little stream is tolerably well wooded, and which, with large expansive summits, grows to the height of sixty or seventy feet.

The bed of the creek is sand and gravel, the water dispersed over the broad bed in several shallow streams. We found here, on the right bank, in the shade of the trees, a fine spring of very cold water. It will be remarked that I do not mention, in this portion of the journey, the temperature of the air, sand, springs, etc.—an omission which will be explained in the course of the narrative. In my search for plants I was well rewarded at this place.

With the change in the geological formation on leaving Fort Laramie the whole face of the country has entirely altered its appearance. Eastward of that meridian the principal objects which strike the eye of a traveler are the absence of timber, and the immense expanse of prairie, covered with the verdure of rich grasses, and highly adapted for pasturage. Wherever they are not disturbed by the vicinity of man, large herds of buffalo give animation to this country. Westward of Laramie River the region is sandy and apparently sterile; and the place of the grass is usurped by the artemisia and other odoriferous plants, to whose growth the sandy soil and dry air of this elevated region seem highly favorable.

One of the prominent characteristics in the face of the country is the extraordinary abundance of the artemisias. They grow everywhere—on the hills, and over the river bottoms, in tough, twisted, wiry clumps; and, wherever the beaten track was left, they rendered the progress of the carts rough and slow. As the country increased in elevation on our advance to the west, they increased in size; and the whole air is strongly impregnated and saturated with the odor of camphor and spirits of turpentine which belongs to this plant. This climate has been found very favorable to the restoration of health, particularly in cases of consumption; and possibly the respiration of air so highly impregnated by aromatic plants may have some influence.

Our dried meat had given out, and we began to be in want of food; but one of the hunters killed an antelope this evening, which afforded some relief, although it did not go far among so many hungry men. At eight o'clock at night, after a march of twenty-seven miles, we reached our proposed encampment on the Fer-à-Cheval, or Horseshoe Creek. Here we found good grass, with a great quantity of *prêle*, which furnished good food for our tired animals. This creek is well timbered, principally with *liard amère,* and, with the exception of Deer Creek, which we had not yet reached, is the largest affluent of the right bank between Laramie and the mouth of the Sweet Water.

July 23d. The present year had been one of unparalleled drought, and throughout the country the water had been almost dried up. By availing themselves of the annual rise, the traders had invariably succeeded in carrying their furs to the Missouri; but this season, as has already been mentioned, on both forks of the Platte they had entirely failed. The greater number of the springs, and many of the streams, which made halting places for the voyageurs, had been dried up. Everywhere the soil looked parched and burnt; the scanty yellow grass crisped under the foot, and even the hardiest plants were destroyed by want of moisture. I think it necessary to mention this fact, because to the rapid evaporation in such an elevated region, nearly five thousand feet above the sea, almost wholly unprotected by timber, should be attributed much of the sterile appearance of the country, in the destruction of vegetation, and the numerous saline efflorescences which covered the ground. Such I afterward found to be the case.

I was informed that the roving villages of Indians and travelers had never met with difficulty in finding an abundance of grass for their horses; and now it was after great search that we were able to find a scanty patch of grass, sufficient to keep them from sinking; and in the course of a day or two they began to suffer very much. We found none today at noon; and, in the course of our search on the Platte, came to a grove of cottonwood where some Indian village had recently encamped. Boughs of the cottonwood, yet green, covered the ground, which the Indians had cut down to feed their horses upon. It is only in the winter that recourse is had to this means of sustaining them; and their resort to it at this time was a striking evidence of the state of the country. We followed their example, and turned our horses into a grove of young poplars. This began to present itself as a very serious evil, for on our animals depended altogether the further prosecution of our journey.

Shortly after we had left this place, the scouts came galloping in with the alarm of Indians. We turned in immediately toward the river, which here had a steep high bank, where we formed with the carts a very close barricade, resting on the river, within which the animals were strongly hobbled and picketed. The guns were discharged and reloaded, and men thrown forward, under cover of the bank, in the direction by which the Indians were expected. Our interpreter, who, with the Indian, had gone to meet them, came in, in about ten minutes, accompanied by two Sioux. They looked sulky, and we could obtain from them only some confused information. We learned that they belonged to the party which had been on the trail of the emigrants, whom they had overtaken at Rock Independence, on the Sweet Water. Here the party had disagreed, and came nigh fighting among themselves. One portion were desirous of attacking the whites, but the others were opposed to it; and finally they had broken up into small bands, and dispersed over the country. The greater portion of them had gone over into the territory of the Crows,[6] and intended to return by way of the Wind River Valley,[7] in the hope of being able to fall upon some small parties of Crow Indians.

The remainder were returning down the Platte in scattered parties of ten and twenty; and those whom we had encountered belonged to the party who had advocated an attack on the emigrants. Several of the men suggested shooting them on the spot; but I promptly discountenanced any such proceeding. They further informed me that buffalo were very scarce, and little or no grass to be found. There had been no rain, and innumerable quantities of grasshoppers had destroyed the grass. This insect had been so numerous since leaving Fort Laramie, that the ground seemed alive with them; and in walking, a little moving cloud preceded our footsteps. This was bad news. No grass, no buffalo—food for neither horse nor man. I gave them some plugs of tobacco, and they went off, apparently well satisfied to be clear of us; for my men did not look upon them very lovingly, and they glanced suspiciously at our warlike preparations, and the little ring of rifles which surrounded them. They were evidently in a bad humor, and shot one of their horses when they had left us a short distance.

We continued our march, and, after a journey of about twenty-one miles, encamped on the Platte. During the day I had occasionally remarked among the hills the *Psoralea esculenta*, the bread-root of the Indians. The Sioux use this root very extensively, and I have frequently met with it among them, cut into thin slices and dried. In the course of the evening we were visited by six Indians, who told us that a larger party was encamped a few miles above. Astronomical observations placed us in longitude 104° 59′ 59″, and latitude 42° 39′ 25″.

We made the next day twenty-two miles, and encamped on the right bank of the Platte, where a handsome meadow afforded tolerably good grass. There were the remains of an old fort here, thrown up in some sudden emergency, and on the opposite side was a picturesque bluff of ferruginous sandstone. There was a handsome grove a little above, and scattered groups of trees bordered the river. Buffalo made their appearance this afternoon, and the hunters came in, shortly after we had encamped, with three fine cows. The night was fine, and observations gave for the latitude of the camp, 42° 47′ 40″.

July 25th. We made but thirteen miles this day, and encamped about noon in a pleasant grove on the right bank. Low scaffolds were erected, upon which the meat was laid, cut up into thin strips, and small fires kindled below. Our object was to profit by the vicinity of the buffalo, to lay in a stock of provisions for ten or fifteen days. In the course of the afternoon the hunters brought in five or six cows, and all hands were kept busily employed in preparing the meat, to the drying of which the guard attended during the night. Our people had recovered their gaiety, and the busy figures around the blazing fires gave a picturesque air to the camp. A very serious accident occurred this morning, in the breaking of one of the barometers. These had been the object of my constant solicitude, and as I had intended them principally for mountain service, I had used them as seldom as possible; taking them always down at night and on the occurrence of storms, in order to lessen the chances of being broken. I was reduced to one, a standard barometer of Troughton's construction. This I determined to preserve, if possible. The latitude is 42° 51′ 35″, and by a mean of the results from chronometer and lunar distances, the adopted longitude of this camp is 105° 50′ 45″.

July 26th. Early this morning we were again in motion. We had a stock of provisions for fifteen days carefully stored away in the carts, and this I resolved should only be encroached upon when our rifles should fail to procure us present support. I determined to reach the mountains, if it were in any way possible. In the meantime buffalo were plenty. In six miles from our encampment (which, by way of distinction, we shall call Dried Meat Camp) we crossed a handsome stream, called La Forche Boisée. It is well timbered, and, among the flowers in bloom on its banks, I remarked several asters.

Five miles farther we made our noon halt, on the banks of the Platte, in the shade of some cottonwoods. There were here, as generally now along the river, thickets of *hippophaæ*, the *grains de bœuf* of the country. They were of two kinds—one bearing a red berry (the *Shepherdia argentea* of Nuttall); the other a yellow berry, of which the Tartars are said to make a kind of rob.

By a meridian observation, the latitude of the place was 42° 50′ 08″. It was my daily practice to take observations of the sun's meridian altitude; and why they are not given will appear in the sequel. Eight miles farther we reached the mouth of Deer Creek, where we encamped. Here was an abundance of rich grass, and our animals were compensated for past privations. This stream was at this time twenty feet broad, and well timbered with cottonwood of an uncommon size. It is the largest tributary of the Platte between the mouth of the Sweet Water and the Laramie. Our astronomical observations gave for the mouth of the stream a longitude of 106° 08′ 24″, and latitude of 42° 52′ 24″.

July 27th. Nothing worthy of mention occurred on this day; we traveled later than usual, having spent some time in searching for grass, crossing and recrossing the river before we could find a sufficient quantity for our animals. Toward dusk, we encamped among some artemisia bushes, two and three feet in height, where some scattered patches of short, tough grass afforded a scanty supply. In crossing, we had occasion to observe that the river was frequently too deep to be forded, though we always succeeded in finding a place where the water did not enter the carts. The stream continued very clear, with two or three hundred feet breadth of water, and the sandy bed and banks were frequently covered with large round pebbles. We had traveled this day twenty-seven miles. The main chain of the Black Hills was here only about seven miles to the south, on the right bank of the river, rising abruptly to the height of eight and twelve hundred feet. Patches of green grass in the ravines on the steep sides marked the presence of springs, and the summits were clad with pines.

July 28th. In two miles from our encampment we reached the place where the regular road crosses the Platte. There was two hundred feet breadth of water at this time in the bed, which has a variable width of eight to fifteen hundred feet. The channels were generally three feet deep, and there were large angular rocks on the bottom, which made the ford in some places a little difficult. Even at its low stages this river cannot be crossed at random, and this has always been used as the best ford. The low stage of the waters the present year had made it fordable in almost any part of its course, where access could be had to its bed.

For the satisfaction of travelers, I will endeavor to give some description of the nature of the road from Laramie to this point. The nature of the soil may be inferred from its geological formation. The limestone at the eastern limit of this section is succeeded by limestone without fossils, a great variety of sandstone, consisting principally of red sandstone and fine conglomerates. The red sandstone is argillaceous, with compact white gypsum, or alabaster, very beautiful. The other sandstones are gray, yellow, and ferruginous, sometimes very coarse. The apparent sterility of the country must therefore be sought for in other causes than the nature of the soil. The face of the country cannot with propriety be called hilly. It is a succession of long ridges, made by the numerous streams which come down from the neighboring mountain range. The ridges have an undulating surface, with some such appearance as the ocean presents in an ordinary breeze.

The road which is now generally followed through this region is, therefore, a very good one, without any difficult ascents to overcome. The principal obstructions are near the river, where the transient waters of heavy rains have made deep ravines with steep banks, which render frequent circuits necessary. It will be remembered that wagons pass this road only once or twice a year, which is by no means sufficient to break down the stubborn roots of the innumerable artemisia bushes. A partial absence of these is often the only indication of the track; and the roughness produced by their roots in many places gives the road the character of one newly opened in a wooded country. This is usually considered the worst part of the road east of the mountains; and as it passes through an open prairie region, may be much improved, so as to avoid the greater part of the inequalities it now presents. From the mouth of the Kansas to the Green River Valley, west of the Rocky Mountains, there is no such thing as a mountain road on the line of communication.

We continued our way, and about four miles beyond the ford Indians were discovered again; and I halted while a party were sent forward to ascertain who they were. In a short time they returned, accompanied by a number of Indians of the Oglala band of Sioux. From them we received some interesting information. They had formed part of the great village, which they informed us had broken up, and was on its way home. The greater part of the village, including the Arapahoes, Cheyennes, and Oglalas, had crossed the Platte eight or ten miles below the mouth of the Sweet Water, and were now behind the mountains to the south of us, intending to regain the Platte by way of Deer Creek. They had taken this unusual route in search of grass and game. They gave us a very discouraging picture of the country. The great drought, and the plague of grasshoppers, had swept it so that scarce a blade of grass was to be seen, and there was not a buffalo to be found in the whole region. Their people, they further said, had been nearly starved to death, and we would find their road marked by lodges which they had thrown away in order to move more rapidly, and by the carcasses of the horses which they had eaten, or which had perished by starvation. Such was the prospect before us.

When he had finished the interpretation of these things, Mr. Bissonette immediately rode up to me, and urgently advised that I should entirely abandon the further prosecution of my exploration. . . . "The best advice I can give you, is to turn back at once." It was his own intention to return, as we had now reached the point to which he had engaged to attend me. In reply, I called up my men, and communicated to them fully the information I had just received. I then expressed to them my fixed determination to proceed to the end of the enterprise on which I had been sent; but as the situation of the country gave me some reason to apprehend that it might be attended with an unfortunate result to some of us, I would leave it optional with them to continue with me or to return.

Among them were some five or six who I knew would remain. We had still ten days' provisions; and, should no game be found, when this stock was expended, we had our horses and mules, which we could eat when other means of subsistence failed. But not a man flinched from the undertaking. "We'll eat the mules," said Basil Lajeunesse; and thereupon we shook hands with our interpreter and his Indians, and parted. With them I sent back one of my men, Dumés, whom the effects of an old wound in the leg rendered incapable of continuing the journey on foot, and his horse seemed on the point of giving out. Having resolved to disencumber ourselves immediately of everything not absolutely necessary to our future operations, I turned directly in toward the river, and encamped on the left bank, a little above the place where our council had been held, and where a thick grove of willows offered a suitable spot for the object I had in view.

The carts having been discharged, the covers and wheels were taken off, and, with the frames, carried into some low places among the willows, and concealed in the dense foliage in such a manner that the glitter of the ironwork might not attract the observation of some straggling Indian. In the sand, which had been blown up into waves among the willows, a large hole was then dug, ten feet square and six deep. In the meantime all our effects had been spread out upon the ground, and whatever was designed to be carried along with us separated and laid aside, and the remaining part carried to the hole and carefully covered up. As much as possible, all traces of our proceedings were obliterated, and it wanted but a rain to render our cache safe beyond discovery. All the men were now set at work to arrange the pack saddles and make up the packs.

The day was very warm and calm, and the sky entirely clear, except where, as usual along the summits of the mountainous ridge opposite, the clouds had congregated in masses. Our lodge had been planted, and, on account of the heat, the ground pins had been taken out, and the lower part slightly raised. Near to it was standing the barometer, which swung in a tripod frame; and within the lodge, where a small fire had been built, Mr. Preuss was occupied in observing the temperature of boiling water. At this instant, and without any warning, until it was within fifty yards, a violent gust of wind dashed down the lodge, burying under it Mr. Preuss and about a dozen men who had attempted to keep it from being carried away. I succeeded in saving the barometer, which the lodge was carrying off with itself, but the thermometer was broken. We had no others of a high graduation, none of those which remained going higher than 135° Fahrenheit. Our astronomical observations gave to this place, which we named Cache Camp, a longitude of 106° 38' 26", latitude 42° 50' 53".

July 29th. All our arrangements having been completed, we left the encampment at seven o'clock this morning. In this vicinity the ordinary road leaves the Platte, and crosses over to the Sweet Water River, which it strikes near Rock Independence. Instead of following this road, I had determined to keep the immediate valley of the Platte so far as the mouth of the Sweet Water, in the expectation of finding better grass. To this I was further prompted by the nature of my instructions. To Mr. Carson was assigned the office of guide, as we had now reached a part of the country with which, or a great part of which, long residence had made him familiar. In a few miles we reached the Red Buttes, a famous landmark in this country, whose geological composition is red sandstone, limestone, and calcareous sandstone and pudding stone.

The river here cuts its way through a ridge; on the eastern side of it are the lofty escarpments of red argillaceous sandstone which are called the Red Buttes. In this passage the stream is not much compressed or pent up, there being a bank of considerable though variable breadth on either side. Immediately on entering, we discovered a band of buffalo. The hunters failed to kill any of them; the leading hunter being thrown into a ravine, which occasioned some delay, and in the meantime the herd clambered up the steep face of the ridge. It is sometimes wonderful to see these apparently clumsy animals make their way up and down the most rugged and broken precipices. We halted to noon before we had cleared this passage, at a spot twelve miles distant from Cache Camp, where we found an abundance of grass. So far, the account of the Indians was found to be false. On the banks were willow and cherry trees. The cherries were not yet ripe, but in the thickets were numerous fresh tracks of the grizzly bear, which are very fond of this fruit. The soil here is red, the composition being derived from the red sandstone. About seven miles brought us through the ridge, in which the course of the river is north and south. Here the valley opens out broadly, and high walls of the red formation present themselves among the hills to the east. We crossed here a pretty little creek, an affluent of the right bank. It is well timbered with cottonwood in this vicinity, and the absinthe has lost its shrublike character, and becomes small trees six and eight feet in height, and sometimes eight inches in diameter. Two or three miles above this creek we made our encampment, having traveled today twenty-five miles. Our animals fared well here, as there is an abundance of grass. The river bed is made up of pebbles, and in the bank, at the level of the water, is a conglomerate of coarse pebbles about the size of ostrich eggs, and which I remarked in the banks of the Laramie Fork. It is overlaid by a soil of mixed clay and sand, six feet thick. By astronomical observations our position is in longitude 106° 54' 32", and latitude 42° 38'.

July 30th. After traveling about twelve miles this morning, we reached a place where the Indian village had crossed the river. Here were the poles of discarded lodges and skeletons of horses lying about. Mr. Carson, who had never been higher up than this point on the river, which has the character of being exceedingly rugged, and walled in by precipices above, thought it advisable to camp near this place, where we were certain of obtaining grass, and tomorrow make our crossing among the rugged hills to the Sweet Water River. Accordingly, we turned back and descended the river to an island near by, which was about twenty acres in size, covered with a luxuriant growth of grass. The formation here I found highly interesting. Immediately at this island the river is again shut up in the rugged hills, which come down to it from the main ridge in a succession of spurs three or four hundred feet high, and alternated with green, level *prairillons* or meadows, bordered on the riverbanks with thickets of willow, and having many plants to interest the traveler. The island lies between two of the ridges, three or four hundred yards apart, of which that on the right bank is composed entirely of red argillaceous sandstone, with thin layers of fibrous gypsum. On the left bank, the ridge is composed entirely of silicious pudding stone, the pebbles in the numerous strata increasing in size from the top to the bottom, where they are as large as a man's head. So far as I was able to determine, these strata incline to the northeast, with a dip of about fifteen degrees. This pudding stone, or conglomerate formation, I was enabled to trace through an extended range of country, from a few miles east of the meridian of Fort Laramie to where I found it superposed on the granite of the Rocky Mountains, in longitude 109°. From its appearance, the main chain of the Laramie Mountains is composed of this rock; and in a number of places I found isolated hills, which served to mark a former level, which had been probably swept away.

These conglomerates are very friable, and easily decomposed; and I am inclined to think this formation is the source from which was derived the great deposit of sand and gravel which forms the surface rock of the prairie country west of the Mississippi.

Crossing the ridge of red sandstone, and traversing the little prairie which lies to the southward of it, we made in the afternoon an excursion to a place which we have called the Hot Spring Gate. This place has much the appearance of a gate, by which the Platte passes through a ridge composed of a white and calcareous sandstone. The length of the passage is about four hundred yards, with a smooth, green prairie on either side. Through this place the stream flows with a quiet current, unbroken by any rapid, and is about seventy yards wide between the walls, which rise perpendicularly from the water. To that on the right bank, which is the lower, the barometer gave a height of three hundred and sixty feet. . . . This place will be more particularly described hereafter, as we passed through it on our return.

We saw here numerous herds of mountain sheep, and frequently heard the volley of rattling stones which accompanied their rapid descent down the steep hills. This was the first place at which we had killed any of these animals; and, in consequence of this circumstance, and of the abundance of these sheep or goats (for they are called by each name), we gave to our encampment the name of Goat Island. Their flesh is much esteemed by the hunters, and has very much the flavor of the Alleghany Mountain sheep. I have seen a horn of this animal three feet long and seventeen inches in circumference at the base, weighing eleven pounds. But two or three of these were killed by our party at this place, and of these the horns were small. The use of these horns seems to be to protect the animal's head in pitching down precipices to avoid pursuing wolves—their only safety being in places where they cannot be followed. The bones are very strong and solid, the marrow occupying but a very small portion of the bone in the leg, about the thickness of a rye straw. The hair is short, resembling the winter color of our common deer, which it nearly approaches in size and appearance. Except in the horns, it has no resemblance whatever to the goat. The longitude of this place, resulting from chronometer and lunar distances, and an occultation of ε Arietis, is 107° 13′ 29″, and the latitude 42° 33′ 72″. One of our horses, which had given out, we left to recover strength on the island, intending to take her, perhaps, on our return.

July 31st. This morning we left the course of the Platte, to cross over to the Sweet Water. Our way, for a few miles, lay up the sandy bed of a dry creek, in which I found several interesting plants. Leaving this, we wound our way to the summit of the hills, of which the peaks are here eight hundred feet above the Platte, bare and rocky. A long and gradual slope led from these hills to the Sweet Water, which we reached in fifteen miles from Goat Island. I made an early encampment here, in order to give the hunters an opportunity to procure a supply from several bands of buffalo which made their appearance in the valley near by. The stream here is about sixty feet wide, and at this time twelve to eighteen inches deep, with a very moderate current.

The adjoining prairies are sandy, but the immediate river bottom is a good soil, which afforded an abundance of soft green grass to our horses, and where I found a variety of interesting plants, which made their appearance for the first time. A rain tonight made it unpleasantly cold; and there was no tree here to enable us to pitch our single tent, the poles of which had been left at Cache Camp. We had, therefore no shelter except what was to be found under cover of the absinthe bushes, which grew in many thick patches, one or two and sometimes three feet high.

August 1st. The hunters went ahead this morning, as buffalo appeared tolerably abundant, and I was desirous to secure a small stock of provisions; we moved about seven miles up the valley, and encamped one mile below Rock Independence.[8] This is an isolated granite rock, about six hundred and fifty yards long, and forty in height. Except in a depression of the summit, where a little soil supports a scanty growth of shrubs, with a solitary dwarf pine, it is entirely bare. Everywhere within six or eight feet of the ground, where the surface is sufficiently smooth, and in some places sixty or eighty feet above, the rock is inscribed with the names of travelers. Many a name famous in the history of this country, and some well known to science, are to be found mixed among those of the traders and of travelers for pleasure and curiosity, and of missionaries among the savages. Some of these have been washed away by the rain, but the greater number are still very legible. The position of this rock is in longitude 107° 26′, latitude 42° 29′ 36″. We remained at our camp of August 1st until noon of the next day occupied in drying meat. By observation, the longitude of the place is 107° 25′ 23″, latitude 42° 29′ 56″.

August 2d. Five miles above Rock Independence we came to a place called the Devil's Gate, where the Sweet Water cuts through the point of a granite ridge.[9] The length of the passage is about three hundred yards, and the width thirty-five yards. The walls of rock are vertical, and about four hundred feet in height; and the stream in the gate is almost entirely choked up by masses which have fallen from above. In the wall, on the right bank, is a dike of traprock, cutting through a fine-grained gray granite. Near the point of this ridge crop out some strata of the valley formation, consisting of a grayish micaceous sandstone, and fine-grained conglomerate, and marl. We encamped eight miles above the Devil's Gate. . . . There was no timber of any kind on the river, but good fires were made of driftwood, aided by the bois de vache.

We had tonight no shelter from the rain, which commenced, with squalls of wind about sunset. The country here is exceedingly picturesque. On either side of the valley, which is four or five miles broad, the mountains rise to the height of twelve and fifteen hundred or two thousand feet. On the south side, the range appears to be timbered, and tonight is luminous with fires—probably the work of the Indians who have just passed through the valley. On the north, broken and granite masses rise abruptly from the greensward of the river, terminating in a line of broken summits. Except in the crevices of the rock, and here and there on a ledge or bench of the mountain, where a few hardy pines have clustered together, these are perfectly bare and destitute of vegetation.

Among these masses, where there are sometimes isolated hills and ridges, green valleys open in upon the river, which sweeps the base of these mountains for thirty-six miles. Everywhere its deep verdure and profusion of beautiful flowers are in pleasing contrast with the sterile grandeur of the rock and the barrenness of the sandy plain, which, from the right bank of the river, sweeps up to the mountain range that forms its southern boundary. The great evaporation on the sandy soil of this elevated plain, and the saline efflorescences which whiten the ground, and shine like lakes reflecting the sun, make a soil wholly unfit for cultivation.

August 3d. We were early on the road the next morning, traveling along the upland part of the valley, which is overgrown with artemisia. Scattered about on the plain are occasional small isolated hills. One of these, which I examined, about fifty feet high, consisted of white clay and marl, in nearly horizontal strata. Several bands of buffalo made their appearance today, with herds of antelope; and a grizzly bear—the only one we encountered during the journey—was seen scrambling up among the rocks. As we passed over a slight rise near the river, we caught the first view of the Wind River Mountains, appearing, at this distance of about seventy miles, to be a low and dark mountainous ridge. The view dissipated in a moment the pictures which had been created in our minds, by many descriptions of travelers, who have compared these mountains to the Alps in Switzerland, and speak of the glittering peaks which rise in icy majesty amidst the eternal glaciers nine or ten thousand feet into the region of eternal snows. The nakedness of the river was relieved by groves of willows, where we encamped at night, after a march of twenty-six miles; and numerous bright-colored flowers had made the river bottom look gay as a garden. We found here a horse, which had been abandoned by the Indians because his hoofs had been so much worn that he was unable to travel; and during the night a dog came into the camp.

August 4th. Our camp was at the foot of the granite mountains, which we climbed this morning to take some barometrical heights; and here among the rocks was seen the first magpie. On our return, we saw one at the mouth of the Platte River. We left here one of our horses, which was unable to proceed farther. A few miles from the encampment we left the river, which makes a bend to the south, and, traversing an undulating country, consisting of a grayish micaceous sandstone and fine-grained conglomerates, struck it again, and encamped, after a journey of twenty-five miles. Astronomical observations placed us in latitude 42° 32′ 30″, and longitude 108° 30′ 13″.

August 5th. The morning was dark, with a driving rain, and disagreeably cold. We continued our route as usual; but the weather became so bad that we were glad to avail ourselves of the shelter offered by a small island, about ten miles above our last encampment, which was covered with a dense growth of willows. There was fine grass for our animals, and the timber afforded us comfortable protection and good fires. In the afternoon the sun broke through the clouds for a short time, and the barometer at 5 P.M. was at 23.713, the thermometer 60°, with the wind strong from the northwest. We availed ourselves of the fine weather to make excursions in the neighborhood. The river, at this place, is bordered by hills of the valley formation. They are of moderate height; one of the highest peaks on the right bank being, according to the barometer, one hundred and eighty feet above the river. On the left bank they are higher. They consist of a fine white clayey sandstone, a white calcareous sandstone, and coarse sandstone or pudding stone.

August 6th. It continued steadily raining all the day; but, notwithstanding, we left our encampment in the afternoon. Our animals had been much refreshed by their repose and an abundance of rich, soft grass, which had been much improved by the rains. In about three miles we reached the entrance of a cañon, where the Sweet Water issues upon the more open valley we had passed over. Immediately at the entrance, and superimposed directly upon the granite, are strata of compact calcareous sandstone and chert, alternating with fine white and reddish-white, and fine gray and red sandstones. These strata dip to the eastward at an angle of about eighteen degrees, and form the western limit of the sand and limestone formations on the line of our route. Here we entered among the primitive rocks.

The usual road passes to the right of this place; but we wound, or rather scrambled, our way up the narrow valley for several hours. Wildness and disorder were the character of this scenery. The river had been swollen by the late rains, and came rushing through with an impetuous current, three or four feet deep, and generally twenty yards broad. The valley was sometimes the breadth of the stream, and sometimes opened into little green meadows, sixty yards wide, with open groves of aspen. The stream was bordered throughout with aspen, beech, and willow; and tall pines grew on the sides and summits of the crags. On both sides the granite rocks rose precipitously to the height of three hundred and five hundred feet, terminating in jagged and broken-pointed peaks; and fragments of fallen rock lay piled up at the foot of the precipices. Gneiss, mica slate, and a white granite, were among the varieties I noticed. Here were many old traces of beaver on the stream; remnants of dams, near which were lying trees which they had cut down, one and two feet in diameter.

The hills entirely shut up the river at the end of about five miles, and we turned up a ravine that led to a high prairie, which seemed to be the general level of the country. Hence, to the summit of the ridge, there is a regular and very gradual rise. Blocks of granite were piled up at the heads of the ravines, and small bare knolls of mica slate and milky quartz protruded at frequent intervals on the prairie, which was whitened in occasional spots with small salt lakes, where the water had evaporated, and left the bed covered with a shining incrustation of salt. The evening was very cold, a northwest wind driving a fine rain in our faces; and at nightfall we descended to a little stream, on which we encamped, about two miles from the Sweet Water. Here had recently been a very large camp of Snake and Crow Indians; and some large poles lying about afforded the means of pitching a tent, and making other places of shelter. Our fires tonight were made principally of the dry branches of the artemisia, which covered the slopes. It burns quickly, with a clear oily flame, and makes a hot fire. The hills here are composed of hard, compact mica slate, with veins of quartz.

August 7th. We left our encampment with the rising sun. As we rose from the bed of the creek, the snow line of the mountains stretched grandly before us, the white peaks glittering in the sun. They had been hidden in the dark weather of the last few days, and it had been snowing on them while it rained in the plains. We crossed a ridge, and again struck the Sweet Water—here a beautiful, swift stream, with a more open valley, timbered with breech and cottonwood. It now began to lose itself in the many small forks which make its head; and we continued up the main stream until near noon, when we left it a few miles, to make our noon halt on a small creek among the hills, from which the stream issues by a small opening. Within was a beautiful grassy spot, covered with an open grove of large beech trees, among which I found several plants that I had not previously seen.

The afternoon was cloudy, with squalls of rain; but the weather became fine at sunset, when we again encamped on the Sweet Water, within a few miles of the South Pass.[10] The country over which we have passed today consists principally of the compact mica slate, which crops out on all the ridges, making the uplands very rocky and slaty. In the escarpments which border the creeks, it is seen alternating with a light-colored granite, at an inclination of 45°; the beds varying in thickness from two or three feet to six or eight hundred. At a distance, the granite frequently has the appearance of irregular lumps of clay, hardened by exposure. A variety of asters may now be numbered among the characteristic plants, and the artemisia continues in full glory; but cacti have become rare, and mosses begin to dispute the hills with them. The evening was damp and unpleasant, the thermometer, at 10 o'clock, being at 36°, and the grass wet with a heavy dew. Our astronomical observations placed this encampment in longitude 109° 21′ 32″, and latitude 42° 27′ 15″.

Early in the morning we resumed our journey, the weather still cloudy, with occasional rain. Our general course was west, as I had determined to cross the dividing ridge by a bridle path over the broken country more immediately at the foot of the mountains, and return by the wagon road, two and a half miles to the south of the point where the trail crosses.

About six miles from our encampment brought us to the summit. The ascent had been so gradual that, with all the intimate knowledge possessed by Carson, who had made this country his home for seventeen years, we were obliged to watch very closely to find the place at which we had reached the culminating point. This was between two low hills, rising on either hand fifty or sixty feet. When I looked back at them, from the foot of the immediate slope on the western plain, their summits appeared to be about one hundred and twenty feet above. From the impression on my mind at this time, and subsequently on our return, I should compare the elevation which we surmounted immediately at the pass, to the ascent of the Capitol Hill from the Avenue, at Washington. It is difficult for me to fix positively the breadth of this pass. From the broken ground where it commences, at the foot of the Wind River chain, the view to the southeast is over a champaign country, broken, at the distance of nineteen miles, by the Table Rock; which, with the other isolated hills in its vicinity, seems to stand on a comparative plain. This I judged to be its termination, the ridge recovering its rugged character with the Table Rock.

It will be seen that it in no manner resembles the places to which the term is commonly applied—nothing of the gorgelike character and winding ascents of the Alleghany passes in America; nothing of the Great St. Bernard and Simplon passes in Europe. Approaching it from the mouth of the Sweet Water, a sandy plain, one hundred and twenty miles long, conducts, by a gradual and regular ascent, to the summit, about seven thousand feet above the sea; and the traveler, without being reminded of any change by toilsome ascents, suddenly finds himself on the waters which flow to the Pacific Ocean. By the route we had traveled, the distance from Fort Laramie is three hundred and twenty miles, or nine hundred and fifty from the mouth of the Kansas.[11]

Continuing our march, we reached, in eight miles from the pass, the Little Sandy, one of the tributaries of the Colorado, or Green River, of the Gulf of California.[12] The weather had grown fine during the morning, and we remained here the rest of the day, to dry our baggage and take some astronomical observations. The stream was about forty feet wide, and two or three deep, with clear water and a full swift current, over a sandy bed. It was timbered with a growth of low, bushy and dense willows, among which were little verdant spots, which gave our animals fine grass, and where I found a number of interesting plants. Among the neighboring hills I noticed fragments of granite containing magnetic iron. Longitude of the camp was 109° 37′ 59″, and latitude 42° 27′ 34.″

August 9th. We made our noon halt today on Big Sandy, another tributary of Green River. The face of the country traversed was of a brown sand of granite materials, the detritus of the neighboring mountains. Strata of the milky quartz cropped out, and blocks of granite were scattered about containing magnetic iron. On Sandy Creek the formation was of particolored sand, exhibited in escarpments fifty to eighty feet high. In the afternoon we had a severe storm of hail, and encamped at sunset on the first New Fork. Within the space of a few miles, the Wind Mountains supply a number of tributaries to Green River, which are all called the New Forks. Near our camp were two remarkable isolated hills, one of them sufficiently large to merit the name of mountain. They are called the Two Buttes, and will serve to identify the place of our encampment, which the observations of the evening placed in longitude 109° 58' 11", and latitude 42° 42' 46". On the right bank of the stream, opposite to the large hill, the strata which are displayed consist of decomposing granite, which supplies the brown sand of which the face of the country is composed to a considerable depth.

August 10th. The air at sunrise is clear and pure, and the morning extremely cold, but beautiful. A lofty snow peak of the mountain is glittering in the first rays of the sun, which has not yet reached us. The long mountain wall to the east, rising two thousand feet abruptly from the plain, behind which we see the peaks, is still dark, and cuts clear against the glowing sky. A fog, just risen from the river, lies along the base of the mountain. A little before sunrise the thermometer was at 35°, and at sunrise 33°. Water froze last night, and fires are very comfortable. The scenery becomes hourly more interesting and grand, and the view here is truly magnificent; but, indeed, it needs something to repay the long prairie journey of a thousand miles. The sun has just shot above the wall, and makes a magical change. The whole valley is glowing and bright, and all the mountain peaks are gleaming like silver. Though these snow mountains are not the Alps, they have their own character of grandeur and magnificence, and will doubtless find pens and pencils to do them justice. In the scene before us, we feel how much wood improves a view. The pines on the mountain seemed to give it much additional beauty. I was agreeably disappointed in the character of the streams on this side of the ridge. Instead of the creeks which description had led me to expect, I find bold broad streams, with three or four feet water and a rapid current. The fork on which we are encamped is upward of a hundred feet wide, timbered with groves or thickets of the low willow.

We were now approaching the loftiest part of the Wind River chain; and I left the valley a few miles from our encampment, intending to penetrate the mountains as far as possible with the whole party. We were soon involved in very broken ground, among long ridges covered with fragments of granite. Winding our way up a long ravine, we came unexpectedly in view of a most beautiful lake, set like a gem in the mountains.[13] The sheet of water lay transversely across the direction we had been pursuing; and, descending the steep, rocky ridge, where it was necessary to lead our horses, we followed its banks to the southern extremity. Here a view of the utmost magnificence and grandeur burst upon our eyes. With nothing between us and their feet to lessen the effect of the whole height, a grand bed of snow-capped mountains rose before us, pile upon pile, glowing in the bright light of an August day. Immediately below them lay the lake, between two ridges covered with dark pines which swept down from the main chain to the spot where we stood. Here, where the lake glittered in the open sunlight, its banks of yellow sand and the light foliage of aspen groves contrasted well with the gloomy pines. "Never before," said Preuss, "in this country or in Europe, have I seen such magnificent, grand rocks."

I was so much pleased with the beauty of the place that I determined to make the main camp here, where our animals would find good pasturage, and explore the mountains with a small party of men. Proceeding a little farther, we came suddenly upon the outlet of the lake, where it found its way through a narrow passage between low hills. Dark pines, which overhung the stream, and masses of rock, where the water foamed along, gave it much romantic beauty. Where we crossed, which was immediately at the outlet, it is two hundred and fifty feet wide, and so deep that with difficulty we were able to ford it. Its bed was an accumulation of rocks, boulders, and broad slabs, and large angular fragments, among which the animals fell repeatedly.

The current was very swift, and the water cold and of a crystal purity. In crossing this stream, I met with a great misfortune in having my barometer broken. It was the only one. A great part of the interest of the journey for me was in the exploration of these mountains, of which so much had been said that was doubtful and contradictory; and now their snowy peaks rose majestically before me, and the only means of giving them authentically to science, the object of my anxious solicitude by night and day, was destroyed. We had brought this barometer in safety a thousand miles, and broke it almost among the snow of the mountains. The loss was felt by the whole camp—all had seen my anxiety, and aided me in preserving it. The height of these mountains, considered by the hunters and traders the highest in the whole range, had been a theme of constant discussion among them; and all had looked forward with pleasure to the moment when the instrument, which they believed to be true as the sun, should stand upon the summits and decide their disputes. Their grief was only inferior to my own.

This lake is about three miles long, and of very irregular width, and apparently great depth, and is the headwater of the third New Fork, a tributary to Green River, the Colorado of the West. On the map and in the narrative I have called it Mountain Lake. I encamped on the north side, about three hundred and fifty yards from the outlet. This was the most western point at which I obtained astronomical observations, by which this place, called Bernier's Encampment, is made in 110° 08′ 03″ west longitude from Greenwich, and latitude 42° 49′ 49″. The mountain peaks, as laid down, were fixed by bearings from this and other astronomical points. We had no other compass than the small ones used in sketching the country; but from an azimuth, in which one of them was used, the variation of the compass is 18° east. The correction made in our field work by the astronomical observations indicates that this is a very correct observation.

As soon as the camp was formed, I set about endeavoring to repair my barometer. As I have already said, this was a standard cistern barometer of Troughton's construction. The glass cistern had been broken about midway; but as the instrument had been kept in a proper position, no air had found its way into the tube, the end of which had always remained covered. I had with me a number of vials of tolerably thick glass, some of which were of the same diameter as the cistern, and I spent the day in slowly working on these, endeavoring to cut them of the requisite length, but as my instrument was a very rough file, I invariably broke them. A groove was cut in one of the trees, where the barometer was placed during the night, to be out of the way of any possible danger, and in the morning I commenced again. Among the powder horns in the camp I found one which was very transparent, so that its contents could be almost as plainly seen as through glass. This I boiled and stretched on a piece of wood to the requisite diameter, and scraped it very thin in order to increase to the utmost its transparency. I then secured it firmly in its place on the instrument, with strong glue made from a buffalo, and filled it with mercury properly heated. A piece of skin which had covered one of the vials furnished a good pocket, which was well secured with strong thread and glue, and then the brass cover was screwed to its place. The instrument was left some time to dry; and when I reversed it, a few hours after, I had the satisfaction to find it in perfect order, its indications being about the same as on the other side of the lake before it had been broken. Our success in this little incident diffused pleasure throughout the camp; and we immediately set about our preparations for ascending the mountains.

As will be seen on reference to a map, on this short mountain chain are the headwaters of four great rivers of the continent; namely, the Colorado, Columbia, Missouri, and Platte rivers. It had been my design after having ascended the mountains, to continue our route on the western side of the range, and, crossing through a pass at the northwestern end of the chain, about thirty miles from our present camp, return along the eastern slope, across the heads of the Yellowstone River, and join on the line to our station of August 7th, immediately at the foot of the ridge. In this way I should be enabled to include the whole chain, and its numerous waters, in my survey; but various considerations induced me, very reluctantly, to abandon this plan.

I was desirous to keep strictly within the scope of my instructions, and it would have required ten or fifteen additional days for the accomplishment of this object; our animals had become very much worn-out with the length of the journey; game was very scarce; and, though it does not appear in the course of the narrative (as I have avoided dwelling upon trifling incidents not connected with the objects of the expedition), the spirits of the men had been much exhausted by the hardships and privations to which they had been subjected. Our provisions had well-nigh all disappeared. Bread had been long out of the question; and of all our stock, we had remaining two or three pounds of coffee and a small quantity of macaroni, which had been husbanded with great care for the mountain expedition we were about to undertake. Our daily meal consisted of dry buffalo meat, cooked in tallow; and, as we had not dried this with Indian skill, part of it was spoiled, and what remained of good was as hard as wood, having much the taste and appearance of so many pieces of bark. Even of this, our stock was rapidly diminishing in a camp which was capable of consuming two buffaloes in every twenty-four hours. These animals had entirely disappeared; and it was not probable that we should fall in with them again until we returned to the Sweet Water.

Our arrangements for the ascent were rapidly completed. We were in a hostile country, which rendered the greatest vigilance and circumspection necessary. The pass at the north end of the mountain was generally infested by Blackfeet [15]; and immediately opposite was one of their forts, on the edge of a little thicket, two or three hundred feet from our encampment. We were posted in a grove of beech, on the margin of the lake and a few hundred feet long, with a narrow *prairillon* on the inner side, bordered by the rocky ridge. In the upper end of this grove we cleared a circular space about forty feet in diameter, and, with the felled timber and interwoven branches, surrounded it with a breastwork five feet in height. A gap was left for a gate on the inner side, by which the animals were to be driven in and secured, while the men slept around the little work. It was half hidden by the foliage; and, garrisoned by twelve resolute men, would have set at defiance any band of savages which might chance to discover them in the interval of our absence. Fifteen of the best mules with fourteen men, were selected for the mountain party. Our provisions consisted of dried meat for two days, with our little stock of coffee and some macaroni. In addition to the barometer and a thermometer, I took with me a sextant and spyglass, and we had, of course, our compasses. In charge of the camp I left Bernier, one of my most trustworthy men, who possessed the most determined courage.

August 12th. Early in the morning we left the camp, fifteen in number, well armed, of course, and mounted on our best mules. A pack animal carried our provisions, with a coffeepot and kettle, and three or four tin cups. Every man had a blanket strapped over his saddle, to serve for his bed, and the instruments were carried by turns on their backs. We entered directly on rough and rocky ground; and, just after crossing the ridge, had the good fortune to shoot an antelope. We heard the roar and had a glimpse of a waterfall as we rode along; and, crossing in our way two fine streams tributary to the Colorado, in about two hours' ride we reached the top of the first row or range of the mountains. Here, again, a view of the most romantic beauty met our eyes. It seemed as if, from the vast expanse of uninteresting prairie we had passed over, nature had collected all her beauties together in one chosen place. We were overlooking a deep valley, which was entirely occupied by three lakes, and from the brink the surrounding ridges rose precipitously five hundred and a thousand feet, covered with the dark green of the balsam pine, relieved on the border of the lake with the light foliage of the aspen. They all communicated with each other; and the green of the waters, common to mountain lakes of great depth, showed that it would be impossible to cross them. The surprise manifested by our guides when these impassable obstacles suddenly barred our progress proved that they were among the hidden treasures of the place, unknown even to the wandering trappers of the region. Descending the hill, we proceeded to make our way along the margin to the southern extremity. A narrow strip of angular fragments of rock sometimes afforded a rough pathway for our mules, but generally we rode along the shelving side, occasionally scrambling up, at a considerable risk of tumbling back into the lake.

The slope was frequently sixty degrees; the pines grew densely together, and the ground was covered with the branches and trunks of trees. The air was fragrant with the odor of the pines; and I realized, this delightful morning, the pleasure of breathing that mountain air which makes a constant theme of the hunter's praise, and which now made us feel as if we had all been drinking some exhilarating gas. The depths of this unexplored forest were a place to delight the heart of a botanist. There was a rich undergrowth of plants, and numerous gay-colored flowers in brilliant bloom. We reached the outlet at length, where some freshly barked willows that lay in the water showed that the beaver had been recently at work. There were some small brown squirrels jumping about in the pines, and a couple of large mallard ducks swimming about in the stream.

The hills on this southern end were low, and the lake looked like a mimic sea as the waves broke on the sandy beach in the force of a strong breeze. There was a pretty open spot, with fine grass for our mules; and we made our noon halt on the beach, under the shade of some large hemlocks. We resumed our journey after a halt of about an hour, making our way up the ridge on the western side of the lake. In search of smoother ground, we rode a little inland, and, passing through groves of aspen, soon found ourselves again among the pines. Emerging from these, we struck the summit of the ridge above the upper end of the lake.

We had reached a very elevated point, and in the valley below, and among the hills, were a number of lakes at different levels; some two or three hundred feet above others, with which they communicated by foaming torrents. Even to our great height, the roar of the cataracts came up, and we could see them leaping down in lines of snowy foam. From this scene of busy waters we turned abruptly into the stillness of a forest, where we rode among the open bolls of the pines, over a lawn of verdant grass having strikingly the air of cultivated grounds. This led us, after a time, among masses of rock which had no vegetable earth but in hollows and crevices, though still the pine forest continued. Toward evening we reached a defile, or rather a hole in the mountains, entirely shut in by dark pine-covered rocks.

A small stream, with a scarcely perceptible current, flowed through a level bottom of perhaps eighty yards' width, where the grass was saturated with water. Into this the mules were turned, and were neither hobbled nor picketed during the night, as the fine pasturage took away all temptation to stray; and we made our bivouac in the pines. The surrounding masses were all of granite. While supper was being prepared I set out on an excursion in the neighborhood, accompanied by one of my men. We wandered about among the crags and ravines until dark, richly repaid for our walk by a fine collection of plants, many of them in full bloom. Ascending a peak to find the place of our camp, we saw that the little defile in which we lay communicated with the long green valley of some stream, which, here locked up in the mountains, far away to the south found its way in a dense forest to the plains.

Looking along its upward course, it seemed to conduct, by a smooth gradual slope, directly toward the peak, which, from long consultation as we approached the mountain, we had decided to be the highest of the range. Pleased with the discovery of so fine a road for the next day, we hastened down to the camp, where we arrived just in time for supper. Our table service was rather scant; and we held the meat in our hands, and clean rocks made good plates on which we spread our macaroni. Among all the strange places on which we had occasion to encamp during our long journey, none have left so vivid an impression on my mind as the camp of this evening. The disorder of the masses which surrounded us; the little hole through which we saw the stars overhead; the dark pines where we slept; and the rocks lit up with the glow of our fires—made a night picture of very wild beauty.

August 13th. The morning was bright and pleasant, just cool enough to make exercise agreeable, and we soon entered the defile I had seen the preceding day. It was smoothly carpeted with a soft grass, and scattered over with groups of flowers of which yellow was the predominant color. Sometimes we were forced, by an occasional difficult pass, to pick our way on a narrow ledge along the side of the defile, and the mules were frequently on their knees; but these obstructions were rare, and we journeyed on in the sweet morning air, delighted at our good fortune in having found such a beautiful entrance to the mountains. This road continued for about three miles, when we suddenly reached its termination in one of the grand views which, at every turn, meet the traveler in this magnificent region. Here the defile up which we had traveled opened out into a small lawn, where, in a little lake, the stream had its source.

There were some fine asters in bloom, but all the flowering plants appeared to seek the shelter of the rocks, and to be of lower growth than below, as if they loved the warmth of the soil and kept out of the way of the winds. Immediately at our feet a precipitous descent led to a confusion of defiles, and before us rose the mountains. . . . It is not by the splendor of far-off views, which have lent such a glory to the Alps, that these impress the mind; but by a gigantic disorder of enormous masses, and a savage sublimity of naked rock, in wonderful contrast with innumerable green spots of a rich floral beauty shut up in their stern recesses. Their wildness seems well suited to the character of the people who inhabit the country.

I determined to leave our animals here, and make the rest of our way on foot. The peak appeared so near that there was no doubt of our returning before night, and a few men were left in charge of the mules with our provisions and blankets. We took with us nothing but our arms and instruments, and as the day had become warm, the greater part left their coats. Having made an early dinner, we started again. We were soon involved in the most rugged precipices, nearing the central chain very slowly, and rising but little. The first ridge hid a succession of others; and when, with great fatigue and difficulty, we had climbed up five hundred feet, it was but to make an equal descent on the other side; all these intervening places were filled with small deep lakes, which met the eye in every direction, descending from one level to another, sometimes under bridges formed by huge fragments of granite, beneath which was heard the roar of the water. These constantly obstructed our path, forcing us to make long detours; frequently obliged to retrace our steps, and frequently falling among the rocks. Maxwell was precipitated toward the face of a precipice, and saved himself from going over by throwing himself flat on the ground. We clambered on, always expecting with every ridge that we crossed to reach the foot of the peaks, and always disappointed, until about four o'clock, when, pretty well worn-out, we reached the shore of a little lake in which there was a rocky island. . . . We remained here a short time to rest, and continued on around the lake, which had in some places a beach of white sand, and in others was bound with rocks, over which the way was difficult and dangerous, as the water from innumerable springs made them very slippery.

By the time we had reached the farther side of the lake, we found ourselves all exceedingly fatigued, and, much to the satisfaction of the whole party, we encamped. The spot we had chosen was a broad flat rock, in some measure protected from the winds by the surrounding crags, and the trunks of fallen pines afforded us bright fires. Near by was a foaming torrent, which tumbled into the little lake about one hundred and fifty feet below us, and which, by way of distinction, we have called Island Lake. We had reached the upper limit of the piny region, as, above this point, no tree was to be seen, and patches of snow lay everywhere around us on the cold sides of the rocks. The flora of the region we had traversed since leaving our mules was extremely rich, and, among the characteristic plants, the scarlet flowers of the *Dodecatheon dentatum* everywhere met the eye in great abundance. A small green ravine, on the edge of which we were encamped, was filled with a profusion of alpine plants in brilliant bloom. From barometrical observations made during our three days' sojourn at this place, its elevation above the Gulf of Mexico is ten thousand feet.

During the day we had seen no sign of animal life, but among the rocks here we heard what was supposed to be the bleat of a young goat, which we searched for with hungry activity, and found to proceed from a small animal of a gray color, with short ears and no tail—probably the Siberian squirrel. We saw a considerable number of them, and, with the exception of a small bird like a sparrow, it is the only inhabitant of this elevated part of the mountains. On our return we saw, below this lake, large flocks of the mountain goat. We had nothing to eat tonight. Lajeunesse, with several others, took their guns and sallied out in search of a goat, but returned unsuccessful. At sunset the barometer stood at 20.522; the attached thermometer, 50°. Here we had the misfortune to break our thermometer, having now only that attached to the barometer. I was taken ill short after we had encamped, and continued so until late in the night, with violent headache and vomiting. This was probably caused by the excessive fatigue I had undergone, and want of food, and perhaps, also, in some measure, by the rarity of the air. The night was cold, as a violent gale from the north had sprung up at sunset, which entirely blew away the heat of the fires. The cold, and our granite beds, had not been favorable to sleep, and we were glad to see the face of the sun in the morning. Not being delayed by any preparations for breakfast, we set out immediately.

On every side as we advanced was heard the roar of water and of a torrent, which we followed up a short distance, until it expanded into a lake about one mile in length. On the northern side of the lake was a bank of ice, or rather of snow covered with a crust of ice. Carson had been our guide into the mountains, and, agreeably to his advice, we left this little valley and took to the ridges again; which we found extremely broken, and where we were again involved among precipices. Here were ice fields, among which we were all dispersed, seeking each the best path to ascend the peak. Preuss attempted to walk along the upper edge of one of these fields, which sloped away at an angle of about twenty degrees; but his feet slipped from under him, and he went plunging down the plane. A few hundred feet below, at the bottom, were some fragments of sharp rock, on which he landed, and, though he turned a couple of somersets, fortunately received no injury beyond a few bruises. Two of the men, Clément Lambert and Descoteaux, had been taken ill, and lay down on the rocks a short distance below; and at this point I was attacked with headache and giddiness, accompanied by vomitting, as on the day before.

Finding myself unable to proceed, I sent the barometer over to Preuss, who was in a gap two or three hundred yards distant, desiring him to reach the peak, if possible, and take an observation there. He found himself unable to proceed farther in that direction, and took an observation where the barometer stood at 19.401; attached thermometer 50°, in the gap. Carson, who had gone over to him, succeeded in reaching one of the snowy summits of the main ridge, whence he saw the peak toward which all our efforts had been directed, towering eight or ten hundred feet into the air above him. In the meantime, finding myself grow rather worse than better, and doubtful how far my strength would carry me, I sent Basil Lajeunesse, with four men, back to the place where the mules had been left.

We were now better acquainted with the topography of the country, and I directed him to bring back with him, if it were in any way possible, four or five mules, with provisions and blankets. With me were Maxwell and Ayot; and after we had remained nearly an hour on the rock, it became so unpleasantly cold, though the day was bright, that we set out on our return to the camp, at which we all arrived safely, straggling in one after the other. I continued ill during the afternoon, but became better toward sundown, when my recovery was completed by the appearance of Basil and four men, all mounted. The men who had gone with him had been too much fatigued to return, and were relieved by those in charge of the horses; but in his powers of endurance Basil resembled more a mountain goat than a man. They brought blankets and provisions, and we enjoyed well our dried meat and a cup of good coffee. We rolled ourselves up in our blankets, and, with our feet turned to a blazing fire, slept soundly until morning.

August 15th. It had been supposed that we had finished with the mountains; and the evening before it had been arranged that Carson should set out at daylight, and return to breakfast at the Camp of the Mules, taking with him all but four or five men, who were to stay with me and bring back the mules and instruments. Accordingly, at the break of day they set out. With Preuss and myself remained Basil Lajeunesse, Clément Lambert, Janisse, and Descoteaux. When we had secured strength for the day by a hearty breakfast, we covered what remained, which was enough for one meal, with rocks, in order that it might be safe from any marauding bird; and, saddling our mules, turned our faces once more toward the peaks. This time we determined to proceed quietly and cautiously, deliberately resolved to accomplish our object if it were within the compass of human means. We were of opinion that a long defile which lay to the left of yesterday's route would lead us to the foot of the main peak. Our mules had been refreshed by the fine grass in the little ravine at the Island Camp, and we intended to ride up the defile as far as possible in order to husband our strength for the main ascent. Though this was a fine passage, still it was a defile of the most rugged mountains known, and we had many a rough and steep slippery place to cross before reaching the end. In this place the sun rarely shone; snow lay along the border of the small stream which flowed through it, and occasional icy passages made the footing of the mules very insecure, and the rocks and ground were moist with the trickling waters in this spring of mighty rivers. We soon had the satisfaction to find ourselves riding along the huge wall which forms the central summits of the chain. There at last it rose by our sides, a nearly perpendicular wall of granite, terminating, from two to three thousand feet above our heads, in a serrated line of broken, jagged cones. We rode on until we came almost immediately below the main peak, which I denominated the Snow Peak, as it exhibited more snow to the eye than any of the neighboring summits. Here were three small lakes of a green color, each of perhaps a thousand yards in diameter, and apparently very deep. These lay in a kind of chasm; and, according to the barometer, we had attained but a few hundred feet above the Island Lake. The barometer here stood at 20.450, attached thermometer, 70°.

We managed to get our mules up to a little bench about a hundred feet above the lakes, where there was a patch of good grass, and turned them loose to graze. During our rough ride to this place, they had exhibited a wonderful surefootedness. Parts of the defile were filled with angular, sharp fragments of rock, three or four and eight or ten feet cube; and among these they had worked their way, leaping from one narrow point to another, rarely making a false step, and giving us no occasion to dismount. Having divested ourselves of every unnecessary encumbrance, we commenced the ascent. This time, like experienced travelers, we did not press ourselves, but climbed leisurely, sitting down so soon as we found breath beginning to fail. At intervals we reached places where a number of springs gushed from the rocks, and about one thousand eight hundred feet above the lakes came to the snow line. From this point our progress was uninterrupted climbing. Hitherto I had worn a pair of thick moccasins, with soles of parfleche; but here I put on a light thin pair, which I had brought for the purpose, as now the use of our toes became necessary to a further advance. I availed myself of a sort of comb of the mountain, which stood against the wall like a buttress, and which the wind and the solar radiation, joined to the steepness of the smooth rock, had kept almost entirely free from snow. Up this I made my way rapidly. Our cautious method of advancing in the outset had spared my strength; and, with the exception of a slight disposition to headache, I felt no remains of yesterday's illness. In a few minutes we reached a point where the buttress was overhanging, and there was no other way of surmounting the difficulty than by passing around one side of it, which was the face of a vertical precipice of several hundred feet.

Putting hands and feet in the crevices between the blocks, I succeeded in getting over it, and, when I reached the top, found my companions in a small valley below. Descending to them, we continued climbing, and in a short time reached the crest. I sprang upon the summit, and another step would have precipitated me into an immense snow field five hundred feet below. To the edge of this field was a sheer icy precipice; and then, with a gradual fall, the field sloped off for about a mile, until it struck the foot of another lower ridge. I stood on a narrow crest, about three feet in width, with an inclination of about 20° N., 51° E. As soon as I had gratified the first feelings of curiosity I descended, and each man ascended in his turn; for I would only allow one at a time to mount the unstable and precarious slab, which it seemed a breath would hurl into the abyss below. We mounted the barometer in the snow of the summit, and, fixing a ramrod in a crevice, unfurled the national flag to wave in the breeze where never flag waved before. During our morning's ascent we had met no sign of animal life, except the small sparrowlike bird already mentioned. A stillness the most profound and a terrible solitude forced themselves constantly on the mind as the great features of the place. Here, on the summit, where the stillness was absolute, unbroken by any sound, and the solitude complete, we thought ourselves beyond the region of animated life; but while we were sitting on the rock, a solitary bee (*Bombus,* the humblebee) came winging his flight from the eastern valley, and lit on the knee of one of the men.

It was a strange place, the icy rock and the highest peak of the Rocky Mountains,[15] for a lover of warm sunshine and flowers; and we pleased ourselves with the idea that he was the first of his species to cross the mountain barrier—a solitary pioneer to foretell the advance of civilization. I believe that a moment's thought would have made us let him continue his way unharmed; but we carried out the law of this country, where all animated nature seems at war, and, seizing him immediately, put him in at least a fit place—in the leaves of a large book, among the flowers we had collected on our way. The barometer stood at 18.293, the attached thermometer at 44°; giving for the elevation of this summit thirteen thousand five hundred and seventy feet above the Gulf of Mexico, which may be called the highest flight of the bee. It is certainly the highest known flight of that insect. From the description given by Mackenzie of the mountains where he crossed them, with that of a French officer still farther to the north, and Colonel Long's measurements to the south, joined to the opinion of the oldest traders of the country, it is presumed that this is the highest peak of the Rocky Mountains.

The day was sunny and bright, but a slight shining mist hung over the lower plains, which interfered with our view of the surrounding country. On one side we overlooked innumerable lakes and streams, the spring of the Colorado of the Gulf of California; and on the other was the Wind River Valley, where were the heads of the Yellowstone branch of the Missouri; far to the north we just could discover the snowy heads of the Trois Tetons, where were the sources of the Missouri and Columbia rivers; and at the southern extremity of the ridge the peaks were plainly visible, among which were some of the springs of the Nebraska, or Platte River. Around us the whole scene had one main striking feature, which was that of terrible convulsion. Parallel to its length, the ridge was split into chasms and fissures, between which rose the thin lofty walls, terminated with slender minarets and columns. . . . According to the barometer, the little crest of the wall on which we stood was three thousand five hundred and seventy feet above that place, and two thousand seven hundred and eighty above the little lakes at the bottom, immediately at our feet. Our camp at the Two Hills (an astronomical station) bore S. 3° E., which, with a bearing afterward obtained from a fixed position, enabled us to locate the peak. The bearing of the Trois Tetons was N. 50° W., and the direction of the central ridge of the Wind River Mountains S. 39° E. The summit rock was gneiss, succeeded by sienitic gneiss. Sienite and feldspar succeeded in our descent to the snow line, where we found a feldspathic granite. I had remarked that the noise produced by the explosion of our pistols had the usual degree of loudness, but was not in the least prolonged, expiring almost instantaneously.

Having now made what observations our means afforded, we proceeded to descend. We had accomplished an object of laudable ambition, and beyond the strict order of our instructions. We had climbed the loftiest peak of the Rocky Mountains, and looked down upon the snow a thousand feet below, and, standing where never human foot had stood before, felt the exultation of first explorers.*

* I received, under date of March 8, 1884, a letter from Mr. H. G. Nickerson, a member of the Eighth Legislative Assembly, Wyoming Territory, informing me that their Legislature had just passed an act to create the county of Frémont; embracing within its limits the headwaters of Wind River and the Peak, the ascent of which, in 1842, is told in the preceding pages.

J. C. F.

It was about two o'clock when we left the summit; and when we reached the bottom the sun had already sunk behind the wall, and the day was drawing to a close. It would have been pleasant to have lingered here and on the summit longer; but we hurried away as rapidly as the ground would permit, for it was an object to regain our party as soon as possible, not knowing what accident the next hour might bring forth.

We reached our cache of provisions at nightfall. Here was not the inn which awaits the tired traveler on his return from Mont Blanc, or the orange groves of South America, with their refreshing juices and soft fragrant air; but we found our little cache of dried meat and coffee undisturbed. Though the moon was bright, the road was full of precipices, and the fatigue of the day had been great. We therefore abandoned the idea of rejoining our friends, and lay down on the rock, and, in spite of the cold, slept soundly.

August 16th. We left our encampment with the daylight. We saw on our way large flocks of the mountain goat looking down on us from the cliffs. At the crack of a rifle they would bound off among the rocks, and in a few minutes make their appearance on some lofty peak, some hundred or a thousand feet above. It is needless to attempt any further description of the country; the portion over which we traveled this morning was rough as imagination could picture it, and to us seemed equally beautiful. A concourse of lakes and rushing waters, mountains of rocks naked and destitute of vegetable earth, dells and ravines of the most exquisite beauty, all kept green and fresh by the great moisture in the air, and sown with brilliant flowers, and everywhere thrown around all the glory of most magnificent scenes—these constitute the features of the place, and impress themselves vividly on the mind of the traveler. It was not until eleven o'clock that we reached the place where our animals had been left when we first attempted the mountains on foot. Near one of the still burning fires we found a piece of meat, which our friends had thrown away, and which furnished us a mouthful—a very scanty breakfast. We continued directly on, and reached our camp on the mountain lake at dusk. We found all well. Nothing had occurred to interrupt the quiet since our departure, and the fine grass and good cool water had done much to re-establish our animals. All heard with great delight the order to turn our faces homeward; and toward sundown of the 17th we encamped again at the Two Buttes.

In the course of this afternoon's march the barometer was broken past remedy. I regretted it, as I was desirous to compare it again with Dr. Engelmann's [16] barometers at St. Louis, to which mine were referred; but it had done its part well, and my objects were mainly fulfilled. It had touched the highest point of its destiny, and would never be put to a less noble use—as the Scandinavians mean when, after drinking the health of the bride, the glass is thrown over the shoulder and shattered that it may never be used again.

August 19th. We left our camp on Little Sandy River at about seven in the morning, and traversed the same sandy, undulating country. The air was filled with the turpentine scent of the various artemisias, which are now in bloom, and, numerous as they are, give much gaiety to the landscape of the plains. At ten o'clock we stood exactly on the divide in the pass, where the wagon road crosses, and, descending immediately upon the Sweet Water, halted to take a meridian observation of the sun. The latitude was 42° 24' 32".

In the course of the afternoon we saw buffalo again, and at our evening halt on the Sweet Water the roasted ribs again made their appearance around the fires, and with them, good humor, and laughter, and song were restored to the camp. Our coffee had been expended, but we now made a kind of tea from the roots of the wild cherry tree. . . .*

FOOTNOTES

1. James Bridger was one of the most picturesque and famous frontiersmen of his day. Born in 1804 in Richmond, Virginia, he had been taken to Missouri as a child, and orphaned at an early age. In 1822 he joined William H. Ashley's fur-trapping expedition to the headwaters of the Missouri; and for the next twenty years he roamed the West from southern Colorado to the Canadian line. He has been generally credited with the first visit (1824) to Great Salt Lake. Living by the fur trade, he was quick to note its decline. He turned instead to the emigrant business, and made Fort Bridger, which he established in south-western Wyoming (on Blacks Fork of the Green River), and its accompanying blacksmith shop, a valuable station for all wayfarers. Long afterward he was to

* Frémont's record of his homeward journey to St. Louis and Washington, which latter city he reached October 29, contains little new, and is omitted.

help the engineers of the Union Pacific find a lower, easier path to the West than South Pass. He died near Kansas City in 1881.

2. Here was a greater frontiersman than Bridger, greater perhaps than even Kit Carson. Born in Ireland about the beginning of the century, Thomas Fitzpatrick came to the United States in youth, went west, and was soon engaged in the fur trade and the Indian trade. He was one of Ashley's men, and with Jedediah S. Smith headed Ashley's party sent in 1823 to tap the Wyoming country. It was this party which in 1824 made the first recorded journey of white men through South Pass. Like Bridger, when the fur trade decayed he turned to guiding various Western parties. In 1841–42 he led groups of emigrants bound for the Pacific slope, and as we shall see, in 1843–44 was a guide to Frémont's second expedition. During the Mexican War he conducted Kearny's army to Santa Fe. Early in the 1850s, he became an extremely effective Indian agent. He was a man of unusual intelligence and fine judgment. His death in 1854, just after he had induced some unruly tribes to make a treaty of peace, was a serious loss to the West.

3. As has been noted, Fort Hall was built by Nathaniel Wyeth in the Idaho country, at the junction of the Snake and Portneuf rivers, in 1834. The Hudson's Bay Company bought it in 1837, and managed it until it was abandoned in 1855. It was an invaluable center for the Indian trade, and for the rest and refitting of emigrant parties along the Oregon Trail.

4. Nicollet had been the first man to use the barometer for ascertaining the altitude of points in the interior of North America, and Frémont had learned from him to set a high value on the instrument.

5. Laramie Peak is actually about ten thousand feet above sea level.

6. The Crow Indians were a specially strong tribe, and especially fond of war, though in general they reserved their hostilities for neighboring nations, especially the Teton Sioux and Blackfeet. They were friendly to the whites, and furnished the army many scouts. Their hunting grounds were the upper Yellowstone region of Wyoming, and Montana. At this time, for some reason, they were in defiant mood; probably the westward emigration had filled them with apprehension.

7. Wind River, rising in western Wyoming, flows into the Big Horn River, and so sends its waters by way of the Yellowstone to the Missouri. The Wind River Range, now Frémont's objective, fills a great part of present-day Frémont County. Not far beyond, to the northwest, lie Jackson's Hole, the Teton Range, and Yellowstone Park. In short, the Wind River Range is in the midst of some of the grandest scenery of the Rockies.

8. Independence Rock was the most noted landmark on the Oregon Trail. So named because some trappers had celebrated the Fourth of July there in or about 1825, it is a huge outcropping of granite, covering about twenty-seven acres and rising 155 feet above the Sweetwater River. It was 838 miles from Kansas City by the trail.

9. Another famous landmark to travelers on the Oregon Trail.

10. This pass was to the Rocky Mountains what the Cumberland Gap was to the Appalachians; the Oregon and California Trail carried multitudes through it, and many pens have described it. Some students have thought that John Colter discovered it in 1807 or 1808. Much better evidence exists that the party which returned from Astoria in 1812 with Robert Stuart crossed it. But, as before noted, the "effective" discovery was by Thomas Fitzpatrick. See

F. S. Dellenbaugh, *Frémont and '49*, pp. 82–83, for a discussion of the various claims to early use of the pass.

11. This was a remarkably accurate estimate; Hiram Chittenden in 1901 reckoned the distance from Kansas City as 947 miles.

12. Frémont's party had left the waters flowing to the east, and was on streams tributary to the Pacific.

13. Frémont identified this body of water, which marked the westernmost point of his expedition, by the prosaic name of Mountain Lake. He was now, as he writes later, in the mountain area whence flow the upper waters of the Colorado, Columbia, Missouri, and Platte; the Snake represented the Columbia and the Big Horn the Missouri. The Wind River Chain thus has title to be called the central range of the Rockies.

14. The Blackfeet were remarkable in that, belonging to the Algonkian family of the Eastern timberlands, they adopted the use of the horse, made a long journey west, and found a home around the head of the Missouri River, from Montana on northward into Saskatchewan. They are said to have gained their name from the fact that when they first appeared on the slopes of the Rockies, their moccasins were black from travel over the recently burned prairie. A powerful and aggressive nation, they often showed hostility to the whites in this period.

15. An unfortunate sentence. Perhaps Frémont meant the highest peak of this particular range, but if so, he was mistaken even in this; for Gannett Peak five miles distant is 13,785 feet high, or fifty-five feet higher than the true figures (13,730 feet) for Frémont's peak. At an earlier date Captain B. L. E. Bonneville, climbing a high peak in this same range, had concluded that it must be the tallest in North America.

16. This was George Engelmann (1809–1884), a graduate of the University of Halle, who had migrated to America, and become the leading physician of St. Louis. He gave his spare time to the study of botany and meteorology, wrote much and ably on botanical topics, gathered a great herbarium, and in 1856 organized the St. Louis Academy of Science. It is probable that during his various sojourns in St. Louis Frémont came to know this eminent savant.

CHAPTER 6

Second Expedition, 1843–44:
Kit Carson and Fitzpatrick:
Journey to Great Salt Lake *

THE winter of 1842–43 was busily occupied in preparing my report of the expedition. To Mr. Preuss was assigned the labor of the maps. In addition to the general map of the country explored, a series of maps representing each a day's journey, a guidebook in atlas form, was prepared for the use of the emigration. This was the suggestion of Mr. Benton. Upon each of the maps the places were indicated for camps where grass and water and wood would be found. The distinguished botanist Professor Torrey kindly undertook the description of the plants collected during the journey. To me fell the labor of the various computations and the writing of the report.

The third life alluded to in the "scope" of this narrative came now in for its portion of work. I write more easily by dictation. Writing myself, I have too much time to think and dwell upon words as well as ideas. In dictation there is not time for this and then, too, I see the face of my second mind, and get there at times the slight dissent confirming my own doubt, or the pleased expression which represents the popular impression of a mind new to the subject. This invites discussion—a form of discussion impossible except with a mind and purpose in harmony with one's own and on the same level— therefore the labor of amanuensis, commencing at this early time, has remained with Mrs. Frémont.

* The first few pages of this chapter are taken from Frémont's *Memoirs,* the remainder from his *Report of the Exploring Expedition to Oregon and North California in the Years 1843–44,* which he dated Washington City, March 1, 1845.

The report was called for by the Senate, and on the motion of Mr. Linn it was printed for the use of the Senate, and a number of extra copies ordered. In support of his motion, Mr. Linn said:

The object of the expedition was to examine and report upon the rivers and country between the frontiers of Missouri and the base of the Rocky Mountains: and especially to examine the character, and ascertain the latitude and longitude, of the South Pass, the great crossing place in those mountains on the way to the Oregon. All the objects of the expedition have been accomplished, and in a way to be beneficial to science and instructive to the general reader as well as useful to the Government. Supplied with the best astronomical and barometrical instruments, well qualified to use them, and accompanied by twenty-five voyageurs enlisted for the purpose at St. Louis, and trained to all the hardships and dangers of the prairies and the mountains, Mr. Frémont left the mouth of the Kansas, on the frontiers of Missouri, on June 10th, and in the incredibly short space of four months returned to the same point without an accident to a man, and with a vast mass of useful observations and many hundred specimens in botany and geology.

In executing his instructions, Mr. Frémont proceeded up the Kansas River far enough to ascertain its character, and then crossed over to the Great Platte and pursued that river to its source in the mountains, where the Sweet Water (a head branch of the Platte) issues from the neighborhood of the South Pass. He reached the pass on August 8th, and described it as a wide and low depression of the mountains, where the ascent is as easy as that of the hill on which this Capitol stands, and where a plainly beaten wagon road leads to the Oregon through the valley of Lewis River, a fork of the Columbia.

He went through the pass and saw the headwaters of the Colorado of the Gulf of California; and, leaving the valleys, to indulge a laudable curiosity and to make some useful observations, and attended by four of his men, he climbed the loftiest peak of the Rocky Mountains, until then untrodden by any known human being; and on August 15th looked down upon ice and snow some thousand feet below, and traced in the distance the valleys of the rivers which, taking their rise in the same elevated ridge, flow in opposite directions to the Pacific Ocean and to the Mississippi. From that ultimate point he returned by the valley of the Great Platte, following the stream in its whole course, and solving all questions in relation to its navigability and the character of the country through which it flows.

The results of all these observations Mr. Frémont has condensed into a brief report—enough to make a document of ninety or one hundred pages; and believing that this document would be of general interest to the whole country, and beneficial to science as well as useful to the Government, I move the printing of the extra number which has been named.

This report proves conclusively that the country for several hundred miles from the frontier of Missouri is exceedingly beautiful and fertile; alternate woodland and prairie, and certain portions well supplied with water. It also proves that the valley of the River Platte has a very rich soil, affording great facilities for emigrants to the west of the Rocky Mountains.

This was the first act done with the, apparent, support of the Government in aid to the Oregon emigration.

Upon this subject Mr. Benton says:

Connected with this emigration, and auxiliary to it, was the first expedition of Lieutenant Frémont to the Rocky Mountains, and undertaken and completed in the summer of 1842—upon its outside view the conception of the Government, but in fact conceived without its knowledge, and executed upon solicited orders, of which the design was unknown.

In the meantime the second expedition had been planned.[1]

Pending the discussion at Washington of the Ashburton Treaty, some propositions concerning Oregon which had been suggested between the negotiators were submitted to the Senators from Missouri, and by them promptly rejected. These suggestions of "a conventional divisional line" forewarned them of a basis of settlement that admitted doubt upon the clear title of the United States to the Valley of the Columbia, which they had resolved to maintain against the field. The divisional line meant the north bank of the Columbia for the boundary, with equal rights of navigation in the river and to the harbor at its mouth. The proposition to surrender simply inspired promptness in the measures projected to commit the Government to their views and render any compromise impossible; and the plans for extending the exploration into Oregon were hurried forward.

A policy of delay suggested in the President's message required that before any title to lands be given to emigrants in Oregon territory, "the respective claims of the two Governments should be settled." The answer to this open proposition for delay, in deference to the claims of England, was made by Senator Linn, of Missouri, who introduced a bill to encourage and protect emigration by stockading the line of travel and providing for grants of land. This bill gave the keynote to the emigration; though the bill passed the Senate, it was not acted on in the House, but the emigrants assumed it to mean government protection.

It was fair to set out distinctly the distorted and absurdly erroneous views entertained concerning the country we had to examine, as a reason for the explorations that brought to common knowledge the inexhaustible riches of the vast region which, through years of obstacle, its friends had struggled to reclaim from the possession of a foreign power. The necessity must be looked at from conditions existing at the time, not by the light thrown back upon them by the conditions of today.

The following extract from the *Athenæum*, London, reviewing, in March, 1844, the first report, shows the undetermined conditions which also existed on the other side of the water at the time. It concludes:

It is said that Lieutenant Frémont has been appointed to the survey of the Oregon Territory. We are heartily glad of it. He will be sure to do his work well, and if our topographical engineers labor in the same style and spirit, we may reckon on obtaining, through their joint efforts, an accurate knowledge of that country, so that we may be able to calculate, on safe grounds, the exact amount of blood and treasure which may be prudently expended in the conquest of it.

The second expedition was to connect with the first expedition at the South Pass, but to approach the mountains on a different line. It was intended to examine the broad region south of the Columbia River, lying between the Rocky Mountains and the Pacific Ocean. In this way the two expeditions would give a connected survey of the interior and western half of the continent.[2]

Early in the spring of 1843, I left Washington with the whole family, Mr. Benton having preceded us to Missouri. Mr. Preuss and Jacob Dodson were with us. Jacob was only eighteen, but strong and active, and nearly six feet in height. He was of the good colored people of the district, born free, but with the feeling of belonging with a family and giving to it unchanging service. Others of his people held lifetime service in the family of Mr. Benton, and it was the ambition of this boy to go with me. About noon the stagecoach was climbing up one of the Pennsylvania mountains—when reaching the summit, it capsized. The driver, too confident of his skill, and disregarding the shouts of the wagoner, attempted to pass one of those huge wagons with its string of horses, with the result of overturning us into a gully, the coach lighting on its roof. Jacob, who was on the box, was at the horses' heads before the coach reached the gully, and the wagoner's men prevented further harm from frightened animals. Inside the coach all was so silent that the first thought was that all had been hurt, but as they were drawn out one by one, Mrs. Benton was found to be the only one injured. She had received a hurt on the head which stunned her, and made rest necessary, so that we remained over until next day.

Preuss, who had gotten out to enjoy a walk up the mountain in the company of his pipe, was not to be consoled because he had not been part of the disaster; it was necessary to remind him that his being away had saved the precious barometer, which he never left out of his care. Chance had given us a good place for the overset. The "wagon stand" near by stood on the stony, bleak mountainside; it was one of the bygone, old-fashioned, Pennsylvania taverns, and the abundant game hanging about gave it now the appearance of a rough hunting lodge. The landlady, who had seen the coach go over, tried to comfort us by loading her table with every good thing she had, or her housewifely skill could prepare. The buckwheat cakes were half an inch thick and porous like a sponge, capable of absorbing enough of the good mountain butter to support a man for a day; with honey from the buckwheat fields, and maple syrup from the forest. The venison steaks were excellent, broiled over wood coals. It was the native abundance of that day.

One may forget many things but it would not be easy to efface from a traveler's memory this contrast to many an aftertime; before a year had passed Preuss and I had recalled the stone house in the mountains with its big fires and lavish abundance of good food.

Mrs. Frémont was to remain in St. Louis during my absence, which was not to be for more than about eight months. Experience enabled me to make my preparations quickly. Among the men engaged at St. Louis for this journey were six who had been with me in the first: Alexis Ayot, François Badeau, Baptiste Bernier, Basil

Lajeunesse, Louis Ménard and Raphael Proue, all good men; together with Louis Zindel, Prussian artillerist, who was one of the party under Mr. Nicollet in his second expedition.

As I expected to be much among Indians who had for many years a known character for audacious bravery and treachery, I applied to Colonel S. W. Kearny,[3] commanding Third Military Division, for a howitzer, which he furnished me from the arsenal at St. Louis.

I had obtained for guide Mr. Thomas Fitzpatrick, well known in the mountains. He was known to be a brave man and had lived through rough experiences in the Indian country. On one occasion, surrounded by Blackfeet in the Wind River Mountains, all his party had been killed except himself, but the peril and excitement of the three days among the rocks while the Indians were searching for him had turned his thick hair entirely white. He was still young, and it made a contrast to the healthy ruddy color of his face.

On May 17th I arrived at the little town of Kansas, near the junction of the Kansas River with the Missouri. Maxwell, who will be remembered as having accompanied me in 1842, joined the camp here to accompany me as far as the Upper Arkansas. Carson joined me as we reached the mountains at a little Mexican pueblo on the Arkansas River.

In setting out on this journey I made the acquaintance of Major Cummins, who had long been Indian agent among the Delawares and other Indians, and a friend of long standing to Senator Benton and valued by him. He was a large, fine-looking man, advanced now in years, but stanch in person as in character. His house was always open to me with a frontier welcome, which means much; and the introduction he gave me to the Shawnee and Delaware Indians gained me their confidence and proved most valuable to me for years afterward.

While engaged in completing my outfit I received from Mrs. Frémont a letter which urged me to set out upon the journey forthwith and make at Bent's Fort the waiting for the grass to get its full strength. Satisfied that there was reason for such urgency, I started on the morning of the 29th, twelve days only after reaching Kansas, and made my first encampment on the verge of the great prairies four miles beyond the frontier. It was not until my return that I learned the reason why this sudden move was required of me.

I had requested Mrs. Frémont to open all my letters, using her discretion in regard to forwarding any of them while I remained on the frontier. But there came an official order from the head of my corps, Colonel Abert, directing me to return to Washington in order to explain why, in addition to ordinary arms, I had taken a howitzer with me: that it was a scientific expedition—not military—and not to be armed as such.[4] The flimsiness of this excuse for breaking up the expedition after it had been planned and ordered, and in movement, was so apparent to Mrs. Frémont, as also was the true reason for it, that she did not hesitate to suppress the order, and write me the letter which caused me to make an immediate start. She did not communicate this proceeding to Colonel Abert until I was far beyond the reach of recall. Mr. Benton was not in St. Louis, and she took council with no one. She acted entirely on her own knowledge, which was full, concerning the expedition, and existing reasons for opposing it.

I never knew where the order originated. It came through Colonel Abert.[5] He was a quiet man, not likely to disturb an expedition gotten up, apparently, under his own direction and, so far as he knew, originating with himself. It was not probable that I would have been recalled from the Missouri frontier to Washington, fifteen hundred miles of water and stagecoach traveling, to explain why I had taken an arm that simply served to increase the means of defense for a small party very certain to encounter Indian hostility, and which involved very trifling expense.

On his return to St. Louis Mr. Benton approved Mrs. Frémont's action, and so wrote to Washington, at the same time asking an explanation, but there the subject rested.

I mention it here to show the compliance of the Administration with the English situation in Oregon. . . .* My party consisted principally of Creole and Canadian French, and Americans, amounting in all to thirty-nine men, among whom will be recognized several of those who were with me in my first expedition, and who have been favorably brought to notice. Mr. Thomas Fitzpatrick, whom many years of hardship and exposure in the Western territories had rendered familiar with a portion of the country it was designed to

---

* Here the material from the *Memoirs* covering events which could not be put into an official report, ends, and that from the *Report* begins.

explore, had been selected as our guide; and Mr. Charles Preuss, who had been my assistant in the previous journey, was again associated with me in the same capacity on the present expedition. Mr. Theodore Talbot,[6] of Washington City, had been attached to the party, with a view to advancement in his profession; and at St. Louis I had been joined by Mr. Frederick Dwight, a gentleman of Springfield, Mass., who availed himself of our overland journey to visit the Sandwich Islands and China, by way of Fort Vancouver.

The men engaged for the service were: Alexis Ayot, François Badeau, Oliver Beaulieu, Baptiste Bernier, John A. Campbell, John G. Campbell, Manuel Chapman, Ransom Clark, Philibert Courteau, Michel Crélis, William Creuss, Clinton Deforest, Baptiste Derosier, Basil Lajeunesse, François Lajeunesse, Henry Lee, Louis Ménard, Louis Montreuil, Samuel Neil, Alexis Pera, François Pera, James Power, Raphael Proue, Oscar Sarpy, Baptiste Tabeau, Charles Taplin, Baptiste Tesson, Auguste Vasquez, Joseph Verrot, Patrick White, Tiery Wright, and Louis Zindel. Two Delaware Indians—a fine-looking old man and his son—were engaged to accompany the expedition as hunters, through the kindness of Major Cummins, the excellent Indian agent.

The party was armed generally with Hall's carbines, which, with a brass twelve-pound howitzer, had been furnished to me by Colonel Kearny. Three men were specially detailed for the management of this piece, under the charge of Zindel, who had been nineteen years a noncommissioned officer of artillery in the Prussian Army, and regularly instructed in the duties of his profession. The camp equipage and provisions were transported in twelve carts, drawn each by two mules; and a light covered wagon, mounted on good springs, had been provided for the safer carriage of the instruments. These were: One refracting telescope, by Frauenhofer; one reflecting circle, by Gambey; two sextants, by Troughton; one pocket chronometer, No. 837, by Goffe, Falmouth; one pocket chronometer, No. 739, by Brockbank; one syphon barometer, by Bunten, Paris; one cistern barometer, by Frye & Shaw, New York; six thermometers, and a number of small compasses.

To make the exploration as useful as possible, I determined, in conformity to my general instructions, to vary the route to the Rocky Mountains from that followed in the year 1842. The route then was up the valley of the Great Platte River to the South Pass, in north latitude 42°; the route now determined on was up the valley of the Kansas River and to the head of the Arkansas, and to some pass in the mountains, if any could be found, at the sources of that river.

By making this deviation from the former route, the problem of a new road to Oregon and California, in a climate more genial, might be solved; and a better knowledge obtained of an important river, and the country it drained; while the great object of the expedition would find its point of commencement at the termination of the former, which was at that great gate in the ridge of the Rocky Mountain called the South Pass.

Resuming our journey on the 31st, after the delay of a day to complete our equipment and furnish ourselves with some of the comforts of civilized life, we encamped in the evening at Elm Grove, in company with several emigrant wagons, constituting a party which was proceeding to Upper California under the direction of Mr. J. B. Childs,[7] of Missouri. The wagons were variously freighted with goods, furniture, and farming utensils, containing among other things an entire set of machinery for a mill which Mr. Childs designed erecting on the waters of the Sacramento River, emptying into the Bay of San Francisco.

We were joined here by Mr. William Gilpin,[8] of Missouri, who, intending this year to visit the settlements in Oregon, had been invited to accompany us, and proved a useful and agreeable addition to the party. From this encampment, our route until June 3d was nearly the same as that described to you in 1842. Trains of wagons were almost constantly in sight giving to the road a populous and animated appearance, although the greater portion of the emigrants were collected at the crossing, or already on their march beyond the Kansas River.

Leaving at the ford the usual emigrant road to the mountains, we continued our line along the southern side of the Kansas. . . .*

---

* Some pages of no special interest on Frémont's journey through present-day Kansas are omitted. His party followed the Oregon Trail (as on the first expedition) as far as the ford of the Kansas River near what is now Topeka; they then diverged from the trail, continuing west along the southern bank of the Kansas until they reached the junction with the Republican River, up which they traveled. On the way they encountered a war party of Osage Indians, who charged their camp and ran off some horses; but Frémont by a hot pursuit

As we were riding quietly along, eagerly searching every hollow in search of game, we discovered, at a little distance in the prairie, a large grizzly bear so busily engaged in digging roots that he did not perceive us until we were galloping down a little hill fifty yards from him, when he charged upon us with such sudden energy that several of us came near losing our saddles. Being wounded, he commenced retreating to a rocky piny ridge near by, from which we were not able to cut him off, and we entered the timber with him. The way was very much blocked up with fallen timber; and we

recovered the stock. Going up the Republican, they saw elk and antelope. The carts found the way rough and toilsome. In order to map more of the country, Frémont divided his expedition. He placed Fitzpatrick in charge of the supply train, to move forward to St. Vrain's Fort in northeastern Colorado, on the upper waters of the Platte. He himself with fifteen men (taking the brass howitzer and the instrument wagon) went across country to the Solomon Fork of the Kansas River. Thence he traveled northwest into a corner of Nebraska and on into the northeastern corner of Colorado.

The country rose as they went, until they were on arid plains about 4000 feet high. On the last day of June they reached the crest of a range of rolling hills: "We found ourselves overlooking a broad and misty valley, where, about ten miles distant, and 1,000 feet below us, the South Fork of the Platte was rolling magnificently along, swollen with the waters of melting snows. It was in strong and refreshing contrast with the parched country from which we had just issued; and when, at night, the broad expanse of water grew indistinct, it almost seemed that we had pitched our tents on the shore of the sea." The following afternoon they had a grander sight: "We caught a far and uncertain view of a faint blue mass in the west, as the sun sank behind it; and from our camp in the morning, at the mouth of Bijou, Long's Peak and the neighboring mountains stood out into the sky, grand and luminously white, covered to their bases with glittering snow."

About noon on July 4 Frémont's party arrived at St. Vrain's Fort, where the hospitable owner invited them to join him at a feast celebrating the day. With his animals worn-out and his stock of provisions exhausted, Frémont had hoped to obtain supplies here; but to his intense disappointment, the fort was so impoverished that he could obtain only a little unbolted Mexican flour, with some salt and a few pounds of powder and lead. He therefore contracted with Lucien Maxwell, who was going on to Taos, New Mexico, to buy ten or a dozen mules at that place, load them with provisions, and meet the party at the mouth of Boiling Spring Creek (Fontaine Qui Bouille) on the Arkansas. At daybreak on the 6th Maxwell was on his way, and a few hours later Frémont started on up the Platte. Within a few miles he reached Fort Lancaster, kept by a trader named Lupton who was establishing a prosperous farm with hogs and cattle. Continuing, Frémont on July 7 camped at a place now within the city limits of Denver. They pushed on along the divide between the Platte and the Arkansas, passing near the strange area of eroded rocks called the Garden of the Gods. The morning of July 11 found them on Bijou Fork, near present-day Sidney, Colorado.

kept up a running fight for some time, animated by the bear charging among the horses. He did not fall until after he had received six rifle balls. He was miserably poor, and added nothing to our stock of provisions.

We followed the stream to its head in a broken ridge, which, according to the barometer, was about seven thousand five hundred feet above the sea. This is a piny elevation into which the prairies are gathered, and from which the waters flow in almost every direction to the Arkansas, Platte, and Kansas rivers, the latter stream having here its remotest sources. Although somewhat rocky and broken, and covered with pines, in comparison with the neighboring mountains it scarcely forms an interruption to the great prairie plains which sweep up to their bases.

We had an excellent view of Pike's Peak from this camp, at the distance of forty miles. This mountain barrier presents itself to travelers on the plains, which sweep almost directly to its bases; an immense and comparatively smooth and grassy prairie, in very strong contrast with the black masses of timber, and the glittering snow above them. . . .

With occasional exceptions, comparatively so very small as not to require mention, these prairies are everywhere covered with a close and vigorous growth of a great variety of grasses, among which the most abundant is the buffalo grass (*Sesleria dactyloides*). Between the Platte and Arkansas rivers, that part of this region which forms the basin drained by the waters of the Kansas, with which our operations made us more particularly acquainted, is based upon a formation of calcareous rocks.

The soil of all this country is excellent, admirably adapted to agricultural purposes, and would support a large agricultural and pastoral population. The plain is watered by many streams. Throughout its western half these are shallow with sandy beds, becoming deeper as they reach the richer lands approaching the Missouri River; they generally have bottom lands bordered by bluffs varying from fifty to five hundred feet in height. In all this region the timber is entirely confined to the streams. In the eastern half, where the soil is a deep, rich vegetable mold, retentive of rain and moisture, it is of vigorous growth, and of many different kinds; and throughout the western half it consists entirely of various species of cottonwood, which deserves to be called the tree of the desert—growing in sandy soils, where no other tree will grow; pointing out the existence of water, and furnishing to the traveler fuel, and food for his animals. Add to this that the western border of the plain is occupied by the Sioux, Arapaho, and Cheyenne nations, and its eastern limits by the Pawnees and other half-civilized tribes for whom the intermediate country is a war ground, and a tolerably correct idea can be formed of the appearance and condition of the country.

Descending a somewhat precipitous and rocky hillside among the pines, which rarely appear elsewhere than on the ridge, we encamped at its foot, where there were several springs, which make one of the extreme sources of the Smoky Hill Fork of the Kansas. From this place the view extended over the Arkansas Valley, and the Spanish peaks in the south beyond. As the greater part of the men continued sick, I encamped here for the day, and ascertained conclusively, from experiments on myself, that their illness was caused by the meat of the buffalo bull.

On the summit of the ridge, near the camp, were several rock-built forts, which in front were very difficult of approach, and in the rear were protected by a precipice entirely beyond the reach of a rifle ball. The evening was tolerably clear, with a temperature at sunset of 63°. Elevation of the camp, seven thousand three hundred feet.

Turning the next day to the southwest, we reached, in the course of the morning, the wagon road to the settlements on the Arkansas River, and encamped in the afternoon on the Fontaine-Qui-bouit (or Boiling Spring) River,[9] where it was fifty feet wide, with a swift current. I afterward found that the spring and river owe their names to the bubbling of the effervescing gas in the former, and not to the temperature of the water, which is cold. During the morning a tall species of *Gilia*, with a slender white flower, was characteristic; and in the latter part of the day, another variety of esparcette (wild clover), having the flower white, was equally so. We had a fine sunset of golden-brown; and in the evening, a very bright moon, with the near mountains, made a beautiful scene. Thermometer, at sunset, was 69°, and our elevation above the sea five thousand eight hundred feet.

July 13th. The morning was clear, with a northwesterly breeze, and the thermometer at sunrise at 46°. There were no clouds along the mountains, and the morning sun showed very clearly their rugged character.

We resumed our journey very early down the river, following an extremely good lodge trail, which issues by the head of this stream from the Bayou Salade, a high mountain valley behind Pike's Peak. The soil along the road was sandy and gravelly, and the river well timbered.

We halted at noon under the shade of some fine large cotton-woods, our animals luxuriating on rushes (*Equisetum hyemale*), which along this river were remarkably abundant. A variety of cactus made its appearance, and among several strange plants were numerous and beautiful clusters of a plant resembling *Mirabilis jalapa,* with a handsome convolvulus I had not hitherto seen (*Calystegia*).

In the afternoon we passed near the encampment of a hunter named Maurice, who had been out on the plains in pursuit of buffalo calves, a number of which I saw among some domestic cattle near his lodge. Shortly afterward, a party of mountaineers galloped up to us—fine-looking and hardy men, dressed in skins and mounted on good, fat horses; among them were several Connecticut men, a portion of Wyeth's party, whom I had seen the year before, and others were men from the Western States.

Continuing down the river, we encamped at noon on the 14th at its mouth, on the Arkansas River. A short distance above our encampment, on the left bank of the Arkansas, is a pueblo [10] (as the Mexicans call their civilized Indian villages), where a number of mountaineers, who had married Spanish women in the valley of Taos, had collected together and occupied themselves in farming, carrying on at the same time a desultory Indian trade. They were principally Americans, and treated us with all the rude hospitality their situation admitted; but as all commercial intercourse with New Mexico was now interrupted, in consequence of Mexican decrees to that effect, there was nothing to be had in the way of provisions. They had, however, a fine stock of cattle, and furnished us an abundance of excellent milk. I learned here that Maxwell, in company with two other men, had started for Taos on the morning of the 9th, but that he would probably fall into the hands of the Utah Indians, commonly called Spanish Utes.

As Maxwell had no knowledge of their being in the vicinity when he crossed the Arkansas, his chance of escape was very doubtful; but I did not entertain much apprehension for his life, having great confidence in his prudence and courage. I was further informed that there had been a popular tumult among the pueblos, or civilized Indians residing near Taos, against the "foreigners" of that place, in which they had plundered their houses and ill-treated their families. Among those whose property had been destroyed was Mr. Beaubien, father-in-law of Maxwell, from whom I had expected to obtain supplies, and who had been obliged to make his escape to Santa Fe.

By this position of affairs our expectation of obtaining supplies from Taos was cut off. I had here the satisfaction to meet our good buffalo-hunter of 1842, Christopher Carson, whose services I considered myself fortunate to secure again; and as a reinforcement of mules was absolutely necessary, I despatched him immediately, with an account of our necessities, to Mr. Charles Bent,[11] whose principal post is on the Arkansas River, about seventy-five miles below Fontaine-Qui-bouit. He was directed to proceed from that post by the nearest route across the country, and meet me with what animals he should be able to obtain at St. Vrain's Fort. I also admitted into the party Charles Towns—a native of St. Louis, a serviceable man, with many of the qualities of a good voyageur.

According to our observations, the latitude of the mouth of the river is 38° 15′ 23″, its longitude 104° 58′ 30″, and its elevation above the sea four thousand eight hundred and eighty feet.

On the morning of the 16th, the time for Maxwell's arrival having expired, we resumed our journey, leaving for him a note in which it was stated that I would wait for him at St. Vrain's Fort until the morning of the 26th, in the event that he should succeed in his commission. Our direction was up the Boiling Spring River, it being my intention to visit the celebrated springs from which the river takes its name, and which are on its upper waters at the foot of Pike's Peak.[12]

Our animals fared well while we were on this stream, there being everywhere a great abundance of *prêle. Ipomea leptophylla,* in bloom, was a characteristic plant along the river, generally in large bunches, with two to five flowers on each. Beautiful clusters of the plant resembling *Mirabilis jalapa* were numerous, and *Glycyrrhiza lepidota* was a characteristic of the bottoms. Currants, nearly ripe, were abundant, and among the shrubs which covered the bottom was a very luxuriant growth of chenopodiaceous shrubs four to six feet high.

On the afternoon of the 17th we entered among the broken ridges at the foot of the mountains, where the river made several forks. Leaving the camp to follow slowly, I rode ahead in the afternoon in search of the springs. In the meantime the clouds, which had been gathered all the afternoon over the mountains, began to roll down their sides, and a storm so violent burst upon me that it appeared I had entered the storehouse of the thunderstorms.

I continued, however, to ride along up the river until about sunset, and was beginning to be doubtful of finding the springs before the next day when I came suddenly upon a large, smooth rock, about twenty yards in diameter, where the water from several springs was bubbling and boiling up in the midst of a white incrustation with which it had covered a portion of the rock. As this did not correspond with a description given me by the hunters, I did not stop to taste the water, but dismounting, walked a little way up the river, and, passing through a narrow thicket of shrubbery bordering the stream, stepped directly upon a huge white rock, at the foot of which the river, already become a torrent, foamed along, broken by a small fall.

A deer which had been drinking at the spring was startled by my approach and, springing across the river, bounded off up the mountain. In the upper part of the rock, which had apparently been formed by deposition, was a beautiful white basin, overhung by current bushes, in which the cold, clear water bubbled up, kept in constant motion by the escaping gas, and overflowing the rock, which it had almost entirely covered with a smooth crust of glistening white. I had all day refrained from drinking, reserving myself for the spring; and as I could not well be more wet than the rain had already made me, I lay down by the side of the basin, and drank heartily of the delightful water. . . . A beautiful spot, immediately at the foot of lofty mountains, beautifully timbered, which sweep closely round, shutting up the little valley in a kind of cove. As it was beginning to grow dark, I rode quickly down the river, on which I found the camp a few miles below.

The morning of the 18th was beautiful and clear, and, all the people being anxious to drink of these famous waters, we encamped immediately at the springs, and spent there a very pleasant day. On the opposite side of the river is another locality of springs, which are entirely of the same nature. The water has a very agreeable taste, which Mr. Preuss found very much to resemble that of the famous Seltzer Springs, in the Grand Duchy Nassau, a country famous for wine and mineral waters; and it is almost of entirely of the same character, though still more agreeable than that of the famous Beer Springs, near Bear River of the Great Salt Lake. . . .*

July 19th. A shaft of the gun carriage was broken in the afternoon; and we made an early halt, the stream being from twelve to twenty feet wide, with clear water. As usual, the clouds had gathered to a storm over the mountains, and we had a showery evening. At sunset the thermometer stood at 62°, and our elevation above the sea was six thousand five hundred and thirty feet.

July 20th. This morning (as we generally found the mornings under these mountains) was very clear and beautiful, and the air cool and pleasant, with the thermometer at 44°. We continued our march up the stream, between pine hills on the one hand and the main Black Hills on the other, along a green sloping bottom, toward the ridge which separates the waters of the Platte from those of the Arkansas.

As we approached the dividing ridge, the whole valley was radiant with flowers; blue, yellow, pink, white, scarlet, and purple vied with each other in splendor. Esparcet was one of the highly characteristic plants, and a bright-looking flower (*Gaillardia aristata*) was very frequent; but the most abundant plant along our road today was *Geranium maculatum*, which is the characteristic plant on this portion of the dividing grounds.

Crossing to the waters of the Platte, fields of blue flax added to the magnificence of this mountain garden; this was occasionally four feet in height, which was a luxuriance of growth that I rarely

---

* Some material on Frémont's chemical analysis of an incrustation left by the spring, and on the geological formations near by, is omitted.

saw this almost universal plant attain throughout the journey. Continuing down a branch of the Platte, among high and very steep timbered hills, covered with fragments of rock, toward evening we issued from the piny region, and made a late encampment near Poundcake Rock, on that fork of the river which we had ascended on July 8th. Our animals enjoyed the abundant rushes this evening, as the flies were so bad among the pines that they had been much harassed. A deer was killed here this evening; and again the evening was overcast, and a collection of brilliant red clouds in the west was followed by the customary squall of rain.

Achillea millefolium (milfoil) was among the characteristic plants of the river bottoms today. This was one of the most common plants during the whole of our journey, occurring in almost every variety of situation. I noticed it on the lowlands of the rivers, near the coast of the Pacific, and near to the snow among the mountains of the Sierra Nevada.

During this excursion we had surveyed to its head one of the two principal branches of the Upper Arkansas, seventy-five miles in length, and entirely completed our survey of the South Fork of the Platte to the extreme sources of that portion of the river which belongs to the plains and heads in the broken hills of the Arkansas dividing ridge at the foot of the mountains. That portion of its waters which were collected among these mountains it was hoped to explore on our homeward voyage.

Reaching St. Vrain's Fort on the morning of the 23d, we found Mr. Fitzpatrick and his party in good order and excellent health, and with him my true and reliable friend Kit Carson, who had brought ten good mules with the necessary pack saddles.

Mr. Fitzpatrick, who had often endured every extremity of want during the course of his mountain life, and knew well the value of provisions in this country, had watched over our stock with jealous vigilance, and there was an abundance of flour, rice, sugar, and coffee in the camp; and again we fared luxuriously. Meat was, however, very scarce; and two very small pigs, which we obtained at the fort, did not go far among forty men. Mr. Fitzpatrick had been here a week, during which time his men had been occupied in refitting the camp; and the repose had been very beneficial to his animals, which were now in tolerably good condition.

I had been able to obtain no certain information in regard to the character of the passes in this portion of the Rocky Mountain Range,[13] which had always been represented as impracticable for carriages, but the exploration of which was incidentally contemplated with the view of finding some convenient point of passage for the road of emigration, which would enable it to reach, on a more direct line, the usual ford of the Great Colorado—a place considered as determined by the nature of the country beyond that river. It is singular that, immediately at the foot of the mountains, I could find no one sufficiently acquainted with them to guide us to the plains at their western base; but the race of trappers who formerly lived in their recesses has almost entirely disappeared— dwindled to a few scattered individuals, some one or two of whom are regularly killed in the course of each year by the Indians.

It will be remembered that in the previous year, I brought with me to their village, near this post, and hospitably treated on the way, several Cheyenne Indians whom I had met on the Lower Platte. Shortly after their arrival here, these were out with a party of Indians (themselves the principal men), which discovered a few trappers in the neighboring mountains, whom they immediately murdered, although one of them had been nearly thirty years in the country, and was perfectly well known, as he had grown gray among them.

Through this portion of the mountains, also, are the customary roads of the war parties going out against the Utah and Shoshone Indians [14]; and occasionally parties from the Crow nation make their way down to the southward along this chain, in the expectation of surprising some straggling lodges of their enemies. Shortly before our arrival, one of their parties had attacked an Arapaho village in the vicinity, which they had found unexpectedly strong; and their assault was turned into a rapid flight, and a hot pursuit, in which they had been compelled to abandon the animals they had ridden, and escape on their war horses.

Into this uncertain and dangerous region small parties of three or four trappers who now could collect together rarely ventured; and consequently it was seldom visited and little known. Having determined to try the passage by a pass through a spur of the mountains made by the Câche à la Poudre River, which rises in the high bed of mountains around Long's Peak, I thought it advisable to avoid any encumbrance which would occasion detention, and accordingly again separated the party into two divisions—one of which, under the command of Mr. Fitzpatrick, was directed to cross the plains to the mouth of the Laramie River, and, continuing thence its route along the usual emigrant road, meet me at Fort Hall, a post belonging to the Hudson's Bay Company, and situated on Snake River, as it is commonly called in the Oregon territory, although better known to us as Lewis' Fork of the Columbia. The latter name is there restricted to one of the upper forks of the river.

Our Delaware Indians having determined to return to their homes, it became necessary to provide this party with a good hunter; and I accordingly engaged in that capacity Alexander Godey,[15] a young man about twenty-five years of age, who had been in this country six or seven years, all of which time he had been actively employed in hunting for the support of the posts, or in solitary trading expeditions among the Indians.

In courage and professional skill he was a formidable rival to Carson, and constantly afterwards was among the best and most efficient of the party, and in difficult situations was of incalculable value. Hiram Powers, one of the men belonging to Mr. Fitzpatrick's party, was discharged at this place.

A French *engagé* at Lupton's Fort had been shot in the back on July 4th, and died during our absence to the Arkansas. The wife of the murdered man, an Indian woman of the Snake nation, desirous, like Naomi of old, to return to her people, requested and obtained permission to travel with my party to the neighborhood of Bear River, where she expected to meet with some of their villages. Happier than the Jewish widow, she carried with her two children, pretty little half-breeds, who added much to the liveliness of the camp. Her baggage was carried on five or six pack horses, and I gave her a small tent, for which I no longer had any use, as I had procured a lodge at the fort.

For my own party I selected the following men, a number of whom old associations rendered agreeable to me:

Charles Preuss, Christopher Carson, Basil Lajeunesse, François Badeau, Jean Baptiste Bernier, Louis Ménard, Raphael Proue,

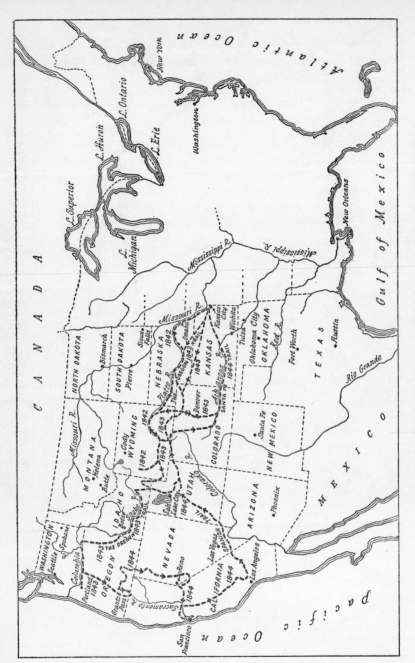

The First and Second Far Western Explorations, 1842 and 1843–1844

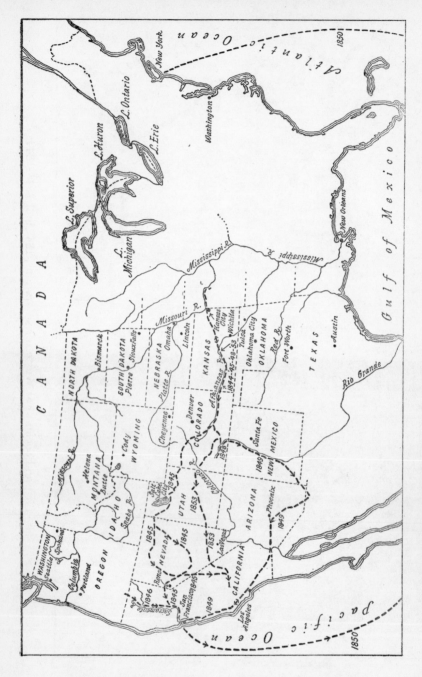

The Third, Fourth, and Fifth Far Western Expeditions, 1845–1846, 1848–1849, and 1853
(Frémont Wrote an Account Only of the 1845–1846 Expedition.)

Jacob Dodson, Louis Zindel, Henry Lee, Jean Baptiste Derosier, François Lajeunesse, and Auguste Vasquez.

By observation, the latitude of the post is 40° 16' 33" and its longitude 105° 12' 23", depending, with all the other longitudes along this portion of the line, upon a subsequent occultation of September 13, 1843, to which they are referred by the chronometer.

Its distance from Kansas Landing, by the road we traveled (which, it will be remembered, was very winding along the Lower Kansas River), was seven hundred and fifty miles. The rate of the chronometer, determined by observations at this place for the interval of our absence, during this month, was 33.72", which you will hereafter see did not sensibly change during the ensuing month, and remained nearly constant during the remainder of our journey across the continent. This was the rate used in referring to St. Vrain's Fort, the longitude between that place and the mouth of the Fontaine-Qui-bouit.

Our various barometrical observations, which are better worthy of confidence than the isolated determination of 1842, give, for the elevation of the fort above the sea, four thousand nine hundred and thirty feet. The barometer here used was also a better one, and less liable to derangement.

At the end of two days, which was allowed to my animals for necessary repose, all the arrangements had been completed, and on the afternoon of the 26th we resumed our respective routes. Some little trouble was experienced in crossing the Platte, the waters of which were still kept up by rains and melting snow; and, having traveled only about four miles, we encamped in the evening on Thompson's Creek, where we were very much disturbed by mosquitoes.

The following days we continued our march westward over comparative plains, and, fording the Câche à la Poudre on the morning of the 28th, entered the Black Hills,* and nooned on this stream in the mountains beyond them. Passing over a fine large bottom in the afternoon, we reached a place where the river was shut up in the hills; and, ascending a ravine, made a laborious and very difficult passage around by a gap, striking the river again about dusk. A little labor, however, would remove this difficulty, and render the

---

* The Laramie Range north of present-day Laramie, Wyoming.

road to this point a very excellent one. The evening closed in dark, with rain, and the mountains looked gloomy.

July 29th. Leaving our encampment about seven in the morning, we traveled until three in the afternoon along the river, which, for this distance of about six miles, runs directly through a spur of the main mountains.

We were compelled by the nature of the ground to cross the river eight or nine times at difficult, deep, and rocky fords, the stream running with great force, swollen by the rains—a true mountain torrent, only forty or fifty feet wide. It was a mountain valley of the narrowest kind—almost a chasm; and the scenery very wild and beautiful. . . .*

August 1st. The beautiful plants of yesterday reappeared occasionally; flax in bloom occurred during the morning, and esparcet in luxuriant abundance was a characteristic of the stony ground in the afternoon. The camp was roused into a little excitement by a chase after a buffalo bull, and an encounter with a war party of Sioux and Cheyenne Indians about thirty strong. Hares and antelope were seen during the day, and one of the latter was killed. The Laramie Peak was in sight this afternoon. The evening was clear, with scattered clouds; temperature 62°. The day's journey was twenty-six miles.

August 2d. Temperature at sunrise 52°, and scenery and weather made our road today delightful. The neighboring mountain is thickly studded with pines, intermingled with the brighter foliage of aspens, and occasional spots like lawns between the patches of snow among the pines, and here and there on the heights. Our route below lay over a comparative plain covered with the same brilliant vegetation, and the day was clear and pleasantly cool.

During the morning we crossed many streams, clear and rocky, and broad grassy valleys, of a strong black soil washed down from the mountains and producing excellent pasturage. These were timbered with the red willow and long-leaved cottonwood, mingled

---

* The material here omitted records some dry details of what Frémont calls "the uninteresting country between Laramie Hills and the Sweet Water Valley"; an area already touched in the first expedition. On July 31 the expedition, to its great relief, emerged on the Laramie River, within sight of the Medicine Bow Mountains. These lie west and northwest of the city of Laramie in southeastern Wyoming (Carbon County).

with aspen, as we approached the mountain more nearly toward noon. Esparcet was a characteristic, and flax occurred frequently in bloom. We halted at noon on the most western fork of Laramie River—a handsome stream about sixty feet wide and two feet deep, with clear water and a swift current over a bed composed entirely of boulders or roll stones. There was a large open bottom here, on which were many lodge poles lying about; and in the edge of the surrounding timber were three strong forts that appeared to have been recently occupied.

At this place I became first acquainted with the yampa (*Anethum graveolens*), which I found our Snake woman engaged in digging in the low-timbered bottom of the creek. Among the Indians along the Rocky Mountains, and more particularly among the Shoshone or Snake Indians, in whose territory it is very abundant, this is considered the best among the roots used for food. To us it was an interesting plant—a little link between the savage and civilized life. Here, among the Indians, its root is a common article of food, which they take pleasure in offering to strangers; while with us, in a considerable portion of America and Europe, the seeds are used to flavor soup. It grows more abundantly and in greater luxuriance on one of the neighboring tributaries of the Colorado than in any other part of this region; and on that stream, to which the Snakes are accustomed to resort every year to procure a supply of their favorite plant, they have bestowed the name of Yampa River. Among the trappers it is generally known as Little Snake River; but in this and other instances where it illustrated the history of the people inhabiting the country, I have preferred to retain the aboriginal name.[16]

In the afternoon we took our way directly across the spurs from the point of the mountain, where we had several ridges to cross; and, although the road was not rendered bad by the nature of the ground, it was made extremely rough by the stiff, tough bushes of *Artemisia tridentata*,* in this country commonly called sage. This shrub now began to make its appearance in compact fields; and we

---

* The greater portion of our subsequent journey was through a region where this shrub constituted the tree of the country; and as it will often be mentioned in occasional descriptions, the word *artemisia* only will be used, without the specific name. [Frémont's note.]

were about to quit for a long time this country of excellent pasturage and brilliant flowers.

Ten or twelve buffalo bulls were seen during the afternoon, and we were surprised by the appearance of a large red ox. We gathered around him as if he had been an old acquaintance, with all our domestic feelings as much awakened as if we had come in sight of an old farmhouse. He had probably made his escape from some party of emigrants on Green River; and, with a vivid remembrance of some old green field, he was pursuing the straightest course for the frontier that the country admitted. We carried him along with us as a prize; and when it was found in the morning that he had wandered off, I would not let him be pursued, for I would rather have gone through a starving time of three entire days than let him be killed after he had successfully run the gantlet so far among the Indians.

I have been told by Mr. Bent's people of an ox, born and raised at St. Vrain's Fort, which made his escape from them at Elm Grove, near the frontier, having come in that year with the wagons. They were on their way out, and saw occasionally places where he had eaten and lain down to rest; but did not see him for about seven hundred miles, when they overtook him on the road, traveling along to the fort, having unaccountably escaped Indians and every other mischance.

We encamped at evening on the principal fork of Medicine Bow River, near to an isolated mountain called the Medicine Butte, which appeared to be about eighteen hundred feet above the plain, from which it rises abruptly, and was still white, nearly to its base, with a great quantity of snow. The streams were timbered with the long-leaved cottonwood and red willow, and during the afternoon a species of onion was very abundant.

I obtained here an immersion of the first satellite of Jupiter, which, corresponding very nearly with the chronometer, placed us in longitude 106° 47′ 25″. The latitude, by observation, was 41° 37′ 16″; elevation above the sea seven thousand eight hundred feet, and distance from St. Vrain's Fort one hundred and forty-seven miles.

August 3d. There was a white frost last night; the morning is clear and cool. We were early on the road, having breakfasted before sunrise, and in a few miles' travel entered the pass of the

Medicine Butte, through which led a broad trail which had been recently traveled by a very large party. Immediately in the pass the road was broken by ravines, and we were obliged to clear a way through groves of aspens, which generally made their appearance when we reached elevated regions. According to the barometer this was eight thousand three hundred feet; and while we were detained in opening a road, I obtained a meridional observation of the sun, which gave 41° 35′ 48″ for the latitude of the pass. The Medicine Butte is isolated by a small tributary of the North Fork of the Platte, but the mountains approach each other very nearly, the stream running at their feet. On the south they are smooth, with occasional streaks of pine; but the butte itself is ragged, with escarpments of red feldspathic granite, and dark with pines, the snow reaching from the summit to within a few hundred feet of the trail.

The granite here was more compact and durable than that in the formation which we had passed through a few days before to the eastward of Laramie. Continuing our way over a plain on the west side of the pass, where the road was terribly rough with artemisia, we made our evening encampment on the creek, where it took a northern direction, unfavorable to the course we were pursuing.

Bands of buffalo were discovered as we came down upon the plain, and Carson brought into the camp a cow which had the fat on the fleece two inches thick. Even in this country of rich pasturage and abundant game it is rare that the hunter chances upon a finer animal. Our voyage had already been long, but this was the first good buffalo meat we had obtained. We traveled today twenty-six miles.

August 4th. The morning was clear and calm; and, leaving the creek, we traveled toward the North Fork of the Platte, over a plain which was rendered rough and broken by ravines. With the exception of some thin grasses the sandy soil here was occupied almost exclusively by artemisia, with its usual turpentine odor. We had expected to meet with some difficulty in crossing the river, but happened to strike it where there was a very excellent ford, and halted at noon on the left bank, two hundred miles from St. Vrain's Fort.

The hunters brought in pack animals loaded with fine meat. According to our imperfect knowledge of the country, there should have been a small affluent to this stream a few miles higher up; and in the afternoon we continued our way among the river hills, in the expectation of encamping upon it in the evening. The ground proved to be so exceedingly difficult, broken up into hills, terminating in escarpments and broad ravines five or six hundred feet deep, with sides so precipitous that we could scarcely find a place to descend, that, toward sunset, I turned directly in toward the river, and, after nightfall, entered a sort of ravine. We were obliged to feel our way and clear a road in the darkness, the surface being much broken, and the progress of the carriages being greatly obstructed by the artemisia, which had a luxuriant growth of four to six feet in height.

We had scrambled along this gully for several hours, during which we had knocked off the carriage lamps, broken a thermometer and several small articles, when, fearing to lose something of more importance, I halted for the night at ten o'clock. Our animals were turned down toward the river, that they might pick up what little grass they could find; and after a little search some water was found in a small ravine, and improved by digging. We lighted up the ravine with fires of artemisia, and about midnight sat down to a supper which we were hungry enough to find delightful, although the buffalo meat was crusted with sand and the coffee was bitter with the wormwood taste of the artemisia leaves.

A successful day's hunt had kept our hunters occupied until late, and they slept out, but rejoined us at daybreak, when, finding ourselves only about a mile from the river, we followed the ravine down, and camped in a cottonwood grove on a beautiful grassy bottom, where our animals indemnified themselves for the scanty fare of the past night. It was quite a pretty and pleasant place; a narrow strip of prairie about five hundred yards long terminated at the ravine where we entered by high precipitous hills closing in upon the river, and at the upper end by a ridge of low, rolling hills.

In the precipitous bluffs were displayed a succession of strata containing fossil vegetable remains and several beds of coal. In some of the beds the coal did not appear to be perfectly mineralized, and in some of the seams it was compact and remarkably lustrous. In these latter places there were, also, thin layers of a very fine white salts, in powder.

As we had a large supply of meat in the camp, which it was necessary to dry, and the surrounding country appeared to be well stocked with buffalo, which it was probable, after a day or two, we would not see again until our return to the Mississippi waters, I determined to make here a provision of dried meat, which would be necessary for our subsistence in the region we were about entering, which was said to be nearly destitute of game. Scaffolds were accordingly soon erected, fires made, and the meat cut into thin slices to be dried, and all were busily occupied, when the camp was thrown into a sudden tumult by a charge from about seventy mounted Indians, over the low hills at the upper end of the little bottom.

Fortunately, the guard, who was between them and our animals, had caught a glimpse of an Indian's head, as he raised himself in his stirrups to look over the hill, a moment before he made the charge, and succeeded in turning the band into the camp, as the Indians charged into the bottom with the usual yell. Before they reached us, the grove on the verge of the little bottom was occupied by our people, and the Indians brought to a sudden halt, which they made in time to save themselves from a howitzer shot, which would, undoubtedly, have been very effective in such a compact body, and further proceedings were interrupted by their signs for peace. They proved to be a war party of Arapaho and Cheyenne Indians, and informed us that they had charged upon the camp under the belief that we were hostile Indians, and had discovered their mistake only at the moment of the attack—an excuse which policy required us to receive as true, though under the full conviction that the display of our little howitzer and our favorable position in the grove certainly saved our horses, and probably ourselves, from their marauding intentions. They had been on a war party, and had been defeated, and were, consequently, in a state of mind which aggravates their innate thirst for plunder and blood. Their excuse, however, was taken in good part, and the usual evidences of friendship interchanged. The pipe went round, provisions were spread, and the tobacco and goods furnished the customary presents, which they look for even from traders, and much more from Government authorities.

They were returning from an expedition against the Shoshone

Indians, one of whose villages they had surprised, at Bridger's Fort, on Ham's Fork of Green River (in the absence of the men, who were engaged in an antelope surround), and succeeded in carrying off their horses, and taking several scalps. News of the attack reached the Snakes immediately, who pursued and overtook them, and recovered their horses; and, in the running fight which ensued, the Arapahoes had lost several men killed, and a number wounded, who were coming on more slowly with a party in the rear. Nearly all the horses they had brought off were the property of the whites at the fort. After remaining until nearly sunset, they took their departure; and the excitement which their arrival had afforded subsided into our usual quiet, a little enlivened by the vigilance rendered necessary by the neighborhood of our uncertain visitors. At noon the thermometer was at 75°, at sunset 70°, and the evening clear. Elevation above the sea, six thousand eight hundred and twenty feet; latitude 41° 36′ 00″; longitude 107° 22′ 27″.

August 6th. At sunrise the thermometer was at 46°, the morning being clear and calm. We traveled today over an extremely rugged country, barren and uninteresting—nothing to be seen but artemisia bushes, and in the evening, found a grassy spot among the hills, kept green by several springs, where we encamped late. Within a few hundred yards was a very pretty little stream of clear cool water, whose green banks looked refreshing among the dry rocky hills. The hunters brought in a fat mountain sheep (*Ovis montana*).

Our road the next day was through a continued and dense field of artemisia, which now entirely covered the country in such a luxuriant growth that it was difficult and laborious for a man on foot to force his way through, and nearly impracticable for our light carriages. The region through which we were traveling was a high plateau, constituting the dividing ridge between the waters of the Atlantic and Pacific oceans, and extending to a considerable distance southward, from the neighborhood of the Table Rock, at the southern side of the South Pass. Though broken up into rugged and rocky hills of a dry and barren nature, it has nothing of a mountainous character, the small streams which occasionally occur belonging neither to the Platte nor the Colorado, but losing themselves either in the sand or in small lakes.

From an eminence, in the afternoon, a mountainous range became visible in the north, in which were recognized some rocky peaks belonging to the range of the Sweet Water Valley; and, determining to abandon any further attempt to struggle through this almost impracticable country, we turned our course directly north, toward a pass in the valley of the Sweet Water River. A shaft of the gun carriage was broken during the afternoon, causing a considerable delay; and it was late in an unpleasant evening before we succeeded in finding a very poor encampment, where there was a little water in a deep trench of a creek, and some scanty grass among the shrubs. All the game here consisted in a few straggling buffalo bulls, and during the day there had been but very little grass, except in some green spots where it had collected around springs or shallow lakes. Within fifty miles of the Sweet Water, the country changed into a vast saline plain, in many places extremely level, occasionally resembling the flat sandy beds of shallow lakes. Here the vegetation consisted of a shrubby growth, among which were several varieties of chenopodiaceous plants; but the characteristic shrub was *Fremontia vermicularis,* with smaller saline shrubs growing with singular luxuriance, and in many places holding exclusive possession of the ground.

On the evening of the 8th, we encamped on one of these freshwater lakes, which the traveler considers himself fortunate to find; and the next day, in latitude by observation 42° 20′ 06″, halted to noon immediately at the foot of the southern side of the range which walls in the Sweet Water Valley, on the head of a small tributary to that river.

Continuing in the afternoon our course down the stream, which here cuts directly through the ridge, forming a very practicable pass, we entered the valley, and, after a march of about nine miles, encamped on our familiar river, endeared to us by the acquaintance of the previous expedition; the night having already closed in with a cold rainstorm. Our camp was about twenty miles above the Devil's Gate, which we had been able to see in coming down the plain; and, in the course of the night, the clouds broke away around Jupiter for a short time, during which we obtained an immersion of the first satellite, the result of which agreed very nearly with the chronometer, giving for the mean longitude 107° 50′ 07″, elevation above the sea, six thousand and forty feet, and distance from St.

Vrain's Fort, by the road we had just traveled, three hundred and fifteen miles.

Here passes the road to Oregon; and the broad, smooth highway, where the numerous heavy wagons of the emigrants had entirely beaten and crushed the artemisia was a happy exchange to our poor animals for the sharp rocks and tough shrubs among which they had been toiling so long; and we moved up the valley rapidly and pleasantly. With very little deviation from our route of the preceding year, we continued up the valley, and on the evening of the 12th, encamped on the Sweet Water, at a point where the road turns off to cross to the plains of Green River. The increased coolness of the weather indicated that we had attained a great elevation, which the barometer here placed at seven thousand two hundred and twenty feet; and during the night water froze in the lodge.

The morning of the 13th was clear and cold, there being a white frost; and the thermometer, a little before sunrise, standing at 26.5°. Leaving this encampment (our last on the waters which flow toward the rising sun) we took our way along the upland, toward the dividing ridge which separates the Atlantic from the Pacific waters, and crossed it by a road some miles farther south than the one we had followed on our return in 1842. We crossed very near the Table Mountain, at the southern extremity of the South Pass, which is near twenty miles in width and already traversed by several different roads.

Selecting as well as I could, in the scarcely distinguishable ascent, what might be considered the dividing ridge in this remarkable depression in the mountain, I took a barometrical observation, which gave seven thousand four hundred and ninety feet for the elevation above the Gulf of Mexico.[17] On my visit of the preceding year, I estimated the elevation of this pass at about seven thousand feet; a correct observation with a good barometer enables me now to give it with more precision. Its importance, as the great gate through which commerce and traveling may hereafter pass between the valley of the Mississippi and the North Pacific, justifies a precise notice of its locality and distance from leading points, in addition to this statement of its elevation. Its latitude at the point where we crossed is 42° 24′ 32″, its longitude, 109° 26′ 00″, its distance from the mouth of the Kansas, by the common traveling route, nine hundred and sixty-two miles; from the mouth of the Great Platte, along the valley of that river, according to our previous survey, eight hundred and eighty-two miles; and its distance from St. Louis about four hundred miles more by the Kansas, and about seven hundred by the Great Platte route—these additions being steamboat conveyance in both instances. From this pass to the mouth of the Oregon is about one thousand six hundred miles by the common traveling route; so that, under a general point of view, it may be assumed to be about halfway between the Mississippi and the Pacific Ocean on the common traveling route.

Following a hollow of slight and easy descent, in which was very soon formed a little tributary to the Gulf of California (for the waters which flow west from the South Pass go to this gulf), we made our usual halt four miles from the pass, in latitude by observation 42° 19′ 53″. Entering here the valley of Green River—the great Colorado of the West—and inclining very much to the southward along the streams which form the Sandy River, the road led for several days over dry and level uninteresting plains, to which a low, scrubby growth of artemisia gave a uniform dull, grayish color; and on the evening of the 15th we encamped in the Mexican territory, on the left bank of the Green River, sixty-nine miles from the South Pass, in longitude 110° 05′ 05″ and latitude 41° 53′ 54″, distant one thousand and thirty-one miles from the mouth of the Kansas. This is the emigrant road to Oregon, which bears much to the southward to avoid the mountains about the western heads of Green River—the Rio Verde of the Spaniards.[18]

August 16th. Crossing the river, here about four hundred feet wide, by a very good ford, we continued to descend for seven or eight miles on a pleasant road along the right bank of the stream, of which the islands and shores are handsomely timbered with cottonwood. The refreshing appearance of the broad river, with its timbered shores and green-wooded islands, in contrast to its dry sandy plains, probably obtained for it the name of Green River, which was bestowed on it by the Spaniards, who first came into this country to trade some twenty-five years ago. It was then familiarly known as the Seeds-kedée-agie, or Prairie Hen (*Tetrao urophasianus*) River, a name which is received from the Crows, to whom its upper waters belong, and on which this bird is still very abundant.

By the Shoshone and Utah Indians, to whom belongs, for a considerable distance below, the country where we were now traveling, it was called the Bitterroot River, from the great abundance in its valley of a plant which affords them one of their favorite roots. Lower down, from Brown's Hole to the southward, the river runs through lofty chasms, walled in by precipices of red rock; and even among the wilder tribes who inhabit that portion of its course I have heard it called by Indian refugees from the Californian settlements, the Rio Colorado.

We halted to noon at the upper end of a large bottom, near some old houses, which had been a trading post, in latitude 41° 46′ 54″. At this place the elevation of the river above the sea is six thousand two hundred and thirty feet; that of Lewis' Fork of the Columbia at Fort Hall is, according to our subsequent observations, four thousand five hundred feet. The descent of each stream is rapid, but that of the Colorado is but little known, and that little derived from vague report. Three hundred miles of its lower part, as it approaches the Gulf of California, is reported to be smooth and tranquil; but its upper part is manifestly broken into many falls and rapids. From many descriptions of trappers, it is probable that in its foaming course among its lofty precipices it presents many scenes of wild grandeur; and though offering many temptations, and often discussed, no trappers have been found bold enough to undertake a voyage which has so certain a prospect of a fatal termination. The Indians have strange stories of beautiful valleys abounding with beaver, shut up among inaccessible walls of rock in the lower course of the river; and to which the neighboring Indians, in their occasional wars with the Spaniards, and among themselves, drive their herds of cattle and flocks of sheep, leaving them to pasture in perfect security.

The road here leaves the river, which bends considerably to the east; and in the afternoon we resumed our westerly course, passing over a somewhat high and broken country; and about sunset, after a day's travel of twenty-six miles, reached Black's Fork of the Green River [19]—a shallow stream, with a somewhat sluggish current, about one hundred and twenty feet wide, timbered principally with willow, and here and there an occasional large tree.

At three in the morning I obtained an observation of an emersion of the first satellite of Jupiter, with other observations. The heavy wagons have so completely pulverized the soil that clouds of fine light dust are raised by the slightest wind, making the road sometimes very disagreeable.

August 17th. Leaving our encampment at six in the morning, we traveled along the bottom, which is about two miles wide, bordered by low hills, in which the strata contained handsome and very distinct vegetable fossils. . . .*

August 18th. We passed on the road this morning the grave of one of the emigrants, being the second we had seen since falling into their trail; and halted to noon on the river a short distance above. The Shoshone woman took leave of us here, expecting to find some of her relations at Bridger's Fort, which is only a mile or two distant, on a fork of this stream. In the evening we encamped on a salt creek, about fifteen feet wide, having today traveled thirty-two miles. I obtained an emersion of the first satellite under favorable circumstances, the night being still and clear.

One of our mules died here, and in this portion of our journey we lost six or seven of our animals. The grass which the country had lately afforded was very poor and insufficient; and animals which have been accustomed to grain become soon weak, and unable to labor, when reduced to no other nourishment than grass. The American horses (as those are usually called which are brought to this country from the States) are not of any serviceable value until after they have remained a winter in the country, and become accustomed to live entirely on grass.

August 19th. Desirous to avoid every delay not absolutely necessary, I sent on Carson in advance to Fort Hall this morning, to make arrangements for a small supply of provisions. A few miles from our encampment the road entered a high ridge, which the trappers called the "little mountain," connecting the Utah with the Wind River chain; and in one of the hills near which we passed I remarked strata of a conglomerate formation, fragments of which were scattered over the surface. We crossed a ridge of this conglomerate, the road passing near a grove of low cedar, and descended upon one of the heads of Ham's Fork, called Muddy, where we made our midday halt.

In the river hills at this place I discovered strata of fossiliferous

* Some geological detail is here omitted.

rock having an oölitic structure, which, in connection with the neighboring strata, authorizes us to believe that here, on the west side of the Rocky Mountains, we find repeated the modern formations of Great Britain and Europe, which have hitherto been wanting to complete the system of North American geology.

In the afternoon we continued our road, and, searching among the hills a few miles up the stream, and on the same bank, I discovered among alternating beds of coal and clay a stratum of white indurated clay containing very clear and beautiful impressions of vegetable remains. This was the most interesting fossil locality I had met in the country, and I deeply regretted that time did not permit me to remain a day or two in the vicinity; but I could not anticipate the delays to which I might be exposed in the course of our journey—or, rather, I knew that they were many and inevitable —and after remaining here only about an hour, I hurried off, loaded with as many specimens as I could conveniently carry. Coal made its appearance occasionally in the hills during the afternoon, and was displayed in rabbit burrows in a kind of gap, through which we passed over some high hills, and we descended to make our encampment on the same stream, where we found but very poor grass.

In the evening a fine cow with her calf, which had strayed off from some emigrant party, were found several miles from the road and brought into camp; and as she gave an abundance of milk, we enjoyed tonight an excellent cup of coffee. We traveled today twenty-eight miles and, as has been usual since crossing the Green River, the road has been very dusty and the weather smoky and oppressively hot. Artemisia was characteristic among the few plants.

August 20th. We continued to travel up the creek by a very gradual ascent and a very excellent grassy road, passing on the way several small forks of the stream. The hills here are higher, presenting escarpments of particolored and apparently clay rocks—purple, dark-red, and yellow—containing strata of sandstone and limestone with shells, with a bed of cemented pebbles, the whole overlaid by beds of limestone. The alternation of red and yellow gives a bright appearance to the hills, one of which was called by our people the Rainbow Hill; and the character of the country became more agreeable, and traveling far more pleasant, as now we found timber and very good grass. Gradually ascending, we reached the lower level of a bed of white limestone, lying upon a white clay, on the upper line of which the whole road is abundantly supplied with beautiful cool springs, gushing out a foot in breadth and several inches deep, directly from the hillside.

At noon we halted at the last main fork of the creek, at an elevation of seven thousand two hundred feet, and in latitude, by observation, 41° 39′ 45″; and in the afternoon continued on the same excellent road, up the left or northern fork of the stream, toward its head, in a pass which the barometer placed at eight thousand two hundred and thirty feet above the sea. This is a connecting ridge between the Utah or Bear River Mountains and the Wind River chain of the Rocky Mountains, separating the waters of the Gulf of California on the east, and those on the west belonging more directly to the Pacific, from a vast interior basin whose rivers are collected into numerous lakes having no outlet to the ocean. From the summit of this pass, the highest which the road crosses between the Mississippi and the western ocean, our view was over a very mountainous region, whose rugged appearance was greatly increased by the smoky weather, through which the broken ridges were dark and dimly seen. The ascent to the summit of the gap was occasionally steeper than the National Road in the Alleghanies; and the descent, by way of a spur on the western side, is rather precipitous, but the pass may still be called a good one. Some thickets of willow in the hollows below deceived us into the expectation of finding a camp at our usual hour at the foot of the mountain; but we found them without water, and continued down a ravine, and encamped about dark at a place where the springs again began to make their appearance, but where our animals fared badly, the stock of the emigrants having grazed the grass as completely as if we were again in the midst of the buffalo.

August 21st. An hour's travel this morning brought us into the fertile and picturesque valley of Bear River, the principal tributary to the Great Salt Lake.[20] The stream is here two hundred feet wide, fringed with willows and occasional groups of hawthorns. We were now entering a region which for us possessed a strange and extraordinary interest. We were upon the waters of the famous lake which forms a salient point among the remarkable geographical features of the country, and around which the vague and superstitious accounts of the trappers had thrown a delightful obscurity, which we anticipated pleasure in dispelling, but which, in the meantime, left a crowded field for the exercise of our imagination. In our occasional conversations with the few old hunters who had visited the region, it had been a subject of frequent speculation; and the wonders which they related were not the less agreeable because they were highly exaggerated and impossible.

Hitherto this lake had been seen only by trappers who were wandering through the country in search of new beaver streams, caring very little for geography; its islands had never been visited; and none were to be found who had entirely made the circuit of its shores; and no instrumental observations, or geographical survey of any description, had ever been made anywhere in the neighboring region. It was generally supposed that it had no visible outlet; but among the trappers, including those in my own camp, were many who believed that somewhere on its surface was a terrible whirlpool, through which its waters found their way to the ocean by some subterranean communication. All these things had made a frequent subject of discussion in our desultory conversations around the fires at night; and my own mind had become tolerably well filled with their indefinite pictures, and insensibly colored with their romantic descriptions, which, in the pleasure of excitement, I was well disposed to believe, and half expected to realize.

Where we descended into this beautiful valley it is three to four miles in breadth, perfectly level, and bounded by mountainous ridges, one above another, rising suddenly from the plain. The emigrant road passes along a portion of the river, which in its character of level bottoms, enclosed between abrupt mountains, presents a type of the streams of this region.

We continued our road down the river, and at night encamped with a family of emigrants—two men, women, and several children— who appeared to be bringing up the rear of the great caravan. I was struck with the fine appearance of their cattle, some six or eight yoke of oxen, which really looked as well as if they had been all the summer at work on some good farm. It was strange to see one small family traveling alone through such a country, so remote from civilization. Some nine years since, such a security might have been a fatal one; but since their disastrous defeats in the country a little north, the Blackfeet have ceased to visit these waters. Indians, however, are very uncertain in their localities; and the friendly feelings, also, of those now inhabiting it may be changed.

According to barometrical observation at noon, the elevation of the valley was six thousand four hundred feet above the sea; and our encampment at night in latitude 42° 03′ 47″ and longitude 111° 10′ 53″, by observation—the day's journey having been twenty-six miles. This encampment was therefore within the territorial limit of the United States, our traveling, from the time we entered the valley of the Green River on August 15th, having been to the south of the forty-second degree of North Latitude, and consequently on Mexican territory; and this is the route all the emigrants now travel to Oregon.* The temperature at sunset was 65°; and at evening there was a distant thunderstorm, with a light breeze from the north. Antelope and elk were seen during the day on the opposite prairie; and there were ducks and geese in the river.

The next morning, in about three miles from our encampment, we reached Smith's Fork,[21] a stream of clear water, about fifty feet in breadth. It is timbered with cottonwood, willow, and aspen, and makes a beautiful debouchment through a pass about six hundred yards wide, between remarkable mountain hills, rising abruptly on either side, and forming gigantic columns to the gate by which it enters Bear River Valley. The bottoms, which below Smith's Fork had been two miles wide, narrowed, as we advanced, to a gap five hundred yards wide; and during the greater part of the day we had a winding route, the river making very sharp and sudden bends, the mountains steep and rocky, and the valley occasionally so narrow as only to leave space for a passage through. We made our halt at noon in a fertile bottom, where the common blue flax was growing abundantly, a few miles below the mouth of Thomas' Fork, one of the larger tributaries of the river.

Crossing, in the afternoon, the point of a narrow spur, we descended into a beautiful bottom, formed by a lateral valley, which presented a picture of home beauty that went directly to our hearts. The edge of the wood, for several miles along the river, was dotted with the white covers of emigrant wagons, collected in groups at different camps, where the smokes were rising lazily from the fires, around which the women were occupied in preparing the evening

* The party had crossed from present-day Wyoming into present-day Idaho, and had camped just north of the present Utah boundary.

meal, and the children playing in the grass; and herds of cattle, grazing about in the bottom, had an air of quiet security and civilized comfort that made a rare sight for the traveler in such a remote wilderness.

In common with all the emigration, they had been reposing for several days in this delightful valley, in order to recruit their animals on its luxuriant pasturage after their long journey, and prepare them for the hard travel along the comparatively sterile banks of the Upper Columbia. At the lower end of this extensive bottom the river passes through an open cañon where there were high vertical rocks to the water's edge, and the road here turns up a broad valley to the right. It was already near sunset; but, hoping to reach the river again before night, we continued our march along the valley, finding the road tolerably good, until we arrived at a point where it crosses the ridge by an ascent of a mile in length, which was so very steep and difficult for the gun and carriage that we did not reach the summit until dark.

It was absolutely necessary to descend into the valley for water and grass, and we were obliged to grope our way in the darkness down a very steep, bad mountain, reaching the river at about ten o'clock. It was late before our animals were gathered into camp, several of those which were very weak being necessarily left to pass the night on the ridge; and we sat down again to a midnight supper. The road, in the morning, presented an animated appearance. We found that we had encamped near a large party of emigrants, and a few miles below another body was already in motion. Here the valley had resumed its usual breadth, and the river swept off along the mountains on the western side, the road continuing directly on.

In about an hour's travel we met several Shoshone Indians, who informed us that they belonged to a large village which had just come into the valley from the mountains to the westward, where they had been hunting antelope, and gathering serviceberries. Glad at the opportunity of seeing one of their villages, and in the hope of purchasing from them a few horses, I turned immediately off into the plain toward their encampment, which was situated on a small stream near the river.

We had approached within something more than a mile of the village when suddenly a single horseman emerged from it at full speed, followed by another, and another, in rapid succession; and then party after party poured into the plain, until, when the foremost rider reached us, all the whole intervening plain was occupied by a mass of horsemen, which came charging down upon us with guns and naked swords, lances, and bows and arrows—Indians entirely naked, and warriors fully dressed for war, with the long red streamers of their war bonnets reaching nearly to the ground—all mingled together in the bravery of savage warfare. They had been thrown into a sudden tumult by the appearance of our flag, which, among these people, is regarded as an emblem of hostility, it being usually borne by the Sioux, and the neighboring mountain Indians, when they come here to war; and we had accordingly been mistaken for a body of their enemies. A few words from the chief quieted the excitement; and the whole band, increasing every moment in number, escorted us to their encampment, where the chief pointed out a place for us to encamp near his own lodge, and made known our purpose in visiting the village.

In a very short time we purchased eight horses, for which we gave in exchange blankets, red and blue cloth, beads, knives, and tobacco, and the usual other articles of Indian traffic. We obtained from them also a considerable quantity of berries of different kinds, among which serviceberries were the most abundant; and several kinds of roots and seeds, which we could eat with pleasure, as any kind of vegetable food was gratifying to us.

I ate here, for the first time, the *kooyah,* or tobaccoroot (*Valeriana edulis*), the principal edible root among the Indians who inhabit the upper waters of the streams on the western side of the mountains. It has a very strong and remarkably peculiar taste and odor, which I can compare to no other vegetable that I am acquainted with, and which to some persons is extremely offensive. It was characterized by Mr. Preuss as the most horrid food he had ever put in his mouth; and when, in the evening, one of the chiefs sent his wife to me with a portion which she had prepared as a delicacy to regale us, the odor immediately drove him out of the lodge; and frequently afterward he used to beg that when those who liked it had taken what they desired, it might be sent away. To others, however, the taste is rather an agreeable one, and I was afterward always glad when it formed an addition to our scanty meals. It is full of nutriment; and in its unprepared state is said by the Indians to have very strong poisonous qualities, of which it is deprived by a peculiar process, being baked in the ground for about two days.

The morning of the 24th was disagreeably cool, with an easterly wind and very smoky weather. We made a late start from the village, and regaining the road (on which, during all the day, were scattered the emigrant wagons), we continued on down the valley of the river, bordered by high and mountainous hills, on which fires are seen at the summit.

The soil appears generally good, although, with the grasses, many of the plants are dried up, probably on account of the great heat and want of rain. The common blue flax of cultivation, now almost entirely in seed—only a scattered flower here and there remaining—is the most characteristic plant of the Bear River Valley. When we encamped at night on the right bank of the river, it was growing as in a sown field. We had traveled during the day twenty-two miles, encamping in latitude (by observation) 42° 36′ 56″, chronometric longitude 111° 42′ 05″.

In our neighborhood, the mountains appeared extremely rugged, giving still greater value to this beautiful natural pass.

August 25th. This was a cloudless but smoky autumn morning, with a cold wind from the southeast, and a temperature of forty-five degrees at sunrise. In a few miles I noticed, where a little stream crossed the road, fragments of scoriated basalt scattered about—the first volcanic rock we had seen, and which now became a characteristic rock along our future road. In about six miles' travel from our encampment, we reached one of the points in our journey to which we had always looked forward with great interest—the famous Beer Springs.[22] It is a basin of mineral waters enclosed by the mountains, which sweep around a circular bend of Bear River here, at its most northern point, and which from a northern, in the course of a few miles acquires a southern, direction toward the Great Salt Lake.

A pretty little stream of clear water enters the upper part of the basin from an open valley in the mountains and, passing through the bottom, discharges into Bear River. Crossing this stream, we descended a mile below, and made our encampment in a grove of cedar immediately at the Beer Springs, which, on account of the effervescing gas and acid taste, have received their name from the voyageurs and trappers of the country, who, in the midst of their rude and hard lives, are fond of finding some fancied resemblance to the luxuries they rarely have the fortune to enjoy.

Although somewhat disappointed in the expectations which various descriptions had led me to form of unusual beauty of situation and scenery, I found it altogether a place of very great interest; and a traveler for the first time in a volcanic region remains in a constant excitement, and at every step is arrested by something remarkable and new. There is a confusion of interesting objects gathered together in a small space. Around the place of encampment the Beer Springs were numerous; but, as far as we could ascertain, were entirely confined to that locality in the bottom. In the bed of the river, in front, for a space of several hundred yards, they were very abundant, the effervescing gas rising up and agitating the water in countless bubbling columns. In the vicinity round about were numerous springs of an entirely different and equally marked mineral character.

In a rather picturesque spot, about thirteen hundred yards below our encampment, and immediately on the riverbank, is the most remarkable spring of the place. In an opening on the rock, a white column of scattered water is thrown up, in form like a jet d'eau, to a variable height of about three feet, and, though it is maintained in a constant supply, its greatest height is attained only at regular intervals, according to the action of the force below. It is accompanied by a subterranean noise, which, together with the motion of the water, makes very much the impression of a steamboat in motion; and, without knowing that it had been already previously so called, we gave to it the name of the Steamboat Spring. The rock through which it is forced is slightly raised in a convex manner, and gathered at the opening into an urn-mouthed form, and is evidently formed by continued deposition from the water, and colored bright red by oxide of iron. . . . *

It is a hot spring, and the water has a pungent and disagreeable metallic taste, leaving a burning effect on the tongue. Within perhaps two yards of the jet d'eau is a small hole of about an inch in

---

* A chemical analysis of the rock, which Frémont found to be 92.55% carbonate of lime, omitted.

diameter, through which, at regular intervals, escapes a blast of hot air with a light wreath of smoke, accompanied by a regular noise. This hole had been noticed by Dr. Wislizenus, a gentleman who several years since passed by this place, and who remarked, with very nice observation, that smelling the gas which issued from the orifice produced a sensation of giddiness and nausea.

Mr. Preuss and myself repeated the observation, and were so well satisfied with its correctness that we did not find it pleasant to continue the experiment, as the sensation of giddiness which it produced was certainly strong and decided. A huge emigrant wagon, with a large and diversified family, had overtaken us and halted to noon at our encampment; and, while we were sitting at the spring, a band of boys and girls, with two or three young men, came up, one of whom I asked to stoop down and smell the gas, desirous to satisfy myself further of its effects. But his natural caution had been awakened by the singular and suspicious features of the place, and he declined my proposal decidedly, adding a few indistinct remarks about the devil, whom he seemed to consider the genius loci. The ceaseless motion and the play of the fountain, the red rock, and the green trees near, make this a picturesque spot.

A short distance above the spring, and near the foot of the same spur, is a very remarkable yellow-colored rock, soft and friable, consisting principally of carbonate of lime and oxide of iron, of regular structure, which is probably a fossil coral. The rocky bank along the shore between the Steamboat Spring and our encampment, along which is dispersed the water from the hills, is composed entirely of strata of a calcareous tufa, with the remains of moss and reedlike grasses, which is probably the formation of springs.

The Beer or Soda Springs, which have given name to this locality, are agreeable, but less highly flavored than the Boiling Springs at the foot of Pike's Peak, which are of the same character. They are very numerous, and half hidden by tufts of grass, which we amused ourselves in removing and searching about for more highly impregnated springs. They are some of them deep and of various sizes —sometimes several yards in diameter, and kept in constant motion by columns of escaping gas. By analysis, one quart of the water contains as follows:

	Grains
Sulphate of magnesia..................	12.10
Sulphate of lime......................	2.12
Carbonate of lime.....................	3.86
Carbonate of magnesia.................	3.22
Chloride of calcium...................	1.33
Chloride of magnesium.................	1.12
Chloride of sodium....................	2.24
Vegetable extractive matter, etc......	0.85
	26.84

The carbonic acid originally contained in the water had mainly escaped before it was subjected to analysis, and it was not therefore taken into consideration.

In the afternoon I wandered about among the cedars, which occupy the greater part of the bottom toward the mountains. The soil here has a dry and calcined appearance; in some places, the open grounds are covered with saline efflorescences, and there are a number of regularly shaped and very remarkable hills, which are formed of a succession of convex strata that have been deposited by the waters of extinct springs, the orifices of which are found on their summits, some of them having the form of funnel-shaped cones.

Others of these remarkably shaped hills are of a red-colored earth, entirely bare, and composed principally of carbonate of lime, with oxide of iron, formed in the same manner. Walking near one of them, on the summit of which the springs were dry, my attention was attracted by an underground noise, around which I circled repeatedly until I found the spot from beneath which it came, and, removing the red earth, discovered a hidden spring, which was boiling up from below, with the same disagreeable metallic taste as the Steamboat Spring.

Continuing up the bottom, and crossing the little stream which has been already mentioned, I visited several remarkable red and white hills, which had attracted my attention from the road in the morning. These are immediately upon the stream, and, like those already mentioned, are formed by the deposition of successive strata from the springs. On their summits, the orifices through which the waters had been discharged were so large that they resembled miniature craters, being some of them several feet in diameter, circular, and regularly formed as if by art. At a former time, when these dried-up fountains were all in motion, they must have made a beautiful display on a grand scale; and nearly all this basin appears to me to have been formed under their action, and should be called the Place of Fountains.

At the foot of one of these hills, or rather on its side near the base, are several of these small limestone columns, about one foot in diameter at the base and tapering upward to a height of three or four feet; and on the summit the water is boiling up and bubbling over, constantly adding to the height of the little obelisks. In some, the water only boils up, no longer overflowing, and has here the same taste as the Steamboat Spring. The observer will remark a gradual subsidence in the water which formerly supplied the fountains, as on all the summits of the hills the springs are now dry, and are found only low down upon their sides or on the surrounding plain.

A little higher up the creek, its banks are formed by strata of a very heavy and hard scoriaceous basalt, having a bright metallic luster when broken. The mountains overlooking the plain are of an entirely different geological character. Continuing on, I walked to the summit of one of them, where the principal rock was a granular quartz. Descending the mountains, and returning toward the camp along the base of the ridge which skirts the plain, I found at the foot of a mountain spur, and issuing from a compact rock of a dark-blue color, a great number of springs having the same pungent and disagreeably metallic taste already mentioned, the water of which was collected into a very remarkable basin, whose singularity, perhaps, made it appear to me very beautiful. It is large —perhaps fifty yards in circumference; and in it the water is contained at an elevation of several feet above the surrounding ground by a wall of calcareous tufa, composed principally of the remains of mosses, three or four, and sometimes ten feet high. The water within is very clear and pure, and three or four feet deep, where it could be conveniently measured near the wall; and, at a considerably lower level, is another pond or basin of very clear water, and apparently of considerable depth, from the bottom of which the gas was escaping in bubbling columns at many places. This water was collected into a small stream which, in a few hundred yards, sank under ground, reappearing among the rocks between the two great springs near the river, which it entered by a little fall.

Late in the afternoon I set out on my return to the camp, and, crossing in the way a large field of a salt that was several inches deep, found on my arrival that our emigrant friends, who had been encamped in company with us, had resumed their journey, and the road had again assumed its solitary character.

The temperature of the largest of the Beer Springs at our encampment was 65° at sunset, that of the air being 62.5°. Our barometric observation gave five thousand eight hundred and forty feet for the elevation above the Gulf, being about five hundred feet lower than the Boiling Springs, which are of a similar nature, at the foot of Pike's Peak. The astronomical observations gave for our latitude 42° 39′ 57″, and 111° 46′ 00″ for the longitude. The night was very still and cloudless, and I sat up for an observation of the first satellite of Jupiter, the emersion of which took place about midnight, but fell asleep at the telescope, awaking just a few minutes after the appearance of the star.

The morning of the 26th was calm, and the sky without clouds, but smoky; and the temperature at sunrise 28.5°. At the same time, the temperature of the large Beer Spring, where we encamped, was 56°; that of the Steamboat Spring 87°; and that of the steam hole near it, 81.5°. In the course of the morning the last wagons of the emigration passed by, and we were again left in our place in the rear.

Remaining in camp until nearly eleven o'clock, we traveled a short distance down the river, and halted to noon on the bank at a point where the road quits the valley of Bear River, and, crossing a ridge which divides the Great Basin from the Pacific waters, reaches Fort Hall by way of the Portneuf River in a distance of probably fifty miles, or two and a half days' journey for wagons.

An examination of the great lake which is the outlet of this river, and the principal feature of geographical interest in the basin, was one of the main objects contemplated in the general plan of our survey; and I accordingly determined at this place to leave the road, and, after having completed a reconnaissance of the lake, regain it subsequently at Fort Hall. But our little stock of provisions had again become extremely low; we had only dried meat sufficient for one meal, and our supply of flour and other comforts was entirely exhausted. I therefore immediately despatched one of the party, Henry Lee, with a note to Carson, at Fort Hall, directing him to load a pack horse with whatever could be obtained there in the way of provisions, and endeavor to overtake me on the river.

In the meantime, we had picked up along the road two tolerably well-grown calves, which would have become food for wolves, and which had probably been left by some of the earlier emigrants, none of those we had met having made any claim to them; and on these I mainly relied for support during our circuit to the lake.

In sweeping around the point of the mountain which runs down into the bend, the river here passes between perpendicular walls of basalt, which always fix the attention, from the regular form in which it occurs and its perfect distinctness from the surrounding rocks among which it has been placed. The mountain, which is rugged and steep, and, by our measurement, one thousand four hundred feet above the river directly opposite the place of our halt, is called the Sheep Rock—probably because a flock of the common mountain sheep (*Ovis montana*) had been seen on the craggy point.

As we were about resuming our march in the afternoon I was attracted by the singular appearance of an isolated hill with a concave summit, in the plain, about two miles from the river, and turned off toward it while the camp proceeded on its way to the southward in search of the lake. I found the thin and stony soil of the plain entirely underlaid by the basalt which forms the river walls; and when I reached the neighborhood of the hill, the surface of the plain was rent into frequent fissures and chasms of the same scoriated volcanic rock, from forty to sixty feet deep, but which there was not sufficient light to penetrate entirely, and which I had not time to descend. Arrived at the summit of the hill, I found that it terminated in a very perfect crater, of an oval or nearly circular form, three hundred and sixty paces in circumference, and sixty feet at the greatest depth. The walls, which were perfectly vertical and disposed like masonry in a very regular manner, were composed of a brown-colored scoriaceous lava, evidently the production of a modern volcano, and having all the appearance of the lighter scoriaceous lavas of Mount Etna, Vesuvius, and other volcanoes. The faces of the walls were reddened and glazed by the fire in which they had been melted, and which had left them contorted and twisted by its violent action.

Our route during the afternoon was a little rough, being (in the direction we had taken) over a volcanic plain, where our progress was sometimes obstructed by fissures, and black beds, composed of fragments of the rock. On both sides the mountains appeared very broken, but tolerably well timbered.

August 26th. Crossing a point of ridge which makes in to the river, we fell upon it again before sunset, and encamped on the right bank, opposite to the encampment of three lodges of Snake Indians.[23] They visited us during the evening, and we obtained from them a small quantity of roots of different kinds in exchange for goods. Among them was a sweet root of very pleasant flavor, having somewhat the taste of preserved quince. My endeavors to become acquainted with the plants which furnish to the Indians a portion of their support were only gradually successful, and after long and persevering attention, and even after obtaining, I did not succeed in preserving them until they could be satisfactorily determined.

In this portion of the journey I found this particular root cut up into such small pieces that it was only to be identified by its taste, when the bulb was met with in perfect form among the Indians lower down on the Columbia, among whom it is the highly celebrated camass. It was long afterward, on our return through Upper California, that I found the plant itself in bloom, which I supposed to furnish the camass root (*Camassia esculenta*). The root diet had a rather mournful effect at the commencement, and one of the calves was killed this evening for food. The animals fared well on rushes.

August 27th. The morning was cloudy, with appearance of rain, and the thermometer at sunrise at 29°. Making an unusually early start, we crossed the river at a good ford and, following for about three hours a trail which led along the bottom, we entered a labyrinth of hills below the main ridge and halted to noon in the ravine of a pretty little stream, timbered with cottonwood of large size, ash-leaved maple, with cherry and other shrubby trees. The hazy weather, which had prevented any very extended views since entering the Green River Valley, began now to disappear. There was a slight rain in the earlier part of the day, and at noon, when the thermometer had risen to 79.5°, we had a bright sun, with blue sky and scattered cumuli. According to the barometer, our halt here among the hills was at an elevation of five thousand three hundred and twenty feet.

Crossing a dividing ridge in the afternoon, we followed down another little Bear River tributary to the point where it emerged on an open green flat among the hills, timbered with groves and bordered with canethickets, but without water. A pretty little rivulet, coming out of the hillside and overhung by tall flowering plants of a species I had not hitherto seen, furnished us with a good camping place. The evening was cloudy, the temperature at sunset 69°, and the elevation five thousand one hundred and forty feet.

Among the plants occurring along the line of road during the day, épinet des prairies (*Grindelia squarrosa*) was in considerable abundance, and is among the very few plants remaining in bloom—the whole country having now an autumnal appearance, in the crisped and yellow plants and dried-up grasses. Many cranes were seen during the day, with a few antelope, very shy and wild.

August 28th. During the night we had a thunderstorm, with moderate rain, which has made the air this morning very clear, the thermometer being at 55.°. Leaving our encampment at the Cane Spring and quitting the trail on which we had been traveling, and which would probably have afforded us a good road to the lake, we crossed some very deep ravines, and in about an hour's traveling again reached the river. We were now in a valley five or six miles wide, between mountain ranges which, about thirty miles below, appeared to close up and terminate the valley, leaving for the river only a very narrow pass, or cañon, behind which we imagined that we should find the broad waters of the lake.

We made the usual halt at the mouth of a small clear stream, having a slightly mineral taste (perhaps of salt), four thousand seven hundred and sixty feet above the gulf. In the afternoon we climbed a very steep sandy hill; and after a slow and winding day's march of twenty-seven miles encamped at a slough on the river. There were great quantities of geese and ducks, of which only a few were shot, the Indians having probably made them very wild.

The men employed themselves in fishing, but caught nothing. A skunk (*Mephitis Americana*) which was killed in the afternoon made a supper for one of the messes. The river is bordered occasionally with fields of cane, which we regarded as an indication of our approach to a lake country. We had frequent showers of rain during the night, with thunder.

August 29th. The thermometer at sunrise was 54°, with air from the northwest, and dark rainy clouds moving on the horizon; rain squalls and bright sunshine by intervals. I rode ahead with Basil to explore the country, and, continuing about three miles along the river, turned directly off on a trail running toward three marked gaps in the bordering range, where the mountains appeared cut through to their bases, toward which the river plain rose gradually.

Putting our horses into a gallop on some fresh tracks which showed very plainly in the wet path, we came suddenly upon a small party of Shoshone Indians who had fallen into the trail from the north. We could only communicate by signs; but they made us understand that the road through the chain was a very excellent one, leading into a broad valley which ran to the southward. We halted to noon at what may be called the gate of the pass, on either side of which were huge mountains of rock, between which stole a little pure-water stream, with a margin just sufficiently large for our passage. From the river the plain had gradually risen to an altitude of five thousand five hundred feet, and by meridian observation the latitude of the entrance was 42°.

In the interval of our usual halt several of us wandered along up the stream to examine the pass more at leisure. Within the gate the rocks receded a little back, leaving a very narrow but most beautiful valley, through which the little stream wound its way, hidden by different kinds of trees and shubs—aspen, maple, willow, cherry, and elder; a fine verdure of smooth, short grass spread over the remaining space to the bare sides of the rocky walls. These were of blue limestone, which constitutes the mountain here; and opening directly on the grassy bottom were several curious caves, which appeared to be inhabited by root-diggers. On one side was gathered a heap of leaves for a bed, and they were dry, open and pleasant. On the roofs of the caves I remarked bituminous exudations from the rock.

The trail was an excellent one for pack horses; but as it sometimes crossed a shelving point, to avoid the shrubbery we were
obliged in several places to open a road for the carriage through
the wood. A squaw on horseback, accompanied by five or six dogs,
entered the pass in the afternoon, but was too much terrified at
finding herself in such unexpected company to make any pause
for conversation, and hurried off at a good pace—being of course no
further disturbed than by an accelerating shout. She was well and
showily dressed, and was probably going to a village encamped
somewhere near, and evidently did not belong to the tribe of root-
diggers.[24]

We had now entered a country inhabited by these people; and
as in the course of our voyage we shall frequently meet with them
in various stages of existence, it will be well to remark that, scattered over the great region west of the Rocky Mountains and south
of the Great Snake River, are numerous Indians whose subsistence
is almost solely derived from roots and seeds, and such small animals as chance and great good fortune sometimes bring within their
reach. They are miserably poor, armed only with bows and arrows,
or clubs; and as the country they inhabit is almost destitute of
game, they have no means of obtaining better arms. In the northern
part of the region just mentioned they live generally in solitary
families; and farther to the south they are gathered together in
villages.

Those who live together in villages, strengthened by association,
are in exclusive possession of the more genial and richer parts of
the country, while the others are driven to the ruder mountains
and to the more inhospitable parts of the country. But simply observing, in accompanying us along our road, will give to the reader
a better knowledge of these people than I could give in any other
than a very lengthened description.

Roots, seeds, and grass, every vegetable that affords any nourishment, and every living animal thing, insect or worm, they eat.
Nearly approaching to the lower animal creation, their sole employment is to obtain food; and they are constantly occupied in a
struggle to support existence.

The most remarkable feature of the pass is the Standing Rock,
which has fallen from the cliffs above, and standing perpendicularly

near the middle of the valley, presents itself like a watchtower in the pass. It will give a tolerably correct idea of the character of the scenery in this country, where generally the mountains rise abruptly up from comparatively unbroken plains and level valleys; but it will entirely fail in representing the picturesque beauty of this delightful place, where a green valley, full of foliage and a hundred yards wide, contrasts with naked crags that spire up into a blue line of pinnacles three thousand feet above, sometimes crested with cedar and pine, and sometimes ragged and bare.

The detention that we met with in opening the road, and perhaps a willingness to linger on the way, made the afternoon's travel short; and about two miles from the entrance we passed through another gate, and encamped on the stream at the junction of a little fork from the southward, around which the mountains stooped more gently down, forming a small open cove.

As it was still early in the afternoon, Basil and myself in one direction, and Mr. Preuss in another, set out to explore the country, and ascended different neighboring peaks in the hope of seeing some indications of the lake; but though our elevation afforded magnificent views, the eye ranging over a long extent of Bear River, with the broad and fertile Cache Valley, in the direction of our search was only to be seen a bed of apparently impracticable mountains. Among these the trail we had been following turned sharply to the northward, and it began to be doubtful if it would not lead us away from the object of our destination; but I nevertheless determined to keep it, in the belief that it would eventually bring us right. A squall of rain drove us out of the mountain, and it was late when we reached the camp. The evening closed in with frequent showers of rain, with some lightning and thunder.

August 30th. We had constant thunderstorms during the night, but in the morning the clouds were sinking to the horizon, and the air was clear and cold, with the thermometer at sunrise at 39°. Elevation by barometer five thousand five hundred and eighty feet. We were in motion early, continuing up the little stream without encountering any ascent where a horse would not easily gallop, and, crossing a slight dividing ground at the summit, descended upon a small stream, along which we continued on the same excellent road. In riding through the pass numerous cranes were seen; and prairie hens, or grouse (*Bonasia umbellus*), which lately had been rare, were very abundant.

This little affluent brought us to a larger stream, down which we traveled through a more open bottom, on a level road where heavily laden wagons could pass without obstacle. The hills on the right grew lower, and, on entering a more open country, we discovered a Shoshone village; and being desirous to obtain information and purchase from them some roots and berries, we halted on the river, which was lightly wooded with cherry, willow, maple, serviceberry, and aspen.

A meridian observation of the sun which I obtained here gave 42° 14' 22" for our latitude, and the barometer indicated a height of five thousand one hundred and seventy feet. A number of Indians came immediately over to visit us, and several men were sent to the village with goods, tobacco, knives, cloth, vermilion, and the usual trinkets, to exchange for provisions. But they had no game of any kind; and it was difficult to obtain any roots from them, as they were miserably poor and had but little to spare from their winter stock of provisions. Several of the Indians drew aside their blankets, showing me their lean and bony figures; and I would not any longer tempt them with a display of our merchandise to part with their wretched subsistence, when they gave as a reason that it would expose them to temporary starvation.

A great portion of the region inhabited by this nation formerly abounded in game, the buffalo ranging about in herds, as we had found them on the eastern waters, and the plains dotted with scattered bands of antelope; but so rapidly have they disappeared within a few years, that now, as we journeyed along, an occasional buffalo skull and a few wild antelope were all that remained of the abundance which had covered the country with animal life.[25]

The extraordinary rapidity with which the buffalo is disappearing from our territories will not appear surprising when we remember the great scale on which their destruction is yearly carried on. With inconsiderable exceptions, the business of the American trading posts is carried on in their skins; every year the Indian villages make new lodges, for which the skin of the buffalo furnishes the material; and in that portion of the country where they are still found, the Indians derive their entire support from them, and slaughter them with a thoughtless and abominable extravagance. Like the Indians themselves, they have been a characteristic of the great West; and as, like them, they are visibly diminishing, it will be interesting to throw a glance backward through the last twenty years, and give some account of their former distribution through the country and the limit of their western range.

The information is derived principally from Mr. Fitzpatrick, supported by my own personal knowledge and acquaintance with the country. Our knowledge does not go farther back than the spring of 1824, at which time the buffalo were spread in immense numbers over the Green River and Bear River valleys, and through all the country lying between the Colorado, or Green River of the Gulf of California, and Lewis' Fork of the Columbia River, the meridian of Fort Hall then forming the western limit of their range.

The buffalo then remained for many years in that country, and frequently moved down the valley of the Columbia, on both sides of the river, as far as the Fishing Falls. Below this point they never descended in any numbers. About the year 1834 or 1835 they began to diminish very rapidly, and continued to decrease until 1838 or 1840, when, with the country we have just described, they entirely abandoned all the waters of the Pacific north of Lewis' Fork of the Columbia. At that time the Flathead Indians were in the habit of finding their buffalo on the heads of Salmon River and other streams of the Columbia; but now they never meet with them farther west than the three forks of the Missouri, or the plains of the Yellowstone River.

In the course of our journey it will be remarked that the buffalo have not so entirely abandoned the waters of the Pacific, in the Rocky Mountain region south of the Sweet Water, as in the country north of the Great Pass. This partial distribution can only be accounted for in the great pastoral beauty of that country, which bears marks of having long been one of their favorite haunts, and by the fact that the white hunters have more frequented the northern than the southern region—it being north of the South Pass that the hunters, trappers, and traders have had their rendezvous for many years past; and from that section also the greater portion of the beaver and rich furs were taken, although always the most dangerous, as well as the most profitable, hunting ground.

In that region lying between the Green or Colorado River and the headwaters of the Rio del Norte, over the Yampa, Kooyah, White, and Grand Rivers—all of which are the waters of the Colorado—the buffalo never extended so far to the westward as they did on the waters of the Columbia; and only in one or two instances have they been known to descend as far west as the mouth of White River.

In traveling through the country west of the Rocky Mountains, observations readily led me to the impression that the buffalo had for the first time crossed that range to the waters of the Pacific only a few years prior to the period we are considering; and in this opinion I am sustained by Mr. Fitzpatrick and the older trappers in that country.

In the region west of the Rocky Mountains we never meet with any of the ancient vestiges which, throughout all the country lying upon their eastern waters, are found in the great highways, continuous for hundreds of miles, always several inches and sometimes several feet in depth, which the buffalo have made in crossing from one river to another, or in traversing the mountain ranges. The Snake Indians, more particularly those low down upon Lewis' Fork, have always been very grateful to the American trappers for the great kindness (as they frequently expressed it) which they did to them in driving the buffalo so low down the Columbia River.

The extraordinary abundance of the buffalo on the east side of the Rocky Mountains, and their extraordinary diminution, will be made clearly evident from the following statement: At any time between the years 1824 and 1836 a traveler might start from any given point, south or north, in the Rocky Mountain Range, journeying by the most direct route to the Missouri River, and during the whole distance his road would be always among large bands of buffalo, which would never be out of his view until he arrived almost within sight of the abodes of civilization.

At this time the buffalo occupy but a very limited space, principally along the eastern base of the Rocky Mountains, sometimes extending at their southern extremity to a considerable distance into the plains between the Platte and Arkansas rivers, and along the eastern frontier of New Mexico as far south as Texas.

The following statement, which I owe to the kindness of Mr.

Sanford, a partner in the American Fur Company, will further illustrate this subject, by extensive knowledge acquired during several years of travel through the region inhabited by the buffalo:

The total amount of robes annually traded by ourselves and others will not be found to differ much from the following statement:

	Robes
American Fur Company	70,000
Hudson's Bay Company	10,000
All other companies, probably	10,000
Making a total of	90,000

as an average annual return for the last eight or ten years.

In the northwest the Hudson's Bay Company purchase from the Indians but a very small number—their only market being Canada, to which the cost of transportation nearly equals the produce of the furs; and it is only within a very recent period that they have received buffalo robes in trade; and out of the great number of buffalo annually killed throughout the extensive regions inhabited by the Comanches and other kindred tribes no robes whatever are furnished for trade. During only four months of the year (from November until March) the skins are good for dressing, those obtained in the remaining eight months being valueless to traders; and the hides of bulls are never taken off or dressed as robes at any season. Probably not more than one-third of the skins are taken from the animals killed, even when they are in good season, the labor of preparing and dressing the robes being very great; and it is seldom that a lodge trades more than twenty skins in a year. It is during the summer months, and in the early part of autumn, that the greatest number of buffalo are killed, and yet at this time a skin is never taken for the purpose of trade.

From these data, which are certainly limited, and decidedly within bounds, the reader is left to draw his own inference of the immense number annually killed.

In 1842 I found the Sioux Indians of the Upper Platte *démontés*, as their French traders expressed it, with the failure of the buffalo; and in the following year large villages from the Upper Missouri came over to the mountains at the heads of the Platte in search of them. The rapidly progressive failure of their principal, and almost their only, means of subsistence has created great alarm among them; and at this time there are only two modes presented to them by which they see a good prospect for escaping starvation: one of these is to rob the settlements along the frontier of the States, and the other is to form a league between the various tribes of the Sioux nation, the Cheyennes, and Arapahoes, and make war against the Crow nation, in order to take from them their country, which is now the best buffalo country in the West. This plan they now have in consideration; and it would probably be a war of extermination, as the Crows have long been advised of this state of affairs, and say that they are perfectly prepared. These are the best warriors in the Rocky Mountains, and are now allied with the Snake Indians; and it is probable that their combination would extend itself to the Utahs, who have long been engaged in war against the Sioux. It is in this section of country that my observation formerly led me to recommend the establishment of a military post.

The further course of our narrative will give fuller and more detailed information of the present disposition of the buffalo in the country we visited.

Among the roots we obtained here I could distinguish only five or six different kinds; and the supply of the Indians whom we met consisted principally of yampa (*Anethum graveolens*), tobacco root (*Valeriana*), and a large root of a species of thistle (*Circium Virginianum*), which now is occasionally abundant, and is a very agreeably flavored vegetable.

We had been detained so long at the village that in the afternoon we made only five miles, and encamped on the same river after a day's journey of nineteen miles. The Indians informed us that we should reach the big salt water after having slept twice and traveling in a southerly direction. The stream had here entered a nearly level plain or valley, of good soil, eight or ten miles broad, to which no termination was to be seen, and lying between ranges of mountains which, on the right, were grassy and smooth, unbroken by rock, and lower than on the left, where they were rocky and bald, increasing in height to the southward.

On the creek were fringes of young willows, older trees being rarely found on the plains, where the Indians burn the surface to produce better grass. Several magpies (*Pica Hudsonica*) were seen on the creek this afternoon; and a rattlesnake was killed here, the first which had been seen since leaving the eastern plains. Our camp tonight had such a hungry appearance that I suffered the little cow to be killed, and divided the roots and berries among the people. A number of Indians from the village encamped near.

The weather the next morning was clear, the thermometer at sunrise at 44.5°, and, continuing down the valley, in about five miles we followed the little creek of our encampment to its junction with a larger stream, called Roseaux, or Reed River. Immediately opposite, on the right, the range was gathered into its highest peak, sloping gradually low, and running off to a point apparently some forty or fifty miles below. Between this (now become the valley stream) and the foot of the mountains we journeyed along a handsome sloping level, which frequent springs from the hills made occasionally miry, and halted to noon at a swampy spring, where there were good grass and abundant rushes. Here the river was forty feet wide, with a considerable current, and the valley a mile and a half in breadth, the soil being generally good, of a dark color, and apparently well adapted to cultivation.*

The day had become bright and pleasant, with the thermometer at 71°. By observation our latitude was 41° 59' 31", and the elevation above the sea four thousand six hundred and seventy feet. On our left, this afternoon, the range at long intervals formed itself into peaks, appearing to terminate about forty miles below, in a rocky cape; beyond which several others were faintly visible; and we were disappointed when at every little rise we did not see the lake. Toward evening our way was somewhat obstructed by fields of artemisia, which began to make their appearance here, and we encamped on the Roseaux, the water of which had acquired a decidedly salt taste, nearly opposite to a cañon gap in the mountains through which the Bear River enters this valley.

As we encamped, the night set in dark and cold, with heavy rain, and the artemisia, which was here our only wood, was so wet that it would not burn. A poor, nearly starved dog, with a wound in his side from a ball, came to the camp, and remained with us until the winter, when he met a very unexpected fate.

September 1st. The morning was squally and cold, the sky scattered over with clouds; and the night had been so uncomfortable that we were not on the road until eight o'clock. Traveling between

---

* Following the Reed (now called the Malade River) from the north, the party was now inside the boundary of present-day Utah.

Roseaux and Bear rivers, we continued to descend the valley, which gradually expanded, as we advanced, into a level plain of good soil, about twenty-five miles in breadth, between mountains three thousand and four thousand feet high, rising suddenly to the clouds, which all day rested upon the peaks. These gleamed out in the occasional sunlight, mantled with the snow which had fallen upon them, while it rained on us in the valley below, of which the elevation here was about four thousand five hundred feet above the sea. . . . *

Among the useful things which formed a portion of our equipage was an indiarubber boat, eighteen feet long, made somewhat in the form of a bark canoe of the northern lakes. The sides were formed by two airtight cylinders, eighteen inches in diameter, connected with others forming the bow and stern. To lessen the danger from accidents to the boat, these were divided into four different compartments, and the interior space was sufficiently large to contain five or six persons, and a considerable weight of baggage. The Roseaux being too deep to be forded, our boat was filled with air, and in about one hour all the equipage of the camp, carriage and gun included, ferried across.

Thinking that perhaps in the course of the day we might reach the outlet at the lake, I got into the boat with Basil Lajeunesse, and paddled down Bear River, intending at night to rejoin the party, which in the meantime proceeded on its way. The river was from sixty to one hundred yards broad, and the water so deep that, even on the comparatively shallow points, we could not reach the bottom within fifteen feet. On either side were alternately low bottoms and willow points, with an occasional high prairie; and for five or six hours we followed slowly the winding course of the river, which crept along with a sluggish current among frequent detours several miles around, sometimes running for a considerable distance directly up the valley.

As we were stealing quietly down the stream, trying in vain to get a shot at a strange large bird that was numerous among the willows, but very shy, we came unexpectedly upon several families of root-diggers, who were encamped among the rushes on the shore, and appeared very busy about several weirs or nets which had been

* Two paragraphs of botanical detail omitted.

rudely made of canes and rushes for the purpose of catching fish. They were very much startled at our appearance, but we soon established an acquaintance; and finding that they had some roots, I promised to send some men with goods to trade with them. They had the usual very large heads remarkable among the Digger tribe, with matted hair, and were almost entirely naked, looking very poor and miserable, as if their lives had been spent in the rushes where they were, beyond which they seemed to have very little knowledge of anything. From the few words we could comprehend, their language was that of the Snake Indians.

Our boat moved so heavily that we had made very little progress, and, finding that it would be impossible to overtake the camp, as soon as we were sufficiently far below the Indians, we put to the shore near a high prairie bank, hauled up the boat, and cached our effects in the willows. Ascending the bank, we found that our desultory labor had brought us only a few miles in a direct line; and, going out into the prairie, after a search we found the trail of the camp, which was now nowhere in sight, but had followed the general course of the river in a large circular sweep which it makes at this place. The sun was about three hours high when we found the trail; and as our people had passed early in the day, we had the prospect of a vigorous walk before us.

Immediately where we landed, the high arable plain on which we had been traveling for several days past, terminated in extensive low flats, very generally occupied by salt marshes, or beds of shallow lakes, whence the water had in most places evaporated, leaving their hard surface encrusted with a shining white residuum, and absolutely covered with very small univalve shells. As we advanced, the whole country around us assumed this appearance; and there was no other vegetation than the shrubby chenopodiaceous and other apparently saline plants, which were confined to the rising grounds.

Here and there on the riverbank, which was raised like a levee above the flats through which it ran, was a narrow border of grass, and short, black-burned willows, the stream being very deep and sluggish, and sometimes six hundred to eight hundred feet wide. After a rapid walk of about fifteen miles, we caught sight of the campfires among clumps of willows just as the sun had sunk behind the mountains on the west side of the valley, filling the clear sky with a golden yellow. These last rays, to us so precious, could not have revealed a more welcome sight. To the traveler, and the hunter, a campfire in the lonely wilderness is always cheering; and to ourselves, in our present situation, after a hard march in a region of novelty, approaching the debouches of a river in a lake of almost fabulous reputation, it was doubly so.

A plentiful supper of aquatic birds, and the interest of the scene, soon dissipated fatigue; and I obtained during the night emersions of the second, third, and fourth satellites of Jupiter, with observations for time and latitude.

September 3d. The morning was clear, with a light air from the north, and the thermometer at sunrise at 45.5°. At three in the morning Basil was sent back with several men and horses for the boat, which, in a direct course across the flats, was not ten miles distant; and in the meantime there was a pretty spot of grass here for the animals. The ground was so low that we could not get high enough to see across the river on account of the willows; but we were evidently in the vicinity of the lake, and the waterfowl made this morning a noise like thunder. A pelican (*Pelecanus onocrotalus*) was killed as he passed by, and many geese and ducks flew over the camp. On the dry salt marsh here is scarce any other plant than *Salicornia herbacea*. In the afternoon the men returned with the boat, bringing with them a small quantity of roots, and some meat, which the Indians had told them was bear meat.

Descending the river for about three miles in the afternoon, we found a bar to any further traveling in that direction—the stream being spread out in several branches and covering the low grounds with water, where the miry nature of the bottom did not permit any further advance. We were evidently on the border of the lake, although the rushes and canes which covered the marshes prevented any view; and we accordingly encamped at the little delta which forms the mouth of Bear River, a long arm of the lake stretching up to the north between us and the opposite mountains. The river was bordered with a fringe of willows and canes, among which were interspersed a few plants; and scattered about on the marsh was a species of *Uniola*, closely allied to *U. spicata* of our seacoast. The whole morass was animated with multitudes of waterfowl, which appeared to be very wild—rising for the space of a mile round about at the sound of a gun, with a noise like distant thunder. Several of the people waded out into the marshes, and we had tonight a delicious supper of ducks, geese, and plover.

Although the moon was bright, the night was otherwise favorable, and I obtained this evening an emersion of the first satellite, with the usual observations. A mean result, depending on various observations made during our stay in the neighborhood, places the mouth of the river in longitude 112° 19′ 30″ west from Greenwich; latitude 41° 30′ 22″; and, according to the barometer, in elevation four thousand two hundred feet above the Gulf of Mexico. The night was clear, with considerable dew, which I had remarked every night since September first.

The next morning, while we were preparing to start, Carson rode into the camp with flour and a few other articles of light provision, sufficient for two or three days—a scanty but very acceptable supply. Mr. Fitzpatrick had not yet arrived, and provisions were very scarce and difficult to be had at Fort Hall, which had been entirely exhausted by the necessities of the emigrants. He brought me also a letter from Mr. Dwight, who, in company with several emigrants, had reached that place in advance of Mr. Fitzpatrick, and was about continuing his journey to Vancouver.

Returning about five miles up the river, we were occupied until nearly sunset in crossing to the left bank—the stream, which in the last five or six miles of its course is very much narrower than above, being very deep immediately at the banks, and we had great difficulty in getting our animals over. The people with the baggage were easily crossed in the boat, and we encamped on the left bank where we crossed the river. At sunset the thermometer was at 75°, and there was some rain during the night, with a thunderstorm at a distance.

September 5th. Before us was evidently the bed of the lake, being a great salt marsh perfectly level and bare, whitened in places by saline efflorescences, with here and there a pool of water, and having the appearance of a very level seashore at low tide. Immediately along the river was a very narrow strip of vegetation, consisting of willows, helianthi, roses, flowering vines, and grass, bordered on the verge of the great marsh by a fringe of singular plants which appear to be a shrubby salicornia, or a genus allied to it.

About twelve miles to the southward was one of those isolated mountains, now appearing to be a kind of peninsula; and toward this we accordingly directed our course, as it probably afforded a good view of the lake; but the deepening mud as we advanced forced us to return toward the river and gain the higher ground at the foot of the eastern mountains. Here we halted for a few minutes at noon, on a beautiful little stream of pure and remarkably clear water, with a bed of rock *in situ*, on which was an abundant water plant with a white blossom. There was good grass in the bottoms; and, amid a rather luxuriant growth, its banks were bordered with a large showy plant (*Eupatorium purpureum*), which I here saw for the first time. We named the stream Clear Creek.

We continued our way along the mountain, having found here a broad plainly beaten trail, over what was apparently the shore of the lake in the spring, the ground being high and firm, and the soil excellent and covered with vegetation, among which a leguminous plant (*Glycyrrhiza lepidota*) was a characteristic. The ridge here rises abruptly to the height of about four thousand feet, its face being very prominently marked with a massive stratum of rose-colored granular quartz, which is evidently an altered sedimentary rock—the lines of deposition being very distinct. It is rocky and steep, divided into several mountains, and the rain in the valley appears to be always snow on their summits at this season. Near a remarkable rocky point of the mountain, at a large spring of pure water, were several hackberry trees (*Celtis*), probably a new species, the berries still green; and a short distance farther, thickets of sumuch (*Rhus*).

On the plain here I noticed blackbirds and grouse. In about seven miles from Clear Creek the trail brought us to a place at the foot of the mountain where there issued, with considerable force, ten or twelve hot springs, highly impregnated with salt.* In one of these the thermometer stood at 136°, and in another at 132.5°; and the water, which spread in pools over the low ground, was colored red.[26]

---

* Frémont's chemical analysis is omitted; 50.43% carbonate of lime, 33.5% peroxide of iron.

At this place the trail we had been following turned to the left, apparently with the view of entering a gorge in the mountain, from which issued the principal fork of a large and comparatively well-timbered stream called Weber's Fork. We accordingly turned off toward the lake and encamped on this river, which was one hundred to one hundred and fifty feet wide, with high banks, and very clear, pure water, without the slightest indication of salt.

September 6th. Leaving the encampment early, we again directed our course for the peninsular butte, across a low shrubby plain, crossing in the way a slough-like creek with miry banks, and wooded with thickets of thorn (*Cratægus*) which were loaded with berries. This time we reached the butte without any difficulty, and, ascending to the summit, immediately at our feet beheld the object of our anxious search—the waters of the inland Sea stretching in still and solitary grandeur far beyond the limit of our vision. It was one of the great points of the exploration; and as we looked eagerly over the lake in the first emotions of excited pleasure, I am doubtful if the followers of Balboa felt more enthusiasm when, from the heights of the Andes, they saw for the first time the great Western Ocean. It was certainly a magnificent object, and a noble terminus to this part of our expedition; and to travelers so long shut up among mountain ranges a sudden view over the expanse of silent waters had in it something sublime. Several large islands raised their high rocky heads out of the waves; but whether or not they were timbered was still left to our imagination, as the distance was too great to determine if the dark hues upon them were woodland or naked rock.

During the day the clouds had been gathering black over the mountains to the westward, and while we were looking a storm burst down with sudden fury upon the lake and entirely hid the islands from our view. So far as we could see, along the shores there was not a solitary tree, and but little appearance of grass; and on Weber's Fork, a few miles below our last encampment, the timber was gathered into groves, and then disappeared entirely. As this appeared to be the nearest point to the lake where a suitable camp could be found, we directed our course to one of the groves, where we found a handsome encampment, with good grass and an abundance of rushes (*Equisetum hyemale*). At sunset the thermometer was at 55°, the evening clear and calm, with some cumuli.

September 7th. The morning was calm and clear, with a temperature at sunrise of 39.5°. The day was spent in active preparation for our intended voyage on the lake. On the edge of the stream a favorable spot was selected in a grove, and, felling the timber, we made a strong corral, or horse pen, for the animals, and a little fort for the people who were to remain. We were now probably in the country of the Utah Indians, though none reside upon the lake. The india-rubber boat was repaired with prepared cloth and gum, and filled with air, in readiness for the next day.

The provisions which Carson had brought with him being now exhausted, and our stock reduced to a small quantity of roots, I determined to retain with me only a sufficient number of men for the execution of our design; and accordingly seven were sent to Fort Hall under the guidance of François Lajeunesse, who, having been for many years a trapper in the country, was considered an experienced mountaineer. Though they were provided with good horses, and the road was a remarkably plain one of only four days' journey for a horseman, they became bewildered (as we afterward learned) and, losing their way, wandered about the country in parties of one or two, reaching the fort about a week afterward. Some straggled in of themselves and the others were brought in by Indians who had picked them up on Snake River, about sixty miles below the fort, traveling along the emigrant road in full march for the Lower Columbia. The leader of this adventurous party was François.

Hourly barometrical observations were made during the day, and after departure of the party for Fort Hall, we occupied ourselves in continuing our little preparations and in becoming acquainted with the country in the vicinity. The bottoms along the river were timbered with several kinds of willow, hawthorn, and fine cottonwood trees (*Populus canadensis*) with remarkably large leaves, and sixty feet in height by measurement.

We formed now but a small family. With Mr. Preuss and myself, Carson, Bernier, and Basil Lajeunesse had been selected for the boat expedition—the first ever attempted on this interior sea and Badeau, with Derosier and Jacob (the colored man), were to be left in charge of the camp. We were favored with most delightful weather.

Tonight there was a brilliant sunset of golden orange and green, which left the western sky clear and beautifully pure; but clouds in the east made me lose an occultation. The summer frogs were singing around us, and the evening was very pleasant, with a temperature of 60°—a night of a more southern autumn. For our supper we had yampa, the most agreeably flavored of the roots, seasoned by a small fat duck which had come in the way of Jacob's rifle. Around our fire tonight were many speculations on what tomorrow would bring forth, and in our busy conjectures we fancied that we should find every one of the large islands a tangled wilderness of trees and shrubbery, teeming with game of every description that the neighboring region afforded, and which the foot of a white man or Indian had never violated.

Frequently during the day, clouds had rested on the summits of their lofty mountains, and we believed that we should find clear streams and springs of fresh water; and we indulged in anticipations of the luxurious repasts with which we were to indemnify ourselves for past privations. Neither, in our discussions, were the whirlpool and other mysterious dangers forgotten which Indian and hunters' stories attributed to this unexplored lake.

The men had discovered that instead of being strongly sewed (like that of the preceding year, which so triumphantly rode the cañons of the Upper Great Platte), our present boat was only pasted together in a very insecure manner, the maker having been allowed so little time in the construction that he was obliged to crowd the labor of two months into several days. The insecurity of the boat was sensibly felt by us; and, mingled with the enthusiasm and excitement that we all felt at the prospect of an undertaking which had never before been accomplished was a certain impression of danger, sufficient to give a serious character to our conversation.

The momentary view which had been had of the lake the day before, its great extent and rugged islands, dimly seen amidst the dark waters in the obscurity of the sudden storm, were well calculated to heighten the idea of undefined danger with which the lake was generally associated.

September 8th. A calm, clear day, with a sunrise temperature of 41°. In view of our present enterprise, a part of the equipment of the boat had been made to consist in three airtight bags, about three feet long, and capable each of containing five gallons. These had been filled with water the night before, and were now placed in the boat, with our blankets and instruments, consisting of a sextant, telescope, spyglass, thermometer, and barometer.

We left the camp at sunrise, and had a very pleasant voyage down the river, in which there was generally eight or ten feet of water, deepening as we neared the mouth in the latter part of the day. In the course of the morning we discovered that two of the cylinders leaked so much as to require one man constantly at the bellows to keep them sufficiently full of air to support the boat. Although we had made a very early start, we loitered so much on the way—stopping every now and then, and floating silently along to get a shot at a goose or a duck—that it was late in the day when we reached the outlet. The river here divided into several branches, filled with fluvials, and so very shallow that it was with difficulty we could get the boat along, being obliged to get out and wade. We encamped on a low point among rushes and young willows, where there was a quantity of driftwood which served for our fires.

The evening was mild and clear; we made a pleasant bed of the young willows; and geese and ducks enough had been killed for an abundant supper at night, and for breakfast next morning. The stillness of the night was enlivened by millions of waterfowl. Latitude (by observation) 41° 11′ 26″ and longitude 112° 11′ 30″.

September 9th. The day was clear and calm; the thermometer at sunrise at 49°. As is usual with the trappers on the eve of any enterprise, our people had made dreams, and theirs happened to be a bad one—one which always preceded evil—and consequently they looked very gloomy this morning; but we hurried through our breakfast in order to make an early start and have all the day before us for our adventure.

The channel in a short distance became so shallow that our navigation was at an end, being merely a sheet of soft mud, with a few inches of water, and sometimes none at all, forming the low-water shore of the lake. All this place ws absolutely covered with flocks of screaming plover. We took off our clothes, and, getting overboard, commenced dragging the boat—making, by this operation, a very curious trail, and a very disagreeable smell in stirring up the mud, as we sank above the knee at every step. The water here was still fresh, with only an insipid and disagreeable taste, probably derived from the bed of fetid mud. After proceeding in this way about a mile we came to a small black ridge on the bottom, beyond which the water became suddenly salt, beginning gradually to deepen, and the bottom was sandy and firm. It was a remarkable division, separating the fresh water of the rivers from the briny water of the lake, which was entirely saturated with common salt. Pushing our little vessel across the narrow boundary, we sprang on board, and at length were afloat on the waters of the unknown sea.

We did not steer for the mountainous islands, but directed our course toward a lower one which it had been decided we should first visit, the summit of which was formed like the crater at the upper end of Bear River Valley. So long as we could touch the bottom with our paddles, we were very gay; but gradually, as the water deepened, we became more still in our frail bateau of gum cloth distended with air, and with pasted seams. Although the day was very calm, there was a considerable swell on the lake; and there were white patches of foam on the surface, which were slowly moving to the southward, indicating the set of a current in that direction and recalling the recollection of the whirlpool stories. The water continued to deepen as we advanced, the lake becoming almost transparently clear, of an extremely beautiful bright-green color; and the spray, which was thrown into the boat and over our clothes, was directly converted into a crust of common salt, which covered also our hands and arms.

"Captain," said Carson, who for some time had been looking suspiciously at some whitening appearances outside the nearest islands, "what are those yonder?—won't you just take a look with the glass?" We ceased paddling for a moment, and found them to be the caps of the waves that were beginning to break under the force of a strong breeze that was coming up the lake. The form of the boat seemed to be an admirable one, and it rode on the waves like a water bird; but, at the same time, it was extremely slow in its progress. When we were a little more than halfway across the reach, two of the divisions between the cylinders gave way, and it required the constant use of the bellows to keep in a sufficient quantity of air. For a long time we scarcely seemed to approach our island, but gradually we worked across the rougher sea of the open channel into the smoother water under the lee of the island,

and began to discover that what we took for a long row of pelicans ranged on the beach were only low cliffs whitened with salt by the spray of the waves; and about noon we reached the shore, the transparency of the water enabling us to see the bottom at a considerable depth.

It was a handsome broad beach where we landed, behind which the hill, into which the island was gathered, rose somewhat abruptly; and a point of rock at one end enclosed it in a sheltering way; and as there was an abundance of driftwood along the shore, it offered us a pleasant encampment. We did not suffer our fragile boat to touch the sharp rocks; but, getting overboard, discharged the baggage, and, lifting it gently out of the water, carried it to the upper part of the beach, which was composed of very small fragments of rock.

Among the successive banks of the beach, formed by the action of the waves, our attention, as we approached the island, had been attracted by one ten to twenty feet in breadth, of a dark-brown color. Being more closely examined, this was found to be composed, to the depth of seven or eight, and twelve inches, entirely of the larvæ of insects, or, in common language, of the skins of worms, about the size of a grain of oats, which had been washed up by the waters of the lake.

Alluding to this subject some months afterward, when traveling through a more southern portion of this region in company with Mr. Joseph Walker, an old hunter, I was informed by him that, wandering with a party of men in a mountain country east of the great Californian range, he surprised a party of several Indian families encamped near a small salt lake, who abandoned their lodges at his approach, leaving everything behind them. Being in a starving condition, they were delighted to find in the abandoned lodges a number of skin bags containing a quantity of what appeared to be fish, dried and pounded. On this they made a hearty supper, and were gathering around an abundant breakfast the next morning when Mr. Walker discovered that it was with these, or a similar worm, that the bags had been filled. The stomachs of the stout trappers were not proof against their prejudices, and the repulsive food was suddenly rejected. Mr. Walker had further opportunities of seeing these worms used as an article of food; and I am inclined to think they are the same as those we saw, and appear to be a product of the salt lakes.

Mr. Walker was associated with Captain Bonneville in his expedition to the Rocky Mountains; and had since that time remained in the country, generally residing in some one of the Snake villages, when not engaged in one of his numerous trapping expeditions, in which he is celebrated as one of the best and bravest leaders who have ever been in the country.

The cliffs and masses of rock along the shore were whitened by an incrustation of salt where the waves dashed up against them; and the evaporating water which had been left in holes and hollows on the surface of the rocks was covered with a crust of salt about one-eighth of an inch in thickness. It appeared strange that, in the midst of this grand reservoir, one of our greatest wants lately had been salt. Exposed to be more perfectly dried in the sun, this became very white and fine, having the usual flavor of very excellent common salt, without any foreign taste; but only a little was collected for present use, as there was in it a number of small black insects.

Carrying with us the barometer and other instruments, in the afternoon we ascended to the highest point of the island—a bare rocky peak, eight hundred feet above the lake. Standing on the summit, we enjoyed an extended view of the lake, enclosed in a basin of rugged mountains, which sometimes left marshy flats and extensive bottoms between them and the shore, and in other places came directly down into the water with bold and precipitous bluffs. Following with our glasses the irregular shores, we searched for some indications of a communication with other bodies of water, or the entrance of other rivers; but the distance was so great that we could make out nothing with certainty. To the southward several peninsular mountains, three thousand or four thousand feet high, entered the lake, appearing, so far as the distance and our position enabled us to determine, to be connected by flats and low ridges with the mountains in the rear.

At the season of high waters in the spring, it is probable that all the marshes and low grounds are overflowed, and the surface of the lake considerably greater.[27] In several places the view was of unlimited extent—here and there a rocky islet appearing above the water at a great distance; and beyond, everything was vague and undefined. As we looked over the vast expanse of water spread out beneath us, and strained our eyes along the silent shores over which hung so much doubt and uncertainty, and which were so full of interest to us, I could hardly repress the almost irresistible desire to continue our exploration; but the lengthening snow on the mountains was a plain indication of the advancing season, and our frail linen boat appeared so insecure that I was unwilling to trust our lives to the uncertainties of the lake. I therefore unwillingly resolved to terminate our survey here, and remain satisfied for the present with what we had been able to add to the unknown geography of the region. We felt pleasure also in remembering that we were the first who, in the traditionary annals of the country, had visited the islands, and broken with the cheerful sound of human voices the long solitude of the place.

From the point where we were standing, the ground fell off on every side to the water, giving us a perfect view of the island, which is twelve or thirteen miles in circumference, being simply a rocky hill, on which there is neither water nor trees of any kind; although at a distance the *Fremontia vermicularis*, which was in great abundance, might easily be mistaken for woods. The plant seemed here to delight in a congenial air, growing in extraordinary luxuriance seven to eight feet high, and was very abundant on the upper parts of the island, where it was almost the only plant. This is eminently a saline shrub; its leaves have a very salt taste, and it luxuriates in saline soils, where it is usually a characteristic. It is widely diffused over all this country. A chenopodiaceous shrub, which is a new species of *Obione* (O. rigida, *Torr. & Frem.*), was equally characteristic of the lower parts of the island. These two are the striking plants on the island, and belong to a class of plants which form a prominent feature in the vegetation of this country. On the lower parts of the island also a prickly pear of very large size was frequent. On the shore, near the water, was a woolly species of *Phaca*; and a new species of umbelliferous plant (*Leptotæmia*) was scattered about in very considerable abundance. These constituted all the vegetation that now appeared upon the island.

I accidentally left on the summit the brass cover to the object end of my spyglass; and as it will probably remain there undisturbed by Indians, it will furnish matter of speculation to some future traveler. In our excursions about the island we did not meet with any kind of animal; a magpie, and another larger bird, probably attracted by the smoke of our fire, paid us a visit from the shore, and were the only living things seen during our stay. The rock constituting the cliffs along the shore where we were encamped is a talcous rock or stealite, with brown spar.

At sunset the temperature was 70°. We had arrived just in time to obtain a meridian altitude of the sun, and other observations were obtained this evening, which place our camp in latitude 41° 10′ 42″, and longitude 112° 21′ 05″ from Greenwich. From a discussion of the barometrical observations made during our stay on the shores of the lake, we have adopted four thousand two hundred feet for its elevation above the Gulf of Mexico. In the first disappointment we felt from the dissipation of our dream of the fertile islands, I called this Disappointment Island.[28]

Out of the driftwood we made ourselves pleasant little lodges, open to the water, and, after having kindled large fires to excite the wonder of any straggling savage on the lake shores, lay down, for the first time in a long journey, in perfect security, no one thinking about his arms. The evening was extremely bright and pleasant; but the wind rose during the night, and the waves began to break heavily on the shore, making our island tremble. I had not expected in our inland journey to hear the roar of an ocean surf; and the strangeness of our situation and the excitement we felt in the associated interests of the place made this one of the most interesting nights I remember during our long expedition.

In the morning the surf was breaking heavily on the shore, and we were up early. The lake was dark and agitated, and we hurried through our scanty breakfast and embarked—having first filled one of the buckets with water from the lake, of which it was intended to make salt. The sun had risen by the time we were ready to start; and it was blowing a strong gale of wind, almost directly off the shore, and raising a considerable sea in which our boat strained very much. It roughened as we got away from the island, and it required all the efforts of the men to make any head against the wind and sea, the gale rising with the sun, and there was danger of being blown into one of the open reaches beyond the island. At the distance of half a mile from the beach the depth of water was sixteen feet, with a clay bottom; but as the working of the boat was very severe labor and during the operation of sounding it was necessary to cease paddling, during which the boat lost considerable way, I was unwilling to discourage the men, and reluctantly gave up my intention of ascertaining the depth, and the character of the bed. There was a general shout in the boat when we found ourselves in one fathom, and we soon after landed on a low point of mud immediately under the butte of the peninsula, where we unloaded the boat, and carried the baggage about a quarter of a mile to firmer ground.

We arrived just in time for meridian observation, and carried the barometer to the summit of the butte, which is five hundred feet above the lake. Mr. Preuss set off on foot for the camp, which was about nine miles distant, Basil accompanying him to bring back horses for the boat and baggage. The rude-looking shelter we raised on the shore, our scattered baggage and boat lying on the beach, made quite a picture; and we called this the Fisherman's Camp. *Lynosiris graveolens,* and another new species of *Obione* (*O. confertifolia—Torr. & Frem.*), were growing on the low grounds, with interspersed spots of an unwholesome salt grass, on a saline clay soil, with a few other plants.

The horses arrived late in the afternoon, by which time the gale had increased to such a height that a man could scarcely stand before it; and we were obliged to pack our baggage hastily, as the rising water of the lake had already reached the point where we were halted. Looking back as we rode off, we found the place of recent encampment entirely covered.

The low plain through which we rode to the camp was covered with a compact growth of shrubs of extraordinary size and luxuriance. The soil was sandy and saline, flat places resembling the beds of ponds, that were bare of vegetation and covered with powdery white salts, being interspersed among the shrubs.

Artemisia tridentata was very abundant, but the plants were principally saline; a large and vigorous chenopodiaceous shrub, five to eight feet high, being characteristic, with *Fremontia vermicularis,* and a shrubby plant which seems to be a new salicornia. We reached the camp in time to escape a thunderstorm which blackened the sky, and were received with a discharge of the howitzer by the people, who, having been unable to see anything of us on the lake, had begun to feel some uneasiness.

September 11th. Today we remained at this camp, in order to obtain some further observations and to boil down the water which had been brought from the lake for a supply of salt. Roughly evaporated over the fire, the five gallons of water yielded fourteen pints of very fine-grained and very white salt, of which the whole lake may be regarded as a saturated solution. A portion of the salt thus obtained has been subjected to analysis—giving, in one hundred parts, the following proportions:

ANALYSIS OF THE SALT

Chloride of sodium (common salt)	97.80
Chloride of calcium	0.61
Chloride of magnesia	0.24
Sulphate of soda	0.23
Sulphate of lime	1.12
	100.00

A small stream entering the Utah Lake, south of the Spanish Fork, is the first water of that lake which our road of 1844 crosses in coming up from the southward.

When I was on this stream with Mr. Walker in that year he informed me that on the upper part of the river are immense beds of rock salt of very great thickness, which he had frequently visited. Farther to the southward the rivers which are affluent to the Colorado, such as the Rio Virgen and Gila River, near their mouths are impregnated with salt by the cliffs of rock salt between which they pass. These mines occur in the same ridge in which, about one hundred and twenty miles to the northward, and subsequently in their more immediate neighborhood, we discovered the fossils belonging to the oölitic period, and they are probably connected with that formation, and are the source from which the Great Lake obtains its salt. Had we remained longer, we should have found them in its bed, and in the mountains around its shores.

By observation, the latitude of this camp is 41° 15′ 50″ and longitude 112° 06′ 43″. The observations made during our stay give for the rate of the chronometer 31″.72, corresponding almost exactly with the rate obtained at St. Vrain's Fort. Barometrical observations were made hourly during the day. This morning we breakfasted on yampa, and had only camass for supper; but a cup of good coffee still distinguished us from our Digger acquaintances.

FOOTNOTES

1. This second expedition, as Frémont indicates, was planned by a Congressional group which was determined to obtain all possible knowledge of the West, to encourage emigration, and to do whatever else they could to promote American expansion to the Pacific. The men who led this group believed that they had a far larger vision than President Tyler or Secretary of State Webster. They were much impressed by Frémont's report on his first expedition, and delighted by the fact that he had emphatically asserted the fertility of the country stretching several hundred miles west from the far boundary of Missouri— a country that some earlier travelers had termed a desert.

2. Lieutenant Charles Wilkes of the Navy (who, like Frémont, had studied under Ferdinand R. Hassler) had headed a notable exploring expedition in 1838–42 which, among other work, had surveyed the northwestern coast of America. Frémont's expedition would in a sense connect with this.

3. Here we meet a man destined to play a malign part in Frémont's life. Stephen Watts Kearny (1794–1848) was a brave, devoted, and skillful frontier officer. He had gone from Columbia College to fight in the War of 1812, had remained in the Army, and in 1819 had been sent to Camp Missouri, north of present-day Omaha. Thereafter he served at a number of Western posts. Now, in 1843, with the rank of colonel, he commanded the Third Military Department, with headquarters in St. Louis. He had married a St. Louis girl, stepdaughter of General William Clark, and was a friend of the Benton family. His energy and ability were great, but he was an excessively strict disciplinarian, harsh and domineering of temper.

4. It is not difficult to understand why the Administration in Washington objected to the howitzer. Relations with Great Britain and Mexico alike were uneasy, and both nations feared American territorial aggression. Their officers would welcome an ordinary exploring expedition, but be highly suspicious of a heavily armed party of Americans entering the Oregon country and California. It is not at all unlikely that the Tyler Administration was itself a bit suspicious of what Senators Linn, Benton, and their colleagues were doing.

5. John James Abert (1788–1863) was the son of one of Rochambeau's officers. Graduating from West Point in 1811, he became a topographical engineer, and in 1829 took charge of the Topographical Bureau in Washington. At this time he held the rank of colonel. A faithful and capable government officer, he helped supervise important Federal activities in the engineering field, and wrote reports of high value. As Frémont suggests, the order for recall probably came from someone higher in rank than Abert, and one more keenly interested in international affairs.

6. Colonel Abert had ordered Talbot taken along. The young man kept a journal which, now in the Library of Congress, is an amusing and useful source of information on the West.

7. The proper spelling is Chiles, and this will be used hereafter.

8. Frémont might well think Gilpin useful and agreeable. He was one of the remarkable Western figures of his time. Born in Pennsylvania of Quaker stock in 1813, he left West Point to study for the bar, but re-entered military life to fight in the Seminole War. Resigning from the Army, he edited the *Missouri Argus* in St. Louis for a time, and practiced law in Independence, Missouri. Later he was to fight under Doniphan in the Mexican War, and to be the first governor of the Territory of Colorado. H. H. Bancroft wrote a biographical account of him.

9. Now called Fountain Creek.

10. This was the village from which grew the present-day city of Pueblo, Colorado. The well-known frontiersman James Beckwourth (1798–1867) was an intermittent resident of the village.

11. Another of the great figures of the early Southwest. Charles Bent, a Virginian by birth, was born in 1799, the son of a judge who presently removed to Missouri. He entered the fur trade along with his younger brother William. In 1824 the two, with Ceran St. Vrain, went on a trapping journey to the Upper Arkansas River, and built a fortified post near what is now Pueblo. The three men soon organized the firm of Bent & St. Vrain, and in 1828–32 built Bent's Fort at present-day La Junta, Colorado, on the Arkansas. Thereafter Charles was an influential personage in both the Upper Arkansas country and New Mexico. He married into a Taos family from which Kit Carson also eventually took a bride. When Kearny occupied New Mexico during the Mexican War he appointed Charles Bent civil governor.

12. The celebrated springs are at present-day Manitou, with the city of Colorado Springs close at hand.

13. This statement, as F. S. Dellenbaugh says in *Frémont and '49,* is almost incredible when we consider that Frémont was accompanied by Kit Carson and Fitzpatrick, whose knowledge of the Rockies, and especially the part south of the present-day Montana boundary, was almost encyclopedic. But there may have been wide gaps in the knowledge even of these men.

14. The Utah or Ute Indians and the Shoshone belonged to the same linguistic family. The Shoshonean stock, which included the Comanche (ultimately a prairie tribe), the Hopi, and the Paiute, at one time controlled most of the region from the central Rockies across the Great Basin to the Sierra Nevada, and from northern Texas across to southern California. The Utes, occupying what is now central and western Colorado and eastern Utah, were especially dangerous. The Cheyenne, named above, were originally a northern plains tribe, confederated with the Arapahoes. But in 1835 William Bent (who had married into the tribe) induced about half of them to move down to an area where Bent's Fort and his trading firm could profit from their hunting and trapping. These became known as the Southern Cheyenne.

15. Frémont formed the highest opinion of Godey, even comparing him to Carson; and Godey for his part never flagged in admiration for Frémont.

16. Frémont's name, placed on his map, has stuck; it is now the Yampa River.

17. A later railroad survey fixed the altitude at 7397 feet; Frémont's figure was close.

18. The usual supposition is that the river was named for a trapper of the name of Green. What is certain is that the Green River Valley, with its fine grass, trees, and water, was long a favorite rendezvous for trappers, fur traders,

and frontiersmen in general. Here Kit Carson had fought and wounded a notorious bully named Shuman. Chapter 20 of Irving's *Adventures of Captain Bonneville* contains a lively description of these trappers' meetings.

19. Actually it was Ham's Fork of the Green River that he reached.

20. It was James Bridger who, arriving on the shore of Great Salt Lake in the winter of 1824–25, dismounted with some other trappers to get a drink, and made the famous remark: "Hell, we are on the shore of the Pacific!" The notion that the lake might somehow be connected with the Pacific lingered until 1826, when some trappers circumnavigated it. As Frémont writes, the waters of the Bear River empty into the lake from the north, as do those of the Jordan River from the south; but the lake has no outlet. By the time he reached the area, the big salt water, visited by Bonneville among others, was famous. But he was the first scientist to describe carefully either the Bear River or the lake; and the account here given of the whole district is still in many ways the best ever written.

21. Named for the noted frontiersman Jedediah Smith.

22. Described briefly in Chapter 28 of Irving's *Adventures of Captain Bonneville*. Bonneville thought that the water really had the taste of beer, and says that his men "drank it with avidity and in copious draughts."

23. Since the late eighteenth century fur traders and others had called the Indians in the Snake River Valley of what is now Idaho, and in the circumjacent areas, the Snake tribe. This was a misnomer; they were actually Shoshone and Paiute.

24. All the tribes in the area mentioned lived largely on roots, seeds, piñon nuts, and the like, for meat was hardly to be had. Frémont was probably speaking of the Paiute tribe, itself a vague term. The so-called Paiutes inhabited a region centering in eastern Utah.

25. The material Frémont here presents on the buffalo is of special value and interest, as it was gathered at a time before other observers had seriously inquired into the subject.

26. This spot was a few miles north of the site of the present city of Ogden, Utah.

27. This was a shrewd observation. Great Salt Lake in fact varies materially in extent as rainfall in the region is slight or copious. Its area in 1850 was about 1750 square miles; in 1869 it was 2170 square miles.

28. It is now called Frémont Island. His figures for altitude were almost precisely correct.

CHAPTER 7

From Great Salt Lake to Fort Vancouver *

SEPTEMBER 14, 1843. . . . We crossed the Roseaux, and encamped on the left bank, halting early for the pleasure of enjoying a wholesome and abundant supper, and were pleasantly engaged in protracting our unusual comfort when Tabeau galloped into the camp with news that Mr. Fitzpatrick was encamped close by us with a good supply of provisions—flour, rice, and dried meat, and even a little butter.

Excitement tonight made us all wakeful; and after a breakfast before sunrise the next morning, we were again on the road, and, continuing up the valley, crossed some high points of hills and halted to noon on the same stream, near several lodges of Snake Indians, from whom we purchased about a bushel of serviceberries,[1] partially dried. By the gift of a knife I prevailed upon a little boy to show me the kooya plant, which proved to be *Valeriana edulis*. The root, which constitutes the kooya is large, of a very bright yellow color, with the characteristic odor, but not so fully developed as in the prepared substance. It loves the rich moist soil of river bottoms, which was the locality in which I always afterward found it. It was now entirely out of bloom, according to my observation flowering in the months of May and June.

In the afternoon we entered a long ravine leading to a pass in the dividing ridge between the waters of Bear River and the Snake River, or Lewis' Fork of the Columbia, our way being very much

* From Frémont's *Report* on his second expedition. His party left Great Salt Lake September 12, 1843, moving out on the first stage "by nearly the same route which we had traveled in coming to the lake." Some matter on the country thus retraversed is omitted. The narrative is resumed September 14, with a passage which drives home Frémont's belief that the fertile Salt Lake Valley and Bear River Valley were eminently fitted for settlement. This passage, read and pondered by the leaders of the Mormons, was to have a great impact on American history.

impeded, and almost entirely blocked up, by compact fields of luxuriant artemisia. Taking leave at this point of the waters of Bear River, and of the geographical basin which encloses the system of rivers and creeks which belong to the Great Salt Lake, and which so richly deserves a future detailed and ample exploration, I can say of it, in general terms, that the bottoms of this river (Bear) and of some of the creeks which I saw, form a natural resting and recruiting station for travelers, now and in all time to come. The bottoms are extensive, water excellent, timber sufficient, the soil good and well adapted to the grains and grasses suited to such an elevated region.

A military post and a civilized settlement would be of great value here; and cattle and horses would do well where grass and salt so much abound. The lake will furnish exhaustless supplies of salt. All the mountainsides here are covered with a valuable nutritious grass—called bunch grass from the form in which it grows—which has a second growth in the fall. The beasts of the Indians were fat upon it; our own found it a good subsistence; and its quantity will sustain any amount of cattle and make this truly a bucolic region.

We met here an Indian family on horseback, which had been out to gather serviceberries, and were returning loaded. This tree was scattered about on the hills, and the upper part of the pass was timbered with aspen (*Populus trem.*); the common blue flowering flax occurring among the plants. . . .

September 17th. About noon we reached the main fork [of the Bannock River, a tributary of the Snake]. The Bannock River was before us, the valley being here one and a half miles wide, fertile, and bordered by high hills, not over five hundred feet high, partly covered with cedar. . . .*

September 18th. The day clear and calm, with a temperature of 25° at sunrise. After traveling seven or eight miles we emerged on the plains of the Columbia, in sight of the famous Three Buttes, a well-known landmark in the country, distant about forty-five miles.

---

* Frémont's *Report* has no entries for September 15 or 16. Some unimportant botanical and astronomical detail is omitted. His spelling for the Bannock River is Pannack, but the correct name will be used in the text. The party was now headed for Fort Hall on the Upper Snake River (Lewis' Fork of the Columbia, as it was then generally called), a great port of call on the Oregon Trail. They were again well inside present-day Idaho.

The French word "butte," which so often occurs in this narrative, is retained from the familiar language of the country, and identifies the objects to which it refers. It is naturalized in the region of the Rocky Mountains; and even if desirable to render it in English, I know of no word which would be its precise equivalent. It is applied to the detached hills and ridges which rise abruptly and reach too high to be called hills or ridges, and not high enough to be called mountains. "Knob," as applied in the Western States, is their most descriptive term in English. "Cerro" is the Spanish term; but no translation or paraphrasis would preserve the identity of these picturesque landmarks, familiar to the traveler, and often seen at a great distance.

Covered as far as could be seen with artemisia, the dark and ugly appearance of this plain obtained for it the name of the Sage Desert; and we were agreeably surprised on reaching the Portneuf River to see a beautiful green valley with scattered timber spread out beneath us on which about four miles distant, were glistening the white walls of the fort. The Portneuf runs along the upland plain nearly to its mouth, and an abrupt descent of perhaps two hundred feet brought us down immediately upon the stream, which at the ford is one hundred yards wide and three feet deep, with clear water, a swift current, and gravelly bed; but a little higher up the breadth was only about thirty-five yards, with apparently deep water.

In the bottom I remarked a very great number of springs and sloughs, with remarkably clear water and gravel beds. At sunset we encamped with Mr. Talbot and our friends who came on to Fort Hall when we went to the lake, and whom we had the satisfaction to find all well, neither party having met with any mischance in the interval of our separation. They, too, had had their share of fatigue and scanty provisions, as there had been very little game left on the trail of the populous emigration; and Mr. Fitzpatrick had rigidly husbanded our stock of flour and light provisions, in view of the approaching winter and the long journey before us.

September 19th. This morning the sky was very dark and gloomy, and at daylight it began snowing thickly, and continued all day, with cold, disagreeable weather. At sunrise the temperature was 43°. I rode up to the fort, and purchased from Mr. Grant (the officer in charge of the post) several very indifferent horses, and five oxen in very fine order, which were received at the camp with great satisfaction; and one being killed at evening, the usual gaiety and good humor were at once restored. Night came in stormy.

September 20th. We had a night of snow and rain, and the thermometer at sunrise was at 34°; the morning was dark, with a steady rain, and there was still an inch of snow on the ground, with an abundance on the neighboring hills and mountains. The sudden change in the weather was hard for our animals, which trembled and shivered in the cold—sometimes taking refuge in the timber, and now and then coming out and raking the snow off the ground for a little grass, or eating the young willows.

September 21st. Ice made tolerably thick during the night, and in the morning the weather cleared up very bright, with a temperature at sunrise of 29°; and I obtained a meridian observation for latitude at the fort, with observations for time. The sky was again covered in the afternoon, and the thermometer at sunset 48°.

September 22d. The morning was cloudy and unpleasant, and at sunrise a cold rain commenced, with a temperature of 41°.

The early approach of winter and the difficulty of supporting a large party determined me to send back a number of the men who had become satisfied that they were not fitted for the laborious service and frequent privation to which they were necessarily exposed, and which there was reason to believe would become more severe in the further extension of the voyage. I accordingly called them together, and, informing them of my intention to continue our journey during the ensuing winter, in the course of which they would probably be exposed to considerable hardship, succeeded in prevailing upon a number of them to return voluntarily. These were: Charles De Forrest, Henry Lee, J. Campbell, William Creuss, A. Vasquez, A. Pera, Patrick White, B. Tesson, M. Creely, François Lajeunesse, Basil Lajeunesse.

Among these I regretted very much to lose Basil Lajeunesse, one of the best men in my party, who was obliged, by the condition of his family, to be at home in the coming winter. Our preparations having been completed in the interval of our stay here, both parties were ready this morning to resume their respective routes.

Except that there is a greater quantity of wood used in its construction, Fort Hall very much resembles the other trading posts

which have been already described, and would be another excellent
post of relief for the emigrant.[2] It is in the low, rich bottom of the
valley, apparently twenty miles long, formed by the confluence of
Portneuf River with Lewis' Fork of the Columbia, which it enters
about nine miles below the fort,* and narrowing gradually to the
mouth of the Bannock River, where it has a breadth of only two or
three miles. Allowing fifty miles for the road from the Beer Springs
of Bear River to Fort Hall, its distance along the traveled road from
the town of Westport, on the frontier of Missouri, by way of Fort
Laramie and the great South Pass, is one thousand three hundred
and twenty-three miles. Beyond this place, on the line of road along
the barren valley of the Upper Columbia, there does not occur, for
a distance of nearly three hundred miles to the westward, a fertile
spot of ground sufficiently large to produce the necessary quantity
of grain, or pasturage enough to allow even a temporary repose to
the emigrants.

On their recent passage they had been able to obtain, at very high
prices and in insufficient quantity, only such assistance as could be
afforded by a small and remote trading post—and that a foreign
one—which, in the supply of its own wants, had necessarily drawn
around it some of the resources of civilization, but which obtained
nearly all its supplies from the distant depot of Vancouver, by a
difficult water carriage of two hundred and fifty miles up the Columbia River and a land carriage by pack horses of six hundred
miles.

An American military post sufficiently strong to give to their road
a perfect security against the Indian tribes, who are unsettled in
locality and very uncertain in their disposition, and which, with the
necessary facilities for the repair of their equipage, would be able
to afford them relief in stock and grain from the produce of the
post, would be of extraordinary value to the emigration. Such a
post (and all others which may be established on the line to Oregon) would naturally form the nucleus of a settlement at which
supplies and repose would be obtained by the emigrant or trading
caravans which may hereafter traverse these elevated and, in many
places, desolate and inhospitable regions.[3]

I subjoin an analysis of the soil in the river bottom near Fort Hall,
which will be of assistance in forming some correct idea of its gen-

* Not far from present-day Pocatello, Idaho.

eral character in the neighboring country. I characterize it as good land, but the analysis will show its precise properties.

ANALYSIS OF SOIL

Silica	68.55
Alumina	7.45
Carbonate of lime	8.51
Carbonate of magnesia	5.09
Oxide of iron	1.40
Organic vegetable matter	4.74
Water and loss	4.26
	100.00

Our observations place this post in longitude 112° 29′ 54″, latitude 43° 01′ 30″, and in elevation above the sea four thousand five hundred feet.

Taking leave of the homeward party, we resumed our journey down the valley, the weather being very cold and the rain coming in hard gusts which the wind blew directly in our faces. We forded the Portneuf in a storm of rain, the water in the river being frequently up to the axles, and about one hundred and ten yards wide.

After the gust the weather improved a little, and we encamped about three miles below, at the mouth of the Bannock River, on Lewis' Fork, which here has a breadth of about one hundred and twenty yards. The temperature at sunset was 42°, the sky partially covered with dark, rainy clouds.

September 23d. The temperature at sunrise was 32°, the morning dark and snow falling steadily and thickly, with a light air from the southward. I profited of being obliged to remain in camp to take hourly barometrical observations from sunrise to midnight. The wind at eleven o'clock set in from the northward in heavy gusts, and the snow changed into rain. In the afternoon, when the sky brightened, the rain had washed all the snow from the bottoms; but the neighboring mountains, from summit to foot, were luminously white—an inauspicious commencement of the autumn, of which this was the first day.

September 24th. The thermometer at sunrise was at 35° and a blue sky in the west promised a fine day. The river bottoms here are narrow and swampy, with frequent sloughs; and after crossing the

Bannock the road continued along the uplands, rendered very slippery by the soil of wet clay, and entirely covered with artemisia bushes, among which occur frequent fragments of obsidian.

At noon we encamped in a grove of willows, at the upper end of a group of islands, about half a mile above the American Falls of Snake River. Among the willows here were some bushes of Lewis and Clark's currant (*Ribes aureum*). The river here enters between low mural banks, which consist of a fine vesicular traprock, the intermediate portions being compact and crystalline. Gradually becoming higher in its downward course, these banks of scoriated volcanic rock form, with occasional interruptions, its characteristic feature along the whole line to the Dalles of the Lower Columbia, resembling a chasm which had been rent through the country and which the river had afterward taken for its bed. The immediate valley of the river is a high plain, covered with black rocks and artemisias.

In the south is a bordering range of mountains which, although not very high, are broken and covered with snow; and at a great distance to the north is seen the high, snowy line of the Salmon River Mountains, in front of which stand out prominently in the plain the three isolated rugged-looking little mountains commonly known as the Three Buttes. Between the river and the distant Salmon River Range the plain is represented by Mr. Fitzpatrick as so entirely broken up and rent into chasms as to be impracticable even for a man on foot. By measurement the river above is eight hundred and seventy feet wide, immediately contracted at the fall, in the form of a lock, by jutting piles of scoriaceous basalt, over which the foaming river must present a grand appearance at the time of high water. The evening was clear and pleasant, with dew, and at sunset the temperature was 54°. By observation, the latitude is 42° 47′ 05″ and the longitude 112° 40′ 13″.

September 25th. Thermometer at sunrise 47°. The day came in clear, with a strong gale from the south, which commenced at eleven of the last night.

The road today led along the river, which is full of rapids and small falls. Grass is very scanty; and along the rugged banks are scattered cedars, with an abundance of rocks and sage. We traveled fourteen miles and encamped in the afternoon near the river, on a rocky creek, the bed of which was entirely occupied with boulders of a very large size. For the last three or four miles the right bank of the river has a palisaded appearance. One of the oxen was killed here for food. The thermometer at evening was at 55°, the sky almost overcast, and the barometer indicated an elevation of four thousand four hundred feet.

September 26th. Rain during the night, and the temperature at sunrise 42°. Traveling along the river, in about four miles we reached a picturesque stream to which we gave the name of Fall Creek. It is remarkable for the many falls which occur in a short distance; and its bed is composed of a calcareous tufa, or vegetable rock, composed principally of the remains of reeds and mosses, resembling that at the Basin Spring on Bear River.

The road along the river bluffs had been occasionally very bad; and imagining that some rough obstacles rendered such a detour necessary, we followed for several miles a plain wagon road leading up this stream until we reached a point whence it could be seen making directly toward a low place in the range on the south side of the valley, and we became immediately aware that we were on a trail formed by a party of wagons, in company with which we had encamped at Elm Grove, near the frontier of Missouri, and which were proceeding to Upper California under the direction of Mr. Joseph Chiles.[4] At the time of their departure, no practicable passes were known in the southern Rocky Mountains within the territory of the United States; and the probable apprehension of difficulty in attempting to pass near the settled frontier of New Mexico, together with the desert character of the unexplored region beyond, had induced them to take a more northern and circuitous route by way of the Sweet Water Pass and Fort Hall. They had still between them and the valley of the Sacramento a great mass of mountains, forming the Sierra Nevada, here commonly known as the Great California Mountain, and which were at this time considered as presenting an impracticable barrier to wheeled carriages.

Various considerations had suggested to them a division of the party; and a greater portion of the camp, including the wagons with the mill and other stores, were now proceeding under the guidance of Mr. Joseph Walker, who had engaged to conduct them, by a long sweep to the southward, around what is called the Point of the

Mountain; and, crossing through a pass known only to himself, gain the banks of the Sacramento by the valley of the San Joaquin. It was a long and hazardous journey for a party in which there were women and children. Sixty days was the shortest period of time in which they could reach the Point of the Mountain, and their route lay through a country inhabited by wild and badly disposed Indians and very poor in game; but the leader was a man possessing great and intimate knowledge of the Indians, with an extraordinary firmness and decision of character.

In the meantime Mr. Chiles had passed down the Columbia with a party of ten or twelve men, with the intention of reaching the settlements on the Sacramento by a more direct course which indefinite information from hunters had indicated in the direction of the headwaters of the Rivière aux Malheurs; and, having obtained there a reinforcement of animals and a supply of provisions, meet the wagons before they should have reached the Point of the Mountain, at a place which had been previously agreed upon. In the course of our narrative we shall be able to give some information of the fortune which attended the movements of these adventurous travelers.

Having discovered our error, we immediately regained the line along the river, which the road quitted about noon, and encamped at five o'clock on a stream called Raft River (Rivière aux Cajeux), having traveled only thirteen miles. In the north, the Salmon River Mountains are visible at a very far distance; and on the left, the ridge in which Raft River heads is about twenty miles distant, rocky, and tolerably high. Thermometer at sunset 44°, with a partially clouded sky, and a sharp wind from the southwest.

September 27th. It was now no longer possible, as in our previous journey, to travel regularly every day and find at any moment a convenient place for repose at noon, or a camp at night; but the halting places were now generally fixed along the road by the nature of the country, at places where, with water, there was a little scanty grass.

Since leaving the American Falls the road had frequently been very bad; the many short, steep ascents exhausting the strength of our worn-out animals, requiring always at such places the assistance of the men to get up each cart, one by one; and our progress with twelve or fourteen wheeled carriages, though light and made for the purpose, in such a rocky country was extremely slow; and I again determined to gain time by a division of the camp. Accordingly, today the parties again separated, constituted very much as before—Mr. Fitzpatrick remaining in charge of the heavier baggage. The morning was calm and clear, with a white frost, and the temperature at sunrise 24°.

Today the country had a very forbidding appearance; and after traveling twenty miles over a slightly undulating plain, we encamped at a considerable spring, called Swamp Creek, rising in low grounds near the point of a spur from the mountain. Returning with a small party in a starving condition from the westward twelve or fourteen years since, Carson had met here three or four buffalo bulls, two of which were killed. They were among the pioneers which had made the experiment of colonizing in the valley of the Columbia, and which had failed, as heretofore stated. At sunset the thermometer was at 46°, and the evening was overcast, with a cold wind from the southeast, and tonight we had only sage for firewood. Mingled with the artemisia was a shrubby and thorny chenopodiaceous plant.

September 28th. Thermometer at sunrise 40°. The wind rose early to a gale from the west, with a very cold, driving rain; and after an uncomfortable day's ride of twenty-five miles we were glad when at evening we found a sheltered camp, where there was an abundance of wood, at some elevated rocky islands covered with cedar, near the commencement of another long cañon of the river.

With the exception of a short detention at a deep little stream called Goose Creek, and some occasional rocky places, we had today a very good road; but the country has a barren appearance, sandy, and densely covered with the artemisias from the banks of the river to the foot of the mountains. Here I remarked among the sage bushes green bunches of what is called the second growth of grass. The river today has had a smooth appearance, free from rapids, with a low, sandy hill slope bordering the bottoms, in which there is a little good soil. Thermometer at sunset 45°, blowing a gale, and disagreeably cold.

September 29th. The thermometer at sunrise 36°, with a bright sun, and appearance of finer weather.

The road for several miles was extremely rocky, and consequently bad; but entering after this a sandy country, it became very good, with no other interruption than the sage bushes which covered the river plain so far as the eye could reach, and, with their uniform tint of dark gray, gave to the country a gloomy and somber appearance. All the day the course of the river has been between walls of the black volcanic rock, a dark line of the escarpment on the opposite side pointing out its course, and sweeping along in foam at places where the mountains which border the valley present always on the left two ranges, the lower one a spur of the higher; and on the opposite side, the Salmon River Mountains are visible at a great distance. Having made twenty-four miles, we encamped about five o'clock on Rock Creek, a stream having considerable water, a swift current, and wooded with willow.

September 30th. Thermometer at sunrise, 28°. In its progress toward the river this creek soon enters a chasm of the volcanic rock, which in places along the wall presents a columnar appearance; and the road becomes extremely rocky whenever it passes near its banks. It is only about twenty feet wide where the road crosses it, with a deep bed and steep banks, covered with rocky fragments, with willows and a little grass on its narrow bottom. The soil appears to be full of calcareous matter, with which the rocks are encrusted. The fragments of rock which had been removed by the emigrants in making a road where we ascended from the bed of this creek were whitened with lime; and during the afternoon's march I remarked in the soil a considerable quantity of calcareous concretions.

Toward evening the sages became more sparse, and the clear spaces were occupied by tufts of green grass. The river still continued its course through a trough or open cañon; and toward sunset we followed the trail of several wagons which had turned in toward Snake River, and encamped, as they had done, on the top of the escarpment. There was no grass here, the soil among the sage being entirely naked; but there is occasionally a little bottom along the river, which a short ravine of rocks at rare intervals leaves accessible; and by one of these we drove our animals down and found some tolerably good grass bordering the water.

Immediately opposite to us a subterranean river bursts out directly from the face of the escarpment, and falls in white foam to the river below.[5] The main river is enclosed with mural precipices, which form its characteristic feature along a great portion of its course. A melancholy and strange-looking country—one of fracture, and violence, and fire.

We had brought with us, when we separated from the camp, a large gaunt ox, in appearance very poor; but, being killed tonight, to the great joy of the people, he was found to be remarkably fat. As usual at such occurrences the evening was devoted to gaiety and feasting; abundant fare now made an epoch among us; and in this laborious life, in such a country as this, our men had but little else to enjoy.

The temperature at sunset was 65°, with a clear sky and very high wind. By the observation of the evening the encampment was in longitude 114° 25' 04" and in latitude 42° 38' 44".

October 1st. The morning clear, with wind from the west, and the thermometer at 55°. We descended to the bottom, taking with us the boat, for the purpose of visiting the fall in the opposite cliffs; and while it was being filled with air we occupied ourselves in measuring the river, which is one thousand seven hundred and eighty-six feet in breadth, with banks two hundred feet high. We were surprised on our arrival at the opposite side to find a beautiful basin of clear water, formed by the falling river, around which the rocks were whitened by some saline incrustation. Here the Indians had constructed wicker dams, although I was informed that the salmon do not ascend the river so far, and its character below would apparently render it impracticable.

The ascent of the steep hillside was rendered a little difficult by a dense growth of shrubs and fields of cane; and there were frequent hidden crevices among the rocks, where the water was heard rushing below; but we succeeded in reaching the main stream, which, issuing from between strata of the traprock in two principal branches, produced almost immediately a torrent twenty-two feet wide and white with foam. It is a picturesque spot of singular beauty, overshaded by bushes, from under which the torrent glances, tumbling into the white basin below, where the clear water contrasted beautifully with the muddy stream of the river. Its outlet was covered with a rank growth of canes, and a variety of unusual plants, and nettles (*Urtica canabina*), which, before they were noticed, had set our hands and arms on fire. The temperature of the spring was 58°, while that of the river was 51°. The perpendicular height of the place at which this stream issues is forty-five feet above the river, and one hundred and fifty-two feet below the summit of the precipice, making nearly two hundred feet for the height of the wall. On the hillside here were obtained specimens consisting principally of fragments of the shells of small crustacea, and which were probably formed by deposition from these springs proceeding from some lake or river in the highlands above.

We resumed our journey at noon, the day being hot and bright; and, after a march of seventeen miles, encamped at sunset on the river, near several lodges of Snake Indians.[6]

Our encampment was about one mile below the Fishing Falls, a series of cataracts with very inclined planes, which are probably so named because they form a barrier to the ascent of the salmon; and the great fisheries, from which the inhabitants of this barren region almost entirely derive a subsistence, commence at this place.

These appeared to be unusually gay savages, fond of loud laughter; and, in their apparent good nature and merry character, struck me as being entirely different from the Indians we had been accustomed to see. From several who visited our camp in the evening we purchased, in exchange for goods, dried salmon. At this season they are not very fat, but we were easily pleased. The Indians made us comprehend that when the salmon came up the river in the spring they are so abundant that they merely throw in their spears at random, certain of bringing out a fish.

These poor people are but slightly provided with winter clothing; there is but little game to furnish skins for the purpose; and of a little animal which seemed to be the most numerous, it required twenty skins to make a covering to the knees. But they are still a joyous, talkative race, who grow fat and become poor with the salmon, which at least never fail them—the dried being used in the absence of the fresh. We are encamped immediately on the river-bank, and with the salmon jumping up out of the water, and Indians paddling about in boats made of rushes, or laughing around the fires, the camp tonight has quite a lively appearance.

The river at this place is more open than for some distance above;

and, for the time, the black precipices have disappeared, and no calcareous matter is visible in the soil. The thermometer at sunset, 74°; clear and calm.

October 2d. The sunrise temperature was 48°, the weather clear and calm. Shortly after leaving the encampment we crossed a stream of clear water with a variable breadth of ten to twenty-five yards, broken by rapids, and lightly wooded with willow, and having a little grass on its small bottom land.

The barrenness of the country is in fine contrast today with the mingled beauty and grandeur of the river, which is more open than hitherto, with a constant succession of falls and rapids. Over the edge of the black cliffs, and out from their faces, are falling number-less streams and springs; and all the line of the river is in motion with the play of the water. In about seven miles we reached the most beautiful and picturesque fall I had seen on the river.

On the opposite side, the vertical fall is perhaps eighteen feet high; and nearer, the sheet of foaming water is divided and broken into cataracts, where several little islands on the brink and in the river above give it much picturesque beauty, and make it one of those places the traveler turns again and again to fix in his memory. There were several lodges of Indians here, from whom we traded salmon.

Below this place the river makes a remarkable bend; and the road, ascending the ridge, gave us a fine view of the river below, intersected at many places by numerous fish dams. In the north, about fifty miles distant, were some high snowy peaks of the Salmon River Mountains;[7] and in the northeast the last peak of the range was visible, at the distance of perhaps one hundred miles or more. The river hills consist of very broken masses of sand, covered every-where with the same interminable fields of sage, and occasionally the road is very heavy.

We now very frequently saw Indians, who were strung along the river at every little rapid where fish are to be caught, and the cry *"Haggai, haggai"* (fish), was constantly heard whenever we passed near their huts or met them in the road. Very many of them were oddly and partially dressed in overcoat, shirt, waistcoat, or panta-loons, or whatever article of clothing they had been able to procure in trade from the emigrants; for we had now entirely quitted the country where hawks' bells, beads, and vermilion were the current coin, and found that here only useful articles, and chiefly clothing, were in great request. These, however, are eagerly sought after, and for a few trifling pieces of clothing travelers may procure food sufficient to carry them to the Columbia.

We made a long stretch across the upper plain, and encamped on the bluff, where the grass was very green and good, the soil of the upper plains containing a considerable proportion of calcareous matter. This green freshness of the grass was very remarkable for the season of the year. Again we heard the roar of a fall in the river below, where the water in an unbroken volume goes over a descent of several feet. The night is clear, and the weather continues very warm and pleasant, with a sunset temperature of 70°.

October 3d. The morning was pleasant, with a temperature at sunrise of 42°. The road was broken by ravines among the hills, and in one of these, which made the bed of a dry creek, I found a fragmentary stratum, or brecciated conglomerate, consisting of flinty slate pebbles, with fragments of limestone containing fossil shells.

On the left the mountains are visible at a distance of twenty or thirty miles, appearing smooth and rather low; but at intervals higher peaks look out from beyond, and indicate that the main ridge, which we are leaving with the course of the river, and which forms the northern boundary of the Great Basin, still maintains its elevation.

About two o'clock we arrived at the ford where the road crosses to the right bank of Snake River. An Indian was hired to conduct us through the ford, which proved impracticable for us, the water sweeping away the howitzer and nearly drowning the mules, which we were obliged to extricate by cutting them out of the harness. The river here is expanded into a little bay in which there are two islands, across which is the road of the ford; and the emigrants had passed by placing two of their heavy wagons abreast of each other, so as to oppose a considerable mass against the body of water.

The Indians informed us that one of the men, in attempting to turn some cattle which had taken a wrong direction, was carried off by the current and drowned. Since their passage the water had risen considerably; but fortunately we had a resource in the boat, which was filled with air and launched; and at seven o'clock we were safely encamped on the opposite bank, the animals swimming across, and the carriage, howitzer, and baggage of the camp being carried over in the boat.

At the place where we crossed, above the islands, the river had narrowed to a breadth of one thousand and forty-nine feet by measurement, the greater portion of which was from six to eight feet deep. We were obliged to make our camp where we landed, among the Indian lodges, which are semicircular huts made of willow, thatched over with straw, and open to the sunny south. By observation, the latitude of our encampment on the right bank of the river was 42° 55′ 58″, chronometric longitude 115° 04′ 46″, and the traveled distance from Fort Hall two hundred and eight miles.

October 4th. Calm, pleasant day, with the thermometer at sunrise at 47°. Leaving the river at a considerable distance to the left, and following up the bed of a rocky creek, with occasional holes of water, in about six miles we ascended by a long and rather steep hill, to a plain six hundred feet above the river over which we continued to travel during the day, having a broken ridge two thousand or three thousand feet high on the right. The plain terminates, where we ascended, in an escarpment of vesicular traprock, which supplies the fragments of the creek below. The sky clouded over, with a strong wind from the northwest, with a few drops of rain and occasional sunlight, threatening a change.

Artemisia still covers the plain, but *Purshia tridentata* makes its appearance here on the hillsides, and on bottoms of the creeks— quite a tree in size, and larger than the artemisia. We crossed several hollows with a little water in them and improved grass; and, turning off from the road in the afternoon in search of water, traveled about three miles up the bed of a willow creek, toward the mountain, and found a good encampment, with wood and grass, and little ponds of water in the bed of the creek; which must be of more importance at other seasons, as we found there several old fixtures for fishing. There were many holes on the creek prairie, which had been made by the Diggers in search of roots. Wind increased to a violent gale from the northwest, with a temperature at sunset of 57°.

October 5th. The morning was calm and clear, and at sunrise the thermometer was at 32°. The road today was occasionally extremely rocky, with hard volcanic fragments, and our traveling very slow. In about nine miles the road brought us to a group of smoking hot springs, with a temperature of 164°.

There were a few helianthi in bloom, with some other low plants, and the place was green round about; the ground warm, and the air pleasant, with a summer atmosphere that was very grateful in a day of high and cold searching wind. The rocks were covered with a white and red encrustation, and the water has on the tongue the same unpleasant effect as that of the Basin Spring on Bear River. They form several branches, and bubble up with force enough to raise the small pebbles several inches. . . .*

These springs are near the foot of the ridge (a dark and rugged-looking mountain), in which some of the nearer rocks have a reddish appearance, and probably consist of a reddish-brown trap, fragments of which were scattered along the road after leaving the spring. The road was now about to cross the Point of this Mountain, which we judged to be a spur from the Salmon River Range.

We crossed a small creek, and encamped about sunset on a stream which is probably Lake River. This is a small stream, some five or six feet broad, with a swift current, wooded principally with willows and some few cottonwoods. Along the banks were canes, rosebushes, and clematis, with *Purshia tridentata* and artemisias on the upper bottom. The somber appearance of the country is somewhat relieved in coming unexpectedly from the dark rocks upon these green and wooded watercourses, sunk in chasms, and in the spring, the contrasted effect must make them beautiful.

The thermometer at sunset 47°, and the night threatening snow.

October 6th. The morning warm, the thermometer 46° at sunrise, and sky entirely clouded. After traveling about three miles over an extremely rocky road, the volcanic fragments began to disappear; and, entering among the hills at the point of the mountain, we found ourselves suddenly in a granite country. Here the character of the vegetation was very much changed; the artemisia disappeared almost entirely, showing only at intervals toward the close of the day, and was replaced by *Purshia tridentata* with flowering shrubs and small fields of *Dieteria divaricata*, which gave bloom and gaiety to the hills. These were everywhere covered with a fresh and green

* Frémont's chemical analysis omitted.

short grass, like that of the early spring. This is the fall or second growth, the dried grass having been burnt off by the Indians; and wherever the fire has passed, the bright-green color is universal. The soil among the hills is altogether different from that of the river plain, being in many places black, in others sandy and gravelly, but of a firm and good character, appearing to result from the decomposition of the granite rocks, which is proceeding rapidly.

In quitting for a time the artemisia (sage) through which we had been so long voyaging, and the somber appearance of which is so discouraging, I have to remark that I have been informed that in Mexico wheat is grown upon the ground which produces this shrub; which, if true, relieves the soil from the character of sterility imputed to it. Be this as it may, there is no dispute about the grass, which is almost universal on the hills and mountains, and always nutritious, even in its dry state.

We passed on the way masses of granite on the slope of a spur, which was very much weathered and abraded. This is a white feldspathic granite, with small scales of black mica; smoky quartz in which there are garnets appear to constitute this portion of the mountain. The road at noon reached a broken ridge, on which were scattered many boulders or blocks of granite; and, passing very small streams, where, with a little more than the usual timber, was sometimes gathered a little wilderness of plants, we encamped on a small stream, after a march of twenty-two miles, in company with a few Indians.

Temperature at sunset, 51°; and the night was partially clear, with a few stars visible through drifting white clouds. The Indians made an unsuccessful attempt to steal a few horses from us—a thing of course with them, and to prevent which the traveler is on perpetual watch.

October 7th. The day was bright, clear, and pleasant, with a temperature of 45°; and we breakfasted at sunrise, the birds singing in the trees as merrily as if we were in the midst of summer. On the upper edge of the hills, on the opposite side of the creek, the black volcanic rock reappears; and ascending these, the road passed through a basin, around which the hills swept in such a manner as to give it the appearance of an old crater. Here were strata and broken beds of black scoriated rock, and hills composed of the same, on the summit of one of which there was an opening resembling a rent.

We traveled today through a country resembling that of yesterday, where, although the surface was hilly, the road was good, being firm and entirely free from rocks and artemisia. To our left, below, was the great sage plain; and on the right were the near mountains, which presented a smoothly broken character or rather a surface waved into numberless hills. The road was occasionally enlivened by meeting Indians, and the day was extremely beautiful and pleasant; and we were pleased to be free from the sage, even for a day. When we had traveled about eight miles we were nearly opposite to the highest portion of the mountains on the left side of the Smoke River Valley; and, continuing on a few miles beyond, we came suddenly in sight of the broad, green line of the valley of the Rivière Boisée (Wooded River), black near the gorge where it debouches into the plains, with high precipices of basalt, between walls of which it passes on emerging from the mountains. Following with the eye its upward course, it appears to be shut in among lofty mountains, confining its valley in a very rugged country.

Descending the hills, after traveling a few miles along the high plain, the road brought us down upon the bottoms of the river, which is a beautiful rapid stream, with clear mountain water, and, as the name indicates, well wooded with some varieties of timber—among which are handsome cottonwoods. Such a stream had become quite a novelty in this country, and we were delighted this afternoon to make a pleasant camp under fine old trees again. There were several Indian encampments scattered along the river; and a number of their inhabitants, in the course of the evening, came to the camp on horseback with dried and fresh fish to trade. The evening was clear, and the temperature at sunset 57°.

At the time of the first occupation of this region by parties engaged in the fur trade, a small party of men, under the command of —— Reid, constituting all the garrison of a little fort on this river, were surprised and massacred by the Indians; and to this event the stream owes its occasional name of Reid's River.

On the 8th we traveled about twenty-six miles, the ridge on the right having scattered pines on the upper parts; and, continuing the next day our road along the river bottom, after a day's travel of twenty-four miles we encamped in the evening on the right bank of the river, a mile above the mouth, and early the next morning arrived at Fort Boisé.[8] This is a simple dwelling house on the right bank of Snake River, about a mile below the mouth of Rivière Boisée; and on our arrival we were received with an agreeable hospitality by Mr. Payette,[9] an officer of the Hudson's Bay Company, in charge of the fort, all of whose garrison consisted in a Canadian *engagé*.

Here the road recrosses the river, which is broad and deep; but with our good boat, aided by two canoes which were found at the place, the camp was very soon transferred to the left bank. Here we found ourselves again surrounded by the sage, *Artemisia tridentata,* and the different shrubs which during our voyage had always made their appearance abundantly on saline soils, being here the prevailing and almost the only plants. Among them the surface was covered with the usual saline efflorescences, which here consist almost entirely of carbonate of soda, with a small portion of chloride of sodium.

Mr. Payette had made but slight attempts at cultivation, his efforts being limited to raising a few vegetables, in which he succeeded tolerably well; the post being principally supported by salmon. He was very hospitable and kind to us, and we made a sensible impression upon all his comestibles; but our principal inroad was into the dairy, which was abundantly supplied, stock appearing to thrive extremely well; and we had an unusual luxury in a present of fresh butter, which was, however, by no means equal to that of Fort Hall—probably from some accidental cause. During the day we remained here there were considerable numbers of miserable half-naked Indians around the fort, who had arrived from the neighboring mountains. During the summer, the only subsistence of these people is derived from the salmon, of which they are not provident enough to lay up a sufficient store for the winter, during which many of them die from absolute starvation.

Many little accounts and scattered histories, together with an acquaintance which I gradually acquired of their modes of life, had left the aboriginal inhabitants of this vast region pictured in my mind as a race of people whose great and constant occupation was the means of procuring a subsistence; and though want of space and other reasons will prevent me from detailing the many incidents which made these things familiar to me, this great feature among the characteristics of the country will gradually be forced upon the mind of the reader.

Pointing to a group of Indians who had just arrived from the mountains on the left side of the valley, and who were regarding our usual appliances of civilization with an air of bewildered curiosity, Mr. Payette informed me that, every year since his arrival at this post, he had unsuccessfully endeavored to induce these people to lay up a store of salmon for their winter provision. While the summer weather and the salmon lasted they lived contentedly and happily, scattered along the different streams where the fish were to be found; and as soon as the winter snows began to fall, little smokes would be seen rising among the mountains, where they would be found in miserable groups, starving out the winter, and sometimes, according to the general belief, reduced to the horror of cannibalism—the strong, of course, preying on the weak. Certain it is they are driven to any extremity for food, and eat every insect, and every creeping thing, however loathsome and repulsive. Snails, lizards, ants—all are devoured with the readiness and greediness of mere animals. In common with all the other Indians we had encountered since reaching the Pacific waters, these people use the Shoshone or Snake language, which, as will be remarked in the course of the narrative, is the universal language over a very extensive region.

On the evening of the 10th I obtained, with the usual observations, a very excellent emersion of the first satellite, agreeing very nearly with the chronometer. From these observations the longitude of the fort is 116° 47' 00", latitude 43° 49' 22", and elevation above the sea two thousand one hundred feet.

Sitting by the fire on the riverbank, and waiting for the immersion of the satellite, which did not take place until after midnight, we heard the monotonous song of the Indians, with which they accompany a certain game of which they are very fond. Of the poetry we could not judge, but the music was miserable.

October 11th. The morning was clear, with a light breeze from the east, and a temperature at sunrise of 33°. A part of a bullock purchased at the fort, together with the boat to assist him in crossing, was left here for Mr. Fitzpatrick, and at eleven o'clock we resumed our journey; and directly leaving the river, and crossing the artemisia plain, in several ascents we reached the foot of a ridge where the road entered a dry, sandy hollow, up which it continued to the head, and, crossing a dividing ridge, entered a similar one.

We met here two poor emigrants (Irishmen) who had lost their horses two days since—probably stolen by the Indians—and were returning to the fort in hopes to hear something of them there. They had recently had nothing to eat; and I halted to unpack an animal, and gave them meat for their dinner. In this hollow the artemisia is partially displaced on the hillsides by grass; and descending it, about sunset we reached the Rivière aux Malheurs (the Unfortunate or Unlucky River), a considerable stream, with an average breadth of fifty feet and, at this time, eighteen inches' depth of water.*

The bottom lands were generally one and a half mile broad, covered principally with long dry grass; and we had difficulty to find sufficient good grass for the camp. With the exception of a bad place of a few hundred yards long, which occurred in rounding a point of hill to reach the ford of the river, the road during the day had been very good.

October 12th. The morning was clear and calm, and the thermometer at sunrise 23°. My attention was attracted by a smoke on the right side of the river, a little below the ford, where I found on the low bank, near the water, a considerable number of hot springs, in which the temperature of the water was 193°. The ground, which was too hot for the naked foot, was covered above and below the springs with an encrustation of common salt, very white and good, and fine-grained.

Leading for five miles up a broad dry branch of the Malheurs River, the road entered a sandy hollow where the surface was rendered firm by the admixture of other rock, being good and level until arriving near the head of the ravine, where it became a little rocky, and we met with a number of sharp ascents over an undulating surface. Crossing here a dividing ridge, it became an excellent road of gradual descent down a very marked hollow, in which, after ten miles, willows began to appear in the dry bed of a head of the Rivière aux Bouleaux (Birch River); and descending seven miles,

---

* The party had now entered present-day Oregon.

we found, at its junction with another branch, a little water, not very good or abundant, but sufficient in case of necessity for a camp.

Crossing Birch River, we continued for about four miles across a point of hill, the country on the left being entirely mountainous, with no level spot to be seen; whence we descended to Snake River—here a fine-looking stream, with a large body of water and a smooth current, although we hear the roar and see below us the commencement of rapids where it enters among the hills. It forms here a deep bay, with a low sand island in the midst; and its course among the mountains is agreeably exchanged for the black volcanic rock. The weather during the day had been very bright and extremely hot; but, as usual, so soon as the sun went down, it was necessary to put on overcoats.

I obtained this evening an observation of an emersion of the first satellite, and our observations place this encampment in latitude 44° 17′ 36″ and longitude 116° 56′ 45″, which is the mean of the results from the satellite and chronometer; the elevation above the sea, one thousand eight hundred and eighty feet. At this encampment the grass is scanty and poor.

October 13th. The morning was bright, with the temperature at sunrise 28°. The horses had strayed off during the night, probably in search of grass; and, after a considerable delay, we had succeeded in finding all but two when, about nine o'clock, we heard the sound of an Indian song and drum approaching, and, shortly after, three Cayuse Indians appeared in sight, bringing with them the two animals. They belonged to a party which had been on a buffalo hunt in the neighborhood of the Rocky Mountains, and were hurrying home in advance. We presented them with some tobacco and other things, with which they appeared well satisfied, and, moderating their pace, traveled in company with us.

We were now about to leave the valley of the great southern branch of the Columbia River,[10] to which the absence of timber and the scarcity of water give the appearance of a desert, to enter a mountainous region where the soil is good and in which the face of the country is covered with nutritious grasses and dense forest—land embracing many varieties of trees peculiar to the country, and on which the timber exhibits a luxuriance of growth unknown to the eastern part of the continent and to Europe.

This mountainous region connects itself in the southward and westward with the elevated country belonging to the Cascade or California range; and, as will be remarked in the course of the narrative, forms the eastern limit of the fertile and timbered lands along the desert and mountainous region included within the Great Basin —a term which I apply to the intermediate region between the Rocky Mountains and the next range, containing many lakes, with their own system of rivers and creeks (of which the Great Salt Lake is the principal), and which have no connection with the ocean or the great rivers which flow into it. This Great Basin is yet to be adequately explored.[11]

And here, on quitting the banks of a sterile river to enter on arable mountains, the remark may be made that, on this western slope of our continent, the usual order of distribution of good and bad soil is often reversed—the river and creek bottoms being often sterile and darkened with the gloomy and barren artemisia, while the mountain is often fertile and covered with rich grass, pleasant to the eye and good for flocks and herds.

Leaving entirely the Snake River, which is said henceforth to pursue its course through cañons amidst rocky and impracticable mountains where there is no possibility of traveling with animals, we ascended a long and somewhat steep hill; and, crossing the dividing ridge, came down into the Valley of Burnt River, which here looks like a hole among the hills. The average breadth of the stream here is thirty feet; it is well fringed with the usual small trees; and the soil in the bottoms is good, with better grass than we had lately been accustomed to see.

We now traveled through a very mountainous country, the stream running rather in a ravine than a valley, and the road is decidedly bad and dangerous for single wagons, frequently crossing the stream where the water is sometimes deep; all the day the animals were fatigued in climbing up and descending a succession of steep ascents, to avoid the precipitous hillsides; and the common trail, which leads along the mountainside at places where the river strikes the base, is sometimes bad even for a horseman.

The mountains along this day's journey were composed, near the river, of a salty calcareous rock in a metamorphic condition. It appears originally to have been a salty sedimentary limestone, but its present condition indicates that it has been altered and has become partially crystalline—probably from the proximity of volcanic rocks. But though traveling was slow and fatiguing to the animals, we were delighted with the appearance of the country, which was green and refreshing after our tedious journey down the parched valley of Snake River.

The mountains were covered with good bunch grass (festuca); the water of the streams was cold and pure; their bottoms were handsomely wooded with various kinds of trees; and huge and lofty and picturesque precipices were displayed where the river cut through the mountains.

We found in the evening some good grass and rushes; and encamped among large timber, principally birch, which had been recently burnt and blackened, and almost destroyed by fire. The night was calm and tolerably clear, with the thermometer at sunset at 59°. Our journey today was about twenty miles.

October 14th. The day was clear and calm, with a temperature at sunrise of 46°. After traveling about three miles up the valley, we found the river shut up by precipices in a kind of cañon, and the road makes a circuit over the mountains. In the afternoon we reached the river again, by another little ravine; and, after traveling along it for a few miles, left it enclosed among rude mountains, and, ascending a smaller branch, encamped on it about five o'clock, very much elevated above the valley.

The view was everywhere limited by mountains, on which were no longer seen the black and barren rocks, but a fertile soil, with excellent grass, and partly well covered with pine. I have never seen a wagon road equally bad, in the same space, as this of yesterday and today. I noticed where one wagon had been overturned twice, in a very short distance; and it was surprising to me that those wagons which were in the rear, and could not have had much assistance, got through at all. Still, there is no mud, and the road has one advantage in being perfectly firm. The day had been warm and very pleasant, and the night was perfectly clear.

October 15th. The thermometer at daylight was 42°, and at sunrise 40°; clouds, which were scattered over all the sky, disappeared with the rising sun. The trail did not much improve until we had crossed the dividing grounds between the Brulé (Burnt) and Powder rivers.*

The rock displayed on the mountains as we approached the sum-

* In what is now Baker County, northeastern Oregon.

mit was a compact trap, decomposing on the exposed surfaces, and apparently an altered argillaceous sandstone, containing small crystalline nodules of anolcime, apparently filling cavities originally existing. From the summit here the whole horizon shows high mountains; no high plain or level is to be seen; and on the left, from south around by the west to north, the mountains are black with pines, while through the remaining space to the eastward they are bald, with the exception of some scattered pines.

We are now entering a region where all the elevated parts are covered with dense and heavy forests. From the dividing grounds we descended by a mountain road to Powder River,[12] on an old bed of which we encamped. Descending from the summit, we enjoyed a picturesque view of high rocky mountains on the right, illuminated by the setting sun.

From the heights we had looked in vain for a well-known landmark on Powder River, which had been described to me by Mr. Payette as *l'arbre seul* (the lone tree); and, on arriving at the river, we found a fine tall pine stretched on the ground, which had been felled by some inconsiderate emigrant ax. It had been a beacon on the road for many years past.

Our Cayuses had become impatient to reach their homes, and traveled on ahead today; and this afternoon we were visited by several Indians who belonged to the tribes on the Columbia. They were on horseback, and were out on a hunting excursion, but had obtained no better game than a large gray hare, of which each had some six or seven hanging to his saddle.

We were also visited by an Indian who had his lodge and family in the mountain to the left. He was in want of ammunition, and brought with him a beaver skin to exchange, which he valued at six charges of powder and ball. I learned from him that there are very few of these animals remaining in this part of the country. . . .*

October 17th. Thermometer at sunrise, 25°. The weather at daylight was fine, and the sky without a cloud; but these came up, or were formed with the sun, and at seven were thick over all the sky. Just now this appears to be the regular course—clear and brilliant during the night, and cloudy during the day.

---

*A brief passage on the weather and some astronomical observations is omitted.

There is snow yet visible in the neighboring mountains, which yesterday extended along our route to the left in a lofty and dark-blue range, having much the appearance of the Wind River Mountains. It is probable that they have received their name of the Blue Mountains from the dark-blue appearance given to them by the pines.

We traveled this morning across the affluents to Powder River, the road being good, firm, and level; and the country became constantly more pleasant and interesting. The soil appeared to be very deep, and is black and extremely good, as well among the hollows of the hills on the elevated plats as on the river bottoms; the vegetation being such as is usually found in good ground. . . .*

From the waters of this stream the road ascended by a good and moderate ascent to a dividing ridge, but immediately entered upon ground covered with fragments of an altered siliceous slate, which are in many places large and render the road racking to a carriage.

In this rock the planes of deposition are distinctly preserved, and the metamorphism is evidently due to the proximity of volcanic rocks. On either side, the mountains here are densely covered with tall and handsome trees; and mingled with the green of a variety of pines is the yellow of the European larch (*Pinus larix*), which loses its leaves in the fall. From its present color we were enabled to see that it forms a large proportion of the forests on the mountains, and is here a magnificent tree, attaining sometimes the height of two hundred feet, which I believe is elsewhere unknown.

About two in the afternoon we reached a high point of the dividing ridge, from which we obtained a good view of the Grand Rond —a beautiful level basin, or mountain valley, covered with good grass on a rich soil, abundantly watered, and surrounded by high and well-timbered mountains; and its name descriptive of its form— the great circle. It is a place—one of the few we have seen in our journey so far—where a farmer would delight to establish himself, if he were content to live in the seclusion which it imposes. It is about twenty miles in diameter, and may in time form a superb county. Probably with the view of avoiding a circuit, the wagons had directly descended into the Rond by the face of a hill so very rocky and continuously steep as to be apparently impracticable;

* A chemical analysis of the soil omitted.

and, following down on their trail, we encamped on one of the branches of the Grand Rond River, immediately at the foot of the hill. I had remarked, in descending, some very white spots glistening on the plain, and, going out in that direction after we had encamped, I found them to be the bed of a dry salt lake, or marsh, very firm and bare, which was covered thickly with a fine white powder containing a large quantity of carbonate of soda (thirty-three in one hundred parts).

The old grass had been lately burnt off from the surrounding hills, and, wherever the fire had passed, there was a recent growth of strong, green, and vigorous grass; and the soil of the level prairie, which sweeps directly up to the foot of the surrounding mountains, appears to be very rich, producing flax spontaneously and luxuriantly in various places. . . .*

October 18th. It began to rain an hour before sunrise, and continued until ten o'clock; the sky entirely overcast, and the temperature at sunrise 48°. We resumed our journey somewhat later than usual, traveling in a nearly north direction across this beautiful valley, and about noon reached a place on one of the principal streams, where I had determined to leave the emigrant trail, in the expectation of finding a more direct and better road across the Blue Mountains.[13] At this place the emigrants appeared to have held some consultation as to their further route, and finally turned directly off to the left, reaching the foot of the mountain in about three miles, and ascending it by a hill as steep and difficult as that by which we had yesterday descended to the Rond.

Quitting, therefore, this road, which, after a very rough crossing, issued from the mountains by the heads of the Umatilah River, we continued our northern course across the valley, following an Indian trail which had been indicated to me by Mr. Payette, and encamped at the northern extremity of the Grand Rond, on a sloughlike stream of very deep water, without any apparent current. There are some pines here on the low hills at the creek, and in the northwest corner of the Rond is a very heavy body of timber, which descends into the plain.

The clouds, which had rested very low along the mountainsides

---

* Again a soil analysis omitted. The proper spellings are Grande Ronde and Umatilla. The party was moving north into what is now southeastern Washington.

during the day, rose gradually up in the afternoon; and in the evening the sky was almost entirely clear, with a temperature at sunset of 47°. Some indifferent observations placed the camp in longitude 117° 28′ 26″, latitude 45° 26′ 47″; and the elevation was two thousand six hundred feet above the sea.

October 19th. This morning the mountains were hidden by fog: there was a heavy dew during the night, in which the exposed thermometer at daylight stood at 32°, and at sunrise the temperature was 35°.

We passed out of the Grand Rond by a fine road along the creek, which, for a short distance, runs in a kind of rocky chasm. Crossing a low point, which was a little rocky, the trail conducted into the open valley of the stream—a handsome place for farms; the soil, even of the hills, being rich and black. Passing through a point of pines, which bore evidences of being much frequented by the Indians and in which the trees were sometimes apparently two hundred feet high and three to seven feet in diameter, we halted for a few minutes in the afternoon at the foot of the Blue Mountains, on a branch of the Grand Rond River, at an elevation of two thousand seven hundred feet.

Resuming our journey, we commenced the ascent of the mountain through an open pine forest of large and stately trees, among which the balsam pine made its appearance, the road being good, with the exception of one steep ascent with a corresponding descent, which might both have been easily avoided by opening a way for a short distance through the timber.

It would have been well had we encamped on the stream where we had halted below, as the night overtook us on the mountain, and we were obliged to encamp without water and tie up the animals to the trees for the night. We had halted on a smooth, open place of a narrow ridge which descended very rapidly to a ravine, or piny hollow, at a considerable distance below, and it was quite a pretty spot, had there been water near. But the fires at night look very cheerless after a day's march when there is no preparation for supper going on; and, after sitting some time around the blazing logs, Mr. Preuss and Carson, with several others, volunteered to take the indiarubber buckets and go down into the ravine in search of water. It was a very difficult way, in the darkness, down the slippery side of the steep mountain, and harder still to climb about half a mile up again; but they found the water, and the cup of coffee, which it enabled us to make, and bread were only enjoyed with greater pleasure. . . .*

October 20th. There was a heavy white frost during the night, and at sunrise the temperature was 37° The animals had eaten nothing during the night; and we made an early start, continuing our route among the pines, which were more dense than yesterday, and still retained their magnificent size.

The larches cluster together in masses on the sides of the mountains, and their yellow foliage contrasts handsomely with the green of the balsam and other pines. After a few miles we ceased to see any pines, and the timber consisted of several varieties of spruce, larch, and balsam pine, which have a regularly conical figure. These trees appeared from sixty to nearly two hundred feet in height, the usual circumference being ten to twelve feet, and in the pines sometimes twenty-one feet. In open places near the summit these trees became less high and more branching, the conical form having a greater base.

The instrument carriage occasioned much delay, it being frequently necessary to fell trees and remove the fallen timber. The trail we were following led up a long spur, with a very gradual and gentle rise. At the end of three miles we halted at an open place near the summit, from which we enjoyed a fine view over the mountainous country where we had lately traveled, to take a barometrical observation at the height of four thousand seven hundred and sixty feet.

After traveling occasionally through open places in the forest we were obliged to cut a way through a dense body of timber, from which we emerged on an open mountainside, where we found a number of small springs, and encamped after a day's journey of ten miles. Our elevation here was five thousand feet.

October 21st. There was a very heavy white frost during the night, and the thermometer at sunrise was 30°.

We continued to travel through the forest, in which the road was rendered difficult by fallen trunks, and obstructed by many small trees which it was necessary to cut down. But these are only accidental difficulties, which could easily be removed, and a very excel-

* Astronomical observations omitted.

lent road may be had through this pass, with no other than very moderate ascents or declivities.

A laborious day, which had advanced us only six miles on our road, brought us in the afternoon to an opening in the forest, in which there was a fine mountain meadow, with good grass and a large clear-water stream; one of the head branches of the Umatilah River.

During this day's journey the barometer was broken, and the elevations above the sea, hereafter given, depend upon the temperature of boiling water. Some of the white spruces which I measured today were twelve feet in circumference, and one of the larches ten; but eight feet was the average circumference of those measured along the road.

I held in my hand a tapeline as I walked along, in order to form some correct idea of the size of the timber. Their height appeared to be from one hundred to one hundred and eighty, and perhaps two hundred feet, and the trunks of the larches were sometimes one hundred feet without a limb; but the white spruces were generally covered with branches nearly to the root. All these trees have their branches, particularly the lower ones, declining.

October 22d. The white frost this morning was like snow on the ground; the ice was a quarter of an inch thick on the creek, and the thermometer at sunrise was at 20°. But in a few hours the day became warm and pleasant, and our road over the mountains was delightful and full of enjoyment.

The trail passed sometimes through very thick young timber, in which there was much cutting to be done; but after traveling a few miles the mountains became more bald, and we reached a point from which there was a very extensive view in the northwest. We were here on the western verge of the Blue Mountains, long spurs of which, very precipitous on either side, extended down into the valley, the waters of the mountain roaring between them.

On our right was a mountain plateau covered with a dense forest; and to the westward, immediately below us, was the great Nez Percé (Pierced Nose) prairie, in which dark lines of timber indicated the course of many affluents to a considerable stream that was seen pursuing its way across the plain toward what appeared to be the Columbia River. This I knew to be the Walla Walla River,[14] and occasional spots along its banks, which resembled clearings, were supposed to be the mission or Indians settlements; but the weather was smoky and unfavorable to far views with the glass.

The rock displayed here in the escarpments is a compact amorphous trap, which appears to constitute the mass of the Blue Mountains in this latitude; and all the region of country through which we have traveled since leaving the Snake River has been the seat of violent and extensive igneous action.

Along the Burnt River Valley the strata are evidently sedimentary rocks, altered by the intrusion of volcanic products, which in some instances have penetrated and essentially changed their original condition. Along our line of route, from this point to the California mountains, there seems but little essential change. All our specimens of sedimentary rocks show them to be much altered, and volcanic productions appear to prevail throughout the whole intervening distance.

The road now led along the mountainside, around heads of the precipitous ravines; and, keeping men ahead to clear a road, we passed alternately through bodies of timber and small open prairies, and encamped in a large meadow, in view of the great prairie below.

At sunset the thermometer was at 40°, and the night was very clear and bright. Water was only to be had here by descending a bad ravine, into which we drove our animals, and had much trouble with them in a very close growth of small pines. Mr. Preuss had walked ahead, and did not get into camp this evening. The trees here maintained their size, and one of the black spruces measured fifteen feet in circumference. In the neighborhood of the camp pines have reappeared here among the timber.

October 23d. The morning was very clear; there had been a heavy white frost during the night, and at sunrise the thermometer was at 31°.

After cutting through two thick bodies of timber, in which I noticed some small trees of hemlock spruce (*perusse*), the forest became more open, and we had no longer any trouble to clear a way. The pines here were eleven or twelve feet in circumference and about one hundred and ten feet high, and appeared to love the open grounds.

The trail now led along one of the long spurs of the mountain, descending gradually toward the plain; and, after traveling a few miles, we emerged finally from the forest, in full view of the plain below, and saw the snowy mass of Mount Hood, standing high out above the surrounding country, at a distance of one hundred and eighty miles.

The road along the ridge was excellent, and the grass very green and good, the old grass having been burnt off early in the autumn. About four o'clock in the afternoon we reached a little bottom on the Walla Walla River, where we found Mr. Preuss, who yesterday had reached this place, and found himself too far in advance of the camp to return. The stream here has just issued from the narrow ravines, which are walled with precipices, in which the rock has a brown and more burnt appearance than above. At sunset the thermometer was at 48°; and our position was in longitude 118° 00′ 39″ and in latitude 45° 53′ 35″.

The morning was clear, with a temperature at sunrise of 24°. Crossing the river, we traveled over a hilly country with good bunch grass; the river bottom, which generally contains the best soil in other countries, being here a sterile level of rock and pebbles. We had found the soil in the Blue Mountains to be of excellent quality, and it appeared also to be good here among the lower hills. Reaching a little eminence, over which the trail passed, we had an extensive view along the course of the river, which was divided and spread over its bottom in a network of water, receiving several other tributaries from the mountains.

There was a band of several hundred horses grazing on the hills about two miles ahead; and as we advanced on the road we met other bands, which Indians were driving out to pasture also on the hills. True to its general character, the reverse of other countries, the hills and mountains here were rich in grass, the bottoms barren and sterile.

In six miles we crossed a principal fork, below which the scattered water of the river was gathered into one channel; and, passing on the way several unfinished houses, and some cleared patches where corn and potatoes were cultivated, we reached, in about eight miles farther, the missionary establishment of Dr. Whitman, which consisted at this time of one adobe house—i.e., built of unburnt bricks, as in Mexico.[15]

I found Dr. Whitman absent on a visit to the Dalles of the Columbia; but had the pleasure to see a fine-looking large family of emigrants—men, women, and children—in robust health, all indemnifying themselves for previous scanty fare in a hearty consumption of potatoes, which are produced here of a remarkably good quality. We were disappointed in our expectation of obtaining corn meal or flour at this station, the mill belonging to the mission having been lately burnt down; but an abundant supply of excellent potatoes banished regrets, and furnished a grateful substitute for bread.

A small town of Nez Percé Indians gave an inhabited and even a populous appearance to the station; and, after remaining about an hour, we continued our route, and encamped on the river about four miles below, passing on the way an emigrant encampment.

Temperature at sunset 49°

October 25th. The weather was pleasant, with a sunrise temperature of 36°. Our road today had in it nothing of interest, and the country offered to the eye only a sandy, undulating plain, through which a scantily timbered river takes its course.

We halted about three miles above the mouth, on account of grass; and the next morning arrived at the Nez Percé Fort, one of the trading establishments of the Hudson's Bay Company, a few hundred yards above the junction of the Walla Walla with the Columbia River.[16] Here we had the first view of this river, and found it about one thousand two hundred yards wide, and presenting the appearance of a fine navigable stream.

We made our camp in a little grove of willows on the Walla Walla, which are the only trees to be seen in the neighborhood, but were obliged to send the animals back to the encampment we had left, as there was scarcely a blade of grass to be found. The post is on the bank of the Columbia, on a plain of bare sands, from which the air was literally filled with clouds of dust and sand during one of the few days we remained here—this place being one of the several points on the river which are distinguished for prevailing high winds, which come from the sea. The appearance of the post and country was without interest, except that we here saw, for the first time, the great river on which the course of events for the last half-century has been directing attention and conferring historical fame.

The river is, indeed, a noble object, and has here attained its full magnitude. About nine miles above, and in sight from the heights about the post, is the junction of the two great forks which constitute the main stream—that on which we had been traveling from Fort Hall, and known by the names of Lewis' Fork, Shoshone, and Snake River; and the North Fork, which has retained the name of Columbia, as being the main stream.

We did not go up to the junction, being pressed for time; but the union of two large streams, coming, one from the southeast and the other from the northeast, and meeting in what may be treated as the geographical center of the Oregon Valley, thence doubling the volume of water to the ocean while opening two great lines of communication with the interior continent, constitutes a feature in the map of the country which cannot be overlooked; and it was probably in reference to this junction of waters and these lines of communication that this post was established. They are important lines, and, from the structure of the country, must forever remain so—one of them leading to the South Pass and to the valley of the Mississippi, the other to the pass at the head of the Athabasca River and to the countries drained by the waters of the Hudson Bay.

The British fur companies now use both lines; the Americans, in their emigration to Oregon, have begun to follow the one which leads toward the United States. Bateaus from tidewater ascend to the junction, and thence high up the North Fork, or Columbia. Land conveyance only is used upon the line of Lewis' Fork. To the emigrants to Oregon the Nez Percé is a point of interest, as being, to those who choose it, the termination of their overland journey. The broad expanse of the river here invites them to embark on its bosom, and the lofty trees of the forest furnish the means of doing so.

From the South Pass to this place is about one thousand miles; and as it is about the same distance from that pass to the Missouri River at the mouth of the Kansas, it may be assumed that two thousand miles is the necessary land travel in crossing from the United States to the Pacific Ocean on this line. From the mouth of the Great Platte it would be about one hundred miles less. Mr. McKinley, the commander of the post, received us with great civility, and both to myself and the heads of the emigrants who were there at the time extended his hospitality in a comfortable dinner to which he invited us. By a meridional altitude of the sun, the only observation that the weather permitted us to obtain, the mouth of the Walla Walla River is in latitude 46° 03′ 46″; and, by the road we had traveled, six hundred and twelve miles from Fort Hall.

At the time of our arrival, a considerable body of the emigrants, under the direction of Mr. Applegate,[17] a man of considerable resolution and energy, had nearly completed the building of a number of Mackinaw boats, in which they proposed to continue their further voyage down the Columbia. I had seen, in descending the Walla Walla River, a fine drove of several hundred cattle, which they had exchanged for Californian cattle, to be received at Vancouver, and which are considered a very inferior breed. The other portion of the emigration had preferred to complete their journey by land along the banks of the Columbia, taking their stock and wagons with them.

Having reinforced our animals with eight fresh horses, hired from the post, and increased our stock of provisions with dried salmon, potatoes, and a little beef, we resumed our journey down the left bank of the Columbia, being guided on our road by an intelligent Indian boy, whom I had engaged to accompany us as far as the Dalles. . . . The basaltic rock, which constitutes the geological formation of the Columbia Valley, now presents itself. From an elevated point to which the road led, we obtained another far view of Mount Hood, one hundred and fifty miles distant. We obtained on the riverbank an observation of the sun at noon, which gave for the latitude 45° 58′ 08″.

The country today was very unprepossessing, and our road bad; and as we toiled slowly along through deep loose sands, and over fragments of black volcanic rock, our laborious traveling was strongly contrasted with the rapid progress of Mr. Applegate's fleet of boats, which suddenly came gliding swiftly down the broad river, which here chanced to be tranquil and smooth. At evening we encamped on the riverbank, where there was very little grass, and less timber. We frequently met Indians on the road, and they were collected at every favorable spot along the river.

October 29th. The road continued along the river, and in the course of the day Mount St. Helens, another snowy peak of the Cascade Range, was visible. We crossed the Umatilah River at a fall near its mouth. This stream is of the same class as the Walla Walla River, with a bed of volcanic rock, in places split into fissures. Our encampment was similar to that of yesterday; there was very little grass, and no wood. The Indian brought us some pieces for sale, which were purchased to make our fires.

October 31st. By observation, our camp is in latitude 45° 50' 05", and longitude 119° 22' 18". The night has been cold, and we have white frost this morning, with a temperature at daylight of 25°, and at sunrise of 24°. The early morning was very clear, and the stars bright; but, as usual since we are on the Columbia, clouds formed immediately with the rising sun. The day continued fine, the east being covered with scattered clouds, but the west remaining clear, showing the remarkable conelike peak of Mount Hood brightly drawn against the sky. This was in view all day in the southwest, but no other peaks of the range were visible. Our road was a bad one, of very loose deep sand.

We met on the way a party of Indians unusually well dressed, wearing clothes of civilized texture and form. They appeared intelligent, and, in our slight intercourse, impressed me with the belief that they possessed some aptitude for acquiring languages.

We continued to travel along the river, the stream being interspersed with many sandbars (it being the season of low water) and with many islands, and an apparently good navigation. Small willows were the only wood, rock and sand the prominent geological feature. The rock of this section is a very compact and tough basalt, occurring in strata which have the appearance of being broken into fragments, assuming the form of columnar hills, and appearing always in escarpments, with the broken fragments strewed at the base and over the adjoining country.

We made a late encampment on the river, and used tonight *Purshia tridentata* for firewood. Among the rocks which formed the bank was very good green grass. Latitude 45° 44' 23", longitude 119° 45' 09"

November 1st. Mount Hood is glowing in the sunlight this morning, and the air is pleasant, with a temperature of 38°. We continued down the river, and, passing through a pretty, green valley bounded by high precipitous rock, encamped at the lower end.

On the right shore, the banks of the Columbia are very high and steep; the river is one thousand six hundred and ninety feet broad, and dark bluffs of rock give it a picturesque appearance.

November 2d. The river here entered among bluffs, leaving no longer room for a road; and we accordingly left it, and took a more inland way among the river hills, on which we had no sooner entered, than we found a great improvement in the country. The sand had disappeared, and the soil was good, and covered with excellent grass, although the surface was broken into high hills, with uncommonly deep valleys.

At noon we crossed John Day's River, a clear and beautiful stream, with a swift current and a bed of rolled stones. It is sunk in a deep valley, which is characteristic of all the streams in this region; and the hill we descended to reach it well deserves the name of mountain. Some of the emigrants had encamped on the river, and others at the summit of the farther hill, the ascent of which had probably cost their wagons a day's labor; and others again had halted for the night a few miles beyond, where they had slept without water. We also encamped in a grassy hollow without water; but as we had been forewarned of this privation by the guide, the animals had all been watered at the river, and we had brought with us a sufficient quantity for the night.

November 3d. After two hours' ride through a fertile, hilly country, covered as all the upland here appears to be with good green grass, we descended again into the river bottom, along which we resumed our sterile road, and in about four miles reached the ford of the Fall River (Rivière aux Chutes), a considerable tributary to the Columbia.* We had heard, on reaching the Nez Percé Fort, a repetition of the account in regard to the unsettled character of the Columbia Indians at the present time; and to our little party they had at various points manifested a not very friendly disposition, in several attempts to steal our horses. At this place I expected to find a badly-disposed band, who had plundered a party of fourteen emigrant men a few days before, and taken away their horses; and accordingly we made the necessary preparations for our security, but happily met with no difficulty.

The river was high, divided into several arms, with a rocky island at its outlet into the Columbia, which at this place it rivaled in size, and apparently deserved its highly characteristic name, which is

---

* Now Deschutes River, draining east central Oregon.

received from one of its many falls some forty miles up the river. It entered the Columbia with a roar of falls and rapids, and is probably a favorite fishing station among the Indians, with whom both banks of the river were populous; but they scarcely paid any attention to us.

The ford was very difficult at this time, and had they entertained any bad intentions, they were offered a good opportunity to carry them out, as I rode directly into the river, and during the crossing the howitzer was occasionally several feet under water, and a number of the men appeared to be more often below than above. Our guide was well acquainted with the ford, and we succeeded in getting everything safe over to the left bank. We delayed here only a short time to put the gun in order, and ascending a long mountain hill, left both rivers, and resumed our route again among the interior hills.

The roar of the Falls of the Columbia is heard from the heights, where we halted a few moments to enjoy a fine view of the river below. In the season of high water it would be a very interesting object to visit, in order to witness what is related of the annual submerging of the fall under the waters which back up from the basin below, constituting a great natural lock at this place. But time had become an object of serious consideration, and the falls, in their present state, had been seen and described by many.

After a day's journey of seventeen miles, we encamped among the hills on a little clear stream, where, as usual, the Indians immediately gathered round us. Among them was a very old man, almost blind from age, with long and very white hair. I happened, of my own accord, to give this old man a present of tobacco, and was struck with the impression which my unpropitiated notice made on the Indians, who appeared in a remarkable manner acquainted with the real value of goods, and to understand the equivalents of trade.

At evening one of them spoke a few words to his people, and, telling me that we need entertain no uneasiness in regard to our animals, as none of them would be disturbed, they went all quietly away. In the morning when they again came to the camp, I expressed to them the gratification we felt at their reasonable conduct, making them a present of some large knives and a few smaller articles.

November 4th. The road continued among the hills, and, reaching an eminence, we saw before us, in a little green valley watered by a clear stream, a tolerably large valley through which the trail passed.

In comparison with the Indians of the Rocky Mountains and the great eastern plain these are disagreeably dirty in their habits. Their huts were crowded with half-naked women and children, and the atmosphere within anything but pleasant to persons who had just been riding in the fresh morning air. We were somewhat amused with the scanty dress of one woman, who, in common with the others, rushed out of the huts on our arrival, and who, in default of other covering, used a child for a fig leaf.

The road in about half an hour passed near an elevated point, from which we overlooked the valley of the Columbia for many miles, and saw in the distance several houses surrounded by fields, which a chief, who had accompanied us from the village, pointed out to us as the Methodist Missionary Station.[18] In a few miles we descended to the river, which we reached at one of its remarkably interesting features, known as the Dalles of the Columbia. The whole volume of the river at this place passed between the walls of a chasm, which has the appearance of having been rent through the basaltic strata which form the valley rock of the region. At the narrowest place we found the breadth, by measurement, fifty-eight yards, and the average height of the walls above the water twenty-five feet; forming a trough between the rocks—whence the name, probably applied by a Canadian voyageur.

The mass of water in the present low state of the river, passed swiftly between, deep and black, and curled into many small whirlpools and countercurrents, but unbroken by foam and so still that scarcely the sound of a ripple was heard. The rock, for a considerable distance from the river, was worn over a large portion of its surface into circular holes and well-like cavities by the abrasion of the river, which, at the season of high waters, is spread out over the adjoining bottoms.

In the recent passage through this chasm, an unfortunate event had occurred to Mr. Applegate's party, in the loss of one of their boats, which had been carried under water in the midst of the Dalles, and two of Mr. Applegate's children and one man drowned.

This misfortune was attributed only to want of skill in the steersman, as at this season there is no impediment to navigation, although the place is entirely impassable at high water, when boats pass safely over the great falls above, in the submerged state in which they then find themselves.

The basalt here is precisely the same as that which constitutes the rock of the valley higher up the Columbia, being very compact, with a few round cavities.

We passed rapidly three or four miles down the level valley, and encamped near the mission. The character of the forest growth here changed, and we found ourselves, with pleasure, again among oaks and other forest trees of the East, to which we had long been strangers; and the hospitable and kind reception with which we were welcomed among our country people at the mission, aided the momentary illusion of home.

Two good-looking wooden dwelling houses and a large schoolhouse, with stables, barn, and garden, and large cleared fields between the houses and the riverbank, on which were scattered the wooden huts of an Indian village, gave to the valley the cheerful and busy air of civilization, and had in our eyes an appearance of abundant and enviable comfort.

Our land journey found here its western termination. The delay involved in getting our camp to the right bank of the Columbia, and in opening a road through the continuous forest to Vancouver, rendered a journey along the river impracticable; and on this side the usual road across the mountain required strong and fresh animals, there being an interval of three days in which they could obtain no food. I therefore wrote immediately to Mr. Fitzpatrick, directing him to abandon the carts at the Walla Walla Missionary Station, and, as soon as the necessary pack saddles could be made which his party required, meet me at the Dalles, from which point I proposed to commence our homeward journey.

The day after our arrival being Sunday, no business could be done at the mission; but on Monday Mr. Perkins [19] assisted me in procuring from the Indians a large canoe, in which I designed to complete our journey to Vancouver, where I expected to obtain the necessary supply of provisions and stores for our winter journey. Three Indians from the family to whom the canoe belonged were engaged to assist in working her during the voyage, and, with them, our water party consisted of Mr. Preuss and myself, with Bernier and Jacob Dodson.

In charge of the party which was to remain at the Dalles I left Carson, with instructions to occupy the people in making pack saddles and refitting their equipage. The village from which we were to take the canoe was on the right bank of the river, about ten miles below, at the mouth of the Tinanens Creek; and while Mr. Preuss proceeded down the river with the instruments in a little canoe paddled by two Indians, Mr. Perkins accompanied me with the remainder of the party by land. The last of the emigrants had just left the Dalles at the time of our arrival, traveling some by water and others by land, making arklike rafts, on which they had embarked their families and household, with their large wagons and other furniture, while their stock were driven along the shore.

For about five miles below the Dalles, the river is narrow and probably very deep; but during this distance, it is somewhat open with grassy bottoms on the left. Entering, then, among the lower mountains of the Cascade Range, it assumes a general character, and high and steep rocky hills shut it in on either side, rising abruptly in places to the height of one thousand five hundred feet above the water, and gradually acquiring a more mountainous character as the river approaches the Cascades.

After an hour's travel, when the sun was nearly down, we searched along the shore for a pleasant place, and halted to prepare supper. We had been well supplied by our friends at the mission with delicious salted salmon, which had been taken at the fattest season; also with potatoes, bread, coffee, and sugar.

We were delighted at a change in our mode of traveling and living. The canoe sailed smoothly down the river; at night we encamped upon the shore, and a plentiful supply of comfortable provisions supplied the first of wants. We enjoyed the contrast which it presented to our late toilsome marchings, our night watchings, and our frequent privation of food. We were a motley group, but all happy: three unknown Indians; Jacob, a colored man; Mr. Preuss, a German; Bernier, Creole French, and myself.

Being now upon the ground explored by the South Sea expedition under Captain Wilkes, and having accomplished the object of uniting my survey with his, and thus presenting a connected exploration from the Mississippi to the Pacific, and the winter being at hand, I deemed it necessary to economize time by voyaging in the night, as is customary here, to avoid the high winds, which rise with the morning, and decline with the day.

Accordingly, after an hour's halt we again embarked, and resumed our pleasant voyage down the river. The wind rose to a gale after several hours; but the moon was very bright and the wind was fair, and the canoe glanced rapidly down the stream, the waves breaking into foam alongside; and our night voyage, as the wind bore us rapidly along between the dark mountains, was wild and interesting. About midnight we put to the shore on a rocky beach, behind which was a dark-looking pine forest. We built up large fires among the rocks, which were in large masses round about; and, arranging our blankets in the most sheltered places we could find, passed a delightful night.

After an early breakfast, at daylight we resumed our journey, the weather being clear and beautiful, and the river smooth and still. On either side of the mountains are all pine-timbered, rocky, and high. We were now approaching one of the marked features of the Lower Columbia, where the river forms a great cascade, with a series of rapids, in breaking through the range of mountains to which the lofty peaks of Mount Hood and St. Helens belong, and which rise as great pillars of snow on either side of the passage.

The main branch of the Sacramento River, and the Klamath,[20] issue in cascades from this range; and the Columbia, breaking through it in a succession of cascades, gives the idea of cascades to the whole range; and hence the name of the Cascade Range, which it bears, and distinguishes it from the Coast Range lower down. In making a short turn to the south, the river forms the cascades in breaking over a point of agglomerated masses of rock, leaving a handsome bay to the right, with several rocky pine-covered islands, and the mountains sweep at a distance around a cove where several small streams enter the bay.

In less than an hour we halted on the left bank, about five minutes' walk above the cascades, where there were several Indian huts, and where our guides signified it was customary to hire Indians to assist in making the portage. When traveling with a boat as light as a canoe, which may easily be carried on the shoulders of the Indians, this is much the better side of the river for the portage, as the ground here is very good and level, being a handsome bottom, which I remarked was covered (as was now always the case along the river) with a growth of green and fresh-looking grass.

It was long before we could come to an understanding with the Indians; but at length, when they had first received the price of their assistance in goods, they went vigorously to work; and in a shorter time than had been occupied in making our arrangements, the canoe, instruments, and baggage were carried through (a distance of about half a mile) to the bank below the main cascade, where we again embarked, the water being white with foam among ugly rocks, and boiling into a thousand whirlpools. The boat passed with great rapidity, crossing and recrossing in the eddies of the current.

After passing through about two miles of broken water, we ran some wild-looking rapids, which are called the Lower Rapids, being the last on the river, which below is tranquil and smooth—a broad, magnificent stream. On a low broad point on the right bank of the river, at the lower end of these rapids, were pitched many tents of the emigrants, who were waiting here for their friends from above, or for boats and provisions which were expected from Vancouver.

In our passage down the rapids, I had noticed their camps along the shore, or transporting their goods across the portage. This portage makes a head of navigation, ascending the river. It is about two miles in length, and above, to the Dalles, is forty-five miles of smooth and good navigation.

We glided on without further interruption between very rocky and high steep mountains, which sweep along the river valley at a little distance, covered with forests of pine, and showing occasionally lofty escarpments of red rock. Nearer, the shore is bordered by steep escarped hills, and huge vertical rocks, from which the waters of the mountain reach the river in a variety of beautiful falls, sometimes several hundred feet in height; occasionally along the river occurred pretty bottoms, covered with the greenest verdure of the spring. To a professional farmer, however, it does not offer many places of sufficient extent to be valuable for agriculture; and after passing a few miles below the Dalles, I had scarcely seen a place on the south shore where wagons could get to the river. The beauty of the scenery was heightened by the continuance of very delightful weather, resembling the Indian summer of the Atlantic.

A few miles below the cascades we passed a singular isolated hill; and in the course of the next six miles occurred five very pretty falls from the heights on the left bank, one of them being of a very picturesque character; and toward sunset we reached a remarkable point of rocks, distinguished, on account of prevailing high winds, and the delay it frequently occasions to the canoe navigation, by the name of Cape Horn. It borders the river in a high wall of rock, which comes boldly down into deep water; and in violent gales down the river, and from the opposite shore, which is the prevailing direction of strong winds, the water is dashed against it with considerable violence. It appears to form a serious obstacle to canoe traveling; and I was informed by Mr. Perkins that in a voyage up the river he had been detained two weeks at this place, and was finally obliged to return to Vancouver.

The winds of this region deserve a particular study. They blow in currents, which show them to be governed by fixed laws; and it is a problem how far they may come from the mountains, or from the ocean, through the breaks in the mountains which let out the river.

The hills here had lost something of their rocky appearance, and had already begun to decline. As the sun went down, we searched along the river for an inviting spot and, finding a clean rocky beach, where some large dry trees were lying on the ground, we ran our boat to the shore; and, after another comfortable supper, plowed our way along the river in darkness.

Heavy clouds covered the sky this evening, and the wind began to sweep in gusts among the trees, as if bad weather were coming. As we advanced, the hills on both sides grew constantly lower; on the right, retreating from the shore, and forming a somewhat extensive bottom of intermingled prairie and wooded land. In the course of a few hours, and opposite to a small stream coming in from the north, called the Tea Prairie River, the highlands on the left declined to the plains, and three or four miles below disappeared entirely on both sides, and the river entered the low country.

The river had gradually expanded; and when we emerged from

the highlands, the opposite shores were so distant as to appear indistinct in the uncertainty of the light. About ten o'clock our pilots halted, apparently to confer about the course, and after a little hesitation, pulled directly across an open expansion of the river, where the waves were somewhat rough for a canoe, the wind blowing very fresh. Much to our surprise, a few minutes afterward we ran aground. Backing off our boat, we made repeated trials at various places to cross what appeared to be a point of shifting sandbars, where we had attempted to shorten the way by a cutoff. Finally, one of our Indians got into the water and waded about until he found a channel sufficiently deep, through which we wound along after him, and in a few minutes again entered the deep water below.

As we paddled rapidly down the river, we heard the noise of a sawmill at work on the right bank; and, letting our boat float quietly down, we listened with pleasure to the unusual sounds; and before midnight encamped on the bank of the river, about a mile above Fort Vancouver. Our fine, dry weather had given place to a dark, cloudy night. At midnight it began to rain; and we found ourselves suddenly in the gloomy and humid season which, in the narrow region lying between the Pacific and the Cascade Mountains, and for a considerable distance along the coast, supplies the place of winter.

In the morning, the first object that attracted my attention was the bark *Columbia,* lying at anchor near the landing. She was about to start on her voyage to England, and was now ready for sea; being detained only in waiting the arrival of the express batteaus—which descend the Columbia and its north fork with the overland mail from Canada and Hudson Bay—which had been delayed beyond their usual time.

I immediately waited upon Dr. McLaughlin,[21] the executive officer of the Hudson's Bay Company in the territory west of the Rocky Mountains, who received me with the courtesy and hospitality for which he has been eminently distinguished, and which makes a forcible and delightful impression on a traveler from the long wilderness from which we had issued. I was immediately supplied by him with the necessary stores and provisions to refit and support my party in our contemplated winter journey to the States; and also with a Mackinaw boat and canoes, manned with Canadian and Iroquois voyageurs and Indians, for their transportation to the Dalles of the Columbia.

In addition to his efficient kindness in furnishing me with these necessary supplies, I received from him a warm and gratifying sympathy in the suffering which his great experience led him to anticipate for us in our homeward journey, and a letter of recommendation and credit for any officers of the Hudson's Bay Company into whose posts we might be driven by unexpected misfortune.

Of course the future supplies for my party were paid for, bills on the Government of the United States being readily taken; but every hospitable attention was extended to me, and I accepted an invitation to take a room in the fort, and to "make myself at home" while I stayed.

I found many American emigrants at the fort; others had already crossed the river into their land of promise—the Willamette Valley. Others were daily arriving; and all of them had been furnished with shelter, so far as it could be afforded by the buildings connected with the establishment. Necessary clothing and provisions (the latter to be afterward returned in kind from the produce of their labor) were also furnished. This friendly assistance was of very great value to the emigrants, whose families were otherwise exposed to much suffering in the winter rains, which had now commenced at the same time that they were in want of all the common necessaries of life.

Those who had taken a water conveyance at the Nez Percé Fort continued to arrive safely, with no other accident than has been already mentioned. The party which had passed over the Cascade Mountains were reported to have lost a number of their animals; and those who had driven their stock down the Columbia had brought them safely in, and found for them a ready and very profitable market, and were already proposing to return to the States in the spring for another supply.

In the space of two days our preparations had been completed, and we were ready to set out on our return. It would have been very gratifying to have gone down to the Pacific, and, solely in the interest and in the love of geography, to have seen the ocean on the western as well as on the eastern side of the continent, so as to give a satisfactory completeness to the geographical picture which had been formed in our minds; but the rainy season had now regularly set in, and the air was filled with fogs and rain, which left no beauty in any scenery, and obstructed observations.

The object of my instructions had been entirely fulfilled in having connected our reconnaissance with the surveys of Captain Wilkes; and although it would have been agreeable and satisfactory to terminate here also our ruder astronomical observations, I was not, for such a reason, justified to make a delay in waiting for favorable weather.

Near sunset of the 10th, the boats left the fort, and encamped after making only a few miles. Our flotilla consisted of a Mackinaw barge and three canoes—one of them that in which we had descended the river; and a party in all of twenty men. One of the emigrants, Mr. Peter H. Burnet, of Missouri, who had left his family and property at the Dalles, availed himself of the opportunity afforded by the return of our boats to bring them down to Vancouver. This gentleman, as well as the Messrs. Applegate, and others of the emigrants whom I saw, possessed intelligence and character, with the moral and intellectual stamina, as well as the enterprise, which give solidity and respectability to the foundation of colonies.

November 11th. The morning was rainy and misty. We did not move with the practiced celerity of my own camp; and it was near nine o'clock when our motley crew had finished their breakfast and were ready to start. Once afloat, however, they worked steadily and well, and we advanced at a good rate up the river; and in the afternoon a breeze sprang up, which enabled us to add a sail to the oars. At evening we encamped on a warm-looking beach, on the right bank, at the foot of the high river hill, immediately at the lower end of Cape Horn.

On the opposite shore is said to be a singular hole in the mountain, from which the Indians believe comes the wind producing these gales. It is called the Devil's Hole, and the Indians, I was told, have been resolving to send down one of their slaves to explore the region below. . . .*

---

* Some detail on the stormy weather of November 12 and 13 is omitted, as is Frémont's brief account of the difficulty of cordelling the boats up the Columbia's swift current on November 13 and 14. During the next three days they laboriously retraced their river path to the Dalles.

FOOTNOTES

1. The Juneberry, shadbush, or serviceberry is not to be confounded with the European serviceberry, which is of the same order of Rosaceae, but larger. The American shrub bears a sweet reddish-purple fruit of huckleberry size, and is often cultivated both for its blossoms and its berries.

2. Fort Hall, as we have said, was now in the hands of the Hudson's Bay Company. Frémont calls it a "foreign" trading post, and he was right; for while the company agents at the fort could not, and did not, treat the now large stream of emigrants with anything but friendliness, they surveyed the new-comers with a somewhat jealous eye. They did not wish to see the Anglo-American control of the Pacific Northwest become a purely American control. Frémont very properly suggested a larger and better-stocked American post at or near this point on the Oregon Trail.

3. Emigrants from the east had until recently been compelled to discard their wagons at or near Fort Hall, and rely on pack horses alone to carry them over the very rough country to the west. Marcus Whitman in 1836 had got a two-wheeled cart three hundred miles farther along to Fort Boisé. In 1840 a small party guided by Dr. Robert Newell tried to get to Oregon proper with wagons, but had to discard the wagon boxes along the way.

4. J. B. Chiles had been with the party of emigrants which in 1841 had crossed the Great Basin on the line of what Frémont later named the Humboldt River, surmounting the Sierra Nevada by the Sonora Pass, and coming down into California. Chiles was now leading another party. It divided at Fort Hall, Chiles himself going to Fort Boisé, and from that point traveling by the Pitt and Malheur rivers to the Sacramento Valley. The other section of the party, under Joseph Walker, went down the Humboldt, over to Walker Lake, and thence into California by Walker Pass. Chiles was a stalwart Missourian, who settled down on a grant from the Mexican Government.

5. Frémont was close here to the magnificent cataract of the Snake called Shoshone Falls, which in height (190 feet) exceeds Niagara, and in volume at times of flood hardly yields to the more famous waterfall. Had he known of it, he would doubtless have deviated to see it.

6. More accurately called Shoshone, and certainly of that family; no Snake tribe existed. Perhaps these belonged to the Bannock tribe.

7. The Salmon River Mountains are mainly in Lemhi County, Idaho, just under the Montana boundary. To the east of Lemhi lies Frémont County.

8. This was another post of the Hudson's Bay Company, and another important stopping place on the Oregon Trail. A fort had first been built in 1834 about seven miles above the point where the Boisé River empties into the Snake; later the fort which Frémont describes was placed at the junction of the two streams. The present-day city of Boisé is of course farther up the river of that name.

9. The Payette River and the town of Payette in Idaho (not to mention the Boisé-Payette Company, one of the Weyerhaeüser interests) commemorate the name of this hospitable French Canadian. T. J. Farnham a few years earlier had described him as "a merry, fat old gentleman of fifty."

10. That is, the party was abandoning the Snake River, so generally barren in its valley, to strike northwest into the well-wooded mountain country of

what is now northeastern Oregon—a shorter route to the Columbia River, and one with much more natural beauty.

11. This is the first use in history of the term Great Basin; one of Frémont's titles to fame is that he first identified and described this great natural feature of the West.

12. The really famous Powder River of course belongs to Wyoming and Montana; the Powder River of northeastern Oregon, which helps drain the Powder River Mountains, empties into the Snake.

13. The Blue Mountains, chiefly in Umatilla County, Oregon, run up to just south of Walla Walla in eastern Washington. They reach a height of 8650 feet.

14. Frémont spells the name Walahwalah.

15. Marcus Whitman (1802–1847), a well-educated physician, had offered his services to the American Board for Foreign Missions, and in 1835 had been sent with the Rev. Samuel Parker to survey the missionary field in the Oregon country. He returned East aflame with enthusiasm, and after marrying a fellow missionary, set out in 1836 with a small party (including two women) for his chosen field. The story of how they founded two missions, one near present-day Lewiston, Idaho, and one in the Walla Walla Valley, is one of the best known in Western history. Whitman exerted himself heroically. His famous winter ride to the East in 1842–43, however, was made for reasons connected with mission activities, and not (as legend has it) for the political object of arousing Americans to the importance of taking over Oregon. He returned to the Walla Walla Valley in the great migration of 1843. As Frémont states, his mission establishment consisted of one adobe house. It was unfortunate that Frémont had no opportunity to talk with this eminent man. A few years later some superstitious Indians who attributed an outbreak of smallpox to his activities murdered him and his wife.

16. This is not far from present-day Wallula. The Nez Percé were the principal tribe of the Shahaptian stock, and had gained their name by their custom of wearing nose ornaments. They occupied eastern Washington and Oregon and central Idaho. Lewis and Clark had found them friendly, and they had sent all the way to St. Louis in 1832 to ask for religious and general instruction. At this time they were still well disposed. Their tragic history when, under Chief Joseph, they long afterward resisted expulsion from their country, and so began the Nez Percé War (1876), is well known.

17. Jesse Applegate (1811–1888), a Kentuckian by birth, a man of superior education, had been a deputy of the surveyor-general's office in St. Louis, and had done much field work in Missouri before he undertook farming in that State. Hard times and dislike of slavery caused him in 1843 to join the great emigration to the Pacific Northwest. He contributed a herd to the movement, and was chosen head of the "cow column." It was largely because of his leadership that the company made so successful a transit, with its wagons, to the Willamette country. Subsequently he played a prominent part in the development of Oregon as a Territory and a State. His spirited narrative called *A Day with the Cow-Column* suggests that had opportunity offered, he might have won distinction as a writer.

18. This station had been established by the Rev. Jason Lee, who had gone out to the Oregon country with N. J. Wyeth's party in 1834, and with other missionaries had settled on the Willamette. Later, with Dr. Elijah White, he established a new mission at the Dalles—the point where the Columbia forces

its way through a narrow channel plowed deep in the basalt rock. Lee had
gone back to New York in 1838, and the following year had brought a large
party (the "Great Reinforcement") out to the Columbia by sea. His mission
at the Dalles exercised a powerful and beneficent influence on the surrounding
Indians.

19. Mr. Perkins was one of the heads of the Methodist mission station at
the Dalles.

20. Frémont, as is noted later, preferred this spelling Flamath, as representing more accurately the pronunciation of the word given by the Indians, but
in the text Klamath is used because it is the current spelling.

21. Frémont pays due tribute to this imposing figure. As the Columbia River
factor of the Hudson's Bay Company, he played a statesmanlike part in the
early history of the Northwest, served his corporation well, and at the same
time made literally hundreds of friends among the American pioneers. He had
been born of Scottish stock in the Province of Quebec in 1784. In 1824, after
experience in charge of the company post at Fort William on Lake Superior,
he was appointed to the Columbia River station, and next year established Fort
Vancouver at what is now Vancouver, Washington. Here he developed farms,
dairies, orchards, a flour mill, a sawmill, a shipyard, and other activities. He
was a helpful friend of American missionaries, while his aid to destitute American emigrants saved many from perishing. He always encouraged settlement
south of the Columbia, while hoping that the country north of the river would
remain in British hands. A man of great height, commanding mien, and stern
integrity, he gained a wide influence among Indians and whites alike simply
through force of character and soundness of judgment. Many travelers had
occasion, like Frémont, to speak of his kindness.

CHAPTER 8

Klamath Falls: Pyramid Lake:
Across the Sierra Nevada in Winter *

NOVEMBER 18, 1843. [At the Dalles again]. . . . Carson had removed the camp a little nearer to the hills, where the animals
had better grass. We found everything in good order, and arrived
just in time to partake of an excellent roast of California beef. My
friend Mr. Gilpin had arrived in advance of the party. His object in
visiting this country had been to obtain correct information of the
Willamette settlements; and he had reached this point in his journey
highly pleased with the country over which he had traveled, and
with invigorated health. On the following day he continued his
journey, in our returning boats, to Vancouver.

The camp was now occupied in making the necessary preparations for our homeward journey, which, though homeward, contemplated a new route, and a great circuit to the south and southeast, and the exploration of the Great Basin between the Rocky
Mountains and the Sierra Nevada. Three principal objects were indicated, by report or by maps, as being on this route, the character
or existence of which I wished to ascertain, and which I assumed as
landmarks, or leading points, on the projected line of return. The
first of these points was the Klamath lake, on the tableland between
the head of Fall River, which comes to the Columbia, and the Sacramento, which goes to the Bay of San Francisco; and from which lake
a river of the same name makes its way westwardly direct to
the ocean. This lake and river are often called Klamath. . . . The
position of this lake, on the line of inland communication between
Oregon and California; its proximity to the demarcation boundary
of latitude 42°; its imputed double character of lake, or meadow,
according to the season of the year; and the hostile and warlike

* From Frémont's *Report* on his second expedition.

character attributed to the Indians about it—all made it a desirable object to visit and examine. From this lake our course was intended to be about southeast, to a reported lake called Mary's, at some days' journey in the Great Basin; and thence, still on southeast, to the reputed Buenaventura River,[1] which has had a place in so many maps, and countenanced the belief of the existence of a great river flowing from the Rocky Mountains to the Bay of San Francisco. From the Buenaventura the next point was intended to be in that section of the Rocky Mountains which includes the heads of Arkansas River, and of the opposite waters of the California Gulf; and thence down the Arkansas to Bent's Fort, and home.

This was our projected line of return—a great part of it absolutely new to geographical, botanical, and geological science—and the subject of reports in relation to lakes, rivers, deserts, and savages hardly above the condition of mere wild animals, which inflamed desire to know what this terra incognita really contained. It was a serious enterprise, at the commencement of winter, to undertake the traverse of such a region, and with a party consisting only of twenty-five persons, and they of many nations—American, French, German, Canadian, Indian, and colored—and most of them young, several being under twenty-one years of age.

All knew that a strange country was to be explored, and dangers and hardships to be encountered; but no one blenched at the prospect. On the contrary, courage and confidence animated the whole party. Cheerfulness, readiness, subordination, prompt obedience, characterized all; nor did any extremity of peril and privation, to which we were afterward exposed, ever belie, or derogate from, the fine spirit of this brave and generous commencement.

The course of the narrative will show at what point, and for what reasons, we were prevented from the complete execution of this plan, after having made considerable progress upon it, and how we were forced by desert plains and mountain ranges, and deep snows, far to the south and near to the Pacific Ocean, and along the western base of the Sierra Nevada; where, indeed, a new and ample field of exploration opened itself before us. For the present, we must follow the narrative, which will first lead us south along the valley of Fall River, and the eastern base of the Cascade Range, to the Klamath Lake, from which, or its margin, three rivers go in three directions—one west, to the ocean; another north, to the Columbia; the third south, to California.*

For the support of the party, I had provided at Vancouver a supply of provisions for not less than three months, consisting principally of flour, peas, and tallow—the latter being used in cooking; and in addition to this, I had purchased at the mission some California cattle, which were to be driven on the hoof. We had one hundred and four mules and horses—part of the latter procured from the Indians about the mission, and for the sustenance of which our reliance was upon the grass which we should find, and the soft porous wood which was to be its substitute when there was none.

Mr. Fitzpatrick, with Mr. Talbot and the remainder of our party, arrived on the 21st; and the camp was now closely engaged in the labor of preparation. Mr. Perkins succeeded in obtaining as guide to the Klamath Lake two Indians—one of whom had been there, and bore the marks of several wounds he had received from some of the Indians in the neighborhood; and the other went along for company. In order to enable us to obtain horses, he despatched messengers to the various Indian villages in the neighborhood, informing them that we were desirous to purchase, and appointing a day for them to bring them in.

We made, in the meantime, several excursions in the vicinity. Mr. Perkins walked with Mr. Preuss and myself to the heights, about nine miles distant on the opposite side of the river, whence, in fine weather, an extensive view may be had over the mountains, including seven great peaks of the Cascade Range; but clouds, on this occasion, destroyed the anticipated pleasure, and we obtained bearings only to three that were visible: Mount Rainier, St. Helen's, and Mount Hood. On the heights, about one mile south of the mission, a very fine view may be had of Mount Hood and St. Helen's. In order to determine their positions with as much accuracy as possible, the angular distances of the peaks were measured with the sextant, at different fixed points from which they could be seen.

The Indians brought in their horses at the appointed time, and we succeeded in obtaining a number in exchange for goods; but they were relatively much higher here, where goods are plenty and at moderate prices, than we had found them in the more eastern part

* Frémont means the Deschutes and Rogue rivers in Oregon and the Pitt River in California.

of our voyage. Several of the Indians inquired very anxiously to know if we had any *dollars;* and the horses we procured were much fewer in number than I had desired, and of thin, inferior quality, the oldest and poorest being those that were sold to us. These horses, as our journey gave constant occasion to remark, are valuable for hardihood and great endurance.

November 24th. At this place one of the men was discharged; and at the request of Mr. Perkins, a Chinook Indian,[2] a lad of nineteen, who was extremely desirous to "see the whites," and make some acquaintance with our institutions, was received into the party, under my especial charge, with the understanding that I would again return him to his friends. He had lived for some time in the household of Mr. Perkins, and spoke a few words of the English language.

November 25th. We were all up early, in the excitement of turning toward home. The stars were brilliant, and the morning cold—the thermometer at daylight 26°.

Our preparations had been finally completed, and today we commenced our journey. The little wagon which had hitherto carried the instruments, I judged it necessary to abandon, and it was accordingly presented to the mission. In all our long traveling, it had never been overturned or injured by any accident of the road; and the only things broken were the glass lamps, and one of the front panels, which had been kicked out by an unruly Indian horse. The howitzer was the only wheeled carriage now remaining. We started about noon, when the weather had become disagreeably cold, with flurries of snow. Our friend Mr. Perkins, whose kindness had been active and efficient during our stay, accompanied us several miles on our road, when he bade us farewell, and consigned us to the care of our guides.

Ascending to the uplands beyond the southern fork of the Tinanens Creek,[3] we found the snow lying on the ground in frequent patches, although the pasture appeared good, and the new short grass was fresh and green. We traveled over high, hilly land, and encamped on a little branch of Tinanens Creek, where there were good grass and timber. The southern bank was covered with snow, which was scattered over the bottom, and the little creek, its borders lined with ice, had a chilly and wintry look.

A number of Indians had accompanied us so far on our road,

and remained with us during the night. Two bad-looking fellows, who were detected in stealing, were tied and laid before the fire, and guard mounted over them during the night. The night was cold and partially clear.

November 26th. The morning was cloudy and misty, and but a few stars visible. During the night water froze in the tents, and at sunrise the thermometer was at 20°. Left camp at ten o'clock, the road leading along tributaries of the Tinanens, and being, so far, very good. We turned to the right at a fork of the trail, ascending by a steep ascent along a spur to the dividing grounds between this stream and the waters of Fall River. The creeks we had passed were timbered principally with oak and other deciduous trees. Snow lies everywhere here on the ground, and we had a slight fall during the morning; but toward noon the gray sky yielded to a bright sun.

This morning we had a grand view of St. Helen's and Rainier; the latter appeared of a conical form, and very lofty, leading the eye far up into the sky.[4] The line of the timberland country is very distinctly marked here, the bare hills making with it a remarkable contrast. The summit of the ridge commanded a fine view of the Taih [Tygh] Prairie, and the stream running through it, which is a tributary to the Fall River, the chasm of which is visible to the right. A steep descent of a mountain hill brought us down into the valley, and we encamped on the stream after dark, guided by the light of fires, which some naked Indians belonging to a village on the opposite side were kindling for us on the bank. This is a large branch of the Fall River. There was a broad band of thick ice some fifteen feet wide on either bank, and the river current is swift and bold.

The night was cold and clear, and we made our astronomical observation this evening with the thermometer at 20°.

In anticipation of coming hardship, and to spare our horses, there was much walking done today; and Mr. Fitzpatrick and myself made the day's journey on foot. Somewhere near the mouth of this stream are the falls from which the river takes its name.

November 27th. A fine view of Mount Hood this morning; a rose-colored mass of snow, bearing S. 85° W. by compass. The sky is clear, and the air cold, the thermometer 2.5° below zero, the trees and bushes glittering white and the rapid stream filled with floating ice.

Stiletsi and the White Crane, two Indian chiefs who had accompanied us thus far, took their leave, and we resumed our journey at ten o'clock. We ascended by a steep hill from the river bottom, which is sandy, to a volcanic plain, around which lofty hills sweep in a regular form. It is cut up by gullies of basaltic rock, escarpments of which appear everywhere in the hills. This plain is called the Tygh Prairie, and is sprinkled with some scattered pines.

The country is now far more interesting to a traveler than the route along the Snake and Columbia rivers. To our right we had always the mountains, from the midst of whose dark pine forests the isolated snowy peaks were looking out like giants. They served us for grand beacons to show the rate at which we advanced in our journey. Mount Hood was already becoming an old acquaintance, and, when we ascended the prairie, we obtained a bearing to Mount Jefferson, S. 23° W.[5]

The Indian superstition has peopled these lofty peaks with evil spirits, and they have never yet known the tread of a human foot. Sternly drawn against the sky, they look so high and steep, so snowy and rocky, that it would appear almost impossible to climb them; but still a trial would have its attractions for the adventurous traveler.

A small trail takes off through the prairie, toward a low point in the range, and perhaps there is here a pass into the Willamette Valley. Crossing the plain, we descended by a rocky hill into the bend of a tributary of Fall River, and made an early encampment. The water was in holes and frozen over, and we were obliged to cut through the ice for the animals to drink. An ox, which was rather troublesome to drive, was killed here for food. . . .*

November 28th. The sky was clear in the morning, but suddenly clouded over, and at sunrise began to snow, with the thermometer at 18°.

We traversed a broken high country partly timbered with pine, and about noon crossed a mountainous ridge, in which, from the rock occasionally displayed, the formation consists of compact lava. Frequent tracks of elk were visible in the snow. On our right, in the afternoon, a high plain, partially covered with pine, extended about ten miles to the foot of the Cascade Mountains.

At evening we encamped in a basin narrowly surrounded by rocky hills, after a day's journey of twenty-one miles. The surround-

* Some astronomical detail omitted.

ing rocks are either volcanic products or highly altered by volcanic action, consisting of quartz and reddish-colored siliceous masses.

November 29th. We emerged from the basin, by a narrow pass, upon a considerable branch of Fall River, running to the eastward through a narrow valley. The trail, descending this stream, brought us to a locality of hot springs, which were on either bank. Those on the left, which were formed into deep, handsome basins, would have been delightful baths if the outer air had not been so keen, the thermometer in these being at 89°. There were others on the opposite side, at the foot of an escarpment, in which the temperature of the water was 134°. These waters deposited around the spring a brecciated mass of quartz and feldspar, much of it of a reddish color.

We crossed the stream here, and ascended again to a high plain, from an elevated point of which we obtained a view of six of the great peaks—Mount Jefferson, followed to the southward by two others of the same class; and succeeding, at a still greater distance to the southward, were three other lower peaks, clustering together in a branch ridge. These, like the great peaks, were snowy masses, secondary only to them; and, from the best examination our time permitted, we are inclined to believe that the range to which they belong is a branch from the great chain which here bears to the westward. The trail during the remainder of the day followed near to the large stream on the left, which was continuously walled in between high rocky banks. We halted for the night on a little bye-stream.

November 30th. Our journey today was short. Passing over a high plain, on which were scattered cedars, with frequent beds of volcanic rock in fragments, interspersed among the grassy grounds, we arrived suddenly on the verge of the steep and rocky descent to the valley of the stream we had been following and which here ran directly across our path, emerging from the mountains on the right. You will remark that the country is abundantly watered with large streams which pour down from the neighboring range.

These streams are characterized by the narrow and chasmlike valleys in which they run, generally sunk a thousand feet below the plain. At the verge of this plain they frequently commence in vertical precipices of basaltic rock, and which leave only casual places at which they can be entered by horses. The road across the country, which would otherwise be very good, is rendered impracticable for wagons by these streams. There is another trail among the mountains, usually followed in the summer, which the snows now compelled us to avoid; and I have reason to believe that this, passing nearer the heads of these streams, would afford a much better road.

At such places, the gun carriage was unlimbered, and separately descended by hand. Continuing a few miles up the left bank of the river, we encamped early in an open bottom among the pines, a short distance below a lodge of Indians. Here, along the river, the bluffs present escarpments seven or eight hundred feet in height, containing strata of a very fine porcelain clay, overlaid, at the height of about five hundred feet, by a massive stratum of compact basalt one hundred feet in thickness, which again is succeeded above by other strata of volcanic rocks.

The clay strata are variously colored, some of them very nearly as white as chalk, and very fine-grained. Specimens brought from these have been subjected to microscopical examination by Professor Bailey, of West Point, and are considered by him to constitute one of the most remarkable deposits of fluviatile infusoria on record. While they abound in genera and species which are common in fresh water, but which rarely thrive where the water is even brackish, not one decidedly marine form is to be found among them, and their fresh-water origin is therefore beyond a doubt. It is equally certain that they lived and died at the situation where they were found, as they could scarcely have been transported by running waters without an admixture of sandy particles; from which, however, they are remarkably free. . . .*

December 1st. A short distance above our encampment we crossed this river, which was thickly lined along its banks with ice. In common with all these mountain streams, the water was very clear, and the current swift. It was not everywhere fordable, and the water was three or four feet deep at our crossing, and perhaps a hundred feet wide. As was frequently the case at such places, one of the mules got his pack, consisting of sugar, thoroughly wet, and turned into molasses.

One of the guides informed me that this was a "salmon water," and pointed out several ingeniously contrived places to catch the fish; among the trees in the bottom I saw an immense pine, about

* Some details on the infusoria, and on latitude and longitude, omitted.

twelve feet in diameter. A steep ascent from the opposite bank delayed us again; and as, by the information of our guides, grass would soon become very scarce, we encamped on the height of land, in a marshy place among the pines, where there was an abundance of grass.

We found here a single Nez Percé family, who had a very handsome horse in their drove, which we endeavored to obtain in exchange for a good cow; but the man "had two hearts," or rather, he had one and his wife had another: she wanted the cow, but he loved the horse too much to part with it. These people attach great value to cattle, with which they are endeavoring to supply themselves.

December 2d. In the first rays of the sun the mountain peaks this morning presented a beautiful appearance, the snow being entirely covered with a hue of rosy gold. We traveled today over a very stony, elevated plain, about which were scattered cedar and pine, and encamped on another large branch of Fall River. We were gradually ascending to a more elevated region, which would have been indicated by the rapidly increasing quantities of snow and ice, had we not known it by other means. A mule which was packed with our cooking utensils wandered off among the pines unperceived, and several men were sent back to search for it.

December 3d. Leaving Mr. Fitzpatrick with the party, I went ahead with the howitzer and a few men, in order to gain time, as our progress with the gun was necessarily slower. The country continued the same—very stony, with cedar and pine; and we rode on until dark, when we encamped on a hillside covered with snow, which we used tonight for water, as we were unable to reach any stream.

December 4th. Our animals had taken the back track, although a great number were hobbled, and we were consequently delayed until noon. Shortly after we had left this encampment the mountain trail from the Dalles joined that on which we were traveling. After passing for several miles over an artemisia plain, the trail entered a beautiful pine forest, through which we traveled for several hours, and about four o'clock descended into the valley of another large branch, on the bottom of which were spaces of open pines, with occasional meadows of good grass, in one of which we encamped. The stream is very swift and deep, and about forty feet wide, and nearly half frozen over. Among the timber here are larches one hundred and forty feet high and over three feet in diameter. We had tonight the rare sight of a lunar rainbow.

December 5th. Today the country was all pine forest, and beautiful weather made our journey delightful. It was too warm at noon for winter clothes; and the snow, which lay everywhere in patches through the forest, was melting rapidly.

After a few hours' ride we came upon a fine stream in the midst of the forest, which proved to be the principal branch of Fall River. It was occasionally two hundred feet wide—sometimes narrowed to fifty feet; the waters very clear, and frequently deep. We ascended along the river, which sometimes presented sheets of foaming cascades, its banks occasionally blackened with masses of scoriated rock, and found a good encampment on the verge of an open bottom, which had been an old camping ground of the Cayuse Indians.[6] A great number of deer horns were lying about, indicating game in the neighborhood. The timber was uniformly large, some of the pines measuring twenty-two feet in circumference at the ground, and twelve to thirteen feet at six feet above.

In all our journeying we had never traveled through a country where the rivers were so abounding in falls, and the name of this stream is singularly characteristic. At every place where we come in the neighborhood of the river is heard the roaring of falls. The rock along the banks of the stream, and the ledge over which it falls, is a scoriated basalt, with a bright metallic fracture. The stream goes over in one clear pitch, succeeded by a foaming cataract of several hundred yards. In the little bottom above the falls a small stream discharges into an *entonnoir,* and disappears below. We had made an early encampment, and in the course of the evening Mr. Fitzpatrick joined us here with the lost mule. Our lodge poles were nearly worn out, and we found here a handsome set leaning against one of the trees, very white, and cleanly scraped. Had the owners been here, we would have purchased them; but as they were not, we merely left the old ones in their place, with a small quantity of tobacco.

December 6th. The morning was frosty and clear. We continued up the stream on undulating forest ground, over which there was scattered much fallen timber. We met here a village of Nez Percé Indians, who appeared to be coming down from the mountains and had with them fine bands of horses. With them were a few Snake Indians of the root-digging species.

From the forest we emerged into an open valley ten or twelve miles wide, through which the stream was flowing tranquilly, upward of two hundred feet broad, with occasional islands, and bordered with fine broad bottoms. Crossing the river, which here issues from a great mountain ridge on the right, we continued up the southern and smaller branch, over a level country, consisting of fine meadowland alternating with pine forests, and encamped on it early in the evening. A warm sunshine made the day pleasant.

December 7th. Today we had good traveling ground, the trail leading sometimes over rather sandy soils in the pine forest, and sometimes over meadowland along the stream. The great beauty of the country in summer constantly suggested itself to our imaginations; and even now we found it beautiful, as we rode along these meadows, from half a mile to two miles wide. The rich soil and excellent water, surrounded by noble forests, make a picture that would delight the eye of a farmer. . . .*

December 8th. Today we crossed the last branch of the Fall River, issuing, like all the others we had crossed, in a southwesterly direction from the mountains. Our direction was a little east of south, the trail leading constantly through pine forests.

The soil was generally bare, consisting, in greater part, of a yellowish-white pumice stone, producing varieties of magnificent pines, but not a blade of grass; and tonight our horses were obliged to do without food, and use snow for water. These pines are remarkable for the red color of the boles, and among them occurs a species, of which the Indians had informed me when leaving the Dalles. The unusual size of the cone (sixteen or eighteen inches long) had attracted their attention; and they pointed it out to me among the curiosities of the country. They are more remarkable for their large diameter than their height, which usually averages only about one hundred and twenty feet. The leaflets are short—only two or three inches long, and five in a sheath—the bark of a red color.

December 9th. The trail leads always through splendid pine forests. Crossing dividing grounds by a very fine road, we descended very gently toward the south. The weather was pleasant, and we

* Data on latitude and longitude omitted.

halted late. The soil was very much like that of yesterday; and on the surface of a hill, near our encampment, were displayed beds of pumice stone; but the soil produced no grass, and again the animals fared badly.

December 10th. The country began to improve; and about eleven o'clock we reached a spring of cold water on the edge of a savannah, or grassy meadow, which our guides informed us was an arm of the Klamath Lake; and a few miles further we entered upon an extensive meadow, or lake of grass, surrounded by timbered mountains. This was the Klamath Lake.[7] It was a picturesque and beautiful spot, and rendered more attractive to us by the abundant and excellent grass, which our animals, after traveling through pine forests, so much needed; but the broad sheet of water which constitutes a lake was not to be seen. Overlooking it, immediately west, were several snowy knobs, belonging to what we have considered a branch of the Cascade Range. A low point covered with pines made out into the lake, which afforded us a good place for an encampment, and for the security of our horses, which were guarded in view on the open meadow.

The character of courage and hostility attributed to the Indians [8] of this quarter induced more than usual precaution, and, seeing smokes rising from the middle of the lake (or savannah) and along the opposite shores, I directed the howitzer to be fired. It was the first time our guides had seen it discharged, and the bursting of the shell at a distance, which was something like the second fire of the gun, amazed and bewildered them with delight. It inspired them with triumphant feelings; but on the camps at a distance the effect was different, for the smokes in the lake and on the shores immediately disappeared.

The point on which we were encamped forms, with the opposite eastern shore, a narrow neck, connecting the body of the lake with a deep cove or bay which receives the principal affluent stream, and over the greater part of which the water (or rather ice) was at this time dispersed in shallow pools. Among the grass, and scattered over the prairie lake, appeared to be similar marshes. It is simply a shallow basin, which, for a short period at the time of melting snows, is covered with water from the neighboring mountains; but this probably soon runs off, and leaves for the remainder of the year a green savannah, through the midst of which the river Klamath, which flows to the ocean, winds its way to the outlet on the south-western side.

December 11th. No Indians made their appearance, and I determined to pay them a visit. Accordingly, the people were gathered together, and we rode out toward the village in the middle of the lake, which one of our guides had previously visited. It could not be directly approached, as a large part of the lake appeared a marsh, and there were sheets of ice among the grass, on which our horses could not keep their footing. We therefore followed the guide for a considerable distance along the forest and then turned off toward the village, which we soon began to see was a few large huts, on the top of which were collected the Indians. When we had arrived within half a mile of the village, two persons were seen advancing to meet us; and, to please the fancy of our guides, we ranged ourselves into a long line, riding abreast, while they galloped ahead to meet the strangers.

We were surprised, on riding up, to find one of them a woman, having never before known a squaw to take any part in the business of war. They were the village chief and his wife, who, in excitement and alarm at the unusual event and appearance, had come out to meet their fate together. The chief was a very prepossessing Indian, with very handsome features, and a singularly soft and agreeable voice—so remarkable as to attract general notice. The huts were grouped together on the bank of the river, which, from being spread out in a shallow marsh at the upper end of the lake, was collected here into a single stream. They were large round huts, perhaps twenty feet in diameter, with rounded tops, on which was the door by which they descended into the interior. Within, they were supported by posts and beams.

Almost like plants, these people seem to have adapted themselves to the soil, and to be growing on what the immediate locality afforded. Their only subsistence at this time appeared to be a small fish, great quantities of which had been smoked and dried, were suspended on strings about the lodge. Heaps of straw were lying around; and their residence in the midst of grass and rushes had taught them a peculiar skill in converting this material to useful purposes. Their shoes were made of straw or grass, which seemed well adapted for a snowy country; and the women wore on their head a closely woven basket, which made a very good cap. Among other things were particolored mats about four feet square, which we purchased to lay on the snow under our blankets, and to use for tablecloths.

Numbers of singular-looking dogs, resembling wolves, were sitting on the tops of the huts, and of these we purchased a young one, which, after its birthplace, was named Klamath.

The language spoken by these Indians is different from that of the Shoshone and Columbia River tribes, and otherwise than by signs they cannot understand each other. They made us comprehend that they were at war with the Modoc who lived to the southward and to the eastward; but I could obtain from them no certain information.

The river on which they live enters the Cascade Mountains on the western side of the lake, and breaks through them by a passage impracticable for travelers; but over the mountains, to the northward, are passes which present no other obstacle than in the almost impenetrable forests. Unlike any Indians we had previously seen, these wore shells in their noses. We returned to our camp, after remaining here an' hour or two, accompanied by a number of Indians.

In order to recruit a little the strength of our animals, and obtain some acquaintance with the locality, we remained here for the remainder of the day. By observation, the latitude of the camp was 42° 56′ 51″, and the diameter of the lake, or meadow, as has been intimated, about twenty miles. It is a picturesque and beautiful spot, and, under the hand of cultivation, might become a little paradise. Game is found in the forest; timbered and snowy mountains skirt it, and fertility characterizes it. Situated near the heads of three rivers, and on the line of inland communication with California, and near to Indians noted for treachery, it will naturally, in the progress of the settlement of Oregon, become a point for military occupation and settlement.

From Klamath Lake, the further continuation of our voyage assumed a character of discovery and exploration, which, from the Indians here, we could obtain no information to direct, and where the imaginary maps of the country, instead of assisting, exposed us to suffering and defeat. In our journey across the desert, Mary's Lake and the famous Buenaventura River were two points on which I relied to recruit the animals, and repose the party.

Forming, agreeably to the best maps in my possession, a connected water line from the Rocky Mountains to the Pacific Ocean, I felt no other anxiety than to pass safely across the intervening desert to the banks of the Buenaventura, where, in the softer climate of a more southern latitude, our horses might find grass to sustain them, and ourselves be sheltered from the rigors of winter and from the inhospitable desert.

The guides who had conducted us thus far on our journey were about to return, and I endeavored in vain to obtain others to lead us, even for a few days, in the direction (east) which we wished to go. The chief to whom I applied alleged the want of horses, and the snow on the mountains across which our course would carry us, and the sickness of his family, as reasons for refusing to go with us.

December 12th. This morning the camp was thronged with Klamath Indians from the southeastern shore of the lake; but, knowing the treacherous disposition, which is a remarkable characteristic of the Indians south of the Columbia, the camp was kept constantly on its guard. I was not unmindful of the disasters which Smith and other travelers had met with in this country, and therefore was equally vigilant in guarding against treachery and violence.[9]

According to the best information I had been able to obtain from the Indians, in a few days' traveling we should reach another large water, probably a lake, which they indicated exactly in the course we were about to pursue.

We struck our tents at ten o'clock, and crossed the lake in a nearly east direction, where it has the least extension—the breadth of the arm being here only about a mile and a half. There were ponds of ice, with but little grass for the greater part of the way; and it was difficult to get the pack animals across, which fell frequently, and could not get up with their loads, unassisted. The morning was very unpleasant, snow falling at intervals in large flakes, and the sky dark.

In about two hours we succeeded in getting the animals over; and, after traveling another hour along the eastern shore of the lake, we turned up into a cove where there was a sheltered place among the timber, with good grass, and encamped. The Indians who had accompanied us so far returned to their village on the southeastern shore. Among the pines here, I noticed some five or six feet in diameter.

December 13th. The night has been cold, the peaks around the lake gleam out brightly in the morning sun, and the thermometer is at zero. We continued up the hollow formed by a small affluent to the lake, and immediately entered an open pine forest on the mountain. The way here was sometimes obstructed by fallen trees, and the snow was four to twelve inches deep. The mules at the gun pulled heavily, and walking was a little laborious.

In the midst of the wood we heard the sound of galloping horses, and were agreeably surprised by the unexpected arrival of our Klamath chief with several Indians. He seemed to have found his conduct inhospitable in letting the strangers depart without a guide through the snow, and had come, with a few others, to pilot us a day or two on the way. After traveling in an easterly direction through the forest, for about four hours, we reached a considerable stream, with a border of good grass; and here, by the advice of our guides, we encamped. It is about thirty feet wide, and two to four feet deep, the water clear, with some current, and, according to the information of our Indians, is the principal affluent to the lake, and the headwater of the Klamath River. . . .*

December 14th. Our road was over a broad mountain, and we rode seven hours in a thick snowstorm, always through pine forests, when we came down upon the headwaters of another stream, on which there was grass. The snow lay deep on the ground, and only the high swamp grass appeared above.

The Indians were thinly clad, and I had remarked during the day that they suffered from the cold. This evening they told me that the snow was getting too deep on the mountain, and I could not induce them to go any farther. The stream we had struck issued from the mountain in an easterly direction, turning to the southward a short distance below; and, drawing its course upon the ground, they made us comprehend that it pursued its way for a long distance in that direction, uniting with many other streams, and gradually becoming a great river.

Without the subsequent information, which confirmed the opinion, we became immediately satisfied that this water formed the

* Material on latitude and longitude omitted.

principal stream of the Sacramento River; and, consequently, that this main affluent of the Bay of San Francisco had its source within the limits of the United States, and opposite a tributary to the Columbia, and near the head of the Klamath River, which goes to the ocean north of 42°, and within the United States.[10]

December 15th. A present consisting of useful goods afforded much satisfaction to our guides; and, showing them the national flag, I explained that it was a symbol of our nation, and they engaged always to receive it in a friendly manner. The chief pointed out a course by following which we would arrive at the big water, where no more snow was to be found.

Traveling in a direction North 60° East by compass, which the Indians informed me would avoid a bad mountain to the right, we crossed the Sacramento where it turned to the southward, and entered a grassy level plain—a smaller Grand Rond—from the lower end of which the river issued into an inviting country of low rolling hills. Crossing a hard frozen swamp on the farther side of the Rond, we entered again the pine forest, in which very deep snow made our traveling slow and laborious. We were slowly but gradually ascending a mountain, and after a hard journey of seven hours, we came to some naked places among the timber, where a few tufts of grass showed above the snow, on the side of a hollow; and here we encamped. Our cow, which every day got poorer, was killed here, but the meat was rather tough.

December 16th. We traveled this morning through snow about three feet deep, which, being crusted, very much cut the feet of our animals. The mountains still gradually rose; we crossed several springheads covered with quaking asp, otherwise it was all pine forest. The air was dark with falling snow, which everywhere weighed down the trees. The depths of the forest were profoundly still, and below, we scarce felt a breath of the wind which whirled the snow through their branches.

I found that it required some exertion of constancy to adhere steadily to one course through the woods, when we were uncertain how far the forest extended, or what lay beyond; and on account of our animals it would be bad to spend another night on the mountain. Toward noon the forest looked clear ahead, appearing suddenly to terminate, and beyond a certain point we could see no trees.

Riding rapidly ahead to this spot, we found ourselves on the verge of a vertical and rocky wall of the mountain.

At our feet—more than a thousand feet below—we looked into a green prairie country, in which a beautiful lake, some twenty miles in length, was spread along the foot of the mountains, its shores bordered with green grass. Just then the sun broke out among the clouds, and illuminated the country below, while around us the storm raged fiercely. Not a particle of ice was to be seen on the lake, or snow on its borders, and all was like summer or spring. The glow of the sun in the valley below brightened up our hearts with sudden pleasure, and we made the woods ring with joyful shouts to those behind; and gradually, as each came up, he stopped to enjoy the unexpected scene. Shivering on snow three feet deep, and stiffening in a cold north wind, we exclaimed at once that the names of Summer Lake and Winter Ridge [11] should be applied to these two proximate places of sudden and violent contrast.

We were now immediately on the verge of the forest land in which we had been traveling so many days, and looking forward to the east, scarce a tree was to be seen. Viewed from our elevation, the face of the country exhibited only rocks and grass, and presented a region in which the artemisia became the principal wood, furnishing to its scattered inhabitants fuel for their fire, building material for their huts, and shelter for the small game which ministers to their hunger and nakedness. Broadly marked by the boundary of the mountain wall, and immediately below us, were the first waters of that Great Interior Basin which has the Wasatch and Bear River mountains for its eastern, and the Sierra Nevada for its western rim, and the edge of which we had entered upward of three months before at the Great Salt Lake.

When we had sufficiently admired the scene below, we began to think about descending, which here was impossible, and we turned toward the north, traveling always along the rocky wall. We continued on for four or five miles, making ineffectual attempts at several places, and at length succeeded in getting down at one which was extremely difficult of descent. Night had closed in before the foremost reached the bottom, and it was dark before we all found ourselves together in the valley. There were three or four half-dead dry cedar trees on the shore, and those who first arrived kindled bright fires to light on the others.

One of the mules rolled over and over two or three hundred feet into a ravine, but recovered himself, without any other injury than to his pack; and the howitzer was left midway the mountain until morning. By observation, the latitude of this encampment is 42° 57′ 22″. It delayed us until near noon the next day to recover ourselves, and put everything in order; and we made only a short camp along the western shore of the lake, which, in the summer temperature we enjoyed today, justified the name we had given it.

Our course would have taken us to the other shore, and over the highlands beyond; but I distrusted the appearance of the country, and decided to follow a plainly beaten Indian trail leading along this side of the lake. We were now in a country where the scarcity of water and of grass makes traveling dangerous, and great caution was necessary.

December 18th. We continued on the trail along the narrow strip of land between the lake and the high rocky wall from which we had looked down two days before. Almost every half-mile we crossed a little spring or stream of pure cold water; and the grass was certainly as fresh and green as in the early spring. From the white efflorescence along the shore of the lake, we were enabled to judge that the water was impure, like that of lakes we subsequently found; but the mud prevented us from approaching it.

We encamped near the eastern point of the lake, where there appeared between the hills a broad and low connecting hollow with the country beyond. From a rocky hill in the rear, I could see, marked out by a line of yellow dried grass, the bed of a stream which probably connected the lake with other waters in the spring. The observed latitude of this encampment is 42° 42′ 37″.

December 19th. After two hours' ride in an easterly direction through a low country, the high ridge with pine forests still to our right, and a rocky and bald but lower one on the left, we reached a considerable fresh-water stream, which issues from the piny mountains. So far as we had been able to judge, between this stream and the lake we had crossed dividing grounds, and there did not appear to be any connection, as might be inferred from the impure condition of the lake water.

The rapid stream of pure water, roaring along between banks

overhung with aspens and willows, was a refreshing and unexpected sight; and we followed down the course of the stream, which brought us soon into a marsh, or dry lake, formed by the expanding waters of the stream. It was covered with high reeds and rushes, and large patches of ground had been turned up by the squaws in digging for roots, as if a farmer had been preparing the land for grain.

I could not succeed in finding the plant for which they had been digging. There were frequent trails, and fresh tracks of Indians; and, from the abundant signs visible, the black-tailed hare appears to be numerous here. It was evident that, in other seasons, this place was a sheet of water. Crossing this marsh toward the eastern hills, and passing over a bordering plain of heavy sands, covered with artemisia, we encamped before sundown on the creek, which here was very small, having lost its water in the marshy grounds. We found here tolerably good grass. The wind tonight was high, and we had no longer our huge pine fires, but were driven to our old resource of small dried willows and artemisia. About twelve miles ahead, the valley appears to be closed in by a high dark-looking ridge.

December 20th. Traveling for a few hours down the stream this morning, we turned a point of the hill on our left, and came suddenly in sight of another and much larger lake, which, along its eastern shore, was closely bordered by the high black ridge which walled it in by a precipitous face on this side. Throughout this region the face of the country is characterized by these precipices of black volcanic rock, generally enclosing the valleys of streams, and frequently terminating the hills.

Often in the course of our journey we would be tempted to continue our road up the gentle ascent of a sloping hill which, at the summit, would terminate abruptly in a black precipice. Spread out over a length of twenty miles, the lake, when we first came in view, presented a handsome sheet of water; and I gave to it the name of Lake Abert, in honor of the chief of the corps to which I belonged.[12]

The fresh-water stream we had followed emptied into the lake by a little fall; and I was doubtful for a moment whether to go on, or encamp at this place. The miry ground in the neighborhood of the lake did not allow us to examine the water conveniently, and, being now on the borders of a desert country, we were moving cautiously. It was, however, still early in the day, and I continued on, trusting either that the water would be drinkable, or that we should find some little spring from the hillside. We were following an Indian trail which led along the steep rocky precipice, a black ridge along the western shore holding out no prospect whatever. The white efflorescences which lined the shore like a bank of snow, and the disagreeable odor which filled the air as soon as we came near, informed us too plainly that the water belonged to one of those fetid salt lakes which are common in this region.

We continued until late in the evening to work along the rocky shore, but, as often afterward, the dry inhospitable rock deceived us; and, halting on the lake, we kindled up fires to guide those who were straggling along behind. We tried the water, but it was impossible to drink it, and most of the people tonight lay down without eating; but some of us, who had always a great reluctance to close the day without supper, dug holes along the shore, and obtained water which, being filtered, was sufficiently palatable to be used, but still retained much of its nauseating taste. There was very little grass for the animals, the shore being lined with a luxuriant growth of chenopodiaceous shrubs, which burned with a quick bright flame, and made our firewood.

The next morning we had scarcely traveled two hours along the shore when we reached a place where the mountains made a bay, leaving at their feet a low bottom around the lake. Here we found numerous hillocks covered with rushes, in the midst of which were deep holes, or springs, of pure water; and the bottom was covered with grass, which, although of a bad and unwholesome quality, and mixed with saline efflorescences, was still abundant, and made a good halting place to recruit our animals; and we accordingly encamped here for the remainder of the day.

I rode ahead several miles to ascertain if there was any appearance of a watercourse entering the lake, but found none, the hills preserving their dry character, and the shore of the lake sprinkled with the same white powdery substance, and covered with the same shrubs. There were flocks of ducks on the lake, and frequent tracks of Indians along the shore, where the grass had been recently burned by their fires.

We ascended the bordering mountain in order to obtain a more perfect view of the lake in sketching its figure; hills sweep entirely around its basin, from which the waters have no outlet.

December 22d. Today we left this forbidding lake. Impassable rocky ridges barred our progress to the eastward, and I accordingly bore off toward the south, over an extensive sage plain. At a considerable distance ahead, and a little on our left, was a range of snowy mountains, and the country declined gradually toward the foot of a high and nearer ridge immediately before us, which presented the feature of black precipices, now becoming common to the country.

On the summit of the ridge, snow was visible; and there being every indication of a stream at its base, we rode on until after dark, but were unable to reach it, and halted among the sage bushes on the open plain, without either grass or water. The two india-rubber bags had been filled with water in the morning, which afforded sufficient for the camp; and rain in the night-formed pools, which relieved the thirst of the animals. Where we encamped on the bleak sandy plain, the Indians had made huts or circular enclosures, about four feet high and twelve feet broad, of artemisia bushes. Whether these had been forts or houses, or what they had been doing in such a desert place, we could not ascertain.

December 23d. The weather is mild, the thermometer at daylight 38°, the wind having been from the southward for several days. The country has a very forbidding appearance, presenting to the eye nothing but sage and barren ridges. We rode up toward the mountain, along the foot of which we found a lake, which we could not approach on account of the mud; and, passing around its southern end, ascended the slope at the foot of the ridge, where in some hollows we had discovered bushes and small trees—in such situations a sure sign of water.

We found here several springs, and the hillside was well sprinkled with a species of festuca—a better grass than we had found for many days. Our elevated position gave us a good view over the country, but we discovered nothing very encouraging. Southward, about ten miles distant, was another small lake, toward which a broad trail led along the ridge, and this appearing to afford the most practicable route, I determined to continue our journey in that direction.

December 24th. We found the water of the lake tolerably pure, and encamped at the farther end. There were some good grass and canes along the shore, and the vegetation at this place consisted principally of chenopodiaceous shrubs.

December 25th. We were roused on Christmas morning, by a discharge from the small arms and howitzer, with which our people saluted the day; and the name of which we bestowed on the lake.[13] It was the first time, perhaps, in this remote and desolate region, in which it had been so commemorated.

Always, on days of religious or national commemoration, our voyageurs expect some unusual allowance; and, having nothing else, I gave to them each a little brandy (which was carefully guarded as one of the most useful articles a traveler can carry), with some coffee and sugar, which here, where every eatable was a luxury, was sufficient to make them a feast. The day was sunny and warm, and, resuming our journey, we crossed some slight dividing grounds into a similar basin, walled in on the right by a lofty mountain ridge. The plainly beaten trail still continued, and occasionally we passed camping grounds of the Indians, which indicated to me that we were on one of the great thoroughfares of the country.

In the afternoon I attempted to travel in a more eastern direction; but after a few laborious miles, was beaten back into the basin by an impassable country. There were fresh Indian tracks about the valley, and last night a horse was stolen. We encamped on the valley bottom, where there was some creamlike water in ponds, colored by a clay soil and frozen over. Chenopodiaceous shrubs constituted the growth, and made again our firewood. The animals were driven to the hill, where there was tolerably good grass.

December 26th. Our general course was again south. The country consists of larger or smaller basins, into which the mountain waters run down, forming small lakes; they present a perfect level, from which the mountains rise immediately and abruptly. Between the successive basins, the dividing grounds are usually very slight; and it is probable that, in the seasons of high water, many of these basins are in communication. At such times there is evidently an abundance of water, though now we find scarcely more than the dry beds.

On either side, the mountains, though not very high, appear to be rocky and sterile. The basin in which we were traveling declined toward the southwest corner, where the mountains indicated a narrow outlet; and, turning round a rocky point or cape, we continued up a lateral branch valley, in which we encamped at night on a rapid, pretty little stream of fresh water, which we found unexpectedly among the sage near the ridge, on the right side of the valley. It was bordered with grassy bottoms and clumps of willows, the water partially frozen. This stream belongs to the basin we had left. By a partial observation tonight, our camp was found to be directly on the forty-second parallel.[14] Tonight a horse belonging to Carson, one of the best we had in the camp, was stolen by the Indians.

December 27th. We continued up the valley of the stream, the principal branch of which here issues from the bed of high mountains. We turned up a branch to the left, and fell into an Indian trail, which conducted us by a good road over open bottoms along the creek, where the snow was five or six inches deep. Gradually ascending, the trail led through a good broad pass in the mountain, where we found the snow about one foot deep.

There were some remarkably large cedars in the pass which were covered with an unusual quantity of frost, which we supposed might possibly indicate the neighborhood of water; and as, in the arbitrary position of Mary's Lake, we were already beginning to look for it, this circumstance contributed to our hope of finding it near. Descending from the mountain we reached another basin, on the flat lake bed of which we found no water, and encamped among the sage on the bordering plain, where the snow was still about one foot deep. Among this the grass was remarkably green, and tonight the animals fared tolerably well.*

December 28th. The snow being deep, I had determined, if any more horses were stolen, to follow the tracks of the Indians into the mountains, and put a temporary check to their sly operations; but it did not occur again.

Our road this morning lay down a level valley, bordered by steep mountainous ridges, rising very abruptly from the plain. Artemisia was the principal plant, mingled with Fremontia and the chenopodiaceous shrubs. The artemisia was here extremely large, being sometimes a foot in diameter and eight feet high.

Riding quietly along over the snow, we came suddenly upon smokes rising among these bushes, and, galloping up, we found two huts open at the top, and loosely built of sage,[15] which ap-

---

* The party had crossed from Oregon into northwestern Nevada, then Mexican territory.

peared to have been deserted at the instant; and, looking hastily around, we saw several Indians on the crest of the ridge near by, and several others scrambling up the side. We had come upon them so suddenly that they had been well-nigh surprised in their lodges. A sage fire was burning in the middle; a few baskets made of straw were lying about, with one or two rabbit skins; and there was a little grass scattered about, on which they had been lying. *"Tabibo—bo!"* they shouted from the hills—a word which, in the Snake language, signifies "white"—and remained looking at us from behind the rocks.

Carson and Godey rode toward the hill, but the men ran off like deer. They had been so much pressed that a woman with two children had dropped behind a sage bush near the lodge, and when Carson accidentally stumbled upon her, she immediately began screaming in the extremity of fear, and shut her eyes fast, to avoid seeing him. She was brought back to the lodge, and we endeavored in vain to open a communication with the men. By dint of presents, and friendly demonstrations, she was brought to calmness; and we found that they belonged to the Snake nation, speaking the language of that people.

Eight or ten appeared to live together, under the same little shelter, and they seemed to have no other subsistence than the roots or seeds they might have stored up, and the hares which live in the sage, and which they are enabled to track through the snow, and are very skillful in killing. Their skins afford them a little scanty covering. Herding together among bushes, and crouching almost naked over a little sage fire, using their instinct only to procure food, these may be considered, among human beings, the nearest approach to the mere animal creation. We have reason to believe that these had never before seen the face of a white man.

The day had been pleasant, but about two o'clock it began to blow; and crossing a slight dividing ground, we encamped on the sheltered side of a hill where there was good bunch grass, having made a day's journey of twenty-four miles. The night closed in, threatening snow; but the large sage bushes made bright fires.

December 29th. The morning mild, and at four o'clock it commenced snowing. We took our way across a plain thickly covered with snow, toward a range of hills in the southeast. The sky soon became so dark with snow that little could be seen of the surrounding country, and we reached the summit of the hills in a heavy snowstorm. On the side we had approached, this had appeared to be only a ridge of low hills, and we were surprised to find ourselves on the summit of a bed of broken mountains, which, as far as the weather would permit us to see, declined rapidly to some low country ahead, presenting a dreary and savage character; and for a moment I looked around in doubt on the wild and inhospitable prospect, scarcely knowing what road to take which might conduct us to some place of shelter for the night.

Noticing among the hills the head of a grassy hollow, I determined to follow it, in the hope that it would conduct us to a stream. We followed a winding descent for several miles, the hollow gradually broadening into little meadows, and becoming the bed of a stream as we advanced; and toward night, we were agreeably surprised by the appearance of a willow grove, where we found a sheltered camp, with water and excellent and abundant grass. The grass, which was covered by the snow on the bottom, was long and green, and the face of the mountain had a more favorable character in its vegetation, being smoother, and covered with good bunch grass.

The snow was deep, and the night very cold. A broad trail had entered the valley from the right, and a short distance below the camp were the tracks where a considerable party of Indians had passed on horseback, who had turned out to the left, apparently with the view of crossing the mountains to the eastward. These Indians were probably Modocs.

December 30th. After following the stream for a few hours in a southeasterly direction it entered a cañon where we could not follow; but determined not to leave the stream, we searched a passage below where we could regain it, and entered a regular narrow valley. The water had now more the appearance of a flowing creek; several times we passed groves of willows, and we began to feel ourselves out of all difficulty. From our position it was reasonable to conclude that this stream would find its outlet in Mary's Lake, and conduct us into a better country.

We had descended rapidly, and here we found very little snow. On both sides the mountains showed often stupendous and curious-looking rocks, which at several places so narrowed the valley, that scarcely a pass was left for the camp. It was a singular place to travel through—shut up in the earth, a sort of chasm, the little strip of grass under our feet, the rough walls of bare rock on either hand, and the narrow strip of sky above. The grass tonight was abundant, and we encamped in high spirits.

December 31st. After an hour's ride this morning our hopes were once more destroyed. The valley opened out, and before us again lay one of the dry basins. After some search, we discovered a high water outlet, which brought us in a few miles, and by a descent of several hundred feet, into another long broad basin, in which we found the bed of a stream, and obtained sufficient water by cutting the ice. The grass on the bottoms was salt and unpalatable.

Here we concluded the year 1843, and our New Year's Eve was rather a gloomy one. The result of our journey began to be very uncertain; the country was singularly unfavorable to travel, the grasses being frequently of a very unwholesome character; and the hoofs of our animals were so worn and cut by the rocks that many of them were lame, and could scarcely be got along.

New Year's Day, 1844. We continued down the valley, between a dry-looking black ridge on the left and a more snowy and high one on the right. Our road was bad, along the bottom being broken by gullies and impeded by sage, and sandy on the hills, where there is not a blade of grass, nor does any appear on the mountains. The soil in many places consists of a fine powdery sand, covered with a saline efflorescence, and the general character of the country is desert. During the day we directed our course toward a black cape, at the foot of which a column of smoke indicated hot springs.

January 2d. We were on the road early, the face of the country hidden by falling snow. We traveled along the bed of the stream, in some places dry, in others covered with ice, the traveling being very bad, through deep fine sand rendered tenacious by a mixture of clay. The weather cleared up a little at noon, and we reached the hot springs of which we had seen the vapor the day before. There was a large field of the usual salt grass here peculiar to such places. The country otherwise is a perfect barren, without a blade of grass, the only plants being some dwarf Fremontias. We passed the rocky cape, a jagged broken point, bare and torn.

The rocks are volcanic, and the hills here have a burnt appearance—cinders and coal occasionally appearing as at a blacksmith's forge. We crossed the large dry bed of a muddy lake in a south-easterly direction, and encamped at night without water and with-

out grass, among sage bushes covered with snow. The heavy road
made several mules give out today; and a horse which had made
the journey from the States successfully thus far was left on the
trail.

January 3d. A fog, so dense that we could not see a hundred yards,
covered the country, and the men that were sent out after the horses
were bewildered and lost; and we were consequently detained at
camp until late in the day.

Our situation had now become a serious one. We had reached
and run over the position where, according to the best maps in my
possession, we should have found Mary's Lake, or River. We were
evidently on the verge of the desert which had been reported to us;
and the appearance of the country was so forbidding that I was
afraid to enter it, and determined to bear away to the southward,
keeping close along the mountains, in the full expectation of reaching the Buenaventura River.[16]

This morning I put every man in the camp on foot—myself, of
course, among the rest—and in this manner lightened, by distribution, the loads of the animals. We traveled seven or eight miles
along the ridge bordering the valley, and encamped where there
were a few bunches of grass on the bed of a hill torrent, without
water. There were some large artemisias but the principal plants are
chenopodiaceous shrubs. The rock composing the mountains is here
changed suddenly into white granite. The fog showed the tops of
the hills at sunset, and stars enough for observations in the early
evening, and then closed over us as before. Latitude by observation,
40° 48′ 15″.

January 4th. The fog today was still more dense, and the people
again were bewildered. We traveled a few miles around the western
point of the ridge, and encamped where there were a few tufts of
grass, but no water. Our animals now were in a very alarming state,
and there was increased anxiety in the camp.

January 5th. Same dense fog continued, and one of the mules
died in camp this morning. I have had occasion to remark, in such
conditions as these, that animals which are about to die leave the
band, and coming into the camp, lie down about the fires. We
moved to a place where there was a little better grass, about two
miles distant. Taplin, one of our best men, who had gone out on a
scouting excursion, ascended a mountain near by, and to his great

surprise emerged into a region of bright sunshine, in which the upper parts of the mountain were glowing, while below all was obscured in the darkest fog.

January 6th. The fog continued the same, and with Mr. Preuss and Carson, I ascended the mountain to sketch the leading features of the country, as some indication of our future route, while Mr. Fitzpatrick explored the country below. In a very short distance we had ascended above the mist, but the view obtained was not very gratifying. The fog had partially cleared off from below when we reached the summit; and in the southwest corner of a basin communicating with that in which we had encamped we saw a lofty column of smoke, sixteen miles distant, indicating the presence of hot springs. There, also, appeared to be the outlet of those draining channels of the country, and as such places afforded always more or less grass, I determined to steer in that direction. The ridge we had ascended, appeared to be composed of fragments of white granite. We saw here traces of sheep and antelope.

Entering the neighboring valley, and crossing the bed of another lake, after a hard day's travel over ground of yielding mud and sand we reached the springs, where we found an abundance of grass, which, though only tolerably good, made this place, with reference to the past, a refreshing and agreeable spot.

This is the most extraordinary locality of hot springs we had met during the journey. The basin of the largest one has a circumference of several hundred feet; but there is at one extremity a circular space, of about fifteen feet in diameter, entirely occupied by the boiling water. It boils up at irregular intervals, and with much noise. The water is clear, and the spring deep; a pole about sixteen feet long was easily immersed in the center, but we had no means of forming a good idea of the depth. It was surrounded on the margin with a border of green grass, and near the shore the temperature of the water was 206°. We had no means of ascertaining that of the center, where the heat was greatest; but, by dispersing the water with a pole, the temperature at the margin was increased to 208°, and in the center it was doubtless higher. By driving the pole toward the bottom, the water was made to boil up with increased force and noise. There are several other interesting places where water and smoke or gas escape, but they would require a long description. The water is impregnated with common salt, but not so much so as to render it unfit for general cooking; and a mixture of snow made it pleasant to drink.

In the immediate neighborhood the valley bottom is covered almost exclusively with chenopodiaceous shrubs of greater luxuriance, and larger growth, than we have seen them in any preceding part of the journey. I obtained this evening some astronomical observations.

Our situation now required caution. Including those which gave out from the injured condition of their feet, and those stolen by Indians, we had lost, since leaving the Dalles of the Columbia, fifteen animals; and of these, nine had been left in the last few days. I therefore determined, until we should reach a country of water and vegetation, to feel our way ahead by having the line of route explored some fifteen or twenty miles in advance, and only to leave a present encampment when the succeeding one was known.

Taking with me Godey and Carson, I made today a thorough exploration of the neighboring valleys,[17] and found in a ravine in the bordering mountains a good camping-place, where was water in springs, and a sufficient quantity of grass for a night. Overshading the springs were some trees of the sweet cottonwood, which, after a long interval of absence, we saw again with pleasure, regarding them as harbingers of a better country. To us they were eloquent of green prairies and buffalo.

We found here a broad and plainly marked trail, on which there were tracks of horses, and we appeared to have regained one of the thoroughfares which pass by the watering places of the country. On the western mountains of the valley, with which this of the boiling spring communicates, we remarked scattered cedars—probably an indication that we were on the borders of the timbered region extending to the Pacific. We reached the camp at sunset, after a day's ride of about forty miles. The horses we rode were in good order, being of some that were kept for emergencies, and rarely used.

Mr. Preuss had ascended one of the mountains, and occupied the day in sketching the country; and Mr. Fitzpatrick had found, a few miles distant, a hollow of excellent grass and pure water, to which the animals were driven, as I remained another day to give them an opportunity to recruit their strength. Indians appear to be every-where prowling about like wild animals, and there is a fresh trail across the snow in the valley near. Latitude of the boiling springs, 40° 39′ 46″.

On the 9th we crossed over to the cottonwood camp. Among the shrubs on the hills were a few bushes of *Ephedra occidentalis*, which we afterward found frequently along our road, and, as usual, the lowlands were occupied with artemisia. While the party pro-ceeded to this place, Carson and myself reconnoitered the road in advance, and found another good encampment for the following day.

January 10th. We continued our reconnaissance ahead, pursuing a south direction in the basin along the ridge, the camp following slowly after. On a large trail there is never any doubt of finding suitable places for encampments. We reached the end of the basin, where we found, in a hollow of the mountain which enclosed it, an abundance of good bunch grass. Leaving a signal for the party to encamp, we continued our way up the hollow,[18] intending to see what lay beyond the mountain. The hollow was several miles long, forming a good pass, the snow deepening to about a foot as we neared the summit. Beyond, a defile between the mountains de-scended rapidly about two thousand feet; and filling up all the lower space was a sheet of green water, some twenty miles broad. It broke upon our eyes like the ocean.

The neighboring peaks rose high above us, and we ascended one of them to obtain a better view. The waves were curling in the breeze, and their dark-green color showed it to be a body of deep water. For a long time we sat enjoying the view, for we had become fatigued with mountains, and the free expanse of moving waves was very grateful. It was set like a gem in the mountains, which, from our position, seemed to enclose it almost entirely. At the western end it communicated with the line of basins we had left a few days since; and on the opposite side it swept a ridge of snowy mountains, the foot of the great Sierra. Its position at first inclined us to believe it Mary's Lake, but the rugged mountains were so entirely dis-cordant with descriptions of its low rushy shores and open country, that we concluded it some unknown body of water, which it after-ward proved to be.[19]

On our road down, the next day, we saw herds of mountain sheep, and encamped on a little stream at the mouth of the defile, about a mile from the margin of the water, to which we hurried down immediately. The water is so slightly salt that, at first, we thought it fresh, and would be pleasant to drink when no other could be had. The shore was rocky—a handsome beach, which reminded us of the sea. On some large granite boulders that were scattered about the shore, I remarked a coating of a calcareous substance, in some places a few inches, and in others a foot in thickness. Near our camp, the hills, which were of primitive rock, were also covered with this substance, which was in too great quantity on the mountains along the shore of the lake to have been deposited by water, and has the appearance of having been spread over the rocks in mass. . . .* Where we had halted appeared to be a favorite camping place for Indians.

January 13th. We followed again a broad Indian trail along the shore of the lake to the southward. For a short space we had room enough in the bottom; but after traveling a short distance, the water swept the foot of precipitous mountains, the peaks of which are about three thousand feet above the lake. The trail wound along the base of these precipices, against which the water dashed below, by a way nearly impracticable for the howitzer. During a greater part of the morning the lake was nearly hid by a snowstorm, and the waves broke on the narrow beach in a long line of foaming surf, five or six feet high.

The day was unpleasantly cold, the wind driving the snow sharp against our faces; and, having advanced only about twelve miles, we encamped in a bottom formed by a ravine, covered with good grass, which was fresh and green. We did not get the howitzer into camp, but were obliged to leave it on the rocks until morning. We saw several flocks of sheep, but did not succeed in killing any. Ducks were riding on the waves, and several large fish were seen. The mountainsides were crusted with the calcareous cement previously mentioned.

There were chenopodiaceous and other shrubs along the beach; and, at the foot of the rocks, an abundance of *Ephedra occidentalis,* whose dark-green color makes them evergreens among the shrubby

* Chemical analysis omitted.

growth of the lake. Toward evening the snow began to fall heavily, and the country had a wintry appearance.

The next morning the snow was rapidly melting under a warm sun. Part of the morning was occupied in bringing up the gun; and, making only nine miles, we encamped on the shore, opposite a very remarkable rock in the lake, which had attracted our attention for many miles. It rose, according to our estimate, six hundred feet above the water; and, from the point we viewed it, presented a pretty exact outline of the great pyramid of Cheops. . . . Like other rocks along the shore, it seemed to be encrusted with calcareous cement. This striking feature suggested a name for the lake, and I called it Pyramid Lake; and though it may be deemed by some a fanciful resemblance, I can undertake to say that the future traveler will find a much more striking resemblance between this rock and the pyramids of Egypt than there is between them and the object from which they take their name.

The elevation of this lake above the sea is four thousand eight hundred and ninety feet, being nearly seven hundred feet higher than the Great Salt Lake, from which it lies nearly west, and distant about eight degrees of longitude. The position and elevation of this lake make it an object of geographical interest. It is the nearest lake to the western rim, as the Great Salt Lake is to the eastern rim, of the Great Basin which lies between the base of the Rocky Mountains and the Sierra Nevada, and the extent and character of which, its whole circumference and contents, it is so desirable to know.

The last of the cattle which had been driven from the Dalles was killed here for food, and was still in good condition.

January 15th. A few poor-looking Indians made their appearance this morning, and we succeeded in getting one into the camp. He was naked, with the exception of a tunic of hare skins. He told us that there was a river at the end of the lake, but that he lived in the rocks near by. From the few words our people could understand, he spoke a dialect of the Snake language; but we were not able to understand enough to know whether the river ran in or out, or what was its course; consequently, there still remained a chance that this might be Mary's Lake.

Groves of large cottonwood, which we could see at the mouth of the river, indicated that it was a stream of considerable size; and, at all events, we had the pleasure to know that now we were in a country where human beings could live. Accompanied by the Indian, we resumed our road, passing on the way several caves in the rock where there were baskets and seeds; but the people had disappeared. We saw also horse tracks along the shore.

Early in the afternoon, when we were approaching the groves at the mouth of the river, three or four Indians met us on the trail.[20] We had an explanatory conversation in signs, and then moved on together toward the village, which the chief said was encamped on the bottom.

Reaching the groves, we found the inlet of a large fresh-water stream, and all at once were satisfied that it was neither Mary's River nor the waters of the Sacramento, but that we had discovered a large interior lake, which the Indians informed us had no outlet. It is about thirty-five miles long; and by the mark of the water line along the shores, the spring level is about twelve feet above its present waters. The chief commenced speaking in a loud voice as we approached, and parties of Indians armed with bows and arrows issued from the thickets.

We selected a strong place for our encampment, a grassy bottom nearly enclosed by the river, and furnished with abundant firewood. The village, a collection of straw huts, was a few hundred yards higher up. An Indian brought in a large fish to trade, which we had the inexpressible satisfaction to find was a salmon trout; we gathered round him eagerly. The Indians were amused with our delight, and immediately brought in numbers, so that the camp was soon stocked. Their flavor was excellent—superior, in fact, to that of any fish I have ever known. They were of extraordinary size—about as large as the Columbia River salmon—generally from two to four feet in length. From the information of Mr. Walker, who passed among some lakes lying more to the eastward, this fish is common to the streams of the inland lakes. He subsequently informed me that he had obtained them weighing six pounds when cleaned and the head taken off; which corresponds very well with the size of those obtained at this place. They doubtless formed the subsistence of these people, who hold the fishery in exclusive possession.

I remarked that one of them gave a fish to the Indian we had first seen, which he carried off to his family. To them it was probably a feast, being of the Digger tribe, and having no share in the fishery, living generally on seeds and roots. Although this was a time of the year when the fish have not yet become fat, they were excellent, and we could only imagine what they are at the proper season. These Indians were very fat, and appeared to live an easy and happy life. They crowded into the camp more than was consistent with our safety, retaining always their arms; and as they made some unsatisfactory demonstrations, they were given to understand that they would not be permitted to come armed into the camp, and strong guards were kept with the horses. Strict vigilance was maintained among the people, and one-third at a time were kept on guard during the night. There is no reason to doubt that these dispositions, uniformly preserved, conducted our party securely through Indians famed for treachery.

In the meantime, such a salmon-trout feast as is seldom seen was going on in our camp; and every variety of manner in which fish could be prepared—boiled, fried, and roasted in the ashes—was put into requisition; and every few minutes an Indian would be seen running off to spear a fresh one.

Whether these Indians had seen whites before, we could not be certain; but they were evidently in communication with others who had, as one of them had some brass buttons, and we noticed several other articles of civilized manufacture. We could obtain from them but little information respecting the country. They made on the ground a drawing of the river, which they represented as issuing from another lake in the mountains three or four days distant, in a direction a little west of south; beyond which they drew a mountain, and further still, two rivers, on one of which they told us that people like ourselves traveled. Whether they alluded to the settlements on the Sacramento, or to a party from the United States which had crossed the Sierra about three degrees to the southward a few years before, I am unable to determine. I tried unsuccessfully to prevail on some of them to guide us for a few days on the road, but they only looked at each other and laughed. The latitude of our encampment, which may be considered the mouth of the inlet, is 39° 51′ 13″ by our observations.

January 16th. This morning we continued our journey along this beautiful stream, which we naturally called the Salmon Trout

River.[21] Large trails led up on either side; the stream was handsomely timbered with large cottonwoods, and the waters were very clear and pure. We were traveling along the mountains of the great Sierra, which rose on our right, covered with snow; but below, the temperature was mild and pleasant. We saw a number of dams which the Indians had constructed to catch fish. After having made about eighteen miles, we encamped under some large cottonwoods on the river bottom, where there was tolerably good grass.

January 17th. This morning we left the river, which here issues from the mountains on the west. With every stream I now expected to see the great Buenaventura; and Carson hurried eagerly to search, on everyone we reached, for beaver cuttings, which he always maintained we should find only on waters that ran to the Pacific; and the absence of such signs was to him a sure indication that the water had no outlet from the Great Basin.

We followed the Indian trail through a tolerably level country, with small sage bushes, which brought us, after twenty miles journey, to another large stream timbered with cottonwood, and flowing also out of the mountains, but running more directly to the eastward.

On the way we surprised a family of Indians in the hills, but the man ran up the mountain with rapidity, and the woman was so terrified, and kept up such a continued screaming, that we could do nothing with her and were obliged to let her go.

January 18th. There were Indian lodges and fish dams on the stream. There were no beaver cuttings on the river; but below, it turned round to the right, and hoping that it would prove a branch of the Buenaventura, we followed it down for about three hours, and encamped.

I rode out with Mr. Fitzpatrick and Carson to reconnoiter the country, which had evidently been alarmed by the news of our appearance. This stream joined with the open valley of another to the eastward; but which way the main water ran, it was impossible to tell. Columns of smoke rose over the country at scattered intervals— signals by which the Indians here, as elsewhere, communicate to each other that enemies are in the country. It is a signal of ancient and very universal application among barbarians.

Examining into the condition of the animals when I returned into the camp, I found their feet so much cut up by the rocks, and so many of them lame, that it was evidently impossible that they could cross the country to the Rocky Mountains. Every piece of iron that could be used for the purpose had been converted into nails, and we could make no further use of the shoes we had remaining. I therefore determined to abandon my eastern course, and to cross the Sierra Nevada into the Valley of the Sacramento, wherever a practical pass could be found. My decision was heard with joy by the people, and diffused new life throughout the camp. Latitude by observation 39° 24' 16".[22]

January 19th. A great number of smokes are still visible this morning, attesting at once the alarm which our appearance had spread among these people, and their ignorance of us. If they knew the whites, they would understand that their only object in coming among them was to trade, which required peace and friendship; but they have nothing to trade—consequently nothing to attract the white man: hence their fear and flight.

At daybreak we had a heavy snow, but set out, and, returning up the stream, went out of our way in a circuit over a little mountain, and encamped on the same stream a few miles above, in latitude 39° 19' 21" by observation.

January 20th. Today we continued up the stream, and encamped on it close to the mountains. The freshly fallen snow was covered with the tracks of Indians, who had descended from the upper waters, probably called down by the smokes in the plain.

We ascended a peak of the range, which commanded a view of the stream behind the first ridge, where it was winding its course through a somewhat open valley,[23] and I sometimes regret that I did not make the trial to cross here; but while we had fair weather below, the mountains were darkened with falling snow, and, feeling unwilling to encounter them, we turned away again to the southward. In that direction we traveled the next day over a tolerably level country, having always the high mountains on the west. There was but little snow or rock on the ground; and, after having traveled twenty-four miles, we encamped again on another large stream, running off to the northward and eastward, to meet that we had left. It ran through broad bottoms having a fine meadowland appearance. Latitude 39° 01' 53".[24]

January 22d. We traveled up the stream for about fourteen miles to the foot of the mountains, from which one branch issued in the southwest, the other flowing from south-southeast along their base.[25] Leaving the camp below, we ascended the range through which the first stream passed, in a cañon; on the western side was a circular valley, about fifteen miles long, through which the stream wound its way, issuing from a gorge in the main mountain, which rose abruptly beyond.

The valley looked yellow with faded grass; and the trail we had followed was visible, making toward the gorge, and this was evidently a pass; but again, while all was bright sunshine on the ridge, and on the valley where we were, the snow was falling heavily in the mountains. I determined to go still to the southward, and encamped on the stream near the forks, the animals being fatigued, and the grass tolerably good.

The rock of the ridge we had ascended is a compact lava, assuming a granitic appearance and structure, and containing, in some places, small nodules of obsidian. So far as composition and aspect are concerned, the rock in other parts of the ridge appears to be granite; but it is probable that this is only a compact form of lava of recent origin. By observation, the elevation of the encampment was five thousand and twenty feet; and the latitude 38° 49′ 54″.

January 23d. We moved along the course of the other branch toward the southeast, the country affording a fine road; and, passing some slight dividing grounds, descended toward the valley of another stream. There was a somewhat rough-looking mountain ahead, which it appeared to issue from, or to enter—we could not tell which; and as the course of the valley and the inclination of the ground had a favorable direction, we were sanguine to find here a branch of the Buenaventura; but were again disappointed, finding it an inland water, on which we encamped after a day's journey of twenty-four miles.[26]

It was evident that, from the time we descended into the plain at Summer Lake, we had been flanking the great range of mountains which divided the Great Basin from the waters of the Pacific; and that the continued succession, and almost connection, of lakes and rivers which we encountered were the drainings of that range. Its rains, springs, and snows would sufficiently account for these lakes and streams, numerous as they were.

January 24th. A man was discovered running toward the camp as we were about to start this morning, who proved to be an Indian of rather advanced age—a sort of forlorn hope, who seemed to have been worked up into the resolution of visiting the strangers who were passing through the country. He seized the hand of the first man he met as he came up, out of breath, and held on as if to assure himself of protection. He brought with him in a little skin bag a few pounds of the seeds of a pine tree, which today we saw for the first time, and which Dr. Torrey has described as a new species, under the name of *Pinus monophyllus*; in popular language, it might be called the nut pine. We purchased them all from him. The nut is oily, of very agreeable flavor, and must be very nutritious, as it constitutes the principal subsistence of the tribes among which we were now traveling. By a present of scarlet cloth, and other striking articles, we prevailed upon this man to be our guide for two days' journey. As clearly as possible by signs, we made him understand our object; and he engaged to conduct us in sight of a good pass which he knew.

Here we ceased to hear the Shoshone language, that of this man being perfectly untelligible.[27] Several Indians who had been waiting to see what reception he would meet with now came into camp, and, accompanied by the newcomers, we resumed our journey.

The road led us up the creek, which here becomes a rather rapid mountain stream fifty feet wide, between dark-looking hills without snow; but immediately beyond them rose snowy mountains on either side, timbered principally with the nut pine. On the lower grounds, the general height of this tree is twelve to twenty feet, and eight inches the greatest diameter; it is rather branching, and has a peculiar and singular but pleasant odor. We followed the river for only a short distance along a rocky trail, and crossed it at a dam which the Indians made us comprehend had been built to catch salmon trout. The snow and ice were heaped up against it three or four feet deep entirely across the stream.

Leaving here the stream, which runs through impassable cañons, we continued our road over a very broken country, passing through a low gap between the snowy mountains. The rock which occurs immediately in the pass has the appearance of impure sandstone, containing scales of black mica. This may be only a stratified lava; on issuing from the gap, the compact lava, and other volcanic products usual in the country, again occurred.

We descended from the gap into a wide valley, or rather basin, and encamped on a small tributary to the last stream, on which there was very good grass. It was covered with such thick ice, that it required some labor with pickaxes to make holes for the animals to drink. The banks are lightly wooded with willow, and on the upper bottoms are sage and Fremontia, with *Ephedra occidentalis*, which begins to occur more frequently.

The day has been a summer one, warm and pleasant; no snow on the trail, which, as we are all on foot, makes traveling more agreeable. The hunters went into the neighboring mountains, but found no game. We have five Indians in camp tonight.

January 25th. The morning was cold and bright, and as the sun rose the day became beautiful. A party of twelve Indians came down from the mountains to trade pine nuts, of which each one carried a little bag.[28] These seemed now to be the staple of the country, and whenever we met an Indian, his friendly salutation consisted in offering a few nuts to eat and to trade; their only arms were bows and flint-pointed arrows.

It appeared that in almost all the valleys the neighboring bands were at war with each other; and we had some difficulty in prevailing on our guides to accompany us on this day's journey, being at war with the people on the other side of a large snowy mountain which lay before us.

The general level of the country appeared to be getting higher, and we were gradually entering the heart of the mountains. Accompanied by all the Indians, we ascended a long ridge and reached a pure spring at the edge of the timber, where the Indians had waylaid and killed an antelope, and where the greater part of them left us. Our pacific conduct had quieted their alarms, and though at war among each other, yet all confided in us, thanks to the combined effects of power and kindness—for our arms inspired respect, and our little presents and good treatment conciliated their confidence. Here we suddenly entered snow six inches deep, and the ground was a little rocky with volcanic fragments, the mountain appearing to be composed of such rock. The timber consists principally of nut pines (*Pinus monophyllus*), which here are of a larger size—twelve to fifteen inches in diameter, heaps of cones lying on the ground where the Indians had gathered the seeds.

The snow deepened gradually as we advanced. Our guides wore

out their moccasins, and putting one of them on a horse, we enjoyed the unusual sight of an Indian who could not ride. He could not even guide the animal, and appeared to have no knowledge of horses. The snow was three or four feet deep on the summit of the pass, and from this point the guide pointed out our future road, declining to go any farther.

Below us was a little valley, and beyond this the mountains rose higher still, one ridge above another, presenting a rude and rocky outline. We descended rapidly to the valley; the snow impeded us but little, yet it was dark when we reached the foot of the mountain.

The day had been so warm that our moccasins were wet with melting snow; but here, as soon as the sun begins to decline, the air gets suddenly cold, and we had great difficulty to keep our feet from freezing—our moccasins being frozen perfectly stiff.

After a hard day's march of twenty-seven miles we reached the river, some time after dark, and found the snow about a foot deep on the bottom—the river being entirely frozen over. We found a comfortable camp where there were dry willows abundant, and we soon had blazing fires.[29]

A little brandy, which I husbanded with great care, remained, and I do not know any medicine more salutary, or any drink (except coffee) more agreeable, than this in a cold night after a hard day's march. Mr. Preuss questioned whether the famed nectar even possessed so exquisite a flavor. All felt it to be a reviving cordial.

The next morning, when the sun had not yet risen over the mountains the thermometer was two degrees below zero; but the sky was bright and pure, and the weather changed rapidly into a pleasant day of summer. I remained encamped, in order to examine the country and allow the animals a day of rest, the grass being good and abundant under the snow.

The river is fifty to eighty feet wide, with a lively current and very clear water. It forked a little above our camp, one of its branches coming directly from the south. At its head appeared to be a handsome pass; and from the neighboring heights we could see, beyond, a comparatively low and open country, which was supposed to form the valley of the Buenaventura.[30] The other branch issued from a nearer pass, in a direction S. 75° W., forking at the foot of the mountain, and receiving part of its waters from a little lake.

I was in advance of the camp when our last guides had left us; but, so far as could be understood, this was the pass which they had indicated, and, in company with Carson, today I set out to explore it.[31] Entering the range, we continued in a northwesterly direction up the valley, which here bent to the right. It was a pretty, open bottom, locked between lofty mountains, which supplied frequent streams as we advanced. On the lower part they were covered with nut-pine trees, and above with masses of pine, which we easily recognized from the darker color of the foliage. From the fresh trails which occurred frequently during the morning, deer appeared to be remarkably numerous in the mountain. We had now entirely left the desert country, and were on the verge of a region which, extending westward to the shores of the Pacific, abounds in large game, and is covered with a singular luxuriance of vegetable life.

The little stream grew rapidly smaller, and in about twelve miles we had reached its head, the last water coming immediately out of the mountain on the right; and this spot was selected for our next encampment. The grass showed well in sunny places, but in colder situations the snow was deep, and began to occur in banks, through which the horses found some difficulty in breaking a way. To the left the open valley continued in a southwesterly direction, with a scarcely perceptible ascent, forming a beautful pass, the exploration of which we deferred until the next day, and returned to the camp.

Today an Indian passed through the valley on his way into the mountains, where he showed us was his lodge. We comprehended nothing of his language; and though he appeared to have no fear, passing along in full view of the camp, he was indisposed to hold any communication with us, but showed the way he was going, and pointed for us to go on our road. By observation, the latitude of this encampment was 38° 18' 01", and the elevation above the sea six thousand three hundred and ten feet.

January 27th. Leaving the camp to follow slowly, with directions to Carson to encamp at the place agreed on, Mr. Fitzpatrick and myself continued the reconnaissance. Arriving at the head of the stream, we began to enter the pass—passing occasionally through open groves of large pine trees on the warm side of the defile, where the snow had melted away, occasionally exposing a large

Indian trail. Continuing along a narrow meadow, we reached in a few miles the gate of the pass, where there was a narrow strip of prairie, about fifty yards wide, between walls of granite rock. On either side rose the mountains, forming on the left a rugged mass, or nucleus, wholly covered with deep snow, presenting a glittering and icy surface. At the time, we supposed this to be the point into which they were gathered between the two great rivers, and from which the waters flowed off to the bay.[32] This was the icy and cold side of the pass, and the rays of the sun hardly touched the snow. On the left, the mountains rose into peaks; but they were lower and secondary, and the country had a somewhat more open and lighter character. On the right were several hot springs, which appeared remarkable in such a place. In going through, we felt impressed by the majesty of the mountain, along the huge wall of which we were riding. Here there was no snow; but immediately beyond was a deep bank, through which we dragged our horses with considerable effort.

We then immediately struck upon a stream which gathered itself rapidly, and descended quickly; and the valley did not preserve the open character of the other side, appearing below to form a cañon. We therefore climbed one of the peaks on the right, leaving our horses below; but we were so much shut up that we did not obtain an extensive view, and what we saw was not very satisfactory, and awakened considerable doubt. The valley of the stream pursued a northwesterly direction, appearing below to turn sharply to the right, beyond which further view was cut off.

It was, nevertheless, resolved to continue our road the next day down this valley, which we trusted still would prove that of the middle stream between the two great rivers. Toward the summit of this peak the fields of snow were four or five feet deep on the northern side; and we saw several large hares, which had on their winter color, being white as the snow around them. The winter day is short in the mountains, the sun having but a small space of sky to travel over in the visible part above our horizon; and the moment his rays are gone the air is keenly cold. The interest of our work had detained us long, and it was after nightfall when we reached the camp.[33]

January 28th. Today we went through the pass with all the camp, and, after a hard day's journey of twelve miles, encamped on a high

point where the snow had been blown off, and the exposed grass
afforded a scanty pasture for the animals. Snow and broken country
together made our traveling difficult; we were often compelled to
make large circuits, and ascend the highest and most exposed
ridges, in order to avoid snow, which in other places was banked up
to a great depth.

During the day a few Indians were seen circling around us on
snowshoes, and skimming along like birds; but we could not bring
them within speaking distance. Godey, who was a little distance
from the camp, had sat down to tie his moccasins, when he heard
a low whistle near, and looking up, saw two Indians half-hiding
behind a rock about forty yards distant; they would not allow him
to approach, but breaking into a laugh, skimmed off over the snow,
seeming to have no idea of the power of firearms, and thinking
themselves perfectly safe when beyond arm's length.

Tonight we did not succeed in getting the howitzer into camp.
This was the most laborious day we had yet passed through, the
steep ascents and deep snow exhausting both men and animals. Our
single chronometer had stopped during the day, and its error in time
occasioned the loss of an eclipse of a satellite this evening. It had not
preserved the rate with which we started from the Dalles, and this
will account for the absence of longitudes along this interval of our
journey.

January 29th. From this height we could see, at a considerable
distance below, yellow spots in the valley, which indicated that
there was not much snow. One of these places we expected to reach
tonight; and some time being required to bring up the gun, I went
ahead with Mr. Fitzpatrick and a few men, leaving the camp to
follow in charge of Mr. Preuss.

We followed a trail down a hollow where the Indians had descended, the snow being so deep that we never came near the
ground; but this only made our descent the easier, and when we
reached a little affluent to the river at the bottom, we suddenly
found ourselves in presence of eight or ten Indians. They seemed
to be watching our motions, and like the others, at first were indisposed to let us approach, ranging themselves like birds on a fallen
log on the hillside above our heads, where, being out of reach, they
thought themselves safe. Our friendly demeanor reconciled them,

and when we got near enough, they immediately stretched out to us handfuls of pine nuts, which seemed an exercise of hospitality. We made them a few presents, and telling us that their village was a few miles below, they went on to let their people know what we were.

The principal stream still running through an impracticable cañon, we ascended a very steep hill, which proved afterward the last and fatal obstacle to our little howitzer, which was finally abandoned at this place. We passed through a small meadow a few miles below, crossing the river, which depth, swift current, and rock made it difficult to ford; and after a few more miles of very difficult trail, issued into a larger prairie bottom, at the farther end of which we encamped, in a position rendered strong by rocks and trees. The lower parts of the mountain were covered with the nut pine.

Several Indians appeared on the hillside, reconnoitering the camp, and were induced to come in; others came in during the afternoon; and in the evening we held a council. They immediately made it clear that the water on which we were also belonged to the Great Basin, in the edge of which we had been since December 17th; and it became evident that we had still the great ridge on the left to cross before we could reach the Pacific waters.

We explained to the Indians that we were endeavoring to find a passage across the mountains into the country of the whites, whom we were going to see, and told them that we wished them to bring us a guide, to whom we would give presents of scarlet cloth and other articles, which were shown to them. They looked at the reward we offered, and conferred with each other, but pointed to the snow on the mountain, and drew their hands across their necks, and raised them above their heads, to show the depth, and signified that it was impossible for us to get through. They made signs that we must go to the southward, over a pass through a lower range, which they pointed out; there, they said, at the end of one day's travel, we would find people who lived near a pass in the great mountain; and to that point they engaged to furnish us a guide. They appeared to have a confused idea, from report, of whites who lived on the other side of the mountain; and once, they told us, about two years ago, a party of twelve men, like ourselves, had ascended their river, and crossed to the other waters. They pointed out to us where they had crossed; but then, they said, it was summertime; now it would be impossible.

I believe that this was a party led by Mr. Chiles,[34] one of the only two men whom I know to have passed through the California mountains from the interior of the Basin—Walker being the other—and both were engaged upward of twenty days, in the summertime, in getting over. Chile's destination was the Bay of San Francisco, to which he descended by the Stanislaus River; and Walker subsequently informed me that, like myself, descending to the southward on a more eastern line, day after day he was searching for the Buenaventura, thinking that he had found it with every new stream, until, like me, he abandoned all idea of its existence, and turning abruptly to the right, crossed the great chain. These were both Western men, animated with the spirit of exploratory enterprise which characterizes that people.

The Indians brought in during the evening an abundant supply of pine nuts, which we traded from them. When roasted, their pleasant flavor made them an agreeable addition to our now scanty store of provisions, which were reduced to a very low ebb. Our principal stock was in peas, which it is not necessary to say contain scarcely any nutriment. We had still a little flour left, some coffee, and a quantity of sugar, which I reserved as a defense against starvation.

The Indians informed us that at certain seasons they have fish in their waters, which we supposed to be salmon trout; for the remainder of the year they live upon the pine nuts, which form their great winter subsistence—a portion being always at hand, shut up in the natural storehouse of the cones. At present they were presented to us as a whole people living upon this simple vegetable.

The other division of the party did not come in tonight, but encamped in the upper meadow, and arrived the next morning. They had not succeeded in getting the howitzer beyond the place mentioned, and where it had been left by Mr. Preuss in obedience to my orders; and, in anticipation of the snowbanks and snowfields still ahead, foreseeing the inevitable detention to which it would subject us, I reluctantly determined to leave it there for the time. It was of the kind invented by the French for the mountain part of their war in Algiers; and the distance it had come with us proved how well it was adapted to its purpose. We left it, to the great sorrow of the whole party, who were grieved to part with a companion which had made the whole distance from St. Louis, and commanded respect for us on some critical occasions, and which might be needed for the same purpose again.

January 30th. Our guide, who was a young man, joined us this morning; and leaving our encampment late in the day, we descended the river, which immediately opened out into a broad valley, furnishing good traveling ground. In a short distance we passed the village, a collection of straw huts; and a few miles below the guide pointed out the place where the whites had been encamped before they entered the mountain.

With our late start we made but ten miles, and encamped on the low river bottom, where there was no snow but a great deal of ice; and we cut piles of long grass to lay under our blankets, and fires were made of large dry willows, groves of which wooded the stream. The river took here a northeasterly direction, and through a spur from the mountains on the left was the gap where we were to pass the next day.

January 31st. We took our way over a gently rising ground, the dividing ridge being tolerably low; and traveling easily along a broad trail, in twelve or fourteen miles reached the upper part of the pass, when it began to snow heavily, with very cold weather. The Indians had only the usual scanty covering, and appeared to suffer greatly from the cold. All left us except our guide. Half-hidden by the storm, the mountains looked dreary; and as night began to approach, the guide showed great reluctance to go forward. I placed him between two rifles, for the way began to be difficult. Traveling a little farther, we struck a ravine, which the Indian said would conduct us to the river; [35] and as the poor fellow suffered greatly, shivering in the snow which fell upon his naked skin, I would not detain him any longer, and he ran off to the mountain, where, he said, there was a hut near by. He had kept the blue and scarlet cloths I had given him tightly rolled up, preferring rather to endure the cold than to get them wet.

In the course of the afternoon, one of the men had a foot frostbitten; and about dark we had the satisfaction of reaching the bottoms of a stream timbered with large trees, among which we found a sheltered camp, with an abundance of such grass as the season afforded for the animals. We saw before us, in descending from the pass, a great continuous range, along which stretched the valley of the river, the lower parts steep, and dark with pines, while, above, it was hidden in clouds of snow. This we felt instantly satisfied was the central ridge of the Sierra Nevada, the great California Mountain, which only now intervened between us and the waters of the bay. We had made a forced march of twenty-six miles, and three mules had given out on the road. Up to this point, with the exception of two stolen by Indians, we had lost none of the horses which had been brought from the Columbia River, and a number of these were still strong and in tolerably good order. We had now sixty-seven animals in the band.

We had scarcely lighted our fires when the camp was crowded with nearly naked [Washo] Indians; some of them were furnished with long nets in addition to bows, and appeared to have been out on the sage hills to hunt rabbits. These nets were, perhaps, thirty to forty feet long, kept upright in the ground by slight sticks at intervals, and were made from a kind of wild hemp, very much resembling, in manufacture, those common among the Indians of the Sacramento Valley. They came among us without any fear, and scattered themselves about the fires, mainly occupied in gratifying their astonishment. I was struck by the singular appearance of a row of about a dozen, who were sitting on their haunches perched on a log near one of the fires, with their quick sharp eyes following every motion.

We gathered together a few of the most intelligent of the Indians, and held this evening an interesting council. I explained to them my intentions. I told them that we had come from a very far country, having been traveling now nearly a year, and that we were desirous simply to go across the mountain into the country of the other whites. There were two who appeared particularly intelligent —one, a somewhat old man. He told me that before the snows fell, it was six sleeps to the place where the whites lived, but that now it was impossible to cross the mountain on account of the deep snow; and showing us, as the others had done, that it was over our heads, he urged us strongly to follow the course of the river, which he said would conduct us to a lake in which there were many large fish. There, he said, were many people; there was no snow on the ground, and we might remain there until the spring.

From their descriptions we were enabled to judge that we had encamped on the upper water of the Salmon Trout River.[36] It is hardly necessary to say that our communication was only by signs, as we understood nothing of their language; but they spoke, notwith-standing, rapidly and vehemently, explaining what they considered the folly of our intentions, and urging us to go down to the lake. *Táh-ve*, a word signifying "snow," we very soon learned to know, from its frequent repetition. I told him that the men and the horses were strong, and that we would break a road through the snow; and spreading before him our bales of scarlet cloth, and trinkets, showed him what we would give for a guide. It was necessary to obtain one, if possible; for I had determined here to attempt the passage of the mountain.

Pulling a bunch of grass from the ground, after a short discussion among themselves, the old man made us comprehend that if we could break through the snow, at the end of three days we would come down upon grass, which he showed us would be about six inches high, and where the ground was entirely free. So far, he said, he had been in hunting for elk; but beyond that (and he closed his eyes) he had seen nothing; but there was one among them who had been to the whites, and, going out of the lodge, he returned with a young man of very intelligent appearance. Here, said he, is a young man who has seen the whites with his own eyes; and he swore, first by the sky, and then by the ground, that what he said was true. With a large present of goods we prevailed upon this young man to be our guide, and he acquired among us the name Mélo—a word signifying friend, which they used very frequently. He was thinly clad, and nearly barefoot, his moccasins being about worn out. We gave him skins to make a new pair, and to enable him to perform his undertaking to us. The Indians remained in the camp during the night, and we kept the guide and two others to sleep in the lodge with us—Carson lying across the door, and having made them com-prehend the use of our firearms.

The snow, which had intermitted in the evening, commenced falling again in the course of the night, and it snowed steadily all day. In the morning I acquainted the men with my decision, and explained to them that necessity required us to make a great effort to clear the mountains. I reminded them of the beautiful valley of the Sacramento, with which they were familiar from the descrip-tions of Carson, who had been there some fifteen years ago, and who, in our late privations, had delighted us in speaking of its rich pastures and abounding game, and drew a vivid contrast between its summer climate, less than a hundred miles distant and the falling snow around us. I informed them (and long experience had given them confidence in my observations and good instruments) that almost directly west, and only about seventy miles distant, was the great farming establishment of Captain Sutter—a gentleman who had formerly lived in Missouri, and, emigrating to this country, had become the possessor of a principality. I assured them that from the heights of the mountain before us we should doubtless see the valley of the Sacramento River, and with one effort place ourselves again in the midst of plenty.*

The people received this decision with the cheerful obedience which had always characterized them; and the day was immediately devoted to the preparations necessary to enable us to carry it into effect. Leggings, moccasins, clothing—all were put into the best state to resist the cold. Our guide was not neglected. Extremity of suffering might make him desert; we therefore did the best we could for him. Leggings, moccasins, some articles of clothing, and a large green blanket, in addition to the blue and scarlet cloth, were lavished upon him, and to his great and evident contentment. He arrayed himself in all his colors, and, clad in green, blue, and scarlet, he made a gay-looking Indian and, with his various presents, was probably richer and better clothed than any of his tribe had ever been before.

I have already said that our provisions were very low; we had neither tallow nor grease of any kind remaining, and the want of salt became one of our greatest privations. The poor dog which had been found in the Bear River Valley, and which had been a *compagnon de voyage* ever since, had now become fat, and the mess to which it belonged requested permission to kill it. Leave was granted. Spread out on the snow, the meat looked very good, and it made a strengthening meal for the greater part of the camp. Indians brought in two or three rabbits during the day, which were purchased from them. The river was forty to seventy feet wide, and now entirely frozen over. It was wooded with large cottonwood, willow,

* That is, they were almost directly across the Sierra from the present-day city of Sacramento; they had crossed from present-day Nevada into California southeast of Lake Tahoe.

and *grains de bœuf.* By observation, the latitude of this encampment was 38° 37' 18".

February 2d. It had ceased snowing, and this morning the lower air was clear and frosty; and six or seven thousand feet above, the peaks of the Sierra now and then appeared among the rolling clouds, which were rapidly dispersing before the sun. Our Indian shook his head as he pointed to the icy pinnacles shooting high up into the sky, and seeming almost immediately above us. Crossing the river on the ice, and leaving it immediately, we commenced the ascent of the mountain along the valley of a tributary stream. The people were unusually silent; for every man knew that our enterprise was hazardous, and the issue doubtful.

The snow deepened rapidly, and it soon became necessary to break a road. For this service, a party of ten was formed, mounted on the strongest horses; each man in succession opening the road on foot, or on horseback, until himself and his horse became fatigued, when he stepped aside; and, the remaining number passing ahead, he took his station in the rear. Leaving this stream, and pursuing a very direct course, we passed over an intervening ridge to the river we had left.

On the way we passed two low huts entirely covered with snow, which might very easily have escaped observation. A family was living in each; and the only trail I saw in the neighborhood was from the door hole to a nut-pine tree near, which supplied them with food and fuel. We found two similar huts on the creek where we next arrived; and, traveling a little higher up, encamped on its banks in about four feet depth of snow. Carson found near an open hillside, where the wind and the sun had melted the snow, leaving exposed sufficient bunch grass for the animals tonight.

The nut pines were now giving way to heavy timber, and there were some immense pines on the bottom, around the roots of which the sun had melted away the snow; and here we made our camps and built huge fires. Today we had traveled sixteen miles, and our elevation above the sea was six thousand seven hundred and sixty feet.[37]

February 3d. Turning our faces directly toward the main chain, we ascended an open hollow along a small tributary to the river, which, according to the Indians, issues from a mountain to the south. The snow was so deep in the hollow that we were obliged to travel along the steep hillsides, and over spurs, where wind and sun had in places lessened the snow, and where the grass, which appeared to be in good quality along the sides of the mountains, was exposed.

We opened our road in the same way as yesterday, but made only seven miles; and encamped by some springs at the foot of a high and steep hill, by which the hollow ascended to another basin in the mountain. The little stream below was entirely buried in snow. The springs were shaded by the boughs of a lofty cedar, which here made its first appearance; the usual height was one hundred and twenty to one hundred and thirty feet, and one that was measured near by was six feet in diameter.

There being no grass exposed here, the horses were sent back to that which we had seen a few miles below. We occupied the remainder of the day in beating down a road to the foot of the hill, a mile or two distant; the snow, being beaten down when moist, in the warm part of the day, and then hard-frozen at night, made a foundation that would bear the weight of the animals the next morning. During the day several Indians joined us on snowshoes. These were made of a circular hoop, about a foot in diameter, the interior space being filled with an open network of bark.

February 4th. I went ahead early with two or three men, each with a led horse, to break the road. We were obliged to abandon the hollow entirely, and work along the mountainside, which was very steep, and the snow covered with an icy crust. We cut a footing as we advanced, and trampled a road through for the animals; but occasionally one plunged outside the trail, and slid along the field to the bottom, a hundred yards below.

Late in the day we reached another bench in the hollow, where in summer the stream passed over a small precipice. Here was a short distance of dividing ground between the two ridges, and beyond an open basin, some ten miles across, whose bottom presented a field of snow. At the further or western side rose the middle crest of the mountain, a dark-looking ridge of volcanic rock.

The summit line presented a range of naked peaks, apparently destitute of snow and vegetation; but below, the face of the whole country was covered with timber of extraordinary size. . . .

Toward a pass which the guide indicated here we attempted in the afternoon to force a road; but after a laborious plunging through two or three hundred yards, our best horses gave out, entirely refusing to make any further effort; and, for the time, we were brought to a stand. The guide informed us that we were entering the deep snow, and here began the difficulties of the mountain; and to him, and almost to all, our enterprise seemed hopeless. I returned a short distance back, to the break in the hollow, where I met Mr. Fitzpatrick.

The camp had been all the day occupied in endeavoring to ascend the hill, but only the best horses had succeeded, the animals, generally, not having sufficient strength to bring themselves up without the packs; and all the line of road between this and the springs was strewed with camp stores and equipage, and horses floundering in snow.

I therefore immediately encamped on the ground with my own mess, which was in advance, and directed Mr. Fitzpatrick to encamp at the springs, and send all the animals in charge of Tableau, with a strong guard, back to the place where they had been pastured the night before. Here was a small spot of level ground, protected on one side by the mountain, and on the other sheltered by a little ridge of rock. It was an open grove of pines, which assimilated in size to the grandeur of the mountain, being frequently six feet in diameter.

Tonight we had no shelter, but we made a large fire around the trunk of one of the huge pines; and covering the snow with small boughs, on which we spread our blankets, soon made ourselves comfortable. The night was very bright and clear, and though the thermometer was only down to 10°, a strong wind which sprang up at sundown made it intensely cold, and this was one of the bitterest nights during the journey.

Two Indians joined our party here; and one of them, an old man, immediately began to harangue us, saying that ourselves and animals would perish in the snow, and that if we would go back, he would show us another and a better way across the mountain. He spoke in a very loud voice, and there was a singular repetition of phrases and arrangement of words which rendered his speech striking and not unmusical.

We had now begun to understand some words, and, with the aid of signs, easily comprehended the old man's simple ideas. "Rock upon rock—rock upon rock—snow upon snow—snow upon snow," said he; "even if you get over the snow, you will not be able to get down from the mountains." He made us the sign of precipices, and showed us how the feet of the horses would slip, and throw them off from the narrow trails which led along their sides.

Our Chinook, who comprehended even more readily than ourselves, and believed our situation hopeless, covered his head with his blanket and began to weep and lament. "I wanted to see the whites," said he; "I came away from my own people to see the whites, and I wouldn't care to die among them; but here"—and he looked around into the cold night and gloomy forest, and, drawing his blanket over his head, began again to lament. Seated around the tree, the fire illuminating the rocks and the tall bolls of the pines round about, and the old Indian haranguing, we presented a group of very serious faces.

February 5th. The night had been too cold to sleep, and we were up very early. Our guide was standing by the fire with all his finery on; and seeing him shiver in the cold, I threw on his shoulders one of my blankets. We missed him a few minutes afterward, and never saw him again. He had deserted. His bad faith and treachery were in perfect keeping with the estimate of Indian character which a long intercourse with this people had gradually forced upon my mind.

While a portion of the camp were occupied in bringing up the baggage to this point, the remainder were busied in making sledges and snowshoes. I had determined to explore the mountain ahead, and the sledges were to be used in transporting the baggage. The mountains here consisted wholly of a white micaceous granite.

The day was perfectly clear, and while the sun was in the sky, warm and pleasant. By observation, our latitude was 38° 42' 26"; and elevation, by the boiling-point, seven thousand four hundred feet.

February 6th. Accompanied by Mr. Fitzpatrick, I set out today, with a reconnoitering party, on snowshoes. We marched all in single file, trampling the snow as heavily as we could. Crossing the open basin, in a march of about ten miles we reached the top of one of the peaks, to the left of the pass indicated by our guide.

Far below us, dimmed by the distance, was a large snowless valley, bounded on the western side, at the distance of about a hundred miles, by a low range of mountains, which Carson recognized with delight as the mountains bordering the coast. "There," said he, "is the little mountain—it is fifteen years ago since I saw it; but I am just as sure as if I had seen it yesterday." Between us, then, and this low coast range, was the valley of the Sacramento; and no one who had not accompanied us through the incidents of our life for the last few months could realize the delight with which at last we looked down upon it. At the distance of apparently thirty miles beyond us were distinguished spots of prairie; and a dark line, which could be traced with the glass, was imagined to be the course of the river; but we were evidently at a great height above the valley, and between us and the plains extended miles of snowy fields, and broken ridges of pine-covered mountains.

It was late in the day when we turned toward the camp; and it grew rapidly cold as it drew toward night. One of the men, Fallon, became fatigued, and his feet began to freeze, and building a fire in the trunk of a dry old cedar, Mr. Fitzpatrick remained with him until his clothes could be dried, and he was in a condition to come on. After a day's march of twenty miles, we straggled into camp, one after another, at nightfall, the greater number excessively fatigued, only two of the party having ever traveled on snowshoes before.

All our energies were now directed to getting our animals across the snow; and it was supposed that, after all the baggage had been drawn with the sleighs over the trail we had made, it would be sufficiently hard to bear our animals. At several places between this point and the ridge we had discovered some grassy spots, where the wind and sun had dispersed the snow from the sides of the hills, and these were to form resting places to support the animals for a night in their passage across. On our way across we had set on fire several broken stumps, and dried trees, to melt holes in the snow for the camps. Its general depth was five feet; but we passed over places where it was twenty feet deep, as shown by the trees.

With one party drawing sleighs loaded with baggage, I advanced today about four miles along the trail, and encamped at the first grassy spot where we expected to bring our horses. Mr. Fitzpatrick, with another party, remained behind, to form an intermediate station between us and the animals.

February 8th. The night had been extremely cold but perfectly still and beautifully clear. Before the sun appeared this morning the thermometer was 3° below zero; 1° higher, when his rays struck the lofty peaks; and 0° when they reached our camp. Scenery and weather combined must render these mountains beautiful in summer; the purity and deep-blue color of the sky are singularly beautiful; the days are sunny and bright, and even warm in the noon hours; and if we could be free from the many anxieties that oppress us, even now we would be delighted here; but our provisions are getting fearfully scant. Sleighs arrived with baggage about ten o'clock; and leaving a portion of it here, we continued on for a mile and a half, and encamped at the foot of a long hill on this side of the open bottom.

Bernier and Godey, who yesterday morning had been sent to ascend a higher peak, got in, hungry and fatigued. They confirmed what we had already seen. Two other sleighs arrived in the afternoon; and the men being fatigued, I gave them all tea and sugar. Snow clouds began to rise in the south-southwest; and, apprehensive of a storm, which would destroy our road, I sent the people back to Mr. Fitzpatrick, with directions to send for the animals in the morning. With me remained Mr. Preuss, Mr. Talbot, and Carson, with Jacob. Elevation of the camp, by the boiling-point, is seven thousand nine hundred and twenty feet.

February 9th. During the night the weather changed, the wind rising to a gale, and commencing to snow before daylight; before morning the trail was covered. We remained quiet in camp all day, in the course of which the weather improved. Four sleighs arrived toward evening, with the bedding of the men. We suffer much from the want of salt; and all the men are becoming weak from insufficient food.

February 10th. Taplin was sent back with a few men to assist Mr. Fitzpatrick; and continuing on with three sleighs carrying a part of the baggage, we had the satisfaction to encamp within two and a half miles of the head of the hollow, and at the foot of the last mountain ridge. Here two large trees had been set on fire, and in the holes, where the snow had been melted away, we found a comfortable camp.

The wind kept the air filled with snow during the day; the sky was very dark in the southwest, though elsewhere very clear. The forest here has a noble appearance: the tall cedar is abundant; its greatest height being one hundred and thirty feet, and circumference twenty, three or four feet above the ground; and here I see for the first time the white pine, of which there are some magnificent trees. Hemlock spruce is among the timber, occasionally as large as eight feet in diameter four feet above the ground; but, in ascending, it tapers rapidly to less than one foot at the height of eighty feet. I have not seen any higher than one hundred and thirty feet, and the slight upper part is frequently broken off by the wind. The white spruce is frequent; and the red pine (*Pinus colorado* of the Mexicans), which constitutes the beautiful forest along the flanks of the Sierra Nevada to the northward, is here the principal tree, not attaining a greater height than one hundred and forty feet, though with sometimes a diameter of ten. Most of these trees appeared to differ slightly from those of the same kind on the other side of the continent.

The elevation of the camp, by the boiling-point, is eight thousand and fifty feet. We are now one thousand feet above the level of the South Pass in the Rocky Mountains; and still we are not done ascending. The top of a flat ridge near was bare of snow, and very well sprinkled with bunch grass, sufficient to pasture the animals two or three days, and this was to be their main point of support. This ridge is composed of a compact trap, or basalt, of a columnar structure; over the surface are scattered large boulders of porous trap. The hills are in many places entirely covered with small fragments of volcanic rock.

Putting on our snowshoes, we spent the afternoon in exploring a road ahead. The glare of the snow, combined with great fatigue, had rendered many of the people nearly blind; but we were fortunate in having some black silk handkerchiefs, which, worn as veils, very much relieved the eyes.

February 11th. High wind continued, and our trail this morning was nearly invisible—here and there indicated by a little ridge of snow. Our situation became tiresome and dreary, requiring a strong exercise of patience and resolution.

In the evening I received a message from Mr. Fitzpatrick, acquainting me with the utter failure of his attempt to get our mules and horses over the snow—the half-hidden trail had proved entirely too slight to support them, and they had broken through, and were plunging about or lying half-buried in snow. He was occupied in endeavoring to get them back to his camp, and in the meantime sent to me for further instructions. I wrote to him to send the animals immediately back to their old pastures; and, after having made mauls and shovels, turn in all the strength of his party to open and beat a road through the snow, strengthening it with branches and boughs of the pines.

February 12th. We made mauls, and worked hard at our end of the road all the day. The wind was high, but the sun bright, and the snow thawing. We worked down the face of the hill, to meet the people at the other end. Toward sundown it began to grow cold, and we shouldered our mauls, and trudged back to camp.

February 13th. We continued to labor on the road, and in the course of the day had the satisfaction to see the people working down the face of the opposite hill, about three miles distant. During the morning we had the pleasure of a visit from Mr. Fitzpatrick, with the information that all was going on well. A party of Indians had passed on snowshoes, who said they were going to the western side of the mountain after fish. This was an indication that the salmon were coming up the streams; and we could hardly restrain our impatience as we thought of them, and worked with increased vigor.

The meat train did not arrive this evening, and I gave Godey leave to kill our little dog (Klamath), which he prepared in Indian fashion—scorching off the hair, and washing the skin with soap and snow, and then cutting it up into pieces, which were laid on the snow. Shortly afterward the sleigh arrived with a supply of horse meat; and we had tonight an extraordinary dinner—pea soup, mule, and dog.

February 14th. With Mr. Preuss, I ascended today the highest peak near us, from which we had a beautiful view of a mountain lake at our feet, about fifteen miles in length, and so entirely surrounded by mountains that we could not discover an outlet.[38] We had taken with us a glass; but though we enjoyed an extended view, the valley was half hidden in mist, as when we had seen it before. Snow could be distinguished on the higher parts of the coast mountains; eastward, as far as the eye could extend, it ranged over a terrible mass of broken snowy mountains, fading off blue in the distance.

The rock composing the summit consists of a very coarse dark volcanic conglomerate; the lower parts appeared to be of a slaty structure. The highest trees were a few scattering cedars and aspens. From the immediate foot of the peak, we were two hours in reaching the summit, and one hour and a quarter in descending. The day had been very bright, still, and clear, and spring seems to be advancing rapidly. While the sun is in the sky, the snow melts rapidly, and gushing springs cover the face of the mountain in all the exposed places; but their surface freezes instantly with the disappearance of the sun. I obtained tonight some observations; and the result from these, and others made during our stay, gives for the latitude 38° 41′ 57″, longitude 120° 25′ 57″, and rate of the chronometer 25.82″.

February 16th. We had succeeded in getting our animals safely to the first grassy hill; and this morning I started with Jacob on a reconnoitering expedition beyond the mountain. We traveled along the crests of narrow ridges, extending down from the mountain in the direction of the valley, from which the snow was fast melting away. On the open spots was tolerably good grass, and I judged we should succeed in getting the camp down by way of these. Toward sundown we discovered some icy spots in a deep hollow; and, descending the mountain, we encamped on the headwater of a little creek, where at last the water found its way to the Pacific.

The night was clear and very long. We heard the cries of some wild animals, which had been attracted by our fire, and a flock of geese passed over during the night. Even these strange sounds had something pleasant to our senses in this region of silence and desolation.

We started again early in the morning. The creek acquired a regular breadth of about twenty feet, and we soon began to hear the rushing of the water below the icy surface, over which we traveled to avoid the snow; a few miles below we broke through where the water was several feet deep, and halted to make a fire and dry our clothes. We continued a few miles farther, walking being very laborious without snowshoes.

I was now perfectly satisfied that we had struck the stream on

which Mr. Sutter lived; and, turning about, made a hard push and
reached the camp at dark. Here we had the pleasure to find all
the remaining animals, fifty-seven in number, safely arrived at the
grassy hill near the camp; and here, also, we were agreeably surprised with the sight of an abundance of salt. Some of the horse
guard had gone to a neighboring hut for pine nuts, and discovered
unexpectedly a large cake of very white, fine-grained salt, which the
Indians told them they had brought from the other side of the mountain; they used it to eat with their pine nuts, and readily sold it
for goods.

On the 19th, the people were occupied in making a road and
bringing up the baggage; and, on the afternoon of the next day,
February 20, 1844, we encamped with the animals and all the matériel of the camp, on the summit of the pass in the dividing ridge,
one thousand miles by our traveled road from the Dalles of the
Columbia. The people, who had not yet been to this point, climbed
the neighboring peak to enjoy a look at the valley.

The temperature of boiling water gave for the elevation of the
encampment nine thousand three hundred and thirty-eight feet
above the sea.[39] This was two thousand feet higher than the South
Pass in the Rocky Mountains, and several peaks in view rose several
thousand feet still higher. Thus, at the extremity of the continent,
and near the coast, the phenomenon was seen of a range of mountains still higher than the great Rocky Mountains themselves. This
extraordinary fact accounts for the Great Basin, and shows that there
must be a system of small lakes and rivers here scattered over a
flat country, and which the extended and lofty range of the Sierra
Nevada prevents from escaping to the Pacific Ocean. Latitude 38°
44'; longitude 120° 28'. Thus this pass in the Sierra Nevada, which
so well deserves its name of Snowy Mountain, is eleven degrees west,
and about four degrees south, of the South Pass.

February 21st. We now considered ourselves victorious over the
mountain; having only the descent before us, and the valley under
our eyes, we felt strong hope that we should force our way down.
But this was a case in which the descent was *not* facile. Still deep
fields of snow lay between, and there was a large intervening space
of rough-looking mountains, through which we had yet to wind our
way.

Carson roused me this morning with an early fire, and we were all up long before day, in order to pass the snow fields before the sun should render the crust soft. We enjoyed this morning a scene at sunrise, which even here was unusually glorious and beautiful. Immediately above the eastern mountains was repeated a cloud-formed mass of purple ranges, bordered with bright yellow-gold; the peaks shot up into a narrow line of crimson cloud, above which the air was filled with a greenish orange; and over all was the singular beauty of the blue sky.

Passing along a ridge which commanded the lake on our right, of which we began to discover an outlet through a chasm on the west, we passed over alternating open ground and hard-crusted snow fields which supported the animals, and encamped on the ridge after a journey of six miles. The grass was better than we had yet seen, and we were encamped in a clump of trees twenty or thirty feet high, resembling white pine. With the exception of these small clumps, the ridges were bare; and, where the snow found the support of the trees, the wind had blown it up into banks ten or fifteen feet high. It required much care to hunt out a practicable way, as the most open places frequently led to impassable banks.

We had hard and doubtful labor yet before us, as the snow appeared to be heavier where the timber began farther down, with few open spots. Ascending a height, we traced out the best line we could discover for the next day's march, and had at least the consolation to see that the mountain descended rapidly. The day had been one of April; gusty, with a few occasional flakes of snow, which, in the afternoon, enveloped the upper mountain in clouds. We watched them anxiously, as now we dreaded a snowstorm.

Shortly afterward we heard the roll of thunder, and looking toward the valley, found it all enveloped in a thunderstorm. For us, as connected with the idea of summer, it had a singular charm; and we watched its progress with excited feelings until nearly sunset, when the sky cleared off brightly, and we saw a shining line of water directing its course toward another, a broader and larger sheet. We knew that these could be no other than the Sacramento and the Bay of San Francisco; but, after our long wandering in rugged mountains, where so frequently we had met with disappointments, and where the crossing of every ridge displayed some unknown lake or river, we were yet almost afraid to believe that we were at last to escape into the genial country of which we had heard so many glowing descriptions, and dreaded again to find some vast interior lake, whose bitter waters would bring us disappointment. On the southern shore of what appeared to be the bay could be traced the gleaming line where entered another large stream; and again the Buenaventura rose up in our minds.

Carson had entered the valley along the southern side of the bay, and remembered perfectly to have crossed the mouth of a very large stream, which they had been obliged to raft; but the country then was so entirely covered with water from snow and rain that he had been able to form no correct impression of watercourses.

We had the satisfaction to know that at least there were people below. Fires were lit up in the valley just at night, appearing to be in answer to ours; and these signs of life renewed, in some measure, the gaiety of the camp. They appeared so near that we judged them to be among the timber of some of the neighboring ridges; but, having them constantly in view day after day, and night after night, we afterward found them to be fires that had been kindled by the Indians among the tulares, on the shore of the bay, eighty miles distant.

Among the very few plants that appeared here was the common blue flax. Tonight a mule was killed for food.

February 22d. Our breakfast was over long before day. We took advantage of the coolness of the early morning to get over the snow, which today occurred in very deep banks among the timber; but we searched out the coldest places, and the animals passed successfully with their loads the hard crust. Now and then the delay of making a road occasioned much labor and loss of time.

In the after part of the day we saw before us a handsome grassy ridge point; and, making a desperate push over a snow field ten to fifteen feet deep, we happily succeeded in getting the camp across, and encamped on the ridge, after a march of three miles. We had again the prospect of a thunderstorm below; and tonight we killed another mule—now our only resource from starvation.

We satisfied ourselves during the day that the lake had an outlet between two ranges on the right; and with this, the creek on which I had encamped, probably effected a junction below. Between these, we were descending. We continued to enjoy the same delightful weather; the sky of the same beautiful blue, and such a sunset and sunrise as on our Atlantic coast we could scarcely imagine. And here among the mountains, nine thousand feet above the sea, we have the deep-blue sky and sunny climate of Smyrna and Palermo, which a little map before me shows are in the same latitude. The elevation above the sea, by the boiling-point, is eight thousand five hundred and sixty-five feet.

February 23d. This was our most difficult day: we were forced off the ridges by the quantity of snow among the timber, and obliged to take to the mountainsides, where, occasionally, rocks and a southern exposure afforded us a chance to scramble along. But these were steep, and slippery with snow and ice; and the tough evergreens of the mountain impeded our way, tore our skins, and exhausted our patience. Some of us had the misfortune to wear moccasins with parfleche soles, so slippery that we could not keep our feet, and generally crawled across the snow beds.

Axes and mauls were necessary today to make a road through the snow. Going ahead with Carson to reconnoiter the road, we reached in the afternoon the river which made the outlet of the lake. Carson sprang over, clear across a place where the stream was compressed among rocks, but the parfleche sole of my moccasin glanced from the icy rock, and precipitated me into the river. It was some few seconds before I could recover myself in the current, and Carson, thinking me hurt, jumped in after me, and we both had an icy bath. We tried to search awhile for my gun, which had been lost in the fall, but the cold drove us out; and making a large fire on the bank, after we had partially dried ourselves we went back to meet the camp. We afterward found that the gun had been slung under the ice which lined the banks of the creek.

Using our old plan of breaking the road with alternate horses, we reached the creek in the evening, and encamped on a dry open place in the ravine. Another branch, which we had followed, here comes in on the left; and from this point the mountain wall on which we had traveled today faces to the south along the right bank of the river, where the sun appears to have melted the snow; but the opposite ridge is entirely covered. Here, among the pines, the hillside produces but little grass—barely sufficient to keep life in the animals. We had the pleasure to be rained upon this afternoon; and grass was now our greatest solicitude. Many of the men looked badly, and some this evening were giving out.

February 24th. We rose at three in the morning, for an astronomical observation, and obtained for the place a latitude of 38° 46′ 58″, longitude 120° 34′ 20″. The sky was clear and pure, with a sharp wind from the northeast, and the thermometer 2° below the freezing point.

We continued down the south face of the mountain; our road leading over dry ground, we were able to avoid the snow almost entirely. In the course of the morning we struck a footpath, which we were generally able to keep; and the ground was soft to our animals' feet, being sandy or covered with mold. Green grass began to make its appearance, and occasionally we passed a hill scatteringly covered with it.

The character of the forest continued the same, and among the trees, the pine with short leaves and very large cones was abundant, some of them being noble trees. We measured one that had ten feet diameter, though the height was not more than one hundred and thirty feet. All along the river was a roaring torrent, its fall very great; and descending with a rapidity to which we had long been strangers, to our great pleasure oak trees appeared on the ridge, and soon became very frequent; on these I remarked unusually great quantities of mistletoe. Rushes began to make their appearance; and at a small creek where they were abundant, one of the messes was left with the weakest horses, while we continued on.

The opposite mountainside was very steep and continuous—unbroken by ravines, and covered with pines and snow; while on the side we were traveling, innumerable rivulets poured down from the ridge. Continuing on, we halted a moment at one of these rivulets, to admire some beautiful evergreen trees, resembling live oak, which shaded the little stream. They were forty to fifty feet high, and two in diameter, with a uniform tufted top; and the summer green of their beautiful foliage, with the singing birds, and the sweet summer wind which was whirling about the dry oak leaves, nearly intoxicated us with delight; and we hurried on, filled with excitement, to escape entirely from the horrid region of inhospitable snow to the perpetual spring of the Sacramento.

When we had traveled about ten miles, the valley opened a little to an oak and pine bottom, through which ran rivulets closely bordered with rushes, on which our half-starved horses fell with avidity; and here we made our encampment. Here the roaring torrent has already become a river,[40] and we had descended to an elevation of three thousand eight hundred and sixty-four feet. Along our road today the rock was a white granite, which appears to constitute the upper part of the mountains on both the eastern and western slopes, while between, the central is a volcanic rock. Another horse was killed tonight, for food.

February 25th. Believing that the difficulties of the road were passed, and leaving Mr. Fitzpatrick to follow slowly, as the condition of the animals required, I started ahead this morning with a party of eight, consisting (with myself) of Mr. Preuss and Mr. Talbot, Carson, Derosier, Towns, Proue, and Jacob. We took with us some of the best animals, and my intention was to proceed as rapidly as possible to the house of Mr. Sutter, and return to meet the party with a supply of provisions and fresh animals.

Continuing down the river, which pursued a very direct westerly course through a narrow valley, with only a very slight and narrow bottom land, we made twelve miles, and encamped at some old Indian huts, apparently a fishing place on the river.

The bottom was covered with trees of deciduous foliage, and overgrown with vines and rushes. On a bench of the hill near by was a field of fresh green grass, six inches long in some of the tufts, which I had the curiosity to measure. The animals were driven here; and I spent part of the afternoon sitting on a large rock among them, enjoying the pauseless rapidity with which they luxuriated in the unaccustomed food.

The forest was imposing today in the magnificence of the trees; some of the pines, bearing large cones, were ten feet in diameter; cedars also abounded, and we measured one twenty-eight and one-half feet in circumference four feet from the ground. This noble tree seemed here to be in its proper soil and climate. We found it on both sides of the Sierra, but most abundant on the west.

FOOTNOTES

1. This mythical Buenaventura River had already been struck from the best maps, such as Albert Gallatin's and B. L. E. Bonneville's; but many still believed in it. According to Senator Benton's *Thirty Years' View,* Dr. McLoughlin credited its existence, and made a sketch to indicate its course. The journeys of Jedediah Smith and Joseph Walker across the Great Basin in 1827 and 1833

respectively should have dispelled the notion that it existed, and Frémont must have heard of at least Walker's trip. But Zebulon M. Pike had reported that the Spaniards spoke of a great inland lake named Timpanagos, and of the river Buenaventura flowing into this lake. And A. Finley, in the map which he published in his *New and General Atlas* (Philadelphia, 1826) had shown the Buenaventura flowing out of a Lake Salado right through the Sierra Nevada into San Francisco Bay! So Frémont thought a good look justified.

2. The Chinook family comprised the Clackama, Clatsop, Wasco, Wistram, and Chinook tribes, all resident in the Columbia River Valley. The Chinook proper, on the lower part of the river, were a relatively advanced folk, who lived in wooden houses, handled canoes skillfully, and traded with some shrewdness.

3. Now Eight Mile Creek.

4. Mt. Rainier (spelled "Regnier" by Frémont) is 14,408 feet high; Mt. St. Helens, 9671 feet high; and Mt. Hood, 11,245 feet high.

5. Mt. Jefferson is 10,200 feet in height. Frémont might well be pleased by the splendid scenery of the Cascade Range, which extends for about five hundred miles from northern California into British Columbia. The highest peaks are all volcanic cones.

6. The Cayuse Indians belonged to the Waiilatpuan family, and it was among them that Marcus Whitman had planted his mission. Their small horses gave a name to the Indian ponies.

7. Actually Klamath Marsh, the lake being about thirty miles farther south. Had Frémont diverged twenty miles to the west, he would have discovered Crater Lake.

8. The Klamath Indians of southwestern Oregon, who belonged to the Lutuamian stock, and who were good hunters and fishermen, were actually rather peaceable toward the whites, but addicted to warfare with other tribes. At this time, as Frémont notes, they were at war with their kinsmen the Modocs.

9. The camp of Jedediah Smith in this region had been attacked on July 14, 1828, by hostile Indians of the Umpqua tribe, and fifteen of his party had been slain. The few survivors were succored at Fort Vancouver by Dr. McLoughlin.

10. The stream Frémont had now reached was the Sycan River in southwestern Oregon. But its waters did not reach the Sacramento, as he shortly surmises; they flow into the Klamath River, a stream 270 miles long, which passed through northwestern California to the Pacific.

11. Summer Lake is still so called.

12. This name also is still preserved.

13. This particular lake was subsequently named in honor of Captain W. H. Warner of the United States Army, who with several soldiers was slain here in 1849 by some Pitt River Indians.

14. The camp, that is, was on the boundary line of the Mexican domains, the northern boundary of present-day Nevada.

15. These huts loosely built of sage or tule reeds are usually called wickiups.

16. F. S. Dellenbaugh, in his *Frémont and '49*, hazards the conjecture that Frémont hoped a fertile Buenaventura Valley might after all exist, and that he might plant a fort in it, on the borders of the Mexican territory. For such a fort, of course, the howitzer would be very valuable.

17. This preliminary exploration for a practicable route was required by the increasingly barren nature of the country. It will be noted that Frémont continued to make these preliminary reconnaissances.

18. Now called Mud Lake.

19. Frémont was the discoverer of Pyramid Lake. This splendid sheet of water in western Nevada is about thirty miles long and ten miles wide, and is fed by the Truckee River. It is a vestige of the prehistoric Lake Lahontan, which with Lake Bonneville covered a large part of the Great Basin after the end of the Pleistocene Era.

20. These were Indians of the Paiute tribe. They were in general root-diggers and grasshopper-eaters, living in wickiups; but they had sufficient imagination later to invent the ghost-dance religion.

21. Now called the Truckee River.

22. Actually Frémont could have spent a pleasant and healthful winter with his party on the Truckee River; but he had his reasons, partly political, for wishing to penetrate into and spy out California. In one sense his was a scientific expedition; in another it was a mission sent by the little group of Senatorial believers in expansion to the Pacific.

23. The stream he saw was the Carson River, winding through the Carson Valley.

24. Here Frémont's party was near present-day Yerington, Nevada; the river flowing northward was the Walker River.

25. They were at the foot of Mt. Wilson, in present-day Nevada.

26. They were on East Walker River just west of the lower point of Walker Lake, and of the present-day town of Montello, Nevada. This entry marks the end of the Buenaventura myth. That ghost river may now be said to disappear from history forever. But how Frémont would have liked to discover it!

27. He was apparently of the Washo tribe, a very small folk who lived about Lakes Washo and Tahoe in western Nevada. Incessantly harassed by the Paiutes, they had diminished to a fragmentary body. They had a language all their own, but Frémont's party was able to communicate with them by the sign language then understood through most of the West.

28. These nuts of which Frémont writes, giving us the first known description, were from the *Pinus monophylla,* and are not to be confused with the edible seeds of the piñon (*Pinus edulis*). When the noted botanist John Torrey of New York came to study and classify the collections which Frémont brought home, he described this new species of pine tree, one much larger than the piñon. As the explorer indicates, pine nuts were very important to the Indians, who still harvest them.

29. This camp was on the East Walker River, not far from what is now Bridgeport, California, at an altitude of about 6500 feet.

30. Even yet a vestige of the Buenaventura dream! The "low and open" country over which they looked contains Mono Lake.

31. Either the Indians had misinformed the party, or they mistook the Indian directions. Faced with a choice of two paths over the Sierra Nevada, they took the harder. They would have done better to take the fork now called Buckeye Creek, which leads into Buckeye Pass; instead, they took Swager Creek, and went on into the more difficult Carson Pass.

32. The "walls of granite rock" were evidently, says F. S. Dellenbaugh, the place now called the Devil's Gate. The two great rivers were of course the San Joaquin and the Sacramento.

33. The Indians meant not the party of Chiles, or of Walker, but the Bartleson-Bidwell group of 1841, which had crossed the Sierra by Sonora Pass.

They, however, made the passage in fair October weather; Frémont was the first to cross in winter.

34. This was the West Walker River.

35. An error; they were now on the East Walker River.

36. The party was close to what is now Markleeville, California. As Dellenbaugh says, "They now had the real snow battle before them."

37. This beautiful mountain lake was Tahoe, and Frémont was its discoverer. Its length is 21.6 miles, width 12 miles.

38. The real height of Carson Pass is 8635 feet. Frémont could now be sure of a safe and relatively easy emergence from the mountains.

39. The South Fork of American River.

CHAPTER 9

Sutter's Fort: The San Joaquin Valley: Return to Utah Lake *

MARCH 6, 1844. . . . We continued on our road through the same surpassingly beautiful country, entirely unequaled for the pasturage of stock by anything we had ever seen. Our horses had now become so strong that they were able to carry us, and we traveled rapidly—over four miles an hour; four of us riding every alternate hour. Every few hundred yards we came upon a little band of deer; but we were too eager to reach the settlement, which we momentarily expected to discover, to halt for any other than a passing shot. In a few hours we reached a large fork, the northern branch of the river, and equal in size to that which we had descended. Together they formed a beautiful stream, 60 to 100 yards wide; which at first, ignorant of the nature of the country through which that river ran, we took to be the Sacramento.

We continued down the right bank of the river, traveling for a while over a wooded upland, where we had the delight to discover tracks of cattle. To the southwest was visible a black column of smoke, which we had frequently noticed in descending, arising from the fires we had seen from the top of the Sierra. From the upland we

* This chapter is from Frémont's *Report* on his second expedition. The entry for March 6 chronicles Frémont's arrival at the junction of the North Fork of the American River with the South Fork which they had been following; the two formed the American, and not, as he at first thought, the Sacramento. The descent from the crest of the Sierra had been fairly rapid, but not without its tribulations. Frémont with seven men had gone ahead of the main party to reach Sutter's Fort and send back provisions. One of these men, his mind affected by the recent hardships, had wandered away for a time; another, Preuss, had got lost for three days, and been reduced to eating raw frogs to sustain himself. But at last they were safe, and able to look forward to the hospitality of Sutter's establishment, where they could get food and fresh mounts.

descended into broad groves on the river, consisting of the ever-green, and a new species of a white oak, with a large tufted top, and three to six feet in diameter. Among these was no brushwood; and the grassy surface gave to it the appearance of parks in an old, settled country. Following the tracks of the horses and cattle in search of people, we discovered a small village of Indians. Some of these had on shirts of civilized manufacture, but were otherwise naked, and we could understand nothing from them; they appeared entirely astonished at seeing us.

We made an acorn meal at noon, and hurried on, the valley being gay with flowers, and some of the banks being absolutely golden with the California poppy (*Eschscholtzia crocea*). Here the grass was smooth and green, and the groves very open, the large oaks throwing a broad shade among sunny spots.

Shortly afterward we gave a shout at the appearance on a little bluff of a neatly built adobe house with glass windows. We rode up, but, to our disappointment, found only Indians. There was no appearance of cultivation, and we could see no cattle, and we supposed the place had been abandoned. We now pressed on more eagerly than ever; the river swept round in a large bend to the right, the hills lowered down entirely; and, gradually entering a broad valley, we came unexpectedly into a large Indian village, where the people looked clean, and wore cotton shirts and various other articles of dress. They immediately crowded around us, and we had the inexpressible delight to find one who spoke a little indifferent Spanish, but who at first confounded us by saying there were no whites in the country; but just then a well-dressed Indian came up, and made his salutations in very well spoken Spanish. In answer to our inquiries he informed us that we were upon the Rio de los Americanos (the River of the Americans), and that it joined the Sacramento River about ten miles below. Never did a name sound more sweetly! We felt ourselves among our countrymen; for the name of "American," in these distant parts, is applied to the citizens of the United States.

To our eager inquiries he answered, "I am a vaquero (cowherd) in the service of Captain Sutter, and the people of this *rancheria* work for him." Our evident satisfaction made him communicative, and he went on to say that Captain Sutter was a very rich man, and always glad to see his country people. We asked for his house. He answered that it was just over the hill before us and offered, if we would wait a moment, to take his horse and conduct us to it. We readily accepted his civil offer. In a short distance we came in sight of the fort, and, passing on the way the house of a settler on the opposite side (a Mr. Sinclair), we forded the river; and in a few miles were met a short distance from the fort by Captain Sutter himself.[1] He gave us a most frank and cordial reception—conducted us immediately to his residence—and under his hospitable roof we had a night of rest, enjoyment, and refreshment, which none but ourselves could appreciate. But the party left in the mountains with Mr. Fitzpatrick were to be attended to; and the next morning, supplied with fresh horses and provisions, I hurried off to meet them. On the second day we met, a few miles below the forks of the Rio de los Americanos; and a more forlorn and pitiable sight than they presented cannot well be imagined. They were all on foot—each man, weak and emaciated, leading a horse or mule as weak and emaciated as themselves. They had experienced great difficulty in descending the mountains, made slippery by rains and melting snows, and many horses fell over precipices and were killed; and with some were lost the packs they carried. Among these was a mule with the plants which we had collected since leaving Fort Hall, along a line of two thousand miles' travel. Out of sixty-seven horses and mules with which we commenced crossing the Sierra only thirty-three reached the Valley of the Sacramento, and they only in a condition to be led along. Mr. Fitzpatrick and his party, traveling more slowly, had been able to make some little exertion at hunting, and had killed a few deer. The scanty supply was a great relief to them; for several had been made sick by the strange and unwholesome food which the preservation of life compelled them to use. We stopped and encamped as soon as we met; and a repast of good beef, excellent bread, and delicious salmon, which I had brought along, were their first relief from the sufferings of the Sierra and their first introduction to the luxuries of the Sacramento. It required all our philosophy and forbearance to prevent plenty from becoming as hurtful to us now as scarcity had been before.

The next day, March 8th, we encamped at the junction of the two rivers, the Sacramento and Americanos; and thus found the whole party in the beautiful valley of the Sacramento. It was a convenient place for the camp; and, among other things, was within reach of the wood necessary to make the pack saddles which we should need on our long journey home, from which we were further distant now than we were four months before, when, from the Dalles of the Columbia, we so cheerfully took up the homeward line of march.

Captain Sutter emigrated to this country from the western part of Missouri in 1838–39, and formed the first settlement in the valley on a large grant of land which he obtained from the Mexican Government. He had, at first, some trouble with the Indians; but by the occasional exercise of well-timed authority, he has succeeded in converting them into a peaceable and industrious people.

The ditches around his extensive wheat fields; the making of the sun-dried bricks of which his fort is constructed; the plowing, harrowing, and other agricultural operations, are entirely the work of these Indians, for which they receive a very moderate compensation—principally in shirts, blankets, and other articles of clothing. In the same manner, on application to the chief of a village, he readily obtains as many boys and girls as he has any use for. There were at this time a number of girls at the fort, in training for a future woolen factory; but they were now all busily engaged in constantly watering the gardens, which the unfavorable dryness of the season rendered necessary. The occasional dryness of some seasons I understood to be the only complaint of the settlers in this fertile valley, as it sometimes renders the crops uncertain. Mr. Sutter was about making arrangements to irrigate his lands by means of the Rio de los Americanos. He had this year sown, and altogether by Indian labor, three hundred fanegas of wheat.

A few years since the neighboring Russian establishment of Ross, being about to withdraw from the country, sold to him a large number of stock, with agricultural and other stores, with a number of pieces of artillery, and other munitions of war; for these a regular yearly payment is made in grain. The fort is a quadrangular adobe structure, mounting twelve pieces of artillery (two of them brass), and capable of admitting a garrison of a thousand men; this, at present, consists of forty Indians, in uniform—one of whom was always found on duty at the gate. As might naturally be expected, the pieces are not in very good order.

The whites in the employment of Captain Sutter, American, French, and German, amount, perhaps, to thirty men. The inner wall is formed into buildings comprising the common quarters, with a blacksmith's and other workshops; the dwelling house, with a large distillery house, and other buildings, occupying more the center of the area.

It is built upon a pondlike stream, at times a running creek communicating with the Rio de los Americanos, which enters the Sacramento about two miles below. The latter is here a noble river, about three hundred yards broad, deep and tranquil, with several fathoms of water in the channel, and its banks continuously timbered. There were two vessels belonging to Captain Sutter at anchor near the landing—one a large two-masted lighter, and the other a schooner, which was shortly to proceed on a voyage to Fort Vancouver for a cargo of goods.

Since his arrival, several other persons, principally Americans, have established themselves in the valley. Mr. Sinclair, from whom I experienced much kindness during my stay, is settled a few miles distant, on the Rio de los Americanos.

Mr. Coudrois, a gentleman from Germany, has established himself on Feather River, and is associated with Captain Sutter in agricultural pursuits. Among other improvements, they are about to introduce the cultivation of rapeseed (*Brassica rapus*), which there is every reason to believe is admirably adapted to the climate and soil. The lowest average produce of wheat, as far as we can at present know, is thirty-five fanegas, for one sown; but, as an instance of its fertility, it may be mentioned that Señor Vallejo obtained, on a piece of ground where sheep had been pastured, eight hundred fanegas for eight sown. The produce being different in various places, a very correct idea cannot be formed.

An impetus was given to the active little population by our arrival, as we were in want of everything. Mules, horses, and cattle were to be collected; the horse mill was at work day and night, to make sufficient flour; the blacksmith's shop was put in requisition for horseshoes and bridle bits; and pack saddles, ropes, and bridles, and all the other little equipments of the camp were again to be provided.

The delay thus occasioned was one of repose and enjoyment, which our situation required, and, anxious as we were to resume our homeward journey, was regretted by no one. In the meantime, I had the pleasure to meet with Mr. Chiles, who was residing at a farm on the other side of the River Sacramento, while engaged in the selection of a place for a settlement, for which he had received the necessary grant of land from the Mexican Government.

It will be remembered that we had parted near the frontier of the States, and that he had subsequently descended the valley of Lewis' Fork, with a party of ten or twelve men, with the intention of crossing the intermediate mountains to the waters of the Bay of San Francisco. In the execution of this design, and aided by subsequent information, he left the Columbia at the mouth of Malheur River; and, making his way to the headwaters of the Sacramento with a part of his company, traveled down that river to the settlements of Nueva Helvetia. The other party, to whom he had committed his wagons and mill irons and saws, took a course farther to the south, and the wagons and their contents were lost.

On the 22d we made a preparatory move, and encamped near the settlement of Mr. Sinclair, on the left bank of the Rio de los Americanos. I had discharged five of the party: Neal, the blacksmith (an excellent workman, and an unmarried man, who had done his duty faithfully and had been of very great service to me) desired to remain, as strong inducements were offered here to mechanics. Although at considerable inconvenience to myself, his good conduct induced me to comply with his request, and I obtained for him, from Captain Sutter, a present compensation of two dollars and a half per diem, with a promise that it should be increased to five if he proved as good a workman as had been represented. He was more particularly an agricultural blacksmith. The other men were discharged with their own consent.

While we remained at this place, Derosier, one of our best men, whose steady good conduct had won my regard, wandered off from the camp and never returned to it again; nor has he since been heard of.[2]

March 24th. We resumed our journey with an ample stock of provisions and a large cavalcade of animals, consisting of one hundred and thirty horses and mules, and about thirty head of cattle, five of which were milch cows. Mr. Sutter furnished us also with an Indian boy who had been trained as a vaquero and who would be serviceable in managing our cavalcade, great part of which were nearly as wild as buffalo; and who was, besides, very anxious to go along with us.

Our direct course home was east; but the Sierra would force us south, above five hundred miles of traveling, to a pass at the head of the San Joaquin River. This pass, reported to be good, was discovered by Mr. Joseph Walker, of whom I have already spoken, and whose name it might, therefore, appropriately bear. To reach it, our course lay along the valley of the San Joaquin—the river on our right, and the lofty wall of the impassable Sierra on the left. From that pass we were to move southeastwardly, having the Sierra then on the right, and reach the Spanish Trail, deviously traced from one watering place to another, which constituted the route of the caravans from Pueblo de los Angeles, near the coast of the Pacific, to Santa Fe of New Mexico. From the pass to this trail was one hundred and fifty miles. Following that trail through a desert, relieved by some fertile plains indicated by the recurrence of the term "vegas," until it turned to the right to cross the Colorado, our course would be northeast until we regained the latitude we had lost in arriving at the Utah Lake, and thence to the Rocky Mountains at the head of the Arkansas.

This course of traveling, forced upon us by the structure of the country, would occupy a computed distance of two thousand miles before we reached the head of the Arkansas, not a settlement to be seen upon it; and the names of places along it, all being Spanish or Indian, indicated that it had been but little trod by American feet. Though long, and not free from hardships, this route presented some points of attraction, in tracing the Sierra Nevada—turning the Great Basin, perhaps crossing its rim on the south—completely solving the problem of any river, except the Colorado, from the Rocky Mountains on that part of our continent—and seeing the southern extremity of the Great Salt Lake, of which the northern part had been examined the year before.

Taking leave of Mr. Sutter,[3] who, with several gentlemen, accompanied us a few miles on our way, we traveled about eighteen miles, and encamped on the Rio de los Cosumnes, a stream receiving its name from the Indians who live in its valley. Our road was through a level country, admirably suited to cultivation, and covered with groves of oak trees, principally the evergreen oak and a large oak already mentioned, in form like those of the white oak. The weather, which here at this season can easily be changed from the summer heat of the valley to the frosty mornings and bright days nearer the mountains, continued delightful for travelers, but unfavorable to the agriculturists, whose crops of wheat began to wear a yellow tinge from want of rain.

March 25th. We traveled for twenty-eight miles over the same delightful country as yesterday, and halted in a beautiful bottom at the ford of the Rio de los Mokelumnes, receiving its name from another Indian tribe living on the river. The bottoms on the stream are broad, rich, and extremely fertile, and the uplands are shaded with oak groves. A showy Lupinus of extraordinary beauty, growing four to five feet in height, and covered with spikes in bloom, adorned the banks of the river and filled the air with a light and grateful perfume.

On the 26th we halted at the Arroyo de las Calaveras (Skull Creek), a tributary to the San Joaquin—the previous two streams entering the bay between the San Joaquin and Sacramento rivers. This place is beautiful, with open groves of oak, and a grassy sward beneath, with many plants in bloom, some varieties of which seem to love the shade of the trees, and grow there in close, small fields.

Near the river, and replacing the grass, are great quantities of amole (soap plant), the leaves of which are used in California for making, among other things, mats for saddlecloths. A vine with a small white flower, called here "yerba buena," and which, from its abundance, gives name to an island and town in the bay, was today very frequent on our road—sometimes running on the ground or climbing the trees.

March 27th. Today we traveled steadily and rapidly up the valley,[4]—for, with our wild animals, any other gait was impossible—and making about five miles an hour. During the earlier part of the day our ride had been over a very level prairie, or rather a succession of long stretches of prairie, separated by lines and groves of oak timber, growing along dry gullies, which are filled with water in seasons of rain; and, perhaps, also by the melting snows. Over much of this extent the vegetation was sparse, the surface showing plainly the action of water, which, in the season of flood, the Joaquin spreads over the valley.

About one o'clock we came again among innumerable flowers; and a few miles farther, fields of the beautiful blue-flowering lupine, which seems to love the neighborhood of water, indicated that we were approaching a stream. We here found this beautiful shrub in thickets, some of them being twelve feet in height. Occasionally three or four plants were clustered together, forming a grand bouquet, about ninety feet in circumference and ten feet high, the whole summit covered with spikes of flowers, the perfume of which is very sweet and grateful. A lover of natural beauty can imagine with what pleasure we rode among these flowering groves, which filled the air with a light and delicate fragrance.

We continued our road for about half a mile, interspersed through an open grove of live oaks, which in form were the most symmetrical and beautiful we had yet seen in this country. The ends of their branches rested on the ground, forming somewhat more than a half-sphere of very full and regular figure, with leaves apparently smaller than usual. The California poppy, of a rich orange color, was numerous today. Elk and several bands of antelope made their appearance.

Our road was now one continued enjoyment; and it was pleasant, riding among this assemblage of green pastures with varied flowers and scattered groves, and out of the warm green spring, to look at the rocky and snowy peaks where lately we had suffered so much. Emerging from the timber, we came suddenly upon the Stanislaus River, where we hoped to find a ford, but the stream was flowing by, dark and deep, swollen by the mountain snows; its general breadth was about fifty yards.

We traveled about five miles up the river, and encamped without being able to find a ford. Here we made a large corral, in order to be able to catch a sufficient number of our wild animals, to relieve those previously packed.

Under the shade of the oaks, along the river, I noticed *Erodium cicutarium* in bloom, eight or ten inches high. This is the plant which we had seen the squaws gathering on the Rio de los Americanos. By the inhabitants of the valley it is highly esteemed for fattening cattle, which appear to be very fond of it. Here, where the soil begins to be sandy, it supplies to a considerable extent the want of grass.

Desirous, as far as possible without delay, to include in our examination the San Joaquin River, I returned this morning down the

Stanislaus for seventeen miles, and again encamped without having found a fording place. After following it for eight miles farther the next morning, and finding ourselves in the vicinity of the San Joaquin, encamped in a handsome oak grove, and, several cattle being killed, we ferried over our baggage in their skins. Here our Indian boy, who probably had not much idea of where he was going, and began to be alarmed at the many streams which we were rapidly putting between him and the village, deserted.

Thirteen head of cattle took a sudden fright, while we were driving them across the river, and galloped off. I remained a day in the endeavor to recover them; but finding they had taken the trail back to the fort, let them go without further effort. Here we had several days of warm and pleasant rain, which doubtless saved the crops below.

On April 1st we made ten miles across a prairie without timber, when we were stopped again by another large river, which is called the Rio de la Merced (River of Our Lady of Mercy).[5] Here the country had lost its character of extreme fertility, the soil having become more sandy and light; but for several days past its beauty had been increased by the additional animation of animal life, and now it is crowded with bands of elk and wild horses; and along the rivers are frequent fresh tracks of grizzly bears, which are unusually numerous in this country. Our route had been along the timber of the San Joaquin, generally about eight miles distant, over a high prairie.

In one of the bands of elk seen today there were about two hundred: but the larger bands, both of these and wild horses, are generally found on the other side of the river, which, for that reason, I avoided crossing. I had been informed below that the droves of wild horses were almost invariably found on the western bank of the river; and the danger of losing our animals among them, together with the wish of adding to our reconnaissance the numerous streams which run down from the sierra, decided me to travel up the eastern bank.

April 2d. The day was occupied in building a boat, and ferrying our baggage across the river, and we encamped on the bank. A large fishing eagle, with white head and tail, was slowly sailing along, looking after salmon; and there were some pretty birds in the timber, with partridges, ducks, and geese innumerable, in the neighborhood. We were struck with the tameness of the latter bird at Helvetia, scattered about in flocks near the wheat fields, and eating grass on the prairie; a horseman would ride by within thirty yards without disturbing them.

April 3d. Today we touched several times the San Joaquin River —here a fine-looking, tranquil stream, with a slight current, and apparently deep. It resembled the Missouri in color, with occasional points of white sand; and its banks, where steep, were a kind of sandy clay; its average width appeared to be about eighty yards. In the bottoms are frequent ponds, where our approach disturbed multitudes of wildfowl, principally geese. Skirting along the timber, we frequently started elk; and large bands were seen during the day, with antelope and wild horses.

The low country and the timber rendered it difficult to keep the main line of the river; and this evening we encamped on a tributary stream, about five miles from its mouth. On the prairie bordering the San Joaquin bottoms we found during the day but little grass, and in its place was a sparse and dwarf growth of plants; the soil, being sandy, with small bare places and hillocks, reminded me much of the Platte bottoms; but, on approaching the timber, we found a more luxuriant vegetation; and at our camp was an abundance of grass and peavines.

The foliage of the oak is getting darker; and everything, except that the weather is a little cool, shows that spring is rapidly advancing; and today we had quite a summer rain.

April 4th. Commenced to rain at daylight, but cleared off brightly at sunrise. We ferried the river without any difficulty, and continued up the San Joaquin. Elk were running in bands over the prairie and in the skirt of the timber. We reached the river again at the mouth of a large slough, which we were unable to ford, and made a circuit of several miles around. Here the country appears very flat; oak trees have entirely disappeared, and are replaced by a large willow nearly equal in size. The river is about a hundred yards in breadth, branching into sloughs, and interspersed with islands. At this time it appears sufficiently deep for a small steamer, but its navigation would be broken by shallows at low water.

Bearing in toward the river, we were again forced off by another slough; and, passing around, steered toward a clump of trees on the river, and, finding there good grass, encamped. The prairies along the left bank are alive with immense droves of wild horses, and they had been seen during the day at every opening through the woods which afforded us a view across the river. Latitude, by observation, 37° 08′ 00″; longitude 120° 45′ 22″.

April 5th. During the earlier part of the day's ride the country presented a lacustrine appearance; the river was deep, and nearly on a level with the surrounding country, its banks raised like a levee, and fringed with willows. Over the bordering plain were interspersed spots of prairie among fields of tule (bulrushes), which in this country are called tulares, and little ponds. On the opposite side a line of timber was visible, which, according to information, points out the course of the slough, which, at times of high water, connects with the San Joaquin River—a large body of water in the upper part of the valley, called the Tulé [Tulare] Lakes.

The river and all its sloughs are very full, and it is probable that the lake is now discharging. Here elk were frequently started, and one was shot out of a band which ran around us.

On our left, the sierra maintains its snowy height, and masses of snow appear to descend very low toward the plains; probably the late rains in the valley were snow on the mountains. We traveled thirty-seven miles, and encamped on the river. Longitude of the camp, 120° 28′ 34″, and latitude 36° 49′ 12″.

April 6th. After having traveled fifteen miles along the river we made an early halt under the shade of sycamore trees. Here we found the San Joaquin coming down from the Sierra with a westerly course, and checking our way, as all its tributaries had previously done. We had expected to raft the river, but found a good ford, and encamped on the opposite bank, where droves of wild horses were raising clouds of dust on the prairie. Columns of smoke were visible in the direction of the Tulare Lakes to the southward—probably kindled in the tulares by the Indians, as signals that there were strangers in the valley.

We made on the 7th a hard march in a cold, chilly rain from morning until night—the weather so thick that we traveled by compass. This was a traverse from the San Joaquin to the waters of the Tulare Lakes, and our road was over a very level prairie country.

We saw wolves frequently during the day, prowling about after the young antelope, which cannot run very fast. These were numerous during the day, and two were caught by the people.

Late in the afternoon we discovered timber, which was found to be groves of oak trees on a dry arroyo. The rain, which had fallen in frequent showers, poured down in a storm at sunset, with a strong wind, which swept off the clouds and left a clear sky. Riding on through the timber, about dark we found abundant water in small ponds, twenty to thirty yards in diameter, with clear, deep water and sandy beds, bordered with bog rushes (*Funcus effusus*) and a tall rush (*Scirpus lacustris*) twelve feet high, and surrounded near the margin with willow trees in bloom; among them one which resembled *Salix myricoides*. The oak of the groves was the same already mentioned, with small leaves, in form like those of the white oak, and forming, with the evergreen oak, the characteristic trees of the valley.

April 8th. After a ride of two miles through brush and open groves we reached a large stream, called the River of the Lake, resembling in size the San Joaquin, and being about one hundred yards broad. This is the principal tributary to the Tulare Lakes, which collect all the waters in the upper part of the valley. While we were searching for a ford some Indians appeared on the opposite bank, and, having discovered that we were not Spanish soldiers, showed us the way to a good ford several miles above.

The Indians of the sierra make frequent descents upon the settlements west of the Coast Range, which they keep constantly swept of horses; among them are many who are called Christian Indians, being refugees from Spanish missions. Several of these incursions occurred while we were at Helvetia. Occasionally parties of soldiers follow them across the Coast Range, but never enter the sierra.

On the opposite side we found some forty or fifty Indians, who had come to meet us from the village below. We made them some small presents and invited them to accompany us to our encampment, which, after about three miles through fine oak groves, we made on the river. We made a fort, principally on account of our animals.

The Indians brought otter skins and several kinds of fish, and bread made of acorns, to trade. Among them were several who had come to live among these Indians when the missions were broken up, and who spoke Spanish fluently. They informed us that they were called by the Spaniards *mansitos* (tame), in distinction from the wilder tribes of the mountains: they, however, think themselves very insecure, not knowing at what unforeseen moment the sins of the latter may be visited on them. They are dark-skinned, but handsome and intelligent Indians, and live principally on acorns and the roots of the tule, of which also their huts are made. By observation, the latitude of the encampment is 36° 24' 50", and longitude 119° 41' 40".

April 9th. For several miles we had very bad traveling over what is called rotten ground, in which the horses were frequently up to their knees. Making toward a line of timber, we found a small fordable stream, beyond which the country improved and the grass became excellent; and, crossing a number of dry and timbered arroyos, we traveled until late through open oak groves, and encamped among a collection of streams. These were running among rushes and willows; and, as usual, flocks of blackbirds announced our approach to water. We have here approached considerably nearer to the eastern Sierra, which shows very plainly, still covered with masses of snow, which yesterday and today has also appeared abundant on the Coast Range.

April 10th. Today we made another long journey of about forty miles, through a country uninteresting and flat, with very little grass and a sandy soil, in which several branches we crossed had lost their water. In the evening the face of the country became hilly; and, turning a few miles up toward the mountains, we found a good encampment on a pretty stream hidden among the hills, and handsomely timbered, principally with large cottonwoods (*populus*, differing from any in Michaux's *Sylva*). The seed vessels of this tree were now just about bursting. Several Indians came down the river to see us in the evening: we gave them supper, and cautioned them against stealing our horses, which they promised not to attempt.

April 11th. A broad trail along the river here takes out among the hills. "*Buen camino*" (good road), said one of the Indians, of whom we had inquired about the pass; and, following it accordingly, it conducted us beautifully through a very broken country, by an excellent way which, otherwise, we should have found extremely bad.

Taken separately, the hills present smooth and graceful outlines, but together, make bad traveling ground.

Instead of grass, the whole face of the country is closely covered with *Erodium cicutarium,* here only two or three inches high. Its height and beauty varied in a remarkable manner with the locality, being, in many low places which we passed during the day, around streams and springs, two and three feet in height. The country had now assumed a character of aridity; and the luxuriant green of these little streams, wooded with willow, oak, or sycamore, looked very refreshing among the sandy hills.

In the evening we encamped on a large creek with abundant water. I noticed here, for the first time since leaving the Arkansas waters, the *Mirabilis jalapa* in bloom.

April 12th. Along our road today the country was altogether sandy, and vegetation meager. *Ephedra occidentalis,* which we had first seen in the neighborhood of the Pyramid Lake, made its appearance here, and in the course of the day became very abundant, and in large bushes.

Toward the close of the afternoon we reached a tolerably large river, which empties into a small lake at the head of the valley; [6] it is about thirty-five yards wide, with a stony and gravelly bed, and the swiftest stream we have crossed since leaving the bay. The bottoms produced no grass, though well timbered with willow and cottonwood; and, after ascending it for several miles, we made a late encampment on a little bottom with scanty grass. In greater part, the vegetation along our road consisted now of rare and unusual plants, among which many were entirely new.

Along the bottoms were thickets consisting of several varieties of shrubs, which made here their first appearance; and among these was *Garrya elliptica* (Lindley), a small tree belonging to a very peculiar natural order, and, in its general appearance (growing in thickets) resembling willow. It now became common along the streams, frequently supplying the place of *Salix longifolia.*

April 13th. The water was low, and a few miles above we forded the river at a rapid, and marched in a southeasterly direction over a less broken country. The mountains were now very near, occasionally looming out through fog. In a few hours we reached the bottom of a creek without water, over which the sandy beds were dispersed in many branches. Immediately where we struck it the timber terminated; and below, to the right, it was a broad bed of dry and bare sands. There were many tracks of Indians and horses imprinted in the sand, which, with other indications, informed us this was the creek issuing from the pass, and which on the map we have called Pass Creek.

We ascended a trail for a few miles along the creek and suddenly found a stream of water, five feet wide, running with a lively current, but losing itself almost immediately. This little stream showed plainly the manner in which the mountain waters lose themselves in sand at the eastern foot of the sierra, leaving only a parched desert and arid plains beyond. The stream enlarged rapidly, and the timber became abundant as we ascended. A new species of pine made its appearance, with several kinds of oaks, and a variety of trees; and the country changing its appearance suddenly and entirely, we found ourselves again traveling among the old orchard-like places. Here we selected a delightful encampment in a handsome, green-oak hollow, where, among the open bolls of the trees, was an abundant sward of grass and peavines.

In the evening a Christian Indian rode into the camp, well dressed, with long spurs and a sombrero, and speaking Spanish fluently. It was an unexpected apparition and a strange and pleasant sight in this desolate gorge of a mountain—an Indian face, Spanish costume, jingling spurs, and horse equipped after the Spanish manner. He informed me that he belonged to one of the Spanish missions to the south, distant two or three days' ride, and that he had obtained from the priests leave to spend a few days with his relations in the sierra. Having seen us enter the pass, he had come down to visit us. He appeared familiarly acquainted with the country, and gave me definite and clear information in regard to the desert region east of the mountains. I had entered the pass with a strong disposition to vary my route, and to travel directly across toward the Great Salt Lake, in the view of obtaining some acquaintance with the interior of the Great Basin, while pursuing a direct course for the frontier; but his representation, which described it as an arid and barren desert that had repulsed by its sterility all the attempts of the Indians to penetrate it determined me for the present to relinquish the plan, and, agreeably to his advice, after crossing the

sierra, continue our intended route along its eastern base to the
Spanish Trail. By this route a party of six Indians, who had come
from a great river in the eastern part of the desert to trade with his
people had just started on their return. He would himself return
the next day to San Fernando; and as our roads would be the same
for two days, he offered his services to conduct us so far on our way.
His offer was gladly accepted.

The fog, which had somewhat interfered with views in the valley,
had entirely passed off and left a clear sky. That which had enveloped us in the neighborhood of the pass proceeded evidently
from fires kindled among the tulares by Indians living near the
lakes, and which were intended to warn those in the mountains that
there were strangers in the valley. Our position was in latitude 35°
17′ 12″, and longitude 118° 35′ 03″. . . .*

April 14th. Our journey today was in the midst of an advanced
spring, whose green and floral beauty offered a delightful contrast
to the sandy valley we had just left. All the day snow was in sight
on the butte of the mountain which frowned down upon us on the
right; but we beheld it now with feelings of pleasant security as we
rode along between green trees and on flowers, with hummingbirds
and other feathered friends of the traveler enlivening the serene
spring air.

As we reached the summit of this beautiful pass, and obtained a
view into the eastern country, we saw at once that here was the
place to take leave of all such pleasant scenes as those around us.
The distant mountains were now bald rocks again; and below, the
land had any color but green.[7] Taking into consideration the nature
of the Sierra Nevada, we found this pass an excellent one for horses;
and with a little labor, or perhaps with a more perfect examination
of the localities, it might be made sufficiently practicable for
wagons. Its latitude and longitude may be considered that of our
last encampment, only a few miles distant. The elevation was not
taken—our half-wild cavalcade making it too troublesome to halt
before night, when once started.

We here left the waters of the bay of San Francisco, and though
forced upon them contrary to my intentions, I cannot regret the
necessity which occasioned the deviation. It made me well ac-

* A paragraph of botanical detail omitted.

quainted with the great range of the Sierra Nevada of the Alta
California, and showed that this broad and elevated snowy ridge
was a continuation of the Cascade Range of Oregon, between which
and the ocean there is still another and a lower range, parallel to
the former and to the coast, and which may be called the Coast
Range. It also made me well acquainted with the basin of the San
Francisco Bay, and with the two fine rivers and their valleys (the
Sacramento and San Joaquin) which are tributary to that bay, and
cleared up some points in geography on which error had long prevailed.

It had been constantly represented, as I have already stated, that
the bay of San Francisco opened far into the interior, by some river
coming down from the base of the Rocky Mountains, and upon
which supposed stream the name of Rio Buenaventura had been
bestowed. Our observations of the Sierra Nevada, in the long distance from the head of the Sacramento to the head of the San
Joaquin, and of the valley below it, which collect all the waters of
the San Francisco Bay, show that this neither is nor can be the case.
No river from the interior does, or can, cross the Sierra Nevada—
itself more lofty than the Rocky Mountains; and as to the Buenaventura, the mouth of which seen on the coast gave the idea and
the name of the reputed great river, it is, in fact, a small stream of
no consequence, not only below the Sierra Nevada, but actually
below the Coast Range—taking its rise within half a degree of the
ocean, running parallel to it for about two degrees, and then falling
into the Pacific near Monterey. There is no opening from the bay
of San Francisco into the interior of the continent. The two rivers
which flow into it are comparatively short, and not perpendicular to
the coast, but lateral to it, and having their heads toward Oregon
and southern California. They open lines of communication north
and south, and not eastwardly; and thus this want of interior communication from the San Francisco Bay, now fully ascertained, gives
great additional value to the Columbia, which stands alone as the
only great river on the Pacific slope of our continent which leads
from the ocean to the Rocky Mountains, and opens a line of communication from the sea to the valley of the Mississippi.

Four *compañeros* joined our guide at the pass; and two going
back at noon, the others continued on in company. Descending from

the hills, we reached a country of fine grass, where the *Erodium cicutarium* finally disappeared, giving place to an excellent quality of bunch grass. Passing by some springs where there was a rich sward of grass among groves of large black oak, we rode over a plain on which the guide pointed out a spot where a refugee Christian Indian had been killed by a party of soldiers which had unexpectedly penetrated into the mountains.

Crossing a low sierra, and descending a hollow where a spring gushed out, we were struck by the sudden appearance of yucca trees, which gave a strange and southern character to the country, and suited well with the dry and desert region we were approaching. Associated with the idea of barren sands, their stiff and ungraceful form makes them to the traveler the most repulsive tree in the vegetable kingdom.[8] Following the hollow, we shortly came upon a creek wooded with large black oak, which yet had not put forth a leaf. There was a small rivulet of running water with good grass.

April 15th. The Indians who had accompanied the guide returned this morning, and I purchased from them a Spanish saddle and long spurs, as reminiscences of the time; and for a few yards of scarlet cloth they gave me a horse, which afterward became food for other Indians.

We continued a short distance down the creek, in which our guide informed us that the water very soon disappeared, and turned directly to the southward along the foot of the mountain, the trail on which we rode appearing to describe the eastern limit of travel, where water and grass terminated.

Crossing a low spur, which bordered the creek, we descended to a kind of plain among the lower spurs, the desert being in full view on our left, apparently illimitable. A hot mist lay over it today, through which it had a white and glistening appearance; here and there a few dry-looking buttes and isolated black ridges rose suddenly upon it. "There," said our guide, stretching out his hand toward it, "there are the great llanos (plains); *no hay agua; no hay zacate—nada* (there is neither water nor grass—nothing); every animal that goes out upon them dies." It was indeed dismal to look upon, and hard to conceive so great a change in so short a distance. One might travel the world over without finding a valley more fresh and verdant, more floral and sylvan, more alive with birds and animals, more bounteously watered, than we had left in the San Joaquin: here, within a few miles' ride, a vast desert plain spread before us, from which the boldest traveler turned away in despair. Directly in front of us, at some distance to the southward, and running out in an easterly direction from the mountains, stretched a sierra having at the eastern end (perhaps fifty miles distant) some snowy peaks, on which, by the information of our guide, snow rested all the year.

Our cavalcade made a strange and grotesque appearance, and it was impossible to avoid reflecting upon our position and composition in this remote solitude. Within two degrees of the Pacific Ocean; already far south of the latitude of Monterey; and still forced on south by a desert on one hand and a mountain range on the other; guided by a civilized Indian, attended by two wild ones from the sierra, a Chinook from the Columbia; and our own mixture of American, French, German—all armed; four or five languages heard at once; above a hundred horses and mules, half-wild; American, Spanish, and Indian dresses and equipments intermingled—such was our composition.

Our march was a sort of procession. Scouts ahead, and on the flanks; a front and rear division; the pack animals, baggage, and horned cattle in the center; and the whole stretching a quarter of a mile along our dreary path. In this form we journey, looking more as if we belonged to Asia than to the United States of America.

We continued in a southerly direction across the plain, to which, as well as to all the country so far as we could see, the yucca trees gave a strange and singular character. Several new plants appeared, among which was a zygophyllaceous shrubs (*Zygophyllum Californicum* Torr. and Frem.) sometimes ten feet in height; in form, and in the pliancy of its branches, it is rather a graceful plant. Its leaves are small, covered with a resinous substance, and, particularly when bruised and crushed, exhale a singular, but very agreeable and refreshing odor. This shrub and the yucca, with many varieties of cactus, make the characteristic features in the vegetation for a long distance to the eastward.

Along the foot of the mountain, twenty miles to the southward, red stripes of flowers were visible during the morning, which we supposed to be variegated sandstones. We rode rapidly during the day, and in the afternoon emerged from the yucca forest at the foot of an outlier of the Sierra before us, and came among the fields of flowers we had seen in the morning, which consisted principally of the rich orange-colored Californian poppy, mingled with other flowers of brighter tints. Reaching the top of this spur, which was covered with fine bunch grass, and where the hills were very green, our guide pointed to a small hollow in the mountain before us, saying, "En esta piedra hay agua." He appeared to know every nook in the country.

We continued our beautiful road, and reached a spring in the slope at the foot of the ridge, running in a green ravine, among granite boulders; here nightshade, and borders of buckwheat, with their white blossoms among the granite rocks, attracted our notice as familiar plants. Several antelopes were seen among the hills, and some large hares. Men were sent back this evening in search of a wild mule with a valuable pack, which had managed (as they frequently do) to hide itself along the road.

By observation, the latitude of the camp is 34° 41' 42" and longitude 118° 20' 00". The next day the men returned with the mule.

April 17th. Crossing the ridge by a beautiful pass of hollows, where several deer broke out of the thickets, we emerged at a small salt lake in a *vallon* lying nearly east and west, where a trail from the mission of San Buenaventura comes in. The lake is about one thousand two hundred yards in diameter; surrounded on the margin by a white salty border, which, by the smell, reminded us slightly of Lake Abert. There are some cottonwoods, with willow and elder, around the lake; and the water is a little salt, although not entirely unfit for drinking.

Here we turned directly to the eastward along the trail, which, from being seldom used, is almost imperceptible; and, after traveling a few miles, our guide halted, and, pointing to the hardly visible trail, "Aqui es camino," said he, "no se pierde—va siempre." He pointed out a black butte on the plain at the foot of the mountain, where we would find water to encamp at night; and, giving him a present of knives and scarlet cloth, we shook hands and parted. He bore off south, and in a day's ride would arrive at San Fernando, one of several missions in this part of California, where the country is so beautiful that it is considered a paradise, and the name of its principal town (Pueblo de los Angeles) would make it angelic.

We continued on through a succession of valleys, and came into a most beautiful spot of flower fields; instead of green, the hills were purple and orange, with unbroken beds, into which each color was separately gathered. A pale straw color, with a bright yellow, the rich red-orange of the poppy mingled with fields of purple, covered the spot with a floral beauty; and, on the border of the sandy deserts, seemed to invite the traveler to go no farther. Riding along through the perfumed air, we soon after entered a defile overgrown with the ominous *Artemisia tridentata*, which conducted us into a sandy plain covered more or less densely with forests of yucca.

Having now the snowy ridge on our right, we continued our way toward a dark butte belong to a low sierra in the plain, and which our guide had pointed out for a landmark. Late in the day the familiar growth of cottonwood, a line of which was visible ahead, indicated our approach to a creek, which we reached where the water spread out into sands, and a little below sank entirely. Here our guide had intended we should pass the night; but there was not a blade of grass, and, hoping to find nearer the mountain a little for the night, we turned up the stream. A hundred yards above we found the creek a fine stream, sixteen feet wide, with a swift current.

A dark night overtook us when we reached the hills at the foot of the ridge, and we were obliged to encamp without grass—tying up what animals we could secure in the darkness, the greater part of the wild ones having free range for the night. Here the stream was two feet deep, swift and clear, issuing from a neighboring snow peak. A few miles before reaching this creek, we had crossed a broad, dry river bed, which, nearer the hills, the hunters had found a bold and handsome stream.

April 18th. Some parties were engaged in hunting up the scattered horses, and others in searching for grass above; both were successful, and late in the day we encamped among some springheads of the river, in a hollow which was covered with only tolerably good grasses, the lower ground being entirely overgrown with large bunches of the coarse stiff grass (*Carex sitchensis*). Our latitude, by observation, was 34° 27' 03", and longitude 117° 43' 21".

Traveling close along the mountain, we followed up, in the afternoon of the 19th, another stream, in hopes to find a grass patch like that of the previous day, but were deceived; except some scattered bunch grass, there was nothing but rock and sand, and even the fertility of the mountain seemed withered by the air of the desert. Among the few trees was the nut pine (*Pinus monophyllus*).

Our road the next day was still in an easterly direction along the ridge, over very bad traveling ground, broken and confounded with crippled trees and shrubs; and, after a difficult march of eighteen miles, a general shout announced that we had struck the great object of our search—the Spanish Trail [9]—which here was running directly north. The road itself and its course were equally happy discoveries to us. Since the middle of December we had continually been forced south by mountains and by deserts, and now would have to make six degrees of northing to regain the latitude on which we wished to cross the Rocky Mountains. The course of the road, therefore, was what we wanted, and, once more, we felt like going homeward. A road to travel on and the right course to go were joyful consolations to us, and our animals enjoyed the beaten track like ourselves.

Relieved from the rocks and brush, our wild mules started off at a rapid rate, and in fifteen miles we reached a considerable river, timbered with cottonwood and willow, where we found a bottom of tolerable grass. As the animals had suffered a great deal in the last few days, I remained here all next day to allow them the necessary repose; and it was now necessary, at every favorable place, to make a little halt. Between us and the Colorado River we were aware that the country was extremely poor in grass, and scarce for water, there being many jornadas (days' journeys), or long stretches of forty to sixty miles, without water, where the road was marked by bones of animals.

Although in Califonia we had met with people who had passed over this trail, we had been able to obtain no correct information about it; and the greater part of what we had heard was found to be only a tissue of falsehoods. The rivers that we found on it were never mentioned, and others, particularly described in name and locality, were subsequently seen in another part of the country. It was described as a tolerably good sandy road, with so little rock as scarcely to require the animals to be shod; and we found it the roughest and rockiest road we had ever seen in the country, and which nearly destroyed our band of fine mules and horses. Many animals are destroyed on it every year by a disease called the foot evil; and a traveler should never venture on it without having his animals well shod, and also carrying extra shoes. Latitude 34° 34' 11" and longitude 117° 13' 00".

The morning of the 22d was clear and bright, and a snowy peak to the southward shone out high and sharply defined. As has been usual since we crossed the mountains and descended into the hot plains, we had a gale of wind. We traveled down the right bank of the stream, over sands which are somewhat loose and have no verdure, but are occupied by various shrubs.

A clear, bold stream, sixty feet wide and several feet deep, had a strange appearance, running between perfectly naked banks of sand. The eye, however, is somewhat relieved by willows, and the beautiful green of the sweet cottonwoods with which it is well wooded. As we followed along its course, the river, instead of growing constantly larger, gradually dwindled away, as it was absorbed by the sand.

We were now careful to take the old camping places of the annual Santa Fe caravans, which, luckily for us, had not yet made their yearly passage. A drove of several thousand horses and mules would have entirely swept away the scanty grass at the watering places, and we should have been obliged to leave the road to obtain subsistence for our animals. After riding twenty miles in a northeasterly direction, we found an old encampment, where we halted. By observation, the elevation of this encampment is two thousand two hundred and fifty feet.

April 23d. The trail followed still along the river, which, in the course of the morning, entirely disappeared. We continued along the dry bed, in which, after an interval of about sixteen miles, the water reappeared in some low places, well timbered with cottonwood and willow, where was another of the customary camping grounds.

Here a party of six Indians came into camp, poor and hungry, and quite in keeping with the character of the country. Their arms were bows of unusual length, and each had a large gourd, strengthened with meshes of cord, in which he carried water. They proved to be the Mohave Indians [10] mentioned by our recent guide; and from one of them, who spoke Spanish fluently, I obtained some interesting information which I would be glad to introduce here.

An account of the people inhabiting this region would undoubtedly possess interest for the civilized world. Our journey homeward was fruitful in incident, and the country through which we traveled, although a desert, offered much to excite the curiosity of the botanist; but limited time and the rapidly advancing season for active operations oblige me to omit all extended descriptions, and hurry briefly to the conclusion of this report.

The Indian who spoke Spanish had been educated for a number of years at one of the Spanish missions, and, at the breaking up of those establishments, had returned to the mountains, where he had been found by a party of Mohave (sometimes called Amuchava) Indians, among whom he had ever since resided.

He spoke of the leader of the present party as *"mi amo"* (my master). He said they lived upon a large river in the southeast, which the "soldiers called the Rio Colorado"; but that formerly a portion of them lived upon this river and among the mountains which had bounded the river valley to the northward during the day, and that here along the river they had raised various kinds of melons. They sometimes came over to trade with the Indians of the sierra, bringing with them blankets and goods manufactured by the Moquis [11] and other Colorado Indians. They rarely carried home horses, on account of the difficulty of getting them across the desert and of guarding them afterward from the Paiute Indians, who inhabit the sierra, at the head of the Rio Virgen (River of the Virgin).

He informed us that, a short distance below, this river finally disappeared. The two different portions in which water is found had received from the priests two different names; and subsequently I heard it called by the Spaniards the Rio de las Animas, but on the map we have called it the Mohave River. [12]

April 24th. We continued down the stream (or rather its bed) for about eight miles, where there was water still in several holes, and encamped. The caravans sometimes continue below to the end of the river, from which there is a very long jornada of perhaps sixty miles without water. . . . *

* A paragraph of botanical detail omitted.

Our cattle had become so tired and poor by this fatiguing traveling that three of them were killed here, and the meat dried. The Indians had now an occasion for a great feast, and were occupied the remainder of the day and all the night in cooking and eating. There was no part of the animal for which they did not find some use, except the bones.

In the afternoon we were surprised by the sudden appearance in the camp of two Mexicans—a man and a boy. The name of the man was Andres Fuentes, and that of the boy (a handsome lad eleven years old) Pablo Hernandez. They belonged to a party consisting of six persons, the remaining four being the wife of Fuentes, the father and mother of Pablo, and Santiago Giacome, a resident of New Mexico. With a cavalcade of about thirty horses they had come out from Pueblo de los Angeles, near the coast, under the guidance of Giacome, in advance of the great caravan, in order to travel more at leisure and obtain better grass. Having advanced as far into the desert as was considered consistent with their safety, they halted at the Archilette—one of the customary camping grounds about eighty miles from our encampment, where there is a spring of good water, with sufficient grass—and concluded to await there the arrival of the great caravan. Several Indians were soon discovered lurking about the camp, who, in a day or two after, came in, and, after behaving in a very friendly manner, took their leave without awakening any suspicions. Their deportment begat a security which proved fatal. In a few days afterward, suddenly a party of about one hundred Indians appeared in sight, advancing toward the camp.

It was too late, or they seemed not to have presence of mind to take proper measures of safety; and the Indians charged down into their camp, shouting as they advanced and discharging flights of arrows. Pablo and Fuentes were on horse guard at the time, and mounted, according to the custom of the country. One of the principal objects of the Indians was to get possession of the horses, and part of them immediately surrounded the band; but, in obedience to the shouts of Giacome, Fuentes drove the animals over and through the assailants, in spite of their arrows, and, abandoning the rest to their fate, carried them off at speed across the plain. Knowing that they would be pursued by the Indians, without making any halt except to shift their saddles to other horses they drove them on

for about sixty miles, and this morning left them at a watering place
on the trail called Agua de Tomaso. Without giving themselves any
time for rest they hurried on, hoping to meet the Spanish caravan,
when they discovered my camp. I received them kindly, taking them
into my own mess, and promised them such aid as circumstances
might put it in my power to give.

April 25th. We left the river abruptly and, turning to the north,
regained in a few miles the main trail (which had left the river
sooner than ourselves) and continued our way across a lower ridge
of the mountain, through a miserable tract of sand and gravel. We
crossed at intervals the broad beds of dry gullies, where in the season of rains and melting snows there would be brooks or rivulets;
and at one of these, where there was no indication of water, were
several freshly dug holes, in which there was water at the depth of
two feet. These holes had been dug by the wolves, whose keen sense
of smell had scented the water under the dry sand. They were nice
little wells, narrow, and dug straight down, and we got pleasant
water out of them.

The country had now assumed the character of an elevated and
mountainous desert, its general features being black, rocky ridges,
bald, and destitute of timber, with sandy basins between. Where
the sides of these ridges are washed by gullies, the plains below are
strewed with beds of large pebbles or rolled stones, destructive to
our soft-footed animals, accustomed to the grassy plains of the Sacramento Valley. Through these sandy basins sometimes struggled a
scanty stream, or occurred a hole of water, which furnished camping
grounds for travelers. Frequently, in our journey across, snow was
visible on the surrounding mountains; but their waters rarely
reached the sandy plain below, where we toiled along oppressed
with thirst and a burning sun.

But throughout this nakedness of sand and gravel were many
beautiful plants and flowering shrubs, which occurred in many new
species, and with greater variety than we had been accustomed to
see in the most luxuriant prairie countries; this was a peculiarity of
this desert. Even where no grass would take root, the naked sand
would bloom with some rich and rare flower, which found its appro-
priate home in the arid and barren spot.

Scattered over the plain, and tolerably abundant, was a handsome
leguminous shrub, three or four feet high, with fine bright-purple

flowers. It is a new *Psoralea,* and occurred frequently henceforward along our road.

Beyond the first ridge our road bore a little to the east of north, toward a gap in a higher line of mountains; and after traveling about twenty-five miles, we arrived at the Agua de Tomaso—the spring where the horses had been left; but, as we expected, they were gone. A brief examination of the ground convinced us that they had been driven off by the Indians. Carson and Godey volunteered with the Mexican to pursue them and, well mounted, the three set off on the trail. At this stopping place there were a few bushes and very little grass. Its water was a pool; but near by was a spring, which had been dug out by Indians or travelers. Its water was cool—a great refreshment to us under a burning sun.

In the evening Fuentes returned, his horse having failed; but Carson and Godey had continued the pursuit. . . .*

In the afternoon of the next day a war whoop was heard, such as Indians make when returning from a victorious enterprise; and soon Carson and Godey appeared, driving before them a band of horses, recognized by Fuentes to be part of those they had lost. Two bloody scalps, dangling from the end of Godey's gun, announced that they had overtaken the Indians as well as the horses.

They informed us that after Fuentes left them, from the failure of his horse, they continued the pursuit alone, and toward night-fall entered the mountains, into which the trail led. After sunset the moon gave light, and they followed the trail by moonshine until late in the night, when it entered a narrow defile and was difficult to follow. Afraid of losing it in the darkness of the defile, they tied up their horses, struck no fire, and lay down to sleep in silence and in darkness. Here they lay from midnight till morning. At daylight they resumed the pursuit, and about sunrise discovered the horses; and, immediately dismounting and tying up their own, they crept cautiously to a rising ground which intervened, from the crest of which they perceived the encampment of four lodges close by. They proceeded quietly, and had got within thirty or forty yards of their object, when a movement among the horses discovered them to the Indians: giving the war shout, they instantly charged into the camp, regardless of the number which the *four* lodges would imply.

The Indians received them with a flight of arrows shot from their

---

* A paragraph of astronomical observations omitted.

long bows, one of which passed through Godey's shirt collar, barely missing the neck; our men fired their rifles upon a steady aim, and rushed in. Two Indians were stretched on the ground, fatally wounded; the rest fled, except a lad, who was captured. The scalps of the fallen were instantly stripped off; but in the process one of them, who had two balls through his body, sprang to his feet, the blood streaming from his skinned head, and uttered a hideous howl. An old squaw, possibly his mother, stopped and looked back from the mountainside she was climbing, threatening and lamenting. The frightful spectacle appalled the stout hearts of our men; but they did what humanity required, and quickly terminated the agonies of the gory savage.

They were now masters of the camp, which was a pretty little recess in the mountain, with a fine spring, and apparently safe from all invasion. Great preparations had been made to feast a large party, for it was a very proper place for a rendezvous and for the celebration of such orgies as robbers of the desert would delight in. Several of the best horses had been killed, skinned, and cut up; for the Indians living in mountains, and only coming into the plains to rob and murder, make no other use of horses than to eat them. Large earthen vessels were on the fire, boiling and stewing the horse beef; and several baskets, containing fifty or sixty pairs of moccasins, indicated the presence, or expectation, of a considerable party. They released the boy, who had given strong evidence of the stoicism, or something else, of the savage character in commencing his breakfast upon a horse's head as soon as he found he was not to be killed, but only tied as a prisoner.

Their object accomplished, our men gathered up all the surviving horses, fifteen in number, returned upon their trail, and rejoined us at our camp in the afternoon of the same day. They had ridden about one hundred miles in the pursuit and return, and all in thirty hours. The time, place, object, and numbers considered, this expedition of Carson and Godey may be considered among the boldest and most disinterested which the annals of Western adventure, so full of daring deeds, can present. Two men, in a savage desert, pursue day and night an unknown body of Indians into the defiles of an unknown mountain—attack them on sight, without counting numbers—and defeat them in an instant—and for what? To punish the robbers of the desert, and to avenge the wrongs of Mexicans whom they did not know. I repeat: it was Carson and Godey who did this—the former an American, born in the Boonslick country of Missouri; the latter a Frenchman, born in St. Louis—and both trained to Western enterprise from early life.

By the information of Fuentes, we had now to make a long stretch of forty or fifty miles across a plain which lay between us and the next possible camp; and we resumed our journey late in the afternoon, with the intention of traveling through the night, and avoiding the excessive heat of the day, which was oppressive to our animals. For several hours we traveled across a high plain, passing, at the opposite side, through a cañon by the bed of a creek running northwardly into a small lake beyond, and both of them being dry.

We had a warm, moonshiny night; and, traveling directly toward the North Star, we journeyed now across an open plain between mountain ridges, that on the left being broken, rocky, and bald, according to the information of Carson and Godey, who had entered here in pursuit of the horses. The plain appeared covered principally with the *Zygophyllum Californicum* already mentioned; and the line of our road was marked by the skeletons of horses, which were strewed to a considerable breadth over the plain. We were afterward always warned on entering one of these long stretches by the bones of these animals, which had perished before they could reach the water. About midnight we reached a considerable stream bed, now dry, the discharge of the waters of this basin (when it collected any), down which we descended in a northwesterly direction. The creek bed was overgrown with shrubbery, and several hours before day it brought us to the entrance of a "cañon," where we found water and encamped. This word "cañon" is used by the Spaniards to signify a defile or gorge in a creek or river, where high rocks press in close, and make a narrow way, usually difficult and often impossible to be passed.

In the morning we found that we had a very poor camping ground: a swampy, salty spot, with a little long, unwholesome grass, and the water which rose in springs, being useful only to wet the mouth, but entirely too salt to drink. All around were sand and rocks, and skeletons of horses which had not been able to find support for their lives. As we were about to start we found, at the distance of a few hundred yards, among the hills to the southward a spring of tolerably good water, which was a relief to ourselves; but the place was too poor to remain long, and therefore we continued on this morning. On the creek were thickets of *Spirolobium odoratum* (acacia) in bloom, and very fragrant. . . .*

April 29th. Today we had to reach the Archilette, distant seven miles, where the Mexican party had been attacked; and, leaving our encampment early, we traversed a part of the desert, the most sterile and repulsive that we had yet seen. Its prominent features were dark sierras, naked and dry; on the plains a few straggling shrubs—among them, cactus of several varieties. Fuentes pointed out one, called by the Spaniards bisnada, which has a juicy pulp, slightly acid, and is eaten by the traveler to allay thirst.

Our course was generally north, and after crossing an intervening ridge, we descended into a sandy plain or basin, in the middle of which was the grassy spot, with its springs and willow bushes, which constitutes a camping place in the desert, and is called the Archilette. The dead silence of the place was ominous, and galloping rapidly up, we found only the corpses of the two men: everything else was gone. They were naked, mutilated, and pierced with arrows. Hernandez had evidently fought, and with desperation. He lay in advance of the willow, half-faced tent, which sheltered his family, as if he had come out to meet danger, and to repulse it from that asylum. One of his hands and both his legs had been cut off. Giacome, who was a large and strong-looking man, was lying in one of the willow shelters, pierced with arrows. Of the women no trace could be found, and it was evident they had been carried off captive. A little lapdog, which had belonged to Pablo's mother, remained with the dead bodies, and was frantic with joy at seeing Pablo; he, poor child, was frantic with grief, and filled the air with lamentations for his father and mother. *Mi padre!—mi madre!*—was his incessant cry. When we beheld this pitiable sight, and pictured to ourselves the fate of the two women, carried off by savages so brutal and so loathsome, all compunction for the scalped-alive Indian ceased; and we rejoiced that Carson and Godey had been alive to give so useful a lesson to these American Arabs, who lie in wait to murder and plunder the innocent traveler.

We were all too much affected by the sad feelings which the

---

* Some topographical detail omitted.

place inspired to remain an unnecessary moment. The night we were obliged to pass there. Early in the morning we left it, having first written a brief account of what had happened, and put it in the cleft of a pole planted at the spring, that the approaching caravan might learn the fate of their friends. In commemoration of the event we called the place Agua de Hernandez—Hernandez' Spring. By observation its latitude was 35° 51′ 21″.

April 30th. We continued our journey over a district similar to that of the day before. From the sandy basin in which was the spring we entered another basin of the same character, surrounded everywhere by mountains. Before us stretched a high range, rising still higher to the left, and terminating in a snowy mountain.

After a day's march of twenty-four miles we reached at evening the bed of a stream from which the water had disappeared; a little only remained in holes, which we increased by digging; and about a mile above, the stream, not yet entirely sunk, was spread out over the sands, affording a little water for the animals. The stream came out of the mountains on the left, very slightly wooded with cottonwood, willow, and acacia, and a few dwarf oaks; and grass was nearly as scarce as water. A plant with showy yellow flowers (*Stanleya integrifolia*) occurred abundantly at intervals for the last two days, and *Eriogonum inflatum* was among the characteristic plants.

May 1st. The air is rough, and overcoats pleasant. The sky is blue, and the day bright. Our road was over a plain, toward the foot of the mountain; *Zygophyllum Californicum*, now in bloom with a small yellow flower, is characteristic of the country; and cacti were very abundant, and in rich fresh bloom, which wonderfully ornaments this poor country.

We encamped at a spring in the pass which had been the site of an old village; here we found excellent grass, but very little water. We dug out the old spring, and watered some of our animals. The mountain here was wooded very slightly with the nut pine, cedars, and a dwarf species of oak; and among the shrubs were *Purshia tridentata*, artemisia, and *Ephedra occidentalis*. The numerous shrubs which constitute the vegetation of the plains are now in bloom, with flowers of white, yellow, red, and purple. The continual rocks, and want of water and grass, begin to be very hard on our mules and horses; but the principal loss is occasioned by their crippled feet, the greater part of those left being in excellent order, and scarcely a day passes without some loss; and, one by one, Fuentes horses are constantly dropping behind. Whenever they give out he dismounts and cuts off their tails and manes to make saddle girths—the last advantage one can gain from them.

The next day, in a short but rough ride of twelve miles, we crossed the mountain and, descending to a small valley-plain, encamped at the foot of the ridge, on the bed of a creek, where we found good grass in sufficient quantity, and abundance of water in holes. The ridge is extremely rugged and broken, presenting on this side a continued precipice, and probably affords very few passes. Many Digger tracks are seen around us, but no Indians were visible.

May 3d. After a day's journey of eighteen miles, in a northeasterly direction, we encamped in the midst of another very large basin, at a camping ground called Las Vegas [13]—a term which the Spaniards use to signify fertile or marshy plains, in contradistinction to llanos, which they apply to dry and sterile plains. Two narrow streams of clear water, four or five feet deep, gush suddenly, with a quick current, from two singularly large springs; these, and other waters of the basin, pass out in a gap to the eastward. The taste of the water is good, but rather too warm to be agreeable, the temperature being 71° in the one and 73° in the other. They, however, afforded a delightful bathing place.

May 4th. We started this morning earlier than usual, traveling in a northeasterly direction across the plain. The new acacia (*Spirolobium odoratum*) has now become the characteristic tree of the country; it is in bloom, and its blossoms are very fragrant. The day was still, and the heat, which soon became very oppressive, appeared to bring out strongly the refreshing scent of the zygophyllaceous shrubs and the sweet perfume of the acacia. The snowy ridge we had just crossed looked out conspicuously in the northwest. In about five hours' ride we crossed a gap in the surrounding ridge, and the appearance of skeletons of horses very soon warned us that we were engaged in another dry jornada, which proved the longest we had made in all our journey—between fifty and sixty miles without a drop of water.

Travelers through countries affording water and timber can have no conception of our intolerable thirst while journeying over the hot yellow sands of this elevated country, where the heated air seems to be entirely deprived of moisture. We ate occasionally the bisnada, and moistened our mouths with the acid of the sour dock (*Rumex venosus*). Hourly expecting to find water, we continued to press on until toward midnight, when, after a hard and uninterrupted march of sixteen hours, our wild mules began running ahead, and in a mile or two we came to a bold running stream—so keen is the sense of that animal, in these desert regions, in scenting at a distance this necessary of life.

According to the information we had received Sevier River was a tributary of the Colorado; and this, accordingly, should have been one of its affluents. It proved to be the Rio de los Angeles (River of the Angels)—a branch of the Rio Virgen (River of the Virgin).

May 5th. On account of our animals, it was necessary to remain today at this place. Indians crowded numerously around us in the morning; and we were obliged to keep arms in hand all day, to keep them out of the camp. They began to surround the horses, which, for the convenience of grass, we were guarding a little above, on the river. These were immediatly driven in, and kept close to the camp.

In the darkness of the night we had made a very bad encampment, our fires being commanded by a rocky bluff within fifty yards; but, notwithstanding, we had the river and small thickets of willows on the other side. Several times during the day the camp was insulted by the Indians; but peace being our object, I kept simply on the defensive. Some of the Indians were on the bottoms, and others haranguing us from the bluffs; and they were scattered in every direction over the hills. Their language being probably a dialect of the Utah, with the aid of signs some of our people could comprehend them very well. They were the same people who had murdered the Mexicans; and toward us their disposition was evidently hostile, nor were we well disposed toward them. They were barefooted and nearly naked, their hair gathered up into a knot behind; and with his bow each man carried a quiver with thirty or forty arrows, partially drawn out. Besides these, each held in his hand two or three arrows for instant service. Their arrows are barbed with a very clear translucent stone, a species of opal [14] nearly as hard as the diamond, and shot from their long bows, are almost as effective as a gunshot. In these Indians I was forcibly struck by an expression of countenance resembling that in a beast of prey, and all their actions are those of wild animals. Joined to the restless motion of the eye there is a want of mind—an absence of thought—and an action wholly by impulse, strongly expressed, and which constantly recalls the similarity.

A man who appeared to be a chief, with two or three others, forced himself into camp, bringing with him his arms, in spite of my orders to the contrary. When shown our weapons, he bored his ears with his fingers, and said he could not hear. "Why," said he, "there are none of you." Counting the people around the camp, and including in the number a mule which was being shod, he made out twenty-two. "So many," said he, showing the number, "and we—we are a great many"; and he pointed to the hills and mountains round about. "If you have your arms," said he, twanging his bow, "we have these." I had some difficulty in restraining the people, particularly Carson, who felt an insult of this kind as much as if it had been given by a more responsible being. "Don't say that, old man," said he; "don't you say that, your life's in danger"—speaking in good English—and probably the old man was nearer to his end than he will be before he meets it.

Several animals had been necessarily left behind near the camp last night, and early in the morning, before the Indians made their appearance, several men were sent to bring them in. When I was beginning to be uneasy at their absence, they returned with information that the animals had been driven off from the trail by Indians; and, having followed the tracks a short distance, they found them cut up and spread out upon bushes.

In the evening I gave a fatigued horse to some of the Indians for a feast; and the village which carried him off refused to share with the others, who made loud complaints from the rocks of the partial distribution. Many of these Indians had long sticks, hooked at the end, which they used in hauling out lizards and other small animals from their holes. During the day they occasionally roasted and ate lizards at our fires. These belong to the people who are generally known under the name of Diggers; and to these I have more particularly had reference when occasionally speaking of a people whose sole occupation is to procure food sufficient to support existence.

The formation here consists of fine yellow sandstone, alternating with a coarse conglomerate, in which the stones are from the size of ordinary gravel to six or eight inches in diameter. This is the formation which renders the surface of the country so rocky, and gives us now a road alternately of loose, heavy sands and rolled stones, which cripple the animals in a most extraordinary manner.

On the following morning we left the Rio de los Angeles, and continued our way through the same desolate and revolting country, where lizards were the only animal, and the tracks of the lizard-eaters the principal sign of human beings. After twenty miles' march through a road of hills and heavy sands we reached the most dreary river I have ever seen—a deep, rapid stream, almost a torrent, passing swiftly by and roaring against obstructions. The banks were wooded with willow, acacia, and a frequent plant of the country already mentioned (*Garrya elliptica*), growing in thickets, resembling willow, and bearing a small pink flower.

Crossing it, we encamped on the left bank, where we found a very little grass. Our three remaining steers, being entirely given out, were killed here. By the boiling-point the elevation of the river here is four thousand and sixty feet, and latitude, by observation, 36° 41′ 33″. The stream was running toward the southwest, and appeared to come from a snowy mountain in the north. It proved to be the Rio Virgen—a tributary to the Colorado.

Indians appeared in bands on the hills, but did not come into camp. For several days we continued our journey up the river, the bottoms of which were thickly overgrown with various kinds of brush; and the sandy soil was absolutely covered with the tracks of Diggers, who followed us stealthily, like a band of wolves; and we had no opportunity to leave behind, even for a few hours, the tired animals, in order that they might be brought into camp after a little repose. A horse or mule left behind was taken off in a moment.

On the evening of the 8th, having traveled twenty-eight miles up the river from our first encampment on it, we encamped at a little grass plat where a spring of cool water issued from the bluff. On the opposite side was a grove of cottonwoods at the mouth of a fork, which here enters the river. On either side, the valley is bounded by ranges of mountains, everywhere high, rocky, and broken. The caravan road was lost and scattered in the sandy country, and we had been following an Indian trail up the river. The hunters the next day were sent out to reconnoiter, and in the meantime we moved about a mile farther up, where we found a good little patch of grass. There being only sufficient grass for the night, the horses were sent with a strong guard in charge of Tabeau to a neighboring hollow, where they might pasture during the day; and to be ready in case the Indians should make any attempt on the animals, several of the best horses were picketed at the camp. In a few hours the hunters returned, having found a convenient ford in the river and discovered the Spanish Trail on the other side.

I had been engaged in arranging plants and, fatigued with the heat of the day, I fell asleep in the afternoon and did not awake until sundown. Presently Carson came to me and reported that Tabeau, who early in the day had left his post, and, without my knowledge, rode back to the camp we had left, in search of a lame mule, had not returned. While we were speaking a smoke rose suddenly from the cottonwood grove below, which plainly told us what had befallen him; it was raised to inform the surrounding Indians that a blow had been struck, and to tell them to be on their guard. Carson, with several men well mounted, was instantly sent down the river, but returned in the night without tidings of the missing man. They went to the camp we had left, but neither he nor the mule was there. Searching down the river, they found the tracks of the mule, evidently driven along by Indians, whose tracks were on each side of those made by the animal. After going several miles they came to the mule itself, standing in some bushes, mortally wounded in the side by an arrow, and left to die, that it might be afterward butchered for food. They also found, in another place, as they were hunting about on the ground for Tabeau's tracks, something that looked like a little puddle of blood, but which the darkness prevented them from verifying. With these details they returned to our camp, and their report saddened all our hearts.

May 10th. This morning, as soon as there was light enough to follow tracks, I set out myself with Mr. Fitzpatrick and several men in search of Tabeau. We went to the spot where the appearance of puddled blood had been seen, and this, we saw at once, had been the place where he fell and died. Blood upon the leaves and beaten-down bushes showed that he had got his wound about twenty paces from where he fell, and that he had struggled for his life. He had probably been shot through the lungs with an arrow. From the place where he lay and bled, it could be seen that he had been dragged to the bank of the river, and thrown into it. No vestige of what had belonged to him could be found, except a fragment of his horse equipment. Horse, gun, clothes—all became the prey of these Arabs of the New World.

Tableau had been one of our best men, and his unhappy death spread a gloom over our party. Men who have gone through such dangers and sufferings as we had seen become like brothers, and feel each other's loss. To defend and avenge each other is the deep feeling of all. We wished to avenge his death; but the condition of our horses, languishing for grass and repose, forbade an expedition into unknown mountains. We knew the tribe who had done the mischief—the same which had been insulting our camp. They knew what they deserved, and had the discretion to show themselves to us no more. The day before, they infested our camp; now, not one appeared; nor did we ever afterward see but one who even belonged to the same tribe, and he at a distance.

Our camp was in a basin below a deep cañon—a gap of two thousand feet deep in the mountain—through which the Rio Virgen passes, and where no man or beast could follow it. The Spanish Trail, which we had lost in the sands of the basin, was on the opposite side of the river. We crossed over to it, and followed it northwardly toward a gap which was visible in the mountain. We approached it by a defile, rendered difficult for our barefooted animals by the rocks strewed along it; and here the country changed its character. From the time we entered the desert, the mountains had been bald and rocky; here they began to be wooded with cedar and pine, and clusters of trees gave shelter to birds—a new and welcome sight—which could not have lived in the desert we had passed.

Descending a long hollow toward the narrow valley of a stream, we saw before us a snowy mountain, far beyond which appeared another, more lofty still. Good bunch grass began to appear on the hillsides, and here we found a singular variety of interesting shrubs.

The changed appearance of the country infused among our people a more lively spirit, which was heightened by finding at evening a halting place of very good grass on the clear waters of the Santa Clara Fork of the Rio Virgen.

May 11th. The morning was cloudy and quite cool, with a shower of rain—the first we have had since entering the desert, a period of twenty-seven days; and we seem to have entered a different climate, with the usual weather of the Rocky Mountains. Our march today was very laborious, over very broken ground, along the Santa Clara River; but then the country is no longer so distressingly desolate.

The stream is prettily wooded with sweet cottonwood trees—some of them of large size; and on the hills, where the nut pine is often seen, a good and wholesome grass occurs frequently. This cottonwood, which is now in fruit, is of a different species from any in Michaux's *Sylva.* Heavy dark clouds covered the sky in the evening, and a cold wind sprang up making fires and overcoats comfortable.

May 12th. A little above our encampment the river forked, and we continued up the right-hand branch, gradually ascending toward the summit of the mountain. As we rose toward the head of the creek the snowy mountains on our right showed out handsomely—high, and rugged with precipices, and covered with snow for about two thousand feet from their summits down.

Our animals were somewhat repaid for their hard marches by an excellent camping ground on the summit of the ridge, which forms here the dividing chain between the waters of the Rio Virgen, which goes south to the Colorado, and those of Sevier River, flowing northwardly, and belonging to the Great Basin. We considered ourselves as crossing the rim of the basin; and, entering it at this point, we found here an extensive mountain meadow, rich in bunch grass, and fresh with numerous springs of clear water, all refreshing and delightful to look upon. It was, in fact, those Las Vegas de Santa Clara,[15] which had been so long presented to us as the terminating point of the desert, and where the annual caravan from California to New Mexico halted and recruited for some weeks. It was a very suitable place to recover from the fatigue and exhaustion of a month's suffering in the hot and sterile desert. The meadow was about a mile wide and some ten miles long, bordered by grassy hills and mountains—some of the latter rising two thousand feet,

and white with snow down to the level of the Vegas. Its elevation
above the sea was five thousand two hundred and eighty feet; latitude, by observation, 37° 28′ 28″; and its distance from where we
first struck the Spanish Trail about four hundred miles.

Counting from the time we reached the desert, and began to
skirt, at our descent from Walker's Pass in the Sierra Nevada, we
had traveled five hundred and fifty miles, occupying twenty-seven
days, in that inhospitable region. In passing before the great caravan we had the advantage of finding more grass, but the disadvantage of finding also the marauding savages who had gathered down
upon the trail, waiting the approach of that prey. This greatly increased our labors, besides costing us the life of an excellent man.
We had to move all day in a state of watch and prepared for combat—scouts and flankers out, a front and rear division of our men,
and baggage animals in the center. At night, camp duty was severe.
Those who had toiled all day had to guard, by turns, the camp and
the horses all night. Frequently one-third of the whole party were
on guard at once; and nothing but this vigilance saved us from
attack. We were constantly dogged by bands, and even whole
tribes of the marauders; and although Tabeau was killed, and our
camp infested and insulted by some, while swarms of them remained on the hills and mountainsides, there was manifestly a consultation and calculation going on to decide the question of attacking us.

Having reached the resting place of the Vegas de Santa Clara
we had complete relief from the heat and privations of the desert,
and some relaxation from the severity of camp duty. Some relaxation, and relaxation only—for camp guards, horse guards, and scouts
are indispensable from the time of leaving the frontiers of Missouri
until we return to them.

After we left the Vegas we had the gratification to be joined by
the famous hunter and trapper Mr. Joseph Walker,[16] whom I have
before mentioned, and who now became our guide. He had left
California with the great caravan; and perceiving, from the signs
along the trail, that there was a party of whites ahead, which he
judged to be mine, he detached himself from the caravan with eight
men (Americans), and ran the gantlet of the desert robbers, killing
two and getting some of the horses wounded, and succeeded in

overtaking us. Nothing but his great knowledge of the country, great courage and presence of mind, and good rifles could have brought him safe from such a perilous enterprise.

May 13th. We remained one day at this noted place of rest and refreshment, and, resuming our progress in a northeastwardly direction, we descended into a broad valley, the water of which is tributary to Sevier Lake. The next day we came in sight of the Wasatch range of mountains on the right, white with snow, and here forming the southeast part of the Great Basin. Sevier Lake, upon the waters of which we now were, belonged to the system of lakes in the eastern part of the basin—of which the Great Salt Lake and its southern limb, the Utah Lake,[17] were the principal—toward the region of which we were now approaching. We traveled for several days in this direction, within the rim of the Great Basin, crossing little streams which bore to the left for Sevier Lake; and plainly seeing, by the changed aspect of the country, that we were entirely clear of the desert and approaching the regions which appertained to the system of the Rocky Mountains. We met, in this traverse, a few mounted Utah Indians, in advance of their main body, watching the approach of the great caravan.

May 16th. We reached a small salt lake, about seven miles long and one broad, at the northern extremity of which we encamped for the night. This little lake, which well merits its characteristic name, lies immediately at the base of the Wasatch range, and nearly opposite a gap in that chain of mountains through which the Spanish Trail passes, and which, again falling upon the waters of the Colorado and crossing the river, proceeds over a mountainous country to Santa Fe.

May 17th. After four hundred and forty miles of traveling on a trail which served for a road, we again found ourselves under the necessity of exploring a track through the wilderness. The Spanish Trail had borne off to the southeast, crossing the Wasatch range. Our course led to the northeast, along the foot of that range, and leaving it on the right. The mountain presented itself to us under the form of several ridges, rising one above the other, rocky, and wooded with pine and cedar, the last ridge covered with snow. Sevier River,[18] flowing northwardly to the lake of the same name, collects its principal waters from this section of the Wasatch chain.

We had now entered a region of great pastoral promise, abounding with fine streams; the rich bunch grass—soil that would produce wheat and indigenous flax—growing as if it had been sown. Consistent with the general character of its bordering mountains, this fertility of soil and vegetation does not extend far into the Great Basin. Mr. Joseph Walker, our guide, and who has more knowledge of these parts than any man I know, informed me that all the country to the left was unknown to him, and that even the Digger tribes, which frequented Lake Sevier, could tell him nothing about it.

May 20th. We met a band of Utah Indians, headed by a chief who had obtained the American or English name of Walker, by which he is quoted and well known. They were all mounted, armed with rifles, and use their rifles well. The chief had a fusee, which he had carried slung, in addition to his rifle. They were journeying slowly toward the Spanish Trail, to levy their usual tribute upon the great Californian caravan. They were robbers of a higher order than those of the desert. They conducted their depredations with form, and under the color of trade, and toll for passing through their country. Instead of attacking and killing, they affect to purchase—taking the horses they like and giving something nominal in return. The chief was quite civil to me. He was personally acquainted with his namesake, our guide, who made my name known to him. He knew of my expedition of 1842; and, as tokens of friendship and proof that we had met, proposed an interchange of presents. We had no great store to choose out of, so he gave me a Mexican blanket, and I gave him a very fine one which I had obtained at Vancouver.

May 23d. We reached Sevier River—the main tributary of the lake of the same name—which, deflecting from its northern course, here breaks from the mountains to enter the lake. It was really a fine river, from eight to twelve feet deep, and after searching in vain for a fordable place, we made little boats (or rather rafts) out of bulrushes, and ferried across. These rafts are readily made, and give a good conveyance across a river. The rushes are bound in bundles and tied hard; the bundles are tied down upon poles, as close as they can be pressed, and fashioned like a boat in being broader in the middle and pointed at the ends. The rushes, being tubular and jointed, are light and strong. The raft swims well, and is shoved along by poles, or paddled, or pushed and pulled by swimmers, or drawn by ropes. On this occasion we used ropes—one at each end—and rapidly drew our little float backward and forward, from shore to shore. The horses swam.

At our place of crossing, which was the most northern point of its bend, the latitude was 39° 22′ 19″. The banks sustained the character of fertility and vegetation which we had seen for some days. The name of this river and lake was an indication of our approach to regions of which our people had been the explorers. It was probably named after some American trapper or hunter, and was the first American name we had met with since leaving the Columbia River. From the Dalles to the point where we turned across the Sierra Nevada, near one thousand miles, we heard Indian names, and the greater part of the distance none; from Nueva Helvetia (Sacramento) to Las Vegas de Santa Clara, about one thousand more, all were Spanish; from the Mississippi to the Pacific, French and American or English were intermixed; and this prevalence of names indicates the national character of the first explorers.

We had here the misfortune to lose one of our people, François Badeau, who had been with me in both expeditions, during which he had always been one of my most faithful and efficient men. He was killed in drawing toward him a gun by the muzzle; the hammer, being caught, discharged the gun, driving the ball through his head. We buried him on the banks of the river.

Crossing the next day a slight ridge along the river, we entered a handsome mountain valley covered with fine grass, and directed our course toward a high snowy peak, at the foot of which lay the Utah Lake. On our right was a ridge of high mountains, their summits covered with snow, constituting the dividing ridge between the basin waters and those of the Colorado. At noon we fell in with a party of Utah Indians coming out of the mountain, and in the afternoon encamped on a tributary to the lake, which is separated from the waters of the Sevier by very slight dividing grounds.

Early the next day we came in sight of the lake; and as we descended to the broad bottoms of the Spanish Fork, three horsemen were seen galloping toward us, who proved to be Utah Indians—scouts from a village which was encamped near the mouth of the river. They were armed with rifles and their horses were in good condition. We encamped near them, on the Spanish Fork, which is one of the principal tributaries to the lake. Finding the Indians troublesome, and desirous to remain here a day, we removed the next morning farther down the lake, and encamped on a fertile bottom near the foot of the same mountainous ridge which borders the Great Salt Lake, and along which we had journeyed the previous September. . . .*

We had now accomplished an object we had in view when leaving the Dalles of the Columbia in November last: we had reached the Utah Lake; but by a route very different from what we had intended, and without sufficient time remaining to make the examinations which were desired. It is a lake of note in this country, under the dominion of the Utahs, who resort to it for fish. Its greatest breadth is about fifteen miles, stretching far to the north, narrowing as it goes, and connecting with the Great Salt Lake. This is the report, and I believe it to be correct; but it is fresh water, while the other is not only salt, but a saturated solution of salt; and here is a problem which requires to be solved. It is almost entirely surrounded by mountains, walled on the north and east by a high and snowy range, which supplies to it a fan of tributary streams. Among these the principal river is the Timpan-ogo [19]—signifying Rock River—a name which the rocky grandeur of its scenery, remarkable even in this country of rugged mountains, has obtained for it from the Indians. In the Utah language, *og-wáhbe*, the term for river, when coupled with other words in common conversation, is usually abbreviated to *ogo, timpan* signifying rock. It is probable that this river furnished the name which on the older maps has been generally applied to the Great Salt Lake; but for this I have preferred a name which will be regarded as highly characteristic, restricting to the river the descriptive term Timpan-ogo, and leaving for the lake into which it flows the name of the people who reside on its shores, and by which it is known throughout the country.

The volume of water afforded by the Timpan-ogo is probably equal to that of the Sevier River; and, at the time of our visit, there was only one place in the lake valley at which the Spanish Fork was fordable. In the range of mountains along its eastern shore the lake is bordered by a plain, where the soil is generally good and in

* A paragraph of botanical detail omitted.

greater part fertile, watered by a delta of prettily timbered streams. This would be an excellent locality for stock farms; it is generally covered with good bunch grass, and would abundantly produce the ordinary grains.

In arriving at the Utah Lake we had completed an immense circuit, of twelve degrees diameter north and south and ten degrees east and west; and found ourselves in May, 1844, on the same sheet of water which we had left in September, 1843. The Utah is the southern limb of the Great Salt Lake; and thus we had seen that remarkable sheet of water both at its northern and southern extremity, and were able to fix its position at these two points.

The circuit which we had made, and which had cost us eight months of time and three thousand five hundred miles of traveling, had given us a view of Oregon and of North California from the Rocky Mountains to the Pacific Ocean, and of the two principal streams which form bays or harbors on the coast of that sea. Having completed this circuit, and being now about to turn the back upon the Pacific slope of our continent and to recross the Rocky Mountains, it is natural to look back upon our footsteps and take some brief view of the leading features and general structure of the country we had traversed.

These are peculiar and striking, and differ essentially from the Atlantic side of our country. The mountains are all higher, more numerous, and more distinctly defined in their ranges and directions; and, what is so contrary to the natural order of such formations, one of these ranges, which is near the coast (the Sierra Nevada and the Coast Range), presents higher elevations and peaks than any which are to be found in the Rocky Mountains themselves. In our eight months' circuit we were never out of sight of snow; and the Sierra Nevada, where we crossed it, was near two thousand feet higher than the South Pass in the Rocky Mountains. In height these mountains greatly exceed those of the Atlantic side, constantly presenting peaks which enter the region of eternal snow; and some of them volcanic and in a frequent state of activity. They are seen at great distances, and guide the traveler in his courses.

The course and elevation of these ranges give direction to the rivers and character to the coast. No great river does, or can, take its rise below the Cascade and Sierra Nevada range; the distance to the sea is too short to admit of it. The rivers of the San Francisco Bay, which are the largest after the Columbia, are local to that bay and lateral to the coast, having their sources about on a line with the Dalles of the Columbia, and running each in a valley of its own, between the Coast Range and the Cascade and Sierra Nevada range. The Columbia is the only river which traverses the whole breadth of the country, breaking through all the ranges, and entering the sea. Drawing its waters from a section of ten degrees of latitude in the Rocky Mountains, which are collected into one stream by three main forks (Lewis', Clark's, and the North Fork) near the center of the Oregon Valley, this great river thence proceeds by a single channel to the sea, while its three forks lead each to a pass in the mountains, which opens the way into the interior of the continent. This fact in relation to the rivers of this region gives an immense value to the Columbia. Its mouth is the only inlet and outlet to and from the sea; its three forks lead to the passes in the mountains; it is, therefore, the only line of communication between the Pacific and the interior of North America; and all operations of war or commerce, of national or social intercourse, must be conducted upon it. This gives it a value beyond estimation, and would involve irreparable injury if lost. In this unity and concentration of its waters the Pacific side of our continent differs entirely from the Atlantic side, where the waters of the Alleghany Mountains are dispersed into many rivers, having their different entrances into the sea, and opening many lines of communication with the interior.

The Pacific coast is equally different from that of the Atlantic. The coast of the Atlantic is low and open, indented with numerous bays, sounds, and river estuaries, accessible everywhere, and opening by many channels into the heart of the country. The Pacific coast, on the contrary, is high and compact, with few bays, and but one that opens into the heart of the country. The immediate coast is what seamen call ironbound. A little within, it is skirted by two successive ranges of mountains, standing as ramparts between the sea and the interior country, and to get through which there is but one gate, and that narrow and easily defended. This structure of the coast, backed by these two ranges of mountains, with its concentration and unity of waters, gives to the country an immense military strength and will probably render Oregon the most impregnable country in the world.

Differing so much from the Atlantic side of our continent, in coast, mountains, and rivers, the Pacific side differs from it in another most rare and singular feature—that of the great interior basin, of which I have so often spoken, and the whole form and character of which I was so anxious to ascertain. Its existence is vouched for by such of the American traders and hunters as have some knowledge of that region; the structure of the Sierra Nevada range of mountains requires it to be there; and my own observations confirm it.

Mr. Joseph Walker, who is so well acquainted in those parts, informed me that, from the Great Salt Lake west, there was a succession of lakes and rivers which have no outlet to the sea, nor any connection with the Columbia, or with the Colorado of the Gulf of California. He described some of these lakes as being large, with numerous streams, and even considerable rivers, falling into them. In fact, all concur in the general report of these interior rivers and lakes; and, for want of understanding the force and power of evaporation, which so soon establishes an equilibrium between the loss and supply of waters, the fable of whirlpools and subterraneous outlets has gained belief as the only imaginable way of carrying off the waters which have no visible discharge.

The structure of the country would require this formation of interior lakes; for the waters which would collect between the Rocky Mountains and the Sierra Nevada, not being able to cross this formidable barrier, nor to get to the Columbia or the Colorado, must naturally collect into reservoirs, each of which would have its little system of streams and rivers to supply it. This would be the natural effect, and what I saw went to confirm it. The Great Salt Lake is a formation of this kind, and quite a large one; having many streams, and one considerable river, four or five hundred miles long, falling into it. This lake and river I saw and examined myself; and also saw the Wasatch and Bear River Mountains, which enclose the waters of the lake on the east and constitute, in that quarter, the rim of the Great Basin.

Afterward, along the eastern base of the Sierra Nevada, where we traveled for forty-two days, I saw the line of lakes and rivers which lie at the foot of that sierra; and which sierra is the western rim of the Basin. In going down Lewis' Fork and the main Columbia, I crossed only inferior streams coming in from the left, such as could draw their water from a short distance only; and I often saw the mountains at their heads, white with snow which, all accounts said, divided the waters of the desert from those of the Columbia, and which could be no other than the range of mountains which form the rim of the basin on its northern side. And in returning from California along the Spanish Trail, as far as the head of the Santa Clara Fork of the Rio Virgen, I crossed only small streams making their way south to the Colorado, or lost in sand—as the Mohave; while to the left, lofty mountains, their summits white with snow, were often visible, and which must have turned water to the north as well as to the south, and thus constituted, on this part, the southern rim of the basin.

At the head of the Santa Clara Fork, and in the Vegas de Santa Clara, we crossed the ridge which parted the two systems of waters. We entered the basin at that point, and have traveled in it ever since, having its southeastern rim (the Wasatch Mountain) on the right, and crossing the streams which flow down into it. The existence of the basin is, therefore, an established fact in my mind; its extent and contents are yet to be better ascertained. It cannot be less than four or five hundred miles each way, and must lie principally in the Alta California; the demarcation latitude of 42° probably cutting a segment from the north part of the rim. Of its interior but little is known. It is called a desert, and from what I saw of it, sterility may be its prominent characteristic; but where there is so much water there must be some oases. The great river and the great lake, reported, may not be equal to the report; but where there is so much snow there must be streams; and where there is no outlet there must be lakes to hold the accumulated waters, or sands to swallow them up. In this eastern part of the basin, containing Sevier, Utah, and the Great Salt lakes, and the rivers and creeks falling into them, we know there is good soil and good grass adapted to civilized settlements. In the western part, on Salmon Trout River and some other streams, the same remark may be made.

The contents of this Great Basin are yet to be examined. That it is peopled we know, but miserably and sparsely. From all that I heard and saw, I should say that humanity here appeared in its lowest form and in its most elementary state. Dispersed in single families; without firearms; eating seeds and insects; digging roots (and hence their name)—such is the condition of the greater part. Others are a degree higher, and live in communities upon some lake or river that supplies fish, and from which they repulse the miserable Digger. The rabbit is the largest animal known in this desert; its flesh affords a little meat, and their baglike covering is made of its skins. The wild sage is their only wood, and here it is of extraordinary size—sometimes a foot in diameter, and six or eight feet high. It serves for fuel, for building material, for shelter to the rabbits, and for some sort of covering for the feet and legs in cold weather. Such are the accounts of the inhabitants and productions of the Great Basin, and which, though imperfect, must have some foundation, and excite our desire to know the whole.

The whole idea of such a desert, and such a people, is a novelty in our country, and excites Asiatic, not American, ideas. Interior basins, with their own systems of lakes and rivers, and often sterile, are common enough in Asia; people still in the elementary state of families, living in deserts, with no other occupation than the mere animal search for food, may still be seen in that ancient quarter of the globe; but in America such things are new and strange, unknown and unsuspected, and discredited when related. But I flatter myself that what is discovered, though not enough to satisfy curiosity, is sufficient to excite it, and that subsequent explorations will complete what has been commenced.

This account of the Great Basin, it will be remembered, belongs to the Alta California, and has no application to Oregon, whose capabilities may justify a separate remark. Referring to my journal for particular descriptions, and for sectional boundaries between good and bad districts, I can only say, in general and comparative terms, that in the branch of agriculture which implies the cultivation of grains and staple crops, it would be inferior to the Atlantic States, though many parts are superior for wheat, while in the rearing of flocks and herds it would claim a high place. Its grazing capabilities are great; and even in the indigenous grass now there, an element of individual and national wealth may be found. In fact, the valuable grasses begin within one hundred and fifty miles of the

Missouri frontier, and extend to the Pacific Ocean. East of the
Rocky Mountains it is the short curly grass on which the buffalo
delight to feed, (whence its name of buffalo) and which is still
good when dry and apparently dead.

West of those mountains it is a larger growth, in clusters, and
hence called bunch grass, and which has a second or fall growth.
Plains and mountains both exhibit them; and I have seen good
pasturage at an elevation of ten thousand feet. In this spontaneous
product, the trading or traveling caravans can find subsistence for
their animals; and in military operations any number of cavalry may
be moved and any number of cattle may be driven; and thus men
and horses be supported on long expeditions, and even in winter in
the sheltered situations.

Commercially, the value of the Oregon country must be great,
washed as it is by the North Pacific Ocean; fronting Asia; producing
many of the elements of commerce; mild and healthy in its climate;
and becoming, as it naturally will, a thoroughfare for the East India
and China trade.

Turning our faces once more eastward, on the morning of the
27th we left the Utah Lake.

FOOTNOTES

1. John Augustus Sutter (1803–1880), whose patronymic when he was born
in Switzerland was Suter, had come to the United States in 1834. After some
years of wandering, which took him to St. Louis, Santa Fe, the Oregon
country, Alaska, and the Hawaiian Islands, he finally established himself on a
large land grant from the Mexican Government in the Sacramento Valley.
The account which Frémont gives of his fort and colony is accurate. It was to
be only a few years until he was literally ruined by the discovery of gold on
his lands, bringing a horde of gold-mad adventurers.

2. This was the man deranged by the hardships of the Sierra crossing.

3. Frémont had stayed at Sutter's Fort twelve days. As Dellenbaugh says,
he had undoubtedly obtained all the information he could get on California,
the political unrest in the province, and the miserable character of the Mexican
soldiers there.

4. That is, the fertile San Joaquin Valley; the river of that name being about
325 miles long. So far as the knowledge of Americans went, this was still
almost unknown territory; no description had ever been given Easterners. The
coast was of course familiar ground. Frémont was eager to see as much new
geography as possible.

5. A mistake; this was the Tuolumne, not the Merced.

6. At a later date Frémont named these waters Kern River and Kern Lake,
appellations which became permanent.

7. As they were at the edge of the Mohave Desert, the prospect was indeed desolate. The pass Frémont mentions was the Tehachapi, now traversed by the Santa Fe Railroad.

8. Frémont is speaking of the Joshua tree, which belongs to the yucca family, and grows in desert regions.

9. The two great southern routes from Santa Fe to California were the Gila Trail and the Spanish Trail. The Spanish Trail was marked out by William Wolfskill in 1830–31. He left Taos in the fall, crossed the Grand and Green rivers and the Wasatch Mountains, reached the Sevier River and followed it for a time, went on southwest on the Virgin River, crossed the Mohave Desert, and proceeded to Los Angeles. This trail soon became a well-known artery of trade. In gold-rush days, many emigrants used both it and the Gila Trail.

10. The Mohave (Frémont's spelling, Mohahve) Indians, of Yuman linguistic stock, lived in the Colorado Valley in California and Arizona, where they carried on agriculture.

11. These are the Hopi Indians, and "Colorado" here of course means the river valley. The Hopi belonged to the Uto-Aztecan family, and lived in mesa villages (pueblos) in northern Arizona.

12. Frémont's name has proved permanent; the Mohave River rises in the San Bernardino Range and flows about a hundred miles before it sinks into the Mohave Desert.

13. Las Vegas, in southern Nevada, near the Colorado River, today famous as an active resort city, was known at this time as a watering place on the Spanish Trail to Los Angeles. It offered the wayfarers good water, grass, and mesquite fuel. Indeed, it was an oasis in an otherwise generally repellent region. Later, in 1855, the Mormons were to build a short-lived fort here, and in 1864 the United States Army was to erect Fort Baker.

14. Obsidian.

15. This "extensive mountain meadow" was later called Mountain Meadows— the site of the infamous massacre of a party of Missouri emigrants in 1857 by Mormons and Indians.

16. Joseph Walker, whose name is sprinkled over the Western map, is remembered chiefly for the expedition he headed in 1833 (at the instance of Captain Bonneville) to explore the West, and especially Great Salt Lake. They traversed an immense amount of territory in the Great Basin and California, crossed the Sierra twice (once by Walker's Pass), and went as far north as the Snake River—but they did not visit the lake! Frémont could have found no better guide.

17. Utah Lake, as Joseph Walker could easily have told Frémont, is not connected with Great Salt Lake.

18. The Sevier River, rising in southwestern Utah, flows northward (as Frémont writes) to escape from the mountains, and southwest to the salt Sevier Lake.

19. Timpanogos is now the accepted spelling.

CHAPTER 10

The Third Expedition: Benton, Bancroft, Buchanan Eager to Gain California: Preparations *

THE eight months that I was to have been absent had extended to fourteen. Mrs. Frémont had been waiting in Saint Louis for me and suspense had deepened into anxiety, for no word had been heard from me after I had left the Lower Columbia in November of '43. The Secretary of War, Mr. Wilkins, had offered to send a party of dragoons to search for me, but naturally it occurred to my friends to reply that if I could not find my way out the dragoons could not do it for me. In those days there was no communication possible to a party involved in the solitudes of the interior country beyond the mountains, and so it was that the first tidings of our safety were brought by myself when I reached Saint Louis in August of '44.[1]

In Saint Louis, where the risks and uncertainties of the mountain country were familiarly known, much sympathy had been felt for Mrs. Frémont as the time wore on and no intelligence came. Many warm expressions of welcome were given me, and we left for Washington animated and gratified by the hearty good wishes of strangers as well as friends.

I arranged for the two Indian boys, Juan and Gregorio, to winter on a property belonging to Mr. Benton, near Lexington, Kentucky. They took with them, to care for, a beautiful saddle horse which I had brought from California. He was to rest for the winter in the blue-grass region. Sacramento, as he was named, was gifted with

* For this chapter, we return again to the *Memoirs,* Vol. I, pp. 411ff., where Frémont takes up the story of the third and most eventful expedition. He prepared no report to the government detailing his travels, but evidently kept notes from which in 1886–87 he wrote this record.

428 NARRATIVES OF EXPLORATION AND ADVENTURE

two fine qualities—courage, and a remarkable power for leaping—a specialty with him. He was beautifully made, an iron-gray of the best California stock, about four years old, well trained, a perfect saddle horse.

Chinook I took with me to Washington. He parted with regret from the other boys, but every feeling was soon absorbed in the delight of "seeing the whites" in their own homes and strange ways of travel.

I found the family well, but several lives had gone out from the circle of our friends. Mr. Nicollet, Mr. Hassler, and Senator Linn had died soon after my leaving in '43. The death of Mr. Nicollet in September, '43, though expected, was sudden. From being restless he had become morbid and solitary, going off alone like a wounded animal trying to escape from its hurt. He had come up to Washington and had gone to a hotel, where he was accidentally found by a friend of the Benton family, Dr. Martin. In his illness former scenes and his own language had taken possession of his mind, and it seems that he had not been able to make himself known to the people of the house. The clerk at the office told Dr. Martin of the unknown French gentleman, and asked him to see who it was. The doctor found him in this condition and arranged to notify his friends and have him removed at once to Baltimore. When he came for him the next morning it was too late. He had died in the night, alone. It was the ending of a good, and useful, and pleasing life. I deeply regretted him, and missed long his friendly and considerate presence.

After all it would have been a fitter end for him to have died under the open sky—and be buried, rolled up in a blanket, by the side of some stream in the mountains—than to have had life close in the night and alone at a hotel.

Mr. Hassler died in Philadelphia in the November of the same year. More fortunate than Mr. Nicollet, he was in the midst of his family. This distinguished man was introduced here by his countryman, Albert Gallatin; and through him was sent as scientific ambassador to London and Paris with the outfit and salary of a foreign minister; so far as I know the only occasion when science has been so honored by this country.

In October, Mr. Benton's friend and colleague, Senator Linn, had also died. His death was a serious loss to the friends of Oregon. Mr. Linn, though of a most pleasing and courteous manner, was unyielding and persistent. This loss was felt, when in the following year a notice to England to terminate the joint occupation was introduced in the Senate. The idea was created by the opposition that this was "a conspiracy to force war" and the Eastern commercial interest was roused to alarm and brought to bear on the Senate—defeating the bill by 28 to 18.

On my arrival at Washington I reported my return to General Scott, and called upon the Secretary of War, Mr. [William] Wilkins, of Pennsylvania, who in his frank quick manner unaffectedly expressed surprise at my apparent youth, but pleasantly qualified this by saying that in my case it was a good failing, as young men never saw the obstacles.

I had now returned to the satisfactions and enjoyment of family life. Living so long on the memory only of this, it had become too unsubstantial. In the first weeks at Washington I had the great pleasure to see my mother again. During recent years this had become rare. To spare my time and be with me in the family surroundings she came to Washington and remained until the cold weather obliged me to take her back to the South. With her presence the past time of careless boyhood was linked in a most satisfied and happy way to the serious labor of the maturer years, which were advancing with their inevitable cares. A responsible Quaker family of Philadelphia asked to have charge of Chinook for the winter, and he was accordingly placed in their care. While settling myself to work in preparing the results of the journey I found my time constantly broken in upon.

To Mr. Preuss had been assigned the congenial labor of making up the maps. He was now owner of a comfortable home of his own, a good house near the Arsenal, which the locality brought within his means. The large front room he converted into his working room, where he had space and good light, and there was a lookout over the river, and a long bit of grassed ground where Preuss made an arbor and where he smoked his pipe as he watched his child playing and the cow grazing.

The interesting character of the regions visited by this expedition, California chiefly, drew much attention and brought me many letters and personal inquiries. It became impossible to reconcile attention to visitors with work in hand; and in order therefore to avoid this serious embarrassment I took for a workshop a small wooden two-story house not far from the residence of Mr. Benton. This was well apart from other buildings and had about it large enclosed grounds. I had here with me as assistant Mr. Joseph C. Hubbard, who, although no older than myself, was already a practical astronomer and a rapid and skillful computer, and with his aid the various calculations went fast. This was the occupation of the daylight. To keep ourselves in practice, both being fond of astronomical observations, we mounted a transit instrument, and the house being isolated, we were able to vary our work and have still an interesting point to it.

Wishing to prove the accuracy of a sextant by trying it against other observations, we went for several nights together quite late, when the streets were quiet and few passers to disturb the mercury, to a church near by where there was a large stone carriage step near the curb on which to set the horizon. Waiting for the stars which I wanted, to come into position, I rested more agreeably on the ground half lying against the stone. A few days afterward a deacon of this church, who lived opposite, called upon Mr. Benton, regretting that he had disagreeable information to give, which still he thought it his duty to impart to him. He said that for several nights he had seen his son-in-law in a state of gross intoxication lying on the pavement in front of the church, and apparently unwilling to allow a more sober companion who was with him to take him to the house.

Mr. Benton did not receive this charitable information in the grateful spirit which the informer had expected. On the contrary the deacon was first frightened and then humiliated. Mr. Benton made him understand that he had converted an honorable fact into a damaging falsehood—in the way that slanders often originate, taking the color of the mind from which engenders them.

After the computations came the writing of the Report. This had its great interest, but was still a task which required concentrated, systematic labor. Mrs. Frémont now worked with me daily at the little wooden house, but for her the work had its peculiar interest. Talking incidents over made her familiar with the minuter details of the journey, outside of those which we recorded, and gave her a realizing sense of the uncertainties and precarious chances that attend such travel, and which day and night lie in wait; and it gave her for every day an object unusual in the life of a woman.

To me, in drawing these results into visible form, there was now the impelling gratification of bringing into clear view the different face which our examination had given to the regions explored—their many points of general interest; their unexpectedly great resources and capacities for population and trade—thus vindicating the West in the importance which they attached to that territory.

There was but brief time in which to do this writing. In the evenings the notebooks were consulted, and the work thought out and prepared for the morning. Jacob kept up the camp habit and very early brought me coffee; and punctually at nine o'clock Mrs. Frémont joined me at the workshop. From that hour until one the writing went on, with seldom anything to break the thread, the dictation sometimes continuing for hours, interrupted only when an occasional point of exceptional interest brought out inquiry or discussion. After the four hours' stretch there was tea with a light luncheon and then a walk to the river; and after, work again until dusk.

Mrs. Benton was alarmed by this pull on her daughter, but Mr. Benton was delighted. He used sometimes to turn into our workroom to enjoy the pleasure he had in seeing the work grow. Another refreshing rest of the day came when we all met in the evening at dinner. Mr. Benton held to some observances in the family life which, though formal, were pleasant. He was fond of that degree of social decorum which respect for others' feelings should always exact, and is grateful to everyone. To him this was habitual. With the dressing for dinner were laid aside any subjects not suited to general harmony. Mr. Benton always relaxed to the enjoyment of the interesting and cheerful dinner table—himself contributing his large share and example, except when, on rare occasions, he came down from the Senate preoccupied by some interesting debate. One day he was so much engrossed that he forgot his office of carver, on which he rather prided himself—but continued biting, as he thought, a piece of bread—until he was roused by the general laugh, and "Father, that's the claret cork you are trying to eat." . . .*

At the instance of General Scott I was given the double brevet of

---

* A long letter Frémont sent the *New York Times* in 1877 on an interview by Brigham Young is omitted. Some passages quoted to show the misleading character of old books of history and travel are also deleted.

first lieutenant and captain. He made my services the subject of a special report, which consisted of two parts: the first, an argument that a double brevet, under existing law, might be granted; the second, that in consideration of services rendered by me it ought to be granted. The fact that General Scott was known to be tenacious of military observances increased the value of his recommendation. Accordingly, I was appointed by President Tyler captain by brevet, "to rank as such from the 31st day of July, 1844: for gallant and highly meritorious services in two expeditions commanded by himself; the first to the Rocky Mountains, which terminated October 17, 1842; and the second beyond those mountains, which terminated July 31, 1844." This brevet has the greater value for me because it is the only recognition for "services rendered" that I have received from my own Government.

After the change of administration in March I accompanied Mr. Benton to visit the President, Mr. Polk. In speaking to him of the interesting facts in the geography of the West I mentioned that I had shortly before, at the Library of Congress, drawn out from the map stand one giving the United States and Territories, and found on it the Great Salt Lake represented as connected with the Pacific Ocean by three great rivers: one discharging into the Columbia River from the northwestern end; another from the southwestern end into the head of the Gulf of California; the third from the middle of the western side of the lake running westward, breaking through the Sierra Nevada and discharging into the Bay of San Francisco. Bearing in mind the account given me at Vancouver of the Buenaventura River, the known fact of the Great Colorado, and the existence of large streams flowing into the lake, it is easy to see how the reports of trappers scattered over that region, who had seen it only in widely separated parts, might be connected together in the compilation of maps so as to give the lake these outlets.

The President seemed for the moment skeptical about the exactness of my information and disposed to be conservative. He evidently "respected that ancient chaos" of the Western geography as it existed on the old maps. Like the Secretary, he found me "young," and said something of the "impulsiveness of young men," and was not at all satisfied in his own mind that those three rivers were not running there as laid down.

It may be remembered that Alexis Ayot was severely wounded at the frontier, just when reaching the end of the journey. As an evidence of the interest felt in the expeditions, I anticipate here to say in what way he was not lost sight of. He was a French Canadian, young, and with simple faith in "government." He believed that, as he had been crippled in its service, he only needed to show himself in Washington to be provided for. To his surprise and distress he was told that as he was not an enlisted soldier the pension laws could not apply to him. "*Je vais mourir de faim*," he said to Mrs. Frémont; "*je ne suis pas clerc, je n'avais que mes jambes.*" That evening Mrs. Frémont was telling of this disappointment to herself as well as to the poor voyageur to Mrs. [John A.] Dix, a charming, sympathetic woman with whom as with her husband the family intimacy was great. A large, rather bashful gentleman waiting to see Mr. Dix sat apart taking no share in the talk of the two ladies; but after he had made his visit to the Senator, Mr. Dix came in from his library to say that this was the chairman of the Committee on Pensions; that he had been so interested for the crippled man that he had asked him to say that if Mrs. Frémont would write out briefly—just as she told it—the man's case, he thought he could help him. This was Preston King, of New York.

He made good his offer. A special act was introduced by Mr. King for his relief, and within a few days it had gone through both houses, received the signature of President Polk, and Ayot found himself with not only his pension, but back pay from the date of his wound. Swaying on his crutches, he tried to thank Mrs. Frémont, and with tears running down his dark face said, "I cannot kneel to thank you—*je n'ai plus de jambes*—but you are my *Sainte Madonne et je vous fais ma prière.*" To draw his pension he had to become an American resident. He was thorough, becoming also a citizen and marrying an American girl. And as a shoemaker in Montpelier, Vermont, I learned of his friendly arguments, and his voting for me there, many years after.

I had returned inspired with California. Its delightful climate and uncommon beauty of surface; the great strength of its vegetation and its grand commercial position—took possession of my mind. My wish when I first saw it settled into intention, and I determined to make there a home.

With all these advantages it was unused. Its great forests and fertile lands, the fish that crowded its waters, the noble harbor and great commerce that waited for it, were all unused; lying waste like an Indian country, as in greater part it was. Its fertile seaboard was one great stock farm and its whole population only a few thousands—so far distant from the Central Government that it was ready at any moment to break off. It had now come to share the great interest which the men in control of affairs at Washington had felt for the more northern coast of the Pacific. Mr. Webster invited me to dine with him "to talk about California." I found that his mind was specially fixed upon the Bay of San Francisco and the commanding advantage it would give us for war and commerce. He drew his line, however, at the coast. Coming as he did from a part of our country where grass contends with rocks for possession of the fields, it was difficult to make him realize the wonderful fertility of the unobstructed soil of California, where wild oats make unbroken fields from valley to mountaintop. For him the Rocky Mountains extended the influence of their name to the sea beaches and mingled their rocks with the sands, making in his mind the picture which he afterward gave of California: "a strip of sandy land along the Pacific Ocean with here and there an oasis of fertile soil; offering no inducements for us except the fine harbors indented upon its coast."

What Mr. Webster thought of these harbors he says in a letter written to his son March 11, 1845, quoted by Mr. George Ticknor Curtis in his well-studied and admirable life of Buchanan. In this letter Mr. Webster is speaking of the improbability that England would go to war with us to prevent the annexation of Texas. "But," he says, "she will now take care that Mexico shall not cede California, or any part thereof, to us. You know my opinion to have been, and now is, that the port of San Francisco would be twenty times as valuable to us as all Texas."

I communicated my inspiration to others. For this Mr. Benton's mind was open. Many clients from among old Spanish families in Florida and Louisiana; his practice in defending their interests; the knowledge acquired of the usage as well as the laws under which their old land grants had been held; his knowledge of the language which led to friendships with his clients—all gave him unusual interest now in Mexico. Out of this had come his sympathy for them as a people. He had always held that toward Mexico our relation should be that of the Great Republic aiding a neighboring state in its early struggles; and he belonged with those who preferred the acquiring of Texas by treaty and purchase, not by war. This he opposed and denounced. He came now to hold the same views concerning California.

President Polk entered on his office with a fixed determination to acquire California, if he could acquire it in an honorable and just manner.[2]

The President and Mr. Bancroft held it impossible for Mexico, situated as things then were, to retain possession of California, and therefore it was right to negotiate with Mexico for the acquisition of that which to her could be of no use. This it was hoped to accomplish by peaceful negotiation; but if Mexico, in resenting our acceptance of the offer of Texas to join us, should begin a war with us, then, by taking possession of the province.

The Secretary of State, Mr. Buchanan, and Senator Dix of New York, came frequently to confer with Senator Benton. As chairman of the Committee on Military Affairs, he was the center of information and conference. . . .*

Concurrently with the *Report* upon the second expedition the plans and scope of a third one had been matured. It was decided that it should be directed to that section of the Rocky Mountains which gives rise to the Arkansas River, the Rio Grande del Norte of the Gulf of Mexico, and the Rio Colorado of the Gulf of California; to complete the examination of the Great Salt Lake and its interesting region; and to extend the survey west and southwest to the examination of the great ranges of the Cascade Mountains and the Sierra Nevada, so as to ascertain the lines of communication through the mountains to the ocean in that latitude. And in arranging this expedition, the eventualities of war were taken into consideration.

The geographical examinations proposed to be made were in greater part in Mexican territory. This was the situation: Texas was gone and California was breaking off by reason of distance; the now increasing American emigration was sure to seek its better climate. Oregon was still in dispute; nothing was settled except the fact of

* A letter by Bancroft to Buchanan, with other irrelevant material, omitted.

a disputed boundary; and the chance of a rupture with Great Britain lent also its contingencies.

Mrs. Frémont was to have accompanied me to the frontier, but the dangerous illness of Mrs. Benton kept her at home. I went off with only Jacob and Chinook, who had been recalled from Philadelphia, and was glad to go back to his people.

The Quaker family had been interested in him and careful to give him such rudiments of practical knowledge as he might be able to put to good use. But he was about twenty years old when he left the Columbia with me; intelligent, with set character formed among the habits of Indian life, as ineradicable from Indian manhood as his love of free range from a wild horse. How far his brief education was likely to influence his life was made strikingly clear to us when on the evening he reached Washington he exhibited the parting gifts which he had received from his friends. Among these was a large Bible which had been made attractive in his eyes by its ornamentation. "Chinook been a Quaker all winter," he said, and opening this at the blank leaves for "Family Record"—"Here," he added, with the short Indian laugh of pleasure, "Chinook put here name all wife, and all horse." The knowledge which his eyes had taken in would be useful among his people. He was the son of a chief, and the stories he could tell of his life among the whites would add to his importance; and the kind treatment he had received would dispose himself and them to be friendly to the Americans.

The Indian boys who had spent a happy winter in Kentucky met me at Saint Louis, bringing with them Sacramento, aggressively well.

On the frontier I formed a camp where my party was quickly organized. For this expedition ampler means had been provided, and in view of uncertain conditions the force suitably increased. In addition to the usual outfit of arms I had procured about a dozen rifles, the best that could be found, with the object of setting them up as prizes for the best marksmen, to be shot for during the journey.[3] Many of my old men joined me. And I had again Godey.

The animals I had left on pasture were in fine condition; hardened by the previous journey and thoroughly rested, they were well fitted

to endure a campaign. From the Delaware nation twelve men had
been chosen to go with me. These were known to be good hunters
and brave men and two of them were chiefs, Swanok and Sagundai.
Mr. Preuss was not with me this time; but was now in assured
employment and preferred in his comfortable home to rest from the
hardships of the last journey. In his place Mr. Edward M. Kern,[4] of
Philadelphia, went with me as topographer. He was besides an accomplished artist; his skill in sketching from nature and in accurately drawing and coloring birds and plants made him a valuable
accession to the expedition. Lieutenants Abert and Peck had been
attached to my command, and also with me were Mr. James
McDowell, a nephew of Mrs. Benton, and Mr. Theodore Talbot,
whose health had been restored by the previous journey.

It was getting late in the year. The principal objects of the expedition lay in and beyond the Rocky Mountains, and for these
reasons no time could be given to examinations of the prairie region.
The line of travel was directed chiefly to pass over such country as
would afford good camping grounds; where water and grass, and
wood and abundant game, would best contribute to maintain the
health of the men and the strength of the animals. Along the route
we met the usual prairie incidents of Indians and large game, which
furnished always wholesome excitement. In those days these broke
pleasantly in upon the silence and uniformity of the prairie and
made a good school for the men. On the high plains we encountered
a Cheyenne village which was out on a hunt. The men came to
meet us on the plain, riding abreast and their drums sounding. They
were in all their bravery, and the formidable line was imposing, and
looked threatening to those of our people who were without experience in an Indian country. Men tried and fearless in accustomed
dangers are often at the first encounter nervous in those that are
unfamiliar. But the Cheyennes were friendly, and we on our side
were too strong for any exhibition of hostility or rudeness; and so
we gave the usual presents in exchange for friendly conduct and
good wishes.

We had lost an animal which in the night had strayed off from
the band, and early on the march next morning Basil, with a companion, had been sent out to look for it. He did not get in at night
nor in the morning. I therefore remained encamped and with a

small party went in turn to look for him. After a search of an hour or two we discovered them halted, and apparently scanning the horizon around, in some uncertainty where to look for us. We were down in a swale in the ground about three hundred yards away, and so out of sight that we had not been seen. We thought to try them, and quickly throwing off the greater part of our clothes we raised an Indian yell and charged. But there was no hesitation with them. They were off their horses in an instant and their leveled pieces brought us to an abrupt halt and a hearty laugh which we all enjoyed in having found them safe and well.

Returning to camp, our first experiment suggested another. The camp lay in a sort of broad gully below the level of the prairie. It was midday and the people were careless and more occupied by getting the dinner than with Indians. Riding quietly down to the hollow which gave an easy approach, we charged them with the usual yell. Our charge gave them a good lesson, though it lasted but a moment. It was like charging into a beehive; there were so many men in the camp ready with their rifles that it was very unsafe to keep up our Indian character beyond the moment of the charge. Still, like all excitement, it stirred the blood pleasantly for the moment.

On the second of August, 1845, we reached Bent's Fort, on the Arkansas River. This was our real point of departure. It was desirable to make a survey of the prairie region to the southward, embracing the Canadian and other rivers.[5] I accordingly formed a detached party, in charge of which I placed Lieutenants Abert and Peck, Lieutenant Abert being in chief command. Including these officers, the command consisted of thirty-three men, and I had the good fortune to secure my friend Mr. Fitzpatrick for their guide. I had endeavored to obtain the services of an Indian who knew well the country, and was a man of great influence, especially among the Comanches, but no offer that I could make him would induce him to go. It happened that the fort was well provisioned, and from its supplies we were able to furnish the party with a good outfit. This consisted principally of coffee and sugar for two months, several boxes of macaroni, and a quantity of rice, together with four fanegas of Mexican flour. In addition, they took with them eight steers brought up on the prairie and therefore easy to drive. They were furnished with four large circular tents, and as the face of the country which was covered by the projected survey was not much broken, four wagons were added for their outfit and camp equipage. This outfit may appear luxurious for the prairie, but provisions go fast where thirty healthy men taking just the right quantity of exercise are to be fed three times a day. Mr. Hatcher, who was a good hunter, was to accompany them as far as Bent's Post on the Canadian.

On the 12th Mr. Fitzpatrick took leave of me and joined the party. On the same day Lieutenant Abert changed his encampment preparatory to making his start, and on the 14th the two officers came to take leave of me. It is well to say here that on the journey to Bent's Fort I had been much prepossessed in their favor. They had shown themselves well qualified for such an expedition, which as of course was entirely new to them. In this journey they had given evidence of the prudence and good judgment which enabled them to carry through successfully the expedition entrusted to their care.

The next day I sent Lieutenant Abert his instructions, which were to survey the Canadian from its source to its junction with the Arkansas, taking in his way the Purgatory River, and the heads of the Washita; and on the 16th he commenced his journey down the Arkansas. With Lieutenant Abert also went Mr. James McDowell,[6] who decided to avail himself of this survey to return for the reason that his work would not be carried into the winter, while my journey to the Pacific was expected to be of long duration.

From the fort I sent an express to Carson at a rancho, or stock farm, which with his friend Richard Owens he had established on the Cimarron, a tributary to the Arkansas River. But he had promised that in the event I should need him, he would join me. And I knew that he would not fail to come. My messenger found him busy starting the congenial work of making up a stock ranch. There was no time to be lost, and he did not hesitate. He sold everything at a sacrifice, farm and cattle; and not only came himself but brought his friend Owens to join the party. This was like Carson, prompt, self-sacrificing, and true. I received them both with great satisfaction.

That Owens was a good man it is enough to say that he and Carson were friends. Cool, brave, and of good judgment; a good hunter and good shot; experienced in mountain life; he was an acquisition, and proved valuable throughout the campaign.

Godey had proved himself during the preceding journey, which had brought out his distinguishing qualities of resolute and aggressive courage. Quick in deciding and prompt in acting he had also the French *élan* and their gaiety of courage. "*Gai, gai, avançons nous.*" I mention him here because the three men come fitly together, and because of the peculiar qualities which gave them in the highest degree efficiency for the service in which they were engaged.

The three, under Napoleon, might have become Marshals, chosen as he chose men. Carson, of great courage; quick and complete perception, taking in at a glance the advantages as well as the chances for defeat; Godey, insensible to danger, of perfect coolness and stubborn resolution; Owens, equal in courage to the others, and in coolness equal to Godey, had the coup-d'æil of a chess-player, covering the whole field with a glance that sees the best move. His dark-hazel eye was the marked feature of his face, large and flat and farsighted.

Godey was a Creole Frenchman of Saint Louis, of medium height with black eyes and silky curling black hair which was his pride. In all situations he had that care of his person which good looks encourage. Once when with us in Washington, he was at a concert; immediately behind him sat the wife of the French Minister, Madame Pageot, who, with the lady by her, was admiring his hair, which was really beautiful, "but," she said, "*c'est une perruque.*" They were speaking unguardedly in French. Godey had no idea of having his hair disparaged and with the prompt coolness with which he would have repelled any other indignity turned instantly to say, "*Pardon, madame, c'est bien à moi.*" The ladies were silenced as suddenly as the touch on a tree trunk silences a katydid.

On the 16th of August I left Bent's Fort with a well-appointed compact party of sixty, mostly experienced and self-reliant men, equal to any emergency likely to occur, and willing to meet it.

On the 20th of August we encamped on the Arkansas at the mouth of the Fontaine qui Bouit River.[7] I had with me good instruments for astronomical observations, among them a portable transit instrument. This I set up, and established here one of the four principal positions on which depend the longitudes of the region embraced in the expeditions. The longitude was determined by moon culminations and the latitude by sextant observations of Polaris and stars in the south. The resulting longitude at this position is 104° 42′ 41″. The latitude 38° 15′ 18″.

On the 26th we encamped at the mouth of the Great Canyon,[8] and next morning, leaving the river, passed in our way over a bench of the mountain which the trappers believed to be the place where Pike was taken prisoner by the Mexicans. But this side of the river was within our territory. He supposed himself to be on the Arkansas when he was taken prisoner on the Rio del Norte, where he had built a stockade.

Crossing various forks of the river, we finally, on September 2d, reached and continued up the main branch, having on our right the naked rock ridge of the mountain, and encamped at night on the headwaters of the Arkansas in Mexican territory; in latitude 39° 20′ 38″, longitude 106° 27′ 15″.

This was pleasant traveling. The weather now was delightful and the country beautiful. Fresh and green, aspen groves and pine woods and clear rushing water, cool streams sparkling over rocky beds.

In a pine grove at the head of the river we came to our delighted surprise upon a small herd of buffalo, which were enjoying themselves in the shade and fresh grass and water. It was now very rare that these animals were found so far west, and this made for us a most pleasant and welcome incident, as it was long now since we had parted from the buffalo. This must have been a stray herd which had found its way into the upper mountains and they had remained for a long time undisturbed. Sometimes in severe winters deer find their way into the highest parts of the wooded mountains, and remain there, keeping fat and sheltered in the aspen groves which furnish them food. Probably this little herd of buffalo had done the same. The Utah Pass was several days' journey to the southeast, and this part of the mountain was out of the way of ordinary travel.

Here along in these mountains was one of the pleasantest grounds in the journey. Game was plenty—deer and elk. We were some days after on the mountain slopes, where a lovely view extended across a broad valley to the opposite ridges. It was so fine a view that Kern sketched it. In looking over the country I had ridden off a mile or two from the party, keeping along the heights to enjoy the air and views, when I came upon a small band of buffalo, doubtless part of the herd which we had found in the pines at the top of the mountain. The ground was rough, but we had a fine race. I had closed up and was about to fire when the pistol which I held raised went off, and the ball passed so close to my head that I reined up in surprise. My holster pistols were a hair-trigger pair, and old companions which I liked for that, and because they were true as a rifle. "Sacré bon coup," Basil said of them once when he saw the head of a quail cut off at long range. This time it was my own head. It is in this way that men have been sometimes lost in the mountains and never found. They lie like the trunk of a fallen tree worn by the snow and rain until the tall, rank grass covers and hides them. My trail would not have been taken in time and it would have been by the merest chance that any hunter would have passed the spot.

One of the Delawares had killed a fat buffalo cow. This singular meeting with the buffalo was our last; and they were probably the last stragglers that ever reached the western slope of the mountains. This was the general opinion of our people, whose experience would be likely to make it correct. The places where I have described them made then the broadest range of the buffalo from east to west, and make a fair exhibit of the abounding animal life of the country.

Passing the night of the 4th on Piny River, an affluent of Grand River, of the Colorado of the Gulf of California, we encamped the next day on the same river at "Williams Fishery," in longitude 106° 44′ 21″, latitude 39° 39′ 12″. We caught here a singular fish, which was called buffalo fish from a hump on the back, rising straight up immediately behind the head.[9]

Between fishermen and hunters the camp was abundantly supplied in all this part of our journey. These wood-clothed ranges, with their abundant game and healthful air, we have seen described as "impenetrable deserts whose rugged inaccessibility barred all passage, amid whose parched sterility unfortunate travelers were exposed to death from thirst and hunger."

The character of the mountain country has been so fully given in the previous journeys that it does not need to be longer dwelt upon here. On the 2d of October I encamped on a branch of the Timpanogos River, and on the 10th reached the shore of the lake, and its outlet at the mouth of Hugh's Creek, on the 12th. The geographical features of the country were carefully sketched; and astronomical observations, for which the continued fine weather favored us, were made on the different affluents to the Grand and Green River forks of the Great Colorado. The next day we encamped at a creek on the shore of the Great Salt Lake, where I made the second principal station for longitude. These observations resulted in longitude 112° 06' 08", and latitude 40° 45' 53".

It will be remarked that our journey from the head of the Arkansas River had been continuously in Mexican territory, as was all of the Salt Lake Valley. Two weeks were spent in this valley and on its tributary streams, during which we were occupied in fixing the positions of various points, and extending our examination into and around the lake.

The rocky shores of its islands were whitened by the spray which leaves salt on everything it touches, and a covering like ice forms over the water which the waves throw among the rocks. This seems to be the dry season when the waters recede; and the shores of the lake, especially on the south side, are whitened with encrustations of fine white salt. The shallow arms of the lake, under a slight covering of briny water, present beds of salt extending for miles. Plants and bushes blown by the winds upon these fields are entirely encrusted with crystallized salt. The stem of a small twig, less than the size of a goose quill, from the southeastern shore, showed a formation of more than an inch think of crystallized salt. The fresh water received by the lake is great in quantity, from the many fresh-water streams flowing into it, but they seem to have no perceptible effect. We could find in it no fish, or animal life of any kind, the larvæ which were accumulated in beds on the shore being found to belong to winged insects. On the contrary, the upper lake—the Timpanogos—which discharges into this by a stream about thirty-five miles long, is fresh water, and affords large trout and other fish in great numbers. These constitute the food of the Indians during the fishing season.

The mineral or rock salt is found in beds of great thickness at the heads of a stream in the mountains to the eastward behind the lakes. These strata probably underlie the bed of the Great Salt Lake, and constitute the deposit from which it obtains its salt. It was found by us in the place marked by Humboldt on his map of New Spain as derived from the journal of the missionary Father Escalante, who toward the close of the last century attempted to penetrate the unknown country from Santa Fe of New Mexico to Monterey of California. But he does not seem to have got farther in his adventurous journey—and this at that time was far—than the south end of the Timpanogos. Southeast of this lake is the chain of the Wasatch Mountains, which make in that part the rim of the Great Basin. In this mountain, at the place where Humboldt has written "Montagnes de Sel Gemme" (Rock Salt Mountain), the strata of salt are found in thick beds of red clay, at the heads of a small stream tributary to the Utah or Timpanogos Lake on its southeasterly side.[10]

FOOTNOTES

1. In his official *Report* of his second expedition, Frémont's final date is August 6, 1844, when he arrived in St. Louis and disbanded his party. His account of his journey from Bent's Fort to St. Louis occupies only four pages, contains nothing of special interest, and is omitted. But it does relate a disaster. About the middle of July, as they traveled down the Smoky Hill Fork of the Kansas River, they encamped for the night on the high prairie not far from the stream, which was only a hundred yards wide. A succession of heavy thunderstorms came up; the river suddenly burst its banks, becoming five or six hundred yards in breadth; and their perishable collections were "almost entirely ruined, and the hard labor of many months destroyed in a moment."

2. In March, 1845, President Polk had told Secretary George Bancroft of the Navy: "There are four great measures which are to be the measures of my Administration: one, a reduction of the tariff; another, the independent treasury; a third, the settlement of the Oregon boundary question; and lastly, the acquisition of California." That month the Mexican Minister in Washington, angered by the annexation of Texas, withdrew.

3. This emphasis on marksmanship suggests that the journey was not purely scientific in its objects.

4. Kern, a man of acute intelligence and perfect honesty, kept a brief journal, which is included as an appendix in Captain J. H. Simpson's *Report of Explorations across the Great Basin of Utah in 1859* (1876).

5. This survey was of course into Mexican territory, which it was no business of American scientists to survey. Evidently the intention was to examine the country for possible military movements.

6. Jessie Benton Frémont's mother was a McDowell, and this young man was her nephew.

7. That is, the site of present-day Pueblo, Colorado.

8. Frémont means the Royal Gorge of the Arkansas River in southern Colorado, where granite walls rise more than a thousand feet above the river bed.

9. Several kinds of the buffalo fish, all belonging to the sucker family and allied to carp, are known; some of them reach three feet in length. The white flesh is usually criticized as coarse, but in the Mississippi Valley it is esteemed by many people.

10. The preliminary stage of the expedition had now been completed. Frémont's intention was to undertake the arduous and dangerous task of exploring the unknown part of the Great Basin.

CHAPTER 11

Crossing the Great Basin:
Indian Fighting: Sutter's Fort Again:
Hostility of Mexicans *

A<small>T THIS</small> point we were to leave the [Great Salt] Lake. From any neighboring mountain height looking westward, the view extended over ranges which occupied apparently the whole visible surface—nothing but mountains, and in wintertime a forbidding prospect. Afterward, as we advanced, we found the lengthening horizon continued the same prospect until it stretched over the waters of the Pacific. Looking across over the crests of these ridges, which nearly all run north and south, was like looking lengthwise along the teeth of a saw.

Some days here were occupied in deciding upon the direction to be taken for the onward journey. The route I wished to take lay over a flat plain covered with sagebrush. The country looked dry and of my own men none knew anything of it—neither Walker nor Carson.[1] The Indians declared to us that no one had ever been known to cross the plain, which was desert; so far as any of them had ventured, no water had been found.[2] It was probably for this reason Father Escalante had turned back. Men who have traveled over this country in later years are familiar with the stony, black, unfertile mountains that so often discouraged and brought them disappointment. Nearly upon the line of our intended travel, and

* From Frémont's *Memoirs*, Vol. I, pp. 432ff. The exploring party, camped on the shores of Great Salt Lake, had found the mid-October weather stormy. The peaks of the Bear River Range were whitened with snow, though the lake shore was never really cold. Some paragraphs on the weather are omitted. When, from any elevation, the party looked westward, where they must go, they saw only desert, bounded by forbidding ranges, serrated like the teeth of a saw.

at the farther edge of the desert, apparently fifty to sixty miles away, was a peak-shaped mountain. This looked to me to be fertile, and it seemed safe to make an attempt to reach it. By some persuasion and the offer of a tempting reward, I had induced one of the local Indians to go as guide on the way to the mountain, willing to profit by any side knowledge of the ground, or water hole that the rains might have left, and about which the Indians always know in their hunts through the sage after small game.

I arranged that Carson, Archambeau, and Maxwell should set out at night, taking with them a man having charge of a pack mule with water and provisions, and make for the mountain. I to follow with the party the next day and make one camp out into the desert. They to make a signal by smoke in case water should be found.

The next afternoon, when the sun was yet two hours high, with the animals rested and well watered, I started out on the plain. As we advanced this was found destitute of any vegetation except sage bushes, and absolutely bare and smooth as if water had been standing upon it. The animals being fresh, I stretched far out into the plain. Traveling along in the night, after a few hours' march, my Indian lost his courage and grew so much alarmed that his knees really gave way under him and he wabbled about like a drunken man. He was not a true Utah, but rather of the Paiutes, a Digger of the upper class, and he was becoming demoralized at being taken so far from his gîte. Seeing that he could be of no possible use, I gave him his promised reward and let him go. He was so happy in his release that he bounded off like a hare through the sagebrush, fearful that I might still keep him.

Sometime before morning I made camp in the sagebrush, lighting fires to signal Carson's party. Before daybreak Archambeau rode in, the jingling of his spurs a welcome sound, indicating as it did that he brought good tidings. They had found at the peak water and grass, and wood abundant. The gearing up was quickly done and in the afternoon we reached the foot of the mountain, where a cheerful little stream broke out and lost itself in the valley. The animals were quickly turned loose, there being no risk of their straying from the grass and water. To the friendly mountain I gave the name of Pilot Peak. From my observation this oasis is in the latitude 41° 00′ 28″ longitude 114° 11′ 09″. Sometime afterward, when our crossing of the desert became known, an emigrant caravan was taken by this route, which then became known as the Hastings Cutoff.[3]

We gave the animals a day's rest here. The crossing of the desert had been a little strain upon them, many of them being grain-fed horses, unused to traveling on grass. These cannot stand being over-fatigued, soon reaching the stage which is called in the language of the country *resté*, from which they cannot recover without time, and must be left on the trail. With a mule it is very different. He may be *resté* at night, but give him plenty of good grass and water and he is ready for service in the morning.

On the 1st of November, 1845, we resumed our journey. The ridges which occupied the basin and which lay across our route are short, being the links which form the ranges; and between their overlapping points were easy passes by which the valleys connect. This is their regular structure.

Through these passes we wound our way and in the evening encamped at a spring in the head of a ravine which my observations put in longitude 114° 26′ 22″, latitude 40° 43′ 29″; and the next day I made camp at a spring to which I gave the name of Whitton, one of my men who discovered it.[4]

In advancing, the country was always carefully examined, so far as the eye could form any judgment upon it; and from the early morning start the men were spread over it to search for a camping place which with water should give the best grass. The winter was now approaching and I had good reason to know what the snow would be in the Great Sierra. It was imprudent to linger long in the examination of the Great Basin.[5] In order therefore to use to the best advantage the interval of good weather I decided to divide my party and run two separate lines across the Basin.

On the evening of the 8th I encamped on a small stream which I called Crane's Branch, after one of my Delaware hunters. Crane was a good judge of country, with a quick eye exercised in hunting. He was one of the men I liked to have near me. He was usually serious and dignified even for an Indian, who are naturally grave men. The objects which furnish ideas to the mind of an Indian are very few and mostly what he sees within a limited range. Within this, the game and other natural objects which come before his eyes; and outside of it, the enemies whom he goes to fight and scalp, if he can. These make his two sets of ideas. Nearer to the whites, other subjects force their way in confused shape through the barriers of an unknown language, but these are quite outside of the usual Indian understanding. The subjects belonging to their manner of life they hesitate to talk about with the whites; this and the difference of language make them reserved to us. With me the Delawares were now making the grand tour.

Crane's Branch led into a larger stream that was one of two forks forming a river to which I gave the name of Humboldt. I am given by himself the honor of being the first to place his great name on the map of the continent.[6] Both the river and mountain to which I gave his name are conspicuous objects, the river stretching across the basin to the foot of the Sierra Nevada, and the mountain standing out in greater bulk and length than its neighbors, and being one of those which I have named fertile mountains, having on it abundant water and grass, and woods. Years after, in traveling through that country I was glad to find that river and mountain held his name, not only on the maps, but in usage by the people.

I now divided the party, giving to Mr. Kern the charge of the main body, with instructions to follow down and survey the Humboldt River and its valley to their termination in what was called the Sink. This is a broad, level bottom of fertile land, probably once the bed of the lake when over all this region, at a time not very remote, the waters were higher. When I passed there two years later it was covered with grass and several varieties of clover. Thence to continue on along the eastern foot of the sierra to a lake to which I have given the name of Walker, who was to be his guide on this survey. I had engaged Mr. Walker for guide in this part of the region to be explored, with which, and the southern part of the "California Mountain," he was well acquainted. The place of meeting for the two parties was to be the lake. This party would have a secure line of travel in following the river, which would furnish grass and water for the entire journey and so keep the greater number of the animals in as good condition as the season admitted.

To accompany myself I selected ten men, among whom were some of the Delawares. I took leave of the main party and set out on a line westward directly across the basin, the look of the country inducing me to turn somewhat to the south. We lost no time in pressing forward; but the tortuous course rendered unavoidable by the necessity of using just such passes as the mountains gave, and in searching for grass and water, greatly lengthened our road. Still, it gave me knowledge of the country. The early morning began the day's work by the usual careful study of the ground ahead for indications to the best line of travel, and so soon as they were ready the hunters started out to the right and left, scouring the country as we advanced. When anything worthy of note was discovered, a shot was fired, or the horseman would make a few short turns backward and forward as a signal that something requiring attention had been found.

We succeeded in finding always good camping grounds, usually availing ourselves of the Indian trails which skirted the foot of the ridges. When well marked, showing use, these never failed to lead to water, and the larger the trail, the more abundant the water. This we always found at the edge of the mountain, generally in some ravine, and quickly sinking into the ground, never reaching the valley except in seasons of rain. Doubtless artesian wells would find it and make fertile these valleys, which now are dry and barren.

Traveling along the foot of a mountain on one of these trails, we discovered a light smoke rising from a ravine, and riding quietly up, found a single Indian standing before a little sagebrush fire over which was hanging a small earthen pot filled with sage-bush squirrels. Another bunch of squirrels lay near it, and close by were his bow and arrows. He was deep in a brown study, thinking perhaps of some game trail which he had seen and intended to follow that afternoon, and did not see or hear us until we were directly upon him, his absorbed thoughts and the sides of the ravine cutting off sounds. Escape for him was not possible and he tried to seem pleased, but his convulsive start and wild look around showed that he thought his end had come. And so it would—abruptly—had the Delawares been alone. With a deprecating smile he offered us part of his pot-au-feu and his bunch of squirrels. I reassured him with a friendly shake of the hand and a trifling gift. He was a good-looking young man, well made, as these Indians usually are, and naked as a worm.

The Delawares lingered as we turned away, but I would not let them remain. Anyhow, they regarded our journey as a kind of war-path, and no matter what kind of path he is upon a Delaware is always ready to take a scalp when he is in a country where there are strange Indians. We had gone but a short distance when I found they had brought away his bow and arrows, but I had them taken immediately back. These were well made, the bow strong, and made still stronger with sinews, and the arrows were all headed with obsidian worked in the usual spear-shape by patient labor, and nearly as sharp as steel. The Delawares took them back will-ingly when I reminded them that they had exposed the poor fellow to almost certain starvation by depriving him at the beginning of winter of his only means to procure food.[7]

At one of our camps on the foot slopes of a ridge we found again springs of boiling water, but a little way distant from the spring of cold water which supplied us.

A day or two after we saw mountain sheep for the first time in crossing the basin. None were killed, but that afternoon Carson killed an antelope. That day we traveled late, making for the point of a wooded mountain where we had expected to find water, but on reaching it found only the dry bed of a creek where there was some-times running water. It was too late to go farther and I turned up the creek bed, taking the chance to find it above, as the mountain looked promising. Well up toward the top of the mountain, nearly two thousand feet above the plain, we came upon a spring where the little basin afforded enough for careful use. A bench of the mountain near by made a good camping ground, for the November nights were cool and newly fallen snow already marked out the higher ridges of the mountains. With grass abundant, and pine wood and cedars to keep up the night fires, we were well provided for.

Sagundai, who had first found the spring, saw fresh tracks made in the sand by a woman's naked foot, and the spring had been re-cently cleaned out. But he saw no other indications of human life. We had made our supper on the antelope and were lying around the fire, and the men taking their great comfort in smoking. A good supper and a pipe make for them a comfortable ending no matter how hard the day has been. Carson, who was lying on his back with his pipe in his mouth, his hands under his head, and his feet to the fire, suddenly exclaimed, half rising and pointing to the other side of the fire, "Good God! look there!" In the blaze of the fire, peering over her skinny, crooked hands, which shaded her eyes from the glare, was standing an old woman apparently eighty years of age, nearly naked, her grizzly hair hanging down over her face and shoulders. She had thought it a camp of her people and had already begun to talk and gesticulate when her open mouth was paralyzed with fright as she saw the faces of the whites. She turned to escape, but the men had gathered about her and brought her around to the fire. Hunger and cold soon dispelled fear, and she made us understand that she had been left by her people at the spring to die, because she was very old and could gather no more seeds and was no longer good for anything.

She told us she had nothing to eat and was very hungry. We gave her immediately about a quarter of the antelope, thinking she would roast it by our fire, but no sooner did she get it in her hand then she darted off into the darkness. Someone ran after her with a brand of fire, but calling after her brought no answer. In the morning, her fresh tracks at the spring showed that she had been there for water during the night. Starvation had driven her to us, but her natural fear drove her away as quickly so soon as she had secured something to eat. Before we started we left for her at the spring a little supply from what food we had. This, with what she could gather from the nut-pine trees on the mountain, together with our fire, which she could easily keep up, would probably prolong her life even after the snows came. The nut pines and cedars extend their branches out to the ground and in one of their thickets, as I have often proved, these make a comfortable shelter against the most violent snowstorms.

This was Sangundai's Spring.[8] The names of my camps here along become the record of the rivalry of the men in finding good camps. It became the recurring interest of each day to prove their judgment of country as well as their skill as hunters.

The region here along had a special interest for me and our progress was slow for the two following days. We had now reached a low valley line that extends along the eastern foot of the ridges which constitute the Sierra Nevada. Into this low ground the rivers from the sierra as well as from the basin gather into a series of lakes extending south toward the head of the Gulf of California. I had a reason for carefully examining this part of the basin, but the time needed for it would interfere with other objects, and the winter was at hand.

The place appointed for meeting the main party was on the eastward shore of Walker's Lake near the point where the river to which I had given the same name empties into it. Making our way along the foot of the mountain toward our rendezvous, we had reached one of the lakes where at this season the scattered Indians of the neighborhood were gathering to fish. Turning a point on the lake shore, the party of Indians some twelve or fourteen in number came abruptly into view. They were advancing along in Indian file, one following the other, their heads bent forward and eyes fixed on the ground. As our party met them the Indians did not turn their heads nor raise their eyes from the ground. Their conduct indicated unfriendliness; but, habituated to the uncertainties of savage life, we too fell readily into their humor, and passed on our way without word or halt. Even to us it was a strange meeting.

It was the solitary occasion where I met with such an instance of sullen and defiant hostility among Indians and where they neither sought nor avoided conflict. I judged that they either regarded us as intruders, or that they had received some recent injury from the whites who were now beginning to enter California, and which they wished but feared to avenge.

In this region the condition of the Indian is nearly akin to that of the lower animals. Here they are really wild men. In his wild state the Indian lives to get food. This is his business. The superfluous part of his life, that portion which can be otherwise employed, is devoted to some kind of warfare. From this lowest condition, where he is found as the simplest element of existence, up to the highest in which he is found on this continent, it is the same thing. In the Great Basin, where nearly naked he traveled on foot and lived in the sagebrush, I found him in the most elementary form, the men living alone, the women living alone, but all after food. Sometimes one man cooking by his solitary fire in the sagebrush which was his home, his bow and arrows and bunch of squirrels by his side; sometimes on the shore of a lake or river where

food was more abundant a little band of men might be found occupied in fishing; miles away a few women would be met gathering
seeds and insects, or huddled up in a shelter of sagebrush to keep
off the snow. And the same on the mountains or prairies where the
wild Indians were found in their highest condition, where they had
horses and lived in lodges. The labor of their lives was to get something to eat. The occupation of the women was in gleaning from the
earth everything of vegetable or insect life; the occupation of the
men was to kill every animal they could for food and every man of
every other tribe for pleasure. And, in every attempt to civilize,
these are the two lines upon which he is to be met.

On the 24th we encamped at our rendezvous on the lake, where
beds of rushes made good pasturage for our animals. Three days
afterward the main party arrived. They were all in good health, and
had met with no serious accident. But the scarcity of game had made
itself felt, and we were now all nearly out of provisions. It was now
almost midwinter, and the open weather could not be expected to
last.

In this journey across the basin, between latitudes 41° and 38°,
during the month of November, from the 5th to the 25th the mean
temperature was 29° at sunrise and 40° at sunset, ranging at noon
between 41° and 60°. There was a snowstorm between the 4th and
7th, snow falling principally at night, and the sun occasionally
breaking out in the day. The lower hills and valleys were covered
only a few inches deep with snow, which the sun carried off in a
few hours after the storm was over. The weather continued uninterruptedly clear and beautiful until the close of the month. But
though the skies were clear, it was colder now that we had come
within the influence of the main sierra.

I was in the neighborhood of the passage which I had forced
across it a year before, and I had it on my mind. Heavy snows might
be daily expected to block up the passes, and I considered that in
this event it would be hopeless to attempt a crossing with the
material of the whole party.

I therefore decided again to divide it, sending the main body
under Kern to continue southward along the lake line and pass
around the Point of the California Mountain into the head of the
San Joaquin Valley. There, as already described, the great Sierra

Nevada comes down nearly to the plain, making a Point, as in the smaller links, and making open and easy passes where there is never or rarely snow. As before, Walker, who was familiar with the southern part of Upper California, was made the guide of the party; and, after considering the advantages of different places, it was agreed that the place of meeting for the two parties should be at a little lake in the valley of a river called the Lake Fork of the Tulare Lake.

With a selected party of fifteen, among whom were some of my best men, including several Delawares, I was to attempt the crossing of the mountain in order to get through to Sutter's Fort before the snow began to fall. At the fort I could obtain the necessary supplies for the relief of the main party. Leaving them in good order, and cheerful at the prospect of escaping from the winter into the beautiful "California Valley," as it was then called, we separated, and I took up my route for the river which flows into Pyramid Lake, and which on my last journey I had named Salmon Trout River. I now entered a region which hardship had made familiar to me, and I was not compelled to feel my way, but used every hour of the day to press forward toward the pass at the head of this river.

On the 1st of December I struck it above the lower cañon, and on the evening of the 4th camped at its head on the east side of the pass in the Sierra Nevada. Our effort had been to reach the pass before a heavy fall of snow, and we had succeeded. All night we watched the sky, ready to attempt the passage with the first indication of falling snow; but the sky continued clear. On our way up, the fine weather which we had left at the foot of the mountain continued to favor us, and when we reached the pass the only snow showing was on the peaks of the mountains.

At three in the afternoon the temperature was 46°, at sunset, 34°. The observations of the night gave for the longitude of the pass, 120° 15′ 20″, and for latitude, 39° 17′ 12″. Early the next morning we climbed the rocky ridge which faces the eastern side, and at sunrise were on the crest of the divide, 7,200 feet above the sea, the sky perfectly clear, and the temperature 22°. There was no snow in the pass, but already it showed apparently deep on higher ridges and mountaintops. The emigrant road now passed here, following down a fork of Bear River, which leads from the pass into the Sacra-

mento Valley.[10] Finding this a rugged way, I turned to the south
and encamped in a mountain meadow where the grass was fresh
and green. We had made good our passage of the mountain and
entered now among the grand vegetation of the California Valley.
Even if the snow should now begin to fall, we could outstrip it
into the valley, where the winter king already shrank from the warm
breath of spring.

The route the next day led over good traveling ground; gaining
a broad leading ridge, we traveled along through the silence of a
noble pine forest where many of the trees were of great height and
uncommon size. The tall red columns standing closely on the clear
ground, the filtered, flickering sunshine from their summits far
overhead, gave the dim religious light of cathedral aisles, opening
out on every side, one after the other, as we advanced. Later, in
early spring, these forest grounds are covered with a blue carpet of
forget-me-nots.

The pines of the European forests would hide their diminished
heads amidst these great columns of the Sierra. A species of cedar
(*Thuya gigantea*) occurred often of extraordinary bulk and height.
Pinus Lambertiani was one of the most frequent trees, distinguished
among cone-bearing tribes by the length of its cones, which are
sometimes sixteen or eighteen inches long. The Indians eat the
inner part of the burr, and I noticed large heaps of them where they
had been collected.

Leaving the higher ridges, we gained the smoother spurs and
descended about 4,000 feet, the face of the country rapidly changing
as we went down. The country became low and rolling; pines began
to disappear, and varieties of oak, principally an evergreen resembling live oak, became the predominating forest growth. The
oaks bear great quantities of acorns, which are the principal food
of all the wild Indians; it is their breadfruit tree. At a village of a
few huts which we came upon there was a large supply of these
acorns: eight or ten cribs of wickerwork containing about twenty
bushels each. The sweetest and best acorns, somewhat resembling
Italian chestnuts in taste, are obtained from a large tree belonging
to the division of white oaks, distinguished by the length of its acorn,
which is commonly an inch and a half and sometimes two inches.
This long acorn characterizes the tree, which is a new species and

is accordingly specified by Dr. Torrey as *Quercus longiglanda* (Torr. and Frem.)—long-acorn oak. This tree is very abundant and generally forms the groves on the bottom lands of the streams, standing apart with a green undergrowth of grass which gives the appearance of cultivated parks. It is a noble forest tree, sixty to eighty feet high, with a summit of widespreading branches, and frequently attains a diameter of six feet; the largest that we measured reached eleven feet. The evergreen oaks generally have a low growth, with long branches and spreading tops.

At our encampment on the evening of the 8th, on a stream which I named Hamilton's Creek, we had come down to an elevation of 500 feet above the sea. The temperature at sunset was 48°, the sky clear, the weather calm and delightful, and the vegetation that of early spring. We were still upon the foothills of the mountains, where the soil is sheltered by woods and where rain falls much more frequently than in the open Sacramento Valley, near the edge of which we then were. I have been in copious continuous rains of eighteen or twenty hours' duration in the oak region of the mountain when none fell in the valley below. Innumerable small streams have their rise through these foothills, which often fail to reach the river of the valley, but are absorbed in its light soil; the large streams coming from the upper part of the mountain make valleys of their own of fertile soil, covered with luxuriant grass and interspersed with groves.

The oak belt of the mountain is the favorite range of the Indians. I found many small villages scattered through it. They select places near the streams where there are large boulders of granite rock that show everywhere holes which they had used for mortars in which to pound the acorns. These are always pretty spots. The clean, smooth granite rocks standing out from the green of the fresh grass over which the great oaks throw their shade, and the clear running water, are pleasant to eye and ear.

After the rough passage and scanty food of the basin these lovely spots, with the delightful spring weather, fresh grass and flowers, and running water, together with the abundant game, tempted us to make early camps, so that we were about four days in coming down to the valley.[11]

Traveling in this way slowly along, taking the usual astronomical observations and notes of the country, we reached on the 9th of December the Grimes rancho on what was then still known as Rio de los Americanos—the American Fork, near Sutter's Fort.

Captain Sutter received me with the same friendly hospitality which had been so delightful to us the year before. I found that our previous visit had created some excitement among the Mexican authorities.[12] But to their inquiries he had explained that I had been engaged in a geographical survey of the interior and had been driven to force my way through the snow of the mountains simply to obtain a refuge and food where I knew it could be had at his place, which was by common report known to me. Being ourselves already recruited by the easy descent into the valley, I did not need to delay long here. A few days sufficed to purchase some animals and a small drove of cattle, with other needed supplies.

Leaving the upper settlements of New Helvetia, as the Sutter settlement was called, on the 14th of December, I started to find my party which I had left in charge of Talbot when we had separated in the basin on Walker Lake. Passing through the groves of oak which border the American Fork, we directed our route in a southeasterly course towards the Cosumne River.

The Cosumne Indians, who have left their name on this river, and which I had preserved on my map of the country, have been driven away from it within a few years and dispersed among other tribes; and several farms of some leagues in extent had already been commenced on the lower part of the stream. At one of these we encamped about eight miles above the junction of the Cosumne with the Mokelumne River, which a few miles below enters a deep slough in the tidewater of the San Joaquin delta.

Our way now lay over the well-remembered plains of the San Joaquin Valley, the direction of our route inclining toward the mountains. We crossed wooded sloughs, with ponds of deep water, which nearer the foothills are running streams with large bottoms of fertile land, the greater part of our way being through evergreen, and other oaks. The rainy season, which commonly begins with November, had not yet commenced, and the streams were at the low stage usual to the dry season and easily forded. The Mokelumne where we crossed it is about sixty yards wide; the broad alluvial bottoms were here about five hundred yards wide. Leaving this river on the morning of the 16th, we traveled about twenty miles through open woods of white oak, crossing in the way several stream beds, among them the Calaveras Creek. These have abundant water with good land nearer the hills; and the Calaveras makes some remarkably handsome bottoms.

Issuing from the woods, we rode about sixteen miles over open prairie partly covered with bunch grass, the timber reappearing on the rolling hills of the river Stanislaus in the usual belt of evergreen oaks. The level valley was about forty feet below the upland, and the stream seventy yards broad, with the usual fertile bottom land, which was covered with green grass among large oaks. We encamped in one of these bottoms, in a grove of the large white oaks previously mentioned. The many varieties of deciduous and evergreen oaks which predominate throughout the valleys and lower hills of the mountains afford large quantities of acorns. Their great abundance in the midst of fine pastureland must make them an important element in the farming economy of the country.

The day had been very warm. At sunset the temperature was 55° and the weather clear and calm.

At sunrise next morning the thermometer was at 22°, with a light wind from the Sierra N. 75° E. and a clear pure sky, against which the blue line of the mountains showed clearly marked. The way for about three miles was through woods of evergreen and other oaks, with some shrubbery intermingled. Among this was a lupine of extraordinary size, not yet in bloom. Emerging from the woods, we traveled in a southeasterly direction, over a prairie of rolling land, the ground becoming more broken as we approached the Tuolumne River, one of the finest tributaries to the San Joaquin.

The hills were generally covered with a species of geranium (*Erodium cicutarium*), in the language of the country alfalfa, a valuable plant for stock and considered very nutritious. With this was frequently interspersed good and green bunch grass, and a plant commonly called bur clover. This plant, which in some places is very abundant, bears a spirally twisted pod, filled with seeds that remain on the ground during the dry season, well preserved. This affords good food for the cattle until with the spring rains new grass comes up.

We started a band of wild horses on approaching the river and the Indians ran off from a village on the bank, the men lurking round to observe us.

The trail led sidling down the steep face of the hill to the river bottom. The horse I was riding, one of those gotten at Sutter's had been reclaimed from the wild herds, and seeing this wild herd scouring off he remembered his own free days and in mid-trail set himself to bucking, in the way a California horse—wild or tame— knows how to do exceptionally. A wild horse broken to the saddle never forgets, and takes advantage of every chance he has to rid himself of his rider. If a girth breaks or a saddle turns, he knows it. A rifle across the saddle and Indians to be watched and a bucking horse on a steep hillside make a complicated situation, but we got to the bottom without parting company and my horse seemed only pleased by the excitement. . . .*

We encamped on the Tuolumne on bottom land, open-wooded with large white oaks of the new species; and excellent grass furnished good food for the animals. The usual order of the camp was enlivened by the Indians, who were soon reconciled to our presence. About their huts were the usual acorn cribs, containing each some twenty or thirty bushels. The sunset temperature was pleasant, at 54°, and a clear atmosphere. Multitudes of geese and other wild fowl made the night noisy.

In the morning the sky was clear, with an air from the southeast and a hoarfrost covering the ground like a light fall of snow. At sunrise the thermometer was at 24°, a difference from the preceding sunset of thirty degrees. Our course now inclined more toward the foot of the mountain and led over a broken country. In about seventeen miles we reached the Auxumne River—called by the Mexicans Mérced—another large affluent of the San Joaquin, and continued about six miles up the stream, intending gradually to reach the heart of the mountains at the head of the Lake Fork of the Tulare. We encamped on the southern side of the river, where broken hills made a steep bluff, with a narrow bottom. On the northern side was a low, undulating wood and prairie land, over which a band of about three hundred elk was slowly coming to water, feeding as they approached.

The next day was December the 19th, the weather continuing

* A paragraph on another bucking horse later in Frémont's career omitted.

clear and pleasant, very unlike the winter days to which we were accustomed. We continued our journey in a southeasterly direction, over a broken and hilly country without timber, and showing only scattered clumps of trees, from which we occasionally started deer. In a few hours we reached a beautiful country of undulating upland, openly wooded with oaks, principally evergreen, and watered with small streams which together make the Mariposas River. Continuing along, we came upon broad and deeply worn trails which had just been traveled by large bands of horses, apparently coming from the San Joaquin Valley. But we had heard enough to know that they came from the settlements on the coast—that we were approaching villages of Horsethief Indians.[13]

December 22d. . . . According to the appointment made when I left my party under Talbot, it was a valley upon the Lake Fork to which the guide Walker was to conduct him. Here I expected to find him. The men, as well as the cattle and horses, needed rest; a strict guard had been necessary, as in the morning Indian sign was always found around our camp. The position was good in the open ground among the oaks, there being no brush for cover to the Indians, and grass and water were abundant. Accordingly we remained here a day, and on the 24th entered the mountain, keeping as nearly as possible the valley ground of the river. While in the oak belt the traveling was easy and pleasant, but necessarily slow in the search for our people, especially here in this delightful part of the mountain where they should be found. Several days were spent here. At the elevation of 3,500 feet the ridges were covered with oaks and pines intermixed, and the bottom lands with oaks, cottonwoods, and sycamores. Continuing upward, I found the general character of the mountain similar to what it was in the more northern part, but rougher, and the timber perhaps less heavy and more open, but some trees extremely large. I began to be surprised at not finding my party, but continued on, thinking that perhaps in some spread of the river branches I was to find a beautiful mountain valley. Small varieties of evergreen oaks were found at the observed height of 9,840 feet above the sea, at which elevation *Pinus Lambertiani* and other varieties of pine, fir, and cypress were large and lofty trees. The distinctive oak belt was left at about 5,000 feet above the sea.

Indians were still around the camp at night and the necessity of keeping the animals closely guarded prevented them from getting food enough and, joined with the rough and difficult country, weakened them. For this, I usually made the day's journey short. I found the mountain extremely rocky in the upper parts, the streams breaking through cañons, but wooded up to the granite ridges which compose its rocky eminences. We forced our way up among the head springs of the river and finally stood upon the flat ridge of naked granite which made the division of the waters and was 11,000 feet above the sea. The day was sunny and the air warm enough to be not only very agreeable, but with exercise exhilarating, even at that height. Lying immediately below, perhaps 1,000 feet, at the foot of a precipitous descent was a small lake, which I judged to be one of the sources of the main San Joaquin. I had grown, by occasional privation, to look upon water as a jewel beyond price, and this was rendered even more beautiful by its rough setting. The great value to us of the first necessaries of life made a reason why we so seldom found gold or silver or other minerals. Ores of iron and copper, and gold and silver, and other minerals we found, but did not look for. A clear cold spring of running water or a good camp, big game, or fossils imbedded in rock, were among the prized objects of our daily life. Owens, after the discovery of the gold in California, reminded me that he had once on the American Fork noticed some little shining grains which he could see from his horse and which afterward we decided were gold, but we were not interested enough at the time to give it attention; and Breckenridge too reminded me that he brought me in his hand some large grains which I carelessly told him were sulphurets of iron. These too were probably gold. As I said, this bed of summit granite was naked. Here and there a pine or two, stunted and twisted and worried out of shape by the winds, and clamping itself to the rock. But immediately below we encamped in the sheltering pinewoods which now were needed, for toward evening the weather threatened change. The sky clouded over and by nightfall was a uniform dull gray, and early in the night the roar of the wind through the pines had at times the sound of a torrent. And the camp was gloomy. We had ridden hard, and toiled hard, and we were all disappointed and perplexed, wondering what had become of our people. During the night the Indians succeeded in killing one of our best mules. He had fed quietly into one of the little ravines, wooded with brush pines, just out of sight of the guard near by, and an Indian had driven an arrow nearly through his body. Apparently he had died without sound or struggle, just as he was about to drink from the little stream.

The next day, December 31st, I made a short camp, the cattle being tender-footed and scarcely able to travel. To descend the mountain we chose a different way from that by which we had come up, but it was rocky and rough everywhere. The old year went out and the new year came in, rough as the country. Toward nightfall the snow began to come down thickly, and by morning all lay under a heavy fall. The chasms through which the rivers roared were dark against the snow, and the fir branches were all weighed down under their load. This was the end of the few remaining cattle. It was impossible to drive them over the treacherous ground. The snow continued falling, changing the appearance of the ground and hiding slippery breaks and little rocky hollows, where horse and man would get bad falls. Left to themselves cattle could easily work their way to the lower grounds of the mountain, if not killed by Indians. We had great trouble in getting out from the snow region. The mountain winter had now set in, and we had some misgivings as we rode through the forest, silent now without a sound except where we came within hearing of water roaring among rocks or muffled under snow. There were three ridges to surmount, but we succeeded in crossing them, and by sunset when the storm ceased we made a safe camp between 9,000 and 10,000 feet above the sea. The temperature at sunset when the sky had cleared was between eight and nine degrees.

The next day we reached the oak region, where spring weather, rain and sunshine, were found again. At an elevation of 4,500 feet the temperature at the night encampment of the 3d of January, 1846, was 38° at sunset and the same at sunrise, the grass green and growing freshly under the oaks. The snow line at this time reached down to about 6,000 feet above the sea. On the 7th of January we encamped again on the Lake Fork in the San Joaquin Valley. Our camp was in a grove of oaks at an Indian village, not far from the lake. These people recognized the horse of the Indian who had been killed among the hills the day after our encounter with the Horsethief village, and which had been captured by the Delawares. It appeared that this Indian had belonged to their village, and they showed unfriendly signs. But nothing took place during the day and at night I had a large oak at the camp felled. We were unencumbered and its spreading summit as it fell made a sufficient barricade in event of any sudden *alerte*.

We found the temperature much the same as in December. Fogs, which rose from the lake in the morning, were dense, cold, and penetrating; but after a few hours these gave place to a fine day. The face of the country had already much improved by the rains which had fallen while we were traveling in the mountains. Several humble plants, among them the golden-flowered violet (*Viola chrysantha*) and *Erodium cicutarium,* the first valley flowers of the spring, and which courted a sunny exposure and warm sandy soil, were already in bloom on the southwestern hill slopes. In the foothills of the mountains the bloom of the flowers was earlier. Descending the valley, we traveled among multitudinous herds of elk, antelope, and wild horses. Several of the latter which we killed for food were found to be very fat. By the middle of January, when we had reached the lower San Joaquin, the new grass had covered the ground with green among the open timber upon the rich river bottoms, and the spring vegetation had taken a vigorous start.

We had now searched the San Joaquin Valley up to the headwaters of the Tulare Lake Fork, and failed to find my party. They were too strong to have met with any serious accident and my conclusion was that they had traveled slowly in order to give me time to make my round and procure supplies, the moderate travel serving meanwhile to keep their animals in good order, and from the moment they would have turned the Point of the California Mountain the whole valley which they entered was alive with game—antelope and elk and bear and wild horses. Accounting in this way for their failure to meet me, I continued on to Sutter's Fort, at which place I arrived on the 15th of the month, and, remaining there four days, I sailed on Sutter's launch for San Francisco, taking with me eight of my party. From Captain Sutter, who was a Mexican magistrate, I had obtained a passport to Monterey for myself and my men. At Yerba Buena, as it was then called, I spent a few days, which Leidesdorff, our vice-consul, and Captain Hinckley made very agreeable to me. With Captain Hinckley I went to visit the quicksilver mine at New Almaden, going by water to please the Captain. . . .[14]

On January 24, I set out toward evening for Monterey with Mr. Leidesdorff, who was kind enough to give me the advantage of his company. His house was one of the best among the few in Yerba Buena—a low bungalow sort of adobe house with a long piazza facing the bay for the sunny mornings, and a cheerful fire within against the fog and chill of the afternoons. His wife, a handsome, girl-like woman, Russian from Sitka, gave the element of home which had been long missing to my experience. He was a cheerful-natured man, and his garden and his wife spoke pleasantly for him.

We had started rather late and on the plain beyond the Mission Dolores in the darkness and the fog we lost our way, but wandering around we were at last rejoiced by hearing the barking of dogs. This soon brought us to the rancho of Don Francisco Sanchez, for which we were looking, and where we were received with the cordial hospitality which in those days assured a good bed and a savory supper to every traveler, and if his horse happened to be tired or hurt by any accident a good one to replace it for the journey.

The next day we rode along the bay shore, the wooded and fertile character of which needs no describing, and stopped for the night with Don Antonio Sunol. This was my first ride down the valley of San José, and I enjoyed even the passing under the oak groves with the branches cut off to a uniform height by the browsing herds of cattle, listening the while to Leidesdorff's account of the fertility of the country's vegetation. His descriptions of this part of the country were especially interesting to me. He was a lover of nature and his garden at San Francisco was, at that time, considered a triumph.

After a half-day's riding from the Gomez rancho, across the Salinas plains, we reached Monterey and went directly to the house of our consul, Mr. Larkin.[15] I had come to Monterey with the object of obtaining leave to bring my party into the settlements in order to refit and obtain the supplies that had now become necessary. All the camp equipment, the clothes of the men and their saddles and horse gear, were either used up or badly in want of repair.

The next morning I made my official visits. I found the governor, Don Pio Pico, absent at Los Angeles. With Mr. Larkin I called upon

the commanding general, Don José Castro, the prefect, alcalde, and
ex-Governor Alvarado.[16] I informed the general and the other officers that I was engaged in surveying the nearest route from the
United States to the Pacific Ocean. I informed them farther that the
object of the survey was geographical, being under the direction of
the Bureau of Topographical Engineers, to which corps I belonged;
and that it was made in the interests of science and of commerce,
and that the men composing the party were citizens and not soldiers.

The permission asked for was readily granted, and during the
two days I stayed I was treated with every courtesy by the general
and other officers. This permission obtained I immediately set about
arranging for supplies of various kinds and for sending fresh horses
to meet our people, with such supplies of lesser luxuries as I knew
would be grateful to them; and by the middle of February we were
all reunited in the valley of San José, about thirteen miles south of
the village of that name on the main road leading to Monterey,
which was about sixty miles distant.

When we separated at the lake which bears his name there was a
singular mistake between Walker and myself. The understanding
was that we were to meet on the Tulare Lake Fork. This is the large
tributary to the lake, which had been known to myself and party
in the campaign of the preceding year as the Lake River. Mr. Walker
apparently did not know this river, but took it for granted that a
much smaller one, coming from the end of the range and discharging where there are two small lakes amidst bulrushes at the head
of the valley, was the river which was intended for the place of
meeting. These lakes are eighty or ninety miles south of the Tulare
Lake. At the end of the mountain there were lower passes which
were used by trappers and others coming from the basin into the
country about Los Angeles, and the rivers there were known to
Mr. Walker, while probably he had never seen the Tulare Lake
Fork.

Mr. Talbot, with the detached party, had crossed the California
Mountain toward the Point and nearly opposite the southern end
of the Tulare Lakes, and remained encamped in a valley or cove,
near the summit of the sierra, at the head of the river, from December 27th to January 17th. The cove was well wooded with evergreen
oaks, some varieties of pine, firs, and cedars, maintaining the usual

majestic growth which characterizes the cone-bearing trees of the sierra. Until the 12th of January the weather was almost that of summer, when the rains commenced, almost three weeks later than in latitude 37°, where I was. On the 17th there was a fall of snow, washed off by a cold fall of rain in the afternoon, the high ranges remaining covered a foot deep. After that, snow and rain alternated with sunshine, snow remaining on the ridges; and winter set in fairly on all the upper half of the mountain. To this river I gave the name of my topographer, Kern.

Finding that I did not arrive, Mr. Talbot, counseling with Walker, judged it expedient to descend into the valley; and on the morning of the 19th resumed his journey down the San Joaquin to the Cosumne River, where they made an encampment to wait until hearing from me. Meantime Mr. Walker, in his turn, set out on a search for me which was happily terminated by meeting Carson and Owens, who were looking for him.

The people were all in good health, having been well supplied with game, and the animals were in improving condition.[17] The route of the party had been an easy one along the base of the sierra and the pass at the head of the river was low, broad, and open, without any impediment. To one of the lakes along their route on the east side of the range I gave Owens' name.

During the stay of the party on the Cosumne a grizzly bear showed the value of a sudden onset. One of these animals ranging the river bottom after acorns had accidentally discovered the camp, which was at breakfast, and charged into it, scattering the men, driving some into trees, and holding possession until some of the men got hold of their guns. The bear treed even the Delawares. He had four inches thickness of fat on his back and on his belly, and was estimated to weigh a thousand pounds. This shows the fine quality of the range.

The place which I had selected for rest and refitting was a vacant rancho called the Laguna, belonging to Mr. Fisher.[18] I remained here until February, in the delightful spring season of a most delightful climate. The time was occupied in purchasing horses, obtaining supplies, and thoroughly refitting the party. . . .*

* Observation on latitude and longitude omitted.

Many Californians visited the camp, and very friendly relations grew up with us. One day amusements were going on as usual, the Californians showing our men their admirable horsemanship. One of the large vultures which are often seen floating about overhead had been brought down with a broken wing by one of our rifles. This was the point on which we excelled, as the others in perfect horsemanship. The vulture was sitting on the frame of a cart to which he had been tied; he had gotten over his hurt and would have been treated as a pet, but his savage nature would not permit of any approach. By accident a Californian had gotten a fall and the whole camp was shouting and laughing, and Owens, his mouth wide open, was backing toward the cart to rest his arm on the wheel, forgetful of the vulture. The vulture with his long, red neck stretched out was seizing the opportunity—we all saw it and Owens saw our amusement, but not quite in time to escape the grip of the vulture. It was quite a picture—the vulture lying in wait, and Owens' unconsciousness, and the hearty laugh which cheered the bird's exploit. Owens got off with a sharp pinch and a torn sleeve.

The fertile valley of San José is a narrow plain of rich soil lying between equally fertile ranges from two thousand to three thousand feet high, covered on one side with wild oats, and wooded on the range toward the sea. The valley is openly wooded with groves of oak free from underbrush, and after the spring rains covered with grass. On the west it is protected from the chilling influence of the northwest winds by the Cuesta de los Gatos—Wildcat Ridge—which separates it from the coast.

Resuming the work of the expedition, on the 22d March we encamped on the Wildcat Ridge on the road to Santa Cruz, and again on the 23d near the summit.[19] The varied character of the woods and shrubbery on this mountain, which lay between my camp and the Santa Cruz shore, was very interesting to me, and I wished to spend some days there, as now the spring season was renewing vegetation, and the accounts of the great trees in the forest on the west slope of the mountain had roused my curiosity. Always, too, I had before my mind the home I wished to make in this country, and first one place and then another charmed me. But none seemed perfect where the sea was wanting, and so far I had not stood by the open waves of the Pacific. The soft climate of the San José Valley was very enticing, and in the interior I had seen lovely spots in the midst of the great pines where the mountains looked down, but the sea was lacking. The piny fragrance was grateful, but it was not the invigorating salt breeze which brings with it renewed strength. This I wanted for my mother. For me, the shore of "the sounding sea" was a pleasure of which I never wearied, and I knew that along this coast the sea broke deep against bold rocks or shining sands. All this I had reason to believe I would find somewhere on the Santa Cruz shore. We remained on the upper portion of the mountain several days. The place of our encampment was two thousand feet above the sea, and was covered with a luxuriant growth of grass a foot high in many places.

At sunrise the temperature was 40°, at noon, 60°, at four in the afternoon, 65°, and 63° at sunset, with very pleasant weather. The mountains were wooded with many varieties of trees, and in some parts with heavy forests. These forests are characterized by a cypress (*Taxodium*) of extraordinary dimensions, which I have already mentioned among the trees in the Sierra Nevada as distinguished among the forest trees of America by its superior size and height. Among many we measured in this part of the mountain a diameter of nine or ten feet was frequent, sometimes eleven; but going beyond eleven only in a single tree, which reached fourteen feet in diameter. Above two hundred feet was a frequent height. In this locality the bark was very deeply furrowed and unusually thick, being fully sixteen inches on some of the trees. It was now in bloom, flowering near the summit, and the flowers consequently difficult to procure.

This is the staple timber tree of the country, being cut into both boards and shingles, and is the principal timber sawed at the mills. It is soft and easily worked, wearing away too quickly to be used for floors; but it seems to have all the durability which anciently gave the cypress so much celebrity. Posts which had been exposed to the weather three-quarters of a century, since the foundation of the Missions, showed no marks of decay in the wood and are now converted into beams and posts for private dwellings. In California this tree is called the *Palo colorado*, redwood.

Among the oaks in this mountain is a handsome, lofty evergreen tree, specifically different from those of the lower grounds, and in its general appearance much resembling hickory. The bark is smooth, of a white color, and the wood hard and close-grained. It seems to prefer the north hillsides, where some were nearly four feet in diameter and a hundred feet high.

Another remarkable tree of these woods is called in the language of the country madrona. It is a beautiful evergreen with large, thick, and glossy digitated leaves; the trunk and branches reddish-colored and having a smooth and singularly naked appearance, as if the bark had been stripped off. In its green state the wood is brittle, very heavy, hard, and close-grained; it is said to assume a red color when dry, sometimes variegated, and susceptible of a high polish. This tree was found by us only in the mountains. Some measured nearly four feet in diameter and were about sixty feet high. A few scattered flowers were now showing throughout the forests, and on the open ridges shrubs were flowering; but the bloom was not yet general.

On the 25th of February we descended to the coast near the northwestern point of Monterey Bay, losing our fine weather, which in the evening changed to a cold southeasterly storm that continued with heavy and constant rains for several days.

The rainstorm closed with February, and the weather becoming fine, on the 1st of March we resumed our progress along the coast. Over the face of the country between Santa Cruz and Monterey, and around the plains of San Juan, the grass, which had been eaten down by the large herds of cattle, was now everywhere springing up, and flowers began to show their bloom. In the valleys of the mountains bordering the Salinas plains wild oats were three feet high and well headed. The Salinas River runs through these plains, which are some fifty miles in length.

Pursuing our course to the southward, I encamped on the afternoon of March 3d at the Hartnell rancho, which is on a small creek bed well out on the plain.[20] We were now passing Monterey, which was about twenty-five miles distant.

The Salinas Valley lay outside of the more occupied parts of the country, and I was on my way to a pass opening into the San Joaquin Valley, at the head of a western branch of the Salinas River.

In the afternoon the quiet of the camp was disturbed by the sudden appearance of a cavalry officer with two men. The officer proved to be Lieutenant [José Antonio] Chavez, with a communication from the commanding general. He seemed disposed to be somewhat rude and abrupt as I have remarked that subalterns usually are when they represent unfriendly masters. This one brought to me peremptory letters from the general and prefect, ordering me forthwith out of the Department, and threatening force in the event that I should not instantly comply with the order.

Surprised both at the message and the terms in which it was worded, I expressed to the envoy my astonishment at General Castro's breach of good faith, and the rudeness with which he committed it; both of which, I remarked to him, were unworthy of an officer in his position. And I desired him to say in reply to General Castro that I peremptorily refused compliance to an order insulting to my Government and myself. And with this message the envoy went off to his general.[21] Like myself, my men were roused by the offense of the message, and were more than ready to support me in any course I saw fit to adopt.

Early in the morning I moved camp a few miles to the foot of the ridge which separates the Salinas from the San Joaquin, at the house of Don Joaquin Gomez. A stream here issues from the mountain which is called the Gavilan Peak. The road from Monterey passes by this place, entering the neighboring San Juan Valley by way of a short pass called the Gomez Pass.

From the Gomez rancho there is a wood road leading up to the top of the ridge; following this in the morning, I moved up the mountain and encamped on a small wooded flat at the summit of the sierra. This was a convenient position. It afforded wood, water, and grass, and commanded a view of the surrounding country, including the valley of San Juan and the Salinas plain. In case of exigency it opened a retreat to the San Joaquin.

Arriving at the summit, I proceeded immediately to build a rough but strong fort of solid logs, for which we found good trees abundant on the ridge. While this was being built a tall sapling was prepared, and on it, when all was ready, the American flag was raised amidst the cheers of the men. The raising of this flag proved to be a premonitory symptom.[22]

Meantime I opened communication with a rancho in the valley and a steer was brought up to me by two Californian vaqueros.

The wild steer never could have been driven up by the vaqueros, but they had made him fast by a riata to a work ox which tugged it up to the camp; they butchered it immediately, and the smell and sight of the blood so excited the "tame" ox that he became wild and commenced hostilities by charging into and scattering the camp.

I remained in position, our flag flying, for three days; during which I received information from Mr. Larkin and from Californians of what was going on below. From the fort by aid of the glass we could see below, at the Mission of San Juan, Castro's troops gathering, and by the vaqueros we were informed that Indians (*mansos*) were being brought into their camp and kept excited by drink.

Late in the afternoon of the second day we discovered a body of cavalry coming up the wood road which led from the Monterey road to our camp. With about forty men I went quickly down the wood road to where a thicket along the creek made a good ambush, and waited for them. They came up to within a few hundred yards, when they halted; but after some consultation they turned back. Had they come on, they would have had to pass within a few paces of us.

Late in the afternoon of the third day the pole bearing our flag fell to the ground. Thinking I had remained as long as the occasion required, I took advantage of the accident to say to the men that this was an indication for us to move camp, and accordingly I gave the order to prepare to move. The protecting favor which the usage of all civilized governments and peoples accords to scientific expeditions imposed on me, even here, a corresponding obligation; and I now felt myself bound to go on my way, having given General Castro sufficient time to execute his threat. Besides, I kept always in mind the object of the Government to obtain possession of California and would not let a proceeding which was mostly personal put obstacles in the way.

FOOTNOTES

1. This statement must refer to the country immediately adjacent to the route which Frémont intended to take. Joseph Walker, as Washington Irving relates in his book on Bonneville, had taken his party in 1833 (the party that was to explore the Great Salt Lake area thoroughly, and which did almost everything else except that) into the Great Basin. He had gone to the head of Ogden's River (now known by Frémont's name as the Humboldt), and followed it to its sink—"until they ascertained that it lost itself in a great swampy lake, to which there was no apparent discharge." That is, Walker

knew this Humboldt section of the Great Basin well; in fact, he recrossed eastward by this line on his return. But Frémont himself now intended to go by a different line, though sending some of his party by the Humboldt.

2. The Indians were wrong; Walker, Peter Skene Ogden (the first to reach the Humboldt), Jedediah Smith (1827), and the Bartleson-Bidwell party (1841) had all crossed the desert.

3. Frémont's appellation of Pilot Peak has endured. The man who, using Frémont's line, gave his name to this short cut to California was Lansford W. Hastings.

4. The camp, as Dellenbaugh states, was near present-day Shafter, Nevada.

5. If the purposes of the party had been purely scientific, it would have been highly prudent and wise to linger long in examining the little-known Great Basin. But its purposes were partly political and military; the Manifest Destiny group in Washington had impressed on Frémont the fact that war with Mexico was imminent, and their belief that when it came, the Mexicans—unless Americans were on hand for forestalling action—would transfer California to British protection.

6. The Humboldt, draining northeastern Nevada, extends west and south some three hundred miles before it falls into the Humboldt Sink. It has been well called the early highroad of the nation from Salt Lake City to central California. Alexander Humboldt (1767-1835), one of the greatest scientists and geographers of his time, had an immense reputation in this period, reflected in the names of towns in Iowa, Kansas, Nebraska, and other States. But Frémont was the first to put his name on our map.

7. This incident, a good illustration of Frémont's humanity (he disliked taking the life of an animal except under necessity, and abhorred the wanton slaying of Indians) contrasts with bloody incidents in the careers of both Kit Carson and Joseph Walker. The Walker party in this area in 1833 had shot about all the Indians they met, twenty-nine in one spot.

8. According to Dellenbaugh, the camp was some fifteen miles southeast of present-day Hawthorne, Nevada.

9. But he could not have been quite at the head of his Salmon Trout River (the Truckee), for it flows out of Lake Tahoe. Dellenbaugh states that he was within a few miles of Donner Lake.

10. Already emigrant wagons had marked a road through this pass!—later named the Donner Pass. They were the wagons of the Stevens-Townsend party of the previous year, the first wagons in history to cross the Sierra Nevada.

11. Frémont's trip from Great Salt Lake to California, now ending, had in large part (though not in the pass used) blazed a new trail. E. L. Sabin remarks in Kit Carson Days that he had found a new joint in the armor of the Great Basin. "Where much had been white, save for the arching legend 'Unknown,' now much was etched with physical symbols and place names. And although the Frémont southern route was improved upon and shortened by later explorations . . . he really pioneered a permanent feasible trail between the Salt Lake and Northern California. Moreover, he and his stalwarts were the first white men, as he rightfully asserts, to make a survey of this, the prospector's end of Nevada, long thereafter to be terra incognita save to the emigrant, the stage, the pack animals, the Mormon station-keepers, the treasure delver, and the wandering Indian."

12. When Frémont first arrived at Sutter's Fort, Sutter himself was absent, and John Bidwell, who had come to California with the Bartleson-Bidwell

party in 1841, was in charge. According to Bidwell's account, written long afterward for the *Century Magazine*, Frémont asked for much more in the way of animals and supplies than the fort could give him; and when Bidwell made this plain, Frémont took offense. It was true that the second expedition had "created some excitement" among the Mexican authorities; they had become alarmed, as the American consul in Monterey, California, had reported to the State Department on April 12, 1844. Their alarm, with war clouds thickening fast, was now to be greater. When Sutter came back to his fort on the day after Frémont's arrival, he was as cheery, bustling, and helpful as ever, finding mules, cattle, horses, and other supplies. He also notified the Mexican commander in northern California, General Mariano Guadelupe Vallejo, that Frémont's party wished merely to refit for further scientific labors. Sutter was both wise and kindly in all his relations with Americans.

13. The Horsethief Indians, as Frémont tells us, had been Christian Indians at the California missions; when the missions were broken up by the Mexican Government, the Indians took to the mountains, and began running off horses from lowland ranches. They lived on horse meat. Some paragraphs here which detail several encounters of Frémont's party with these thievish tribesmen are omitted. They suggest that Frémont was willing to show a certain aggressiveness in behalf of the American ranchers, who had been losing many horses.

14. These quicksilver mines were later to be the subject of a famous litigation. Frémont says merely that he found them "very interesting," and that they could have been bought at this time for $30,000. He paused at Yerba Buena (now San Francisco) to write his wife a letter, here omitted, in which he states that the existing descriptions of the Great Basin, representing it as a barren plain, were all wrong. Crossing it between the 28th and 39th parallels, he found it traversed by parallel ranges of mountains, "covered with grasses of the best quality, wooded with several varieties of trees, and containing more deer and mountain sheep than we had seen in any previous part of our voyage." He added that he could offer much important new geographical information: "I find the theory of our Great Basin fully confirmed in having for its southern boundary ranges of lofty mountains." He expected to turn homeward at the proper season: "Many months of hardships, close trials, and anxieties have tried me severely, and my hair is turning gray before its time. But all this passes, *et la bon temps viendra*." This letter was dated January 24, 1846. Much was to happen, and some very bad times were to come, before he saw Jessie again.

15. Thomas O. Larkin is called by his discerning biographer, Reuben L. Underhill, an "influential trader; prosperous merchant; first press agent; first and only United States consul; political power among officials of an alien race and creed; first real-estate agent, speculator, and subdivider; reputedly the first millionaire" of his adopted land. Born in Massachusetts in 1832, he had arrived in California thirty years later, and settled at Monterey. A genial, witty man, he made friends easily with the native Californians. He remained a loyal friend to the people even when Mexican and American interests clashed, and did what he could to soften the rigors of the conflict. As able and influential as Sutter, he was shrewder and better balanced. He died in 1858.

16. In the fall of 1844 a revolt against the Mexican governor, Micheltorena, had broken out in California, and he had been forced to surrender in February, 1845. When he departed, California became practically an independent republic. Its government was divided between a civil chief in Los Angeles, Pio

Pico, and a military commandant in Monterey, José Castro. As southern and northern California regarded each other with jealousy and dislike, and as Pico and Castro soon quarreled over revenues, civil war seemed probable. The Americans in California, and particularly those in the Upper Sacramento Valley, regarded the situation uneasily. Castro had warned the Americans that unless they obtained licenses to hold lands as Mexican citizens, they would have to leave. Of the uneasy political situation Frémont would have heard a great deal.

17. Frémont now had a formidable little body—sixty-two well-armed men well trained in marksmanship.

18. William Fisher's ranch was some thirteen miles southeast of San José, between Monterey and San Francisco. It is but a few miles from the spot later chosen for the Lick Observatory.

19. The mountains about here are the Calaveras and Santa Cruz ranges.

20. The E. P. Hartnell ranch was owned by an immigrant from England. It is to be noted that Frémont's expedition was moving at a very leisurely pace, as if waiting on events. It is also to be noted that he had not set out northeast toward the San Joaquin for the Oregon country, nor toward the southeast toward the Colorado River. On the contrary, he had moved toward the southwest. His line of march would take his sixty-two well-armed men through the best settled parts of California.

21. Frémont did not like the language of the message; he did not like the fact that Castro, after promising him protection, should now suddenly order him to get out under threat of forcible expulsion. But Frémont was wrong and Castro in the right. The Mexican authorities had the right to order him from the country at any time they pleased; and his march down alongside the coast settlements, toward the southwest, strongly indicated that his party was not a mere peaceable scientific expedition.

22. Frémont was putting himself still more clearly in the wrong; he should have communicated in writing with Castro. Instead, he was offering battle. He seemed ready to provoke a war. Probably he was actuated by a desire to maintain his prestige with his own men, and with the American settlers; and as the paragraphs below indicate, he gave way in time. But he had acted in an unwarranted manner.

CHAPTER 12

To the Shasta Country: Klamath Lake: Gillespie's Arrival: The Recall to California *

MARCH 11, 1846. Descending the southeastern side of the ridge, we halted for the night on a stream about three miles from the camp of General Castro, a few miles from our fort. The next day we resumed our route, and emerging into the valley of the San Joaquin on the 11th, we found almost a summer temperature and the country clothed in the floral beauty of spring. Traveling by short stages, we reached the Tuolumne River on the evening of the 14th. By observation, in latitude 37° 25′ 53″ and longitude 120° 35′ 55″.

* This chapter is taken from Frémont's *Memoirs*, Vol. I, pp. 470ff. Eight pages of letters which Consul T. O. Larkin sent from Monterey, March 4–March 27, 1846, dealing with Frémont's movements and his clash with Castro, are omitted; they are almost purely political in content. These letters are addressed to various persons, but the most important are to the Secretary of State, Buchanan. Larkin, anxious to keep the peace, must have been much irritated by Frémont's conduct, but his letters betray a certain sympathy with the explorer. He was disgusted by the proclamation which Castro posted after Frémont's departure bragging of the way in which he had driven out this gang of American "bandits." Mexican officers boasted that the Yankees had fled in such haste as to leave their best horses behind. "The horses proved to be those belonging to the Californians themselves," Larkin commented to Buchanan; and he added that the Americans, far from being driven headlong, had moved from four to six miles a day to rest their men.

Larkin also added that many English and American settlers had wished to join Frémont, who could thus have mustered a force as large as that of the Californians. When Frémont reached Fort Sutter, the settlers there gathered around him with noisy congratulations on the firmness of his stand. At that moment General Zachary Taylor, under orders from Polk, had led his army to within thirty miles of the Rio Grande, on disputed territory, despite written warning from the Mexican troops that this advance would be deemed equivalent to a declaration of war. At that moment, too, a lieutenant of the Marine Corps, Archibald H. Gillespie, was at sea, nearing California, with instructions for Larkin and messages and papers for Frémont.

476

On the 21st we entered the Sacramento Valley, and on the 22d encamped at a favorite spot opposite the house of Mr. Grimes. As already mentioned, his house was not far from Sutter's Fort. We remained several days here on the American River, to recruit our animals on the abundant range between the Sacramento and the hills.

On the 24th we broke up camp with the intention of making an examination of the Lower Sacramento Valley, of which I had seen but little above Sutter's Fort. I left the American River ten miles above its mouth, traveling a little east of north in the direction of the Bear River settlements. The road led among oak timber, over ground slightly undulating, covered with grass intermingled with flowers.

At sunrise on the 25th the temperature was a few degrees above the freezing-point, with an easterly wind and a clear sky.

In about thirty miles' travel to the north, we reached the Keyser rancho, on Bear River; an affluent to Feather River, the largest tributary of the Sacramento. The route lay over an undulating country—more so as our course brought us nearer the mountains—wooded with oaks and shrubbery in blossom, with small prairies intervening. Many plants were in flower, and among them the California poppy, unusually magnificent. It is the characteristic bloom of California at this season, and the Bear River bottoms, near the hills, were covered with it. The blue fields of the nemophyla and this golden poppy represent fairly the skies and gold of California.

I was riding quietly along with Godey through the oak groves, the party being several miles off nigher to the hills, when we discovered two Indian women busily occupied among the trees on the top of a hill, gathering plants or clover grass into their conical baskets. Taking advantage of the trees, we had nearly reached the top of the hill, thinking to surprise these quick-eyed beings. Reaching the top, we found nothing there except the baskets—apparently suddenly dropped and the grass spilled out. There were several bushes of a long-stemmed, grasslike shrub, and searching around to see what had become of them, we discovered two pairs of naked feet sticking out just above the top of the bushes.

At the shout we raised two girls to whom the feet belonged rolled out of the bushes into which they had only time to dive as we neared the top of the hill, thinking perhaps that we had not seen them. They were but little alarmed and joined in the laugh we had at their ostrichlike idea of hiding. It appeared that they belonged to a village not far away toward the hills. Ranging around in that beautiful climate, gathering where they had not the trouble to sow, these people had at that time their life of thorough enjoyment. The oaks and pines and grasses gave them abundant vegetable food, and game was not shy. We crossed several small streams, and found the ground miry from the recent rains. The temperature at four in the afternoon was 70°, and at sunset 58°, with an easterly wind, and the night bright and clear.

The morning of the 26th was clear, and warmer than usual; the wind southeasterly, and the temperature 40°. We traveled across the valley plain, and in about sixteen miles reached Feather River at twenty miles from its junction with the Sacramento, near the mouth of the Yuba, so called from a village of Indians who live on it. The river has high banks—twenty or thirty feet—and was here one hundred and fifty yards wide, a deep, navigable stream. The Indians aided us across the river with canoes and small rafts. Extending along the bank in front of the village was a range of wicker cribs, about twelve feet high, partly filled with what is there the Indians' staff of life—acorns. A collection of huts, shaped like beehives, with naked Indians sunning themselves on the tops, and these acorn cribs, are the prominent objects in an Indian village.

There is a fine farm, or rancho, on the Yuba,[1] stocked with about three thousand head of cattle, and cultivated principally in wheat, with some other grains and vegetables, which are carried by means of the river to a market at San Francisco. Mr. Cordua, a native of Germany, who is proprietor of the place, informed me that his average harvest of wheat was twenty-five bushels to the acre, which he supposed would be about the product of the wheatlands in the Sacramento valley. The labor on this and other farms in the valley is performed by Indians. The temperature here was 74° at two in the afternoon, 71° at four, and 69° at sunset, with a northeasterly wind and a clear sky.

At sunrise of the 27th the temperature was 42°, clear, with a northeasterly wind. We traveled northwardly, up the right bank of the river, which was wooded with large white and evergreen oaks, interspersed with thickets of shrubbery in full bloom. This was a pleasant journey of twenty-seven miles, and we encamped at the bend of the river, where it turns from the course across the valley to run southerly to its junction with the Sacramento. The thermometer at sunset was 67°, sky partially clouded, with southerly wind.

The thermometer at sunrise on the 28th was at 45° 5', with a northeasterly wind. The road was over an open plain, with a few small sloughs or creeks that do not reach the river. After traveling about fifteen miles, we encamped on Butte Creek, a beautiful stream of clear water about fifty yards wide, with a bold current running all the year. It has large, fertile bottoms, wooded with open groves, and having a luxuriant growth of peavine among the grass. The oaks here were getting into general bloom. Fine ranchos have been selected on both sides of the stream, and stocked with cattle, some of which were now very fat. A rancho here is owned by Neal, who formerly belonged to my exploring party. It may be remembered that in my last expedition I had acceded to his request to be left at Sutter's, where he was offered high wages, with a certain prospect of betterment, where good mechanics were in great request. He was a skillful blacksmith, and had been and was very useful to me, as our horses' feet were one of the first cares. But his uniform good conduct rendered him worthy of any favor I could grant, and he was accordingly left at Sutter's when we resumed our march homeward. In the brief time which had elapsed he had succeeded in becoming a prospering stockman, with a good rancho. There is a *rancheria* (Indian village) near by, and some of the Indians gladly ran races for the head and offals of a fat cow which had been presented to us. They were *entirely* naked. . . .*

The temperature at sunrise the next day was 50°, with cumuli in the south and west, which left a clear sky at nine, with a northwest wind, and temperature of 64°. We traveled twenty miles, and encamped on Pine Creek, another fine stream, with bottoms of fertile land wooded with groves of large and handsome oaks, some attaining to six feet in diameter, and forty to seventy feet in height. At four in the afternoon the thermometer showed 74° and 64° at sunset, and the sky clear, except in the horizon.

March 30th. The sun rose in masses of clouds over the eastern mountains. A pleasant morning, with a sunrise temperature of 46° 5', and some mosquitoes—never seen, it is said, in the coast country; but at seasons of high water abundant and venomous in the bot-

* Weather detail omitted.

toms of the Joaquin and Sacramento. On the tributaries nearer the mountains but few are seen, and those go with the sun. Continuing up the valley, we crossed in a short distance a large wooded creek, having now about thirty-five feet breadth of water. Our road was over an upland prairie of the Sacramento, having a yellowish, gravelly soil, generally two or three miles from the river, and twelve or fifteen from the foot of the eastern mountains. On the west it was twenty-five or thirty miles to the foot of the mountains, which here make a bed of high and broken ranges. In the afternoon, about half a mile above its mouth, we encamped on Deer Creek, another of these beautiful tributaries to the Sacramento. It has the usual broad and fertile bottom lands common to these streams, wooded with groves of oak and a large sycamore (*Platanus occidentalis*), distinguished by bearing its balls in strings of three to five, and peculiar to California. Mr. Lassen, a native of Germany,[2] has established a rancho here, which he has stocked, and is gradually bringing into cultivation. Wheat, as generally throughout the north country, gives large returns; cotton, planted in the way of experiment, was not injured by frost, and succeeded well; and he has lately planted a vineyard, for which the Sacramento valley is considered to be singularly well adapted. The seasons are not yet sufficiently understood, and too little has been done in agriculture, to afford certain knowledge of the capacities of the country. This farm is in the 40th degree of latitude, our position on the river being in 39° 57' 00" and longitude 121° 56' 44" west from Greenwich, and elevation above the sea five hundred and sixty feet. About three miles above the mouth of this stream are the first rapids—the present head of navigation—in the Sacramento River, which, from the rapids to its mouth in the bay, is more than two hundred miles long, and increasing in breadth from one hundred and fifty yards to six hundred yards in the lower part of its course. . . .*

Much cloudy weather and some showers of rain, during this interval, considerably reduced the temperature, which rose with fine weather on the 5th. Salmon was now abundant in the Sacramento. Those which we obtained were generally between three and four feet in length, and appeared to be of two distinct kinds. It is said that as many as four different kinds ascend the river at different periods. The great abundance in which this fish is found gives it

---

* Some detail on temperature omitted.

an important place among the resources of the country. The salmon crowd in immense numbers up the Umpqua, Klamath, and Trinity rivers, and into every little river and creek on the coast north of the Bay of San Francisco; and up the San Joaquin River, into the Stanislaus, beyond which the Indians say they do not go. Entering all the rivers of the coast far to the north, and finding their way up into the smaller branches which penetrate the forests of the interior country, climbing up cataracts and lesser falls, this fish had a large share in supporting the Indians—who raised nothing, but lived on what Nature gave. A "salmon water," as they named it, was a valuable possession to a tribe or village, and jealously preserved as an inheritance. I found the "salmon waters" in the forests along the eastern flank of the Cascade Range below the Columbia River.

In the evening of the 5th we resumed our journey northward, and encamped on a little creek near the Sacramento, where an emigrant from "the States" was establishing himself, and had already built a house. It is a handsome place, wooded with groves of oak, and along the creek are sycamore, ash, cottonwood, and willow. The day was fine, with a northwest wind.

The temperature at sunrise the next day (April 6th) was 42°, with a northeasterly wind. We continued up the Sacramento, which we crossed in canoes at a farm on the right bank of the river. The Sacramento was here about one hundred and forty yards wide, and with the actual stage of water, which I was informed continued several months, navigable for a steamboat. We encamped a few miles above, on a creek wooded principally with large oaks. Grass was good and abundant, with wild oats and peavine in the bottoms. The day was fine, with a cool northwesterly breeze, which had in it the air of the high mountains. The wild oats here were not yet headed.

The snowy peak of Shasta bore directly north, showing out high above the other mountains. Temperature at sunset 57°, with a west wind and sky partly clouded.

April 7th. The temperature at sunrise was 37°, with a moist air; and a faintly clouded sky indicated that the wind was southerly along the coast.

We traveled toward the Shasta peak, the mountain ranges on both sides of the valleys being high and rugged, and snow-covered. Some remarkable peaks in the sierra, to the eastward, are called The

Sisters, and, nearly opposite, the Coast Range shows a prominent peak, to which in remembrance of my friend Senator Linn, I gave the name Mount Linn, as an enduring monument to recall the prolonged services rendered by him in securing to the country our Oregon coast.[3] I trust this reason will protect it from change. These giant monuments, rising above the country and seen from afar, keep alive and present with the people the memory of patriotic men, and so continue their good services after death. Mount Linn and Mount Shasta keep open to the passing glance each an interesting page of the country's history—the one recording a successful struggle for the ocean boundary which it overlooks, the other the story of a strange people passed away. And so, too, these natural towers call attention from the detail of daily occupation to the larger duties which should influence the lives of men.

Leaving the Sacramento at a stream called Red Bank Creek, we entered on a high and somewhat broken upland, timbered with at least four varieties of oaks, with manzanita (*Arbutus menziesii*) and other shubbery interspersed. The manzanita is the strange shrub which I met in March of '44 in coming down from the Sierra Nevada to Sutter's Fort, and which in my journal of that time I described as follows: "A new and singular shrub, which had made its appearance since crossing the mountain, was very frequent today. It branched out near the ground, forming a clump eight to ten feet high, with pale green leaves of an oval form, and the body and branches had a naked appearance as if stripped of the bark, which is very smooth and thin, of a chocolate color, contrasting well with the pale green of the leaves." Out of its red berries the Indians make a cider which, put to cool in the running streams, makes a pleasant, refreshing drink.

A remarkable species of pine, having leaves in threes (sometimes six to nine inches long), with bluish foliage, and a spreading, oak-shaped top, was scattered through the timber. I have remarked that this tree grows lower down the mountains than the other pines, being found familiarly associated with oaks, the first met after leaving the open valleys, and seeming to like a warm climate. It seems that even among inanimate things association levels differences. This tree, growing among oaks, forgets its narrow piny form and color, and takes the spreaded shape of the oaks, their broad summits, and lesser heights. Flowers were as usual abundant. The splendid California poppy characterized all the route along the valley. A species of clover was in bloom, and the berries of the manzanita were beginning to redden on some trees, while others were still in bloom. We encamped, at an elevation of about one thousand feet above the sea, on a large stream called Cottonwood Creek, wooded on the bottoms with oaks, and with cottonwoods along the bed, which is sandy and gravelly. The water was at this time about twenty yards wide, but is frequently fifty. The face of the country traversed during the day was gravelly, and the bottoms of the creek where we encamped have a sandy soil.

There are six or seven *rancherias* of Indians on the Sacramento River between the farm where we had crossed the Sacramento and the mouth of this creek, and many others in the mountains about the heads of these streams.

The next morning was cloudy, threatening rain, but the sky grew brighter as the sun rose, and a southerly wind changed to northwest, which brought, as it never fails to bring, clear weather.

We continued sixteen miles up the valley, and encamped on the Sacramento River. In the afternoon (April 8th) the weather again grew thick, and in the evening rain began to fall in the valley and snow on the mountains. We were now near the head of the lower valley, and the face of the country and the weather began sensibly to show the influence of the rugged mountains which surround and terminate it.

The valley of the Sacramento is divided into upper and lower—the lower two hundred miles long, the upper known to the trappers as Pitt River, about one hundred and fifty; and the latter not merely entitled to the distinction of upper, as being higher up the river, but also as having a superior elevation of some thousands of feet above it. The division is strongly and geographically marked. The Shasta peak stands at the head of the lower valley, rising from a base of about one thousand feet out of a forest of heavy timber. It ascends like an immense column upward of fourteen thousand feet (nearly the height of Mont Blanc), the summit glistening with snow, and visible, from favorable points of view, at a distance of one hundred and forty miles down the valley. The river here, in descending from the upper valley, plunges down through a cañon, falling two thousand feet in twenty miles. This upper valley is one hundred and fifty miles long, heavily timbered, the climate and productions modified by its altitude, its more northern position, and the proximity and elevation of the neighboring mountains covered with snow. It contains valleys of arable land, and is deemed capable of settlement. Added to the lower valley, it makes the whole valley of the Sacramento three hundred and fifty miles long,

April 9th. At ten o'clock the rain which commenced the previous evening had ceased, and the clouds clearing away, we boated the river, and continued our journey eastward toward the foot of the Sierra. The Sacramento bottoms here are broad and prettily wooded, with soil of a sandy character. Our way led through very handsome, open woods, principally of oaks, mingled with a considerable quantity of the oak-shaped pine. Interspersed among these were boskets or thickets of manzanita, and an abundant white-flowering shrub, now entirely covered with small blossoms. The head of the valley here (lower valley) is watered by many small streams, having fertile bottom lands, with a good range of grass and acorns. In about six miles we crossed a creek twenty or twenty-five feet wide, and several miles farther descended into the broad bottoms of a swift stream, about twenty yards wide, called Cow Creek, so named as being the range of a small band of cattle, which ran off here from a party on their way to Oregon. They are entirely wild, and are hunted like other game. A large band of antelope was seen in the timber, and five or six deer came darting through the woods. An antelope and several deer were killed. There appear to be two species of these deer—both of the kind generally called black-tailed; one, a larger species frequenting the prairies and lower grounds, the other much smaller, and found in the mountains only. The mountains in the northeast were black with clouds when we reached the creek, and very soon a fierce hailstorm burst down on us, scattering our animals and covering the ground an inch in depth with hailstones about the size of wild cherries. The face of the country appeared as whitened by a fall of snow, and the weather became unpleasantly cold. The evening closed in with rain, and thunder rolling around the hills. Our elevation here was between one thousand and eleven hundred feet.

At sunrise the next morning the thermometer was at 33°. The surrounding mountains showed a continuous line of snow, and the high peaks looked wintry. Turning to the southward, we retraced our steps down the valley, and reached Lassen's, on Deer River, on the evening of the 11th. The Sacramento bottoms between Antelope and Deer River were covered with oats, which had attained their full height, growing as in sown fields. The country here exhibited the maturity of spring. The California poppy was everywhere forming seed pods, and many plants were in flower and seed together. Some varieties of clover were just beginning to bloom. By the middle of the month the seed vessels of the California poppy, which, from its characteristic abundance, is a prominent feature in the vegetation, had attained their full size; but the seeds of this and many other plants, although fully formed, were still green-colored, and not entirely ripe. At this time I obtained from the San Joaquin Valley seeds of the poppy, and other plants, black and fully ripe, while they still remained green in this part of the Sacramento—the effect of a warmer climate in the valley of the San Joaquin. . . .*

Here at Lassen's I set up the transit and during the nights of the 14th and 16th (April) obtained good observations of moon culminations which established the longitude of the place in 120° 56′ 44″, latitude obtained 39° 57′ 04″. This was the third of my main stations and the place of observation was upon Deer River half a mile above its mouth in the Sacramento and opposite Lassen's house.

On the 24th I left Lassen's,[4] intending to penetrate the country along the Cascade Ranges north into Oregon, and connect there with the line of my journey of '43, which lay up the Fall River of the Columbia and south to the great savannah, or grassy meadow-lake through which flows from among the ridges of the Cascade Mountains the principal tributary, or rather the main stream, of the waters which make the Klamath Lake and River. It is a timbered country, clothed with heavy pine forests that nourish many streams.

Traveling up the Sacramento over ground already described, we reached the head of the lower valley in the evening of the second day, and in the morning of the 26th left the Sacramento, going up one of the many pretty little streams that flow into the main river around the head of the lower valley. On either side low, steep ridges were covered along their summits with pines, and oaks occupied the somewhat broad bottom of the creek. Snowy peaks which made the horizon on the right gave a cool tone to the landscape, and the thermometer showed a temperature of 71°, but there was no breeze and the air was still and hot. There were many runs

* Some detail on weather omitted.

and small streams, with much bottom land, and the abundant grass and acorns, both of excellent quality, made it a favorite resort for game. The frequent appearance of game furnished excitement, and together with the fine weather, which made mere breathing an enjoyment, kept the party in exhilarated spirits. At our encampment among oak groves in the evening, we found ourselves apparently in a bear garden, where the rough denizens resented our intrusion and made a lively time for the hunters, who succeeded in killing four of them after we had encamped. During our skirmishing among the bear this afternoon we had overtaken and slightly wounded one, just enough to irritate him. At this moment Delaware Charley's horse fell near by the bear. To save Charley we had all to close in on the bear, who was fortunately killed before he could get the Delaware. In his fall the hammer of his gun struck Charley on the bridge of his nose and broke it in the middle. We had no surgeon, but I managed to get it into good shape and it healed without trace of injury. I was always proud of this surgical operation, and the Delaware was especially pleased. He was a fine-looking young man, and naïvely vain of his handsome face, which now had a nose unusual among his people; the aquiline arch had been broken to knit into a clear straight line, of which he became very vain.

At sunset the weather was pleasant, with a temperature of 56°. I had only an observation for latitude, which put the camp in 40° 38' 58", and the elevation above the sea was one thousand and eighty feet. The day following we found a good way along a flat ridge; there was a pretty stream in a mountain valley on the right, and the face of the country was already beginning to assume a mountainous character, wooded with mingled oak and long-leaved pine, and having a surface of scattered rocks, with grass or flowers, among them the three-leaved poppy, its particolored blossoms waving on the long stem above the grass, and gaining for itself the name *Mariposa*, already mentioned because of its resembling living butterflies. I speak often of the grass and the flowers, but I have learned to value the one and the other lend a beauty to the scenery which I do not like to omit, and the reader can always imagine for himself the brightness they give when once he has had described the glorious flowers of this country, where the most lovely hues are spread in fields over both hill and plain. At noon, when we were crossing a high ridge, the temperature was down to 61°, and where we encamped at an elevation of two thousand four hundred and sixty feet, on a creek that went roaring into the valley, the sunset temperature was 52°.

The next day I continued up the stream on which we had slept, and with it the mountain slope rose rapidly, clothed with heavy timber. On crossing one of the high ridges, snow and the great pine *Lambertiani* appeared together, and an hour before noon we reached a pass in the main ridge of the Sierra Nevada, in an open pine forest at an elevation of only four thousand six hundred feet, where the snow was in patches and the deciduous oaks were mingled with the pines. The thermometer was at 50°, and we were not above the upper limit of the oak region. This pass is in about the fortieth degree of latitude, and is in the terminating point of the northern link of the Sierra Nevada chain, which the Cascade Range takes up with the link of the Shasta peak. Between the points of these links the Upper Sacramento River [5] breaks down on its way to the Bay of San Francisco, and the Klamath River to the sea.

Going through this pass and descending the mountain, we entered into what may be called a basin or mountain valley, lying north and south along the ranges of the Cascade Mountains. Here we found a region very different from the Valley of California. We had left behind the soft, delightful climate of the coast, from which we were cut off by the high, snowy mountains, and had ascended into one resembling that of the Great Basin, and under the influence of the same elevation above the sea; but more fertile and having much forest land, and well watered. The face of the country was different from that of the valley which we had just left, being open and more spread into plain, in which there were frequent lakes as well as rivers. The soil itself is different, sometimes bare. At times we traveled over stretches in the forest where the soil was a gray or yellowish-white pumice stone, like that which I have seen along the Cascade Range in traveling south from the Columbia River, where the soil was covered with splendid pine forests, but where there was hardly a blade of grass to be found. Very different from this the compact growth of grass and flowers which belong to the California Valley, where the rich soil had accumulated the wash of ages from the mountains, and where the well-watered land and moisture of the air combine to cover the country with its uncommon and profuse vegetation. The country where we now were was not known to any of the men with me, and I was not able to communicate with any of the Indians, who in this region were unfriendly—from these I might have learned the names by which the natural features were known to them. Except in some of its leading features I regarded this district as not within the limits of fixed geography, and therefore I thought it well to give names to these—to some at the time, and to others afterward, when I came to making up a map of the country. And this was also necessary, as otherwise I could not conveniently refer to them.

On the 29th of April I encamped on the upper Sacramento, above Fall River, which is tributary to it. I obtained observations here, which gave for longitude 121° 07′ 59″ and for latitude 40° 58′ 43″; and the next day again encamped on it at the upper end of a valley, to which, from its marked form, I gave the name Round Valley.⁶ By observation, the longitude here is 121° 01′ 23″, latitude 41° 17′ 17″. On the first of May I encamped on the southeastern end of a lake, which afterward I named Lake Rhett in friendly remembrance of Mr. Barnwell Rhett, of South Carolina, who is connected with one of the events of my life which brought with it an abiding satisfaction. I obtained observations here which placed this end of the lake in longitude 121° 15′ 24″ and latitude 41° 48′ 49″.

This camp was some twenty-five or thirty miles from the lava beds near which Major-General Canby was killed by the Modocs ⁷ twenty-seven years later; and when there was some of the hardest fighting known in Indian history between them and our troops.

This Indian fighting is always close, incurring more certain risk of life and far more sanguinary, than in the ordinary contests between civilized troops. Every Indian fights with intention, and for all that is in him; he waits for no orders, but has every effort concentrated on his intention to kill. And, singularly, this Indian fighting, which calls for the utmost skill and courage on the part of men, is not appreciated by the Government, or held worthy of the notice given to the milder civilized warfare.

When we left Round Valley in the morning Archambeau, who was an inveterate hunter, had gone off among the hills and toward the mountain in search of game. We had now entered more into the open country, though still a valley or high upland along the foot of the main ridge, and were traveling north; but the route of the day is often diverted from its general course by accidents of country and for convenient camping grounds. Archambeau did not come in at night, and when the morning came and did not bring him I did not move camp, but sent out men to look for him. Since leaving the California mountains we had seen no Indians, though frequently we came upon their tracks and other sign. All through this country there were traces of them. Doubtless our campfires had discovered us to them, but they hovered around out of our way and out of sight.

The second day passed and still no trace of Archambeau had been found, and the greater part of the third was passed in scouring the country. There would have been little difficulty in a prairie region, but in a broken or hilly country much ground cannot be covered and the search is restricted to a small area. We had now been in camp three days and I began to be seriously disturbed by his absence. Game had been found scarce in the immediate neighborhood. He had nothing with him but a little dried meat when he turned off from the party, expecting to rejoin us before night, and the Indians in the region through which we were traveling were known to be hostile and treacherous, with a fixed character for daring. Parties from as far north as the Hudson's Bay Company's post who had penetrated here had met with some rough experiences, and the story of trapper adventure hereabout was full of disaster. On one occasion a large party of trappers from the north were encamped on one of the streams of the Cascade Range, and having been led into carelessness by the apparent friendly conduct of the Indians, were every man killed. It was easy to waylay a single man, especially if he were intent on game. I had always been careful of my men, and in all my journeyings lost but few, and with rare exceptions those were by accident or imprudence. Naturally disposed that way, I had always endeavored to provide for their safety so far as the nature of our exposed life permitted, for in case of accident, as we had no surgeon, I was myself the only resource.

A man lost from camp was likely also to lose his life. In such circumstances every hour increases the danger of his situation. And so about sunset we were greatly relieved when a shout from the men on guard roused the camp and we saw Archambeau creeping slowly in, man and horse equally worn-out. Searching for game, he had been led off and entangled among the hills until the coming night roused him and the darkness cut off all chance of reaching camp. His search was as fruitless on the following days. He did not meet game, and his horse being kept close at hand at night had no chance to feed, and was nearly as tired as himself. And he had probably owed his life to his good eyes. These were unusually fine, with an instant quickness to catch a moving object or any slight difference in color or form of what lay before him. I was riding with him on the prairie one day, off from the party, when he suddenly halted. "Stop," he said, "I see an antelope's horns." About fifty steps away an antelope was lying in the tall grass, and the tip of its horn was barely visible above it, but he not only saw it but shot and killed it.

And this time his eyes had served him well again. They were ranging around taking in all before him when he caught sight of a party of Indians. They were traveling directly across his line of way, making toward the coast mountains, probably going to some river in which there were salmon. If they had been coming toward him they would have seen him, or if they had crossed his trail behind him his life would have been lost. He saw them as they were coming up out of a broad ravine and in the instant got his horse out of sight down the slope of a hill. "My heart was in my mouth for a moment," he said. The danger of his situation had already brought on the hurry and excitement which often deprives a man of all prudence. In such mishaps a man quickly loses his head, but at this stage, happily, he struck our trail.

The arrival of Archambeau relieved and spread pleasure through the camp, where he was a general favorite. He was Canadian, tall, fine-looking, very cheerful, and with all the gaiety of the voyageur before hard work and a rough life had driven it out. He had that light, elastic French temperament that makes a cheerful companion in traveling; which in my experience brings out all there is of good or bad in a man. I loved to have my camp cheerful and took care always for the health and comfort which carry good temper with them. Usually, on leaving the frontier, I provided the men with tents or lodges, but by the time we had been a month or two on the road, they would come to me to say that it was hard on them to have to put up their lodge at night when they were tired, and that they made a delay in the morning when starting. So usually their shelters were gladly left behind and they took the weather as it came.

Meantime the days while we had been waiting here were not lost. Our animals had been resting on good grass, and in the morning the welcome order was given to move camp. . . . This was an order which the animals were always prone to resist promptly, and their three days' rest made them do it now with unusual vigor. But the men, too, refreshed by rest and cheered by the recovery of their companion, entered with equal spirit into the fray, and soon we were again on the trail, the animals settled down to their orderly work.

Archambeau was himself again in the morning after a night's rest, and good meals among companions, but his horse was let to run loose for some days, in order to recover its useful strength. With the animals refreshed, we made a long stretch and encamped on a stream flowing into Lake Rhett, which I called McCrady. This was the name of one of my boyhood's friends, living in Charleston, who came this evening into my mind, and I left his memory on the stream.[8] In such work as I was engaged in there is always much time for thinking—or ruminating, as it may better be called—not upon the road, but often at night, waiting for the hour when the work belonging to it may begin.

In the forenoon of the sixth we reached the Klamath Lake at its outlet, which is by a fine, broad stream, not fordable. This is a great fishing station for the Indians, and we met here the first we had seen since leaving the lower valley. They have fixed habitations around the shores of the lake, particularly at the outlet and inlet, and along the inlet up to the swamp meadow, where I met the Klamaths in the winter of '43–'44, and where we narrowly escaped disaster. Our arrival took them by surprise, and though they received us with apparent friendship, there was no warmth in it, but a shyness which came naturally from their habit of hostility.

At the outlet here were some of their permanent huts. From the lake to the sea I judged the river to be about two hundred miles long; it breaks its way south of the huge bulk of Shasta Peak between the points of the Cascade and Nevada ranges to the sea. Up this river the salmon crowd in great numbers to the lake, which is more than four thousand feet above the sea. It was a bright spring morning, and the lake and its surrounding scenery looked charming. It was inviting, and I would have been glad to range over it in one of the Indian canoes. The silent shores and unknown mountains had the attraction which mystery gives always. It was all wild and unexplored, and the uninvaded silence roused curiosity and invited research. Indigenous, the Indians like the rocks and trees seemed part of the soil, growing in a state of rude nature like the vegetation, and like it nourished and fed by nature. And so it had been back to a time of which nothing was known. All here was in the true aboriginal condition, but I had no time now for idling days, and I had to lose the pleasure to which the view before me invited. . . .

The Indians made me understand that there was another large river which came from the north and flowed into the lake at the northern end, and that the principal village was at its mouth, where also they caught many fish. Resuming our journey, we worked our way along between the lake and the mountain, and late in the day made camp at a run, near where it issued from the woods into the lake and where our animals had good feed. For something which happened afterward, I gave this run the name of Denny's Branch.[9] Animals and men all fared well here.

May 7th. The weather continued refreshingly cool. Our way led always between the lake and the foot of the mountains, frequently rough and blocked by decaying logs and fallen trees, where patches of snow still remained in the shade, over ground rarely trodden even by an Indian foot. In the timber the snow was heavy, and naturally much heavier toward the summits and in the passes of the mountains, where the winter still held sway. This year it had continued late and rough. In the late afternoon we reached a piece of open ground through which a steam ran toward the lake. Here the mountain receded a little, leaving a flat where the wood which still occupied the ground left us a convenient open space by the water, and where there was grass abundant. On the way along from the outlet no Indians had been seen and no other sign of life, but now and then when the lake was visible a canoe might be seen glancing along. But in the morning, as we were about to leave camp, a number of them came in. I could not clearly find where they had come from, though they pointed up the lake. Perhaps from some valley in the mountain on this stream, or perhaps they had followed our trail. This was most likely, but if so they were not willing to tell. They would not have done so with any good intent, and they knew well enough that we were aware of it. They said that they were hungry, and I had some mules unpacked and gave them part of our remaining scanty supply of dried meat and the usual present which an Indian, wild or tame, always instinctively expects.

We continued our route over the same kind of ground, rendered difficult by the obstructions which the wash of the rain and snow, and the fallen timber, the undisturbed accumulations of the many years, had placed in these forests. Crossing spurs of mountains and working around the bays or coves between the ridges or winding among the hills, it is surprising how a long day's march dwindles away to a few miles when it comes to be laid down between the rigorous astronomical stations. We had traveled in this direction many such days when we encamped in the afternoon of the 8th of May. A glance at the mountains . . . gives some idea of the character of this unexplored region. By unexplored, I wish to be understood to say that it had never been explored or mapped, or in any way brought to common knowledge, or rarely visited except by strong parties of trappers, and by those at remote intervals, doubtless never by trappers singly. It was a true wilderness. There was the great range of mountains behind the coast, and behind it the lakes and rivers known to the trappers, and that was all, and the interest attached to it was chiefly from the disasters which had befallen them. And from their reports, rude and exaggerated outlines Turtle Lake and Buenaventura River, had been marked down at the stations of the Fur Company. All this gave the country a charm for me. It would have been dull work if it had been to plod over a safe country and here and there to correct some old error.

And I had my work all planned. The friendly reader—and I hope that no unfriendly eyes will travel along with me over these lines; the friends may be few and the many are the neutral minds who read without reference to the writer, solely for the interest they find. To these I write freely, letting the hues of my mind color the paper, feeling myself on pleasant terms with them, giving to them in a manner a life confession in which I hope they find interest, and expecting to find them considerate and weighing fairly, and sometimes condoning, the events as we pass them in review. My reading friend, then, who has traveled with me thus far will remember that some seventeen months before this time, in the December of '43, in coming south from the Colombia, I encamped on a large savannah,

or meadow lake, which made the southern limit of my journey. I
met there a Klamath chief and his wife, who had come out to meet
me and share his fate, whether good or bad, and the chief had
afterward accompanied me and piloted me on my way through the
forest and the snow. Where I had encamped this night I was only
some twenty miles in an air line from their village and I was promising myself some pleasure in seeing them again. According to what
the Indians at the south end of the lake had told me, I had only to
travel eastward a short march and I would find a large village at
the inlet of the river, which I knew must be that on which my
friendly chief lived, some twenty miles above. And his Indians, too,
like all the others along these mountains, had the character of normal
hostility to the whites.

My plans when I started on my journey into this region were to
connect my present survey of the intervening country with my camp
on the savannah, where I had met the Klamaths in that December;
and I wished to penetrate among the mountains of the Cascade
Range. As I have said, except for the few trappers who had
searched the streams leading to the ocean for beaver, I felt sure
that these mountains were absolutely unknown. No one had penetrated their recesses to know what they contained, and no one had
climbed to their summits; and there remained the great attraction
of mystery in going into unknown places—the unknown lands of
which I had dreamed when I began this life of frontier travel. And
possibly, I thought, when I should descend their western flanks,
some safe harbor might yet be found by careful search along that
coast, where harbors were so few; and perhaps good passages from
the interior through these mountains to the sea. I thought that until
the snow should go off the lower part of the mountains I might
occupy what remained of the spring by a survey of the Klamath
River to its heads, and make a good map of the country along the
base of the mountains.

And if we should not find game enough to live upon, we could
employ the Indians to get supplies of salmon and other fish. But I
felt sure that there was game in the woods of these mountains as
well as in those more to the south. Traveling along the northern part
of this range in December of '43, I had seen elk tracks in the snow,
and at an old Cayuse village in the pine forest at the foot of the

mountains, only about sixty miles farther north, there were many deer horns lying around. This showed that we should probably find both elk and deer, and bear, in the mountains, and certainly on the slope toward the sea, where every variety of climate would be found, and every variety of mast-bearing trees, as in the oak region of the Sierra Nevada. And I had not forgotten how fascinated I had been with the winter beauty of the snowy range farther north when at sunrise and at sunset their rose-colored peaks stood up out of the dark pine forests into the clear light of the sky. And my thoughts took the same color when I remembered that Mr. Kern, who had his colors with him, could hold these lovely views in all their delicate coloring.

How fate pursues a man! Thinking and ruminating over these things, I was standing alone by my campfire, enjoying its warmth, for the night air of early spring is chill under the shadows of the high mountains. Suddenly my ear caught the faint sound of horses' feet,[10] and while I was watching and listening as the sounds, so strange hereabout, came nearer, there emerged from the darkness— into the circle of the firelight—two horsemen, riding slowly as though horse and man were fatigued by long traveling. In the foremost I recognized the familiar face of Neal, with a companion whom I also knew. They had ridden nearly a hundred miles in the last two days, having been sent forward by a United States officer who was on my trail with despatches for me; but Neal doubted if he would get through.

After their horses had been turned into the band and they were seated by my fire, refreshing themselves with good coffee while more solid food was being prepared, Neal told me his story. The officer who was trying to overtake me was named Gillespie. He had been sent to California by the Government and had letters for delivery to me. Neal knew the great danger from Indians in this country, and his party becoming alarmed and my trail being fresh, Mr. Gillespie had sent forward Neal and Sigler upon their best horses to overtake me and inform me of his situation. They had left him on the morning of the day before, and in the two days had ridden nearly a hundred miles, and this last day had severely tried the strength of their horses. When they parted from him they had not reached the lake, and for greater safety had not kept my trail quite to the outlet, but crossed to the right bank of the river, striking my trail again on the lake shore. They had discovered Indians on my trail after they had left Gillespie, and on the upper part of the lake the Indians had tried to cut them off, and they had escaped only by the speed and strength of their horses, which Neal had brought from his own rancho. He said that in his opinion I could not reach Gillespie in time to save him, as he had with him only three men and was traveling slow.

A quick eye and a good horse mean life to a man in an Indian country. Neal had both. He was a lover of horses and knew a good one, and those he had with him were the best on his rancho. He had been sent forward by the messenger to let me know that he was in danger of being cut off by the Indians. The trail back along the shore at the foot of the mountains was so nearly impassable at night that nothing could be gained by attempting it, but everything was made ready for an early start in the morning. For the relief party, in view of contingencies, I selected ten of the best men, including Carson, Stepp, Dick Owens, Godey, Basil, and Lajeunesse, with four of the Delawares.

When the excitement of the evening was over I lay down, speculating far into the night on what could be the urgency of the message which had brought an officer of the Government to search so far after me into these mountains. At early dawn we took the backward trail. Snow and fallen timber made the ride hard and long to where I thought to meet the messenger. On the way no Indians were seen and no tracks later than those where they had struck Neal's trail. In the afternoon, having made about forty-five miles, we reached the spot where the forest made an opening to the lake, and where I intended to wait. This was a glade, or natural meadow, shut in by the forest, with a small stream and good grass, where I had already encamped. I knew that this was the first water to which my trail would bring the messenger, and that I was sure to meet him here if no harm befell him on the way. The sun was about going down when he was seen issuing from the wood, accompanied by three men. He proved to be an officer of the Navy, Lieutenant Archibald Gillespie of the Marine Corps. We greeted him warmly. All were glad to see him, whites and Indians. It was long since any news had reached us, and everyone was as pleased to see him as if he had come freighted with letters from home, for all. It was now eleven months since any tidings had reached me.

Mr. Gillespie informed me that he had left Washington under orders from the President and the Secretary of the Navy, and was directed to reach California by the shortest route through Mexico to Mazatlan. He was directed to find me wherever I might be, and was informed that I would probably be found on the Sacramento River. In pursuance of his instructions he had accordingly started from Monterey to look for me on the Sacramento. Learning upon his arrival at Sutter's Fort that I had gone up the valley, he made up a small party at Neal's rancho and, guided by him, followed my trail and had traveled six hundred miles to overtake me, the latter part of the way through great dangers.[11]

The mission on which I had been originally sent to the West was a peaceful one, and Mr. Bancroft had sent Mr. Gillespie to give me warning of the new state of affairs and the designs of the President. Mr. Gillespie had been given charge of despatches from the Secretary of the Navy to Commodore Sloat, and had been purposely made acquainted with their import. Known to Mr. Bancroft as an able and thoroughly trustworthy officer, he had been well instructed in the designs of the Department and with the purposes of the Administration, so far as they related to California. Through him I now became acquainted with the actual state of affairs and the purposes of the Government. The information through Gillespie had absolved me from my duty as an explorer, and I was left to my duty as an officer of the American Army, with the further authoritative knowledge that the Government intended to take California. I was warned by my Government of the new danger against which I was bound to defend myself; and it had been made known to me now on the authority of the Secretary of the Navy that to obtain possession of California was the chief object of the President.

He brought me also a letter of introduction from the Secretary of State, Mr. Buchanan, and letters and papers from Senator Benton and family. The letter from the Secretary was directed to me in my private or citizen capacity, and though importing nothing beyond the introduction, it accredited the bearer to me as coming from the Secretary of State, and in connection with the circumstances and place of delivery it indicated a purpose in sending it. From the letter itself I learned nothing, but it was intelligibly explained to me by the accompanying letter from Senator Benton and by communications from Lieutenant Gillespie.

This officer informed me that he had been directed by the Secretary of State to acquaint me with his instructions, which had for their principal objects to ascertain the disposition of the California people, to conciliate their feelings in favor of the United States; and to find out, with a view to counteracting, the designs of the British Government upon that country. The letter from Senator Benton, while apparently of friendship and family details, contained passages and suggestions which, read by the light of many conversations and discussions with himself and others at Washington, clearly indicated to me that I was required by the Government to find out any foreign schemes in relation to California and, so far as might be in my power, to counteract them.

Neal had much to talk over with his old companions and pleasurable excitement kept us up late; but before eleven o'clock all were wrapped in their blankets and soundly asleep except myself. I sat by the fire in fancied security, going over again the home letters. These threw their own light upon the communication from Mr. Gillespie, and made the expected signal. In substance, their effect was: The time has come. England must not get a foothold. We must be first. Act—discreetly, but positively.

Looking back over the contingencies which had been foreseen in the discussions at Washington, I saw that the important one which carried with it the hopes of Senator Benton and the wishes of the Government was in the act of occurring, and it was with thorough satisfaction I now found myself required to do what I could to promote this object of the President. Viewed by the light of these deliberations in Washington, I was prepared to comprehend fully the communications brought to me by Mr. Gillespie. Now it was officially made known to me that my country was at war, and it was so made known expressly to guide my conduct. I had learned with certainty from the Secretary of the Navy that the President's plan of war included the taking possession of California, and under his confidential instructions I had my warrant. Mr. Gillespie was directed to act in concert with me. Great vigilance and activity were expected of us both, for it was desired that possession should be had of California before the presence in her ports of any foreign vessel of war might make it inconvenient.

I had about thought out the situation when I was startled by a sudden movement among the animals. Lieutenant Gillespie had told me that there were no Indians on his trail, and I knew there were none on mine. This night was one of two when I failed to put men on guard in an Indian country—this night and one spent on an island in the Great Salt Lake. The animals were near the shore of the lake, barely a hundred yards away. Drawing a revolver I went down among them. A mule is a good sentinel, and when he quits eating and stands with his ears stuck straight out taking notice, it is best to see what is the matter. The mules knew that Indians were around, but nothing seemed stirring, and my presence quieting the animals I returned to the fire and my letters.

I saw the way opening clear before me. War with Mexico was inevitable; and a grand opportunity now presented itself to realize in their fullest extent the farsighted views of Senator Benton, and make the Pacific Ocean the western boundary of the United States. I resolved to move forward on the opportunity and return forthwith to the Sacramento Valley in order to bring to bear all the influences I could command. Except myself, then and for nine months afterward, there was no other officer of the Army in California. The citizen party under my command was made up of picked men, and although small in number, constituted a formidable nucleus for frontier warfare, and many of its members commanded the confidence of the emigration.

This decision was the first step in the conquest of California. My mind having settled into this conclusion, I went to my blankets under a cedar. The camp was divided into three fires, and near each one, but well out of the light, were sleeping the men belonging to it. Close up along the margin of the wood which shut us in on three sides were some low cedars, the ends of their boughs reaching nearly to the ground. Under these we made our beds.

One always likes to have his head sheltered, and a rifle with a ramrod or a branch or bush with a blanket thrown over it answers very well where there is nothing better. I had barely fallen to sleep when I was awakened by the sound of Carson's voice, calling to Basil to know "what the matter was over there?" No reply came, and immediately the camp was roused by the cry from Kit and Owens, who were lying together—"Indians." Basil and the half-breed, Denny, had been killed. It was the sound of the ax being driven into Basil's head that had awakened Carson. The half-breed had been killed with arrows, and his groans had replied to Carson's call, and told him what the matter was. No man with an Indian experience jumps squarely to his feet in a night attack, but in an instant every man was at himself. The Delawares who lay near their fire on that side sprang to cover, rifle in hand, at the sound of the ax. We ran to their aid, Carson and I, Godey, Stepp, and Owens, just as the Klamaths charged into the open ground. The fires were smoldering, but gave light enough to show Delaware Crane jumping like a brave as he was from side to side in Indian fashion, and defending himself with the butt of his gun. By some mischance his rifle was not loaded when he lay down. All this was quick work. The moment's silence which followed Carson's shout was broken by our rifles. The Klamath chief, who was at the head of his men, fell in front of Crane, who was just down with five arrows in his body— three in his breast. The Klamaths, checked in their onset and disconcerted by the fall of their chief, jumped back into the shadow of the wood. We threw a blanket over Crane and hung blankets to the cedar boughs and bushes near by, behind my campfire, for a defense against the arrows.

The Indians did not dare to put themselves again in the open, but continued to pour in their arrows. They made no attempt on our animals, which had been driven up by Owens to be under fire of the camp, but made frequent attempts to get the body of their chief. We were determined they should not have it, and every movement on their part brought a rifle shot; a dozen rifles in such hands at short range made the undertaking too hazardous for them to persist in it. While both sides were watching each other from under cover, and every movement was followed by a rifle shot or arrow, I heard Carson cry out: *"Look at the fool. Look at him, will you?"* This was to Godey, who had stepped out to the light of my fire to look at some little thing which had gone wrong with his gun; it was still bright enough to show him distinctly, standing there—a fair mark to the arrows—turning resentfully to Carson for the epithet bestowed on him, but in no wise hurrying himself. He was the most thoroughly insensible to danger of all the brave men I have known.

All night we lay behind our blanket defenses with our rifles cocked in our hands, expecting momentarily another attack, until the morning light enabled us to see that the Indians had disappeared. By their tracks we found that fifteen or twenty Klamaths had attacked us. It was a sorrowful sight that met our eyes in the gray of the morning. Three of our men had been killed: Basil, Crane, and the half-breed Denny, and another Delaware had been wounded—one-fourth of our number. The chief who had been killed was recognized to be the same Indian who had given Lieutenant Gillespie a salmon at the outlet of the lake. Hung to his wrist was an English half-ax. Carson seized this and knocked his head to pieces with it, and one of the Delawares, Sagundai, scalped him. He was left where he fell. In his quiver were forty arrows—as Carson said, "the most beautiful and warlike arrows" he had ever seen. We saw more of them afterward. These arrows were all headed with a lancet-like piece of iron or steel—probably obtained from the Hudson's Bay Company's traders on the Umpqua—and were poisoned for about six inches. They could be driven that depth into a pine tree.

This event cast an angry gloom over the little camp. For the moment I threw all other considerations aside and determined to square accounts with these people before I left them. It was only a few days back that some of these same Indians had come into our camp and I divided with them what meat I had, and unpacked a mule to give them tobacco and knives.

On leaving the main party I had directed it to gear up as soon as the men had breakfasted and follow my trail to a place where we had encamped some days back. This would put them now about twenty-five miles from us. Packing our dead men on the mules, we started to rejoin the main camp, following the trail by which we had come. Before we had been two hours on the way many canoes appeared on the lake, coming from different directions and apparently making for a point where the trail came down to the shore. As we approached this point the prolonged cry of a loon told us that their scout was giving the Indians warning of our approach. Knowing that if we came to a fight the care of our dead men would prove a great hindrance and probably cost more lives, I turned sharply off into the mountain, and buried, or cached them in a close laurel thicket.

With our knives we dug a shallow grave, and wrapping their blankets round them, left them among the laurels. There are men above whom the laurels bloom who did not better deserve them than my brave Delaware and Basil. I left Denny's name on the creek where he died.

The Indians, thrown out by our sudden movement, failed in their intended ambush, and in the afternoon we found our people on the stream where we had encamped three days before. All were deeply grieved by the loss of our companions. The Delawares were filled with grief and rage by the death of Crane and went into mourning, blackening their faces. They were soothed somewhat when I told them that they should have an opportunity to get rid of their mourning and carry home scalps enough to satisfy the friends of Crane and the Delaware nation. With blackened faces, set and angry, they sat around brooding and waiting for revenge.

The camp was very quiet this evening, the men looking to their arms, rubbing and coaxing them. Toward evening I went over to the Delaware fire and sat down among them. They were sitting around their fire, smoking and silent. I did not need to speak; our faces told what we were all thinking about. After a pause I said, "Swonok, bad luck come this time. Crane was a brave. Good man, too. I am very sorry." "Very sick here," he said, striking his hand against his breast; "these Delaware all sick." "There are Indians around the camp, Swonok," I replied. "Yes, I see him. Me and Sagundai and Charley gone out and see him in woods." "How many?" "Maybe ten, maybe twenty, maybe more." "Where did they go?" "Up mountain. He not long way." "Listen, Swonok, we kill some. These same men kill Crane. How best kill him?" The chief's eyes glittered and his face relaxed, and all the Delawares raised their heads. "You go in morning? Which way?" "Only three, four mile, to creek which you know over there," said I pointing up the lake; "next day, big Indian village." Swonok turned to Sagundai and the two chiefs spoke earnestly together for a few moments, the others deeply interested, but gravely listening without speaking. "Captain," said Sagundai, "in the morning you go little way, stop. These Delaware stay here. Indian come in camp, Delaware kill him."

In the morning, when we were ready to start, the Delawares rode out some moments ahead, halting after a few hundred yards until we came up; then, leaving their horses with us, they returned on foot and got into a thicket among some young pines near the camp ground. We continued our way and halted, no one dismounting, at a little run about a quarter of a mile distant. It was not long before the stillness was broken by a scattered volley, and after that, nothing. Shortly Swonok came up. "Better now," he said; "very sick before, better now." They had taken two scalps. The Klamaths, as expected, had rushed into the camp ground, so soon as they thought it safe, and met the rifles of the Delawares. Two were killed and others wounded, but these were able to get away. Fortunately for them, the cracking of a dry branch startled the Klamaths and the Delawares were too eager to shoot as well as usual. I moved on about three miles to a stream where the grass was good and encamped. Choosing an open spot among the pines we built a solid corral of pine logs and branches. It was six feet high and large enough to contain all our animals. At nightfall they were driven into it, and we took up our quarters outside, against the corral, the fires being at a little distance farther out and lighting up, while they lasted, the woods beyond. I obtained observations which put this camp in longitude 121° 58' 45" and latitude 42° 36' 45".

Continuing our route along the lake, we passed around the extreme northwestern bay and after a hard day's march encamped in the midst of woods, where we built again a corral for the night. In the morning there were many canoes on the lake, and Indians had been about during the night, but the lesson they had learned served to keep them warily aloof in daylight. We were not very far from the principal village at the inlet which the Indians whom I had met when I first reached the lake had described to me; and the arms being all carefully examined and packs made secure, we started for it. When within a few miles I sent Carson and Owens ahead with ten men, directing them to reconnoiter the position of the Indians, but if possible to avoid engaging them until we could come up. But as we neared the mouth of the river, the firing began. The party was discovered and had no choice but to open the fight, driving the Indians who were on this side to the other side of the river. As I rode up I saw a dead Indian sitting in the stern of a canoe, which the current had driven against the bank. His hand was still grasping the paddle. On his feet were shoes which I thought Basil wore when he was killed.

The stream was about sixty yards wide and a rapid just above the mouth made it fordable. Without drawing rein we plunged in and crossed to the farther side and joined our men, who were pressed by a large body of Indians. They had abandoned their village and were scattered through a field of sagebrush, in front of the woods. But this time the night was not on their side and the attack was with us. Their arrows were good at close quarters, but the range of the rifle was better. The firing was too severe for them to stand it in open ground and they were driven back into the pinewoods with a loss of fourteen killed. They had intended to make a hard fight. Behind the sage bushes where they had taken their stand every Indian had spread his arrows on the ground in fanlike shape, so that they would be ready to his hand. But when our close fire drove them from the brush they were compelled to move so quickly that many did not have time to gather up their arrows and they lay on the ground, the bright, menacing points turned toward us. Quantities of fish were drying, spread on scaffolds, or hung up on frames. The huts, which were made of tall rushes and willow, like those on the savannah above, were set on fire, and the fish and scaffolds were all destroyed.

About a mile from the village I made my camp on a *clairière* in the midst of woods, where were oaks intermingled with pines, and built a strong corral. Meantime I kept out scouts on every side and horses were kept ready saddled. In the afternoon Indians were reported advancing through the timber; and taking with me Carson, Sagundai, Swonok, Stepp, and Archambeau, I rode out to see what they were intending. Sacramento knew how to jump and liked it. Going through the wood at a hand gallop, we came upon an oak tree which had been blown down; its summit covered quite a space, and being crowded by the others so that I was brought squarely in front of it, I let Sacramento go and he cleared the whole green mass in a beautiful leap. Looking back, Carson called out, "Captain, that horse will break your neck someday." It never happened to Sacramento to hurt his rider, but afterward, on the Salinas plain, he brought out from fight and back to his camp his rider who had been shot dead in the saddle.

In the heart of the wood we came suddenly upon an Indian scout. He was drawing his arrow to the head as we came upon him, and Carson attempted to fire, but his rifle snapped, and as he swerved away the Indian was about to let his arrow go into him; I fired, and in my haste to save Carson, failed to kill the Indian, but Sacramento, as I have said, was not afraid of anything, and I jumped him directly upon the Indian and threw him to the ground. His arrow went wild. Sagundai was right behind me, and as I passed over the Indian he threw himself from his horse and killed him with a blow on the head from his war club. It was the work of a moment, but it was a narrow chance for Carson. The poisoned arrow would have gone through his body.

Giving Sacramento into the care of Jacob, I went into the lodge and laid down on my blankets to rest from the excitement of which the day had been so full. I had now kept the promise I made to myself and had punished these people well for their treachery; and now I turned my thoughts to the work which they had delayed. I was lost in conjectures over this new field when Gillespie came in, all roused into emotion. "By Heaven, this is rough work," he exclaimed. "I'll take care to let them know in Washington about it." "Heaven don't come in for much about here, just now," I said; "and as for Washington, it will be long enough before we see it again, time enough to forget about this."

He had been introduced into an unfamiliar life in joining me and had been surprised into continued excitements by the strange scenes which were going on around him. My surroundings were very much unlike the narrow space and placid uniformity of a man-of-war's deck, and to him the country seemed alive with unexpected occurrences. Though himself was not, his ideas were very much at sea. He was full of admiration for my men and their singular fitness for the life they were leading. He shared my lodge, but this night his excitement would not let him sleep, and we remained long awake, talking over the incidents of the day and speculating over what was to come in the events that seemed near at hand. Nor was there much sleeping in the camp that night, but nothing disturbed its quiet. No attack was made.

The night was clear and I obtained observations here which gave what may be assumed for the longitude of the outlet 121° 52' 08", and for its latitude 42° 41′ 30″. To this river I gave the name of my friend Professor Torrey, who, with all the enthusiasm that goes with a true love of science, had aided me in determining the botany of the country.

The next day we moved late out of camp and traveled to the southward along the lake. I kept the ground well covered with scouts, knowing the daring character of the Klamaths. We made a short day's march and encamped in woods and built a corral. On the following day we continued the march, still in the neighborhood of the lake, and in the evening made camp at its southeastern end, on a creek to which I gave the name of one of the Delaware, We-to-wah. Indians were seen frequently during the day. Observations placed the mouth of this creek in longitude 121° 41′ 23″, latitude 42° 21′ 43″. As had become usual we made a corral to secure the safety of the animals. This was our last camp on the lake. Here I turned away from our comrades whom I had left among the pines. But they were not neglected. When the Klamaths tell the story of the night attack where they were killed, there will be no boasting. They will have to tell also of the death of their chief and of our swift retaliation; and how the people at the fishery had to mourn for the loss of their men and the destruction of their village. It will be a story for them to hand down while there are any Klamaths on their lake.

The pines in these forests were mostly full-grown trees, and for many a year our log forts around the lake will endure, and other travelers may find refuge in them, or wonder, in the present quiet, what had once broken the silence of the forest. Making open spots in the woods where the sunshine can rest longest, the trees that encircle them will be fuller-headed, and grass and flowers will be more luxuriant in the protection of their enclosure, so that they may long remain marked places.

The next day brought no unusual incident. On the day following I was traveling along a well-worn trail when I came upon a fresh scalp on an arrow which had been stuck up in the path. Maxwell and Archambeau were ahead, and in the evening they reported that riding along the trail they met an Indian who, on seeing them, laid down a bunch of young crows which he had in his hand, and forthwith and without parley let fly an arrow at Maxwell, who was foremost. He threw himself from his horse just in time to escape the arrow, which passed over the seat of his saddle, and, after a brief interchange of rifle balls and arrows, the Indian was killed and his scalp put up in the trail to tell the story. We were getting roughened into Indian customs.

Our route was now among the hills over ground where we had already just traveled in going north, and bordering the valley of the upper Sacramento, which, as I have said, was known to trappers under the name of Pitt River. The spring now gave its attraction and freshness to the whole region. The rolling surface of the hills was green up to the timbered ridges of the Cascade Range which we were skirting along; but above, the unconquerable peaks still were clothed with snow, and glittered cool in their solitary heights.[12]

＊　＊　＊　＊　＊

Editor's Note.—Frémont's days of exploration, so full of romance and delight to him, so useful to his country, were temporarily ended. He turned back to California, to the Bear Flag revolt, to the march of the California Battalion under his command against Los Angeles, and to immersion in the full tide of the Mexican War. The high peaks glittering cold along the Cascades and the Sierra Nevada soon looked down on a land filled with the turmoil of the American conquest. That controversial story has nothing to do with the theme of this book. In due course Frémont was to lead two other notable exploring expeditions, privately equipped; but of neither did he pen an account. For that matter, he wrote no report to the government on his third expedition. But he did pen a "Geographical Memoir" in illustration of the Frémont-Preuss map; and the important part of this is appended.

FOOTNOTES

1. The Yuba River flows from the east into the Feather River at what is now the town of Yuba, in Yuba County; they were not far from Marysville and Grass Valley, destined to fame in gold-rush days. The Yuba Indians were of the Maidu family.

2. Peter Lassen was really a Dane by origin. His career was almost as romantic as Sutter's, and he had less of the visionary quality which marked the operations of the Swiss. Lassen's Peak, 10,577 feet, perpetuates his name.

3. Mt. Shasta, in the Cascade Range, is 14,162 feet high. It had been dis-

covered by Peter Skene Ogden about 1827. Mt. Linn, in the Coast Range, is 8604 feet high. Both names have been retained. The name "Shasta" comes from the Shasta Indians, who occupied northern California and southwestern Oregon. Frémont spells it "Shastl."

4. Though Frémont did not know of it for weeks, nor did Washington, April 24–25 was a momentous date; Mexican forces crossed the Rio Grande, and killed or wounded sixteen American dragoons. But both Frémont and Washington fully expected to hear soon of such news.

5. Today called the Pitt River.

6. Now Big Valley.

7. The Modoc Indians of northern California and southern Oregon were, like the Klamaths, of Lutuamian stock. They were placed on a reservation in 1864, but were unhappy; and in 1870 their chief, Captain Jack, led some of them back from the Klamath country into California, thus bringing on the Modoc War. General E. R. S. Canby was slain while trying to arrange a peace.

8. This was Edward McCrady, father of the Confederate officer and historian of the same name. In the campaign of 1856 he defended Frémont from certain false charges, but at the same time broke with him completely on the slavery issue. Lake Rhett, previously mentioned, is now called Tule Lake. Frémont continues to spell Klamath "Tlamath," which is no doubt closer to the Indian pronunciation.

9. Now called Rock Creek.

10. Linsy Sissemore and Ralph Applegate Good, in their history of Klamath County, Oregon, have identified this spot where Frémont heard the fateful news that an officer of Marines was hard on his trail with messages and papers as being probably "near the mouth of Wood Creek." Frémont, as he here relates, then turned about and traveled forty-five miles posthaste to meet Gillespie and his escort of three men on "Denny's Branch" or Rock Creek.

11. We here reach one of the most controversial episodes of California's history. What were the messages which Gillespie brought to Frémont? Did he bring secret instructions? Apparently the one really official document he carried was a copy of Secretary Buchanan's despatch of October 17, 1845, to Consul Larkin, which instructed him to carry on a peaceful intrigue for the separation of California from Mexico, and to be sleeplessly active in counteracting British or French machinations in that province. But he also brought private letters, and oral information; what were they? For an analysis of this question see my *Frémont: Pathmarker of the West,* pp. 236–52.

APPENDIX

GEOGRAPHICAL MEMOIR

Upon Upper California in Illustration of His Map of Oregon and California
By John C. Frémont *

On the second day of February, in the year 1847, during my absence on my third expedition of topographical survey in the western
part of this continent, a resolve was passed by the Senate directing the
construction of two maps—one of the central section of the Rocky Mountains, and the other of Oregon and Upper California—from the materials
collected by me in the two previous expeditions, and with the additions
which the then existing expedition might furnish; and Mr. Charles Preuss,
my assistant in the first and second expeditions, was employed to commence the work.

On my return to the United States in the month of September last, I
found Mr. Preuss closely engaged upon the work on which the Senate
had employed him; and, from that time to the present, I have myself
given all the time that could be spared from other engagements to supply
the additions which the last expedition has enabled me to make. Con-
ceiving that the map of Oregon and California was of the most immediate
and pressing importance, I first directed my attention to its preparation,
in order to bring it into a condition as soon as possible to be laid before
the Senate; which is now done.

In laying this map of Oregon and Upper California before the Senate,
I deem it proper to show the extent and general character of the work,
and how far it may be depended on as correct, as being founded on my
own or other surveys, and how far it is conjectural, and only presented
as the best that is known.

In extent, it embraces the whole western side of this continent between
the eastern base of the Rocky Mountains and the Pacific Ocean, and between the straits of Fuca and the Gulf of California, taking for its outline
on the north the boundary line with Great Britain, and on the south,
including the Bay of San Diego, the head of the Gulf of California, the
rivers Colorado and Gila, and all the country through which the line of
the late treaty with Mexico would run, from El Paso del Norte to the sea.

* Washington, 1848.

509

To complete the view in that quarter, the valley of the Rio del Norte is added, from the head of the river to El Paso del Norte, thereby including New Mexico. The map has been constructed expressly to exhibit the two countries of Oregon and the Alta California together. It is believed to be the most correct that has appeared of either of them; and it is certainly the only one that shows the structure and configuration of the interior of Upper California.

The part of the map which exhibits Oregon is chiefly copied from the works of others, but not entirely, my own explorations in that territory having extended to nearly two thousand miles. The part which exhibits California, and especially the Great Basin, the Sierra Nevada, the beautiful valleys of Sacramento and San Joaquin, is chiefly from my own surveys or personal view, and in such cases is given as correct. Where my own observations did not extend, the best authorities have been followed.

The profile view in the margin, on the north side of the map, exhibits the elevations of the country from the South Pass in the Rocky Mountains to the Bay of San Francisco, passing the Utah and the Great Salt lakes, following the river Humboldt through the northern side of the Great Basin, crossing the Sierra Nevada into the valley of the Sacramento, where the emigrant road now crosses that sierra forty miles north of Nueva Helvetia. This line shows the present traveling route to California. The profile on the south side of the map exhibits the elevations of the country on a different line—the line of exploration in the last expedition—from the head of the Arkansas by the Utah and Great Salt lakes, and through the interior of the Great Basin, crossing the Sierra Nevada into the Sacramento Valley at the head of the Rio de los Americanos. These profile views are given merely for their outlines, to show the structure of the country between the Rocky Mountains and the sea, and the rise and fall occasioned by mountains and valleys. Full and descriptive profile views on a large scale are wanted, marking the geological structure of the country, and exhibiting at their proper altitudes the different products of the vegetable kingdom. Some material is already collected for such a purpose, extending on different lines from the Mississippi to the Pacific, but not sufficient to complete the work.

The Arabic figures on different parts of the map indicate the elevation of places above the level of the sea, a knowledge of which is essential to a just conception of the climate and agricultural capacities of a country.

The longitudes established on the line of exploration of the last expedition are based on a series of astronomical observations, resting on four main positions, determined by lunar culminations. The first of these main positions is at the mouth of the Fontaine Qui Bouit river, on the Upper Arkansas; the second is on the eastern shore of the Great Salt Lake, and two in the valley of the Sacramento, at the western base of the Sierra Nevada. This line of astronomical observations, thus carried across the continent, reaches the Pacific Ocean on the northern shore of the Bay of Monterey.

In my published map of the year 1845, the line of the western coast was laid down according to Vancouver. When the newly established positions were placed on the map now laid before the Senate, it was found that they carried the line of the coast about fourteen miles west, and the valleys of the Sacramento and San Joaquin about twenty miles east, making an increase of more than thirty miles in the breadth of the country below the Sierra Nevada. Upon examination, it was found that these positions agreed, nearly, with the observations of Captain Beechey, at Monterey. The corrections required by the new positions were then accordingly made; the basin of the Sacramento and San Joaquin valleys was removed to the eastward, and the line of the coast projected farther west, conformably to my observations, retaining the configuration given to it by the surveys of Vancouver.

The error in the position of the San Joaquin, Sacramento, and Wahlah-math valleys still exists upon the most authentic maps extant; and it appears that upon the charts in general use a greatly erroneous position is still given to the coast.

By the return of the United States sloop of war *Portsmouth,* Commander Montgomery, from the Pacific Ocean, it is learned that two British ships of war are now engaged in making a new survey of the gulf and coast of California. It is also known that an American whale ship was recently lost on the coast of California in consequence of the errors in the charts now in general use, locating the coast and islands, from Monterey south, too far east.[*]

The astronomical observations made by me across the continent, in this my third expedition, were calculated by Professor Hubbard, of the National Observatory (Washington City) during the present winter; and a note from him on the subject of these observations is added as an appendix to this memoir.[**] My attention having been recently called to this

[*] Naval.—The United States sloop of war *Portsmouth,* Commander John B. Montgomery, arrived at Boston on Friday, from the Pacific Ocean, last from Valparaiso, February 23. Commander Montgomery states that the British frigate *Herald,* and the brig *Pandora,* are engaged in making a new survey of the gulf and coast of California.

The whale ship *Hope,* of Providence, was recently lost on the coast, in consequence of an error in the charts now in general use, which locate the coast and islands from Monterey to Cape St. Lucas from fifteen to forty miles too far to the eastward.—*National Intelligencer.*

[**] Omitted.

subject, (the true position of the coast of California,) I find it worthy of remark that the position given to this coast on the charts of the old Spanish navigators agrees nearly with that which would be assigned to it by the observations of the most eminent naval surveyors of the present day. The position adopted for Monterey and the adjacent coast, on the map now laid before the Senate, agrees nearly with that in which it had been placed by the observations of Malaspina,† in 1791.

In constructing this map it became necessary to adopt the coast line of the Pacific, as found in maps in general use, to give it completeness. It was no part of my design to make a chart of the coast. Finding an error when I came to lay down the Bay of Monterey, I altered my map to suit it. I knew nothing then of any errors in the coast. It is satisfactory now to find that my astronomical observations correspond with those previously made by Beechey and Belcher, and very gratifying to be able to add some testimonial to the correctness of those made by Malaspina long before either of them. Vancouver removed the coast line as fixed by Malaspina, and the subsequent observations carry it back.

In laying this map before the Senate, and in anticipation of the full work which my explorations (with some further examinations) may enable me to draw up hereafter, I deem it a proper accompaniment to the map to present some brief notices of California, with a view to show the character of the country, and its capability or otherwise to sustain a considerable population. In doing this, no general remarks applicable to the whole of California can be used. The diversity in different parts is too great to admit of generalization in the description. Separate views of different parts must be taken; and in this brief sketch, the design is to limit the view to the two great divisions of the country which lie on the opposite sides of the Sierra Nevada, and to the character of that mountain itself, so prominent in the structure of the country, and exercising so great an influence over the climate, soil, and productions of its two divisions.

SIERRA NEVADA

This sierra is part of the great mountain range which, under different names and with different elevations, but with much uniformity of direc-

† Of this skillful, intrepid, and unfortunate navigator, Humboldt (Essay on New Spain) says: "The peculiar merit of his expedition consists not only in the number of astronomical observations, but principally in the judicious method which was employed to arrive at certain results. The longitude and latitude of four points on the coast (Cape San Lucas, Monterey, Nootka, and Fort Mulgrave) were fixed in an absolute manner.

tion and general proximity to the coast, extends from the peninsula of California to Russian America, and without a gap in the distance through which the water of the Rocky Mountains could reach the Pacific Ocean, except at the two places where the Columbia and Frazer's river respectively find their passage. This great range is remarkable for its length, its proximity and parallelism to the seacoast, its great elevation, often more lofty than the Rocky Mountains, and its many grand volcanic peaks, reaching high into the region of perpetual snow. Rising singly, like pyramids, from heavily timbered plateaux, to the height of fourteen and seventeen thousand feet above the sea, these snowy peaks constitute the characterizing feature of the range, and distinguish it from the Rocky Mountains and all others on our part of the continent.

That part of this range which traverses the Alta California is called the Sierra Nevada, (Snowy Mountain)—a name in itself implying a great elevation, as it is only applied, in Spanish geography, to the mountains whose summits penetrate the region of perpetual snow. It is a grand feature of California, and a dominating one, and must be well understood before the structure of the country and the character of its different divisions can be comprehended. It divides California into two parts, and exercises a decided influence on the climate, soil, and productions of each. Stretching along the coast, and at the general distance of 150 miles from it, this great mountain wall receives the warm winds, charged with vapor, which sweep across the Pacific Ocean, precipitates their accumulated moisture in fertilizing rains and snows upon its western flank, and leaves cold and dry winds to pass on to the east. Hence the characteristic differences of the two regions—mildness, fertility, and a superb vegetable kingdom on one side, comparative barrenness and cold on the other.

The two sides of the sierra exhibit two distinct climates. The state of vegetation, in connection with some thermometrical observations made during the recent exploring expedition to California, will establish and illustrate this difference. In the beginning of December, 1845, we crossed this sierra, at latitude 39° 17' 12", at the present usual emigrant pass, at the head of the Salmon Trout River, 40 miles north of New Helvetia, and made observations at each base, and in the same latitude, to determine the respective temperatures, the two bases being, respectively, the western about 500, and the eastern about 4,000 feet above the level of the sea; and the pass, 7,200 feet. The mean results of the observations were, on the eastern side, at sunrise, 9°, at noon, 44°, at sunset, 30°, the state of vegetation and the appearance of the country being at the same time (second week of December) that of confirmed winter; the rivers frozen over, snow on the ridges, annual plants dead, grass dry, and deciduous trees stripped of their foliage. At the western base, the mean temperature during a corresponding week was at sunrise 29°, and at sunset 52°, the state of the atmosphere and of vegetation that of advancing spring; grass fresh and green, four to eight inches high, vernal plants in bloom, the air soft, and all the streams free from ice. Thus December, on one side of the mountain, was winter; on the other it was spring.

THE GREAT BASIN

East of the Sierra Nevada, and between it and the Rocky Mountains, is that anomalous feature in our continent, the Great Basin, the existence of which was advanced as a theory after the second expedition, and is now established as a geographical fact. It is a singular feature: a basin of some five hundred miles diameter every way, between four and five thousand feet above the level of the sea, shut in all around by mountains, with its own system of lakes and rivers, and having no connection whatever with the sea. Partly arid and sparsely inhabited, the general character of the Great Basin is that of desert, but with great exceptions, there being many parts of it very fit for the residence of a civilized people; and of these parts, the Mormons have lately established themselves in one of the largest and best. Mountain is the predominating structure of the interior of the Basin, with plains between—the mountains wooded and watered, the plains arid and sterile. The interior mountains conform to the law which governs the course of the Rocky Mountains and of the Sierra Nevada, ranging nearly north and south, and present a very uniform character of abruptness, rising suddenly from a narrow base of ten to twenty miles, and attaining an elevation of two to five thousand feet above the level of the country. They are grassy and wooded, showing snow on their summit peaks during the greater part of the year, and affording small streams of water from five to fifty feet wide, which lose themselves, some in lakes, some in the dry plains, and some in the belt of alluvial soil at the base; for these mountains have very uniformly this belt of alluvion, the wash and abrasion of their sides, rich in excellent grass, fertile, and light and loose enough to absorb small streams. Between these mountains are the arid plains which receive and deserve the name of desert. Such is the general structure of the interior of the Great Basin, more Asiatic than American in its character, and much resembling the elevated region between the Caspian sea and northern Persia. The rim of this basin is massive ranges of mountains, of which the Sierra Nevada on the west, and the Wasatch and Timpanogos chains on the east, are the most conspicuous. On the north, it is separated from the waters of the Columbia by a branch of the Rocky Mountains, and from the Gulf of California, on the south, by a bed of mountainous ranges, of which the existence has been only recently determined. Snow abounds on them all; on some, in their loftier parts, the whole year, with wood and grass; with copious streams of water, sometimes amounting to considerable rivers, flowing inward, and forming lakes or sinking in the sands. Belts or benches of good alluvion are usually found at their base.

Lakes in the Great Basin. The Great Salt Lake and the Utah Lake are in this basin, toward its eastern rim, and constitute its most interesting feature—one, a saturated solution of common salt, the other, fresh—the Utah about one hundred feet above the level of the Salt Lake, which is itself four thousand two hundred above the level of the sea, and connected by a strait, or river, thirty-five miles long.

These lakes drain an area of ten or twelve thousand square miles, and have, on the east, along the base of the mountain, the usual bench of alluvion, which extends to a distance of three hundred miles, with wood and water, and abundant grass. The Mormons have established themselves on the strait between these two lakes, and will find sufficient arable land for a large settlement—important from its position as intermediate between the Mississippi Valley and the Pacific Ocean, and on the line of communication to California and Oregon.

The Utah is about thirty-five miles long, and is remarkable for the numerous and bold streams which it receives, coming down from the mountains on the southeast, all fresh water, although a large formation of rock salt, imbedded in red clay, is found within the area on the southeast, which it drains. The lake and its affluents afford large trout and other fish in great numbers, which constitute the food of the Utah Indians during the fishing season. The Great Salt Lake has a very irregular outline, greatly extended at times of melting snows. It is about seventy miles in length, both lake ranging nearly north and south, in conformity to the range of the mountains, and is remarkable for its predominance of salt. The whole lake waters seem thoroughly saturated with it, and every evaporation of the water leaves salt behind. The rocky shores of the islands are whitened by the spray, which leaves salt on everything it touches, and a covering like ice forms over the water, which the waves throw among the rocks. The shores of the lake in the dry season, when the waters recede, and especially on the south side, are whitened with encrustations of fine white salt; the shallow arms of the lake, at the same time, under a slight covering of briny water, present beds of salt for miles, resembling softened ice, into which the horses' feet sink to the fetlock. Plants and bushes, blown by the wind upon these fields, are entirely encrusted with crystallized salt, more than an inch in thickness. Upon this lake of salt the fresh water received, though great in quantity, has no perceptible effect. No fish, or animal life of any kind, is found in it, the larvæ on the shore being found to belong to winged insects. A geological examination of the bed and shores of this lake is of the highest interest.

Five gallons of water taken from this lake in the month of September, and roughly evaporated over a fire, gave fourteen pints of salt, a part of which, being subjected to analysis, gave the following proportions:

Chloride of sodium (common salt) .... 97.80 parts.
Chloride of calcium .... 0.61   "
Chloride of magnesium .... 0.24   "
Sulphate of soda .... 0.23   "
Sulphate of lime .... 1.12   "

                                                       100.00

Southward from the Utah is another lake of which little more is now known than when Humboldt published his general map of Mexico. It is the reservoir of a handsome river, about two hundred miles long, rising in the Wasatch mountains, and discharging a considerable volume of water. The river and lake were called by the Spaniards Severe, corrupted by the hunters into Sevier. On the map, they are called Nicollet, in honor of J. N. Nicollet, whose premature death interrupted the publication of the learned work on the physical geography of the basin of the Upper Mississippi, which five years of labor in the field had prepared him to give.

On the western side of the basin, and immediately within the first range of the Sierra Nevada, is the Pyramid Lake, receiving the water of Salmon Trout River. It is thirty-five miles long, between four and five thousand feet above the sea, surrounded by mountains, is remarkably deep and clear, and abounds with uncommonly large salmon trout. Southward, along the base of the Sierra Nevada, is a range of considerable lakes, formed by many large streams from the sierra. Lake Walker, the largest among these, affords great numbers of trout similar to those of the Pyramid Lake, and is a place of resort for Indians in the fishing season.

There are probably other collections of water not yet known. The number of small lakes is very great, many of them more or less salty, and all, like the rivers which feed them, changing their appearance and extent under the influence of the season, rising with the melting of the snows, sinking in the dry weather, and distinctly presenting their high- and low-water mark. These generally afford some fertile and well-watered land, capable of settlement.

Rivers of the Great Basin. The most considerable river in the interior of the Great Basin is the one called on the map Humboldt River, as the mountains at its head are called Humbolt Mountains—so called as a small mark of respect to the "Nestor of scientific travelers," who has done so much to illustrate North American geography, without leaving his name upon any one of its remarkable features. It is a river long known to hunters, and sometimes sketched on maps under the name of Mary's, or Ogden's, but now for the first time laid down with any precision. It is a very peculiar stream, and has many characteristics of an Asiatic river—the Jordan, for example, though twice as long—rising in mountains and losing itself in a lake of its own, after a long and solitary course. It rises in two streams in mountains west of the Great Salt Lake, which unite, after some fifty miles, and bears westwardly along the northern side of the basin toward the great Sierra Nevada, which it is destined never to reach, much less to pass. The mountains in which it rises are round and handsome in their outline, capped with snow the greater part of the year, well clothed with grass and wood, and abundant in water. The stream is a narrow line, without affluents, losing by absorption and evaporation as it goes, and terminating in a marshy lake, with low shores fringed with bulrushes, and whitened with saline encrustations. It has a moderate current, is from two to six feet deep in the dry season, and probably not fordable anywhere below the junction of the forks during the time of melting snows, when both lake and river are considerably enlarged. The country through which it passes (except its immediate valley) is a dry sandy plain, without grass, wood, or arable soil; from about 4,700 feet (at the forks) to 4,200 feet (at the lake) above the level of the sea, winding among broken ranges of mountains, and varying from a few miles to twenty in breadth. Its own immediate valley is a rich alluvion, beautifully covered with blue grass, herd grass, clover, and other nutritious grasses; and its course is marked through the plain by a line of willow and cottonwood trees, serving for fuel. The Indians in the fall set fire to the grass and destroy all trees except in low grounds near the water.

This river possesses qualities which, in the progress of events, may give it both value and fame. It lies on the line of travel to California and Oregon, and is the best route now known through the Great Basin, and the one traveled by emigrants. Its direction, nearly east and west, is the right course for that travel. It furnishes a level unobstructed way for nearly three hundred miles, and a continuous supply of the indispensable articles of water, wood, and grass. Its head is toward the Great Salt Lake, and consequently toward the Mormon settlement, which must become a point in the line of emigration to California and the Lower Columbia. Its termination is within fifty miles of the base of the Sierra Nevada, and opposite the Salmon Trout River Pass—a pass only seven thousand two hundred feet above the level of the sea, and less than half that above the level of the basin, and leading into the valley of the Sacramento some forty miles north of Nueva Helvetia. These properties give to this river a prospective value in future communications with the Pacific Ocean, and the profile view on the north of the map shows the elevations of the present traveling route, of which it is a part, from the South Pass, in the Rocky Mountains, to the Bay of San Francisco.

The other principal rivers of the Great Basin are found on its circumference, collecting their waters from the snowy mountains which surround it, and are, 1. Bear River, on the east, rising in the massive range of the Timpanogos Mountains and falling into the Great Salt Lake, after a doubling course through a fertile and picturesque valley two hundred miles long. 2. The Utah River and Timpanaozu or Timpanogos, discharging themselves into the Utah Lake on the east, after gathering their copious streams in the adjoining parts of the Wasatch and Timpanogos mountains. 3. Nicollet River, rising south in the long range of the Wasatch Mountains, and falling into a lake of its own name, after making an arable and grassy valley, two hundred miles in length, through mountainous country. 4. Salmon Trout River, on the west, running down from the Sierra Nevada and falling into Pyramid Lake, after a course of about one hundred miles. From its source, about one-third of its valley is through a pine-timbered country, and for the remainder of the way through very rocky, naked ridges. It is remarkable for the abundance and excellence of its salmon trout, and presents some ground for cultivation. 5. Carson and Walker rivers, both handsome clear-water streams nearly one hundred miles long, coming, like the preceding, down the eastern flank of the Sierra Nevada and forming lakes of their own name at its base. They contain salmon trout and other fish, and form some large bottoms of good land. 6. Owens River, issuing from the Sierra Nevada on the south, is a large bold stream about one hundred and twenty miles long, gathering its waters in the Sierra Nevada, flowing to the southward, and forming a lake about fifteen miles long at the base of the mountain. At a medium stage it is generally four or five feet deep, in places fifteen, wooded with willow and cottonwood, and makes continuous bottoms of fertile land, at intervals rendered marshy by springs and small affluents from the mountain. The water of the lake in which it terminates has an unpleasant smell and bad taste, but around its shores are found small streams of pure water with good grass. On the map this has been called Owens River.

Besides these principal rivers issuing from the mountains on the circumference of the Great Basin, there are many others, all around, all obeying the general law of losing themselves in sands, or lakes, or belts of alluvion, and almost all of them an index to some arable land, with grass and wood.

Interior of the Great Basin. The interior of the Great Basin, so far as explored, is found to be a succession of sharp mountain ranges and naked plains, such as have been described. These ranges are isolated, presenting summit lines broken into many peaks, of which the highest are between ten and eleven thousand feet above the sea. They are thinly wooded with some varieties of pine (*Pinus monophyllus* characteristic), cedar, aspen, and a few other trees, and afford an excellent quality of bunch grass, equal to any found in the Rocky Mountains. Black-tailed deer and mountain sheep are frequent in these mountains; which, in consideration of their grass, water, and wood, and the alluvion at their base, may be called fertile, in the radical sense of the word, as signifying a capacity to produce, or bear, and in contradistinction to sterility. In this sense these interior mountains may be called fertile. Sterility, on the contrary, is the absolute characteristic of the valleys between the mountains—no wood, no water, no grass, the gloomy artemisia the prevailing shrub—no animals, except the hares, which shelter in these shrubs, and fleet and timid antelope, always on the watch for danger, and finding no place too dry and barren which gives it a wide horizon for its view and a clear field for its flight. No birds are seen in the plains, and few on the mountains. But few Indians are found, and those in the lowest state of human existence, living not even in communities, but in the elementary state of families, and sometimes a single individual to himself—except about the lakes stocked with fish, which become the property and resort of a small tribe. The abundance and excellence of the fish in most of these lakes is a characteristic; and the fishing season is to the Indians the happy season of the year.

Climate of the Great Basin. The climate of the Great Basin does not present the rigorous winter due to its elevation and mountainous structure. Observations made during the last expedition show that around the southern shores of the Salt Lake, latitude 40° 30′ to 41″ for two weeks of the month of October, 1845, from the 13th to the 27th, the mean temperature was 40° at sunrise, 70° at noon, and 54° at sunset—ranging at sunrise from 28° to 57°; at noon, from 62° to 76°; at four in the afternoon, from 58° to 69°; and at sunset, from 47° to 57°.

Until the middle of the month the weather remained fair and very pleasant. On the 15th, it began to rain in occasional showers, which whitened with snow the tops of the mountains on the southeast side of the lake valley. Flowers were in bloom during all the month. About the

18th, on one of the large islands in the south of the lake, helianthus, several species of aster, *Erodium cicutarium*, and several other plants were in fresh and full bloom; the grass of the second growth was coming up finely, and vegetation generally betokened the lengthened summer of the climate.

The 16th, 17th, and 18th, stormy with rain; heavy at night; peaks of the Bear River Range and tops of the mountains covered with snow. On the 18th, cleared with weather like that of late spring, and continued mild and clear until the end of the month, when the fine weather was again interrupted by a day or two of rain. No snow within 2,000 feet above the level of the valley.

Across the interior, between latitudes 41° and 38°, during the month of November (5th to 25th) the mean temperature was 29° at sunrise and 40° at sunset, ranging at noon (by detached observations) between 41° and 60°. There was a snowstorm between the 4th and 7th, the snow falling principally at night, and sun occasionally breaking out in the day. The lower hills and valleys were covered a few inches deep with snow, which the sun carried off in a few hours after the storm was over.

The weather then continued uninterruptedly open until the close of the year, without rain or snow, and during the remainder of November, generally clear and beautiful; nights and mornings calm, a light breeze during the day, and strong winds of very rare occurrence. Snow remained only on the peaks of the mountains.

On the western side of the basin, along the base of the Sierra Nevada, during two weeks from the 25th November to the 11th December, the mean temperature at sunrise was 11° and at sunset 34°, ranging at sunrise from zero to 21°, and at sunset from 23° to 44°. For ten consecutive days of the same period, the mean temperature at noon was 45°, ranging from 33° to 56°. The weather remained open, usually very clear, and the rivers were frozen.

The winter of '43–'44, within the basin, was remarkable for the same open, pleasant weather, rarely interrupted by rain or snow. In fact, there is nothing in the climate of this great interior region, elevated as it is, and surrounded and traversed by snowy mountains, to prevent civilized man from making it his home, and finding in its arable parts the means of a comfortable subsistence; and this the Mormons will probably soon prove in the parts about the Great Salt Lake. The progress of their settlement is already great. On the first of April of the present year, they had 3,000 acres in wheat, seven saw and grist mills, seven hundred houses in a fortified enclosure of sixty acres, stock, and other accompaniments of a flourishing settlement.

Such is the Great Basin, heretofore characterized as a desert, and in some respects meriting that appellation, but already demanding the qualification of great exceptions, and deserving the full examination of a thorough exploration.

MARITIME REGION WEST OF THE SIERRA NEVADA

West of the Sierra Nevada, and between that mountain and the sea, is the second grand division of California, and the only part to which the name applies in the current language of the country. It is the occupied and inhabited part, and so different in character—so divided by the mountain wall of the sierra from the Great Basin above—as to constitute a region to itself, with a structure and configuration—a soil, climate, and productions—of its own; and as northern Persia may be referred to as some type of the former, so may Italy be referred to as some point of comparison for the latter. North and south, this region embraces about ten degrees of latitude—from 32°, where it touches the peninsula of California, to 42°, where it bounds on Oregon. East and west, from the Sierra Nevada to the sea, it will average, in the middle parts, 150 miles, in the northern parts 200—giving an area of above one hundred thousand square miles. Looking westward from the summit of the sierra, the main feature presented is the long, low, broad valley of the Joaquin and Sacramento rivers—the two valleys forming one—five hundred miles long and fifty broad, lying along the base of the sierra and bounded to the west by the low Coast Range of mountains, which separates it from the sea. Long dark lines of timber indicate the streams, and bright spots mark the intervening plains. Lateral ranges, parallel to the Sierra Nevada and the coast, make the structure of the country and break it into a surface of valleys and mountains—the valleys a few hundred, and the mountains two to four thousand, feet above the sea. These form greater masses, and become more elevated in the north, where some peaks, as the Shasta, enter the regions of perpetual snow. Stretched along the mild coast of the Pacific, with a general elevation in its plains and valleys of only a few hundred feet above the level of the sea—and backed by the long and lofty wall of the sierra—mildness and geniality may be assumed as the characteristic of its climate. The inhabitant of corresponding latitudes on the Atlantic side of this continent can with difficulty conceive of the soft air and southern productions under the same latitudes in the maritime region of Upper California. The singular beauty and purity of the sky in the south of this region is characterized by Humboldt as a rare phenomenon, and all travelers realize the truth of his description.

The present condition of the country affords but slight data for forming correct opinions of the agricultural capacity and fertility of the soil. Vancouver found, at the mission of San Buenaventura, in 1792, latitude 34° 16', apples, pears, plums, figs, oranges, grapes, peaches, and pomegranates growing together with the plantain, banana, coconut, sugar cane, and indigo, all yielding fruit in abundance and of excellent quality. Humboldt mentions the olive oil of California as equal to that of Andalusia, and the wine like that of the Canary Islands. At present, but little remains of the high and various cultivation which had been attained at the missions. Under the mild and paternal administration of the "Fathers," the docile character of the Indians was made available for labor, and thousands were employed in the fields, the orchards, and the vineyards. At present, but little of this former cultivation is seen. The fertile valleys are overgrown with wild mustard; vineyards and olive orchards, decayed and neglected, are among the remaining vestiges; only in some places do we see the evidences of what the country is capable. At San Buenaventura we found the olive trees, in January, bending under the weight of neglected fruit; and the mission of San Luis Obispo (latitude 35°) is still distinguished for the excellence of its olives, considered finer and larger than those of the Mediterranean.

The productions of the south differ from those of the north and of the middle. Grapes, olives, Indian corn, have been its staples, with many assimilated fruits and grains. Tobacco has been recently introduced; and the uniform summer heat which follows the wet season, and is uninterrupted by rain, would make the southern country well adapted to cotton. Wheat is the first product of the north where it always constituted the principal cultivation of the missions. This promises to be the grain-growing region of California. The moisture of the coast seems particularly suited to the potato and to the vegetables common to the United States, which grow to an extraordinary size.

Perhaps few parts of the world can produce in such perfection a great variety of fruits and grains as the large and various region enclosing the Bay of San Francisco and drained by its waters. A view of the map will show that region and its great extent, comprehending the entire valleys of the Sacramento and San Joaquin, and the whole western slope of the Sierra Nevada. General phrases fail to give precise ideas, and I have recourse to the notes in my journal to show its climate and productions by the test of the thermometer and the state of the vegetable kingdom.

Editor's Note.—The remainder of the *Geographical Memoir* contains little of interest to the general reader or student of the present day. It comprehends brief descriptions of the San Joaquin and Sacramento valleys as Frémont found them, some notes on the western slope of the Sierra Nevada, and several almost ecstatic paragraphs of praise on San Francisco Bay and the dependent country. But much the most striking part of the *Memoir* is the account of the Great Basin, which Frémont was the first to delineate.

Index

525